A Concise Introduction to American Politics

SEVENTH EDITION

Thomas E. Patterson
Bradlee Professor of Government and the Press
John F. Kennedy School of Government
Harvard University

Boston   Burr Ridge, IL   Dubuque, IA   Madison, WI   New York
San Francisco   St. Louis   Bangkok   Bogotá   Caracas   Kuala Lumpur
Lisbon   London   Madrid   Mexico City   Milan   Montreal   New Delhi
Santiago   Seoul   Singapore   Sydney   Taipei   Toronto

The McGraw·Hill Companies

Higher Education

Published by McGraw-Hill, an imprint of The McGraw-Hill Companies, Inc., 1221 Avenue of the Americas, New York, NY 10020. Copyright © 2008. All rights reserved. No part of this publication may be reproduced or distributed in any form or by any means, or stored in a database or retrieval system, without the prior written consent of The McGraw-Hill Companies, Inc., including, but not limited to, in any network or other electronic storage or transmission, or broadcast for distance learning.

This book is printed on acid-free paper.

1 2 3 4 5 6 7 8 9 0 DOC/DOC 0 9 8 7

ISBN: 978-0-07-340386-1
MHID: 0-07-340386-5

Editor in Chief: *Emily Barrosse*
Publisher: *Frank Mortimer*
Sponsoring Editor: *Monica Eckman*
Marketing Manager: *Simon Heathcote*
Director of Development: *Rhona Robbin*
Development Editor: *Nancy Crochiere*
Editorial Coordinator: *Jessica Badiner*
Production Editor: *Christina Gimlin*
Manuscript Editor: *Mary Roybal*
Art Director: *Jeanne Schreiber*
Cover and Interior Designer: *Kay Fulton*
Art Editor: *Emma Ghiselli*
Photo Research Coordinator: *Alexandra Ambrose*
Photo Research: *PhotoFind, LLC*
Permissions Editor: *Marty Moga*
Media Project Manager: *Ron Nelms*
Print Supplements Producer: *Louis Swaim*
Production Supervisor: *Randy Hurst*
Composition: *10.5/13 Janson by Aptara, Inc.*
Printing: *45# Pub Matte, R. R. Donnelley Crawfordsville*
Cover: © Randy Wells/Stone/Getty Images

Credits: The credits section for this book begins on page C-1 and is considered an extension of the copyright page.

Library of Congress Cataloging-in-Publication Data

Patterson, Thomas E.
 We the people: a concise introduction to American politics/Thomas E. Patterson.—7th ed.
  p. cm.
 Includes bibliographical references and index.
 ISBN-13: 978-0-07-340386-1 (alk. paper)
 ISBN-10: 0-07-340386-5 (alk. paper)
 1. United States—Politics and government. I. Title.
JK274.P36 2007
320.473—dc22

2007010338

The Internet addresses listed in the text were accurate at the time of publication. The inclusion of a Website does not indicate an endorsement by the authors or McGraw-Hill, and McGraw-Hill does not guarantee the accuracy of the information presented at these sites.

www.mhhe.com

To My Children,
Alex and Leigh

ABOUT THE AUTHOR

Thomas E. Patterson is Bradlee Professor of Government and the Press in the John F. Kennedy School of Government at Harvard University. He was previously Distinguished Professor of Political Science in the Maxwell School of Citizenship at Syracuse University. Raised in a small Minnesota town near the Iowa and South Dakota borders, he attended South Dakota State University as an undergraduate and served in the military in Vietnam before enrolling at the University of Minnesota, where he received his Ph.D. in 1971.

He is the author of numerous book and articles, which focus mainly on elections and the media. His book *The Vanishing Voter* (2002) describes and explains the long-term decline in Americans' electoral participation. An earlier book, *Out of Order* (1994), received national attention when President Clinton said every politician and journalist should be required to read it. In 2002, *Out of Order* received the American Political Science Association's Graber Award for the best book of the past decade in political communication. Another of Patterson's books, *The Mass Media Election* (1980), received a *Choice* award as Outstanding Academic Book, 1980-1981. Patterson's first book, *The Unseeing Eye* (1976), was selected by the American Association for Public Opinion Research as one of the fifty most influential books of the past half century in the field of public opinion.

His research has been funded by major grants from the National Science Foundation, the Markle Foundation, the Smith-Richardson Foundation, the Ford Foundation, the Knight Foundation, The Carnegie Corporation, and the Pew Charitable Trusts.

CONTENTS

CHAPTER THREE

FEDERALISM: FORGING A NATION   73

CHAPTER FOUR

CIVIL LIBERTIES: PROTECTING INDIVIDUAL RIGHTS   109

CHAPTER FIVE

EQUAL RIGHTS: STRUGGLING TOWARD FAIRNESS   151

CHAPTER SIX

CHAPTER SEVEN

Contents

CHAPTER EIGHT

POLITICAL PARTIES, CANDIDATES, AND CAMPAIGNS: DEFINING THE VOTER'S CHOICE

CHAPTER NINE

INTEREST GROUPS: ORGANIZING FOR INFLUENCE   293

CHAPTER TEN

THE NEWS MEDIA: COMMUNICATING POLITICAL IMAGES

CHAPTER ELEVEN

CONGRESS: BALANCING NATIONAL GOALS AND LOCAL INTERESTS

CHAPTER TWELVE

THE PRESIDENCY: LEADING THE NATION   407

CHAPTER THIRTEEN

THE FEDERAL BUREAUCRACY: ADMINISTERING
THE GOVERNMENT   449

CHAPTER FOURTEEN

THE FEDERAL JUDICIAL SYSTEM: APPLYING THE LAW   487

CHAPTER FIFTEEN

CHAPTER SIXTEEN

CHAPTER SEVENTEEN

FOREIGN AND DEFENSE POLICY: PROTECTING THE AMERICAN WAY — 605

Recent years have brought changes barely imaginable not so long ago—the war on terrorism, economic globalization, and soaring budget deficits to name a few. In this text, I have sought to capture these and other dynamic features of American politics.

REACHING OUT TO THE STUDENT

This text is dedicated to helping students learn, including nurturing their capacity for critical thinking and civic participation. I have tried to write a text that expands students' horizons as well as one that informs their thinking, a text that they will want to read as opposed to one they are simply required to read. Four features of the text support this effort:

Narrative Style

This is a narrative-based text. Unlike a text that piles fact upon fact and thereby squeezes the life out of its subject, the narrative style aims to bring the subject to life. Politics doesn't have to be dull. Politics has all the elements of drama with the added feature of affecting the lives of real people.

The narrative style is an expository form that allows for the presentation of a lot of material but always as part of a larger point. The details buttress the narrative, highlighting the main ideas. Pedagogical studies have shown that the narrative style is a superior method for teaching a complex science such as political science. It promotes student learning by bringing the key points squarely into view.

Studies also show that students read attentively for a longer period of time when a text is narrative in form. In contrast with a text that compartmentalizes its material, a narrative text draws students into the material, piquing their interest. The strength of a narrative text, however, is not simply that it is more interesting to read. Its deep strength is that it disciplines the writer. Nothing is more discouraging to students than to encounter material of uncertain significance. The narrative form forces the writer to organize the materials so that every piece has a purpose. The fact that partisanship affects Supreme Court appointments is an important fact in its own right but gains significance when explained in the context of the openness of the American legal system, whereby political controversies often become also judicial ones.

Critical Thinking

A pedagogical goal of this text is to help students think critically. Critical thinking is the most important skill that a student can acquire from exposure to the social sciences. Students cannot learn to think critically by engaging in list making or rote memorization. Critical thinking is a cultivated skill that students develop by reflecting on what they have read, by resolving challenges to their assumptions, and by confronting difficult issues. To this end, I have structured the discussion in ways that encourage students to reflect as they read. In the first chapter, for example, I discuss the inexact meanings, conflicting implications, and unfinished promise of Americans' most cherished ideals, including liberty and equality. The discussion includes the "Chinese Exclusion," a grotesque and not widely known chapter in our history that can lead students to think about what it means to be an American.

Two of the book's boxed features have critical thinking as their purpose. Each chapter has a "How the United States Compares" box and a "States in the Nation" box. The United States is the world's oldest democracy but also one of its most distinctive. America's political processes and policies are different in many respects from those found elsewhere. The American states, too, differ from each other, despite being part of the same union. Students invariably gain a better understanding of their nation or state when they become aware of how it differs from others. When students discover, for example, that the United States has a higher child poverty rate than other Western democracies, they naturally want to know why this is the case.

Citizen Involvement

Of the academic disciplines, political science is most closely connected to a role that Americans share—that of citizen. Citizenship is a right and entails a duty. Young Americans recognize the responsibility of citizenship but do not always know how to act on it. Many of them also do not see what theorists like Aristotle and John Stuart Mill saw: that acts of citizenship enlarge the individual as well as the community.

The chapters of this text include two participation suggestions. The first is a "Participating" idea at the end of each chapter. The second is a more substantial "Get Involved" box found in several chapters. Citizenship is partly a state of mind, and the initial "Get Involved!"

boxes seek to foster this outlook. In Chapter 5, for example, the student is urged to "speak out," building on Tocqueville's observation that, if citizens fail to speak for themselves, government will presume to speak for them.

Politics as Discipline and Practice

I have attempted in this book to present American government through the analytical lens of political science but in a way that captures the vivid world of politics. I regularly reminded myself while writing the book that only a tiny percentage of introductory students are interested in an academic political science career. Most students take the course because they are required to do so or because they like politics. I have sought to write a book that will deepen political interest in the second type of student and kindle it in the first type. I had a model for this kind of book in mind: V.O. Key's absorbing *Politics, Parties, and Pressure Groups*, which I had read years earlier as an undergraduate. Professor Key was a consummate scholar with a deep love of politics who gently chided scholars whose interest in political science was confined to the "science" part.

My hope is that the readers of this text will learn, as I did as an undergraduate, to value what political science provides, and to relish what politics offers. The body of this book is shaped by the systematic knowledge that political science has developed. The spirit of this book is defined by the challenging nature of politics—the ongoing struggle of Americans to find agreeable ways to govern themselves.

POLITICAL CULTURE AND OTHER REGULARITIES IN AMERICAN POLITICS

Political science is a complex science in the sense that the objects of study are too intricate and fluid to be reduced to a few mathematical formulas. Indeed, politics includes such a wide range of human activity that political scientists have studied it through a variety of analytical tools: legal analysis, historical analysis, cultural analysis, political psychology, political sociology, rational choice, institutional analysis, organizational analysis, and so on.

Nonetheless, the systematic study of American politics has yielded an impressive body of knowledge. Political scientists have identified several tendencies that are a basis for a systematic understanding of the U.S. political system. These tendencies are introduced in the first chapter and developed in subsequent ones. If students can be expected to forget many of the smaller points made in this book, they may at least come away with an understanding of the regularities of American politics:

- Enduring ideals that are the basis of Americans' political identity and culture and that are a source of many of their beliefs, aspirations, and conflicts.
- Extreme fragmentation of governing authority that is based on an elaborate system of checks and balances that serves to protect against abuses of political power but also makes it difficult for political majorities to assert power when confronting an entrenched or intense political minority.
- Many competing groups, which are a result of the nation's great size, population diversity, and economic complexity and which exercise considerable influence—sometimes to society's benefit and sometimes to its detriment—on public policy.
- Strong emphasis on individual rights, which results in substantial benefits to the individual and places substantial restrictions on majorities.
- Preference for the marketplace as a means of allocating resources, which has the effect of placing many economic issues beyond the reach of political majorities.

All these regularities figure prominently in this book, but the first one on the list has a special place. As Tocqueville, Bryce, Hartz, Rossiter, and other observers have stressed, Americans' deep-rooted political beliefs are the basis of their unity. Americans are a diverse people with origins in many lands. Their nation was founded on a set of principles—including liberty, self-government, equality, and individualism—that became the people's unifying bond. When an American confronts an everyday situation and responds by saying "It's my right," he or she is responding in a way that is distinctly if not uniquely American. And when all such patterned behaviors are taken into account, they constitute a unique political perspective—an *American* political perspective.

Although this text's primary focus is U.S. political institutions and processes, they operate within the context of the nation's political culture. How might one explain the fact that the United States is the only affluent democracy without government-provided medical care for all? Or why Americans, though divided over the conflict in Iraq, universally believe the Iraqi people would be better off if they lived in a democracy? Or why issues such as stem-cell research and biological evolution are larger controversies in the United States than in other Western democracies? Or, as a final example, why lobbying groups have more political clout in the United States than virtually anywhere else?

No analysis of American institutions or processes can fully answer these questions. Americans' deep-rooted beliefs about politics must also be taken into account. Government-provided health care for all, as an example, is at odds with American individualism, which emphasizes self-reliance—a reason why Presidents Roosevelt and Johnson backed away from proposing such a program and why Presidents Truman and Clinton failed miserably when they did so. Americans govern themselves differently than do other people because they have different beliefs about the purposes of government. Indeed, each of the other regularities on the list above is a prominent feature of U.S. politics *because* they stem from cultural beliefs. The prominence in U.S. politics of the marketplace, of interest groups, of individual rights, and of checks and balances owes in significant part to Americans' deep-seated ideas about the proper way to govern.

This fact is one of the major lessons students can derive from a course on U.S. government because it is the link between today's politics and those of the past and the future. What is it—if not a desire for a fuller measure of liberty, equality, self-government, and self-realization—that connects today's citizens with other generations of Americans? This recognition can also lead students to seek a more active part in civic life. America's principles—and the political, economic, and social relationships they idealize—must be constantly renewed and enlarged through principled leadership and citizen action.

The significance of political culture in this text is apparent in the "Political Culture" boxes contained in some of the chapters. These boxes challenge students to think about the encompassing nature of America's political culture. The box in the opening chapter, for example, examines the connection between Americans' political ideals and their religious practices.

NEW TO THIS EDITION

The chapters have been thoroughly updated to include recent scholarship and the latest developments at home and abroad. The largest changes were occasioned by the 2006 midterm election and the Iraq conflict, which have altered American politics far more than anyone would have predicted two years ago, when the previous edition was published. The role of the Internet in American politics continues to feature ever more prominently in the text's instructional content. Each chapter includes one or more World Wide Web icons (identified by a computer mouse alongside which "WWW" appears). Each icon indicates the presence on the text's website of material (self-tests, simulations, and graphics) that is relevant to the topic being discussed.

The chapters also include Historical Background icons that signal content on key historical moments. "Learning from history" contributes to student's understanding of contemporary politics and to their development as citizens. The Cold War was ending as today's undergraduates were being born but its impact on American politics did not expire with the death of the Soviet Union. Students also learn when asked to think more deeply about things they have experienced. Every student is familiar with the war on terrorism, but not all of them have thought about its impact on civil liberties, foreign relations, or the constitutional balance between Congress and the presidency.

This edition includes several new box features. The "Get Involved!" and "Political Culture" boxes mentioned earlier are new. So, too, are the "Media and Politics" boxes. The extraordinary changes in how we get our news are addressed in these boxes. Jon Stewart's "The Daily Show" is examined in one of these boxes; Christian broadcasting is discussed in another. A box feature entitled "Leaders" is also new. Each chapter has one or more of these boxes, which highlight the contributions of exemplary Americans. The text's other box features—"How the United States Compares" and "States in the Nation"—are holdovers from the previous edition.

Finally, in response to suggestions from instructors who have found many of today's students to be less than voracious readers, I have shortened this edition of the text, not by cutting content but by tightening the discussion. I did a line-by-line edit of the entire book, looking to take out words, phrases, examples, or sentences that could be excised without loss of meaning. I also rewrote and tightened whole sections of several chapters. In doing this, I came to understand the truth in Thomas Jefferson's apology to John Adams for writing him a lengthy letter. Wrote Jefferson: "I didn't have time to write a short letter, so I wrote a long one instead." Streamlining takes more time, but the result is a clearer, more vigorous rendition.

Your Suggestions are Invited

We the People has been in use in college classrooms for more than a decade. During that time, the text (including its full-length version, *The American Democracy*) has been adopted at more than eight hundred colleges and universities. I am extremely grateful to all who have used it. I am particularly indebted to the many instructors and students over the years who have sent me recommendations or corrections. You can contact me at the John F. Kennedy School, Harvard University, Cambridge, MA 02138, or by e-mail: thomas_patterson@harvard.edu.

Thomas E. Patterson

Supplements Package

This text is accompanied by supplementary materials. Please contact your local McGraw-Hill representative or McGraw-Hill Customer Service (800-338-3987) for details concerning policies, prices, and availability, as some restrictions may apply.

For Students and Instructors

Online Learning Center

Visit our website at www.mhhe.com/pattersonwtp7.

This website contains separate instructor and student areas. The instructor area contains the instructor's manual, test bank, PowerPoints, and CPS questions, while the student area hosts a wealth of materials including information on career opportunities, the Vanishing Voter Project, presidential timelines and links, and debate topics. It also includes study materials such as additional Internet resources, chapter summaries, practice tests, essay quizzes, and flashcards. All chapter-by-chapter material has been updated for the new edition.

PoliCentral Introducing **PoliCentral!** McGraw-Hill is excited to bring you www.mhhe.com/policentral, a new dynamic, interactive site filled with simulations, debate tools, participation activities, and video, audio, and speech activities.

For Instructors

Instructor's Manual/Test Bank

Available online, the instructor's manual includes the following for each chapter: learning objectives, focus points and main points, a discussion of the readings, supplemental lectures, alternative lecture topics and class discussion topics. The test bank consists of multiple-choice questions and suggested essay topics with answers given alongside the questions and page references provided. Also available is a computerized version of the test bank, PowerPoint presentations and CPS questions.

McGraw-Hill American Government Lecture Launchers

Lecture Launches provide approximately two to three minutes of chapters-specific video to help instructors "launch" their lecture. Round-table discussions, famous speeches, and everyday stories are followed by two "Pause and Think" questions per clip aimed at the heart of new debate. These invite students to consider who sets policy and how they can get involved. In addition to reinforcing the basics, these short video clips focus on civic involvement and consider the Framers of the Constitution. Available in VHS and DVD, with selected clips also available on PoliCentral.com.

PRIMIS ONLINE

Instructors can use this text as a whole, or they can select specific chapters and customize the text to suit their specific classroom needs. The customized text can be created as a hardcopy or as an e-book. Also available in this format are custom chapters on **"California Government"** and **"Texas Government."**

DISTANCE LEARNING

A one-semester American government telecourse using material from *We the People* is available through Intelecom (www.intelecom.org). A correlated study guide is available from McGraw-Hill. Contact your local McGraw-Hill representative for more information.

For Students

STUDY GUIDE

Each chapter includes the following: learning objectives, analytical-thinking exercises, and test review questions—approximately ten true-false, fifteen multiple-choice, and five essay topics. The answers are provided at the end of each chapter.

2006 MIDTERM ELECTION UPDATE
by Richard Semiatin of American University

This supplement details the 2006 election. Richard Semiatin analyzes the context of the election and the role of the Bush administration. This supplement also contains information on major election issues, on the media campaign, on money and fund-raising, on voter participation, and finally on the results and implications of the election.

ACKNOWLEDGMENTS

For this new, seventh edition of *We the People*, I received an enormous amount of sound advice. Reviewers are the lifeblood of a text, and I was fortunate to have the assistance of a skilled group of scholars. I am deeply grateful to each and all of them for their help:

Ole J. Forsberg, *The University of Tennessee*
Adrienne M. Holloway, *North Harris Montgomery Community College*
Murel M. Jones, *Virginia State University*
Richard Kiefer, *Waubonsee Community College*
John Linantud, *University of Houston, Downtown*
Timothy Martinez, *Black Hills State University*
Lauri McNown, *University of Colorado, Boulder*
Mark J. O'Gorman, *Maryville College*
Forest W. Redding, Jr., *Connors State College*
Gregory Schaller, *Villanova University*
Stephen K. Shaw, *Northwest Nazarene University*
Patrick Smith, *Northern Virginia Community College*
Kevin Spiker, *Ohio University*
Thomas C. Sutton, *Baldwin-Wallace College*
Ursula C. Tafe, *University of Massachusetts, Boston*
Paul Weizer, *Fitchburg State College*

I also want to thank those at McGraw-Hill who contributed to the seventh edition. Monica Eckman, my editor, always at the top of her game, topped even that this time. If this edition is the best yet, Monica deserves the credit. Her professional skill and inspired ideas over the past few editions have exceeded what any author could reasonably expect. Nancy Crochiere, Senior Development Editor, contributed throughout the editing process, from the first meeting onward, offering keen suggestions on content and timing. Jessica Badiner provided able assistance throughout.

I would also like to thank my project manager Christina Gimlin, who brought this book to a sound conclusion. Mary Roybal was, once again, a copyeditor with a deft and seamless touch. Toni Michaels did the photo research, providing a marvelous set of choices. I would also like to thank

Randy Hurst, production supervisor; Preston Thomas, designer; and Ron Nelms, media project manager.

At Harvard, I had the diligent and cheerful support of my extraordinary faculty assistant, Kate Tighe, who helped update the text and copied endless drafts of it. Alex Patterson was my photo advisor; his keen eye is behind the final photo selections in this edition. I owe them both a deep thanks.

Thomas Patterson

CHAPTER 1

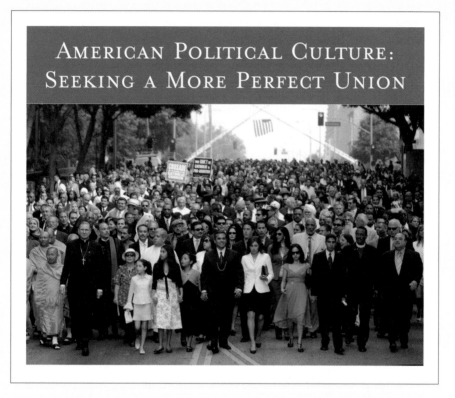

AMERICAN POLITICAL CULTURE:
SEEKING A MORE PERFECT UNION

❝One hears people say that it is inherent in the habits and nature of
democracies to change feelings and thoughts at every moment. . . . But
I have never seen anything like that happening in the great democracy on
the other side of the ocean. What struck me most in the United States
was the difficulty experienced in getting an idea, once conceived, out of
the head of the majority.❞

ALEXIS DE TOCQUEVILLE[1]

At 8:47 A.M. on September 11, 2001, a hijacked American Airlines passenger jet slammed into one of the twin towers of New York City's World
Trade Center. Twenty minutes later, a second hijacked passenger jet hit
the other tower. A third hijacked jet then plowed into the Pentagon building in Washington, D.C. Within two hours, the World Trade Center
towers collapsed, killing all still inside, including police and firefighters
who had rushed bravely into the buildings to help in the evacuation.
Three thousand Americans were murdered that September morning,
the highest death toll ever from an attack on American soil by a foreign

adversary. The toll would have been even higher if not for the bravery of passengers aboard United Airlines flight 93, who fought with its hijackers, causing the plane—which was aimed toward Washington, D.C.—to crash in a barren Pennsylvania field.

That evening, a somber George W. Bush addressed the nation. Urging Americans to stay calm and resolute, President Bush said: "America was targeted for an attack because we're the brightest beacon for freedom and opportunity in the world." Sprinkled throughout his speech were allusions to time-honored American ideals: liberty, the will of the people, justice, and the rule of law. "No one will keep that light from shining," said Bush.

The ideals that guided Bush's speech would have been familiar to any generation of Americans. These ideals have been invoked when Americans have gone to war, declared peace, celebrated national holidays, launched major policy initiatives, and asserted new rights.[2] The ideals contained in Bush's speech were the same ones that had punctuated the speeches of George Washington and Abraham Lincoln, Susan B. Anthony and Franklin D. Roosevelt, Dr. Martin Luther King Jr. and Ronald Reagan.

The ideals were also there at the nation's beginning, when they were put into words in the Declaration of Independence and the Constitution. Of course, the practical meaning of these words has changed greatly during the more than two centuries the United States has been a sovereign nation. When the writers of the Constitution began the document with the words "We the People," they did not have all Americans equally in mind. Black slaves, women, and men without property did not have the same rights as propertied white men.

Nevertheless, America's ideals have been remarkably enduring. Throughout their history, Americans have embraced the same set of core values. They have quarreled over the meaning and practice of these ideals, but they have never seriously questioned the principles themselves. As historian Clinton Rossiter concluded, "There has been in a doctrinal sense, only one America."[3]

This book is about contemporary American politics, not U.S. history or culture. Yet American politics today cannot be understood apart from the nation's heritage. Government does not begin anew with each generation; it builds on the past. In the case of the United States, the most significant link between past and present lies in the nation's founding ideals. The Frenchman Alexis de Tocqueville was among the first to see that the main tendencies of American politics cannot be explained without taking into account the country's core beliefs. "Habits of the heart" was Tocqueville's description of Americans' ideals.[4]

This chapter briefly examines the principles that have helped shape American politics since the country's earliest years. The chapter also explains basic concepts—such as power, pluralism, and constitutionalism—that are important in the study of American politics. The main points made in this chapter are these:

★ *The American political culture centers on a set of core ideals—liberty, equality, self-government, individualism, diversity, and unity—that serve as the people's common bond.* These mythic principles have a substantial influence on what Americans will regard as reasonable and acceptable and on what they will try to achieve.

★ *Politics is the process that determines whose values will prevail in society.* The play of politics in the United States takes place in the context of democratic procedures, constitutionalism, and capitalism and involves elements of majority, pluralist, bureaucratic, and elitist rule.

★ *Politics in the United States is characterized by a number of major patterns, including a highly fragmented governing system, a high degree of pluralism, an extraordinary emphasis on individual rights, and a pronounced separation of the political and economic spheres.*

POLITICAL CULTURE: THE CORE PRINCIPLES OF AMERICAN GOVERNMENT

The people of every nation have a few great ideals that characterize their political life, but, as James Bryce observed, Americans are a special case.[5] Their ideals are the basis of their national identity. Other people take their identity from the common ancestry that led them gradually to gather under one flag. Thus, long before there was a France or a Japan, there were French and Japanese people, each a kinship group united through blood. Even today, it is kinship that links them. There is no way to become fully Japanese except to be born of Japanese parents. Not so for Americans. They are a multitude of people from different lands—England, Germany, Ireland, Africa, Italy, Poland, Mexico, and China, to name just a few (see Figure 1–1). Americans are linked not by blood but by allegiance to a set of commonly held ideals such as liberty and equality.

These ideals are habits of mind, a customary way of thinking about the world. They help Americans live and work together harmoniously. They are part of what social scientists call **political culture,** a term that refers to the characteristic and deep-seated beliefs of a particular people about government and politics.[6]

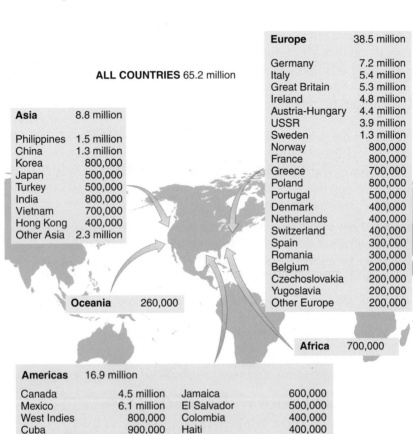

Europe	38.5 million
Germany	7.2 million
Italy	5.4 million
Great Britain	5.3 million
Ireland	4.8 million
Austria-Hungary	4.4 million
USSR	3.9 million
Sweden	1.3 million
Norway	800,000
France	800,000
Greece	700,000
Poland	800,000
Portugal	500,000
Denmark	400,000
Netherlands	400,000
Switzerland	400,000
Spain	300,000
Romania	300,000
Belgium	200,000
Czechoslovakia	200,000
Yugoslavia	200,000
Other Europe	200,000

ALL COUNTRIES 65.2 million

Asia	8.8 million
Philippines	1.5 million
China	1.3 million
Korea	800,000
Japan	500,000
Turkey	500,000
India	800,000
Vietnam	700,000
Hong Kong	400,000
Other Asia	2.3 million

Oceania	260,000

Africa	700,000

Americas	16.9 million		
Canada	4.5 million	Jamaica	600,000
Mexico	6.1 million	El Salvador	500,000
West Indies	800,000	Colombia	400,000
Cuba	900,000	Haiti	400,000
Dominican Republic	800,000	Other Americas	1.9 million

FIGURE 1-1   TOTAL IMMIGRATION TO THE UNITED STATES, 1820–2000, BY CONTINENT AND COUNTRY OF ORIGIN

Source: U.S. Immigration and Naturalization Service.

America's core ideals are rooted in the European heritage of the first white settlers. They arrived during the Enlightenment period, when people were awakening to the idea of human progress. These settlers were not, as is sometimes claimed, seeking to create in America an entirely new way of life. Their ideas about society were shaped by the European culture they had experienced. But the settlers also did not seek to reproduce in America exactly what they had known in Europe. Rather, they wanted to build on that which they admired about the Old World and leave behind that which they disliked.[7] Many of them, for example, were trying to escape religious persecution and came to America for the chance to worship freely.

The settlers' vision of society changed as they discovered the possibilities America offered. The opportunities provided by the New World's vast open lands and its great distance from European rulers gave ordinary people a level of personal freedom unthinkable in the Old World. There was in America no titled nobility that held nearly all the power and nearly all the wealth. Ordinary Americans acquired land and acted independently. In the end, the colonists revolted against their European masters, engaging in the first successful large-scale rebellion in human history driven largely by a vision of a wholly different society. The United States was a nation founded abruptly in 1776 on a set of principles proclaimed in the Declaration of Independence:[8]

> We hold these truths to be self-evident, that all men are created equal; that they are endowed by their Creator with certain unalienable rights; that among these, are life, liberty, and the pursuit of happiness. That, to secure these rights, governments are instituted among men, deriving their just powers from the consent of the governed; that, whenever any form of government becomes destructive of these ends, it is the right of the people to alter or to abolish it, and to institute a new government, laying its foundation on such principles, and organizing its powers in such form, as to them shall seem most likely to effect their safety and happiness.

Subsequent generations of Americans have embraced these principles while discovering that they require constant renewal and rethinking. The principles themselves are timeless. Their meaning in practice is not. The Great Depression of the 1930s, for example, forced Americans to reconsider the everyday realities of personal liberty. One-fourth of the labor force lost their jobs, and another one-fourth could not find full-time employment. Homes were lost to creditors, and food was scarce. It became harder for Americans to think of personal freedom as simply a matter of freedom *from* government, and they turned *to* government for help in dealing with economic hardship. In his 1941 State of the Union Address, President Franklin D. Roosevelt spoke to people's hopes when he declared that "freedom from want" was among Americans' fundamental liberties.

The September 11, 2001, terrorist attacks on U.S. soil challenged Americans once again to rethink the practice of liberty. How much leeway should they give their government in its war on terrorism? How much personal freedom should they surrender to ensure that the nation is never again attacked on such a massive scale? Should Americans allow their government to search citizens' telephone records in the hope of identifying those individuals who might seek to harm the country? Should Americans allow their government to search citizens' bank accounts and travel records in the hope of finding indicators of suspicious behavior?

U.S. politics is remarkable for its historical continuity, which is celebrated here in a ceremony at the Capitol in Washington, D.C.

Questions like these have shaped the American governing experience since the nation's beginning. *A defining characteristic of the U.S. political system is Americans' pursuit of the political ideals on which the nation was founded and that continue to serve as Americans' common bond.*

AMERICA'S CORE VALUES: LIBERTY, EQUALITY, AND SELF-GOVERNMENT

An understanding of America's ideals begins with the recognition that the individual, rather than the government, is the cornerstone of society. Government exists to serve the people. No clearer statement of this principle exists than the reference in the Declaration of Independence to "unalienable rights"—freedoms that belong to each and every person and that cannot lawfully be denied by government.

Liberty, equality, and self-government are widely regarded as America's core political ideals (see Table 1–1). **Liberty** is the principle that individuals should be free to act and think as they choose, provided they do not infringe unreasonably on the freedom and well-being of others. The United States, as historian Louis Hartz said, was "born free."[9] The Declaration of Independence rings with the proclamation that people are entitled

| TABLE 1-1 | AMERICA'S CORE POLITICAL IDEALS |

The United States was founded on a set of political ideals that have served as its people's common bond. Foremost among these ideals are liberty, equality, and self-government.

Ideal	Description	Origin (in part)
Liberty	The principle that individuals should be free to act and think as they choose, provided they do not infringe unreasonably on the rights and freedoms of others.	Colonial America's vast open lands offered a degree of liberty unattainable in Europe; the American Revolution was fought over liberty.
Equality	The notion that all individuals are equal in their moral worth, in their treatment under the law, and in their political voice.	Colonial America's openness made Europe's aristocratic system unenforceable; greater personal opportunity in America fostered a sense of social equality.
Self-government	The principle that the people are the ultimate source and proper beneficiary of governing authority and must have a voice in how they are governed.	Colonial America had a degree of self-government; Americans' sense of personal freedom and equality led them to want self-determination in public affairs as well.

to "Life, Liberty and the Pursuit of Happiness." The preamble to the Constitution declares that the U.S. government was founded to secure "the Blessings of Liberty to ourselves and our Posterity." The Statue of Liberty stands in New York harbor as the symbol of the American people, and the "Star-Spangled Banner" rings out with the words "land of the free."

For early Americans, liberty was nearly a birthright. Ordinary people did not have to accept the European system of absolute government and aristocratic privilege when greater personal liberty was as close as the next area of unsettled land. Not surprisingly, they were determined, when forming their own government, to protect personal liberty. The First Amendment to the Constitution prohibits laws that would infringe on individual freedom: "Congress shall make no law respecting the establishment of religion, or prohibiting the free exercise thereof; or abridging the freedom of speech, or of the press; or the right of the people to peaceably assemble, and to petition the Government for a redress of grievances."

Americans' demand for liberty has persisted throughout the country's history. Observers from Tocqueville onward have seen fit to note that liberty in America, as in no other country, is ingrained in people's thinking. Americans' chief concern, wrote Tocqueville, "is to remain their own masters."

A second American political ideal is **equality**—the notion that all individuals are equal in their moral worth and so are entitled to equal treatment under the law. America provided its white settlers a new level of equality. Europe's rigid aristocratic system based on land ownership was unenforceable in frontier America. Almost any free citizen who wanted to own land could obtain it. It was this natural sense of equality that Thomas Jefferson expressed so forcefully in the Declaration of Independence: "We hold these truths to be self-evident, that all men are created equal."

Equality, however, has always been a less clearly defined concept than liberty. Even Jefferson professed not to know its exact meaning. A slave owner, Jefferson distinguished between free citizens, who were entitled to equal rights, and slaves, who were not. After slavery was abolished, Americans continued to argue over the meaning of equality, and the debate continues today. Does equality require that wealth and opportunity be widely shared? Or does it merely require that artificial barriers to advancement be removed? Despite differing opinions about such questions, an insistence on equality is a distinctive feature of the American experience. Americans, said Bryce, reject "the very notion" that some people might be "better" than others merely because of birth or position.[10] And perhaps no ideal has so inspired Americans to political action as has their desire for fuller equality. The abolition and suffrage movements were rooted in this ideal. The more recent civil rights movements of black Americans, women, Hispanics, gays, and other groups also are testaments to the power of the ideal of equality.

Self-government, America's third great political ideal, is the principle that people are the ultimate source of governing authority and must have a voice in how they are governed. "Governments," the Declaration of Independence proclaims, "deriv[e] their just powers from the consent of the governed." In his Gettysburg address, Lincoln extolled a government "of the people, by the people, for the people."

Americans' belief in self-government originated in colonial America. The Old World was an ocean away, and European governments had no option but to allow the American colonies a degree of self-determination. Out of this experience came the dream of a self-governing nation. It was

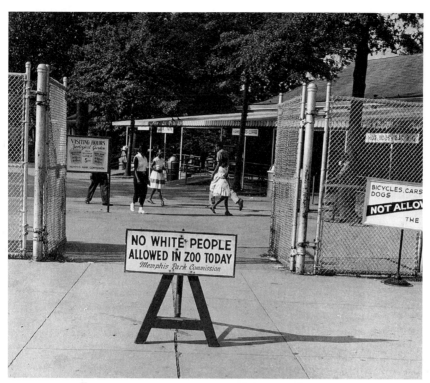

During the era of racial segregation in the South, this sign at the entrance to the Memphis public zoo meant that it was Tuesday—the only day black people were allowed to go to the zoo. On the other six days of the week, the sign excluded black people from entering. The Memphis zoo was typical of life in the South during the so-called Jim Crow era that followed the Civil War. Such policies were pursued despite Americans' professed commitment to equality and were upheld by federal courts despite prohibitions against discrimination set forth in the U.S. Constitution.

an ideal that captured the imagination even of those in the lower ranks of society. Ordinary people willingly risked their lives in the cause of self-government during the American Revolution. The ensuing federal and state constitutions were based on the idea that government is properly founded on the will of the people. "We the People" is the opening phrase of the Constitution of the United States.

At no time in the nation's history has national leadership been conferred except through the vote. At various times and places elsewhere in the world, governing power has been seized by brute force. The United States has an unbroken history of free elections as the legitimate means of acquiring governmental power. Etched in a corridor of the nation's Capitol building are the words Alexander Hamilton spoke when asked about the foundation of the nation's government: "Here, sir, the people govern."

Although liberty, equality, and self-government are the core American political ideals, the American Creed—the set of core values that define the nation's political culture—also includes other principles. **Individualism** is a commitment to personal initiative, self-sufficiency, and material accumulation. It is related to the idea of liberty, which makes the individual the foundation of society, and is buttressed by the idea of equality, which holds that everyone should be given a fair chance to succeed. Individualism stems from the belief that people who are free to pursue their own path and are not unfairly burdened can attain their fullest potential. Individualism has roots in the country's origins as a wilderness society. The early Americans developed a pride in their "rugged individualism," and from this experience grew the idea that people ought to try to make it on their own.

Unity and diversity are also part of the American creed. **Unity** is the principle that Americans are one people and form an indivisible union. **Diversity** holds that individual and group differences should be respected and that these differences are themselves a source of strength. These two principles, which acknowledge at once both the differences and the oneness that are part of the American experience, are expressed in the phrase *E pluribus unum* ("One out of many").

The Power of Ideals

Ideals serve to define the boundaries of action. They do not determine exactly what people will do, but they affect what people will regard as reasonable and desirable. Why, for example, does the United States spend relatively less money on government programs for the poor than do other fully industrialized democracies, including Germany, France, Switzerland, the Netherlands, Spain, Britain, Sweden, Italy, and Japan? Are Americans so much better off than these other people that they have less need for welfare programs? The answer is no. Of all these countries, the United States has the most poverty, in both relative and absolute terms. The United States spends less on social welfare chiefly because of its cultural emphasis on liberty and individualism. Americans have resisted giving government a larger social welfare role because of their deep-seated belief in self-reliance and limited government (see "How the United States Compares").

Of course, social welfare policy is not simply an issue of cultural differences. The welfare issue, like other issues, is part of the rough-and-tumble of everyday politics. There are always powerful interests aligned on both sides of important issues. In the United States, the Republican party, business groups, antitax groups, and others have resisted the expansion of the government's social welfare role, while the Democratic party, unions, minority groups, and others have from time to time argued for

HOW THE UNITED STATES COMPARES

Personal Freedom and Self-Reliance

The United States was labeled "the country of individualism *par excellence*" by William Watts and Lloyd Free in their book *State of the Nation*. They were referring to the emphasis Americans place on self-reliance and personal freedom.

In European democracies, such views also prevail but are moderated by a greater acceptance of welfare programs. The difference between the American and European cultures reflects their differing political traditions. America was an open country ruled by a foreign power, and its revolution was fought largely over the issue of personal liberty. In European revolutions, equality was also at issue, because wealth was held by hereditary aristocracies. Europeans' concern with equality was gradually translated into a willingness to use government as a means of redistributing wealth. An example is government-paid medical care for all citizens.

Even today, Americans are more likely than Europeans (and Canadians as well) to rank personal freedom ahead of economic security, as indicated by a multination survey released in 2004 by the Pew Research Center for the People and the Press. Respondents were asked, "What's more important in society today—that everyone be free to pursue their life's goals without interference from government, or that government play an active role in society so as to guarantee that nobody is in need?" Following are the percentages of respondents in each country who said "free to pursue their life's goals" was the higher priority:

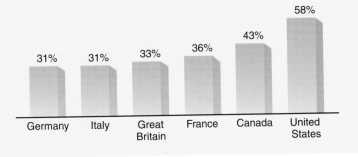

greater intervention. Nevertheless, Americans' belief in individualism, which has no exact equivalent in European society, has played a defining role in shaping U.S. welfare policy.

The distinctiveness of this cultural belief is clear from a recent survey that asked respondents in different countries whether it is more important "that everyone be free to pursue their life's goals without interference from government" or "that government play an active role in society so as to guarantee that nobody is in need." Americans were much less likely than Europeans to say that it is more important to ensure that "nobody is in need."[11] Americans do not necessarily have less sympathy for the poor; rather, they place more emphasis on personal responsibility than do Europeans.[12]

The importance of individualism to American society also is evident in the emphasis on equal opportunity. If individuals are to be entrusted with their own welfare, they must be given a fair chance to succeed on their own. Nowhere is this philosophy more evident than in the country's elaborate system of higher education, which includes nearly three thousand two-year and four-year institutions and is designed to accommodate nearly every individual who wants to pursue a college education. About a fourth of the nation's adult citizens have a college degree, the world's highest rate. Even the American state that has the lowest proportion (see "States in the Nation")—West Virginia, where one in every six adults has a degree—has a higher percentage of college graduates than does the typical European country.

Of course, the idea that success is within equal reach of all Americans who strive for it is far from accurate. Young people who grow up in abject poverty and without adequate guidance know all too well the limits on opportunity. In some inner-city areas, teenage boys are more likely to spend time in jail than to spend time in college.

The Limits of Ideals

Cultural beliefs originate in a country's political and social practices, but they are not perfect representatives of these practices. They are mythic ideas—symbolic positions taken by a people to justify and give meaning to their way of life.[13] Myths contain elements of truth, but they are not the full truth.

High ideals do not come with a guarantee that a people will live up to them. The clearest proof of this failing in the American case is the human tragedy that began nearly four centuries ago and continues today. In 1619 the first black slaves were brought in chains to America. Slavery lasted 250 years. Slaves in the field worked from dawn to dark (from "can see, 'til can't"), in both the heat of summer and the cold of winter. The Civil War brought an end to slavery but not to racial oppression. Slavery was followed by the

Historical
Background

A College Education

Reflecting their cultural beliefs of individualism and equality, Americans have developed the world's most extensive college system. Every state has at least eight colleges within its boundaries. No European democracy has as many colleges as either California (322) or New York (320). The extensive U.S. college system has enabled large numbers of Americans to earn a college degree. About one in four American adults is a college graduate. Even the states that rank low on this indicator have a higher percentage of college graduates than do most European countries.

Q: Why do the northeastern and western coastal states have a higher percentage of adults with college degrees?

A: The northeastern and western coastal states are more affluent and urbanized than most states. Thus, young people in these states can better afford the costs of college and are more likely to need a college degree for the work they intend to pursue.

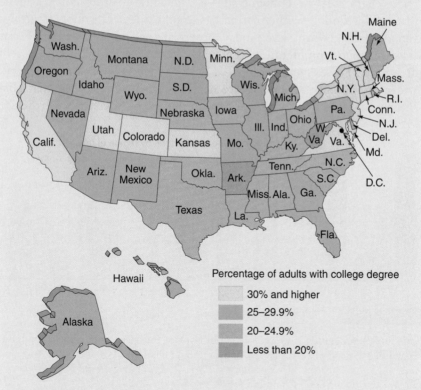

Percentage of adults with college degree

- 30% and higher
- 25–29.9%
- 20–24.9%
- Less than 20%

Source: U.S. Bureau of the Census, 2006. Based on percentage of adults twenty-five years of age or older with a college degree.

Jim Crow era of legal segregation: black people in the South were forbidden by law to use the same schools, hospitals, restaurants, and restrooms as white people. Those who spoke out against this system were subjected to beatings, firebombings, castrations, rapes, and worse—hundreds of African Americans were lynched by white vigilantes in the early 1900s. Today African Americans have equal rights under the law, but in fact they are far from equal. Compared with whites, blacks are twice as likely to live in poverty, twice as likely to be unable to find a job, and twice as likely to die in infancy.[14] There have always been at least two Americas, one for whites and one for blacks.

Despite the lofty claim that "all men are created equal," equality has never been an American birthright. In 1882, Congress suspended Chinese immigration on the assumption that the Chinese were an inferior people. Calvin Coolidge in 1923 asked Congress for a permanent ban on Chinese immigration, saying that people "who do not want to be partakers of the American spirit ought not to settle in America."[15] Not until 1965 was discrimination against the Chinese and other Asians (and Hispanics as well) effectively eliminated from U.S. immigration laws (Figure 1–2).

The claim that the United States is a gigantic melting pot is a blend of fact and fiction. No other nation has so fully opened its doors to groups from around the world. Even today, Americans are more likely than Europeans to support immigration. They also have a better opinion of recent immigrants. For example, compared with French people's view of North African immigrants, Americans are nearly twice as likely to say that Hispanic immigrants are having a positive influence on society. Nevertheless,

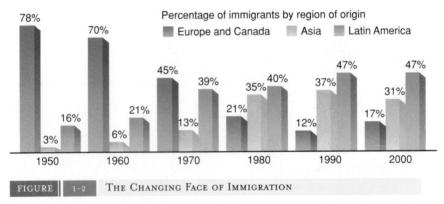

FIGURE 1-2   THE CHANGING FACE OF IMMIGRATION

Until 1965, immigration laws were biased in favor of European immigrants. The laws enacted in 1965 increased the proportion of immigrants from Asia and Latin America. *Source: U.S. Immigration and Naturalization Service, 2006. Percentages are totals for each decade; e.g., the 2000 figures are for the period 1991–2000.*

established groups in America have never fully embraced new arrivals. When Irish, Italian, and Eastern European immigrants reached this country's shores in large numbers in the nineteenth and early twentieth centuries, they encountered nativist elements that assailed their customs and religions. Many Americans, including some members of Congress, wanted Catholics and Jews completely barred from entry. During the last third of the twentieth century, Asian and Hispanic immigrants encountered stiff opposition in some parts of the country. After the September 11, 2001, terrorist attacks on the World Trade Center and the Pentagon, polls indicated that most Americans wanted Middle East immigration sharply reduced or stopped entirely.

Resistance to immigrant groups is not among the stories that Americans like to tell about themselves.[16] Such lapses of historical memory can be found among all peoples, but the tendency to rewrite history is perhaps exaggerated in the American case because Americans' beliefs are so idealistic (see Table 1–2). How could a nation that upholds the ideal of human equality have barred the Chinese, enslaved the blacks, betrayed the Indians, and subordinated women?

One reason why America's ideals do not match reality is that they are general principles, not fixed rules of conduct. They derive from somewhat different experiences and philosophical traditions, and there are points at which they conflict. Equality, for instance, emphasizes fairness and the opportunity for all to partake of society's benefits, whereas liberty emphasizes personal freedom and threats posed to it by political power. Conflict between these ideals is inevitable. Take the issue of affirmative action. Proponents say that only through aggressive affirmative action programs will women and minorities receive the equal treatment in the job market to which they are entitled. Opponents say that aggressive affirmative action infringes unreasonably on the liberty of the employer and the initiative of the work force. Each group can say that it has America's ideals on its side, and no resort to logic can persuade either side that the opposing viewpoint should prevail.

Americans' ideals, despite their inexact meanings, conflicting implications, and unfulfilled promise, have had a strong impact on Americans' politics. If racial, gender, ethnic, and other forms of intolerance constitute the sorriest chapter in the nation's history, the centuries-old struggle of Americans to create a more equal society is among the finest chapters. Few nations have battled so relentlessly against the insidious discrimination that stems from superficial human differences such as the color of one's skin. High ideals are more than mere abstractions. They are a source of human aspiration and, ultimately, of political and social change.

| TABLE | 1-2 | TELLING THE AMERICAN STORY TO CHILDREN |

Americans' values and myths are reflected in their preferences in teaching children about the nation's history. The stories that adults regard as least important are those that reflect unfavorably on the country's idealized image.

In teaching the American story to children, how important is the following theme?	Essential/ Very important	Somewhat important	Somewhat unimportant/ Very unimportant/ Leave it out of the story
With hard work and perseverance, anyone can succeed in America.	83%	14%	4%
Our founders limited the power of government so government would not intrude too much into the lives of its citizens.	74	19	8
America is the world's greatest melting pot in which people from different countries are united into one nation.	73	21	5
America's contribution is one of expanding freedom for more and more people.	71	22	6
Our nation betrayed its founding principles by cruel mistreatment of blacks and American Indians.	59	24	17
Our founders were part of a male-dominated culture that gave important roles to men while keeping women in the background.	38	28	35

Source: Used by permission of the Survey of American Political Culture, James Davison Hunter and Carol Bowman, directors, Institute for Advanced Studies in Culture, University of Virginia.

POLITICS: THE RESOLUTION OF CONFLICT

Cultural ideals help shape what people expect from politics and inspire people to work together for a collective purpose. Politics, however, is more than shared ideals and common efforts. Politics is also a struggle for power and advantage. Commenting on the competitive nature of politics, political scientist Harold Lasswell described it as the struggle over "who gets what, when, and how."[17] **Politics is the process through which a society settles its conflicts.**

Political conflict has two primary sources. One is *scarcity*. Even the richest societies do not have enough wealth to satisfy everyone's desires. Conflict over the distribution of resources is the predictable result. Consider, for example, the issue of school quality. Affluent suburban districts have better schools than do poor inner-city districts. Lacking a strong local tax base, inner-city residents have pressured state governments to provide equal funding to all schools. Residents of suburban communities have fought this arrangement, fearing that it would increase their taxes and weaken their local schools.

Differences in values are the other main source of political conflict. People see issues differently as a result of differences in their beliefs, experiences, and interests. Abortion is an issue of freedom of choice for some and an issue of murder for others. People bring to politics a wide range of conflicting standards—about abortion, the environment, crime and punishment, the poor, the economy, and countless other issues.

The Social Contract

Politics operates by a set of "rules" that determine whose voice will prevail when conflict arises over resources and values. Without such rules, people would be constantly at each other's throats, and society would dissolve into chaos and lawlessness.

For a long period of world history, the rules of politics were stacked against ordinary people. They had no say in their governing and were at the mercy of those in authority. Government was controlled by absolute monarchs, whose word was law. Some of these rulers were tyrants, and many taxed their subjects heavily to raise large armies and erect great palaces.

Roughly four centuries ago, ideas about the proper form of government began to change. Ironically, one of the theorists who contributed to this development was an advocate of absolute rule. In *Leviathan* (published in 1651), the English philosopher Thomas Hobbes argued that government rests on a **social contract** in which ordinary people surrender the freedom they would have in a state of nature in return for the protection that a sovereign ruler can provide. People give up their freedom, Hobbes said, because life in its natural state is "nasty, brutish, and short"—the weak are constantly preyed upon by the strong. Thus, people seek the protection of a strong ruler whom they must obey, even if a particular ruler turns out to be cruel or capricious. The alternative—an endless "war of all against all"—is worse.

Forty years later, the English philosopher John Locke used Hobbes's idea of a social contract to argue *against* absolutism. In his *Second Treatise on Civil Government* (1690), Locke claimed that all individuals have certain natural (or inalienable) rights, including those of life, liberty, and property. Such rights, Locke wrote, belonged to people in their natural state before government was created. When people come together in order to have the protection that only organized government can provide, they retain these rights. People enter into the social contract—they agree to be governed—in order to safeguard their rights. Accordingly, government is obliged to provide this protection. If it fails to do so, Locke argued, the people can rightfully rebel against it and create a new government.

Three-quarters of a century later, the French philosopher Jean Jacques Rousseau extended the idea of a social contract to include popular rule. Like Locke, Rousseau despised absolute government. "Man was born free, but everywhere he is in chains" are the opening words of Rousseau's *Social Contract* (1762). Rousseau claimed that people in their natural state are innocent and happy. Accordingly, the only legitimate government is one that governs in their interest and with their consent. The people, in Rousseau's view, were sovereign. Government was not the sovereign authority but merely the instrument for carrying out the people's laws. Rousseau worried, however, that the people would act selfishly, and he proposed a limit on popular sovereignty. It would be legitimate only if people acted in the common interest—what Rousseau called "the general will."

These ideas—that people have individual rights and should have a say in their government—sparked the American Revolution of 1776. The basic principle of contract theory—that the power of leaders is limited by a set of rules—was embodied in the Constitution of the United States, written in 1787.

The Rules of American Politics

The major rules of American politics—democracy, constitutionalism, and capitalism—establish a political process that is intended to promote self-government, defend individual rights, and protect property.

Democracy   Democracy is a set of rules intended to give ordinary people a significant voice in government. The word *democracy* comes from the Greek words *demos*, meaning "the people," and *kratis*, meaning "to rule." In simple terms, **democracy** is a form of government in which the people govern, either directly or through elected representatives (see Chapter 2). A democracy thus is different from an **oligarchy** (in which control rests with a small group, such as top-ranking military officers or a few wealthy families) and from an **autocracy** (in which control rests with a single individual, such as a king or dictator).

Democratic government rests on the Rousseauist idea that legitimate authority stems from the consent of the governed, which in practice has come to mean majority rule through voting in elections. More direct forms of democracy exist, such as the town meeting in which citizens vote directly on issues affecting them, but the impracticality of such an arrangement at the national level has made majority rule through elections the operating principle of modern democracies.

Majority rule through the vote does not take the same form in all democracies. The U.S. electoral system was established in a period when the power of government—whether it rested with a king or the majority—was greatly feared. To protect against abuses of power, the writers of the U.S. Constitution devised an elaborate system of checks and balances. Authority was divided among the executive, legislative, and judicial branches so that each branch could serve as a check on the power of the others and could balance their power with its own power (see Chapter 2). Indeed, *extreme fragmentation of governing authority is a defining characteristic of the American political system.* One result of this constitutional arrangement is that majority rule is less direct in the United States than in many democratic countries, including those of Europe. In the European democracies, a majority has the power in a single election to place executive and legislative power in the hands of a single group of representatives (see Chapter 2). In the United States, however, elections for the president, the Senate, and the House of Representatives are separate, and the terms of office for these officials are staggered. Thus, for a majority to exercise control in the United States, it must have enough strength and lasting power to dominate a series of elections. *all elected at different times*

Constitutionalism   The concept of democracy implies that the will of the majority should prevail over the wishes of the minority. If taken to the extreme, however, this principle would allow a majority to ride roughshod over the minority. Such action could deprive the minority even of its

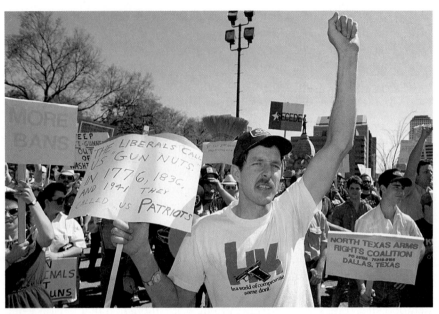

Free speech is a familiar feature of constitutionalism. This anti–gun control rally took place in Austin, Texas.

liberty, a clearly unacceptable outcome. Individuals have rights and freedoms that cannot lawfully be denied by the majority.

Constitutionalism is a set of rules that restricts the lawful uses of power. In its original sense, constitutionalism in Western society referred to a government based on laws and constitutional powers.[18] **Constitutionalism** has since come to refer specifically to the Lockean idea that there are limits to the rightful power of government over citizens. In a constitutional system, officials govern according to law, and citizens have basic rights that government cannot take away or deny.[19] Free speech is an example. Government is prohibited by the First Amendment from interfering with the lawful exercise of free speech. No right is absolute, which means that some restrictions are allowed. No student, for example, has a First Amendment right to shout loudly and disrupt a classroom. Nevertheless, free speech is broadly protected by the courts. During the buildup to war with Iraq in 2003, tens of thousands of antiwar demonstrators took to the streets. Despite instances in which protesters were intimidated by police or arrested for disorderly conduct, those who opposed the government's pursuit of the war had the opportunity to express their views freely without the threat of being sent to prison.

The constitutional tradition in the United States is at least as strong as the democratic tradition. In fact, *a defining characteristic of the American political system is its extraordinary emphasis on individual rights.* Issues that in other democracies would be resolved through elections and in legislative bodies are, in the United States, decided in courts of law as well. As Tocqueville noted, there is hardly a political issue in the United States that does not sooner or later become also a judicial issue.[20] Abortion rights, nuclear power, busing, toxic waste disposal, and welfare services are among the scores of issues that in recent years have

 LEADERS

Sandra Day O'Connor
(1930–)

In 1981, Sandra Day O'Connor became the first woman to be appointed to the U.S. Supreme Court, where she served for a quarter century before retiring in 2006. Toward the end of her tenure, she was widely regarded as the Court's most influential member. A pragmatic jurist, she was the swing vote on an ideologically divided Court. She cast the deciding vote in many 5-4 decisions, usually but not consistently siding with its more conservative members. A graduate of Stanford Law School, O'Connor faced discrimination because of her gender. One firm offered her a job as a legal secretary but not as an attorney. She eventually started her own practice and later served as assistant attorney general in Arizona. She ran successfully for a seat in the Arizona legislature and subsequently was appointed to the Arizona Court of Appeals before being nominated by President Ronald Reagan for a seat on the U.S. Supreme Court. As a member of the Court, O'Connor cast the deciding vote in leading cases involving key issues such as affirmative action, federalism, and abortion. O'Connor's policy influence reflects Tocqueville's observation that sooner or later most political issues in America become also judicial issues. O'Connor's career is testament to the importance in America of constitutionalism—the idea that the power of government over individuals is subject to judicial oversight.

played out in part as questions of rights to be settled through the courts.

Capitalism   Just as democracy and constitutionalism are systems of rules for allocating costs and benefits in American society, so too is capitalism. Societies have adopted alternative ways of organizing their economies. One way is **socialism,** which assigns government a large role in the ownership of the means of production, in regulating economic decisions, and in providing for the economic security of the individual. Under the form of socialism practiced in democratic countries, such as Sweden, the government does not attempt to manage the overall economy. Under **communism,** the government owns most or all major industries and also takes responsibility for overall management of the economy, including production quotas, supply points, and pricing.

Capitalism, an alternative method for distributing economic costs and benefits, holds that the government should interfere with the economy as little as possible. Firms are allowed to operate in a free and open marketplace, and individuals are expected to rely on their own initiative to establish their economic security. Firms decide what they will produce and the price they will charge for their goods, while consumers decide what they will buy at what price. Meanwhile, following a Lockean principle, private property rights are vigorously protected through government action.

Like the rules of democracy and constitutionalism, the rules of capitalism are not neutral. Whereas democracy responds to numbers and constitutionalism responds to individual rights, capitalism responds to wealth. "Money talks" in a capitalist system, which means, among other things, that wealthier people will have by far the greater say not only in economic matters but in political ones as well. Most Americans see nothing wrong with this arrangement and, compared with Europeans, are more likely to accept limits on government action in the area of the economy.

For all practical purposes, this outlook places many kinds of choices that in other countries are decided collectively beyond the reach of political majorities in the United States. Although Americans complain that their taxes are too high, they are taxed at substantially lower rates than are Europeans (see Figure 1–3). This situation testifies to the extent to which Americans believe wealth to be more properly allocated through the economic marketplace than through government policy. *A major characteristic of the American system is a relatively sharp distinction between*

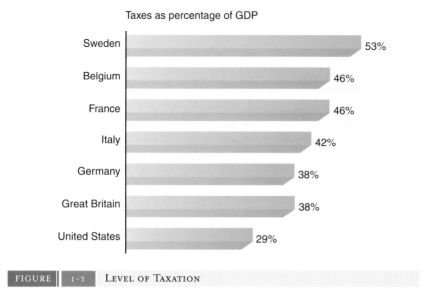

Taxes as percentage of GDP

Sweden	53%
Belgium	46%
France	46%
Italy	42%
Germany	38%
Great Britain	38%
United States	29%

FIGURE **1-3** LEVEL OF TAXATION

Americans pay less in taxes than Europeans do. *Source: OECD, 2006. Percentages based on all taxes (national and subnational) relative to a country's Gross Domestic Product (GDP).*

what is political, and therefore to be decided in the public arena, and what is economic, and therefore to be settled in the private realm.

POLITICAL POWER: THE CONTROL OF POLICY

Rules are necessary in politics because the stakes are high. Individuals who decide how society will be governed have **power,** a term that refers to the ability of persons or institutions to control public policy.[21] **Public policy** is a decision by government to follow a course of action designed to produce a particular outcome. Persons or institutions with sufficient power can determine which side will prevail in policy disputes.

Some governments exercise absolute power. **Totalitarian governments** assert complete dominance over individuals and the institutions of society. They determine the culture, control the media, direct the economy, dictate what can and cannot be taught in schools, define family relations, and decide which religions—if any—can be practiced openly. In fact, virtually no area of life is beyond their sphere of control, which leads them to one-party rule and the use of fear, intimidation, and force to subdue the population.

Germany under Adolf Hitler and the Soviet Union under Josef Stalin were totalitarian regimes. Millions of people in both countries were deemed enemies of the state and were imprisoned, tortured, or murdered.

Harsh rule is also characteristic of **authoritarian governments.** Although authoritarian governments include totalitarian ones, it is useful to distinguish regimes such as Nazi Germany from regimes that, though they admit to no limits on their power, are effectively limited by other strong institutions in the society, such as churches, corporations, or wealthy families. The governments that have resulted periodically from military coups in Africa and South America usually are authoritarian in form. Although authoritarian regimes repress political opponents and restrict free expression, they refrain from asserting full authority, recognizing that any such claim could antagonize powerful institutions that might drive them out of office.

Unlike authoritarian governments, democratic governments are characterized by ongoing competition for power among a range of interests. This tendency is particularly pronounced in the case of the United States. The country's settlement by people of different lands and religions, its great size and geographical variation, and its economic complexity have made the United States a diverse nation. Perhaps no country has more competing interests than the United States. *Competition for power among a great many interests of all kinds is a major characteristic of American politics.* Indeed, America's great diversity helps explain why its political life is not a life-and-death struggle. In *Federalist* No. 10, James Madison argued that government is most dangerous when a single group is powerful enough to gain full political control. In such cases, the group will use government to further its interests at the expense of all others in society. Because the United States is so diverse, however, no single group can hope to achieve full control. This forces groups to work together to exercise power, a process that requires each group to accommodate the interests of others.

Nevertheless, as in every society, power in America is the means of controlling public policy. Americans who have enough power can levy or cut taxes, permit or prohibit abortions, protect or take away private property, provide or refuse health benefits, impose or relax trade barriers, make war or declare peace. With so much at stake, it is not surprising that Americans, like people elsewhere, seek power as a means of achieving their policy goals.

Authority

Political power can reside with private individuals and organizations as well as in the hands of those who occupy government positions. A case in point

🎙 MEDIA AND POLITICS

JON STEWART'S The Daily Show

Long before baseball or football enjoyed its reputation as America's national pastime, political humor occupied that spot. The United States was founded on a rejection of political authority—that of the British monarch—and poking fun at the nation's leaders is nearly an American birthright. Every generation could relate to these words of humorist Will Rogers: "I don't make jokes. I just watch the government and report the facts." Writer Mark Twain echoed this sentiment: "Reader, suppose you were an idiot, and suppose you were a member of Congress. But I repeat myself."

The acknowledged king of political comedy today is Jon Stewart. His program, *The Daily Show*, attracts roughly 1.5 million viewers, ranking it near the top of the ratings for a cable news program. Like Rush Limbaugh's radio talk show (see Chapter 18), which soared in the ratings during the 1990s when the conservative Limbaugh feasted off the actions of Democrat President Bill Clinton, the liberal Stewart's television show has risen in popularity based on his swipes at Republican President George W. Bush. In one telling moment, Stewart looked blankly at the television screen for seemingly endless seconds before blurting out "Please say, please say, you're kidding me." This followed a videotape of National Security Advisor Condoleezza Rice admitting to Congress that she had read a classified briefing titled "Bin Laden Determined to Attack Inside the United States" a month before the September 11, 2001, terrorist attacks on the World Trade Center and the Pentagon. Rice had earlier claimed that no one in the Bush administration could possibly have foreseen the attacks.

Unlike most hosts of shows with a partisan twist, Stewart takes occasional potshots at his preferred party. Following a report about prisoner abuse by U.S. military personnel, Stewart commented: "The prisoner scandal is yet another election year problem for President Bush. And, with the economy still struggling, combat operations in Iraq dragging on, and the 9-11 hearings revealing damning information, even an opponent of limited political skill should be able to capitalize on those problems. The Democrats, however, chose to nominate John Kerry."

(continued)

The Daily Show's formula is a mixture of comedy and the day's news events. More than half the program's audience is under age 40, the opposite of the age distribution of the audience for broadcast network newscasts. But while *The Daily Show* might be helpful in getting today's young adults to pay attention to news, it might not be helpful in getting them involved in politics. A recent study by Jody Baumgartner and Jonathan Morris, political scientists at East Carolina University, found that youthful viewers of *The Daily Show* had more negative views of candidates and of the electoral process than did youthful viewers of broadcast network news.

Political humor dates to the Greeks, but few societies have embraced it as fully as have Americans. Part of the reason is rooted in the American political culture. Liberty, equality, and self-government are assertions of individualism as pitted against traditional deference to the high, the mighty, the rich, and the well-born. As Mark Twain noted of arrogant leaders, "Against the assault of laughter nothing can stand."

is the power exercised by the National Rifle Association (NRA) over gun control policy. NRA members are strongly opposed to restrictions on gun ownership and back up their position through the power of their votes and their money. Although Congress has the authority to enact stricter controls on guns, many of its members are reluctant to antagonize the NRA.

Nevertheless, U.S. officials do have a special kind of power as a result of the positions they hold. When government officials exercise power, it is called **authority,** defined as the recognized right of an individual, organization, or institution to make binding decisions. By this definition, government is not the only source of authority: parents have authority over their children; professors have authority over their students; firms have authority over their employees. However, government is a special case. Government's authority extends to all people within its geographical boundaries and can be used to redefine the authority of the parent, the professor, or the firm. Government's authority is also the most coercive. It includes the power to arrest and imprison, and even to legally punish by death those who violate its rules.

Government needs coercive power to ensure that its laws will be obeyed. Without this power, lawlessness would prevail—as it does in Colombia, where drug lords control large areas of the country. Yet this power can itself be abused, as when government uses force to intimidate opponents. The challenge, as Madison noted, is to grant government the authority necessary to prevent lawlessness while confining its authority to lawful purposes.

Theories of Power

Who has power in America? Who, in the end, decides the policies that the U.S. government pursues? Do the people themselves hold this power, or does it reside in the hands of a relatively small group of influential people, either within or outside of government?

This issue is compelling because the ultimate question of any political system is the question of who governs. Is power widely shared and used for the benefit of the many, or is it narrowly held and used to the advantage of the few? The issue is compelling for a second reason: power is easy to define but hard to locate. Consider, for example, the votes that a member of Congress casts. Are these votes an expression of the member's power, or are they an expression of the power of groups on whom the member depends for reelection?

The pattern of political power in America has been shown to differ substantially across individuals, institutions, and policy areas. As a result, there is no single theory of how power in America is held and exercised. Instead, four broad theories predominate (see Table 1–3). None of these theories describes every aspect of American politics, but each applies in some situations.

Know for quiz

| TABLE | 1-3 | THEORIES OF POWER: WHO GOVERNS AMERICA? |

There are four theories of power in America, each of which must be taken into account in any full explanation of the nation's policies.

Theory	Description
Majoritarianism	Holds that numerical majorities determine issues of policy
Pluralism	Holds that policies are effectively decided through power wielded by special interests that dominate particular policy areas
Elitism	Holds that policy is controlled by a small number of well-positioned, highly influential individuals
Bureaucratic rule	Holds that policy is controlled by well-placed administrators within the government bureaucracy

Majoritarianism: Government by the People   A basic principle of democracy is the idea of majority rule. **Majoritarianism** is the notion that the majority prevails not only in the counting of votes but also in the determination of public policy.

Majorities do sometimes rule in America. Their power is perhaps most evident in those states that offer voters the opportunity to decide directly on policy initiatives, which then become law if they receive a majority vote. The majority's influence is also felt indirectly through the decisions of elected representatives. When Congress in 1996 passed a welfare reform bill that included provisions requiring able-bodied welfare recipients to accept a job or job training after a two-year period or face the loss of their welfare benefits, it was acting in accord with the thinking of a majority of Americans who believed that employable individuals should be self-reliant. A more systematic assessment of the power of majorities is provided by Benjamin Page and Robert Shapiro's study of the relationship between majority opinions and more than three hundred policy issues. On major issues particularly, the researchers found that when majority opinion changed, policy tended to change in the same direction.[22]

Majorities do not always rule in America, however. In many policy areas, majority opinion is either nonexistent or ignored by policymakers. There are only a few issues at any moment that have the broad public's attention and an even smaller number that it really cares about. Thus, majoritarianism cannot account for most government policies. Other explanations are required in these instances.

Pluralism: Government by Groups   One such explanation is provided by the theory of **pluralism,** which focuses on group activity and holds that many policies are effectively decided through power wielded by diverse (plural) interests.

Many policies are in fact more responsive to the interests of particular groups than to majority opinion. Farm subsidies, for example, are determined more by pressures from agricultural groups than by the opinions of the general public. For pluralists, the issue of whether interest-group politics serves the public good centers on whether a diverse range of interests is served. Pluralists contend that it is misleading to view society only in terms of majorities. They see society as primarily a collection of separate interests. Farmers, broadcasters, college students, and multinational corporations have different needs and, according to the pluralist view, should have a disproportionate say in policies that directly affect them. Thus, as long as many groups have influence in their own area of interest, government is responding to the interests of most Americans. Pluralists such as Robert Dahl have argued that this is in fact the way the American political system operates most of the time.[23]

Critics argue that pluralists wrongly assume that the public interest is somehow represented in a system that allows special interests, each in its own sphere, to set public policy (see Chapter 9). Any such outcome, they say, represents the triumph of minority rule over majority rule. Critics also say that society's underprivileged groups are unable to compete effectively because of their lack of organization and money. They see a group system biased in favor of wealthy interests.

Elitism: Government by a Few   Elite theory offers in varying degrees a pessimistic view of the U.S. political system. **Elitism** holds that power in America is held by a small number of well-positioned, highly influential individuals. A leading proponent of elite theory was sociologist C. Wright Mills, who argued that key policies are decided by an overlapping coalition of select leaders, including corporate executives, top military officers, and centrally placed public officials.[24] Other proponents of elite theory have defined the core group somewhat differently, but their contention is the same: America is governed not by majorities or by a plurality of groups but by a small number of well-placed and privileged individuals.

The Federal Reserve Board of Governors is a government body that through its interest-rate policies exerts a substantial influence on the American economy. The board, which meets in secrecy, is an example of the influence of political elites.

Proponents of elite theory differ, however, in the extent to which they believe elites control policy for their own purposes. Some theorists, including G. William Domhoff, hold the view that elites operate behind the scenes in order to manipulate government for selfish ends.[25] Other theorists claim that elites, in part to protect their privileged positions and in part out of a sense of obligation, pursue policies that serve others' interests as well as their own. One such view holds that competing elites appeal to voters for support and, in the process, adopt policy positions favored by large blocs of voters.[26]

Unquestionably, certain policies are effectively controlled by a tiny circle of influential people. The nation's monetary policy, for example, is set by the decisions of the Federal Reserve Board ("the Fed"), which meets in secrecy and decides the interest rates that banks pay for the loans they receive from the Federal Reserve. These rates in turn affect the interest rates that banks charge for their loans to customers. The Fed is very responsive to the concerns of bankers. What is less clear is the Fed's responsiveness to the concerns of consumers.

Bureaucratic Rule: Government by Administrators   A fourth theory holds that power resides in the hands of career government bureaucrats. The leading proponent of the theory of **bureaucratic rule** was the German sociologist Max Weber, who argued that all large organizations tend toward the bureaucratic form, with the result that decision-making power devolves to career administrators whose experience and knowledge of policy issues exceed those of elected officials.[27] Another sociologist, Roberto Michels, propounded the "iron law of oligarchy," concluding that power inevitably gravitates toward experienced administrators at the top of large-scale organizations, even in the case of organizations that aim to be governed democratically.[28]

Bureaucratic politics raises the possibility of a large, permanent government run by unaccountable administrators. Elections come and go, but the bureaucrats who staff executive agencies stay on. As public policy issues have become increasingly complex, these bureaucrats often are the most knowledgeable on those issues and also are well-positioned to influence their resolution. Modern government could not function without career bureaucrats, but in most cases they are not instruments of the majority. They tend instead to act in ways that will promote their own agency and its programs (see Chapter 13).

Who Does Govern?   The perspective of this book is that each of these theories—majoritarianism, pluralism, elitism, and bureaucratic rule—must be taken into account in any full explanation of politics and power in America. As subsequent chapters will demonstrate, some policies are decided by majority influence, whereas others reflect the influence of special interests, bureaucrats, or elites.

THE CONCEPT OF A POLITICAL SYSTEM AND THIS BOOK'S ORGANIZATION

As the foregoing discussion suggests, American government is based on a great many related parts. It is useful to regard these components as constituting a **political system.** The parts are separate, but they connect with one another, affecting how each performs. Political scientist David Easton, who was a pioneer in this conception of politics, said that it makes little sense to study political relations piecemeal when they are, in reality, "interrelated."[29]

The complexity of government has kept political scientists from developing a fully explanatory model of the political system, but the concept of politics as a system is useful for instructional purposes. To view politics as a system is to emphasize the connections between the parts and the ways change in one area affects the others. It is a dynamic conception in that the political system is constantly changing in response to new conditions and to the interplay of its various parts.

The political-system approach characterizes this book, beginning with the organization of its chapters (see Figure 1–4). The political system

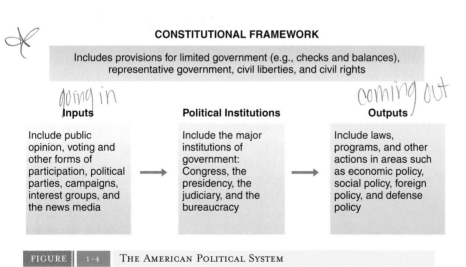

CONSTITUTIONAL FRAMEWORK

Includes provisions for limited government (e.g., checks and balances), representative government, civil liberties, and civil rights

Inputs

Include public opinion, voting and other forms of participation, political parties, campaigns, interest groups, and the news media

Political Institutions

Include the major institutions of government: Congress, the presidency, the judiciary, and the bureaucracy

Outputs

Include laws, programs, and other actions in areas such as economic policy, social policy, foreign policy, and defense policy

FIGURE 1-4   THE AMERICAN POLITICAL SYSTEM

This book's chapters are organized within a political-system framework.

operates against the backdrop of a constitutional framework that defines how power is to be obtained and exercised. This structure is the focus of the opening chapters, which examine how the Constitution defines, in theory and practice, the institutions of government and the rights of individuals. Another part of the political system is *inputs:* the demands people and organizations place on government and the support they provide for institutions, leaders, and policies. These inputs are explored in chapters on public opinion, political participation, political parties, interest groups, and the news media. The functioning of governing officials is addressed in chapters on the nation's *political institutions*—Congress, the presidency, the federal bureaucracy, and the federal courts. Some of the discussion in these chapters is devoted simply to describing these institutions, but most of the discussion explores their interrelationships and how their actions are affected by inputs and by the constitutional system in which they operate. Throughout the book, but particularly in the closing chapters, attention is given to the political system's *outputs*—policy decisions that are binding on society. These decisions, which are made by political institutions in response to inputs, affect American life in many areas, including the economy, the environment, social welfare, education, foreign affairs, and national defense.

The chapters are collectively designed to convey a reliable body of knowledge that will enable the reader to think systematically about the nature of the American political system. This body of knowledge derives from the full range of methodological approaches that political scientists have applied to the study of politics. Political science, unlike some academic disciplines, has been defined more by its subjects of inquiry than by a particular methodology. Normative theory, historical reasoning, legal analysis, and cultural analysis are among the strains, along with political psychology, political sociology, and political economy. Rational choice theory, organizational theory, and institutional analysis are other strains. Each approach can illuminate certain aspects of politics. For example, rational choice theory is based on the assumption that actors pursue their interests rationally and has proved to be a powerful model to describe, for instance, the behavior of elected officials as they seek to position themselves for reelection. As another example, cultural analysis is a powerful lens through which to view the values that motivate political action.

Political scientists have uncovered numerous tendencies in American political behavior, institutions, and processes. Five of these tendencies have been identified in this opening chapter as deserving special attention:

- Enduring cultural ideals that are Americans' common bond and a source of their political goals
- Extreme fragmentation of governing authority that is based on an elaborate system of checks and balances
- Many competing interests that are the result of the nation's great size, population diversity, and economic complexity
- A strong emphasis on individual rights, which is a consequence of the nation's political traditions
- A relatively sharp separation of the political and economic spheres that has the effect of placing many economic issues outside the reach of political majorities

Underlying this book's concern with the broad patterns of the American political system is a question that must be asked of any democracy: what is the relationship of the people to their government? The answer to this question is the foundation not only of a reasonable assessment of the state of American democracy but also of good citizenship. Responsible citizenship depends finally on an informed perspective, on a recognition of how difficult it is to govern effectively and yet how important it is to try. It cannot be said too often that the issue of governing is the most difficult issue facing any society. Nor can it be said too often that governing is a quest and a search, not a resolved issue. The Constitution's opening phrase, "We the People," is a call to Americans to join in that quest. E. E. Schattschneider said it clearly: "In the course of centuries, there has come a great deal of agreement about what democracy is, but nobody has a monopoly on it and the last word has not been spoken."[30]

SUMMARY

The United States is a nation that was formed on a set of ideals. Liberty, equality, and self-government are foremost among these ideals, which also include the principles of individualism, diversity, and unity. These ideals became Americans' common bond and today are the basis of their political culture. Although they are mythic, inexact, and conflicting, these ideals have had a powerful effect on what generation after generation of Americans has tried to achieve politically for themselves and others.

Politics in the United States plays out through rules of the game that include democracy, constitutionalism, and capitalism. Democracy is rule by the people, which in practice refers to a representative system of government in which the people rule through their elected officials. Constitutionalism refers to rules that limit the rightful power of government over citizens. Capitalism is an economic system based on a free-market principle that allows the government only a limited role in determining how economic costs and benefits will be allocated.

Politics is the process by which it is determined whose values will prevail in society. The basis of politics is conflict over scarce resources and competing values. Those who have power win out in this conflict and are able to control governing authority and policy choices. In the United States, no one faction controls all power and policy. Majorities govern on some issues, while groups, elites, and bureaucrats each govern on other issues.

KEY TERMS

authoritarian government (*p. 24*)
authority (*p. 26*)
autocracy (*p. 19*)
bureaucratic rule (*p. 30*)
capitalism (*p. 22*)
communism (*p. 22*)
constitutionalism (*p. 20*)
democracy (*p. 19*)
diversity (*p. 10*)
elitism (*p. 29*)
equality (*p. 8*)
individualism (*p. 10*)
liberty (*p. 6*)

majoritarianism (*p. 28*)
oligarchy (*p. 19*)
pluralism (*p. 28*)
political culture (*p. 3*)
political system (*p. 31*)
politics (*p. 17*)
power (*p. 23*)
public policy (*p. 23*)
self-government (*p. 8*)
social contract (*p. 17*)
socialism (*p. 22*)
totalitarian government (*p. 23*)
unity (*p. 10*)

SUGGESTED READINGS

Dahl, Robert. *On Democracy.* New Haven, Conn.: Yale University Press, 1998. A handbook on democracy by a leading advocate of pluralism.

Domhoff, G. William. *Who Rules America? Power and Politics*, 4th ed. New York: McGraw-Hill, 2002. A critical assessment of American government by a leading proponent of elite theory.

Ferguson, Robert A. *Reading the Early Republic.* Cambridge, Mass.: Harvard University Press, 2004. Argues that America has always been a country trying to reach its ideals.

Katz, Michael B., and Mark J. Stern. *One Nation Divisible: What America Was and What It's Becoming.* New York: Russell Sage Foundation, 2006. A penetrating look at the transformation of American society during the twentieth century.

Lipset, Seymour Martin. *American Exceptionalism: A Double-Edged Sword.* New York: Norton, 1996. Argues that Americans' tendency to view society in idealized terms is a source of both alienation and progress.

Schuck, Peter H. *Diversity in America: Keeping Government at a Safe Distance.* Cambridge, Mass.: Belknap Press of Harvard, 2003. A far-reaching analysis of when diversity does and does not serve America's interests.
Stout, Jeffrey. *Democracy and Tradition.* Princeton, N.J.: Princeton University Press, 2004. An analysis of the moral claims associated with democracy.
White, John Kenneth. *The Values Divide.* Washington, D.C.: CQ Press, 2002. A look at Americans' values in a time of change.

LIST OF WEBSITES

http://www.conginst.org/ A site that provides up-to-date survey data on the American political culture.

http://www.loc.gov/ The Library of Congress website; it provides access to over seventy million historical and contemporary U.S. documents.

http://www.stateline.org/ A University of Richmond/Pew Charitable Trusts site dedicated to providing citizens with information on major policy issues.

http://www.tocqueville.org/ Includes biographical and other references to Alexis de Tocqueville and his writings.

POLITICS IN THEORY AND PRACTICE

Thinking: How are Americans' beliefs about liberty, equality, and self-government related to their preference for constitutionalism? For capitalism? For democracy?
Participating: The American political culture includes a belief in liberty, equality, and self-government. As a prelude to getting involved in public affairs, reflect on what these ideals mean to you. What types of political activity are associated with each of these ideals? Thinking of your own experiences, what have you done to promote these ideals? What might you consider doing in the future to promote them?

ADDITIONAL RESOURCES

For quizzes, interactive simulations, games, graphics, and other study tools, visit the book's Online Learning Center at **www.mhhe.com/pattersonwtp7.**

What We Love About America

By James Carroll

A defining feature of American politics is the nation's founding ideals. For more than two centuries, they have served as Americans' common bond and their vision of a more perfect union. These ideals are invoked particularly during times of national crisis or triumph and also— as in the case of this essay by Boston Globe *columnist James Carroll—on national holidays.*

IT IS BETTER to be a half-formed and rough idea than a brilliant cliché. Such preference for the imperfect new defines America. As we celebrate the birth of our nation, can we put words on the reason we love it? Let me try.

Because Europeans measured what they found here against what they had left behind, newness was the main note of the settled land. In the beginning, religiously inflamed politics had made life intolerable in the old country, a story that achieved its master form with the coming to Virginia and Massachusetts of the English dissidents. But even the mythic 1492 had carried an implication of the New World's liberating significance, for in addition to sponsoring Christopher Columbus, monarchs Ferdinand and Isabella chose that year to expel Jews and Muslims from Spain, establishing the totalitarian principle in Europe. Even as Spaniards then wreaked purposeful and accidental havoc in the New World, they opened an unforeseen escape route from the old.

America, for all of its nascent idealism, began as an instance of brutal European imperialism, with the exterminating of indigenous peoples and the enslavement of Africans as essential elements. But because that nascent idealism found articulation in the solemn compacts of the early generations—culminating first in the Declaration of Independence that we commemorate tomorrow, then in the US Constitution, then in the Bill of Rights—American imperialism contained principles of its own self-criticism. Slavery came to be seen as an abomination less in contrast to the practice of other nations than to the establishing theory of this one. America began, that is, as a half-formed and rough idea, but that idea became the meaning against which all life in this country has been measured ever since. That idea has been a perpetual source of newness, even as it has become more fully formed and clearly articulated.

And what is that idea? It comes to us by now as the brilliant cliché of the Fourth of July, but with stark simplicity it still defines the ground of our being: "All men are created equal." That the idea is dynamic, propelling a permanent social transformation, is evident even in the way that word "men" strikes the ear as anachronistic now. That Jefferson and the others were not thinking of women matters less than the fact that they established a principle that made the full inclusion of women inevitable. And so with those who owned no property, and those who were *themselves* owned property.

How new is this idea today? Its transforming work continues all around us. Last week, the US Supreme Court faulted the Bush administration for its treatment of detainees in Guantanamo, implicitly affirming that one need not be a citizen of this nation to claim basic rights. The foundational principle extends to enemy combatants. They, too, are created equal. And so in other areas. US politics is obsessed with the question of the place of immigrants, legal and illegal. The mainstream argument takes for granted that even here liberalizing change is underway. Confronted with an "illegal" person, the law must still give primacy to personhood. And, on another front, is it an accident that American Episcopalians are the ones challenging the world Anglican body on the question of equality for gays and lesbians?

America is by definition unfinished, because it forever falls short of itself. Not that this nation is more moral than others, but its half-formed foundational ideal required a moral purpose at the start—and a moral purpose to the end. That is both creative and creatively undermining. Born

in a challenge to authority, American authority continually inhibits its own exercise (what the Supreme Court did last week in challenging the executive and legislative branches over Guantanamo). Recognitions of personal alienation inevitably open into demands for the reform of alienating systems—and in America that is the work of politics. It never stops.

Contention is essential to such a social dynamic. Much as the polarized character of national life is bemoaned, the red state/blue state acrimony reveals the genius of what the founders began, for the structures of this public order evolve within a framework that continually transforms conflict into energy for change. The irony, of course, is that those who declare their loyalty to the brilliant cliché of an unchanging past are themselves at the service of the imperfect new. After all, to be an American traditionalist—and isn't this what we universally celebrate tomorrow?—is to affirm the revolution.

What's Your Opinion?

Do you think that America's founding principles are still the glue that holds Americans together and defines their aspirations? Or, as some suggest, are Americans bound together and driven largely by a shared culture of consumerism?

CHAPTER 2

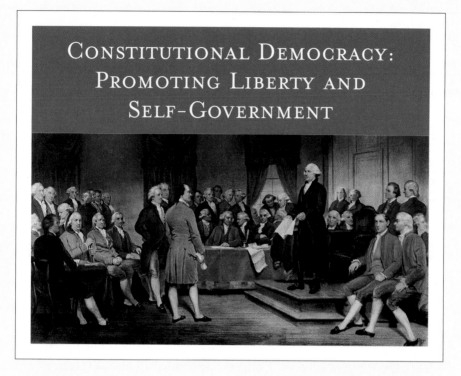

CONSTITUTIONAL DEMOCRACY: PROMOTING LIBERTY AND SELF-GOVERNMENT

66The people must be governed by a majority, with whom all power resides. But how is the sense of this majority to be obtained? 99

FISHER AMES (1788)[1]

On the night of June 17, 1972, a security guard at the Watergate apartment-office complex in Washington, D.C., noticed that the latch on the door to the Democratic party's national headquarters had been taped open. He called the police, who captured the five burglars inside. As it turned out, the men had links to Republican President Richard Nixon's Committee to Re-elect the President. Nixon called the incident "bizarre" and denied that anyone on his staff was involved in the break-in.

The reality was that the Watergate break-in was part of an orchestrated campaign of "dirty tricks" designed to ensure Nixon's reelection. The dirty-tricks campaign included wiretaps, tax audits, and burglaries of Nixon's political opponents (the "enemies list"), who included journalists and antiwar activists in addition to Democrats. Although the Nixon White House managed for a time to hide the truth, the facts of the dirty-tricks campaign gradually became known. During Senate investigative hearings, a White House assistant revealed that Nixon had tape-recorded all his

The Senate Judiciary Committee holds hearings on allegations of illegal acts by President Richard Nixon. The congressional investigation led to Nixon's resignation.

telephone calls and personal conversations in the Oval Office. Nixon at first refused to release the tapes but then made public what he claimed were "all the relevant" ones. Congress demanded additional tapes, as did the special prosecutor who had been appointed to investigate criminal aspects of the Watergate affair. In late July the U.S. Supreme Court, which included four justices appointed by Nixon, unanimously ordered the president to supply sixty-four additional tapes. The tapes were incriminating, and two weeks later, on August 9, 1974, Richard Nixon resigned from office, the first president in U.S. history to do so.

Nixon's downfall was owed in no small measure to the handiwork two centuries earlier of the writers of the Constitution. They were well aware that power could never be entrusted to the goodwill of leaders. "If angels were to govern men," James Madison wrote in *Federalist* No. 51, "neither external nor internal controls on government would be necessary." Madison's point, of course, was that leaders are not angels and, as mere mortals, are subject to temptation and vice, including a lust for power—hence the Framers' insistence on constitutional checks on power, as when they gave Congress the authority to impeach and remove the president from office.

The writers of the Constitution were determined through their system of checks and balances to protect liberty from the threat of a too powerful government. The Framers sought a **limited government,** one subject to strict limits on its lawful uses of power. They also had a second and somewhat competing objective. They wanted **self-government,** government based on the people and subject to their control. Self-government requires that the majority, through its representatives, has the power to rule. However, limited government requires that majority rule stop at the point where it infringes on the legitimate rights and interests of the minority. This consideration led the Framers to forge a Constitution that provides for majority rule but has built-in restrictions on the majority's power.

This chapter describes how the principles of self-government and limited government are embodied in the Constitution and explains the tension between them. The chapter also indicates how these principles have been modified in practice in the course of American history. The main points of this chapter are these:

★ *America during the colonial period developed traditions of limited government and self-government.* These traditions were rooted in governing practices, philosophy, and cultural values.

★ *The Constitution provides for limited government mainly by defining lawful powers and by dividing those powers among competing institutions.* The Constitution, with its Bill of Rights, also prohibits government from infringing on individual rights. Judicial review is an additional safeguard of limited government.

★ *The Constitution in its original form provided for self-government mainly through indirect systems of popular election of representatives.* The Framers' theory of self-government was based on the notion that political power must be separated from immediate popular influences if sound policies are to result.

★ *The idea of popular government—in which the majority's desires have a more direct and immediate impact on governing officials—has gained strength since the nation's beginning.* Originally, the House of Representatives was the only institution subject to direct vote of the people. This mechanism has been extended to other institutions and, through primary elections, even to the nomination of candidates for public office.

BEFORE THE CONSTITUTION: THE COLONIAL AND REVOLUTIONARY EXPERIENCES

Early Americans' admiration for limited government was based partly on their British heritage. Unlike other European governments of the time, Britain did not have an absolute monarchy. The Parliament was an independent body with lawmaking powers, and British subjects had certain rights, including that of jury trial. This tradition carried over to the American colonies. In each colony there was a right to trial by jury. There was also freedom of expression, although of a limited kind. Not all colonies, for example, granted freedom to all religions. The colonies also had a degree of self-government. Each had an elected representative assembly, which was subject to British oversight but nonetheless had substantial legislative powers.

The colonists also had the example of Native American governments, particularly that of the Iroquois Confederacy. The Confederacy was a union of the Mohawk, Oneida, Onondaga, Cayuga, and Seneca tribes, governed by a fifty-member council made up of representatives of the five tribes. To protect each tribe's interest, the confederacy's constitution included a system of checks and balances—a feature that would become a hallmark of the U.S. Constitution. Historians disagree over the influence of the Iroquois Confederacy on colonial thought, but Benjamin Franklin and Thomas Jefferson were among the colonial leaders who wrote approvingly of its governing system.

"The Rights of Englishmen"

The Revolutionary War was partly a rebellion against Britain's failure to respect its own tradition of limited government in the colonies. Many of the colonial charters had conferred upon Americans "the rights of

Englishmen," but Britain showed progressively less respect for these rights as time went on. Until the period after the French and Indian War (1755–63), the colonists had viewed themselves as loyal subjects of the British king. In fact, the colonists had fought alongside British soldiers to drive the French out of the western territories. At the end of the war, however, Britain for the first time imposed heavy taxes on the colonies. The war with France, which was also waged in Europe, had created a budget crisis in Britain. Taxing the colonies was a way to reduce Britain's debt. The first such tax was a stamp tax on colonial newspapers and business documents. The colonists, who were not represented in the British Parliament that imposed the tax, responded angrily. "No taxation without representation" became their rallying cry.

Historical Background

Although Parliament backed down and repealed the Stamp Act, it then passed the Townshend Act, which imposed taxes on all glass, paper, tea, and lead. The colonists again responded angrily, and Parliament again backed down—except for a tax on tea, which was kept to show the colonies that Britain was still in charge of their affairs. The tea tax sparked an act of defiance that became known as the "Boston Tea Party." In December 1773, under the cover of darkness, a small band of patriots disguised as Native

POLITICAL CULTURE

Religion and American Ideals

The United States is a nation established in 1776 on a set of principles—liberty, equality, and self-government. These ideals derived in part from broad lessons of history, the direct experiences of the colonists, and treatises such as those of Locke and Rousseau. Religious beliefs also played a major part.

Many of the early colonists came to America in order to practice their religions freely. Church and state in Europe were joined. Government there sided with a particular religion—Roman Catholicism in France and Spain, Anglicanism in England. Rhode Island's founder, the Reverend Roger Williams, was a Calvinist who left his native England for reasons of religious freedom. Williams was the first to assert that church and state in America ought to be separate. Williams argued that salvation required an acceptance of God, which is meaningful only if it is an act of free will—and this is impossible if religion is imposed on the individual by the state. To Williams and others, religious liberty and political liberty were inseparable. The prevalence of this view is apparent in the First Amendment to the Constitution, which at once provides for freedom of political expression *and* for religious freedom.

Liberty is not the only American ideal with a religious basis. Equality was considered God's work: "all men are created equal." Every individual was a child of God and thus equal in His eyes. (This belief posed a dilemma for slaveholders, who finessed it by claiming that slaves either were soulless or were secondary beings in God's "natural order.") Self-government, too, had a religious foundation, though a Protestant one. Unlike the Catholic Church, which was hierarchical in its organization, with the Pope and bishops at its head, many Protestant sects had self-governing congregations. Their democratic operation affected their members' views on the proper form of government.

America, said the British writer G. K. Chesterton, is "a nation with the soul of a church" and "the only country founded on a creed." He could have added that America is also a nation that emulated a religious model in its governing document. The first colonists formed religious communities governed by written covenant, a model for the written Constitution drafted and ratified by Americans more than a century later.

Americans boarded an English ship in Boston Harbor and dumped its cargo of tea overboard.

After Britain retaliated by closing the port of Boston, the colonists convened the First Continental Congress to decide what they would demand from Britain. Meeting in Philadelphia, they called for free assembly, an end to the British military occupation, their own councils for the imposition of taxes, and trial by local juries. (British authorities had resorted to shipping "troublemakers" to London for trial.) King George III rejected their demands, and in 1775 British troops and colonial minutemen clashed at Lexington and Concord. Eight colonists died on the Lexington green in what became known as "the shot heard 'round the world." The American Revolution had begun.

The Declaration of Independence

Although grievances against Britain were the immediate cause of the American Revolution, ideas about the proper form of government were also on the colonists' minds.[2] The century-old theory of John Locke was particularly influential. Locke held that people have **inalienable rights** (or **natural rights**)—including those of life, liberty, and property—and can rebel against a ruler who tramples on these rights (see Chapter 1).

Thomas Jefferson declared that Locke "was one of the three greatest men that ever lived, without exception," and Jefferson paraphrased Locke's ideas in key passages of the Declaration of Independence:

> We hold these truths to be self-evident, that all men are created equal, that they are endowed by their Creator with certain unalienable rights, that among these are life, liberty and the pursuit of happiness.
>
> That to secure these rights, governments are instituted among men, deriving their just powers from the consent of the governed.
>
> That whenever any form of government becomes destructive of these ends, it is the right of the people to alter or to abolish it, and to institute a new government.

The Declaration was a call to revolution rather than a framework for a new form of government, but the ideas it contained—liberty, equality, individual rights, self-government, lawful powers—became the basis, eleven years later, for the Constitution of the United States. (The Declaration of Independence and the Constitution are reprinted in their entirety in the appendixes of this book.)

The Articles of Confederation

The first government of the United States was based not on the Constitution but on the Articles of Confederation. The Articles, which were

[Handwritten draft of the Declaration of Independence by Thomas Jefferson, with numerous edits and crossed-out words. The legible text reads in part:]

A Declaration by the Representatives of the UNITED STATES OF AMERICA, in General Congress assembled.

When in the course of human events it becomes necessary for one people to dissolve the political bands which have connected them with another, and to assume among the powers of the earth the separate and equal station to which the laws of nature & of nature's god entitle them, a decent respect to the opinions of mankind requires that they should declare the causes which impel them to the separation.

We hold these truths to be self-evident; that all men are created equal & independent; that from that equal creation they derive rights inherent & inalienable, among which are the preservation of life, & liberty, & the pursuit of happiness; that to secure these ends, governments are instituted among men, deriving their just powers from the consent of the governed; that whenever any form of government shall becomes destructive of these ends, it is the right of the people to alter or to abolish it, & to institute new government, laying its foundation on such principles & organising its powers in such form, as to them shall seem most likely to effect their safety & happiness. prudence indeed will dictate that governments long established should not be changed for light & transient causes; and accordingly all experience hath shewn that mankind are more disposed to suffer while evils are sufferable, than to right themselves by abolishing the forms to which they are accustomed but when a long train of abuses & usurpations [begun at a distinguished period & pursuing invariably the same object, evinces a design to reduce them under absolute Despotism] it is their right, it is their duty to throw off such government & to provide new guards for their future security. such has been the patient sufferance of these colonies & such is now the necessity which constrains them to [expunge] their former systems of government. the history of the present king of Great Britain is a history of unremitting injuries and usurpations [among which appears no solitary fact to contradict the uniform tenor of the rest, all of which have] in direct object the establishment of an absolute tyranny over these states. to prove this, let facts be submitted to a candid world [for the truth of which we pledge a faith yet unsullied by falsehood]

he has refused his assent to laws the most wholesome and necessary for the public good:

he has forbidden his governors to pass laws of immediate & pressing importance unless suspended in their operation till his assent should be obtained

This is a portion of Thomas Jefferson's handwritten draft of the Declaration of Independence, a formal expression of America's governing ideals.

adopted during the Revolutionary War, created a very weak national government that was subordinate to the states. The colonies had always been governed separately, and their people considered themselves Virginians, New Yorkers, or Pennsylvanians as much as they thought of themselves as Americans. Moreover, they were leery of a powerful central government. The American Revolution was sparked by grievances against the arbitrary policies of King George III, and Americans were in no mood to replace him with a strong national authority of their own making.

Under the Articles of Confederation, each state retained its "sovereignty, freedom and independence." There was a national Congress, but its members were appointed and paid by their respective state governments. Each of the thirteen states had one vote in Congress, and the agreement of nine states was required to pass legislation. Moreover, any state could block constitutional change: the Articles of Confederation could be amended only by unanimous approval of the states.

Historical Background

The American union held together during the Revolutionary War out of necessity. The states had either to cooperate or to surrender to the British. But once the war ended, the states felt free to go their separate ways. Several states sent representatives abroad to negotiate their own trade agreements with foreign nations. New Hampshire, with its eighteen-mile coastline, even established its own navy. In a melancholy letter to Thomas Jefferson, George Washington wondered whether the United States deserved to be called a nation.

Congress was expected to provide for the nation's defense and establish the basis for a general economy, but the Articles of Confederation did not give it the powers necessary to achieve these goals. The Articles prohibited Congress from interfering in the states' commerce policies, and the states were soon engaged in ruinous trade wars. The Articles also denied to Congress the power to tax, and as a result it had no money with which to build a navy or hire an army.

Shays's Rebellion: A Nation Dissolving

By 1784, the nation was unraveling. Congress was so weak that many of its members did not bother to attend its sessions.[3] Finally, in late 1786, a revolt in western Massachusetts prompted leading Americans to conclude that the country's government had to be changed. A ragtag army of two thousand farmers armed with pitchforks marched on county courthouses to prevent foreclosures on their land. Many of the farmers were veterans of the Revolutionary War; their leader, Daniel Shays, had been a captain in the Revolutionary army. They had been given assurances during the Revolution that their land, which lay fallow because they were away at war, would not be confiscated for unpaid debts and taxes. They had also been promised the back pay owed to them for their military service. (Congress had run out of money during the Revolution.) Instead, they received no back pay, and heavy new taxes were levied on their farms. Many farmers faced the loss of their property and even jail because they could not pay their creditors.

Shays's Rebellion frightened wealthy interests, who called on the governor of Massachusetts to put down the revolt. He in turn asked Congress for help, but it had no army to send. The governor finally raised enough money to hire a militia that put down the revolt, but Shays's Rebellion made it clear that Congress and the army were weak and that civil unrest was spreading. Fear that anarchy would overtake the country was widespread. An emergency meeting of five states, held in Annapolis, led to a plea to Congress to authorize a constitutional convention of all the states to be held the following spring in Philadelphia. Congress authorized the convention but placed a restriction on it: the delegates were to meet for "the sole and express purpose of revising the Articles of Confederation."

NEGOTIATING TOWARD A CONSTITUTION

The delegates to the Philadelphia constitutional convention ignored the instructions of Congress. They drafted a plan for an entirely new form of government. Prominent delegates (among them George Washington, Benjamin Franklin, and James Madison) were determined from the outset to establish an American nation built on a strong central government.

The Great Compromise: QUIZ
A Two-Chamber Congress

Debate at the constitutional convention of 1787 began over a plan put forward by the Virginia delegation, which was dominated by strong nationalists. The **Virginia Plan** (also called the **large-state plan**) called for a two-chamber Congress that would have supreme authority in all areas "in which the separate states are incompetent," particularly defense and interstate trade. The Virginia Plan also provided that representation in both chambers would be based on size. Small states such as Delaware and Rhode Island would be allowed only one representative in the lower chamber, while large states such as Massachusetts and Virginia would have more than a dozen.

The Virginia Plan was sharply attacked by delegates from the smaller states. They rallied around a counterproposal made by New Jersey's William Paterson. The **New Jersey Plan** (also called the **small-state plan**) called for a stronger national government with the power to tax and to regulate commerce among the states; in most other respects, however, the Articles would remain in effect. Congress would have a single chamber in which each state, large or small, would have a single vote.

The debate over the New Jersey and Virginia Plans dragged on for weeks before the delegates reached what is now known as the **Great**

Compromise. It provided for a bicameral (two-chamber) Congress: the House of Representatives would be apportioned among the states on the basis of population, and the Senate would be apportioned on the basis of an equal number of votes (two) for each state. This compromise was critically important. The small states would not have agreed to join a union in which their vote was always weaker than that of large states, a fact reflected in Article V of the Constitution: "No state, without its consent, shall be deprived of its equal suffrage in the Senate."

The North-South Compromise: The Issue of Slavery

The separate interests of the states were also the basis for a second major agreement: the **North-South Compromise** on economic issues. The southern states feared that the northern states, which were more numerous and had a larger population, would use their numerical majority in Congress to tax the South unfairly. If Congress imposed high tariffs on manufactured goods imported from Europe in order to protect domestic manufacturers, the South would be disadvantaged because U.S. manufacturing was based largely in the North. If Congress also imposed high tariffs on agricultural exports, the South again would be disadvantaged because it was the prime source of agricultural exports, which, if taxed, would be more expensive and of less interest to European buyers. The South's delegates were also concerned that northern representatives in Congress would tax or even bar the importation of slaves.

After extended debate, a compromise was reached. Congress was to be prohibited by the Constitution from taxing exports but could tax imports. In addition, Congress would be prohibited until 1808 from passing laws to end the slave trade. However, the most controversial trade-off was the so-called "Three-Fifths Compromise." For purposes of apportionment of taxes and seats in the U.S. House of Representatives, each slave was to count as less than a full person. Northern delegates had argued against the counting of slaves because they did not enjoy legal rights. Southern delegates wanted to count them as full persons for purposes of apportioning House seats (which would have the effect of increasing the number of southern representatives) and to count them as nonpersons for purposes of apportioning taxes (which would have the effect of decreasing the amount of federal taxes levied on the southern states). The delegates finally settled on a compromise that included both taxation and apportionment but counted each slave as three-fifths of a person. Although the southern states did not get all that they wanted, they got the better end of the bargain. If slaves had not been counted at all, the southern states would have had only slightly more than 35 percent of House seats. With the compromise, they held nearly 45 percent of the seats, giving them considerable power over national policy.

These compromises have led critics to claim that the Framers of the Constitution had no objections to slavery. In fact, most of the delegates were deeply troubled by it, recognizing the stark inconsistency between the practice of slavery and the Lockean ideals that all persons are entitled to liberty and equality. "[Slavery] is inconsistent with the principles of the Revolution," Maryland's Luther Martin stated. George Mason, a Virginian and a slaveholder, said: "[Slaveholders] bring the judgment of heaven on a country."[4] Benjamin Franklin and Alexander Hamilton were among the delegates who were involved in antislavery organizations.

Yet the southern states' dependence on slavery was a reality that the delegates had to confront if there was to be a union of the states. The North had few slaves, whereas the South's economy was based on slave labor (see Figure 2–1). John Rutledge of South Carolina asked during the convention debate whether the North regarded southerners as "fools." Southern delegates declared that they would form their own union rather than join one that banned slavery.

A Strategy for Ratification

The compromises over slavery and the structure of the Congress took up most of the four months that the convention was in session. Some of the other issues, such as the structure and powers of the federal judiciary, were the subject of remarkably little debate.

There remained a final issue, however: would those Americans not attending the convention support the proposed Constitution? The delegates realized that ratification was not a sure thing. Congress had not authorized a wholesale restructuring of the federal government and had in fact created a barrier to any such plan. In authorizing the Philadelphia convention, Congress had stated that any proposed change in the Articles would have to be "agreed to in Congress" and then "confirmed by [all of] the states." The delegates recognized that if unanimous consent was required, the Constitution had no chance of ratification. Rhode Island had refused even to send a delegation to the convention. In a bold move, the delegates established their own ratification process. They instructed Congress to send the proposed Constitution directly to the states, where it would become law if approved by at least nine states in special ratifying conventions of popularly elected delegates. It was a masterful strategy. There was little hope that all thirteen state legislatures would approve the Constitution, but nine states through conventions might be persuaded to

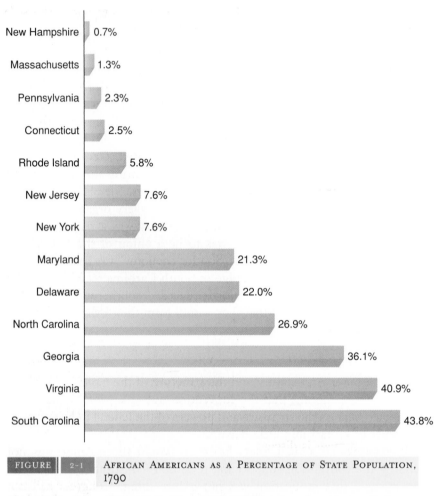

New Hampshire 0.7%

Massachusetts 1.3%

Pennsylvania 2.3%

Connecticut 2.5%

Rhode Island 5.8%

New Jersey 7.6%

New York 7.6%

Maryland 21.3%

Delaware 22.0%

North Carolina 26.9%

Georgia 36.1%

Virginia 40.9%

South Carolina 43.8%

FIGURE 2-1 AFRICAN AMERICANS AS A PERCENTAGE OF STATE POPULATION, 1790

At the time of the writing of the Constitution, African Americans (most of whom were slaves) were concentrated in the southern states. *Source: U.S. Bureau of the Census.*

ratify it. Indeed, North Carolina and Rhode Island were steadfastly opposed to the new union and did not ratify the Constitution until the eleven other states had ratified it and begun the process of establishing the new government.

The Ratification Debate

The debate over ratification was contentious. The **Anti-Federalists** (as opponents of the Constitution were labeled) raised arguments that still echo in American politics. They claimed that the national government would be too powerful and would threaten self-government in the separate states and the liberty of the people. Many Americans had an innate distrust of centralized power and worried that the people's liberty could be eclipsed as easily by a distant American government as it had been by the British king. The fact that the Constitution contained no bill of rights heightened this concern. Did its absence indicate that the central government would be free to define for itself what the people's rights would be?

The presidency was another source of contention. No such office had existed under the Articles, and some worried that it would lead to the creation of an American monarchy. The fact that the president would be chosen by electors appointed by the states lessened but did not eliminate this concern.

Even the motives of the men who wrote the Constitution came under attack. They were men of wealth and education and had acted in response to debtors' riots. Would the Constitution become a tool by which the wealthy ruled over those with little or no money? And who would bear the burden of additional taxation? For Americans struggling with local and state tax payments, the thought of paying national taxes as well was not appealing.

Most Anti-Federalists acknowledged a need to strengthen national commerce and defense. What they opposed was the creation of a powerful national government as the mechanism. They favored a revision of the Articles of Confederation, which in their opinion could accomplish these goals without the risk of establishing a government that could threaten their liberties, their livelihoods, and their local interests. (The Anti-Federalist argument is discussed further in Chapter 3.)

The **Federalists** (as the Constitution's supporters called themselves) responded with a persuasive case of their own. Their strongest arguments were set forth by James Madison and Alexander Hamilton, who along with John Jay wrote a series of essays that were published in a New York City newspaper under the pen name Publius. (The essays, collectively referred to as *The Federalist Papers*, are widely acknowledged as a brilliant political treatise.) Madison and Hamilton argued that the government of the Constitution would correct the defects of the Articles; it would have the power necessary to forge a secure and prosperous union. At the same time, because of restrictions on its powers, the new government would endanger neither the states nor personal liberty. In *Federalist* Nos. 47, 48, 49, 50, and 51, for example, Madison explained how the separation of national institutions was designed to both empower and restrict the federal government. (The Federalist argument is discussed further in Chapter 3.)

Whether the ratification debate changed many minds is unclear. Historical evidence suggests, however, that a majority of ordinary Americans opposed the Constitution's ratification. But their voice in the state ratifying conventions was smaller than that of wealthier interests, which in the main supported the change. The pro-ratification forces were also bolstered by the widespread assumption that George Washington, the most trusted and popular American leader, would become the first president. In the view of historians, the fact that Washington had presided over the Philadelphia convention and the assumption that he would become the chief executive tipped the balance in favor of ratification.

Delaware was the first state to ratify the Constitution, and Connecticut, Georgia, and New Jersey followed, an indication that the Great Compromise had satisfied several of the small states. In the early summer of 1788, New Hampshire became the ninth state to ratify. The Constitution was law. But neither Virginia nor New York had ratified it, and a stable union without these major states was almost unthinkable. As large in area as many European countries, they conceivably could survive as independent nations. They nearly did choose a separate course. In both states, the Constitution barely passed, and then only after the Federalists promised to support a bill of rights designed to protect individual liberty from the power of the central government.

The Framers' Goals

The Englishman James Bryce ranked America's written constitution as its greatest contribution to the practice of government. The Constitution offered the world a new model of government in which a written document defining the state's lawful powers would be a higher authority than the actions of any political leader or institution.

A **constitution** is the fundamental law that defines how a government will legitimately operate—the method for choosing its leaders, the institutions through which these leaders will work, the procedures they must follow in making policy, and the powers they can lawfully exercise. The U.S. Constitution is exactly such a law. It is the highest law of the land. Its provisions define how power is to be acquired and how it can be used.

The Constitution embodied the Framers' vision of a proper government for the American people (see Table 2–1). One of the Framers' goals was the creation of a national government strong enough to meet the nation's needs, particularly in the areas of defense and commerce. Another goal was to preserve the states as governing entities. Accordingly, the Framers established a system of government (federalism) in which power

TABLE	2-1	MAJOR GOALS OF THE FRAMERS OF THE CONSTITUTION

1. To establish a government strong enough to meet the nation's needs—an objective sought through substantial grants of power to the federal government in areas such as defense and commerce (see Chapter 3)
2. To establish a government that would not threaten the existence of the separate states—an objective sought through federalism (see Chapter 3) and through a Congress connected to the states through elections
3. To establish a government that would not threaten liberty—an objective sought through an elaborate system of checks and balances
4. To establish a government based on popular consent—an objective sought through provisions for the direct and indirect election of public officials

is divided between the national government and the states. Federalism is discussed at length in Chapter 3, which also explains how the Constitution laid the foundation for a strong national government.

The Framers' other goals were to establish a national government that was restricted in its lawful uses of power (limited government) and that gave the people a voice in their governance (self-government). These two goals and the story of how they were written into the Constitution are the focus of the rest of this chapter.

PROTECTING LIBERTY: LIMITED GOVERNMENT Quiz

A challenge facing the Framers of the Constitution was how to control the coercive force of government. Government's unique characteristic is that it alone can legally arrest, imprison, and even kill people who break its rules. Force is not the only basis of effective government, but government must be able to use force to prevent lawless elements from taking over society. The dilemma is that government itself can use its force to brutalize and intimidate its opponents. "It is a melancholy reflection," James Madison wrote to Thomas Jefferson shortly after the Constitution's ratification, "that liberty should be equally exposed to danger whether the government has too much or too little power."[5]

The men who wrote the Constitution sought to establish a government strong enough to enforce national interests, including defense and

TABLE 2-2 CONSTITUTIONAL PROVISIONS FOR LIMITED GOVERNMENT

The U.S. Constitution creates an elaborate governing structure designed to protect against the abusive exercise of power—in short, to create a limited government.

Mechanism	Purpose
Grants of power	Powers granted to the national government; accordingly, powers not granted to it are denied to it unless they are necessary and proper to the carrying out of the granted powers.
Separated institutions sharing power	The division of the national government's power among three branches, each of which is to act as a check on the powers of the other two.
Federalism	The division of political authority between the national government and the states, enabling the people to appeal to one authority if their rights and interests are not respected by the other authority.
Denials of power	Powers expressly denied to the national and state governments by the Constitution.
Bill of Rights	The first ten amendments to the Constitution, which specify rights of citizens that the national government must respect.
Judicial review	The power of the courts to declare governmental action null and void when it is found to violate the Constitution.
Elections	The power of the voters to remove officials from office.

commerce among the states (see Chapter 3), but not so strong as to destroy liberty. Limited government is built into the Constitution through both grants of political power and restrictions on that power (see Table 2–2).

Grants and Denials of Power

The Framers chose to limit the national government in part by confining its scope to constitutional **grants of power.** Congress's lawmaking powers are specifically listed in Article I, Section 8 of the Constitution. Seventeen in number, these listed powers include, for example, the powers to tax, to establish an army and navy, to declare war, to regulate commerce among the states, to create a national currency, and to borrow money. Powers *not* granted to the government by the Constitution are in theory denied to it. In a period when other governments had unrestricted powers, this limitation was remarkable.

The Framers also used **denials of power** as a means to limit government, prohibiting certain practices that European rulers had routinely used to intimidate political opponents. The French king, for example, could imprison a subject indefinitely without charge. The U.S. Constitution prohibits such action: citizens have the right to be brought before a court under a writ of habeas corpus for a judgment as to the legality of their confinement. The Constitution also forbids Congress and the states from passing ex post facto laws, under which citizens can be prosecuted for acts that were legal at the time they were committed.

As a further denial of power, the Framers made the Constitution difficult to amend, thereby making it hard for those in power to increase their lawful authority by changing the Constitution. An amendment could be proposed only by a two-thirds majority in both chambers of Congress or by a national constitutional convention called by two-thirds of the state legislatures. Such a proposal would then become law only if ratified by three-fourths of state legislatures or state conventions. In all but one case (the Twenty-first Amendment), state legislatures have done the ratifying. The national constitutional convention as a means of proposing amendments has never been used.

Using Power to Offset Power

Although the Framers believed that grants and denials of power could act as controls on government, they had no illusion that written words alone would suffice. As a consequence, they sought to control government by dividing its powers among separate institutions.[6]

The idea of a **separation of powers** had been proposed decades earlier by the French theorist Montesquieu. His reasoning was widely accepted in America, and when the states drafted new constitutions after the start of the Revolutionary War, they built their governments around this concept. Pennsylvania was an exception, and its experience only seemed to prove the necessity of separated powers. Unrestrained by an independent judiciary or executive, Pennsylvania's all-powerful legislature ignored basic rights and freedoms: Quakers were disenfranchised for their religious beliefs, conscientious objectors to the Revolutionary War were prosecuted, and the right of trial by jury was eliminated.

In *Federalist* No. 10, Madison asked why majorities, once in control of government, had so often used it to oppress their opponents. He attributed the problem to "the mischiefs of faction." People, he argued, are divided into opposing religious, geographical, ethnic, economic, and other factions. These divisions are natural and desirable in that free people have a right to their personal opinions and interests. Yet factions can themselves be a source of oppressive government. If a faction gains full power, it will use its control of government to advance itself at the expense of all others. (*Federalist* No. 10 is widely regarded as the finest political essay ever written by an American. It is reprinted in the reading at the end of this chapter.)

Out of this concern came the Framers' special contribution to the doctrine of the separation of powers. They did not believe that it would be enough, as Montesquieu had suggested, to divide the government's authority strictly along institutional lines, granting all legislative power to the legislature, all judicial power to the courts, and all executive power to the presidency. This total separation would make it too easy for a single faction to exploit a particular type of political power. A faction that controlled the legislature, for example, could enact laws that promoted its interests at the expense of all others. A better system of divided government would be one in which political power could be applied forcibly only when all the institutions supported a course of action. This system would require separate but overlapping powers. Because no one faction could easily gain control over all institutions, factions would be forced to work together, a process that would require each of them to respect the interests of the others.[7]

Separated Institutions Sharing Power: Checks and Balances

The Framers' concept of divided powers has been described by political scientist Richard Neustadt as the principle of **separated institutions sharing power.**[8] The separate branches are interlocked in such a way that an elaborate system of **checks and balances** is created (see Figure 2–2). No institution can act decisively without the support or acquiescence of the other institutions. Legislative, executive, and judicial powers in the American system are divided in such a way that they overlap: each of the three branches of government checks the others' powers and balances those powers with powers of its own. As natural as this system

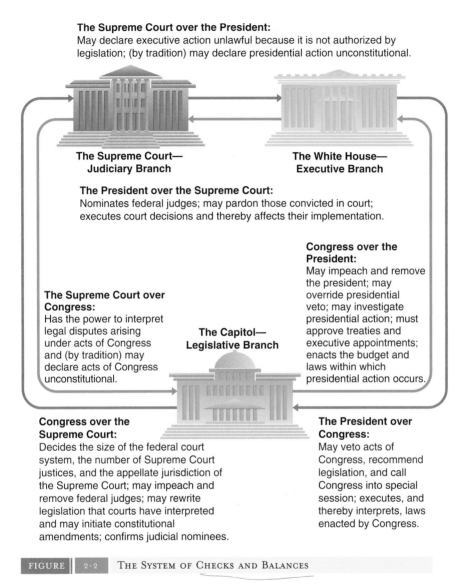

The Supreme Court over the President:
May declare executive action unlawful because it is not authorized by legislation; (by tradition) may declare presidential action unconstitutional.

The Supreme Court—
Judiciary Branch

The White House—
Executive Branch

The President over the Supreme Court:
Nominates federal judges; may pardon those convicted in court; executes court decisions and thereby affects their implementation.

Congress over the President:
May impeach and remove the president; may override presidential veto; may investigate presidential action; must approve treaties and executive appointments; enacts the budget and laws within which presidential action occurs.

The Supreme Court over Congress:
Has the power to interpret legal disputes arising under acts of Congress and (by tradition) may declare acts of Congress unconstitutional.

The Capitol—
Legislative Branch

Congress over the Supreme Court:
Decides the size of the federal court system, the number of Supreme Court justices, and the appellate jurisdiction of the Supreme Court; may impeach and remove federal judges; may rewrite legislation that courts have interpreted and may initiate constitutional amendments; confirms judicial nominees.

The President over Congress:
May veto acts of Congress, recommend legislation, and call Congress into special session; executes, and thereby interprets, laws enacted by Congress.

FIGURE 2-2 THE SYSTEM OF CHECKS AND BALANCES

now might seem to Americans, most democracies are of the parliamentary type, with executive and legislative power combined in a single institution rather than vested in separate ones. In a parliamentary system, the majority in the legislature selects the prime minister, who then serves as both the legislative leader and the chief executive (see "How the United States Compares").

Shared Legislative Powers   Under the Constitution, Congress has legislative authority, but that power is partly shared with the other branches and thus checked by them. The president can veto acts of Congress, recommend legislation, and call special sessions of Congress. The president also has the power to execute—and thereby interpret—the laws Congress makes.

The Supreme Court has the power to interpret acts of Congress that are disputed in legal cases. The Court also has the power of judicial review: it can declare laws of Congress void when it finds that they are not in accord with the Constitution.

Within Congress, there is a further check on legislative power: for legislation to be passed, a majority in each house of Congress is required. Thus, the Senate and the House of Representatives can block each other from acting.

Shared Executive Powers   Executive power is vested in the president but is constrained by legislative and judicial checks. The president's power to make treaties and appoint high-ranking officials, for example, is subject to Senate approval. Congress also has the power to impeach and remove the president from office. In practical terms, Congress's greatest checks on executive action are its lawmaking and appropriations powers. The executive branch cannot act without laws that authorize its activities or without the money that pays for these activities. Congress allowed it to happen

The judiciary's major check on the presidency is its power to declare an action unlawful because it is not authorized by the legislation that the executive claims to be implementing.

 ## HOW THE UNITED STATES COMPARES

Checks and Balances

All democracies place constitutional limits on the power of government. The concept of rule by law, for example, is characteristic of democratic governments but not of authoritarian regimes. Democracies differ, however, in the extent to which political power is restrained through constitutional mechanisms. The United States is an extreme case in that its government rests on an elaborate system of constitutional checks and balances. The system employs a separation

(continued)

of powers among the executive, legislative, and judicial branches. It also includes judicial review, the power of the courts to invalidate actions of the legislative or executive branch. These constitutional restrictions on power are not part of the governing structure of all democracies.

Most democracies have parliamentary systems, which invest both executive and legislative leadership in the office of prime minister. Britain is an example of this type of system. Parliament under the leadership of the prime minister is the supreme authority in Britain. Its laws are not subject to override by Britain's high court, which has no power to review the constitutionality of parliamentary acts.

In parliamentary systems, moreover, either there is only one legislative chamber or, if there are two, power resides primarily in one chamber. The British House of Lords, for example, has only a limited ability to check the actions of the British House of Commons, which the prime minister heads. In the United States, the two legislative chambers—the House and the Senate—are coequal bodies. Because legislation can be enacted only with the approval of both houses, each serves as a check on the other.

Country	Separation of Executive & Legislative Powers?	Judicial Review?
Belgium	No	Yes
Canada	No	Yes
France	Yes	No
Germany	No	Yes
Great Britain	No	No
Italy	No	Yes
Japan	No	Yes
Mexico	Yes	Yes
United States	Yes	Yes

Shared Judicial Powers   Judicial power rests with the Supreme Court and with lower federal courts, which are subject to checks by the other branches of the federal government. Congress is empowered to establish the size of the federal court system, to restrict the Supreme Court's appellate jurisdiction in some circumstances, and to impeach and remove federal judges from office. More important, Congress can rewrite legislation that it believes the courts have misinterpreted and can initiate amendments when it disagrees with court rulings on constitutional issues.

The president has the power to appoint federal judges with the consent of the Senate and to pardon persons convicted in the courts. The president also is responsible for executing court decisions, a function that provides opportunities to influence the way rulings are carried out.

The Bill of Rights

Although the delegates to the Philadelphia convention discussed the possibility of placing a list of individual rights (such as freedom of speech and the right to a fair trial) in the Constitution, they ultimately decided that such a list was unnecessary because of the doctrine of expressed powers: government could not lawfully engage in actions, such as the suppression of speech, that were not authorized by the Constitution. Moreover, the delegates argued that a bill of rights was undesirable because government might feel free to disregard any right that was inadvertently left off the list or that emerged at some future time.

These arguments did not persuade leading Americans who believed that no possible safeguard of liberty should be omitted. "A bill of rights," Jefferson argued, "is what the people are entitled to against every government on earth, general or particular, and what no just government should refuse or rest on inference." Jefferson had included a bill of rights in the constitution he wrote for Virginia at the outbreak of the Revolutionary War, and all but four states had followed Virginia's example.

Opposition to the exclusion of a bill of rights led to its addition to the Constitution. Madison himself introduced a series of amendments during the First Congress, ten of which were soon ratified by the states. These amendments, traditionally called the **Bill of Rights,** include rights such as freedom of speech and religion and due process protections (such as jury trial and legal counsel) for persons accused of crimes. (These rights, termed *civil liberties,* are discussed at length in Chapter 4.)

The Bill of Rights is a precise expression of the concept of limited government. In consenting to be governed, the people agree to accept the authority of government in certain areas but not in others; the people's constitutional rights cannot lawfully be denied by governing officials.

Judicial Review

The writers of the Constitution both empowered and limited government. But who was to decide whether officials were operating within the limits of their constitutionally authorized powers? The Constitution does not specifically entrust this power to a particular branch of government, although it does grant the Supreme Court the authority to decide on "all cases arising under this Constitution." Moreover, at the ratifying conventions of at least eight of the thirteen states, it was argued that the judiciary would have the power to nullify actions that violated the Constitution.[9]

Nevertheless, because the Constitution did not explicitly grant the judiciary this authority, the principle had to be established in practice. The opportunity arose with an incident that occurred after the election of 1800, in which John Adams lost his bid for a second presidential term after a bitter campaign against Jefferson.

Historical Background

Between November 1800, when Jefferson was elected, and March 1801, when he was inaugurated, the Federalist-controlled Congress created fifty-nine additional lower-court judgeships, enabling Adams to appoint loyal Federalists to those positions before he left office. However, Adams's term expired before his secretary of state could deliver the judicial commissions to all the appointees. Without this authorization, an appointee could not take office. Knowing this, Jefferson told his secretary of state, James Madison, not to deliver the commissions. William Marbury was one of those who did not receive his commission, and he asked the Supreme Court to issue a writ of mandamus (a court order directing an official to perform a specific act) that would force Madison to deliver it.

Marbury v. Madison (1803) became the foundation for judicial review by the federal courts. Chief Justice John Marshall wrote the *Marbury* opinion, which declared that Marbury had a legal right to his commission. The opinion also said, however, that the Supreme Court could not issue him a writ of mandamus because it lacked the constitutional authority to do so. Congress had passed ordinary legislation in 1789 that gave the Court this power, but Marshall noted that the Constitution prohibits Congress from expanding the Supreme Court's authority except through a constitutional amendment. That being the case, Marshall argued, the legislation that provided the authorization was constitutionally invalid.[10] In striking down this act of Congress on constitutional grounds, the Court asserted its power of **judicial review**—that is, the power of the judiciary to decide whether a

★ LEADERS

Thomas Jefferson
(1743–1826)

Thomas Jefferson was the principal author of the Declaration of Independence. It was Jefferson who at age thirty-three coined the renowned words "Life, Liberty and the Pursuit of Happiness." A man of contradictions, Jefferson owned slaves while arguing for human equality and liberty. Elected to the presidency in 1800, Jefferson was a proponent of states' rights and of a strict interpretation of the national government's constitutional powers. Yet he overlooked the Constitution, which had no authorization for such an act, in purchasing the Louisiana Territory from the French Emperor Napoleon in 1803, doubling the area of the United States. A reserved man who was a better writer than public speaker, Jefferson dedicated much of his life to the betterment of his home state of Virginia. He drafted the state's Bill of Rights, which included a provision for religious freedom—a right not guaranteed in all states at the time. After retiring to his Monticello estate following his two terms as president, Jefferson designed and founded the University of Virginia, calling it one of his greatest achievements. To Jefferson, the success of the American experiment in self-government rested ultimately on an educated citizenry.

government official or institution has acted within the limits of its constitutional authority and, if not, to declare its action null and void.

Marshall's decision was ingenious because it asserted the power of judicial review without creating the possibility of its rejection by either the executive or the legislative branch. In declaring that Marbury had a right to his commission, the Court in effect said that President Jefferson had failed in his constitutional duty to execute the laws faithfully. But because it did not order Jefferson to deliver the commission, he had no opportunity to refuse to comply with the Court's judgment. At the same time, the Court reprimanded Congress for passing legislation that exceeded its constitutional authority. Congress also had no way to retaliate. It could not force the Court to accept the authority to issue writs of mandamus if the Court itself refused to do so.

Providing for Self-Government

"We the People" is the opening phrase of the Constitution. It expresses the idea that in the United States the people will have the power to govern themselves. In a sense, there is no contradiction between this idea and the Constitution's provisions for limited government, because individual *liberty* is an essential element of *self-government*. If people cannot express themselves freely, they cannot be self-governing. In another sense, however, the contradiction is clear: restrictions on the power of the majority are a denial of its right to govern society in whatever way it chooses.

The Framers believed that the people deserved and required a voice in their government, but they worried that the people would become inflamed by a passionate issue or fiery demagogue and act rashly. To the Framers, the great risk of popular government was **tyranny of the majority:** the people acting as an irrational mob that tramples on the rights of the minority. Their fear was not without foundation. The history of democracies was filled with examples of majority tyranny, and there were even examples from the nation's brief history. In 1786, for instance, debtors had gained control of Rhode Island's legislature and made paper money a legal means of paying debts, even though existing contracts called for payment in gold. Creditors were then hunted down and held captive in public places so that debtors could come and pay them in full with worthless paper money. A Boston newspaper wrote that Rhode Island should be renamed Rogue Island.

Democracy Versus Republic

No form of self-government could eliminate completely the threat to liberty of majority tyranny, but the Framers believed that the danger would be greatly diminished by creating a republican government as opposed to a democratic government.[11] Today, the terms **democracy, republic,** and **representative democracy** are often used interchangeably to refer to a system of government in which political power rests with the people through their ability to choose representatives in free and fair elections. To the writers of the Constitution, however, a *democracy* and a *republic* were different forms of government.

By the term *democracy*, the Framers meant a government in which the power of the majority is unlimited, whether exercised directly (as in the case of town meetings open to all citizens) or through a representative body. The majority's rule is absolute. Should it decide to act tyrannically—to run roughshod over the minority—there is nothing in the laws to stop it. By the term *republic*, the Framers meant a government that is based on majority rule but protects the minority through a guarantee of individual rights and other checks on majority power. The purpose of republican government is to limit the power of the majority—not as a means of preventing the people from governing themselves but as a means of safeguarding minority rights and interests. The majority rules, but it rules within prescribed limits.[12]

The Framers believed that a republican government is superior to a democratic one. They also believed that a republic, to work well in practice, requires virtuous representatives—lawmakers who have an enlightened sense of the public interest. In this respect, their outlook was similar to that of the English theorist Edmund Burke (1729–97). In his *Letter to the Sheriffs of Bristol*, Burke argued that representatives should act as public **trustees:** they are obliged to serve the interest of those who elect them, but the nature of this interest, Burke said, is for the representatives, not the voters, to decide. Burke was concerned with the ease with which a majority can think like a mob, and he claimed that representatives should not surrender their judgment to reckless ideas.

Limited Popular Rule

The Constitution provided that all power would be exercised through representative institutions. There was no provision for any form of direct popular participation in the making of policy decisions. In view of the fact

Rhode Island was nicknamed "Rogue Island" for its disregard of property rights. Shown here is the Rhode Island three-dollar bank note, which came to be worth no more than the paper it was written on and yet was used to pay off gold debts.

that the United States was much too large to be governed directly by the people in popular assemblies, a representative system was necessary. The Framers went beyond what was necessary, however, and placed officials at a considerable distance from the people they represented (see Table 2–3).

The House of Representatives was the only institution that would be based on direct popular election—its members would be elected to serve for two years by a vote of the people. Frequent and direct election of House members was intended to make government sensitive to the concerns of popular majorities.

U.S. senators would be appointed by the legislatures of the states they represented. Because state legislators were popularly elected, the people would be choosing their senators indirectly. Every two years, a third of the senators would be appointed to six-year terms. The Senate was expected to check and balance the House, which, by virtue of the more frequent and direct election of its members, presumably would be more responsive to popular opinion.

Presidential selection was an issue of considerable debate at the Philadelphia convention. Direct election of the president was twice proposed and twice rejected because it linked executive power directly to popular majorities. The Framers finally chose to have the president selected by the votes of electors (the so-called **Electoral College**). Each state would have as many **electoral votes** as it had members in Congress and could select its electors by any method it chose. The president would serve four years and be eligible for reelection.

The Framers decided that federal judges and justices would be appointed rather than elected. They would be nominated by the president

TABLE | **2-3** METHODS OF CHOOSING NATIONAL LEADERS

Fearing the concentration of political power, the Framers devised alternative methods of selection and terms of service for national officials.

Office	Method of Selection	Term of Service
President	Electoral College	4 years
U.S. senator	State legislature	6 years (1/3 of senators' terms expire every 2 years)
U.S. representative	Popular election	2 years
Federal judge	Nominated by president, approved by Senate	Indefinite (subject to "good behavior")

and confirmed through approval by the Senate. Once confirmed, they would "hold their offices during good behavior." In effect, they would be allowed to hold office for life unless they committed a crime. The judiciary was a "guardian" institution that would uphold the rule of law and serve as a check on the elected branches of government.[13]

These differing methods of selecting national officeholders would not prevent a determined majority from achieving unchecked power, but control could not be attained quickly. Unlike the House of Representatives, institutions such as the Senate, presidency, and judiciary would not yield to an impassioned majority in a single election. The delay would reduce the likelihood that government would degenerate into mob rule driven by momentary passions.

Altering the Constitution: More Power to the People

The Framers' conception of self-government was at odds with what the average American in 1787 had come to expect. Every state but South Carolina held annual legislative elections, and several states also chose their governors through direct annual election. Not long after ratification of the Constitution, Americans began to challenge the Constitution's restrictions on majority rule (see Table 2–4).

TABLE 2-4 MEASURES TAKEN TO MAKE GOVERNMENT MORE RESPONSIVE TO POPULAR MAJORITIES

The U.S. Constitution created barriers designed to limit direct popular influence on government. Subsequent changes were designed to lower these barriers and increase the power of voting majorities.

Earlier Situation	Subsequent Development
Separation of powers, as a means of dividing authority and blunting passionate majorities	Political parties, as a means of uniting authorities and linking them with popular majorities
Indirect election of all national officials except House members, as a means of buffering officials from popular influence	Direct election of U.S. senators and popular voting for president (linked to electoral votes), as a means of increasing popular control of officials
Nomination of candidates for public office through political party organizations	Primary elections, as a direct means of selecting party nominees

Jeffersonian Democracy: A Revolution of the Spirit Thomas Jefferson, who otherwise admired the Constitution, was among the prominent Americans who questioned its provisions for self-government—and it was Jefferson who may have spared the nation a bloody conflict over the issue of popular sovereignty. Under John Adams, the second president, the national government increasingly favored the nation's wealthy interests. Adams publicly indicated that the Constitution was designed for a governing elite, while Alexander Hamilton suggested that Adams might have to use force to suppress radical dissent.[14] Jefferson asked whether Adams, with the aid of a strong army, planned soon to deprive ordinary Americans of their liberty. Jefferson challenged Adams in the next presidential election and, upon defeating him, hailed his victory as the "Revolution of 1800."

Although Jefferson was a champion of the common people, he had no clear vision of how a popular government might work in practice. Jefferson saw Congress, not the presidency, as the institution better suited to representing majority opinion.[15] Jefferson also had no illusions about a largely uneducated population's readiness for playing a large governing role and feared the consequences of inciting the masses to confront the moneyed class. But Jefferson did found the nation's first political party (the forerunner of today's Democratic party), which served to link like-minded leaders and thus act as a bridge across divided institutions of power. By and large, however, Jeffersonian democracy was a revolution of the spirit. Jefferson taught Americans to look on national government institutions as belonging to all, not just to the privileged few.[16]

Jacksonian Democracy: Linking the People and the Presidency Not until the election of Andrew Jackson in 1828 did the country have a powerful president who was willing and able to involve the public more fully in government. Jackson carried out the constitutional revolution that Jeffersonian democracy had foreshadowed.

Jackson recognized that the president was the only official who could legitimately claim to represent the people as a whole. Unlike the president, members of Congress were elected from separate states and districts rather than from the entire country. Yet the president's claim to popular leadership was weakened by the fact that the president was chosen by electors rather than by the voters. Jackson's ingenious solution was to have each state give its electoral votes to whichever candidate received the most popular votes in the state. This arrangement, still in effect, places the selection of the president in the voters' hands in most elections. The candidate who receives the most popular votes nationally also is likely to finish first in enough states to win a majority of electoral votes. Since Jackson's time, only three candidates—Rutherford B. Hayes in 1876, Benjamin Harrison in 1888, and George W. Bush in 2000—have won the presidency after losing the popular vote. (The Electoral College is discussed further in Chapter 12.)

The Progressives: Senate and Primary Elections   The Progressive era of the early 1900s brought another wave of democratic reforms. The Progressives rejected the Burkean idea of representatives as trustees, instead embracing the idea of representatives as **delegates**—officeholders who are obligated to respond directly to the expressed opinions of the people they represent.

The Progressives sought to place power more directly in the hands of the people.[17] They succeeded in changing the way some state and local governments operate. Progressive reforms at state and local levels included the initiative and the referendum, which enable citizens to vote directly on legislative issues (see "States in the Nation"). Another Progressive reform was the recall election, which enables citizens through petition to force an officeholder to submit to reelection before the regular expiration of his or her term. (In 2003 a recall election in California resulted in the election of actor Arnold Schwarzenegger as the state's new governor.)

The Progressives also instigated two changes in federal elections. One was the direct election of U.S. senators, who before the Seventeenth Amendment was ratified in 1913 had been chosen by state legislatures and were widely perceived as agents of big business (the Senate was nicknamed the "Millionaires' Club"). Senators who stood to lose their seats in a direct popular vote had blocked earlier attempts to change the Constitution. However, the Senate was persuaded to support an amendment following pressure from the Progressives and revelations that corporate bribes had influenced the selection of several senators. The second change was the **primary election,** which gives rank-and-file voters the power to select party nominees. In the early 1900s, nearly all states adopted the primary election as a means of choosing nominees for at least some federal and state offices. Before this change, nominees were selected by party leaders.

The Progressive era spawned attacks on the Framers. A prominent criticism was laid out in historian Charles S. Beard's *An Economic Interpretation of the Constitution.*[18] Arguing that the Constitution grew out of wealthy Americans' fears of the debtor rebellions and noting that many of the Framers were themselves wealthy men, Beard claimed that the Constitution's

Direct Democracy: The Initiative and Referendum

In some states, citizens through their votes can directly enact or reject legislation. Legislation may be placed on the ballot through either the referendum (in which the state legislature places a legislative proposal on the ballot) or the initiative (in which citizens by gathering enough signatures on petitions place a legislative proposal on the ballot).

Q: Why are southern and northeastern states less likely to have the initiative and referendum than states in other areas?

A: The initiative and referendum were introduced in the early 1900s by the Progressives, who sought to weaken the power of political bosses and give voters a larger voice in their governance. In the Northeast, party machines had enough strength in state legislatures to block their enactment. In the South, these devices were blocked by the white establishment, which feared that blacks and poor whites would make use of them.

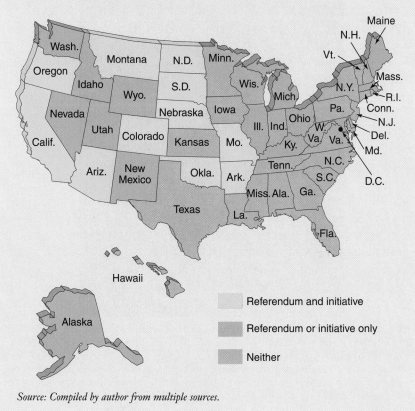

Referendum and initiative

Referendum or initiative only

Neither

Source: Compiled by author from multiple sources.

67

elaborate systems of power and representation were devices for keeping power in the hands of the rich. Beard's thesis was challenged by other historians, and he later acknowledged that he had not taken the Framers' full array of motives into account. Their conception of separation of powers, for example, was a governing principle that had earlier been incorporated into state constitutions. Although the Framers did not have great trust in popular rule, to conclude that they were foes of democracy would be a mistake. They were intent on balancing the demand for self-government with the requirement for limited government, believing that unchecked majority rule could lead to oppressive government.

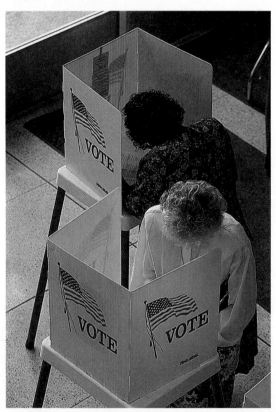

The Constitution originally provided for direct popular election only in the case of the House of Representatives. Not until the 1830s was popular voting for the office of president pervasive, even though then, as today, the choice of a president rested with electors. In 1914, for the first time in all states holding congressional elections, U.S. senators were chosen by popular vote. At roughly the same time, primary elections were widely adopted as a means of nominating candidates for public office. Today, the United States holds elections more often and for more offices than virtually any other nation—a development that is contrary to what the writers of the Constitution believed was proper.

Since the Progressive era, no major structural changes have taken place in the process by which Americans elect their leaders. Nevertheless, the question of how best to achieve self-government in practice continues to engage Americans. During the 1960s, for example, public demands led to fairer voter-registration laws, including the elimination of literacy tests and poll taxes, which were devices designed to keep minorities and poor people from voting. More recent efforts include the term-limit movement, which seeks to limit the length of time an individual can hold the same public office. Through the relationships they build with powerful groups, incumbent officeholders today enjoy a huge advantage over their electoral challengers (see Chapters 8 and 11). Congressional incumbents are able to raise far more money for their campaigns than can their challengers. One result has been increasingly lopsided election outcomes, with more than 95 percent of congressional incumbents winning reelection—most by margins of two to one or greater. Term limits reduce the advantage of incumbency and shift power in election campaigns from moneyed interests to the voters.

CONSTITUTIONAL DEMOCRACY TODAY

The type of government created in the United States in 1787 is today called a **constitutional democracy.** It is *democratic* in its provisions for majority influence through elections and *constitutional* in its requirement that power gained through elections be exercised in accordance with law and with due respect for individual rights.

By some standards, the American system of today is a model of *self-government*.[19] The United States schedules the election of its larger legislative chamber (the House of Representatives) and its chief executive more frequently than does any other democracy. In addition, it is the only major democracy to rely extensively on primary elections rather than party organizations for the selection of party nominees. The principle of popular election to office, which the writers of the Constitution regarded as a prerequisite of popular sovereignty but a method to be used sparingly, has been extended further in the United States than anywhere else.

By other standards, however, the U.S. system is less democratic than many others. Popular majorities must work against the barriers to influence devised by the Framers—the elaborate system of divided powers, staggered terms of office, and separate constituencies. In fact, the link between an electoral majority and a governing majority is less direct in the American system than in nearly all other democratic systems. In the European parliamentary democracies, for example, legislative and executive power are not separated, are not subject to close check by the judiciary, and are acquired through the winning of a legislative majority in national elections. The Framers' vision was a different one, dominated by a concern with *liberty* and therefore with controls on political power. It was a response to the experiences they brought with them to Philadelphia in the summer of 1787.

SUMMARY

The Constitution of the United States is a reflection of the colonial and revolutionary experiences of the early Americans. Freedom from abusive government was a reason for the colonies' revolt against British rule, but the English tradition also provided ideas about government, power, and freedom that were expressed in the Constitution and, earlier, in the Declaration of Independence.

The Constitution was designed in part to provide for a limited government in which political power would be confined to proper uses. The Framers wanted to ensure that the government they were creating would not itself be a threat to freedom. To this end, they confined the national government to expressly granted powers and also denied it certain specific powers. Other prohibitions on government were later added to the Constitution in the form of stated guarantees of individual liberties in the Bill of Rights. The most significant constitutional provision for limited government, however, was a separation of powers among the three branches. The powers given to each branch enable it to act as a check on the exercise of power by the other two, an arrangement that during the nation's history has in fact served as a barrier to abuses of power.

The Constitution, however, made no mention of how the powers and limits of government were to be judged in practice. In its historic ruling in *Marbury v. Madison*, the Supreme Court assumed the authority to review the constitutionality of legislative and executive actions and to declare them unconstitutional and thus invalid.

The Framers of the Constitution, respecting the idea of self-government but distrusting popular majorities, devised a system of government that they felt would temper popular opinion and slow its momentum so that the public's "true interest" (which includes a regard for the rights and interests of the minority) would guide public policy. Different methods were established for selecting the president, the members of the House and Senate, and federal judges as a means of insulating political power against momentary majorities.

Since the adoption of the Constitution, the public gradually has assumed more direct control of its representatives, particularly through measures that affect the way officeholders are chosen. Presidential popular voting (linked to the Electoral College), direct election of senators, and primary elections are among the devices aimed at strengthening the majority's influence. These developments are rooted in the idea, deeply held by ordinary Americans, that the people must have substantial direct influence over their representatives if government is to serve their interests.

KEY TERMS

Anti-Federalists *(p. 49)*
Bill of Rights *(p. 59)*
checks and balances *(p. 55)*
constitution *(p. 51)*
constitutional democracy *(p. 70)*
delegates *(p. 67)*
democracy *(p. 62)*
denials of power *(p. 54)*
Electoral College *(p. 64)*
electoral votes *(p. 64)*
Federalists *(p. 50)*
grants of power *(p. 53)*
Great Compromise *(p. 46-47)*
inalienable (natural) rights *(p. 43)*

judicial review *(p. 60)*
limited government *(p. 39)*
New Jersey (small-state) Plan *(p. 46)*
North-South Compromise *(p. 47)*
primary election *(p. 67)*
representative democracy *(p. 62)*
republic *(p. 62)*
self-government *(p. 39)*
separated institutions sharing
  power *(p. 55)*
separation of powers *(p. 54)*
trustees *(p. 63)*
tyranny of the majority *(p. 62)*
Virginia (large-state) Plan *(p. 46)*

SUGGESTED READINGS

Beard, Charles S. *An Economic Interpretation of the Constitution.* New York: Macmillan, 1941. Argues that the Framers had selfish economic interests uppermost in their minds when they wrote the Constitution.

Edling, Max M. *A Revolution in Favor of Government.* New York: Oxford University Press, 2003. Argues that the Framers intended the Constitution to create a strong government.

Ellis, Joseph J. *Founding Brothers: The Revolutionary Generation.* New York: Vintage, 2002. A riveting account of the lives of America's leading Founders.

Federalist Papers. Many editions, including a one-volume paperback version edited by Isaac Kramnick (New York: Penguin, 1987). A series of essays written by Alexander Hamilton, James Madison, and John Jay under the pseudonym Publius. The essays, published in a New York newspaper in 1787–88, explain the Constitution and support its ratification.

Hardin, Russell. *Liberalism, Constitutionalism, and Democracy.* New York: Oxford University Press, 1999. Analysis of the great ideas that underlie the Constitution.

Holcombe, Randall G. *From Liberty to Democracy.* Ann Arbor: University of Michigan Press, 2002. An interpretive history of the transformation of American government.

McGerr, Michael. *A Fierce Discontent: The Rise and Fall of the Progressive Movement in America, 1870–1920.* New York: Free Press, 2005. Assessment of the Progressive movement's contribution to American democracy.

Tocqueville, Alexis de. *Democracy in America,* vols. 1 and 2, ed. J. P. Mayer. New York: Doubleday/Anchor, 1969. A classic analysis (originally published 1835–40) of American democracy by an insightful French observer.

Wilentz, Sean. *The Rise of American Democracy: Jefferson to Lincoln.* New York: W. W. Norton, 2005. An account of how democratic ideas triumphed over aristocratic ones.

List of Websites

http://www.nara.gov/ The National Archives site; includes an in-depth look at the history of the Declaration of Independence.

http://odur.let.rug.nl/~usa/P/aj7/about/bio/jackxx.htm A site that focuses on Andrew Jackson and his role in shaping U.S. politics.

http://www.yale.edu/lawweb/avalon/constpap.htm Includes documents on the Constitution, the American Revolution, and the constitutional convention.

http://www.yale.edu/lawweb/avalon/presiden/jeffpap.htm A site that includes the papers of Thomas Jefferson. His autobiography is among the available materials.

Politics in Theory and Practice

Thinking: How does the division of power in the U.S. political system contribute to limited government? How do the provisions for representative government (the various methods of choosing national officials) contribute to limited government?

Participating: In recent years, as a means of checking the power of elected officials, a number of states and localities have imposed a limit on the number of terms that representatives can serve. Although the term-limit movement has slowed, there are still opportunities to get involved on either side of the issue. If you favor term limits and want to get involved, you might start by examining the website of U.S. Term Limits (www.termlimits.org). If you oppose term limits, you could begin by looking at the Common Cause site (www.commoncause.org).

Additional Resources

For quizzes, interactive simulations, games, graphics, and other study tools, visit this book's Online Learning Center at **www.mhhe.com/pattersonwtp7.**

The Mischiefs of Faction

By James Madison

James Madison wrote Federalist *No. 10 during the debate over ratification of the Constitution. It has been described as the finest political essay ever written by an American. In it, Madison argues that a "republican" form of government is the surest protection against abuse of political power. He argues that people naturally and passionately pursue their self-interest and, therefore, that power placed directly in the hands of a popular majority is likely to be directed against minority interests. Madison's solution, as described in this chapter, is a constitutional system in which popular influence works through, and is moderated by, representative institutions.*

Among the numerous advantages promised by a well-constructed Union, none deserves to be more accurately developed than its tendency to break and control the violence of faction. . . .

By a faction I understand a number of citizens, whether amounting to a majority or minority of the whole, who are united and actuated by some common impulse of passion, or of interest, adverse to the rights of other citizens, or to the permanent and aggregate interests of the community.

There are two methods of curing the mischiefs of faction: the one, by removing its causes; the other, by controlling its effects.

There are again two methods of removing the causes of faction: the one, by destroying the liberty which is essential to its existence; the other, by giving to every citizen the same opinions, the same passions, and the same interests.

It could never be more truly said than of the first remedy that it was worse than the disease. Liberty is to faction what air is to fire, an ailment without which it instantly expires. But it could not be a less folly to abolish liberty, which is essential to political life, because it nourishes faction than it would be to wish the annihilation of air, which is essential to animal life, because it imparts to fire its destructive agency.

The second expedient is as impracticable as the first would be unwise. As long as the reason of man continues fallible, and he is at liberty to exercise it, different opinions will be formed. As long as the connection subsists between his reason and his self-love, his opinions and his passions will have a reciprocal influence on each other; and the former will be objects to which the latter will attach themselves. The diversity in the faculties of men, from which the rights of property originate, is not less an insuperable obstacle to a uniformity of interest. The protection of these faculties is the first object of government. From the protection of different and unequal faculties of acquiring property, the possession of different degrees and kinds of property immediately results; and from the influence of these on the sentiments and views of the respective proprietors ensues a division of the society into different interests and parties.

The latent causes of faction are thus sown in the nature of man; and we see them everywhere brought into different degrees of activity, according to the different circumstances of civil society. A zeal for different opinions concerning religion, concerning government, and many other points, as well of speculation as of practice; an attachment to different leaders ambitiously contending for pre-eminence and power; or to persons of other descriptions whose fortunes have been interesting to the human passions, have, in turn, divided mankind into parties, inflamed them with mutual animosity, and rendered them much more disposed to vex and oppress each other than to cooperate for their common good. So strong is this propensity of mankind to fall into mutual animosities that where no substantial occasion presents itself the most frivolous and fanciful distinctions have been sufficient to kindle their unfriendly passions and excite their most violent conflicts. But the most common and durable source of factions has been the various and unequal distribution of property. Those who hold and those who are without property have ever formed distinct interests in society. . . .

The inference to which we are brought is that the *causes* of faction cannot be removed and that relief is only to be sought in the means of controlling its *effects*.

If a faction consists of less than a majority, relief is supplied by the republican principle, which enables the majority to defeat its sinister views by regular vote. . . . When a majority is included in a faction, the form of popular government, on the other hand, enables it to sacrifice to its ruling passion or interest both the public good and the rights of other citizens. To secure the public good and private rights against the danger of such a faction, and at the same time to preserve the spirit and the form of popular government, is then the great object to which our inquiries are directed.

By what means is this object attainable? Evidently by one of two only. Either the existence of the same passion or interest in a majority at the same time must be prevented, or the majority, having such coex-

istent passion or interest, must be rendered, by their number and local situation, unable to concert and carry into effect schemes of oppression. If the impulse and the opportunity be suffered to coincide, we well know that neither moral nor religious motives can be relied on as an adequate control. They are not found to be such on the injustice and violence of individuals, and lose their efficacy in proportion to the number combined together, that is, in proportion as their efficacy becomes needful.

From this view of the subject it may be concluded that a pure democracy, by which I mean a society consisting of a small number of citizens, who assemble and administer the government in person, can admit of no cure for the mischiefs of faction. A common passion or interest will, in almost every case, be felt by a majority of the whole, a communication and concert results from the form of government itself; and there is nothing to check the inducements to sacrifice the weaker party or an obnoxious individual. Hence it is that such democracies have ever been spectacles of turbulence and contention; have ever been found incompatible with personal security or the rights of property; and have in general been as short in their lives as they have been violent in their deaths. . . .

A republic, by which I mean a government in which the scheme of representation takes place, opens a different prospect and promises the cure for which we are seeking. Let us examine the points in which it varies from pure democracy, and we shall comprehend both the nature of the cure and the efficacy which it must derive from the Union.

The two great points of difference between a democracy and a republic are: first, the delegation of the government, in the latter, to a small number of citizens elected by the rest; secondly, the greater number of citizens and greater sphere of country over which the latter may be extended.

The effect of the first difference is, on the one hand, to refine and enlarge the public views by passing them through the medium of a chosen body of citizens, whose wisdom may best discern the true interest of their country and whose patriotism and love of justice will be least likely to sacrifice it to temporary or partial considerations. Under such a regulation it may well happen that the public voice, pronounced by the representatives of the people, will be more consonant to the public good than if pronounced by the people themselves, convened for the purpose. . . .

The other point of difference is the greater number of citizens and extent of territory which may be brought within the compass of republican than of democratic government; and it is this circumstance principally which renders factious combinations less to be dreaded in the former than in the latter. The smaller the society, the fewer probably will be the distinct parties and interests composing it; the fewer the distinct parties and interests, the more frequently will a majority be found of the same party; and the smaller the number of individuals composing a majority, and the smaller the compass within which they are placed, the more easily will they concert and execute their plans of oppression. Extend the sphere and you take in a greater variety of parties and interests; you make it less probable that a majority of the whole will have a common motive to invade the rights of other citizens; or if such a common motive exists, it will be more difficult for all who feel it to discover their own strength and to act in unison with each other. . . .

Hence, it clearly appears that the same advantage which a republic has over a democracy in controlling the effects of faction is enjoyed by a large over a small republic—is enjoyed by the Union over the States composing it.

What's Your Opinion?

Do you agree with Madison's assumption and argument? If given a chance, will society's factions use the power of government to promote their selfish interests at the expense of those of society as a whole? Has the American system of checks and balances served to reduce the ability of powerful factions to exploit other interests?

CHAPTER 3

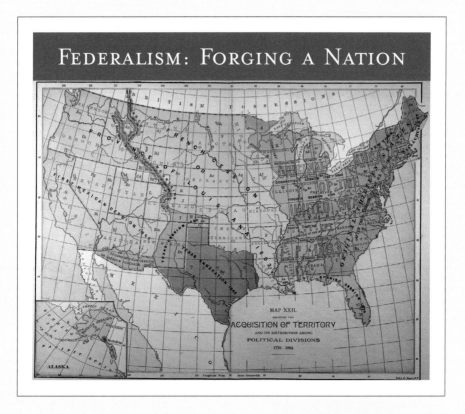

FEDERALISM: FORGING A NATION

MAP XXII.
DEPICTING THE
ACQUISITION OF TERRITORY
AND ITS DISTRIBUTION AMONG
POLITICAL DIVISIONS
1776–1884.

"The question of the relation of the states to the federal government is the
cardinal question of our Constitutional system. It cannot be settled by the
opinion of one generation, because it is a question of growth, and each
successive stage of our political and economic development gives it a new
aspect, makes it a new question."

WOODROW Wilson[1]

In late 2001, Attorney General John Ashcroft directed federal agents to
take action that would stop Oregon physicians from prescribing federally
controlled drugs to assist terminally ill patients in committing suicide.
Ashcroft sought to void the Oregon law that permits physician assistance in
cases where a patient, in the judgment of at least two doctors, has less than
six months to live, is suffering painfully, and is mentally competent to decide
whether to end his or her life. Ashcroft's action was not the first federal
attempt to nullify the Oregon law. Congressional Republicans had twice initiated legislation that would ban physician-assisted suicide—in one instance,
a bill passed in the House but failed to come up for a vote in the Senate.

Oregon's voters had approved the assisted-suicide law in a statewide referendum, becoming the first state (and, as of 2007, the only state) to do so. A majority of Oregon's voters had been persuaded by the argument that no public benefit derives from requiring the dying to accept prolonged suffering. Opponents had countered that society's interest in preserving life outweighs a patient's desire to die, that doctors and relatives in some instances might persuade terminally ill patients to accept death against their will, and that depressed patients who have asked to die should be treated for their depression (after which they might choose to live). In filing suit against the Oregon law, the U.S. Department of Justice argued that "there are important medical, ethical and legal distinctions between intentionally causing a patient's death and providing sufficient dosages of pain medications to eliminate or alleviate pain."

In 2006, the U.S. Supreme Court decided the issue in Oregon's favor, ruling that its physicians could not be punished for prescribing the drugs in question. The Court held in *Gonzales v. Oregon* that federal law did not grant Ashcroft "the extraordinary authority" he had claimed in trying to regulate medical practice. The Court did not repudiate Congress's power to regulate drugs, but it did reject Ashcroft's claim to that authority in the area of physician-assisted suicide.[2]

The controversy surrounding Oregon's Death with Dignity Act is one of thousands of disagreements over the course of American history that have hinged on whether national or state authority should prevail. Americans possess what amounts to dual citizenship: they are citizens both of the United States and of the state where they reside. The American political system is a *federal system*, in which constitutional authority is divided between a national government and state governments: each government is assumed to derive its powers directly from the people and therefore to have sovereignty (final authority) over the policy responsibilities assigned to it. The federal system consists of nation *and* states, indivisible yet separate.[3]

This chapter on American constitutionalism focuses on federalism. The nature of the relationship between the nation and the states was the most pressing issue when the Constitution was written in 1787. This chapter describes how that issue helped shape the Constitution. The chapter's closing sections discuss how federalism has changed throughout the nation's history and conclude with a brief overview of contemporary federalism. The main points presented in the chapter are these:

★ *The power of government must be equal to its responsibilities.* The Constitution was needed because the nation's preceding system (under

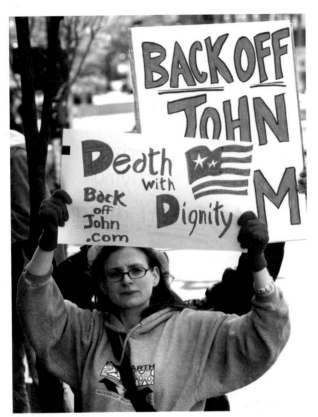

A supporter of Oregon's Death with Dignity law holds a sign outside the federal courthouse in Portland, Oregon, where a hearing on the U.S. Justice Department's challenge to the law is being held. The struggle between the power of the federal government and the power of a state government has been repeated countless times in American history and reflects the U.S. federal system, which vests sovereignty in both the national and state governments. In this particular case, the state, Oregon, prevailed. The U.S. Supreme Court ruled in 2006 that Attorney General John Ashcroft had exceeded his authority in seeking to invalidate the Oregon law.

the Articles of Confederation) was too weak to accomplish its expected goals, particularly those of a strong defense and an integrated economy.

★ *Federalism—the Constitution's division of governing authority between two levels, nation and states—was the result of political bargaining.* Federalism was not a theoretical principle, but a compromise made necessary in 1787 by the prior existence of the states.

★ *Federalism is not a fixed principle for allocating power between the national and state governments, but a principle that has changed over time in response to new political needs.* Federalism has passed through several distinct stages in the course of the nation's history.

★ *Contemporary federalism tilts toward national authority, reflecting the increased interdependence of American society.* However, there is a current trend toward reducing slightly the scope of federal authority.

FEDERALISM: NATIONAL AND STATE *revolution* SOVEREIGNTY

At the time of the writing of the Constitution, some of America's top leaders were dead set against the creation of a strong national government. When rumors circulated that the delegates to the constitutional convention were planning to propose such a government, Patrick Henry, an ardent believer in state-centered government, said that he "smelt a rat." After the convention had adjourned, he realized that his fears were justified. "Who authorized them," he asked, "to speak the language of 'We, the People,' instead of 'We, the States'?"

The question of "people versus states" was precipitated by the failure of the Articles of Confederation. The government under the Articles (see Chapter 2) was a union of states rather than also a union of people. For example, the government had no power to tax citizens, the states alone had this power. Congress had the power to pass laws affecting the states, but although the states were obliged in principle to obey, they were independent enough to ignore national laws that they deemed disagreeable or inconvenient. When Georgia and North Carolina contributed no money to the national treasury between 1781 and 1786, for example, the national government could do little more than beg them to pay their allotted share of the costs of defense, diplomacy, and other national functions.

The only realistic solution to this problem—if the United States was to be a nation in more than name only—was a government that had direct power over the people. If individuals were ordered to pay taxes, for example, they ordinarily would do so. The alternatives—imprisonment or loss of property—were even less appealing.

Although the creation of a national government based directly on the people was therefore a goal of the writers of the Constitution, they also wanted to preserve the states as governing bodies. The states were already in existence, had their own constitutions, and enjoyed popular support. When Virginia's George Mason said he would never agree to a union that abolished the states, he was speaking for virtually all the delegates. The Philadelphia convention therefore devised a system of government

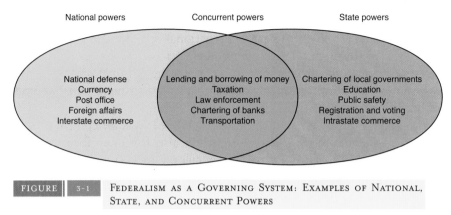

National powers   Concurrent powers   State powers

National defense	Lending and borrowing of money	Chartering of local governments
Currency	Taxation	Education
Post office	Law enforcement	Public safety
Foreign affairs	Chartering of banks	Registration and voting
Interstate commerce	Transportation	Intrastate commerce

FIGURE | **3-1**   FEDERALISM AS A GOVERNING SYSTEM: EXAMPLES OF NATIONAL, STATE, AND CONCURRENT POWERS

The American federal system divides sovereignty between a national government and state governments. Each is constitutionally protected in its existence and authority, although their powers overlap somewhat even in areas granted to one level (for example, the federal government has a role in education policy).

that came to be known as **federalism.** Federalism is the division of **sovereignty,** or ultimate governing authority, between a national government and regional (that is, state) governments. Each directly governs the people and derives its powers from them.

American federalism is basically a system of divided authority (see Figure 3–1). The system gives states the power to address local issues in ways of their own choosing. At the same time, federalism gives the national government the power to decide matters of national scope. Although there is some overlap between state and national action, there is also a division of responsibilities. The national government has primary responsibility for national defense and the currency, among other things, while the states have primary responsibility for policy areas such as public education and police protection. The national and state governments also have some concurrent powers (that is, powers exercised over the same policy areas); for example, each has the power to raise taxes and borrow money.

A federal system is different from a **confederacy,** the type of government established by the Articles. A confederacy is a union in which the states alone are sovereign—the authority of the central government is derived from the states, which can, at will, redefine its authority. Federalism is also different from a **unitary system,** in which sovereignty is vested solely in the national government. Under a unitary system, the people are citizens or subjects only of the national government. The other governments in such a system have only as much authority as the national government allows them to have. The national government even has the power to abolish them as governing bodies. A federal system, in contrast, invests sovereignty—final authority—in both the national and the state governments. Each level of government has a permanent existence and authority independent of those of the other level.

Federalism was invented in America in 1787. It was different not only from a confederate or a unitary system but also from any form of government the world had known. The ancient Greek city-states and the medieval Hanseatic League were confederacies. The governments of Europe were unitary in form. The United States of America would be the first nation to be governed through a true federal system.

The Argument for Federalism

Unlike many other decisions made at the Philadelphia convention, the choice of federalism had no clear basis in political theory. Federalism was a practical necessity: there was a need for a stronger national government, and yet the states existed and were intent on retaining their sovereignty. Nevertheless, the Framers developed arguments for the superiority of this type of political system. Federalism, they said, would protect liberty, moderate the power of government, and provide the foundation for an effective national government.

 ## HOW THE UNITED STATES COMPARES

Federal Versus Unitary Governments

Federalism involves the division of sovereignty between a national government and subnational (such as state) governments. It was invented in 1787 in order to maintain the preexisting American states while establishing an effective central government. Since then a number of other countries have established a *federal* government, but most countries have a *unitary* government, in which all sovereignty is vested in the national government.

However, even within these alternative political systems there are important differences. In Germany's federal system, for example, the states have limited lawmaking powers but do have broad authority in determining how national laws are implemented. By comparison,

(continued)

the U.S. federal system grants substantial lawmaking powers to the states except in specified areas such as national defense and currency.

Unitary systems also differ. In Britain, the national government has delegated substantial authority to regions; Scotland, for example, has its own parliament, which exercises lawmaking powers. In France, on the other hand, political authority is highly centralized.

In nearly all federal systems, the national legislature has two chambers—one apportioned by population (as in the case of the U.S. House of Representatives) and one apportioned by geographical area (as in the case of the U.S. Senate). The U.S. Senate is a pure federal institution in the sense that each state has the same number of senators. In some federal systems, such as Germany's, the states are not equally represented even in the geographically apportioned chamber.

Unitary systems typically have but a single national legislative chamber, which is apportioned by population—there is no constitutional justification for a second chamber based on geography.

Country	Form of Government
Canada	Federal
France	Unitary
Germany	Federal
Great Britain	Modified unitary
Italy	Modified unitary
Japan	Unitary
Mexico	Modified federal
Sweden	Unitary
United States	Federal

Protecting Liberty   Theorists such as Locke and Montesquieu had not proposed a division of power between national and local authorities as a means of protecting liberty. Nevertheless, the Framers came to look upon federalism as part of the Constitution's system of checks and balances (see Chapter 2). Alexander Hamilton argued in *Federalist* No. 28 that the American people could shift their loyalties back and forth between the national and state governments in order to keep each under control. "If [the people's] rights are invaded by either," Hamilton wrote, "they can make use of the other as the instrument of redress."

Moderating the Power of Government   To the Anti-Federalists (opponents of the Constitution), the sacrifice of the states' power to the nation was as unwise as it was unnecessary. They claimed that a distant national government could never serve the people's interests as well as the states could. Liberty *and* self-government, they argued, were enhanced by state-centered government. In support of their contention, the Anti-Federalists turned to Montesquieu, who had concluded that a small republic is more likely than a large one to respect and respond to the people it governs. When government encompasses a small area, he argued, its leaders are in closer touch with the people and have a greater concern for their welfare.

James Madison took issue with this claim. In *Federalist* No. 10, Madison argued that whether a government serves the common good is a function not of its size but of the range of interests that share political power. The problem with a smaller republic, Madison claimed, is that it is likely to have a dominant faction—whether it be large landholders, financiers, an impoverished majority, or some other group—that is strong enough to take full control of government and to use this power to advance its selfish interests. A large republic is less likely to have such an all-powerful faction. If financiers are strong in one area of a large republic, they are likely to be weaker elsewhere. The same will be true of farmers, merchants, laborers, and other interests. A large republic, Madison concluded, would impede the efforts of any single group to gain control and would force groups to compromise and work together. "Extend the sphere," said Madison, "and you take in a greater variety of parties and interests; you make it less probable that a majority of the whole will have a common motive to invade the rights of other citizens."

Strengthening the Union   The most telling argument in 1787 for a federal system, however, was that it would overcome the deficiencies of the Articles. The Articles had numerous flaws (including a very weak executive and a judiciary subservient to the state courts), and two of them were

★ ‖ LEADERS

James Madison
(1751–1836)

James Madison is called the "father of the Constitution." Madison himself rejected the label, saying that the Constitution was the work of "many heads and many hands." Nevertheless, Madison had the clearest idea of how to structure the U.S. government, and he guided the debate at the constitutional convention of 1787. Later, his *Federalist Papers* contributed to the Constitution's ratification. Madison then helped Thomas Jefferson form a political party—one that sought to promote ordinary citizens as opposed to the rich and powerful—that is the forerunner of today's Democratic party He served as secretary of state during Jefferson's presidency and in 1808 succeeded him as president. Europe was in the midst of the Napoleonic Wars, and Madison was not adept at asserting America's neutrality. In 1812, the British invaded Washington, D.C., burning the Capitol and forcing Madison to flee to Maryland. The British withdrew and later were defeated by General Andrew Jackson at New Orleans, leading Americans to claim victory in the War of 1812. After completing his second presidential term in 1817, Madison spoke out against the growing states-rights sentiment that eventually would plunge the nation into the Civil War over the issue of slavery. His dying wish was for the preservation of the Union.

fatal: the government had neither the power to tax nor the power to regulate commerce.

Under the Articles, Congress was given responsibility for national defense but was not granted the power to tax, so it had to rely on the states for the money to maintain an army and a navy. During the first six years under the Articles, Congress asked the states for $12 million but received only $3 million—not even enough to pay the interest on Revolutionary War debts. By 1786 the national government was so desperate for funds that it sold the navy's ships and had fewer than a thousand soldiers in uniform—this at a time when England had an army in Canada and when Spain occupied Florida.

Historical
Background

Congress also was expected to shape a national economy, yet it was powerless to do so because the Articles prohibited it from interfering with the states' commerce policies. States were free to do whatever they wanted, and they took advantage of the situation by imposing trade barriers on each other. Connecticut, for example, placed a higher tariff on manufactured goods made by its trading rival Massachusetts than it placed on the same goods made in England.

The Articles of Confederation showed the fallacy of the adage "That government is best which governs least." The consequences of an overly weak government were abundantly clear: public disorder, economic chaos, and an inadequate national defense.

The Powers of the Nation

The Philadelphia convention met to decide the powers of the national government. The delegates had not been sent to determine how state government should be structured. Accordingly, the U.S. Constitution focuses on the lawful authority of the national government, which is provided through *enumerated and implied powers.* Authority that is not granted to the national government is left—or "reserved"—to the states. Thus, the states have *reserved powers.*

Enumerated Powers   Article I of the Constitution grants to Congress seventeen **enumerated (expressed) powers.** These powers were intended by the Framers to be the basis for a government strong enough to forge a union that was secure in its defense and stable in its commerce. Congress's powers to regulate commerce among the states, to create a national currency, and to borrow money, for example, would provide a foundation for a sound national economy. Its power to tax, combined with its authority to declare war and establish an army and a navy, would enable it to provide for the common defense. In addition, the Constitution prohibits the states from actions that would interfere with the national government's exercise of its lawful powers. Article I, Section 10 forbids the states to make treaties with other nations, raise armies, wage war, print money, or make commercial agreements with other states without the approval of Congress.

The writers of the Constitution recognized that the lawful exercise of national authority would at times conflict with the actions of the states. In such instances, national law was intended to prevail. Article VI of the Constitution grants this dominance in the so-called **supremacy clause,** which provides that "the laws of the United States . . . shall be the supreme law of the land."

Patrick Henry was a leading figure in the American Revolution ("Give me liberty or give me death!"). He later opposed ratification of the Constitution on grounds that the national government should be a union of states and not also of people.

Implied Powers The Framers of the Constitution also recognized that a narrow definition of national authority would result in a government incapable of adapting to change. Under the Articles of Confederation, Congress was strictly confined to those powers expressly granted to it, which limited its ability to respond effectively to the country's changing needs after the Revolutionary War. Concerned that the enumerated powers by themselves might be too restrictive of national authority, the Framers added the **"necessary and proper" clause** or, as it later came to be known, the **elastic clause.** Article I, Section 8 gives Congress the power "to make all laws which shall be necessary and proper for carrying into execution the foregoing [enumerated] powers." This grant gave the national government **implied powers:** the authority to take action that is not expressly authorized by the Constitution but that supports actions that are so authorized.

The Powers of the States

The Framers' preference for a sovereign national government was not shared in 1787 by all Americans. Although Anti-Federalists recognized a need to strengthen defense and interstate commerce, they feared the consequences of a strong central government. The interests of the people of New

Hampshire were not identical to those of Georgians or Pennsylvanians, and the Anti-Federalists argued that only state-centered government would protect the differences. Self-government, they claimed, would be weakened if a powerful national government was created.

The Federalists responded by saying that the national government would have no interest in depriving the states of their liberty or of their right to self-government in local matters.[4] The national government would take responsibility for establishing a strong defense and for promoting a sound economy, while the states would retain nearly all other governing functions, including oversight of public morals, education, and safety.

This argument did not persuade the Anti-Federalists that their fear of an overly powerful national government was baseless. The supremacy and "necessary and proper" clauses were particularly worrisome, because they provided a constitutional basis for future expansions of national authority. Such concerns led to demands for a constitutional amendment that would protect the states against encroachment by the national government. Ratified in 1791 as the Tenth Amendment to the Constitution, it reads: "The powers not delegated to the United States by the Constitution, nor prohibited by it to the States, are reserved to the States." The states' powers under the U.S. Constitution are thus called **reserved powers.**

FEDERALISM IN HISTORICAL PERSPECTIVE

Since ratification of the Constitution over two centuries ago, no aspect of it has provoked more frequent or bitter conflict than federalism. By establishing two levels of sovereign authority, the Constitution created competing centers of power and ambition, each of which was sure to claim disputed areas as belonging within its realm of authority.

Conflict between national and state authority was also ensured by the brevity of the Constitution. The Framers deliberately avoided detailed provisions, recognizing that brief phrases would lend flexibility to the government they were creating. The document does not define, for example, the difference between *inter*state commerce (which the national government is empowered to regulate) and *intra*state commerce (which is reserved for regulation by the states).

Not surprisingly, federalism has been a contentious and dynamic system, its development determined less by constitutional language than by the strength of contending interests and by the country's changing needs. Federalism can be viewed as having progressed through three historical eras, each of which has involved a different relationship between the nation and the states.

GET INVOLVED!
Step Up

The U.S. federal system of government offers an array of channels for political participation. Vital governing decisions are made at the national, state, and local levels, all of which provide opportunities for citizens to make a difference.

Another participatory arena is close at hand: the college campus. Most colleges and universities support a variety of activities in which students can engage. Student government is one such opportunity; another is the student newspaper. Most colleges and universities offer a wide range of groups and sponsored programs, from debate clubs to fraternal organizations. However, many students do not take advantage of these opportunities, and among those who do, many see the opportunities as offering only a temporary benefit.

The theorist John Stuart Mill (1806–73) thought differently, arguing that public involvement has several benefits. One benefit is that people are better able to promote and protect their interests when they are actively involved. Participation also enables people to contribute to their community. Mill suggested yet a third benefit—the one for which he is noted. Mill contended that the active individual is the more virtuous citizen in that he or she will be more socially skilled, more personally assured, and more ethically aware. Community participation helps individuals develop their abilities and understand the interests of others. In a word, the active citizen is more enlightened than the passive one. Mill's belief in the role of participation in personal development led him to support women's rights. In an era when women enjoyed few rights, Mill was a passionate advocate of sexual equality.

If you are not now active in campus groups, consider joining one. If you join—or if you already belong to such a group—take full advantage of the participatory opportunities it provides. The benefits will extend beyond your college years.

An Indestructible Union (1789–1865)

The issue during the first era, which lasted from the Constitution's beginnings in 1789 through the end of the Civil War in 1865, was the Union's survival. Given the state-centered history of America before the

Constitution, it was inevitable that the states would dispute national policies that threatened their particular interests.

The Nationalist View: McCulloch v. Maryland   A first dispute over federalism arose when President George Washington's secretary of the treasury, Alexander Hamilton, proposed that Congress establish a national bank. Thomas Jefferson, Washington's secretary of state, opposed the bank on the grounds that its activities would benefit the interests of the rich at the expense of the interests of ordinary people. Jefferson claimed that the bank was unlawful because the Constitution did not expressly authorize the creation of a national bank. Hamilton and his supporters claimed that because the federal government had constitutional authority to regulate currency, it had the "implied power" to establish a national bank.

Hamilton's view prevailed when Congress in 1791 established the First Bank of the United States, granting it a twenty-year charter. Although Congress did not renew the charter when it expired in 1811, it established the Second Bank of the United States in 1816. State and local banks did not want competition from a national bank and persuaded several state legislatures, including Maryland's, to levy a tax on the national bank's operations within their borders, hoping to drive it out of existence by making its operations unprofitable. Edwin McCulloch, who was in charge of the Maryland branch of the national bank, refused to pay the Maryland tax. The resulting dispute was heard by the U.S. Supreme Court.

Historical
Background

Chief Justice John Marshall was a strong nationalist, and in *McCulloch v. Maryland* (1819) the Supreme Court ruled decisively in favor of national authority. It was reasonable, Marshall concluded, to infer that a government with powers to tax, borrow money, and regulate commerce could establish a bank in order to exercise those powers properly. Marshall's argument was a clear statement of *implied powers*—the idea that through the "necessary and proper" clause the national government's powers extend beyond a narrow reading of its enumerated powers.

Marshall also addressed the meaning of the Constitution's supremacy clause. The state of Maryland argued that, even if the national bank was a legal entity, it had the sovereign authority to tax it. The Supreme Court rejected Maryland's position, concluding that valid national law prevailed over conflicting state law. Because the national government had the power to create the bank, it also could protect the bank against actions by the states, such as taxation, that might destroy it.[5]

A first dispute over federalism was whether the Constitution allowed the creation of a Bank of the United States (shown here in an early-nineteenth-century painting). The Constitution had a clause authorizing the printing of currency but not the establishment of a bank itself.

The *McCulloch* decision served as precedent for later rulings in support of national power. In *Gibbons v. Ogden* (1824), for example, the Marshall-led Court rejected a New York law granting a monopoly to a ferry operating between New York and New Jersey, concluding that New York had encroached on Congress's power to regulate commerce among the states. The Court also ruled that Congress's commerce power extended *into* a state when commerce between two or more states was at issue.[6]

Marshall's opinions asserted that legitimate uses of national power took precedence over state authority and that the "necessary and proper" clause and the commerce clause were broad grants of national power. As a nationalist, Marshall was providing the U.S. government the legal justification for expanding its power in ways that fostered the development of the United States as a nation rather than as a collection of states. This constitutional vision was of utmost significance. As Justice Oliver Wendell Holmes Jr. noted a century later, the Union could not have survived if each state had been allowed to determine for itself the extent to which it would accept national authority.[7]

The States'-Rights View: The Dred Scott *Decision* Although John Marshall's rulings helped strengthen national authority, the issue of slavery posed a growing threat to the Union's survival. Fearing that northern members of Congress might move to abolish slavery, southern leaders did what others have done throughout American history: they devised a constitutional argument to fit their political desires. John C. Calhoun of South Carolina argued that the Constitution had created "a government of states . . . not a government of individuals."[8] This line of reasoning led Calhoun to his famed "doctrine of nullification," which declared that each state had the constitutional right to nullify a national law.

In 1832 South Carolina invoked this doctrine, declaring "null and void" a tariff law that favored northern interests. President Andrew Jackson retorted that South Carolina's action was "incompatible with the existence of the Union," a position that was strengthened when Congress authorized Jackson to use military force if necessary against South Carolina. The state backed down when Congress amended the tariff act to reduce its impact on the South.

The clash foreshadowed a confrontation of far greater scope and consequence: the Civil War. It would not break out for another thirty years, but in the interim, conflicts over states' rights intensified. Westward expansion and immigration into the northern states were tilting power in Congress toward the free states, which increasingly signaled their determination to outlaw slavery in the United States at some future time. Attempts to find a compromise acceptable to both the North and the South were fruitless.

The Supreme Court's infamous *Dred Scott* decision (1857), written by Chief Justice Roger Taney, an ardent states'-rights advocate, intensified the conflict. Dred Scott, a slave who had lived in the North for four years, applied for his freedom when his master died, citing a federal law—the Missouri Compromise of 1820—that made slavery illegal in a free state or territory. The Supreme Court ruled against Scott, claiming that slaves were "property" and that persons of African descent were barred from citizenship and thereby could not sue for their freedom in federal courts. The Court also invalidated the Missouri Compromise. The Court ruled that, because slaves were property and because property could be taken into any state or territory, Congress could not outlaw slavery in any part of the United States.[9]

The Taney Court's decision drew an angry response from the North and contributed to a sectional split within the nation's majority party, the Democrats. In 1860, the Democratic party's northern and southern wings nominated separate candidates for the presidency, which split the Democratic vote and enabled the Republican candidate, Abraham Lincoln, to win the presidency with only 40 percent of the popular vote. Lincoln had campaigned on a platform that called not for an immediate end to slavery but for its gradual abolition through payments to slaveholders. Nevertheless, the southern states saw Lincoln's election as a grave threat to their sovereignty. By the time Lincoln assumed office, seven southern states—led by South Carolina—had left the Union. Four more states were to follow. In justifying his decision to wage war against the secessionists, Lincoln said, "The Union is older than the states." In 1865, the superior strength of the Union army settled by force the question of whether the states are required to accept national authority.

Dual Federalism and Laissez-Faire Capitalism (1865–1937)

Although the Civil War preserved the Union, new challenges to federalism were surfacing. Constitutional doctrine held that certain policy areas, such as interstate commerce and defense, belonged exclusively to the national government, whereas other policy areas, such as public health and intrastate commerce, belonged exclusively to the states. This doctrine, known as *dual federalism*, was based on the idea that a precise separation of national and state authority was both possible and desirable. "The power which one possesses," said the Supreme Court, "the other does not."[10]

American society, however, was in the midst of changes that raised questions about the suitability of dual federalism as a governing concept. The Industrial Revolution had given rise to large business firms, which were using their economic power to dominate markets and exploit workers. Government was the logical counterforce to this economic power. Which level of government—state or national—would regulate business?

There was also the issue of the former slaves. The white South had lost the war but was hardly of a mind to share power with newly freed slaves. Would the federal government be allowed to intervene in state affairs to ensure the fair treatment of African Americans?

Dual federalism became a barrier to an effective response to these issues. From the 1860s through the 1930s, the Supreme Court held firm to the idea that there was a sharp line between national and state authority and, in both areas, a high wall of separation between government and the economy. This era of federalism was characterized by state supremacy in racial policy and business supremacy in commerce policy.

The Fourteenth Amendment and State Discretion Ratified after the Civil War, the Fourteenth Amendment was intended to protect the newly freed slaves from discriminatory actions by state governments. A state was prohibited from depriving "any person of life, liberty, or property without due process of law," from denying "any person within its jurisdiction the equal protection of the laws," and from abridging "the privileges or immunities of citizens of the United States."

Historical Background

Supreme Court rulings during subsequent decades, however, helped to undermine the Fourteenth Amendment's promise of liberty and equality for all. The Court held, for example, that the Fourteenth Amendment did not substantially limit the power of the states to determine the rights to which their residents were entitled.[11] Then, in *Plessy v. Ferguson* (1896), the Court issued its infamous "separate but equal" ruling. A black man, Homer Adolph Plessy, had been convicted of violating a Louisiana law that required white and black citizens to ride in separate railroad cars. The Supreme Court upheld his conviction, concluding that state governments could require blacks to use separate railroad cars and other accommodations as long as those facilities were "equal" in quality to those reserved for use by whites. "If one race be inferior to the other socially," the Court concluded, "the Constitution of the United States cannot put them on the same plane." The lone dissenting justice in the case, John Marshall Harlan, had harsh words for his colleagues: "Our Constitution is color-blind and neither knows nor tolerates classes among citizens. . . . The thin disguise of 'equal' accommodations . . . will not mislead anyone nor atone for the wrong this day done."[12]

With its *Plessy* decision, the Court undercut the Fourteenth Amendment and allowed southern states to segregate the races. Black children were forced into separate schools that seldom had libraries and usually had few teachers. Hospitals for blacks had few doctors and nurses and almost no medical supplies or equipment. Legal challenges to these discriminatory practices were generally unsuccessful. The *Plessy* ruling had become a justification for the separate and *unequal* treatment of black Americans.

Judicial Protection of Business Through its rulings after the Civil War, the Supreme Court also provided a constitutional basis for uncontrolled economic power. A majority of the Court's justices believed in laissez-faire capitalism (which holds that business should be "allowed to act" without interference) and interpreted the Constitution in ways that frustrated government's attempts to regulate business activity. In 1886, for example, the Court decided that corporations were "persons" within the meaning of the Fourteenth Amendment and thus their property rights were protected from substantial regulation by the states.[13] The irony was inescapable. A constitutional amendment that had been enacted to protect the liberty of newly freed slaves was ignored for this purpose but used instead to protect fictitious persons—business corporations.

The Court also weakened the national government's regulatory power by narrowly interpreting its commerce power. The Constitution's

POLITICAL CULTURE
Large Versus Small Republics

During the debate over ratification of the Constitution, Americans argued over whether liberty, equality, and self-government would be better protected by the states or by the nation. The Anti-Federalists argued that a small republic was closer to the people and therefore would do more to protect individuals' rights. Arguing for the Federalists, James Madison countered by saying that a large republic was preferable because its wide diversity of interests would require compromise and tolerance among various groups.

Which view—that of the Anti-Federalists or that of the Federalists—is better supported by history? Have America's founding ideals been better nurtured through state governments or through the national government? For a long period in U.S. history, the answer was one-sided. As political scientist William Riker noted, state-centered government before and after the Civil War was the tool by which white Americans dominated black Americans, first through slavery and later through institutionalized racism (for example, the separation by law of black and white children attending public schools). As Madison prophesied, a smaller republic makes it easier for a particular faction to run roughshod over another.

Legal racial discrimination is now a thing of the past, and state governments are much less likely to side with one faction against others. How would you judge today's situation? In your view, which level of government—federal or state—is more likely to protect and enhance the ideals of liberty, equality, and self-government? Which level of government is more likely to promote the interests of a particular group at the expense of other groups? In what areas of public policy—taxation, education, public safety, and so on—do you think your opinion is most supported?

commerce clause says that Congress shall have the power "to regulate commerce" among the states but does not spell out the economic activities included in the grant of power. When the federal government invoked the Sherman Antitrust Act (1890) in an attempt to break up a monopoly on the manufacture of sugar, the Supreme Court blocked the action, claiming that interstate commerce covered only the "transportation" of goods, not their "manufacture."[14] Manufacturing was deemed part of

Between 1865 and 1937, the Supreme Court's rulings severely restricted national power. Narrowly interpreting Congress's constitutional power to regulate commerce, the Court forbade Congress to regulate child labor and other aspects of manufacturing.

intrastate commerce and thus, according to the dual federalism doctrine, subject to state regulation only. However, because the Court had previously decided that the states' regulatory powers were restricted by the Fourteenth Amendment, the states for the most part were also denied authority to regulate manufacturing activity.

Although the national government subsequently made some headway in business regulation, the Supreme Court remained an obstacle. An example is the case of *Hammer v. Dagenhart* (1918), which arose from a 1916 federal act that prohibited the interstate shipment of goods produced by child labor. The act was popular because factory owners were exploiting children, working them for long hours at low pay. Citing the Tenth Amendment, the Court invalidated the law, ruling that factory practices could be regulated only by the states.[15] However, in an earlier case, *Lochner v. New York* (1905), the Court had prevented a state from regulating labor practices, concluding that such action was a violation of firms' property rights.[16]

In effect, the Court had negated the principle of self-government. The people, through their representatives, were denied the power to act decisively in the economic realm—neither Congress nor the state legislature was allowed to regulate the marketplace. America's corporations, with the Supreme Court as their shield, were the governing authority.[17]

National Authority Prevails   Judicial supremacy in the economic sphere ended abruptly in 1937. For nearly a decade, the United States had been mired in the Great Depression, which President Franklin D. Roosevelt's New Deal was designed to alleviate. The Supreme Court, however, had ruled much of the New Deal's economic recovery legislation unconstitutional. A constitutional crisis of historic proportions seemed inevitable until the Court suddenly reversed its position. In the process, American federalism was fundamentally and forever changed.

Historical
Background

The Great Depression revealed clearly that Americans had become a national community with national economic needs. By the 1930s, more than half the population lived in cities (compared to a fifth in 1860), and more than ten million workers were employed by industry (compared to one million in 1860). Urban workers typically were dependent on landlords for their housing, on farmers and grocers for their food, and on corporations for their jobs. Farmers were more independent, but they too were increasingly a part of a larger economic network. Farmers' income depended on market prices and shipping and equipment costs.[18]

This economic interdependence meant that no area of the economy was immune from damage if things went wrong. When the depression hit in 1929, its effects could not be contained. In the depths of the Great Depression, one-fourth of the nation's work force was unemployed, and another one-fourth could find only part-time work.

The states by tradition had responsibility for helping the unemployed, but they were nearly penniless due to declining tax revenues and the growing need of the population for welfare assistance. Roosevelt's New Deal programs were intended to alleviate Americans' suffering. The National Industry Recovery Act (NIRA), for example, called for coordinated action by major industries and for a federal jobs program. Economic conservatives strenuously opposed such programs, accusing Roosevelt of trying to lead the country into communism. They found an ally in the Supreme Court. In *Schecter v. United States,* just as in previous New Deal cases, the Supreme Court in a 5-4 ruling held that the NIRA was unconstitutional.[19]

Frustrated by the Court's opposition, Roosevelt in 1937 proposed that Congress expand the Supreme Court by passing legislation that would permit an additional justice to be appointed whenever a seated member passed the age of seventy. Roosevelt would then be able to appoint enough new justices to swing the Court to his side. Although Congress rejected Roosevelt's plan, the controversy ended with "the switch in time that saved nine." For reasons that have never been made fully clear, Justice Owen Roberts switched sides on New Deal cases, giving the president a 5-4 majority on the Court.

Within months, the Court upheld the 1935 National Labor Relations Act, which gave employees the right to organize and bargain collectively.[20] In passing the act, Congress had claimed that labor-management disputes disrupted the nation's economy and therefore could be regulated through the commerce clause. In upholding the act, the Supreme Court in effect granted Congress the authority to apply its commerce powers broadly.[21] During this same period, the Court also loosened its restrictions on Congress's use of its taxing and spending powers.[22] These decisions removed the constitutional barrier to increased federal authority, a change the Court later acknowledged when it said that Congress's commerce power is "as broad as the needs of the nation."[23]

In effect, the Supreme Court had finally recognized the obvious: that an industrial economy is not confined by state boundaries and must be subject to national regulation. It was a principle that business itself also increasingly accepted. The nation's banking industry, for example, was saved in the 1930s from almost complete collapse by the creation of a federal regulatory agency, the Federal Deposit Insurance Corporation (FDIC). By insuring depositors' savings against loss, the FDIC stopped the panic withdrawals that had forced many banks to close.

Toward National Citizenship

The fundamental change in the constitutional doctrine of federalism as applied to economic issues that took place in the 1930s was paralleled by similar changes in other areas, including civil rights and civil liberties. In *Brown v. Board of Education* (1954), for example, the Supreme Court held that states could not require black children to attend separate public schools from those attended by white children (see Chapter 5).[24] Another example is the Supreme Court's 1967 *Miranda* ruling, which requires police officers in all states to inform crime suspects of their rights at the time of arrest (see Chapter 4).[25]

Of course, important differences remain in the rights and privileges of the residents of the separate states, as could be expected in a federal system. The death penalty, for example, is legal in some states but not others, and states differ greatly in terms of their services, such as the quality of their public schools. Nevertheless, national citizenship—the notion that Americans should be equal in their rights and opportunities regardless of the state in which they live—is a more encompassing idea today than it was in the past.

FEDERALISM TODAY

Since the 1930s, the relation of the nation to the states has changed so fundamentally that dual federalism is no longer even a roughly accurate description of the American situation.

An understanding of the nature of federalism today requires a recognition of two countervailing trends. The first trend is a long-term *expansion* of national authority that began in the 1930s and continued for the next half century. The national government now operates in many policy areas that were once almost exclusively within the control of states and localities. The national government does not dominate in these policy areas, but it does play a significant role. Much of this national influence stems from social welfare policies enacted in the 1960s as part of President Lyndon Johnson's Great Society program, which included initiatives in health care, public housing, nutrition, welfare, urban development, and other areas previously reserved to states and localities.

The second, more recent trend involves a partial *contraction* of national authority. Known as *devolution,* this trend involves the "passing down" of authority from the national government to the state and local levels. Devolution has reversed the decades-long increase in federal authority, but only in some areas and then only to a moderate degree.

In short, the national government's policy authority has expanded greatly since the 1930s, even though that authority has been reduced somewhat in recent years. We will explain each of these two trends in more detail.

Interdependency and Intergovernmental Relations

Interdependency is a reason that national authority increased dramatically in the twentieth century. Modern systems of transportation, commerce, and communication transcend local and state boundaries. These systems are national—and even international—in scope, which means that problems affecting Americans living in one part of the country are likely to affect Americans living elsewhere. This situation has required Washington to assume a larger policy role. National problems typically require national solutions.

Interdependency has also encouraged national, state, and local policymakers to work together to solve policy problems. This collaborative effort has been described as **cooperative federalism.**[26] The difference between this system of federalism and the older dual federalism has been likened to the difference between a marble cake, whose levels flow together, and a layer cake, whose levels are separate.[27]

Cooperative federalism is based on shared policy responsibilities rather than sharply divided ones. An example is the Medicaid program, which was created in 1965 as part of President Johnson's Great Society initiative and provides health care for the poor. The Medicaid program is jointly funded by the national and state governments, operates within eligibility standards set by the national government, and gives states some latitude in determining the benefits that recipients receive. The Medicaid program is not an isolated example. Literally hundreds of policy programs today are run jointly by the national and state governments. In many cases, local governments are also involved. The following characteristics describe these programs:

- Jointly funded by the national and state governments (and sometimes by local governments)
- Jointly administered, with the states and localities providing most of the direct service to recipients and a national agency providing general administration
- Jointly determined, with both the state and national governments (and sometimes the local governments) having a say in eligibility and benefit levels and with federal regulations, such as those prohibiting discrimination, providing a degree of uniformity to the various state and local efforts

Cooperative federalism should not be interpreted to mean that the states are powerless and dependent. States have retained most of their traditional authority. Nearly 95 percent of the funding for public schools, for example, is provided by states and localities, which also set most of the education standards, from teachers' qualifications to course requirements to the length of the school day. Moreover, the policy areas dominated by the states—such as education, law enforcement, and transportation—tend to be those that have the most direct impact on people's daily lives. Finally, contrary to what many Americans might think, state and local governments have six times as many employees as the federal government.

Nevertheless, the federal government's involvement in policy areas traditionally reserved for the states has increased its influence on policy and diminished state-to-state policy differences. Before the enactment of the federal Medicaid program in 1965, for example, poor people in many states were not entitled to government-paid health care. Now most poor people are eligible for health benefits regardless of where in the United States they live.

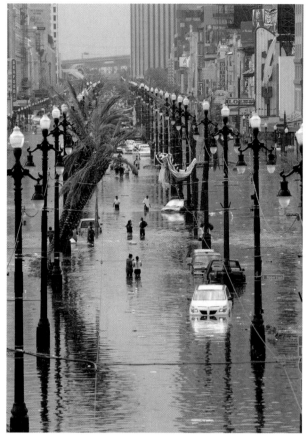

The devastation caused by Hurricane Katrina in 2005 predictably brought federal, state, and local governments together in the reconstruction effort. Cooperative federalism is a term used to describe such joint efforts. Like any governing arrangement, however, cooperative federalism does not ensure success. In the case of Katrina, the scope of the natural disaster overwhelmed the capacity of the nation's governments, leading to widespread criticism of officials at all levels. Shown here is New Orleans' famed Canal Street, covered by floodwaters.

Government Revenues and Intergovernmental Relations

The interdependency of American society—the fact that developments in one area affect what happens elsewhere—is one of two major reasons why the federal government's policy role has expanded greatly since the early twentieth century. The other reason is the federal government's superior taxing capacity. States and localities are in an inherently competitive situation with regard to taxation. A state that raises taxes too high will lose residents and firms to states where taxes are lower. People and businesses

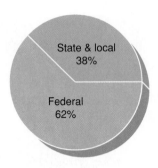

FIGURE   3-2   FEDERAL, STATE, AND LOCAL SHARES OF GOVERNMENT
TAX REVENUE

The federal government raises more tax revenues than all state and local governments combined. *Source: U.S. Department of Commerce, 2006.*

are much less likely to move to another country in search of a lower tax
rate. The result is that the federal government raises more tax revenues
than do all fifty states and the thousands of local governments combined
(see Figure 3–2).

Fiscal Federalism   The federal government's revenue-raising advantage
has helped make money the basis for many of the relations between the
national government and the states and localities. **Fiscal federalism** refers
to the expenditure of federal funds on programs run in part through state
and local governments.[28] The federal government provides some or all of
the money for a program through **grants-in-aid** (cash payments) to states
and localities, which then administer the program.
    The pattern of federal assistance to states and localities during the last
half-century is shown in Figure 3–3. Federal grants-in-aid increased dramatically during this period. A sharp rise occurred in the late 1960s and
early 1970s as a result of President Johnson's Great Society programs.
Roughly one in every five dollars spent by local and state governments in
recent decades has been raised not by them, but by the government in
Washington (see "States in the Nation").
    Cash grants to states and localities have extended Washington's influ-
ence on policy decisions. State and local governments can reject a grant-
in-aid, but if they accept it they must spend it in the way specified by
Congress. Also, because most grants require states to contribute matching funds, the federal programs in effect determine how states will allocate some of their own tax dollars. Federal grants have also pressured state
and local officials to accept broad national goals, such as the elimination

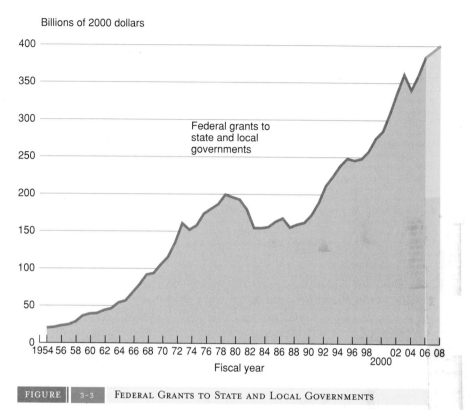

Billions of 2000 dollars

Federal grants to
state and local
governments

Fiscal year

| FIGURE | 3-3 | FEDERAL GRANTS TO STATE AND LOCAL GOVERNMENTS |

Federal aid to states and localities has increased dramatically since the 1950s.
*Source: Office of Management and Budget, 2006. Figure is based on constant (2000)
dollars in order to control for the effects of inflation.*

of racial and other forms of discrimination. A building constructed with
the help of federal funds, for example, must be accessible to persons with
disabilities.

Nevertheless, federal grants-in-aid also serve the policy interests of
state and local officials. While these officials have often complained that
federal grants contain too many restrictions and infringe too much on
their authority, they have been eager to obtain the money because it permits them to offer services they could not otherwise afford. An example
is a 1994 federal grant program that enabled local governments to put
seventy-five thousand additional police officers on the streets.

Categorical and Block Grants State and local governments receive two
major types of assistance, categorical grants and block grants. These differ in the extent to which Washington defines the conditions of their use.

★ | STATES IN THE NATION

Federal Grants-in-Aid to the States

Federal assistance accounts for a significant share of state revenue, but the variation is considerable. New Mexico (with a third of its total revenue coming from federal grants-in-aid) is at one extreme. Nevada (a seventh of its revenue) is at the other.

Q: Why do states in the South, where anti-Washington sentiment is relatively high, get more of their revenue from the federal government than most other states?

A: Many federal grant programs are designed to assist low-income people, and poverty is more widespread in the South. Moreover, southern states traditionally have provided fewer government services, and federal grants therefore constitute a larger proportion of their budgets.

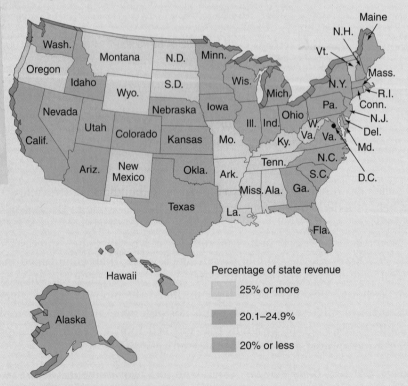

Percentage of state revenue

25% or more

20.1–24.9%

20% or less

Source: U.S. Bureau of the Census, 2006.

Categorical grants are more restrictive. They can be used only for a designated activity. An example is funds directed for use in school lunch programs. These funds can be used only in support of school lunches; they cannot be diverted for other school purposes, such as the purchase of textbooks or the hiring of teachers. **Block grants** are less restrictive. The federal government specifies the general area in which the funds must be used, but state and local officials select the specific projects. A block grant targeted for the health area, for example, might give state and local officials leeway in deciding whether to use the money for hospital construction, medical equipment, or some other health care activity.

State and local officials naturally prefer federal money that comes with fewer strings attached and thus have favored block grants. On the other hand, members of Congress have at times preferred categorical grants, because this form of assistance gives them more control over how state and local officials spend federal funds. Recently, however, officials at all levels have looked to block grants as the key to a more workable form of federalism. This tendency is part of a larger trend—devolution.

A New Federalism: Devolution

Devolution embodies the idea that American federalism will be strengthened by a partial shift in authority from the federal government to the state and local governments. Devolution is attributable to both practical and political developments.[29]

Budgetary Pressures and Public Opinion As a practical matter, the growth in federal assistance had slowed by the early 1980s. The federal government was facing huge budget deficits, and awarding large new grants-in-aid to states and localities was not feasible. As budgetary pressures intensified, relations among national, state, and local officials became increasingly strained. A slowdown in the annual increase in federal assistance had forced states and localities to pay an increasingly larger share of the costs of joint programs. As state and local governments raised taxes or cut other services to meet the costs of joint programs, taxpayer anger intensified. Some grant programs that had not been very popular before the budget crunch, such as food stamps and public housing, now came under even heavier criticism.

By the early 1990s, American federalism was positioned for a change. Two decades earlier, three-fourths of Americans had expressed confidence in Washington's ability to govern effectively. Less than half the public now held this view. A 1993 CBS News/New York Times survey indicated that 69 percent of Americans believed that "the federal government creates more problems than it solves."

In 1994

The Republican Revolution   When the Republican party scored a decisive victory in the 1994 congressional elections, Newt Gingrich declared that "1960s-style federalism is dead." Republican lawmakers proposed to cut some programs, but, even more, they sought to increase state and local control.

That Republicans would lead the move to a more decentralized form of federalism was no surprise. Although members of both parties had supported expansions of federal authority, Republicans had more often questioned the overall result. Republican presidents Richard Nixon and Ronald Reagan, for example, proposed versions of a "new federalism" in which some areas of public policy for which the federal government had assumed responsibility would be returned to states and localities.

Upon taking control of Congress in 1995, Republican lawmakers acted to reduce *unfunded mandates*, federal programs that require action by states or localities but provide no or insufficient funds to pay for it. For example, states and localities are required by federal law to make their buildings accessible to the physically handicapped, but Washington pays only part of the cost of these accommodations. In the Unfunded Mandates Reform Act of 1995, Congress eliminated some of these mandates, although under threat of a presidential veto it exempted those that deal with civil rights. The GOP-controlled Congress also took action to lump additional categorical grants into block grants, thereby giving states more control over how federal money would be spent.

The most significant legislative change came in 1996, when the Republican Congress enacted the sweeping Welfare Reform Act. Its key element, the Temporary Assistance for Needy Families block grant (TANF), ended the decades-old program that granted cash assistance to every poor family with children. TANF restricts a family's eligibility for federal assistance to five years, and after two years a family head normally has to go to work for the benefits to continue. Moreover, TANF gives states wide latitude in setting benefit levels, eligibility criteria, and other regulations affecting aid to poor families. TANF also places states in charge of developing training and education programs that will move people off welfare and into jobs. (TANF and other aspects of the 1996 welfare reform legislation are discussed further in later chapters.)

After passage of the 1996 Welfare Reform Act, congressional efforts to reduce federal authority declined sharply. Welfare had been the main target of Republican lawmakers, and other large changes were politically more difficult to achieve. Nevertheless, devolution had enabled states and localities to recapture some of the authority they had lost since the 1930s. Yet devolution had not succeeded in rolling back the great majority of the federal domestic programs instituted since that time. The fact remains that there are substantial limits on the amount of power that reasonably can be returned to the states. Because of the increased interdependency of American society, the states will never again have the level of autonomy that they enjoyed until the early twentieth century.

Devolution, Judicial Style In the five decades after the 1930s, the Supreme Court granted Congress broad discretion in the enactment of policies affecting state and local governments. In *Garcia v. San Antonio Authority* (1985), for example, the Court held that federal minimum wage standards apply to employees of state and local governments.[30] States and localities are prohibited from paying their own workers less than the federally mandated minimum wage.

In recent years, however, the Supreme Court has moved to restrict somewhat Congress's power to enact laws binding on the states. Turnover in the Court's membership has placed control in the hands of Republican-appointed conservative justices who believe Congress has overstepped its constitutional authority in some areas.[31] In *United States v. Lopez* (1995), for example, the Court cited the Tenth Amendment in striking down a federal law that prohibited the possession of guns within 1,000 feet of a school. Congress had justified the law as an exercise of its commerce power, but the Court stated that the ban had "nothing to do with commerce, or any sort of economic activity."[32] Two years later, in *Printz v. United States* (1997), the Court struck down that part of the federal Handgun Violence Prevention Act (the so-called Brady bill) that required local law-enforcement officers to conduct background checks on prospective handgun buyers. The Court concluded that the provision violated the Tenth Amendment in that it ordered state officials, in this case police officers, to "enforce a federal regulatory program."[33] Congress can require federal officials to take such action, but it cannot order state officials to do so.

The Supreme Court also has used the Eleventh Amendment to trim Congress's authority over state governments. The Eleventh Amendment protects a state from being sued without its consent in federal court by a private citizen. In *Kimel v. Florida Board of Regents* (2000)[34] and *Board of Trustees of the University of Alabama v. Garrett* (2002),[35] the Supreme Court held that states cannot be sued by their own employees for violations of federal age and disability discrimination laws. The Court ruled that, although states must comply with these laws and can be sued by the federal government for violating them, they cannot be sued by their own employees because age and disability discrimination are not among the forms of discrimination protected from state action by the Fourteenth

The terrorist attacks of September 11, 2001, led to the creation of a new federal agency, the Department of Homeland Security. The attacks also led Americans to look to the federal government for leadership. State and local governments would take their cues from Washington.

Amendment. On the other hand, gender is a protected category, which is why the Supreme Court in *Nevada Department of Human Resources v. Hibbs* (2003) held that state governments can be sued for violations of the federal Family and Medical Leave Act (FMLA), which provides unpaid leave and job retention to employees caring for a new baby or a seriously ill family member. The Court said that FMLA was enacted primarily to protect women employees from discrimination and accordingly was "appropriate legislation" under the Fourteenth Amendment.[36]

Although recent Court rulings have limited Congress's discretion to some extent, they have not fundamentally rolled back the increase in federal authority that began during the 1930s. The Supreme Court has not retreated from the principle established then that Congress's commerce and spending powers are broad and substantial.[37] This principle has enabled the federal government, through its grants-in-aid and its regulatory policies, to exercise its authority in policy areas once reserved for the states. American federalism, even with devolution, is a far different governing system today than it was prior to the 1930s.[38] The states remain powerful governing bodies, but they operate within a system in which federal authority is pervasive. In 2005, for example, the Supreme Court upheld the power of Congress to prohibit marijuana use even for medical purposes. Nearly a dozen states, including California, had passed laws enabling patients, with a physician's prescription, to grow and use marijuana. Although the marijuana was not shipped across state lines, the Supreme Court in *Gonzales v. Raich* (2005) held that the commerce clause allows Congress to ban marijuana even in states that have authorized it for medical use only.[39]

THE PUBLIC'S INFLUENCE: SETTING THE BOUNDARIES OF FEDERAL-STATE POWER

Public opinion had a decisive influence on the ebb and flow of federal power during the twentieth century. As changes occurred in Americans' attitudes toward the federal government and the states, the balance of power between these two levels of government also shifted.

During the Great Depression, when it was clear that the states would be unable to help, Americans turned to Washington for relief. For people without jobs, the fine points of the Constitution were of little consequence. President Roosevelt's programs, though a radical departure from the past, quickly gained public favor. A 1936 Gallup poll indicated, for example, that 61 percent of Americans supported Roosevelt's social security program, whereas only 27 percent opposed it. This support reflected a new public attitude: the federal government, not the states, was expected to take the lead in protecting Americans from economic hardship.[40]

The second great wave of federal social programs—Lyndon Johnson's Great Society—was also driven by public demands. Income and education levels had risen dramatically after the Second World War, and Americans wanted more and better services from government.[41] When the states were slow to respond, Americans pressured federal officials to act. The Medicare and Medicaid programs, which were created in 1965 and provide health care for the elderly and the poor, respectively, are examples of Washington's response. So, too, is increased federal aid in areas such as education, housing, and transportation.

Public opinion was also behind the rollback of federal authority in the 1990s. Americans' dissatisfaction with federal deficits and policies provided the springboard for the Republican takeover of Congress in the 1994 midterm election, which led to policies aimed at devolving power to the states.[42] The capstone program of this devolution was the widely popular 1996 Welfare Reform Act.

The public's role in defining the boundaries between federal and state power would come as no surprise to the Framers of the Constitution. For

them, federalism was a pragmatic issue, one to be decided by the nation's
needs rather than by inflexible rules. James Madison predicted as much
when he said Americans would look to whichever level of government was
more responsive to their interests. Indeed, each succeeding generation of
Americans has seen fit to devise a balance of federal and state power that
would serve its needs. Historian Daniel Boorstin said that the true genius
of the American people is their pragmatism, their willingness to try new
approaches to self-government when the old ones stop working.[43] In few
areas of governing has Americans' pragmatism been more apparent than
in their approach to federalism.

SUMMARY

A foremost characteristic of the American political system is its division of
authority between a national government and state governments. The first
U.S. government, established by the Articles of Confederation, was essentially a union of the states.

In establishing the basis for a stronger national government, the
U.S. Constitution also made provision for safeguarding state interests.
The result was the creation of a federal system in which sovereignty
was vested in both national and state governments. The Constitution
enumerates the general powers of the national government and grants it
implied powers through the "necessary and proper" clause. Other powers
are reserved to the states by the Tenth Amendment.

From 1789 to 1865, the nation's survival was at issue. The states found
it convenient at times to argue that their sovereignty took precedence
over national authority. In the end, it took the Civil War to cement the
idea that the United States was a union of people, not of states. From
1865 to 1937, federalism reflected the doctrine that certain policy areas
were the exclusive responsibility of the national government whereas
responsibility in other policy areas belonged exclusively to the states. This
constitutional position validated the laissez-faire doctrine that big business was largely beyond governmental control. It also allowed the states
to discriminate against African Americans in their public policies. Federalism in a form recognizable today began to emerge in the 1930s.

In the areas of commerce, taxation, spending, civil rights, and civil liberties, among others, the federal government now plays an important role, one
that is the inevitable consequence of the increasing complexity of American
society and the interdependence of its people. National, state, and local officials now work closely together to solve the country's problems, a situation
described as cooperative federalism. Grants-in-aid from Washington to the

states and localities have been the chief instrument of national influence. States and localities have received billions in federal assistance; in accepting federal money, they also have accepted both federal restrictions on its use and the national policy priorities that underlie the granting of the money.

The issue of the relationship between the nation and the states has changed somewhat as a result of devolution—a shift of power downward to the states. This change, like changes throughout U.S. history, sprang from the demands of the American people.

KEY TERMS

block grants (*p. 105*)
categorical grants (*p. 105*)
commerce clause (*p. 95*)
confederacy (*p. 81*)
cooperative federalism (*p. 99*)
devolution (*p. 105*)
dual federalism (*p. 93*)
enumerated (expressed) powers (*p. 86*)
federalism (*p. 81*)

fiscal federalism (*p. 102*)
grants-in-aid (*p. 102*)
implied powers (*p. 87*)
"necessary and proper" (elastic) clause (*p. 87*)
reserved powers (*p. 88*)
sovereignty (*p. 81*)
supremacy clause (*p. 86*)
unitary system (*p. 81*)

SUGGESTED READINGS

Beer, Samuel H. *To Make a Nation: The Rediscovery of American Federalism.* Cambridge, Mass.: The Belknap Press of Harvard University, 1993. An innovative interpretive framework for understanding the impact of federalism and nationalism on the nation's development.

Chopra, Pran. *Supreme Court Versus the Constitution: A Challenge to Federalism.* Thousand Oaks, Calif.: Sage Publications, 2006. A look at the Supreme Court's view of federalism.

Cornell, Saul. *The Other Founders: Anti-Federalism and the Dissenting Tradition in America.* Chapel Hill: University of North Carolina Press, 1999. An analysis of Anti-Federalist thought, its origins, and its legacy.

Elkins, Stanley, and Eric McKitrick. *The Age of Federalism: The Early American Republic, 1788–1800.* New York: Oxford University Press, 1993. An award-winning book on the earliest period of American federalism.

Ross, William G. *A Muted Fury: Populists, Progressives, and Labor Unions Confront the Courts, 1890–1937.* Princeton, N. J.: Princeton University Press, 1993. A valuable study of the political conflict surrounding the judiciary's laissez-faire doctrine in the period 1890–1937.

Teaford, John. *The Rise of the States: Evolution of American State Government.* Baltimore, Md.: Johns Hopkins University Press, 2002. A historical assessment of state government that spans the past century.

Walker, David B. *The Rebirth of Federalism*, 2d ed. Chatham, N. J.: Chatham House Publishers, 2000. An optimistic assessment of the state of today's federalism.

LIST OF WEBSITES

http://lcweb2.loc.gov/ammem/amlaw/lawhome.html A site containing congressional documents and debates from 1774 to 1873.

http://www.csg.org/ The site of the Council of State Governments; includes current news from each of the states and basic information about their governments.

http://www.temple.edu/federalism The site of the Center for the Study of Federalism, located at Temple University; offers information and publications on the federal system of government.

http://www.yale.edu/lawweb/avalon/federal/fed.htm A documentary record of the *Federalist Papers*, the Annapolis convention, the Articles of Confederation, the Madison debates, and the U.S. Constitution.

POLITICS IN THEORY AND PRACTICE

Thinking: How have interdependency and the federal government's superior taxing power contributed to a larger policy role for the national government? Do you think these factors will increase or decrease in importance in the future? What will this trend mean for the future of American federalism? (You might find it helpful to think about these questions in the context of a specific policy area, such as the terrorist threat facing the country.)

Participating: Federalism can be a contentious system in that a policy outcome may depend on whether the issue is settled at the national or the state level. Oregon's physician-assisted suicide law (see the chapter's opening example) is a case in point. Consider writing a letter to your representative in Congress expressing your view of what ought to be done in this case. In preparing your letter, you will need to address two questions: What is your opinion on the issue of physician-assisted suicide? What is your opinion on the question of whether an issue of this type should properly be decided at the state or the federal level? Note that your opinion on the issue may be at odds with your opinion on whether state or federal authority should prevail—for example, you may conclude that the issue should be decided by Oregon even though you personally oppose physician-assisted suicide.

ADDITIONAL RESOURCES

For quizzes, interactive simulations, games, graphics, and other study tools, visit the book's Online Learning Center at **www.mhhe.com/pattersonwtp7.**

The National Idea in American Politics

By Samuel H. Beer

*In his essay, retired Harvard profes-
sor Samuel Beer discusses the
"national idea" as a prevailing
theme of American politics. He
focuses on two aspects of federalism
that were discussed in Chapter 3:
the distribution of power between
the two levels of government and
the use of power at each level. By
contrasting Hamilton with Jefferson
and Johnson with Reagan, he shows
the persistent nature of the conflict
between those Americans who favor
activist national government and
those who oppose what they regard
as excessive centralization. Beer's
accounting is a capsule summary of
federalism—a system of government
in which sovereign power is simultaneously invested in two levels of
government, resulting in a dynamic
system in which competing visions
of America are played out.*

The national idea is a way of looking at
American government and American society. It embraces a view of where the authority of government comes from and a view
of what it should be used for. As a concept
of authority, it identifies the whole people
of the nation as the source of the legitimate
powers of any and all governments. As a
concept of purpose, it tells us that we are

one people and guides us toward what we
should make of ourselves as a people. The
national idea envisions one people, at once
sovereign and subject, source of authority
and substance of history, affirming, through
conflict and in diversity, our unity of being
and becoming.

Because the national idea is also a democratic idea, these concepts of authority and
purpose are interdependent. Self-government
is reflexive. The people who govern are also
the object of government. A government of
the people, therefore, gets its legitimacy both
from being a government by the people and
from being a government for the people.

This theory of legitimacy is national and
democratic. It is also federal. In the national
perspective, although we are one people who
enjoy a common life as one nation, we have
set up not a unitary but a dual system of
government. In establishing this system, the
American people authorized and empowered
two sets of governments: a general government for the whole, and state governments
for the parts. The constitutional authority for
the two sets of government is therefore
coordinate. Neither created the other, and
both are subject to the same ultimate legiti-
mating power, the sovereign people. And
periodically the people in this constituent
capacity amend these institutions, by which
in their governing capacity they direct the
day-to-day affairs of the nation.

From our revolutionary beginnings the
national idea has been widely accepted as a
description of historical fact and a theory of
legitimacy of American federalism. The
American political tradition, however, has
also sustained another view. In this opposing view, one of these levels of government,

the federal government, was brought into existence not by the act of a sovereign people but by a compact among sovereign states. From this compact theory inferences follow that radically contradict the conclusions of the national theory. While the national theory has, on balance, had much the greater influence on thought and action, the compact theory has survived and continues even today to show itself in the feelings of citizens, the rhetoric of politicians, and the actions of governments.

When President Reagan took office in 1981, for instance, he proclaimed a "new federalism." Its central thrust was to cut back on the activities of the federal government by reducing or eliminating a vast number of programs, the principal cuts falling on federal aid to state and local governments. The President wished to do this because he judged these activities to be inefficient, unnecessary, and sometimes positively harmful. He also claimed that they were improper under the Constitution. . . .

In his first inaugural address on January 20, 1981, accordingly, President Reagan promised to "restore the balance between levels of government." And while he did not elaborate his political philosophy, he made clear in a phrase or two his reliance upon the compact theory of the Constitution to justify his new federalism. "The Federal government," he declared at one point in his address, "did not create the states; the states created the Federal government."

This allegation did not pass without comment. In response to President Reagan's use of the compact theory, eminent academic critics counterattacked in terms of the national theory. Richard P. Morris of Columbia University called the President's view of the historical facts "a hoary myth about the origins of the Union" and went on to summarize the evidence showing that "the United States was created by the people in collectivity, not by the individual states." No less bluntly, Henry Steele Commager of Amherst College said President Reagan did not understand the Constitution, which in its own words asserts that it was ordained by "We, the People of the United States," not by the states severally. . . .

The argument between the President and the professors was not simply about history. Nor was it mainly about the constitutional authority of the federal and state governments. Their primary disagreement was over public policy, specifically, the use of federal authority in recent years to expand the social and economic programs of the welfare state, especially those dating from the "new federalism" of Lyndon Johnson. President Reagan had taken office as the champion of conservative attitudes that had been gathering force around the country for a generation. He articulated these attitudes in a distinctive vision of American society at home and abroad and in a set of strategies for realizing that vision. Expressing in a new public philosophy the old and familiar values of rugged individualism, he sought to cut back the welfare state and to restore the free market—or in the language of political economy, to shift social choice from public choice toward market choice. Declaring in his first inaugural address that the excessive growth of the public sector in recent years meant that "government is not the solution to our problem; government is the problem," he proposed to "reverse" that growth. Intrinsic to this goal was his promise of another "new federalism" which would "restore the balance between levels of government." The reduction of federal grant programs would at once help restore the federal-state balance and promote the free market.

Some critics called him insincere, claiming that when he said he wanted to restore the federal-state balance, what he really wanted to do was to cut federal spending on social and economic programs. No doubt he was mainly interested in the impact of his policies on American society. But that is no reason for saying that he was not also interested in reducing what he thought was excessive centralization of power in the federal system. In American politics, thinking about federalism has usually had those two aspects: a concern with both the pattern of authority and the pattern of purpose, with the balance of power between levels of government and with the policies for which that power is used. When President Reagan called in the compact theory to lend support to his views on public policy, he was doing what its adherents before him had often done. In their way the nationalists had done the same, right from the days when Alexander Hamilton, as Secretary of the Treasury, set the course of the first administration of George Washington. . . .

Hamilton's nationalism was expressed not only in his belief that Americans were "one people" rather than thirteen separate peoples but even more emphatically in his commitment to governmental activism. This concern that the American people must make vigorous use of their central government for the tasks of nation-building separated him sharply from Thomas Jefferson,

Washington's Secretary of State, who leaned toward the compact theory. . . .

Hamilton is renowned for his statecraft—for his methods of using the powers of government for economic, political, and social ends. But that emphasis obscures his originality, which consisted in his conceptualization of those ends. . . . [E]arlier craftsmen of the modern state in Bourbon France or Hohenzollern Prussia or Whig Britain could take for granted the established authority of a monarchic and aristocratic regime. They too had their techniques for enhancing the attachment of the people to the prince. But in America the people *were* the prince. To enhance their attachment to the ultimate governing power, therefore, meant fortifying the bonds that united them as a people. If the authority of this first nation-state was to suffice for its governance, the purpose of the state would have to become the development of the nation. This was the essential Hamiltonian end: to make the nation more of a nation.

What's Your Opinion?

Which interpretation of the Constitution do you find more convincing, that of Alexander Hamilton or that of Ronald Reagan? If you had a choice of a nation of states or a nation of people, which would you choose? Explain in terms of the impact on how Americans would be governed.

CHAPTER 4

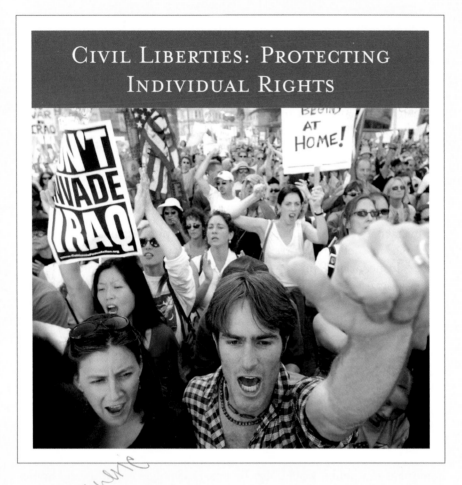

CIVIL LIBERTIES: PROTECTING INDIVIDUAL RIGHTS

❝A bill of rights is what the people are entitled to against every
government on earth, general or particular, and what no just government
should refuse, or rest on inference.**❞**

THOMAS JEFFERSON[1]

Robert and Sarisse Creighton and their three children were asleep
when FBI agents and local police broke into their home in the middle of
the night. Brandishing guns, the officers searched the house for a relative
of the Creightons who was suspected of bank robbery. When asked to
show a search warrant, the officers said, "You watch too much TV." The
suspect was not there, and the officers left as abruptly as they had entered.
The Creightons sued the FBI agent in charge, Russell Anderson, for violating their Fourth Amendment right against unlawful search.

The Creightons won a temporary victory when the U.S. Circuit Court of Appeals for the Eighth Circuit—noting that individuals are constitutionally protected against warrantless searches unless officers have good reason ("probable cause") for a search and unless they have good reason ("exigent circumstances") for conducting that search without a warrant—concluded that Anderson had been derelict in his duty. In the judgment of the appellate court, Anderson should have sought a warrant from a judge, who would have decided whether a search of the Creightons' home was justified.

The Supreme Court of the United States overturned the lower court's ruling. The Court's majority opinion stated: "We have recognized that it is inevitable that law enforcement officials will in some cases reasonably but mistakenly conclude that probable cause is present, and we have indicated that in such cases those officials . . . should not be held personally liable." Justice John Paul Stevens and two other justices sharply dissented. Stevens accused the Court's majority of showing "remarkably little fidelity" to the Fourth Amendment.[2] Civil liberties groups claimed that the Court's decision gave police an open invitation to invade people's homes on the slightest pretext. On the other hand, law enforcement officials praised the decision, saying that a ruling in the Creightons' favor would have made them hesitant to pursue suspects for fear of a lawsuit whenever the search failed to produce the culprit.

As this case illustrates, issues of individual rights are complex and political. No right is absolute. For example, the Fourth Amendment protects Americans not from *all* searches but from *unreasonable* searches. The public would be unsafe if law officials could never pursue a suspect into a home. Yet the public would also be unsafe if police could invade homes anytime they wanted. The challenge for a civil society is to establish a level of police authority that balances the demands of public safety with those of personal freedom. The balance point, however, is always subject to dispute. Did FBI agent Anderson have sufficient cause for a warrantless search of the Creightons' home? Or was his evidence so weak that his forcible entry constituted an unreasonable search? Not even the justices of the Supreme Court could agree on these questions. Six justices sided with Anderson, and three backed the Creightons' position.

This chapter examines issues of **civil liberties,** specific individual rights, such as freedom of speech and protection against self-incrimination, that are constitutionally protected against infringement by government. As seen in Chapter 2, the Constitution's failure to enumerate individual freedoms led to demands for the **Bill of Rights** (see Table 4–1). Enacted in 1791, these first ten amendments to the Constitution specify

| TABLE | 4-1 | THE BILL OF RIGHTS: A SELECTED LIST OF CONSTITUTIONAL PROTECTIONS |

The Bill of Rights refers to the first ten amendments to the Constitution, which include protections of individual rights.

First Amendment

Speech: You are free to say almost anything except that which is obscene, slanders another person, or has a high probability of inciting others to take imminent lawless action.

Assembly: You are free to assemble, although government may regulate the time and place for reasons of public convenience and safety, provided such regulations are applied evenhandedly to all groups.

Religion: You are protected from having the religious beliefs of others imposed on you, and you are free to believe what you like.

Fourth Amendment

Search and seizure: You are protected from unreasonable searches and seizures, although you forfeit that right if you knowingly waive it.

Arrest: You are protected from arrest unless authorities have probable cause to believe you have committed a crime.

Fifth Amendment

Self-incrimination: You are protected against self-incrimination, which means that you have the right to remain silent and to be protected against coercion by law enforcement officials.

Double jeopardy: You cannot be tried twice for the same crime if the first trial results in a verdict of innocence.

Due process: You cannot be deprived of life, liberty, or property without proper legal proceedings.

Sixth Amendment

Counsel: You have a right to be represented by an attorney and can demand to speak first with an attorney before responding to questions from law enforcement officials.

Prompt and reasonable proceedings: You have a right to be arraigned promptly, to be informed of the charges, to confront witnesses, and to have a speedy and open trial by an impartial jury.

Eighth Amendment

Bail: You are protected against excessive bail or fines.

Cruel and unusual punishment: You are protected from cruel and unusual punishment, although this provision does not protect you from the death penalty or from a long prison term for a minor offense.

certain rights of life, liberty, and property that the national government is obliged to respect. A later amendment, the Fourteenth, became the basis for protecting these rights from actions by state and local governments.

Rights have full meaning only as they are protected in law. A constitutional guarantee of free speech, for example, is worth no more than the paper on which it is written if authorities can stop people from speaking freely. Judicial action is important in defining what people's rights mean in practice and in setting limits on official action. In some areas, the judiciary devises a specific test to determine whether government action is lawful. A test applied in the area of free speech, for example, is whether general rules (such as restrictions on the time and place of a public gathering) are applied fairly. Government officials do not meet this test if they apply one set of rules for groups they like and a harsher set of rules for those they dislike.

Issues of individual rights have become increasingly complex. The writers of the Constitution could not possibly have foreseen the United States of the early twenty-first century, with its huge national government, enormous corporations, pervasive mass media, urban crowding, and vulnerability to terrorist acts. These developments are potential threats to personal liberty, and the judiciary in recent decades has seen fit to expand the rights to which individuals are entitled. However, these rights are constantly being balanced against competing rights and society's collective interests. The Bill of Rights operates in an untidy world where people's highest aspirations collide with their worst passions, and it is at this juncture that issues of civil liberties arise. Should an admitted murderer be entitled to recant a confession? Should the press be allowed to print military secrets whose publication might jeopardize national security? Should extremist groups be allowed to publicize their messages of prejudice and hate? Such questions are among the subjects of this chapter, which focuses on these points:

★ *Freedom of expression is the most basic of democratic rights, but, like all rights, it is not unlimited.* Free expression recently has been strongly supported by the Supreme Court.

★ *"Due process of law" refers to legal protections (primarily procedural safeguards) designed to ensure that individual rights are respected by government.*

★ *During the last half-century particularly, the civil liberties of individual Americans have been substantially broadened in law and given greater judicial protection from action by all levels of government.* Of special significance has been the Supreme Court's use of the Fourteenth Amendment to protect these individual rights from action by state and local governments.

★ *Individual rights are constantly being weighed against the demands of majorities and the collective needs of society.* All political institutions are involved in this process, as is public opinion, but the judiciary plays the central role in it and is the institution that is most partial to the protection of civil liberties.

FREEDOM OF EXPRESSION

Freedom of political expression is the most basic of democratic rights. Unless citizens can openly express their political opinions, they cannot properly influence their government or act to protect their other rights. As the Supreme Court concluded in 1984, "The freedom to speak one's mind is not only an aspect of individual liberty—and thus a good unto itself—but also is essential to the common quest for truth and the vitality of society as a whole."[3]

The First Amendment provides the foundation for **freedom of expression**—the right of individual Americans to hold and communicate views of their choosing. For many reasons, such as a desire to conform to social pressure or a fear of harassment, Americans do not always choose to express themselves freely. Moreover, freedom of expression, like other rights, is not absolute. It does not entitle individuals to say or do whatever they want, to whomever they want, whenever they want. Free expression can be denied, for example, if it endangers national security, wrongly damages the reputations of others, or deprives others of their basic freedoms. Nevertheless, the First Amendment provides for freedom of expression by prohibiting laws that would abridge the freedoms of conscience, speech, press, assembly, and petition.

Free expression is vigorously protected by the courts. Today, under most circumstances, Americans can freely express their political views without fear of governmental interference. In earlier times, however, Americans were less free to express their opinions.

The Early Period: The Uncertain Status of the Right of Free Expression

The first attempt by the U.S. government to restrict free expression was the Sedition Act of 1798, which made it a crime to print harsh criticisms of the president or other national officials. Thomas Jefferson called the Sedition Act an "alarming infraction" of the Constitution

Exercising their right of free speech and assembly, antiabortion protesters gather outside a government building. Individuals do not have a constitutional right to demonstrate in any place at any time, but government is required to accommodate requests for marches and other displays of free expression.

Historical Background

and, upon replacing John Adams as president in 1801, pardoned the newspaper publications who had been convicted under it. Because the Supreme Court did not review the sedition cases, however, the judiciary's position on free expression was an open question. The Court also did not rule on free speech during the Civil War era, when the government severely restricted individual rights.

In 1919 the Court finally ruled on a free-expression case. The defendant had been convicted under the 1917 Espionage Act, which prohibited forms of dissent, including the distribution of antiwar leaflets, that could harm the nation's effort in World War I. In *Schenck v. United States* (1919), the Court unanimously upheld the constitutionality of the Espionage Act. In the opinion written by Justice Oliver Wendell Holmes, the Court said that Congress could restrict speech that was "of such a nature as to create a clear and present danger" to the nation's security. In a famous passage, Holmes argued that not even the First Amendment would permit a person to falsely yell "Fire!" in a crowded theater and create a panic that could kill or injure innocent people.[4]

Although the *Schenck* decision upheld a law that limited free expression, it also established a standard—the **clear-and-present-danger test**—for determining when government had exceeded its constitutional authority to restrict speech. Political speech that was a clear and present danger could be banned by government. Speech that did not pose such a danger could *not* be banned. (The clear-and-present-danger test was later replaced by the imminent-lawless-action test, which is discussed later in the chapter.)

The Modern Period: Protecting Free Expression

Until the twentieth century, the tension between national security interests and free expression was not a pressing issue in the United States. The country's great size and ocean barriers provided protection from potential enemies, minimizing concerns about internal subversion. World War I, however, intruded on America's isolation, and World War II brought it to an abrupt end. Since then, Americans' rights of free expression have been defined largely in the context of national security concerns.

Free Speech   During the cold war that developed after World War II, many Americans believed that the Soviet Union was bent on destroying the United States, and the Supreme Court allowed government to limit certain types of expression. In 1951, for example, the Court upheld the convictions of eleven members of the U.S. Communist party who had been prosecuted under a law that made it illegal to express support for the forceful overthrow of the U.S. government.[5] By the late 1950s, however, fear of internal communist subversion was subsiding, and the Supreme Court expanded the scope of free speech.[6] The Court implicitly embraced a legal doctrine first outlined by Justice Harlan Fiske Stone in 1938. Stone argued that First Amendment rights of free expression are the basis of Americans' liberty and ought to have a "preferred position" in the

Historical
Background

law. If government can control what people know and say, it can manipulate their opinions and thereby deprive them of the right to govern themselves. Therefore, government should be broadly prohibited from restricting free expression.[7]

This philosophy has led the Supreme Court to rule that government officials must show that national security is directly and substantially imperiled before they can lawfully prohibit citizens from speaking out. For example, during the Vietnam era, despite the largest sustained protest movement in America's history, not a single individual was convicted solely for criticizing the government's war policy. (Some dissenters were found guilty on other grounds, such as inciting riots and assaulting the police.)

The Supreme Court's protection of **symbolic speech** has been less substantial than its protection of verbal speech. For example, the Court in 1968 upheld the conviction of a Vietnam protester who had burned his draft registration card. The Court concluded that the federal law prohibiting the destruction of draft cards was intended primarily to protect the military's need for soldiers, not to prevent people from criticizing government policy.[8]

The Supreme Court, however, has not granted the government broad power to restrict symbolic speech. In 1989, for example, the Court ruled that the symbolic burning of the American flag is a lawful form of expression. The ruling came in the case of Gregory Lee Johnson, who had set fire to a U.S. flag outside the hall in Dallas where the 1984 Republican National Convention was being held. The Supreme Court rejected the state of Texas's argument that flag burning is, in every instance, an imminent danger to public safety. "If there is a bedrock principle underlying the First Amendment," the Court ruled in the *Johnson* case, "it is that the Government may not prohibit the expression of an idea simply because society finds the idea itself offensive or disagreeable."[9] (A year later the Court struck down a new federal statute that would have made it a federal crime to burn or deface the flag.[10])

Press Freedom and Prior Restraint   Freedom of the press has also received strong judicial protection in recent decades. In *New York Times Co. v. United States* (1971), the Court ruled that the *Times*'s publication of the "Pentagon papers" (secret government documents revealing that officials had deceived the public about aspects of the Vietnam War) could not be blocked by the government, which claimed that publication would hurt the war effort. The documents had been illegally obtained by antiwar activists, who then gave them to the *Times*. The Court ruled that "any system of prior restraints" on the press is unconstitutional unless the government can clearly justify the restriction.[11]

The unacceptability of **prior restraint**—government prohibition of speech or publication before the fact—is basic to the current doctrine of free expression. The Supreme Court has said that any attempt by government to prevent expression carries "a 'heavy presumption' against its constitutionality."[12] News organizations are legally responsible after the fact for what they report or say (for example, they can be sued by an individual whose reputation is wrongly damaged by their words), but generally

★ LEADERS

Oliver Wendell Holmes Jr.
(1841–1935)

Oliver Wendell Holmes Jr. was nominated for the Supreme Court in 1901 by President Theodore Roosevelt and served for more than three decades. The son of a famous writer and physician, Holmes was a leading intellectual force on the Court. An advocate of judicial restraint, he nonetheless argued that the law had to keep pace with society. He helped lay the foundation for an interpretation of the First Amendment that limited government's ability to restrict free expression. Holmes famously wrote that the First Amendment would not protect a person "falsely shouting fire in a theater and causing a panic" but that government also did not have blanket authority to limit free speech. Upon his death, Holmes left his estate to the U.S. government. In one of his Court opinions, he had written: "Taxes are the price we pay for civilization."

government cannot stop the media in advance from reporting their views. One exception is the reporting on U.S. military operations during wartime. The courts have allowed the government to censor reports filed by journalists who are granted access to the battlefront. The courts have also upheld the government's authority to ban uncensored publications by certain past and present government employees, such as CIA agents, who have knowledge of classified information and programs.

Free Expression and State Governments

In 1790 Congress rejected a proposed constitutional amendment that would have applied the Bill of Rights to the states. Thus, the freedoms provided in the Bill of Rights initially were protected only from action by the national government.[13] The effect was that the Bill of Rights had limited meaning for ordinary Americans because state and local governments carry out most of the activities, such as law enforcement, in which people's rights are at issue.

Not until the twentieth century did the Supreme Court begin to protect individual rights from infringement by state and local governments.

The instrument for this change was the **due process clause of the Four-teenth Amendment** to the Constitution.

The Fourteenth Amendment and Selective Incorporation   The Four-teenth Amendment, ratified in 1868, includes a clause that forbids a state from depriving any person of life, liberty, or property without due process of law (due process refers to the legal procedures, such as the right to a lawyer, that have been established as a means of protecting individuals' rights). Six decades later, the Supreme Court in *Gitlow v. New York* (1925) decided that the Fourteenth Amendment applied to state action in the area of free expression. Although the Court upheld Benjamin Gitlow's conviction for violating a New York law making it illegal to advocate the violent overthrow of the U.S. government, the Court said that the states were not completely free to limit expression:

> For present purposes we may and do assume that freedom of speech and of the press—which are protected by the First Amendment from abridge-ment by Congress—are among the fundamental personal rights and "liberties" protected by the due process clause of the Fourteenth Amend-ment from impairment by the states.[14]

There is no indication that Congress, when it passed the Fourteenth Amendment after the Civil War, meant it to protect First Amendment rights from state action. The Supreme Court justified its new inter-pretation in the *Gitlow* case by referring to **selective incorporation**—the incorporation into the Fourteenth Amendment of certain provisions of the Bill of Rights so that these rights can be protected by the fed-eral courts from infringement by the states. The Court reasoned that the Fourteenth Amendment's due process clause would be largely meaningless if states had the power to stop their residents from speak-ing openly.

This interpretation of the Fourteenth Amendment provided the Court with a legal basis for striking down state laws that infringed unreasonably on other forms of free expression. But the Supreme Court can act only in the context of specific cases; it does not have the constitutional authority to issue blanket rulings. Accordingly, the incorporation of additional rights by the Court did not occur until appropriate cases arose and reached the Court on appeal from lower courts. Within a dozen years (see Table 4–2), the Court had received four cases that enabled it to invalidate state laws restricting expression in the areas of speech (*Fiske v. Kansas*), press (*Near v. Minnesota*), religion (*Hamilton v. Regents, University of California*), and assembly and petition (*DeJonge v. Oregon*).[15]

| TABLE 4-2 | SELECTIVE INCORPORATION OF RIGHTS OF FREE EXPRESSION |

In the 1920s and 1930s, the Supreme Court selectively incorporated the free-expression provisions of the First Amendment into the Fourteenth Amendment so that these rights would be protected from infringement by the states.

Supreme Court Case	Year	Constitutional Right at Issue
Gitlow v. New York	1925	Fourteenth Amendment protection of free expression
Fiske v. Kansas	1927	Free speech
Near v. Minnesota	1931	Free press
Hamilton v. Regents, U. of California	1934	Religious freedom
DeJonge v. Oregon	1937	Freedom of assembly and of petition

The *Near* decision is the best known of these rulings. Jay Near was the publisher of a Minneapolis weekly newspaper that regularly made defamatory attacks on blacks, Jews, Catholics, and labor union leaders. His paper was closed down on authority of a state law banning "malicious, scandalous, or defamatory" publications. Near appealed the shutdown, and the Supreme Court ruled in his favor, saying that the Minnesota law was "the essence of censorship."[16]

Limiting the Authority of the States to Restrict Expression Since the 1930s, the Supreme Court has broadly protected freedom of expression from action by the states and by local governments, which derive their authority from the states. The Court has held that the states cannot restrict free expression except when it is almost certain to provoke immediate lawless action such as a rampage or riot. A leading free speech case was *Brandenburg v. Ohio* (1969). The appellant was a Ku Klux Klan member who, in a speech delivered at a Klan rally, said that "revenge" might have to be taken if the national government "continues to suppress the white Caucasian race." He was convicted under an Ohio law, but the Supreme Court reversed the conviction, saying that the First Amendment prohibits a state from suppressing speech that advocates the unlawful use of force "except where such advocacy is directed to inciting or producing imminent lawless action, and is likely to produce such action."[17]

clear and present danger

This test—the likelihood of **imminent lawless action**—is a severe limit on the government's power to restrict expression. It is rare for words alone to incite others to engage in immediate unlawful action. In effect, Americans are free to say almost anything they want on political issues.

This protection includes hate speech. In a unanimous 1992 opinion, the Court struck down a St. Paul, Minnesota, ordinance making it a crime to engage in speech likely to arouse "anger or alarm" on the basis of "race, color, creed, religion or gender." The Court said that the First Amendment prohibits government from "silencing speech on the basis of its content."[18] This protection of hate *speech* does not, however, extend to hate *crimes*, such as assault, motivated by racial or other prejudice. A Wisconsin law that provided for increased sentences for hate crimes was challenged as a violation of the First Amendment. In a unanimous 1993 opinion, the Court said that the law was aimed at "conduct unprotected by the First Amendment" rather than the defendant's speech.[19]

In a key case involving freedom of assembly, the U.S. Supreme Court in 1977 upheld a lower-court ruling against local ordinances of Skokie, Illinois, that had been invoked to prevent a parade there by the American Nazi party.[20] Skokie had a large Jewish population, including many survivors of Nazi Germany's concentration camps. The Supreme Court held that the right of free expression takes precedence over the mere *possibility* that the exercise of that right might have undesirable consequences. Before government can lawfully prevent a speech or rally, it must demonstrate that the event will cause harm and also must demonstrate the lack of alternative ways (such as assigning police officers to control the crowd) to prevent the harm from happening.

The Supreme Court has recognized that freedom of speech and assembly may conflict with the routines of daily life. Accordingly, individuals do not have the right to hold a public rally at a busy intersection during rush hour, nor do they have the right to immediate access to a public auditorium. The Court has held that public officials can regulate the time, place, and conditions of public assembly, provided that these regulations are reasonable and are applied evenhandedly to all groups, including those that hold unpopular views.[21]

In general, the Supreme Court's position is that the First Amendment makes any government effort to regulate the *content* of a message highly suspect. In the flag-burning case, Texas was regulating the content of the message—contempt for the flag and the principles it represents. Texas could not have been regulating the act itself, for the Texas government's

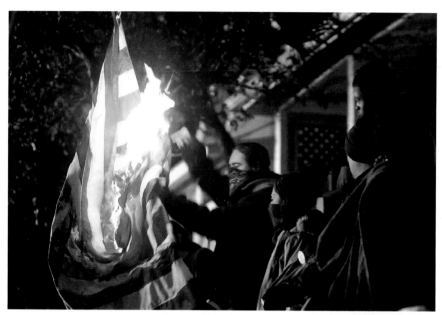

The Supreme Court has ruled that flag burning is a constitutionally protected form of free expression. Shown here is a scene outside California's San Quentin Prison in 2005. The crowd is burning the American flag to protest the execution of convicted murderer Stanley Williams, whose case attracted national attention.

own method of disposing of worn-out flags is to burn them. But a content-neutral regulation (no public rally can be held at a busy intersection during rush hour) is acceptable as long as it is reasonable and does not discriminate against certain groups or ideas.

Libel and Slander

The constitutional right of free expression is not a legal license to avoid responsibility for the consequences of what is said or written. If false information that greatly harms a person's reputation is published (**libel**) or spoken (**slander**), the injured party can sue for damages. If it were easy for public officials to claim defamation and win large amounts of money, individuals and organizations would be reluctant to criticize those in power. As it stands, U.S. slander and libel law is based on the assumption that society has an interest in encouraging citizens and news organizations to speak out. Accordingly, writers and speakers can attack public officials nearly at will without fear that they will have to pay damages for slander or libel. (The courts are less protective of the writer or speaker when allegations are made about a private citizen. What is said about private individuals is considered to be less basic to the democratic process than what is said about public officials.)

The Supreme Court has held that true statements disseminated by the media have "full constitutional protection."[22] In other words, factually accurate statements, no matter how damaging they might be to a public official's career or reputation, are a protected form of expression. Even false statements or conjectures enjoy considerable legal protection. In *New York Times Co. v. Sullivan* (1964), the Supreme Court overruled an Alabama state court that had found the *New York Times* guilty of libel for printing an advertisement that criticized Alabama officials for mistreating student civil rights activists. Even though some of what was alleged was false, the Supreme Court ruled in favor of the *Times*, saying that libel of a public official requires proof of actual malice, which was defined as a knowing or reckless disregard for the truth.[23] It is very difficult to prove that a publication has acted with reckless or deliberate disregard for the truth. In fact, no federal official has won a libel judgment against a news organization in the four decades since the *Sullivan* ruling.

Obscenity

Obscenity is a form of expression that is not protected by the First Amendment and thus can be prohibited by law. However, the Supreme Court has found it difficult to define with precision the criteria by which material is to be judged obscene. The Court set forth the first explicit test for obscenity in *Roth v. United States* (1957) by saying that material is obscene if "taken as a whole" it appeals to "prurient interest" and has no "redeeming social value." This assessment was to be made from the standpoint of "the average person, applying contemporary community standards."[24] However, the test proved unworkable in practice. Even the justices of the Supreme Court, when they personally examined allegedly obscene material, argued over whether it appealed to prurient interest and was without redeeming social value. In the end, they usually concluded that the material at issue had at least some social significance.

In *Miller v. California* (1973), the Court narrowed "contemporary community standards" to the local level. The Court said that what might offend residents of "Mississippi might be found tolerable in Las Vegas."[25] But even this test proved too restrictive. The Court subsequently ruled that material cannot be judged obscene simply because the "average" local resident might object to it. "Community standards" were to be judged in the context of a "reasonable person"—someone whose outlook is broad enough to evaluate the material on its overall merit rather than its most

Justin Timberlake and Janet Jackson during their performances at Super Bowl XXXVIII in Houston, on Sunday, February 1, 2004, just before he pulled off part of her clothing. The incident prompted the Federal Communications Commission to fine the CBS network for violating broadcast decency standards.

objectionable feature. The Court later also modified its content standard, saying that the material must be of a "particularly offensive type."[26] These efforts illustrate the difficulty of defining obscenity and, even more, of establishing a clear-cut legal standard that the courts can apply consistently when obscenity cases arise.

The Supreme Court has distinguished between obscene materials in public places and those in the home. A unanimous ruling in 1969 held that what adults read and watch in the privacy of their homes cannot be made a crime.[27] The Court created an exception to this rule in 1990 by upholding an Ohio law making it a crime to possess pornographic photographs of children.[28] The Court reasoned that the purchase of such material encourages producers to use children in the making of pornographic materials, which is a crime. Consistent with this reasoning, the Court in *Ashcroft v. Free Speech Coalition* (2002) held that pictures of adults digitally altered to look like children cannot be banned because children are not used in the production of this type of material.[29]

Children have also been a consideration in court cases involving material transmitted on cable television or over the Internet. On several occasions, Congress has passed legislation (for example, the 1998 Child Online Protection Act) that would restrict the transmission of sexually explicit material that children can access. The Supreme Court has held that the restrictions, though well intentioned, have been so broad that they would ban material adults have a constitutional right to view if they so choose.[30] The Court has directed officials to find less restrictive ways to keep such material from being seen by children. An example is the federal requirement that cable operators must scramble the signal of channels that convey sexually explicit material if a subscriber requests it.

FREEDOM OF RELIGION

Free religious expression is the precursor of free political expression, at least within the English tradition of limited government. England's Glorious, or Bloodless, Revolution of 1689 centered on the issue of religion and resulted in the Act of Toleration, which gave members of all Protestant sects the right to worship freely and publicly. The English philosopher John Locke (1632–1704) extended this principle, arguing that legitimate government could not inhibit free expression, religious or otherwise. The First Amendment

Historical
Background reflects this tradition, providing for freedom of religion along with freedom of speech, press, assembly, and petition.

In regard to religion, the First Amendment reads: "Congress shall make no law respecting an establishment of religion, or prohibiting the free exercise thereof." The prohibition on laws aimed at "establishment of religion" (the establishment clause) and its "free exercise" (the free-exercise clause) applies to states and localities through the Fourteenth Amendment.

The Establishment Clause

The **establishment clause** has been interpreted by the courts to mean that government may not favor one religion over another or support religion over no religion. (This position contrasts with that of a country such as England, where Anglicanism is the official, or "established," state religion, though no religion is prohibited.) The Supreme Court's interpretation of the establishment clause has been described as maintaining a "wall of separation" between church and state. The Court held in *Engel v. Vitale* (1962) that the establishment clause prohibits the reciting of prayers in public schools.[31] A year later the Court struck down Bible readings in public schools.[32]

MEDIA AND POLITICS

Christian News Broadcasting

Until the 1930s, when the Great Depression altered the nation's course, religion was a powerful force in American politics. The Protestant-Catholic divide was embedded in the conflict between the major parties, and religious impulses inspired many of the great political movements, including the abolitionist and suffragist movements. The severe economic downturn that occurred during the 1930s shifted politics squarely toward economic issues, and the resulting party realignment blurred many long-standing religious splits.

Stirrings of a new politics of religion began in the 1960s, when the Supreme Court held that the First Amendment's ban on the establishment of religion precluded prayer and Bible readings in public schools. When the Supreme Court in 1973 declared that the right to privacy permitted a woman to choose abortion in the first trimester of pregnancy, religion once again took a place at the center of American politics.

This trend can be seen in the spread of Christian-format news broadcasting—news with a religious point of view, typically that of Christian fundamentalism. Christian broadcasting is one of the most rapidly growing forms of media and dominates some media markets in the South. There are now more than two thousand self-described Christian radio stations, double the level of a decade ago. Audience ratings for Christian radio have increased markedly. Although Christian programming is less evident on television, it can be found there as well—most notably in the Pat Robertson–founded Christian Broadcasting Network. The network's main news program is Robertson's *700 Club*, a mix of news, interviews, and religious messages. Robertson's program attracts roughly one million viewers, a large audience by the standards of cable television.

Whether aired on radio or television, Christian news broadcasting differs from traditional news. Top stories are covered but are given a religious slant. In an interview on PBS's *The News Hour with Jim Lehrer*, Ed Sossen of KIXL, a Christian radio station in Austin, Texas, said: "We do the same kinds of things—traffic, news, weather, sports—that another radio station would give, we just do it from a

(continued)

Christian perspective and hopefully people find that comforting."
Sossen commented about judicial appointment hearings: "[We don't
advocate] fair, impartial Supreme Court justices. We want somebody
who agrees with us." On the abortion issue, Christian news broadcasts side openly with the pro-life position. Marvin Olasky, a Christian news journalist who was interviewed on the same *News Hour*
program as Sossen, said: "We won't try to balance a story between
the abortionists and a pro-life person."

What's your awareness and opinion of Christian broadcasting?
Have you listened often enough to have an opinion about whether
its news programming, in addition to serving religious purposes, also
meets people's information needs? Why do you think it does or does
not?

Religion is a powerful force in American life, and the Supreme Court's
ban on religious teaching in public school classrooms has evoked strong
opposition. An Alabama law attempted to circumvent the prayer ruling
by permitting public schools to set aside one minute each day for silent
prayer or meditation. In 1985 the Court declared the law unconstitutional, ruling that "government must pursue a course of complete neutrality toward religion."[33] The Court in 2000 reaffirmed the ban by
extending it to include organized student-led prayer at public school
football games.[34]

The Supreme Court also has banned religious displays on public property when the purpose of such a display is overtly religious and lacks a
historical context. Because of the prominence of religion in American life,
many public buildings sport religious symbolism. For instance, a statue of
Moses holding the Ten Commandments stands in the rotunda of the
Library of Congress building, which opened in 1897. Legal challenges to
such displays are unlikely to succeed. In *Van Orden v. Perry* (2005), for
example, the Supreme Court rejected a suit asking for the dismantling of
a display of the Ten Commandments on a monument on the grounds of
the Texas State Capitol. The Court noted that the display had been
installed nearly a half-century earlier, had been paid for by a nonreligious
group, and had not previously been the subject of dispute.[35] On the other
hand, in *McCreary County v. American Civil Liberties Union* (2005), the
Supreme Court struck down displays of the Ten Commandments on the
walls of two Kentucky courthouses. The displays were recent and had

initially hung by themselves on the courtroom walls. Only after county officials were sued were a few historical displays mounted alongside the religious ones. The Supreme Court concluded that the officials had religious purposes in mind when they erected the displays and thus had to remove them.[36]

The Supreme Court generally has taken a pragmatic approach to religious controversies, permitting some establishment activities while disallowing others. For instance, the Court has allowed states to pay for secular textbooks used in church-affiliated schools[37] but has not allowed them to pay part of the salaries of the teachers in such schools.[38] Such distinctions are based on judgments of whether government action involves "*excessive* entanglement with religion."[39] In allowing public funds to be used by religious schools for secular textbooks but not for teachers' salaries, the courts have indicated that, whereas it is relatively easy to determine whether the content of a particular textbook promotes religion, it would be much harder to determine whether a particular teacher was promoting religion in the classroom.[40]

In a key 2002 decision, however, the Supreme Court upheld an Ohio law that allows students in Cleveland's failing public schools to receive a tax-supported voucher to attend private or parochial school. The Court's majority argued in *Zelman v. Simmons-Harris* that the program did not violate the establishment clause because students had a choice between secular and religious education. Four members of the Court dissented sharply with the majority's reasoning. Justice Stevens said the ruling had removed a "brick from the wall that was once designed to separate religion from government."[41] A piece of the brick was restored in 2004 when the Court in *Locke v. Davey* held that publicly funded scholarships can be denied to students pursuing religious careers. At issue was a state of Washington scholarship program that excluded otherwise eligible students who were studying for the ministry. The state justified the exclusion on grounds that the use of public funds to educate ministers would involve it in the establishment of religion.[42]

The Free-Exercise Clause

The First and Fourteenth Amendments also prohibit government interference with the free exercise of religion. The idea underlying the **free-exercise clause** is clear: Americans are free to believe what they want. However, they are not always free to act on their beliefs. The courts have allowed government interference in the exercise of religious beliefs when such interference is the secondary result of an overriding social goal. An example is the legal protection of children with life-threatening illnesses

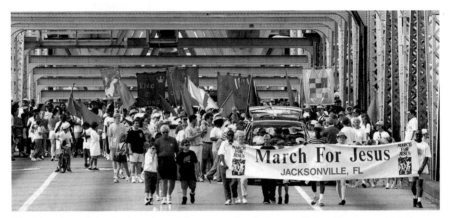

The First Amendment's protection of free expression includes religious freedom, which has led the courts to hold that government in most instances should not promote or interfere with religious practices.

whose parents refuse to permit medical treatment on religious grounds. A court may order that such children be given medical assistance because the social good of saving their lives overrides their parents' free-exercise rights.

In a few circumstances, the free-exercise clause has been the basis for allowing certain individuals to disobey otherwise valid laws. The Supreme Court ruled in 1972 that Amish families did not have to abide by a state law requiring children to attend school until age sixteen because the law conflicted with a centuries-old Amish religious practice of having children leave school and begin work at an early age.[43] In upholding the free exercise of religion in such cases, the Court may be said to have violated the establishment clause by granting preferred treatment to people who hold a particular religious belief. The Court has recognized the potential conflict between the free-exercise and establishment clauses and, as in other such situations, has tried to strike a reasonable balance between the competing claims.

When the free-exercise and establishment clauses cannot be balanced, the Supreme Court has been forced to choose. In 1987 the Court overturned a Louisiana law requiring that creationism (the Bible's account of how the world was created) be taught along with the theory of evolution in public school science courses. Creationism, the Court concluded, is a religious doctrine, not a scientific theory; thus, its inclusion in public school curricula violates the establishment clause by promoting a religious belief.[44] In 2005 a federal judge barred a Pennsylvania public school district from requiring that intelligent design (the belief that God has guided evolution) be taught in science classes along with evolution. The judge concluded that the theory of intelligent design is a disguised version of creationism, has no basis in science, and violates the First Amendment's establishment clause. Some religious groups argue that such decisions trample on the free exercise of religion because children are required to study the theory of evolution even though it conflicts with their belief about creation.

The Right of Privacy

Until the 1960s, Americans' constitutional rights were confined largely to those listed in the Bill of Rights. This situation prevailed despite the Ninth Amendment, which reads "The enumeration in the Constitution, of certain rights, shall not be construed to deny or disparage others retained by the people." In 1965, however, the Supreme Court added to the list of individual rights, declaring that Americans have "a right of privacy." This judgment arose from the case of *Griswold v. Connecticut*, which challenged a state law prohibiting the use of birth control devices, even by married couples. The Supreme Court struck down the statute, concluding that a state had no business interfering with a married couple's decision regarding contraception. The Court did not invoke the Ninth Amendment but reasoned instead that the freedoms in the Bill of Rights imply an underlying right of privacy. The Court held that individuals have a "zone of [personal] privacy" that government cannot lawfully infringe upon.[45]

Abortion

The right of privacy was the basis for the Supreme Court's ruling in *Roe v. Wade* (1973), which gave women full freedom to choose abortion during the first three months of pregnancy.[46] In overturning a Texas law banning abortion except to save the life of the mother, the Court said that the right to privacy is "broad enough to encompass a woman's decision whether or not to terminate her pregnancy."

After *Roe*, antiabortion activists sought to reverse the Court's ruling. Attempts at a constitutional amendment that would ban abortions were unsuccessful, which prompted abortion foes to seek other ways to restrict the practice. They campaigned successfully to prohibit the use of government funds to pay for abortions for poor women. Then, in *Webster v. Reproductive Health Services* (1989), the Supreme Court upheld a Missouri law that prohibits abortions from being performed in Missouri's public hospitals and by its public employees.[47]

Abortion rights activists demonstrate outside the Supreme Court while the justices inside hear arguments on Pennsylvania's controversial abortion law. By a 5-4 vote, the Court narrowly reaffirmed the principle that a woman has the right to choose abortion during the early months of pregnancy.

The *Webster* decision was followed in 1992 by the Pennsylvania abortion case *Planned Parenthood v. Casey*, which antiabortion advocates had hoped would reverse the *Roe* precedent. Instead, by a 5-4 margin, the Supreme Court upheld the principle that a woman has a right to abortion in the earliest months of pregnancy. The Court said that "the essential holding of *Roe v. Wade* should be retained and once again reaffirmed."[48]

The Court also said, however, that a state can impose regulations that do not place an "undue burden" on women seeking an abortion. Accordingly, the Court upheld a provision of the Pennsylvania law that requires parental or judicial consent before a minor can obtain an abortion. Although the Court applied its "undue burden" standard in 2006 to strike down by unanimous vote a New Hampshire law that had no medical emergency exception to its parental-consent requirement,[49] the question of what constitutes a medical emergency remains a subject of dispute among the Court's justices. In *Stenberg v. Carhart* (2000), the Court invalidated a Nebraska law that prohibited so-called partial-birth abortion (in which the fetus's life is terminated during delivery) even in cases where the mother's life or health is in danger.[50] The Court's majority said that the procedure sometimes is the most appropriate way to protect the mother's health. However, the case was decided by a narrow 5-4 margin, prompting congressional Republicans to pass a federal law banning partial-birth abortion and holding doctors criminally liable if they perform the procedure, even when a woman's health is at risk. In 2006 the Supreme Court accepted for review two cases in which the federal law on partial-birth abortions was at issue. The fact that Justice Sandra Day O'Connor, the swing vote in the Nebraska case, had been replaced on the Supreme Court by the more conservative Samuel Alito led some observers to speculate that the Court would reverse its position on partial-birth abortion.

Sexual Relations Among Consenting Adults

Although it was widely said at the time that the Supreme Court's 1965 *Griswold* ruling on contraceptive use took "government out of people's bedrooms," a clear exception remained. All states prohibited sexual relations between consenting adults of the same sex. A number of states eliminated this prohibition over the next two decades, and others stopped enforcing it. Nevertheless, in a 1986 Georgia case, *Bowers v. Hardwick*, the Supreme Court held that the right of privacy did not extend to homosexual acts among consenting adults.[51]

In 2003, however, the Court reversed itself and in the process struck down the sodomy laws of the thirteen states that still had them. The ruling came in response to a Texas law prohibiting consensual sex between adults of the same sex. In *Lawrence v. Texas*, the Court in a 6-3 vote concluded that the Texas sodomy law violated privacy rights protected by the due process clause of the Fourteenth Amendment. The Court said: "The petitioners are entitled to respect for their private lives. The State cannot demean their existence or control their destiny by making their private sexual conduct a crime."[52] The decision was hailed by gay and lesbian rights groups but condemned by some religious leaders, who said that it would open the door to same-sex marriage (see Chapter 5).

The Continuing Issue of Privacy Rights

The right of privacy is a broad issue that extends into many areas, including but not limited to personal medical and financial records. In most of these areas, the "zone of privacy" that is constitutionally protected has yet to be defined and likely will be subject to adjustment as technology and lifestyles change. The Supreme Court undoubtedly will extend privacy protection into new areas and deny it in others, as it did with the issue of "the right to die." In a 1997 case involving a Washington state law that prohibited physician-assisted suicide, the Court held that "liberty" in the Fourteenth Amendment does not include the constitutional right to doctor-assisted suicide.[53] At the same time, the Court hinted that states have the authority to permit physician-assisted suicide if they should decide to do so. Oregon has such a law, which the Court upheld in a 2005 ruling (see Chapter 3).

Privacy questions are among the most contentious in American politics because of the moral issues they raise. The abortion issue, for example, has provoked intense debate for more than three decades. The American public is divided on the issue, and there are many activists on both sides. As with other rights, the abortion issue is not only, or even primarily, fought out in the courts. Abortion opponents have waged demonstrations outside clinics in an effort to stop the practice. Some of these protests have erupted in violent acts against women trying to enter the clinics. In 1994, Congress passed a law making it illegal to block the entrance to abortion clinics or otherwise prevent people from entering. (The Supreme Court upheld the law, concluding that it regulated abortion protesters' actions as opposed to their words and thus did not violate their right to free speech.)[54]

RIGHTS OF PERSONS ACCUSED OF CRIMES

Due process refers to legal protections that have been established to preserve the rights of individuals. The most significant form of these protections is **procedural due process;** the term refers primarily to procedures that authorities must follow before a person can legitimately be punished for an offense.

The U.S. Constitution provides for several procedures designed to protect a person from wrongful arrest, conviction, and punishment. According to Article I, Section 9, any person taken into police custody is entitled to seek a writ of habeas corpus, which requires law enforcement officials to bring the suspect into court and to specify the legal reason for the detention. The Fifth and Fourteenth Amendments provide generally that no person can be deprived of life, liberty, or property without due process of law. Specific procedural protections for the accused are spelled out in the Fourth, Fifth, Sixth, and Eighth Amendments:

- *The Fourth Amendment* forbids the police to conduct searches and seizures unless they have probable cause to believe that a crime has been committed.

- *The Fifth Amendment* protects against double jeopardy (being prosecuted twice for the same offense); self-incrimination (being compelled to testify against oneself); indictment for a crime except through grand jury proceedings; and loss of life, liberty, and property without due process of law.
- *The Sixth Amendment* provides the right to have legal counsel, to confront witnesses, to receive a speedy trial, and to have a trial by jury in criminal proceedings.
- *The Eighth Amendment* protects against excessive bail or fines and prohibits the infliction of cruel and unusual punishment on those convicted of crimes.

These protections have been subject to interpretation. The Sixth Amendment, for example, provides the right to have legal counsel. But what if a person cannot afford a lawyer? For most of the nation's history, poor people had virtually no choice but to act as their own attorney. They had a right to a lawyer but no money with which to hire one. Today, if a person is accused of a serious crime and cannot afford a lawyer, the government must provide one. This change came about not through a constitutional amendment but through Supreme Court rulings that expanded the protections provided by the Sixth Amendment.

Selective Incorporation of Procedural Rights

For most of the nation's history, the procedural protections in the Bill of Rights applied only to the actions of the national government. States in their criminal proceedings were not bound by them. There were limited exceptions, such as a 1932 Supreme Court ruling that a defendant charged in a state court with a crime carrying the death penalty had to be provided with an attorney.[55] Nevertheless, even as the Court was moving to protect free-expression rights from state action in the 1930s, it held back on doing the same for the rights of the accused. The Court claimed that free-expression rights were more deserving of federal protection because they are "the indispensable condition of nearly every other form of freedom."[56]

This view changed abruptly in the 1960s when the Supreme Court broadly required states also to safeguard procedural rights. Changes in public education and communication had made Americans more aware of their rights, and the civil rights movement dramatized the fact that rights were administered unequally: the poor and minority group members had many fewer rights in practice than did other Americans. In response, the Supreme Court in the 1960s "incorporated" Bill of Rights protections for the accused by ruling that these rights are protected

| TABLE | 4-3 | SELECTIVE INCORPORATION OF RIGHTS OF THE ACCUSED |

In the 1960s, the Supreme Court selectively incorporated the fair-trial provisions of the Fourth through Eighth Amendments into the Fourteenth Amendment so that these rights would be protected from infringement by the states.

Supreme Court Case	Year	Constitutional Right (Amendment) at Issue
Mapp v. Ohio	1961	Unreasonable search and seizure (Fourth)
Robinson v. California	1962	Cruel and unusual punishment (Eighth)
Gideon v. Wainwright	1963	Right to counsel (Sixth)
Malloy v. Hogan	1964	Self-incrimination (Fifth)
Pointer v. Texas	1965	Right to confront witnesses (Sixth)
Miranda v. Arizona	1966	Self-incrimination and right to counsel (Fifth and Sixth)
Klopfer v. North Carolina	1967	Speedy trial (Sixth)
Duncan v. Louisiana	1968	Jury trial in criminal cases (Sixth)
Benton v. Maryland	1969	Double jeopardy (Fifth)

against state action by the Fourteenth Amendment's guarantee of due process of law (see Table 4–3).

The selective incorporation process began with *Mapp v. Ohio* (1961). Dollree Mapp's home had been entered by Cleveland police, who, though they failed to find what they were seeking, happened to discover some pornographic material. Mapp's conviction for its possession was overturned by the Supreme Court on the grounds that she had been subjected to unreasonable search and seizure.[57] The Court ruled that illegally obtained evidence could not be used in state courts. Two years later, the Court's decision in *Gideon v. Wainwright* (1963) required the states to furnish attorneys for poor defendants in all felony cases. Clarence Gideon, an indigent drifter, had been convicted and sentenced to prison in Florida for breaking into a poolroom. He successfully appealed on the grounds that he had been denied due process because he could not afford to pay an attorney.[58]

During the 1960s, the Court also ruled that defendants in state criminal proceedings cannot be compelled to testify against themselves,[59] have the right to remain silent and to have legal counsel when arrested,[60] have the right to confront witnesses who testify against them,[61] must be granted a speedy trial,[62] have the right to a jury trial,[63] and cannot be subjected to double jeopardy.[64] The best known of these cases is *Miranda v. Arizona* (1966), which arose when Ernesto Miranda confessed during police interrogation to kidnap and rape. The Supreme Court overturned his conviction on the grounds that he had not been informed of his rights to remain silent and to have legal assistance. This ruling led to the development of the "Miranda warning" that police are now required to read to suspects: "You have the right to remain silent. . . . Anything you say can and will be used against you in a court of law. . . . You have the right to an attorney." (Miranda was subsequently retried and convicted on the basis of evidence other than his confession.)

In a 2000 case, *Dickerson v. United States*, the Supreme Court reaffirmed the *Miranda* decision, saying that it was an established "constitutional rule" that could not be eliminated by ordinary legislation.[65] The Court further strengthened the Miranda precedent in *Missouri v. Siebert* (2004). This ruling came in response to a police strategy of questioning suspects first and then reading them their Miranda rights, followed by a second round of questioning. In such instances, suspects who admitted wrongdoing in the first round of questioning tended also to do so in the second round. The Court concluded that the strategy was intended "to undermine the Miranda warnings" and was not permissible.[66]

Limits on Defendants' Rights

In the courtroom, the rights to counsel, to confront witnesses, and to remain silent are of paramount importance. Before the courtroom phase in a criminal proceeding, the main protection is the Fourth Amendment's restriction on illegal search and seizure. This restriction holds that police must have suspicion of wrongdoing (and, sometimes, a judge's permission) before they can search your person, your car, or your residence, although involvement in an offense (such as driving faster than the speed limit) can lead to a permissible search that uncovers wrongdoing of another kind (such as drug possession). Without search and seizure protection, individuals could be subject to unrestricted police harassment and intimidation, which are characteristics of a totalitarian state, not a free society.

The Fourth Amendment, however, does not provide blanket protection against searches. In 1990, for example, the Supreme Court held that police roadblocks to check drivers for signs of intoxication are legal as long as the action is systematic and not arbitrary (for example, stopping only young drivers would be unconstitutional). The Court justified its decision by saying that roadblocks serve a public safety purpose.[67]

However, the Court does not allow the same types of roadblocks to check for drugs. In *Indianapolis v. Edmund* (2001), the Court held that narcotics roadblocks, because they serve a general law enforcement purpose rather than one specific to highway safety, violate the Fourth Amendment's requirement that police have suspicion of wrongdoing before they can search an individual's auto.[68] The Court has also held that police may not use a thermal-imaging device in order to detect the presence in a home of heat sources that might reveal the production of illegal drugs. Police cannot enter a home without a warrant based on suspicion of wrongdoing, and the Court said that searches based on modern technology must meet the same standard.[69]

The Fourth Amendment protects individuals in their persons as well as in their homes and vehicles. In *Ferguson v. Charleston* (2001), for example, the Court held that patients in public hospitals cannot be forced to take a test for illegal drugs if the purpose is to turn over to the police those patients who test positive. Such action, said the Court, constitutes an illegal search of the person.[70] The rule is somewhat different when it comes to students in public schools. Authorities have more latitude in this situation. For example, the Court in *Board of Education of Independent School District No. 92 of Pottawatomie County v. Earls* (2002) held that random drug testing of high school students involved in extracurricular activities does not violate the ban on unreasonable searches.[71]

The Exclusionary Rule   In general, the Supreme Court in recent decades has reduced but not eliminated the protections afforded to the accused by *Mapp* and other 1960s rulings. The 1960s Court was dominated by liberal justices who saw fit to expand individual rights. Turnover in the Court's membership moved it in a conservative direction and toward positions that give law enforcement officials more leeway in their handling of criminal suspects. The change can be seen in the application of the exclusionary rule, which bars the use in trials of evidence obtained in violation of a person's constitutional rights. The rule was formulated in a 1914 Supreme Court decision,[72] and its application was expanded in federal cases. The *Mapp* decision extended the exclusionary rule to state trial proceedings. Subsequent decisions of the Supreme Court broadened its application to the point where almost any type of illegally obtained evidence was considered inadmissible in a criminal trial. In the 1980s, the Supreme Court reversed the trend by placing restrictions on the rule's application, concluding that illegally obtained evidence can sometimes be admitted in trials if the procedural errors are inadvertent or if the prosecution can show that it would have discovered the evidence anyway.[73]

In recent decades, the Supreme Court has restricted the scope of the "exclusionary rule." This rule excludes from use in court proceedings any evidence that is obtained illegally by law enforcement officials.

Recent decisions have also lowered the standard that must be met for a lawful search and seizure to occur. In the 1960s, the Court developed the principle that police had to have a solid basis ("probable cause") for believing that an individual was involved in a specific crime before they could stop a person and engage in search-and-seizure activity. This principle has been modified, as illustrated by *Whren v. United States* (1996), which upheld the conviction of an individual who had been found with drugs in the front seat of his car. The police had no evidence (no "probable cause") indicating that drugs were in the car, but they suspected that the driver was involved in drug dealing and used a minor traffic infraction as a pretext to stop and check him. The Supreme Court accepted defense arguments that the police had no clear evidence to back their suspicion, that the traffic infraction was not the real reason the individual was stopped, and that police usually do not stop a person for the infraction in question (turning a corner without signaling). However, the Court concluded that the officers' motive was irrelevant, as long as an officer in some situations might reasonably stop a car for the infraction that occurred. Thus, the stop-and-search action was deemed to meet the Fourth Amendment's reasonableness standard.[74]

In general, the Court's goal has been to weaken the exclusionary rule without giving police unduly broad discretion. However, the current Court appears to be in the process of narrowing the exclusionary rule to the point where it would apply only to the most egregious instances of police misconduct. In *Hudson v. Michigan* (2006), the Court overthrew the "knock-and-announce" rule, which began in thirteenth-century England. Under this rule, police officers armed with a search warrant are supposed to knock on the door and announce their presence before entering a suspect's house. Detroit police did not do this when they entered the home of Booker Hudson, and he sought to have his conviction for drug possession tossed out on grounds that the evidence had been obtained illegally. In rejecting his position in a 5-4 ruling, the Court's majority argued that the knock-and-announce rule no longer is necessary because police today are more professional and because individuals whose homes or persons are illegally searched can bring civil suit against the police. In a dissenting opinion, Justice Stephen Breyer ridiculed this idea, saying that the Court's majority could not "cite a single reported case" in which someone whose home had been wrongly entered by police had been awarded damages worth noting.[75]

Habeas Corpus Appeals   Legal protection for the accused has also been reduced by a restriction on habeas corpus appeals to federal courts by individuals who have been convicted of crimes in state courts. (Habeas corpus gives defendants access to federal courts in order to argue that their rights under the Constitution of the United States were violated when they were convicted in a state court.) A 1960s Supreme Court precedent gave prisoners the right to have their appeal heard in federal court unless they had "deliberately bypassed" the opportunity to first make their appeal in state courts.[76]

This precedent was overturned in 1992 when the Court held that inmates can lose the right to a federal hearing even if a lawyer's mistake is the reason they failed to first present their appeal properly in state courts.[77] Another significant habeas corpus setback for inmates occurred in 1993 when the Supreme Court held that federal courts cannot overturn a state conviction on the basis of constitutional error unless the prisoner can demonstrate that the error contributed to the conviction.[78] Previously, the burden of proof had been on the state: it had to prove that the error did not affect the case's outcome. In *Felker v. Turpin* (1996), the Court upheld a recently enacted federal law that prohibited in most cases federal habeas corpus appeals by state prison inmates who have already filed one such appeal.[79]

Through these decisions, the Supreme Court has sought to prevent frivolous and multiple federal court appeals. State prisoners had used habeas corpus appeals to contest even small issues, and some inmates—particularly those on death row—had filed appeal after appeal. An effect was the clogging of the federal courts and a delay in hearing other cases.

A majority of Supreme Court justices concluded that a more restrictive policy toward these appeals was required. They held that it is fair to ask inmates to first pursue their options in state courts and then, except in unusual cases,[80] to confine themselves to a single federal appeal. At the same time, the Court has taken steps to ensure that meritorious appeals are heard. In two 2003 cases, for example, the Court expressed concern that lower federal courts in some instances were not being sufficiently careful in identifying legitimate appeals.[81]

Despite modifications of the appeal process and the exclusionary rule, there has not been a return to the lower procedural standards that prevailed before the 1960s. Many of the vital precedents established in that decade remain in effect, including the most important one of all: the principle that procedural protections guaranteed to the accused by the Bill of Rights must be observed by the states as well as by the federal government.

Crime, Punishment, and Police Practices

The theory and practice of procedural guarantees are often two quite different things, as Adrienne Cureton discovered on January 2, 1995. She is a plainclothes police officer who, with a uniformed partner, was called to the scene of a domestic dispute. A struggle ensued, and her partner radioed for help. When the officers arrived, Cureton and her partner had already handcuffed the homeowner. The officers barged in and mistook Cureton, an African American, for the other person involved in the dispute. They grabbed her by the collar, dragged her by the hair onto the porch, and clubbed her repeatedly with flashlights, despite her screams that she was a police officer.[82]

There is no reliable estimate of how often Americans' rights are violated in practice, but infringements of one sort or another are commonplace. Minorities and the poor are the more likely victims. *Racial profiling* (the assumption that certain groups are more likely to commit particular crimes) is a common police practice and results in the unequal treatment of minorities. An American Civil Liberties Union study found that 80 percent of the motorists stopped and searched by Maryland State Police on Interstate 95 were minorities and only 20 percent were white, despite the fact that white motorists constituted 75 percent of all drivers and were just as likely as minority motorists to violate the traffic laws. A 1999 report by the New Jersey Attorney General's Office revealed a similar pattern in that state. African Americans refer mockingly to a traffic infraction they call DWB—"driving while black."

Another issue of justice in America is whether adherence to proper legal procedures produces reasonable outcomes. The Eighth Amendment

★ STATES IN THE NATION

The Death Penalty

Most crimes and punishments in the United States are defined by state law. Nowhere is this more obvious than in the application of the death penalty. Some states prohibit it, and others apply it liberally. Texas, Florida, and Virginia are far and away the leaders in its application. Roughly a third of all executions in the past quarter-century have taken place in Texas alone.

Q: What do many of the states that prohibit capital punishment have in common?

A: States without the death penalty are concentrated in the North. Most of these states are relatively affluent, rank high on indicators of educational attainment, and have a small minority-group population.

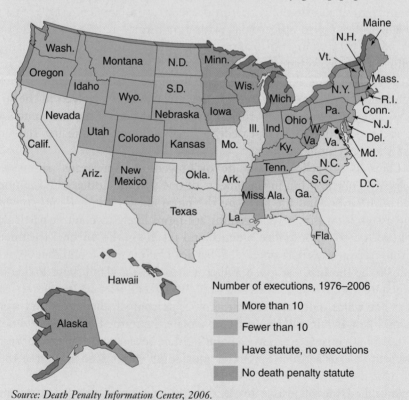

Number of executions, 1976–2006

More than 10

Fewer than 10

Have statute, no executions

No death penalty statute

Source: Death Penalty Information Center, 2006.

prohibits "cruel and unusual punishment" of those convicted of crime, but judgments in this area are subjective. Although the Supreme Court has ordered officials to relieve inmate overcrowding and to improve prison facilities in a few instances, it has concluded that inmates cannot sue over prison conditions unless prison officials show "deliberate indifference" to the conditions.[83] The severity of a sentence can also be an Eighth Amendment issue. The Supreme Court in 1991 upheld a conviction under a Michigan law that mandated life imprisonment without parole for a non-violent first offense involving 1.5 pounds of cocaine.[84] More recently, the Court upheld a conviction under California's "three strikes and you're out" law that sent a twice previously convicted felon to prison for life without parole for shoplifting videotapes worth $100.[85] Although many people would regard such penalties as too severe, the Supreme Court has seldom invoked the Eighth Amendment's prohibition on cruel and unusual punishment. The Court has allowed Congress and the state legislatures to decide the appropriate penalties for crime, believing that it lacks the capacity to devise consistent rules that would differentiate between acceptable and unacceptable levels of punishment.

However, the Supreme Court in two recent decisions did invoke the Eighth Amendment to narrow the use of the death penalty. In *Atkins v. Virginia* (2002), the Court outlawed the death penalty for the mentally retarded, saying that it constitutes "cruel and unusual punishment." The Court noted that nearly all countries in the world prohibit such executions.[86] In 2005, the Court also cited global practices in declaring it unconstitutional to put juveniles to death. The Court's majority wrote in *Roper v. Simmons* that "the United States is the only country in the world that [gave] official sanction to the juvenile death penalty."[87]

Recently, the Supreme Court left open an Eighth Amendment challenge to how states carry out executions.[88] At issue is the mix of chemicals used in lethal injection. Studies indicate that the current mix can cause excruciating pain before death occurs. Visible signs of the prisoner's pain are masked by a paralyzing drug that is part of the mix. If this challenge is upheld, states could still use lethal injection to execute prisoners but would have to devise an acceptable chemical mix before being permitted to do so.

Sentencing issues have also arisen in the context of the Sixth Amendment's guarantee of trial by jury. Until recently, the courts applied the right of jury trial only to the question of a defendant's guilt or innocence and not also to sentencing. However, in *Ring v. Arizona* (2002), the Supreme Court held that the right of jury trial prohibits a judge from deciding whether the death penalty will be imposed in a capital case.

The Court ruled that only a jury could make this determination.[89] This principle was expanded in *Blakley v. Washington* (2004) to include sentences that are longer than the law prescribes. The Supreme Court held that the Sixth Amendment requires that a jury decide whether aggravating factors, such as the cruelty of a crime, justify a harsh sentence.[90] The *Blakley* ruling was widely criticized on grounds that it would overburden the legal system by requiring a second jury trial whenever the prosecution seeks to imprison someone for an unusually long period.

However, the issue of punishment is primarily a political one as opposed to a judicial one. The pressure for harsher sentences has come mainly from elected officials rather than from judges. Being "tough on crime" is a popular political stance, and Congress and most state legislatures during the past two decades have enacted stiffer penalties for crimes while also limiting the ability of judges to reduce the penalties, as in cases where the defendant has no prior criminal record. As a result, the number of federal and state prisoners has more than doubled since 1990. In fact, the United States has the largest per capita prison population in the world (see "How the United States Compares") Russia is the only country that is even close to the United States in terms of the number of its people who are imprisoned. On a per capita basis, the United States has five times as many of its people in jail as Great Britain does.

As the prison population has increased and sentencing has become more severe, debate over America's criminal justice system has intensified. The severest criticisms have been directed at the death penalty and the incarceration of nonviolent drug users. In these areas, U.S. policies are at odds with those of other industrialized countries, nearly all of which

 ## HOW THE UNITED STATES COMPARES

Law and Order

Individual rights are a cornerstone of the American governing system and receive strong protection from the courts. The government's ability to restrict free expression is severely limited, and the individual's right to a fair trial is protected through elaborate due process guarantees.

According to Amnesty International, a watchdog group that monitors human rights achievements and violations around the world, the United States has a good record in terms of its constitutional

(continued)

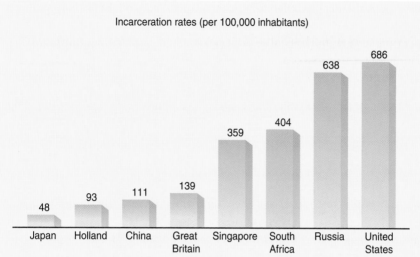

Incarceration rates (per 100,000 inhabitants)

Japan	Holland	China	Great Britain	Singapore	South Africa	Russia	United States
48	93	111	139	359	404	638	686

Source: The Sentencing Project, 2004.

protection of civil liberties. A number of countries in Asia, Africa, Eastern Europe, the Middle East, and Latin America are accused by Amnesty International of "appalling human rights catastrophes" that include the execution, torture, and rape of persons accused of crime or regarded as opponents of the government. Amnesty International does not rank the United States as high as the countries of northern Europe in terms of respect for human rights. Among other problems, Amnesty International faults police in the United States for "excessive force" in their treatment of prisoners and faults U.S. immigration officials for the forcible return of asylum seekers to their country of origin without granting them a hearing.

Although human rights groups admire America's elaborate procedural protections for those accused of crime, they are critical of its sentencing and incarceration policies. The United States is the world leader in the number of people it places behind bars and in the length of sentences for various categories of crime. Defenders of U.S. policy say that although overall crime rates are about the same here as elsewhere, there is more violent crime in America. Critics reply that although the murder rate is high in the United States, it is also true that more than half of the people in prison were convicted of nonviolent offenses, such as drug use or a crime against property. Whatever the reasons, the United States is rivaled only by Russia in the proportion of its people who are in prison.

prohibit the death penalty and rely more heavily on treatment programs than on prisons in dealing with drug offenders. Critics also cite studies showing that minorities and the poor receive harsher sentences than do middle-class whites convicted of comparable crimes.

RIGHTS AND THE WAR ON TERRORISM

In time of war, the courts have allowed government to exercise authority that would not be permitted in peacetime. After the Japanese attack on Pearl Harbor in 1941, for example, President Franklin D. Roosevelt ordered the forced relocation of tens of thousands of Japanese Americans living on the West Coast to detention camps in Arizona, Utah, and other inland locations. Congress endorsed the policy, and the Supreme Court upheld it.[91] Another Supreme Court ruling during World War II denied a U.S. citizen arrested as a Nazi collaborator a court trial after the government decided to try him before a military tribunal.[92]

After the terrorist attacks of September 11, 2001, precedents such as these were invoked by the Bush administration, which declared that customary legal protections must be altered if the war on terrorism was to be waged successfully. "[There is] the necessity for certain types of action . . . when we are in danger," said Solicitor General Theodore Olson.

Detention of Enemy Combatants

The Bush administration soon announced its policy for handling "enemy combatants"—individuals judged to be engaged in terrorism directed at the United States. They were to be detained without access to lawyers or family members until the president chose to release them. The Administration also claimed the authority to round up and hold in secret any individuals living in the United States who were suspected of having terrorist ties. Hundreds of individuals, nearly all of Middle Eastern descent, were taken into custody. Although nearly all of them eventually were cleared of wrongdoing by the FBI, some were held for months and others were deported for immigration violations. A lawsuit forcing the government to explain why these individuals had been detained was dismissed by the Supreme Court; the Bush administration claimed that release of the information would divulge the methods by which U.S. agencies identify suspected terrorists.[93]

As the war on terrorism shifted into military operations in Afghanistan and then Iraq, the United States needed to detain and interrogate the enemy soldiers it captured. Some prisoners were sent to a detention facility created at the U.S. Naval Base at Guantanamo Bay, on the tip of Cuba. Others were imprisoned in Afghanistan, Iraq, and elsewhere. Requests by lawyers and international agencies such as the Red Cross to see the detainees were denied or strictly limited. President Bush claimed that the detainees were enemy combatants rather than prisoners of war and accordingly did not enjoy the legal protections provided by U.S. law or by the Geneva Conventions. Bush did not publicly announce that prisoners would be subjected to harsh interrogation, but such treatment in fact was practiced at Abu Ghraib prison in Iraq and at Guantanamo Bay and was alleged to have taken place at secret CIA prisons in undisclosed locations.

In 2004, the Supreme Court issued its first ruling on these various practices, holding that the Guantanamo Bay detainees had the right to challenge their detention in court. The Court reasoned that the naval base, though in Cuba, is on land leased to the United States and therefore is under the jurisdiction of U.S. courts.[94] In a second 2004 case, *Hamdi v. Rumsfeld*, the Court ruled that one of the Guantanamo Bay detainees—who was a U.S. citizen by virtue of having been born in the United States although he was raised in Saudi Arabia—had the right to be heard in U.S. courts. The Court said that, though the government could hold the prisoner as an enemy combatant, he had the constitutional right to use the U.S. courts to challenge his detention. The Court said that a citizen was entitled to a "fair opportunity to rebut the government's factual assertions before a neutral [judge]" and that "essential constitutional promises may not be eroded" because of the security situation. The Court went on to say: "As critical as the government's interest may be in detaining those who actually pose an immediate threat to the national security of the United States during ongoing international conflict, history and common sense teach us that an unchecked system of detention carries the potential to become a means of oppression and abuse of others who do not present that sort of threat."[95]

Two years later, the Court issued its sharpest rebuke yet of the Bush administration's detention policies. In a ruling almost unprecedented in its challenge to a president's wartime authority, the Court held that the Guantanamo Bay detainees were protected by both the U.S. Uniform Code of Military Justice and the Geneva Conventions. At issue was the Bush administration's use of secret military tribunals to try detainees. In these trials, detainees would have no right to see the evidence against them or to call witnesses who might exonerate them. The Court held in *Hamdan v. Rumsfeld* (2006) that the tribunals were unlawful. In its majority

The war on terrorism has led U.S. soldiers into combat in Iraq (pictured here) and Afghanistan. The war has raised important civil liberties issues, including the question of the president's authority to conduct wiretaps without a judicial warrant and to deny enemy combatants the protection of U.S. law and the Geneva Conventions. Although the courts have deferred in some cases to President Bush's wartime authority as commander-in-chief, they have also overruled some of his policies.

opinion, the Court wrote that "the Executive is bound to comply with the Rule of Law."[96] In response to the ruling, President Bush negotiated legislation, which Congress enacted in 2006, that grants legal protections to detainees held by the U.S. military. However, at Bush's insistence, the legislation excluded CIA interrogations conducted overseas, an exception that the Supreme Court could conceivably rule upon in the future.

Surveillance of Suspected Terrorists

In response to the Bush administration's request for expanded surveillance powers following the September 11 terrorist attacks, Congress passed the USA Patriot Act of 2001, which lowered the standard for judicial approval of wiretaps when terrorist activity was at issue. The law also allowed the sharing of information gained from intelligence surveillance with criminal investigators when evidence was found of criminal activity unrelated to terrorism. Previously, such information could be shared only if it was obtained by the stricter standards officials must follow in criminal investigations. The Patriot Act also gave government increased authority to examine medical, financial, and student records and allowed, in specified situations, secret government searches of homes and offices.

Critics claimed that the USA Patriot Act was at odds with America's constitutional tradition. "No one is questioning the government's authority to prosecute spies and terrorists," said Ann Beeson of the American Civil Liberties Union, "but we do not need to waive the Constitution to do so."[97] For their part, Administration officials said that the September 11 attacks had forced a change in the rules. "The danger that darkened the United States and the civilized world on September 11 did not pass with the atrocities committed that day," stated Attorney General John Ashcroft.

The Bush administration promised to act with restraint in its exercise of the new powers, and congressional oversight committees generally were satisfied with its actions. Then, in late 2005, the *New York Times* revealed that President Bush without judicial approval had secretly authorized the National Security Agency (NSA) to wiretap international phone calls and e-mail messages originating in the United States. Such wiretaps are expressly prohibited by the Foreign Intelligence Surveillance Act (FISA) of 1978. Bush rejected allegations that he had broken the law, saying that he had acted legally under his wartime powers as commander-in-chief and under authority implicitly granted him by the Patriot Act.

In early 2007, the Bush administration abruptly reversed course. Although continuing to claim that President Bush could order wiretaps on his own authority, the Administration announced it would henceforth seek judicial approval because an acceptable "process" for obtaining this approval had been developed. Some pundits suggested that the real reason for the change was a desire to avoid congressional and judicial rebuke. The new Democratic-controlled Congress had scheduled hearings on the Bush administration's wiretap program, and federal courts were hearing cases challenging the program's legality.

Other surveillance issues are certain to be reviewed by the judiciary in the coming years. Lower-court decisions on various aspects of the USA Patriot Act so far have been mixed. One ruling held, for example, that crime-related information obtained in domestic intelligence operations could be shared with law-enforcement officials. However, another ruling held that government without judicial consent cannot require Internet or telephone companies to turn over customer records and then block them from revealing publicly that they have done so.[98]

THE COURTS AND A FREE SOCIETY

The United States was founded on the idea that individuals have an innate right to liberty—to speak their minds, to worship freely, to be secure in their homes and persons, and to be assured of a fair trial. Americans embrace these freedoms in the abstract. In particular situations, however, many Americans tend to prefer policies that diminish the freedom of those who hold minority views or who look and act differently than the majority of Americans. After the September 11, 2001, terrorist attacks, for example, polls indicated that one-third of Americans felt Arab Americans should be placed under special surveillance and that half felt Arab Americans should be required to carry special identification cards. Two-fifths said they would ban college lectures by speakers who argue that certain aspects of U.S. foreign policy have contributed to terrorist activity.

The judiciary is not isolated from the public mood. Judges inevitably are required to balance society's need for security and public order against the rights of the individual. Nevertheless, judges ordinarily can be expected to be more protective of individual rights than are either elected officials or the general public. How far the courts will go in protecting a person's rights depends on the facts of the case, the existing status of the law, prevailing social needs, and the personal views of the judges. Nevertheless, most judges and justices regard the protection of individual rights as a constitutional imperative, which is how the Framers saw the issue. The Bill of Rights was created in order to transform the abstract idea that individuals have inalienable rights to life, liberty, and the pursuit of happiness into a set of specified constitutional rights, thereby bringing them under the protection of courts of law.[99]

Summary

In their search for personal liberty, Americans added the Bill of Rights to the Constitution shortly after its ratification. These amendments guarantee certain political, procedural, and property rights against infringement by the national government. Freedom of expression is the most basic of democratic rights. People are not free unless they can freely express their views. Nevertheless, free expression may conflict with the nation's security needs during times of war and insurrection. The courts at times have allowed government to limit expression substantially for purposes of national security. In recent decades, however, the courts have protected a wide range of free expression in the areas of speech, press, and religion.

The guarantees embodied in the Bill of Rights originally applied only to the national government. Under the principle of selective incorporation of these guarantees into the Fourteenth Amendment, the courts extended them to state governments, though the process was slow and uneven. In the 1920s and 1930s, First Amendment guarantees of freedom of expression were given protection from infringement by the states. The states continued to have wide discretion in criminal proceedings until the early 1960s, when most of the fair-trial rights in the Bill of Rights were given federal protection.

Due process of law refers to legal protections that have been established to preserve individual rights. The most significant form of these protections consists of procedures or methods (for example, the right of an accused person to have an attorney present during police interrogation) designed to ensure that an individual's rights are upheld. A major controversy in this area is the breadth of the exclusionary rule, which bars the use in trials of illegally obtained evidence. The right of privacy, particularly as it applies to the abortion issue, is also a source of controversy, as is the issue of constitutional rights in the pursuit of the war on terrorism.

Civil liberties are not absolute but must be balanced against other considerations (such as national security or public safety) and against one another when different rights conflict. The judicial branch of government, particularly the Supreme Court, has taken on much of the responsibility for protecting and interpreting individual rights. The Court's positions have changed with time and conditions, but the Court has generally been more protective of and sensitive to civil liberties than have elected officials or popular majorities.

KEY TERMS

Bill of Rights (*p. 110*)
civil liberties (*p. 110*)
clear-and-present-danger test (*p. 115*)
due process clause of the Fourteenth
  Amendment (*p. 118*)
establishment clause (*p. 124*)
exclusionary rule (*p. 136*)
freedom of expression (*p. 113*)

free-exercise clause (*p. 127*)
imminent-lawless-action test (*p. 120*)
libel (*p. 121*)
prior restraint (*p. 116*)
procedural due process (*p. 132*)
selective incorporation (*p. 118*)
slander (*p. 121*)
symbolic speech (*p. 116*)

SUGGESTED READINGS

Abraham, Henry J. *Freedom and the Court.* New York: Oxford University Press, 2003. A comprehensive analysis of the Supreme Court's work on civil rights and civil liberties.

Cohen, David B., and John W. Wells, eds. *American National Security and Civil Liberties in an Era of Terrorism.* New York: Palgrave Macmillan, 2004. A balanced set of essays on the current tensions between national security and civil liberties.

Epstein, Lee, and Thomas G. Walker. *Constitutional Law for a Changing America,* 5th ed. Washington, D.C.: Congressional Quarterly Press, 2004. An accessible introduction to U.S. constitutional law.

Hull, N. E. H., and Peter Charles Hoffer. *Roe v. Wade: The Abortion Rights Controversy in American History.* Lawrence: University Press of Kansas, 2001. A thorough assessment of both sides of the abortion conflict, beginning with the *Roe v. Wade* decision.

Perry, Michael J. *Religion in Politics: Constitutional and Moral Perspectives.* New York: Oxford University Press, 1997. A legal and philosophical analysis of the role of religion in politics.

Schwarz, John E. *Freedom Reclaimed: Rediscovering the American Vision.* Baltimore, Md.: Johns Hopkins University Press, 2005. An impassioned argument for an expansive view of liberty, both from and through government action.

Vestal, Theodore H. *The Eisenhower Court and Civil Liberties.* Westport, Conn.: Praeger, 1993. A look at the Supreme Court that greatly expanded the rights of the criminally accused.

LIST OF WEBSITES

http://www.fepproject.org/ Includes information and opinions on a wide range of free-expression policy issues.

http://www.aclu.org/ The American Civil Liberties Union site; provides information on current civil liberties and civil rights issues, including information on recent and pending Supreme Court cases.

http://www.findlaw.com/casecode/supreme.html An excellent source of information on Supreme Court and lower-court rulings.

http://www.ncjrs.org/ The site of the National Criminal Justice Reference Service, a federally funded organization that compiles information on a wide range of criminal-justice issues.

POLITICS IN THEORY AND PRACTICE

Thinking: What is the process of selective incorporation, and why is it important to the rights you possess today?

Participating: Although their right of free expression is protected by law, Americans often choose not to exercise this right for fear of social pressure or official reprisal. Yet constitutional rights tend to wither when people fail to exercise them. Think of an issue that you favor but that is unpopular on your campus or in your community. Consider writing a letter expressing your opinion to the editor of your college or local newspaper. (Practical advice: Keep the letter short and to the point; write a lead sentence that will get readers' attention; provide a convincing argument for your position; be sure to sign the letter and provide a return address so the editor can contact you if there are questions.)

ADDITIONAL RESOURCES

For quizzes, interactive simulations, games, graphics, and other study tools, visit the book's Online Learning Center at **www.mhhe.com/pattersonwtp7**.

A Constitutional Amendment to Ban Flag Burning

By Sam Brownback/Russell Feingold

The Supreme Court has held that free expression is the most fundamental of civil liberties, a position that has led it to strike down most laws that would restrict expression. The Court has even ruled that the burning of the American flag is protected speech. This ruling has prompted several attempts by Congress to pass a constitutional amendment that would ban flag burning. In 2006 Congress came within a single Senate vote of obtaining the two-thirds majority required in each chamber. The Senate debate was marked by thoughtful statements from both advocates and opponents of the amendment. The statements of two of the senators who participated in that debate are given here. Senator Sam Brownback argued for the amendment, and Senator Russell Feingold argued against it.

Senator Sam Brownback (R-Kans.): I was preparing for this debate and thinking about the Lincoln Memorial. What if somebody today, yesterday, or some other time had taken spray paint and sprayed on the Lincoln Memorial: "We want freedom" or "Death to tyrants" or "Down with the flag"? Let's say they wrote that in big spray paint on the Lincoln Memorial and defaced the memorial and then [were] caught and brought to trial and claimed: Wait a minute, I have a first amendment right to say what I want to say, and I believe it is important that I say it anywhere, and I want to say it on the Lincoln Memorial. I want to make my message known, and I am going to spray-paint it all over here; this is free speech, and I ought to be able to do that and this is the place to do it, and Lincoln would approve of that; he believed in free speech, so he wouldn't mind that the memorial was sprayed upon, that it was defaced.

We would all recognize that as being something wrong, violating the law, and something there should be a law against. We don't have a problem with a person standing on the Lincoln Memorial and shouting at the top of his lungs for as long as he wants whatever he wants to say—if it is about the war in Iraq, if it is about the President, if it is about somebody in the Senate, if it is about myself, if it is about the Chair, if it is about anything he wants. We don't have any problem with that. But if he defaces the memorial, we do.

It is interesting, that was the dissent Justice Stevens used in the *Texas v. Johnson* case. He made that same point. We have no problem with a person speaking on the Lincoln Memorial. We have a problem with him defacing the Lincoln Memorial. We have no problem with people speaking against the flag. We have a problem with them defacing the flag. Justice Stevens in his dissent—which I think was rightly said—said: "Had he chosen to spray-paint or perhaps convey with a motion picture projector his message of dissatisfaction on the facade of the Lincoln Memorial, there would be no question about the power of Government to prohibit this means of expression. The prohibition will be supported by the legitimate interests in preserving the quality of an important national asset."

That is what we are talking about today: preserving the quality of an important national asset that people follow into battle, that we have had and honored for years and years, and until recently the court has held up as saying: Yes, this is something that should be protected and is protected by the laws of the land, and these laws are appropriate and are not limitations on free speech.

I think if you follow this court ruling, where does it end? If you say actions are speech, wouldn't you have a legitimate objective in defacing the Lincoln Memorial, particularly if it was some form of political free speech that you wanted to express and put forward? . . . . This is not a complicated issue. It is about whether we are going to have some authority and ability to be able to limit and to be able to honor and to uphold something so precious as our American flag. I think we should do that. I think because of the people who follow this flag and because we are a nation of symbols, and symbols are what unite us, and because of the words and thought that are conveyed by this flag, we should be able to uphold this mighty national asset.

Senator Russell Feingold (D-Wisc.): Let me make one thing clear at the outset. Not a single Senator who opposes the proposed constitutional amendment, as I do, supports burning or otherwise showing disrespect to the flag. Not a single one. None of us think it is "OK" to burn the flag. None of us view the flag as "just a piece of cloth." On those rare occasions when some malcontent defiles or burns our flag, I join everyone in this Chamber in condemning that action.

But we must also defend the right of all Americans to express their views about their Government, however hateful or spiteful or disrespectful those views may be, without fear of their Government putting them in jail for those views. America is not simply a Nation of symbols, it is a Nation of principles. And the most important principle of all, the principle that has made this country a beacon of hope and inspiration for oppressed peoples throughout the world, is the right of free expression. This amendment threatens that right, so I must oppose it.

We have heard at various times over the years that this amendment has been debated that permitting protestors to burn the American flag sends the wrong message to our children about patriotism and respect for our country. I couldn't disagree more with that argument. We can send no better, no stronger, no more meaningful message to our children about the principles and the values of this country than if we oppose efforts to undermine freedom of expression, even expression that is undeniably offensive. When we uphold first amendment freedoms despite the efforts of misguided and despicable people who want to provoke our wrath, we explain what America is really about. Our country and our people are far too strong to be threatened by those who burn the flag. That is a lesson we should proudly teach our children. . . .

It has been almost exactly 17 years since the Supreme Court ruled that flag burning is a form of political speech protected by the first amendment. Proposals to amend the Constitution arose almost immediately and have continued unabated. But while the interest of politicians in this course of action seems as strong as ever, public interest in it seems to be waning. Opinion polls show support for the amendment has fallen. Amending the Constitution to prohibit flag desecration is just not the foremost thing on the minds of the American people. Perhaps that is because it is long since clear that our Republic can survive quite well without this amendment. Nearly a generation has passed since the *Texas v. Johnson* decision, and our Nation is still standing strong. . . .

Indeed, outward displays of patriotism are greater today than they were in 2000. We all know why that is. Our country was viciously attacked on September 11, 2001, and America responded. We didn't need a constitutional amendment to teach Americans how to love their country. They showed us how to do it by entering burning buildings to save their fellow citizens who were in danger, by standing in line for hours to give blood, by driving hundreds of miles to search through the rubble for survivors and to help in cleanup efforts, by praying in their houses of worship for the victims of the attacks and their families.

September 11 inspired our citizens to perform some of the most selfless acts of bravery and patriotism we have seen in our entire history. No constitutional amendment could ever match those acts as a demonstration of patriotism, or create similar acts in the future. We do not need a constitutional amendment to teach Americans how to love their country or how to defend it from our enemies.

What's Your Opinion?

Which argument—Brownback's or Feingold's—do you find more persuasive? What additional claims might you make to support your position on the constitutional issue of flag burning?

Civil rights

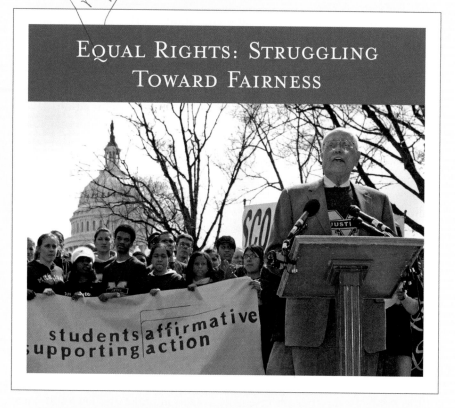

EQUAL RIGHTS: STRUGGLING TOWARD FAIRNESS

> **❝**I have a dream that one day this nation will rise up and live out the true meaning of its creed: 'We hold these truths to be self-evident: that all men are created equal.'**❞**
>
> MARTIN LUTHER KING JR.[1]

The producers of ABC television's *Primetime Live* put hidden cameras on two young men, equally well dressed and groomed, and then sent them on different routes to do the same things—search for an apartment, shop for a car, look at albums in a record store. The cameras recorded people's reactions to the two men. One was usually greeted with smiles and quick service. The other man was more often greeted with suspicious looks and was sometimes made to wait. Why the difference? The explanation was straightforward: the young man who was routinely well received was white; the young man who was sometimes treated poorly was an African American.

The Urban Institute conducted a more substantial experiment. It included pairs of specially trained white and black male college students who were the same in all respects—education, work experience, speech patterns, physical builds—except for their race. The students responded individually to nearly five hundred classified job advertisements in Chicago and Washington, D.C. The black applicants got fewer interviews and received fewer job offers than did the white applicants. An Urban Institute spokesperson said, "The level of reverse discrimination [favoring blacks over whites] that we found was limited, was certainly far lower than many might have been led to fear, and was swamped by the extent of discrimination against black job applicants."[2]

These two experiments suggest why some Americans are still struggling to achieve equal rights. In theory Americans have equal rights, but in reality they are not now equal nor have they ever been. African Americans, women, Hispanic Americans, the disabled, Jews, Native Americans, Catholics, Asian Americans, gays and lesbians, and members of other minority groups have been victims of discrimination in fact and in law. The nation's creed—"all men are created equal"—has encouraged minorities to demand equal treatment. But inequality is built into almost every aspect of U.S. society. For example, compared with whites, African Americans with correctable health problems are significantly less likely to receive coronary-artery bypass surgery, to receive a kidney transplant, or to undergo surgery for early-stage lung cancer.[3]

This chapter focuses on **equal rights, or civil rights**—terms that refer to the right of every person to equal protection under the laws and equal access to society's opportunities and public facilities. Chapter 4 explained that civil liberties refer to specific *individual* rights, such as freedom of speech, that are protected from infringement by government. Equal rights, or civil rights, have to do with whether individual members of differing *groups*—racial, sexual, and the like—are treated equally by government and, in some areas, by private parties. To oversimplify, civil liberties deal with issues of personal freedom, and civil rights deal with issues of equality.

Although the law refers to the rights of individuals first and to those of groups in a secondary and derivative way, this chapter concentrates on groups because the history of civil rights has been largely one of group claims to equality. The chapter emphasizes these points:

★ *Disadvantaged groups have had to struggle for equal rights.* African Americans, women, Native Americans, Hispanic Americans, Asian Americans, and others have all had to fight for their rights in order to come closer to equality with white males.

★ *Americans have attained substantial equality under the law.* They have, in legal terms, equal protection under the laws, equal access to accommodations and housing, and an equal right to vote. Discrimination by law against persons because of race, sex, religion, or ethnicity is now ~~almost~~ nonexistent.

★ *Legal equality for all Americans has not resulted in de facto equality.* African Americans, women, Hispanic Americans, and other traditionally disadvantaged groups have a disproportionately small share of America's opportunities and benefits. Existing inequalities, discrimination, and political pressures still are major barriers to their full equality. Affirmative action is a policy designed to help the disadvantaged achieve a fuller degree of equality.

THE STRUGGLE FOR EQUALITY

Equality has always been the least fully developed of America's founding concepts. Not even Thomas Jefferson, who had a deep admiration for the "common man," believed that a precise meaning could be given to the claim of the Declaration of Independence that "all men are created equal."[4]

The history of America shows that disadvantaged groups have rarely achieved a greater measure of justice without a struggle.[5] Their gains have nearly always followed intense and sustained political action, such as the civil rights movement of the 1960s, that has forced entrenched interests to relinquish or share their privileged status (see Chapter 7).

Disadvantaged groups have a shared history of political exclusion, struggles for empowerment, and policy triumphs, but each has a distinctive history as well, as is evident in a brief review of the equal rights efforts of African Americans, women, Native Americans, Hispanic Americans, Asian Americans, and other groups.

African Americans

No Americans have faced greater hardship than have black Americans. Their ancestors came to this country as slaves after having been captured in Africa, shipped in chains across the Atlantic, and sold in open markets in Charleston, Boston, and other seaports.

The Civil War ended slavery—but not racism. When federal troops withdrew from the South in 1877, the region's white majority took over the state governments, passing laws that kept blacks from voting. Even more punitive were laws that prohibited black citizens from using the same public facilities as whites.[6] In *Plessy v. Ferguson* (1896), the Supreme Court endorsed these laws, ruling that "separate" facilities for the two races did not violate the Constitution as long as the facilities were

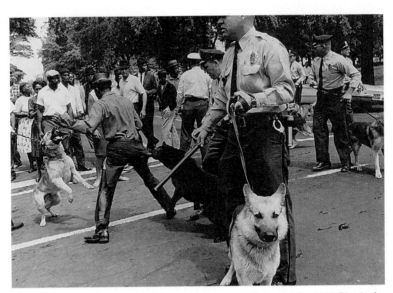

Two police dogs attack a black civil rights activist (*center left*) during the 1963 Birmingham demonstrations. Such images of hatred and violence shook many white Americans out of their complacency about the plight of African Americans.

"equal."[7] The *Plessy* decision became a justification for the separate and *unequal* treatment of African Americans. For example, black children were forced into separate schools that rarely had libraries and had few teachers.

Black Americans challenged these discriminatory practices through legal action, but not until the late 1930s did the Supreme Court begin to respond. The Court began modestly by ruling that where no separate public facilities existed for African Americans, they must be allowed to use those reserved for whites. When Oklahoma, which had no law school for blacks, was ordered to admit Ada Sipuel as a law student in 1949, it created a separate law school for her—she sat alone in a roped-off corridor of the state capitol building. The white students, meanwhile, continued to meet at the University of Oklahoma's law school in Norman, twenty miles away. The Supreme Court then ordered the law school to admit her to regular classes. The law school did so but roped off her seat from the rest of the class and stenciled the word "colored" on it. She was also forced to eat alone in a roped-off area of the law school's cafeteria.[8]

The Brown Decision   Substantial judicial intervention on behalf of African Americans finally occurred in 1954 with *Brown v. Board of*

Education of Topeka. The case began when Linda Carol Brown, a black child in Topeka, Kansas, was denied admission to an all-white elementary school that she passed every day on her way to her all-black school, which was twelve blocks farther. In its decision, the Court reversed its *Plessy* doctrine by declaring that racial segregation of public schools "generates [among black children] a feeling of inferiority as to their status in the community that may affect their hearts and minds in a way unlikely ever to be undone. . . . Separate educational facilities are inherently unequal."[9]

A 1954 Gallup poll indicated that a substantial majority of southern whites opposed the *Brown* decision. The same poll found that a slim majority of whites outside the South agreed with the decision.

The Black Civil Rights Movement   After *Brown*, the struggle of African Americans for their rights became a political movement. Perhaps no single event turned national public opinion so dramatically against segregation as a 1963 march led by Dr. Martin Luther King Jr. in Birmingham, Alabama. As the nation watched on television in disbelief, police officers led by Birmingham's sheriff, Eugene "Bull" Connor, attacked King and his followers with dogs, cattle prods, and fire hoses.

The modern civil rights movement peaked with the triumphant March on Washington for Jobs and Freedom of August 2, 1963. It attracted 250,000 marchers, one of the largest gatherings in the history of the nation's capital. "I have a dream," the Reverend King told the gathering, "that my four little children will one day live in a nation where they will not be judged by the color of their skin but by the content of their character." A year later, after a months-long fight in Congress marked by every parliamentary obstacle that racial conservatives could muster, the Civil Rights Act of 1964 was enacted. The legislation provided African Americans and other minorities with equal access to public facilities and prohibited job discrimination. President Lyndon Johnson, who had been a decisive force in the battle to pass the Civil Rights Act, called for new legislation that would also end racial barriers to voting. Congress answered with the 1965 Voting Rights Act.

The Aftermath of the Civil Rights Movement   Although the most significant progress in history toward the legal equality of all Americans occurred during the 1960s, Dr. King's dream of a color-blind society has remained elusive.[10] Even the legal rights of African Americans do not, in practice, match the promise of the civil rights movement. Studies have found that African Americans accused of crime are more likely to be convicted and to receive stiff sentences than are white Americans on trial for comparable offenses. Federal statistics indicate, for example, that black Americans account for more than 75 percent of crack cocaine convictions but only about 35 percent of crack cocaine users.[11] It is hardly surprising that many African Americans believe that the nation has two standards of justice, with a harsher standard for blacks than for whites.

One area in which African Americans have made substantial progress since the 1960s is elective office (see "States in the Nation"). Although the percentage of black elected officials is still far below the proportion of African Americans in the population, it has risen sharply over recent decades.[12] As of 2006, there were more than four hundred black mayors, more than forty black members of the U.S. House of Representatives, and one black U.S. senator, Barack Obama of Illinois.

Women

The United States carried over from English common law a political disregard for women, forbidding them to vote, hold public office, or serve on juries.[13] Upon marriage, a woman essentially lost her identity as an individual and could not own and dispose of property without her husband's consent. Even a wife's body was not fully hers. A wife's adultery was declared by the Supreme Court in 1904 to be a violation of the husband's property rights![14]

The first women's rights convention in America was held in 1848 in Seneca Falls, New York, after Lucretia Mott and Elizabeth Cady Stanton had been barred from the main floor of an antislavery convention. Thereafter, the struggle for women's rights became closely aligned with the abolitionist movement. However, when the Fifteenth Amendment was ratified after the Civil War, women were not included; the amendment said that the right to vote could not be abridged on account of race or color but said nothing about sex. Not until passage of the Nineteenth Amendment in 1920 did women gain the right to vote.

Women's Legal and Political Gains   Ratification of the Nineteenth Amendment encouraged leaders of the women's movement to propose in 1923 a constitutional amendment that would guarantee equal rights for women. Congress rejected that proposal and several subsequent ones. In 1973, however, Congress approved the Equal Rights Amendment (ERA) and submitted it to the states for ratification or rejection. The ERA failed by three states to receive the three-fourths majority required for ratification.[15] Nevertheless, the ERA helped bring women's rights to the forefront at a time when developments in Congress and the courts were

Black and Latino Representation in State Legislatures

For a long period in U.S. history, there were almost no minorities among the ranks of state legislators. Minorities are still underrepresented relative to their numbers in the population. Although one in every three Americans is a minority-group member, only one in eight state legislators comes from a minority group.

Q: What accounts for differences between the states in the percentage of minority-group members in their legislatures?

A: States with large populations of minorities tend to have a larger percentage of legislators from minority groups. Alabama and Mississippi have large black populations and have the highest proportion of African American legislators. New Mexico, with its large Hispanic population, has the highest proportion of Latino lawmakers.

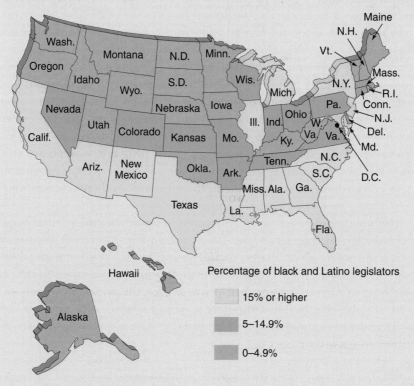

Percentage of black and Latino legislators

15% or higher

5–14.9%

0–4.9%

Source: National Conference of State Legislatures, 2006.

contributing significantly to legal equality for women. Among the congressional initiatives were the Equal Pay Act of 1963, which prohibits sex discrimination in salary and wages by some categories of employers; Title IX of the Education Amendment of 1972, which prohibits sex discrimination in education; and the Equal Credit Act of 1974, which prohibits sex discrimination in the granting of financial credit.

Women are also protected by Title VII of the Civil Rights Act of 1964, which bans gender discrimination in employment. This protection extends to sexual harassment. Lewd comments and unwelcome advances are part of the workplace reality for many American women. However, the courts have held—with increasing firmness—that companies and government agencies can be sued if they do not make an effort to prevent this type of behavior.[16] In a 2006 decision, the Supreme Court strengthened employees' protection by making it easier for them to sue an organization that retaliates against them for filing a sexual harassment complaint. The case involved a woman who, after filing a complaint against her supervisor, was removed from her job as a forklift operator and assigned a less desirable position.[17]

Women have made substantial gains in the area of appointive and elective offices.[18] In 1981, President Reagan appointed the first woman to serve on the Supreme Court, Sandra Day O'Connor. When the Democratic party in 1984 chose Geraldine Ferraro as its vice presidential nominee, she became the first woman to run on the national ticket of a major political party. The elections of California's Dianne Feinstein and Barbara Boxer in 1992 marked the first time that women occupied both U.S. Senate seats of a state. Despite such signs of progress, women are still a long way from political equality with men.[19] Women occupy roughly one in six congressional seats and one in five statewide and city council offices (see "How the United States Compares").

Although women are underrepresented in political office, their vote is increasingly powerful. Until the 1970s, the voting patterns of women and men were nearly alike. Today, there is a substantial **gender gap:** women and men differ in their opinions and their votes. Women are more supportive than men of government programs for the poor, minorities, children, and the elderly. They also have a greater tendency to cast their votes for Democratic candidates (see Figure 5–1). The gender gap is discussed further in Chapter 6.

Job-Related Issues: Family Leave and Comparable Worth   In recent decades, increasing numbers of women have sought employment outside the home. Government statistics indicate that employment-age women

HOW THE UNITED STATES COMPARES

Inequality and Women

The one form of inequality common to all nations is that of gender: nowhere are women equal to men in law or in fact. But there are large differences between countries. A study by the Population Crisis Committee ranked the United States third overall in women's equality, behind only Sweden and Finland. Based on five measures—jobs, education, social relations, marriage and family, and health—the study rated the status of U.S. women at 82.5 percent that of men.

The inequality of women is underscored by their underrepresentation in public office. In no country do women comprise as many as half the members of the national legislature. The Scandinavian countries rank highest in terms of the percentage of female lawmakers. Other northern European countries have lower levels, but their levels are higher than in the United States. The accompanying figure indicates the approximate percentage of seats held by women in the largest chamber of each country's national legislature.

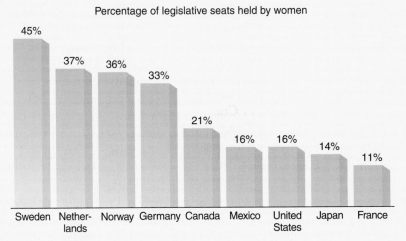

Percentage of legislative seats held by women

Sweden 45%, Netherlands 37%, Norway 36%, Germany 33%, Canada 21%, Mexico 16%, United States 16%, Japan 14%, France 11%

Source: For non–U.S. countries, Inter-Parliamentary Union; for United States, U.S. House of Representatives.

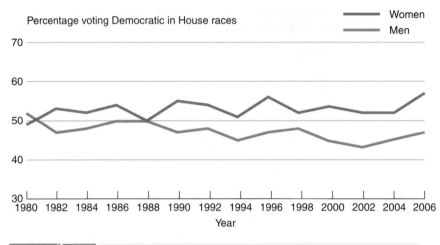

FIGURE | 5-1 | THE GENDER GAP IN CONGRESSIONAL VOTING

Women and men differ, on average, in their political behavior. For example, women are more likely than men to vote Democratic, as shown by the difference between the women's vote and the men's vote for Democratic candidates in U.S. House races. *Source: National Election Studies (1988–98); estimated from multiple polls (2000–2004); 2006 figures based on preliminary data.*

are six times more likely to work outside the home than they were a half-century ago. Women have made gains in many traditionally male-dominated fields. For example, women now make up more than a third of the new lawyers and physicians that graduate each year. The change in women's work status is also reflected in education statistics. A few decades ago, more white, black, and Hispanic men than women were enrolled in college. Today, the reverse is true, with more women than men of each group enrolled. A U.S. Education Department report issued in 2006 showed that women are ahead of men in more than just college enrollment. Compared with men, they are more likely to complete their degree, to do so in less time, and to earn better grades.[20]

Although women have made gains in the workplace, they have not achieved equality with men. Women increasingly hold managerial positions, but as they rise through the ranks, many encounter the so-called *glass ceiling*—the invisible but nonetheless real barrier that women encounter when firms decide who to appoint to the top positions. Of the 500 largest U.S. corporations, only 2 percent are headed by women. Women also earn less than men. The average pay for full-time female employees is about three-fourths that of full-time male employees. One reason is that many jobs traditionally held by women, such as office secretary, pay less than many jobs traditionally held by men, such as truck driver. Attempts by women's groups to change this tendency have been largely unsuccessful. Only a tiny percentage of firms and municipalities have instituted a policy of *comparable worth*. Under this policy, wage scales are set such that women and men receive equal pay for jobs that involve a similar level of difficulty and require a similar level of training or education.[21]

Women gained a major victory in the workplace when Congress passed the Family and Medical Leave Act in 1993. It provides for up to twelve weeks of unpaid leave for employees to care for a new baby or a seriously ill family member. Upon return from leave, the employee ordinarily must be given the original or an equivalent job position with equivalent pay, benefits, and other employment terms. These provisions apply to men as well as women, but women were the instigating force behind the legislation and are its primary beneficiaries because they still bear the larger share of responsibility for sick and young family members.

Traditional practices are reflected in Americans' attitudes toward the role of women in society. Roughly two in five adults say that the preferred marriage is one where the wife stays home to take care of the house. This opinion is more prevalent in the United States than in Europe (see Figure 5–2), even though women's legal and employment gains in the United States have been at least as impressive as those in Europe.

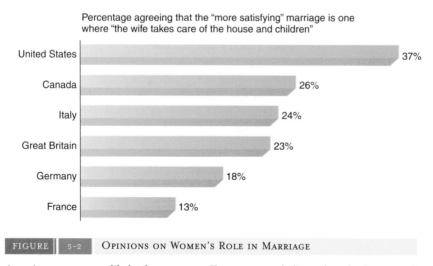

Percentage agreeing that the "more satisfying" marriage is one where "the wife takes care of the house and children"

United States — 37%
Canada — 26%
Italy — 24%
Great Britain — 23%
Germany — 18%
France — 13%

FIGURE 5-2 OPINIONS ON WOMEN'S ROLE IN MARRIAGE

Americans are more likely than western Europeans to believe that the "more satisfying" marriage is one where "the wife takes care of the house and children" rather than one where "the husband and wife both have jobs." *Source: Global Attitudes Survey (2002) by the Pew Research Center for the People and the Press.*

Native Americans

When white settlers began arriving in America in large numbers during the seventeenth century, an estimated ten million Native Americans were living in the territory that would become the United States. By 1900, the Native American population had plummeted to less than one million. No people in human history suffered a steeper loss. Diseases brought by white settlers took the largest toll on the various Indian tribes, but wars and massacres contributed. "The only good Indian is a dead Indian" is not simply a hackneyed expression from cowboy movies. It was part of a strategy of westward expansion, as settlers and U.S. troops alike mercilessly drove the eastern Indians from their ancestral lands to the Great Plains and later took those lands as well. Even well-intentioned policies failed. Reservation lands in some instances were divided into farming plots in the naive belief that Native Americans would readily adjust to an agricultural life based on private property rights.

Today, Native Americans number more than one million, about half of whom live on or close to reservations set aside for them by the federal government. Reservations are governed by treaties signed when they were established. State governments have no direct authority over federal reservations, and the federal government's authority is limited by the terms of a particular treaty. Although U.S. policy toward the reservations has varied over time, the current policy is to promote self-government and economic self-sufficiency.[22] Preservation of Native American cultures is also a policy goal. For example, Native American children can now be taught in their own languages; at an earlier time in schools run by the Bureau of Indian Affairs, children were required to use English.

Native Americans are less than half as likely to attend college as other Americans, their life expectancy is more than ten years lower than the national average, and their infant mortality rate is more than three times higher than that of white Americans. In recent years, some Native American tribes have erected gaming casinos on reservation land. The casinos have brought jobs and income to the reservations but have also brought controversy—traditionalists argue that the casinos are destroying tribal cultures.

The civil rights movement of the 1960s at first did not include Native Americans. Then, in the early 1970s, militant Native Americans occupied the Bureau of Indian Affairs in Washington, D.C., and later seized control of the village of Wounded Knee on a Sioux reservation in southwestern South Dakota, exchanging gunfire with U.S. marshals. These episodes highlighted the grievances of Native Americans and may have contributed to legislation that in 1974 granted Native Americans living on reservations greater control over federal programs that affect them. Native Americans had already benefited from the legislative climate created by the 1960s civil rights movement: in 1968, Congress enacted the Indian Bill of Rights, which gives Native Americans on reservations constitutional guarantees similar to those given to other Americans.

In recent years Native Americans have filed suit to reclaim lost ancestral lands and have won a few settlements. But they stand no realistic chance of getting back even those lands that had been granted to them by federal treaty but later were sold off or seized forcibly by federal authorities. Native Americans were not even official citizens of the United States until passage of an act of Congress in 1924. Their citizenship status came too late to be of much help; their traditional way of life had already largely disappeared.

Hispanic Americans

The fastest-growing minority in the United States is Hispanic Americans, that is, people of Spanish-speaking background. Hispanics recently surpassed African Americans as the nation's largest racial or ethnic minority group. More than 35 million Hispanics live in the United States, an increase of 40 percent over the 1990 census. They have emigrated to the United States primarily from Mexico and the Caribbean islands, mainly Cuba and Puerto Rico. About half of all Hispanics in the United States were born in Mexico or claim a Mexican ancestry. Hispanics are concentrated in their states of entry; thus Florida, New York, and New Jersey have large numbers of Caribbean Hispanics, while California, Texas, Arizona, and New Mexico have many immigrants from Mexico. More than half the population of Los Angeles is of Hispanic—mostly Mexican—descent.

Legal and Political Action Hispanic Americans have benefited from laws and court rulings aimed primarily at protecting other groups. Although the Civil Rights Act of 1964 was largely a response to the condition of black people, its provisions against discrimination apply broadly to other groups.

Nevertheless, Hispanics had their own civil rights movement. Its most publicized actions were the farm workers' strikes of the late 1960s and the 1970s that aimed at achieving basic labor rights for migrant workers. Migrants were working long hours for low pay, were living in shacks without electricity or plumbing, and were unwelcome in many local schools

★ | LEADERS

Cesar Estrada Chavez
(1927–93)

Cesar Chavez led the first successful farm workers' strike in U.S. history. Founder of the United Farm Workers of America, Chavez was called "one of the heroic figures of our time" by Robert F. Kennedy and is widely regarded as the most influential Latino leader in modern U.S. history. A migrant worker as a child, Chavez knew firsthand the deprivations suffered by farm laborers. Like Martin Luther King Jr., Chavez was an advocate of nonviolent protest, and he organized food boycotts that eventually caused agricultural firms to improve wages and working conditions for farm workers. In 1994, Chavez was posthumously awarded the Presidential Medal of Freedom, the highest civilian honor an American can receive.

as well as in some local hospitals. Farm owners at first refused to bargain with the workers, but a well-organized national boycott of California grapes and lettuce forced that state to pass a law giving migrant workers the right to bargain collectively. The strikes were led in California by Cesar Chavez, who himself grew up in a Mexican American migrant family. Chavez's tactics were copied in other states, particularly Texas, but the results were less successful.

The Hispanic civil rights movement has also pursued social and political goals. Hispanics have had some success, for example, in pressuring federal, state, and local governments to increase spending on bilingual education programs. They have also succeeded in getting Congress to enact legislation requiring states to provide bilingual ballots in localities with a sizable concentration of non–English-speaking residents.

Hispanics are one of the country's oldest ethnic groups. Some Hispanics are the descendants of people who helped colonize the areas of California, Texas, Florida, New Mexico, and Arizona before those areas were annexed by the United States. However, most Hispanics are recent immigrants or their descendants. A significant number—roughly ten million by some estimates—are in the United States illegally. In past eras, immigration authorities could more easily control new arrivals because most arrived by ship through a port of entry, such as Ellis Island. Most Hispanics have arrived in the United States by land, many of them crossing illegally from Mexico. U.S. authorities have had little success in stopping this influx. Most illegal aliens come to America seeking jobs, and they now make up an estimated 5 percent of the U.S. work force. They have had broad support in the Hispanic community, which has sought to ease immigration restrictions and to expand the rights and privileges of illegal aliens—positions at odds with those held by many Americans.

In response to growing political pressure over the issue of illegal aliens, President George W. Bush in 2006 urged Congress to enact a guest worker program. Under Bush's plan, workers who are in the United States illegally could enroll in the program, which would allow them to work in the country for up to six years. Other noncitizens could enter the United States as guest workers if they had a job waiting for them. The program was intended to address the nation's labor needs and simultaneously reduce illegal immigration by increasing border surveillance and raising penalties on employers who hire undocumented aliens. Bush's plan had business community support and was backed by many congressional Democrats, although some Democrats wanted the granting of citizenship at the end of six years for guest workers who held jobs and stayed free of crime. Bush's plan won the backing of the Senate but was derailed in the House of Representatives. As a precondition of support for a guest worker program, House Republicans insisted that U.S. borders first be secured against illegal entry, that current laws against hiring illegal aliens be enforced rigorously, and that illegal residents be identified and deported.

As Congress was debating the legislation, large rallies reminiscent of those of the 1960s civil rights movement were taking place in nearly every American city with a sizable Hispanic population. The rally in Los Angeles drew an estimated half million marchers, reputedly the largest such gathering in the city's history. The mostly Hispanic demonstrators took to the streets to protest what they feared was a pending crackdown on illegal immigrants. The scale and spontaneity of the rallies surprised even seasoned political observers; it was a demonstration of Hispanic political solidarity unlike anything previously seen.

Growing Political Power   More than four thousand Hispanic Americans nationwide hold public office. Hispanics have been elected to statewide office in several states, including New Mexico and Arizona. About twenty Hispanic Americans currently serve in the House of Representatives.

Hispanic Americans are a growing political force. By the middle of the century, Hispanics are projected to become the largest racial or ethnic group in California. Their political involvement, like that of other immigrant

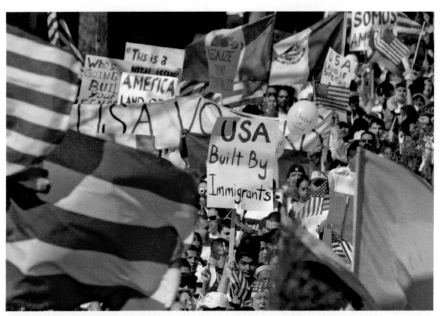

When Congress in 2006 seemed on the verge of enacting legislation that would crack down on illegal immigrants, most of whom are from Mexico, pro-immigrant rallies were held in nearly every American city with a sizable Hispanic population. The rally in Los Angeles was the largest in the city's history. Even in locations more distant from Mexico, the rallies were large and enthusiastic. Shown here is the rally in Lincoln, Nebraska, where the flags of both the United States and Mexico were readily visible.

groups, will increase as they become more firmly rooted in society. At present, about half of all Hispanics are not registered to vote, and only about a third actually vote, limiting the group's political power. Nevertheless, the sheer size of the Hispanic population in states such as Texas and California makes the group a potent force, as was evident in the 2006 election when both the Republicans and the Democrats mounted massive efforts to woo Hispanic voters.

With the exception of the conservative Republican–leaning Cuban Americans of southern Florida, Hispanics lean toward the Democratic party (see Figure 5–3). However, Hispanics are not a cohesive voting bloc in the same way that African Americans are. Blacks of all income levels are solidly Democratic; among Hispanics, Democratic support is concentrated among those of lower income. Opinion surveys show that Hispanics tend to be relatively liberal on economic issues and relatively conservative on social issues. These tendencies suggest that Hispanics will lean Democratic in the near future but divide more evenly between the parties as their average income rises.[23]

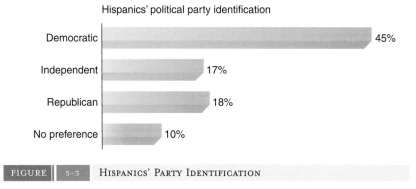

FIGURE 5-3 HISPANICS' PARTY IDENTIFICATION

Hispanics' party loyalties lean heavily toward the Democratic party. *Source: "2005 National Latino Survey," Latino Coalition, December, 2005.*

Asian Americans

Chinese and Japanese laborers were brought into western states during the late 1800s to work in mines and to build railroads. When the need for this labor declined, Congress in 1892 ordered a temporary halt to Asian immigration. Over the next three decades, informal agreements kept all but a few Asians from entering the country. In 1930, Congress completely blocked the entry of Japanese. Japan had protested a California law that prohibited persons of Japanese descent from buying property in the state. Rather than finesse what was called "the California problem," Congress bluntly told Japan that its people were not wanted in the United States.[24]

Discrimination against Asians did not ease substantially until 1965, when Congress enacted legislation that adjusted the immigration quotas to favor those who had previously been assigned very small numbers. This change in the law was a product of the 1960s civil rights movement, which increased public awareness of all forms of discrimination. Asian Americans now number about twelve million, or roughly 4 percent of the total U.S. population. Most Asian Americans live on the West Coast, particularly in California. China, Japan, Korea, India, Vietnam, and the Philippines are the ancestral homes of most Asian Americans.

The rights of Asian Americans have been expanded primarily by court rulings and legislation, such as the Civil Rights Act of 1964, that were initiated in response to the demands of other minorities. In some instances, however, the actions of Asian Americans have strengthened the rights of other minorities. In *Lau v. Nichols* (1974), a case initiated by a Chinese American family, the Supreme Court ruled unanimously that

Chinese workers were brought to the United States in the late 1800s to work on railroads and in mines, but when the need for their labor diminished, they were discouraged from staying in America. Immigration policies that discriminated against Asians lasted until the 1960s.

placing public school children for whom English is a second language in regular classrooms without special assistance is a violation of the Fourteenth Amendment's equal protection clause, because it denies them an equal educational opportunity.[25] Although the Court did not mandate bilingual instruction as the form of that assistance and later held that bilingual courses are not required, the *Lau* decision did lead many schools to establish bilingual instruction. Since then, some states have restricted its use. In California, the limitation was enacted in 1998 through Proposition 227, which requires children for whom English is a second language to take their courses in English after their first year in school, though other forms of assistance and waivers are permitted in some cases.

Asian Americans are an upwardly mobile group. The values of most Asian cultures include family-oriented self-reliance, which, in the American context, has included an emphasis on academic attainment. For example, Asians make up a disproportionate share of the students at California's leading public universities, which base admission primarily on high school grades and standardized test scores. However, Asian Americans are still underrepresented in certain areas of the workplace. According to U.S. government figures, Asian Americans account for about 5 percent of professionals and technicians, slightly more than their percentage of the total population. Yet they hold less than 2 percent of managerial jobs; past and present discrimination has kept them from obtaining their fair share of top business positions. They are also underrepresented politically.[26] Not until 1996, for example, was an Asian American elected governor of a state other than Hawaii.

Other Groups and Their Rights

The 1964 Civil Rights Act (discussed further later in the chapter) prohibits discrimination by sex, race, or national origin. This act classified women and racial and ethnic minorities as legally protected groups, enabling them to pursue their rights in court. As these minority groups gained success, other groups began to demand protection against discrimination rooted in prejudicial attitudes or assumptions.

Older Americans   Older Americans are one such group. The Age Discrimination Act of 1975 and the Age Discrimination in Employment Act of 1967 prohibit discrimination against older workers in hiring for jobs in which age is not clearly a crucial factor in job performance. More recently, mandatory retirement ages for most jobs have been eliminated by law. However, forced retirement for reasons of age is permissible if it is justified by the nature of a particular job or by the performance of a particular employee. As these exceptions to federal age–discrimination laws indicate, older Americans are not as fully protected by law as women and minority-group members are. Age discrimination is not among the forms of discrimination prohibited by the U.S. Constitution.[27] As a result, although the federal government has provided substantial legal protections for older residents, it is not bound by the Constitution to do so.

Disabled Americans   Disabled Americans are also protected from discrimination. Roughly forty million Americans have a physical or mental disability that prevents them from performing a critical function, such as seeing, hearing, or walking. A goal of the disabled is equal access to society's opportunities. This was facilitated by the 1990 Americans with

Disabilities Act, which grants the disabled the same employment and other protections enjoyed by other disadvantaged groups. In addition, the Education for All Handicapped Children Act of 1975 mandates that all children, however severe their disability, must receive a free, appropriate education. Before the legislation, four million children with disabilities were getting either no education or an inappropriate one (as in the case of a blind child who is not taught Braille). Although the disabled have substantial legal protections, they, like the elderly, are not a constitutionally protected group. Accordingly, government actions that have the effect of discriminating against the disabled, are in some cases legal, although the courts have required governments to take reasonable steps to provide the disabled with access to public services and facilities.[28]

Gays and Lesbians   A group that historically has been the object of hostility and discrimination is gays and lesbians. Until recently, they typically responded by trying to hide their sexual orientation. While some still do so, many gays and lesbians now openly pursue a claim to equal protection under the law.

Gays and lesbians gained a significant legal victory when the Supreme Court in *Romer v. Evans* (1996) struck down a Colorado constitutional amendment banning legal protections for homosexuals. In a 6-3 ruling, the Court said that the Colorado law violated the Constitution's guarantee of equal protection because it subjected individuals to employment and other discrimination simply because of their sexual preference. The Court concluded that the law had no reasonable purpose but was instead motivated by hostility toward homosexuals.[29] In *Lawrence v. Texas* (2003), the Court handed gays and lesbians another victory by invalidating state laws that prohibited sexual relations between consenting adults of the same sex (see Chapter 4).[30]

These gains have been partially offset by setbacks. In 2000, for example, the Supreme Court held that the Boy Scouts, as a private organization with a right to free association, can ban gays because the Scout creed forbids homosexuality.[31] Gays and lesbians who are open about their sexual preference are also barred from serving in the U.S. military. However, they can serve under the military's "don't ask, don't tell" (or "don't harass, don't pursue") policy. As long as they do not by words or actions reveal their sexual preference, they are allowed to enlist and remain in the service. In turn, soldiers are instructed not to inquire about others' sexual orientation, nor are they to try to entrap those whom they suspect of being gay or lesbian. The courts have upheld the military's ban, citing the unusually close physical proximity and minimal privacy that typify life in the military. An attempt by U.S. law schools to force a change in the policy by prohibiting the military from recruiting on their premises collapsed when the Supreme Court in 2006 upheld a law that withholds federal funds from colleges that do not give military recruiters the same access to students that they give to recruiters of other employers.[32]

Gay and lesbian couples currently are seeking the same legal status the law extends to opposite-sex married couples. During the past decade, same-sex couples have succeeded in getting some states, cities, and firms to extend employee benefits such as health care insurance to their employees' same-sex partners. These arrangements, however, do not extend to rights such as inheritance and hospital visitation privileges, which are reserved by state law for married couples and their families. In 2000 Vermont legalized the civil union of same-sex couples, thereby granting them the same legal rights as those held by opposite-sex married couples. In 2004, by order of the state's high court, Massachusetts gave same-sex couples the right to marry.

The claim that gay and lesbian couples should have the same legal rights as opposite-sex married couples has been strongly contested. Even before Vermont authorized same-sex unions, Congress passed the Defense of Marriage Act, which defines marriage as "a legal union of one man and one woman as husband and wife." This 1996 law authorizes states to deny marital rights to a same-sex couple that has been granted these rights by another state. Under the U.S. Constitution's "full faith and credit clause," states are required to recognize the laws and contracts of other states, although Congress can create exceptions, as it did with the Defense of Marriage Act.

Social conservatives have sponsored ballot initiatives to prohibit same-sex marriage. In 2004, voters in eleven states overwhelmingly approved bans on such marriages. Voting in the eight states that considered the ban in 2006 was less one-sided. The margin of victory was less than 60 percent in some states, and Arizona voters rejected a same-sex marriage ban, becoming the first electorate to do so.

Aside from the issue of same-sex marriage, Americans have become more accepting of gay and lesbian relationships. Support for civil unions has been increasing gradually in opinion polls, which also indicate most Americans now believe that partners in same-sex relationships should get the same employee benefits as spouses do.[33] For its part, Congress has not taken the issue of same-sex unions beyond the Defense of Marriage Act. An attempt by congressional conservatives in 2006 to initiate a

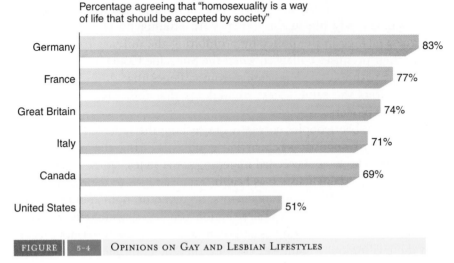

Percentage agreeing that "homosexuality is a way
of life that should be accepted by society"

Germany — 83%

France — 77%

Great Britain — 74%

Italy — 71%

Canada — 69%

United States — 51%

FIGURE 5-4 OPINIONS ON GAY AND LESBIAN LIFESTYLES

Americans are less likely than western Europeans to believe that society should accept gay and lesbian lifestyles. *Source: Global Attitudes Survey (2002) by the Pew Research Center for the People and the Press.*

constitutional amendment to ban same-sex marriage fell far short of the required two-thirds vote in the House and Senate. Yet Americans, perhaps because of their deeper religious beliefs (see Chapter 6), are less supportive of gay and lesbian lifestyles than are Europeans (see Figure 5–4). One thing is sure: issues of gay and lesbian rights, including same-sex marriage and civil union, will be a focus of political action and controversy for the foreseeable future.

EQUALITY UNDER THE LAW

The catchphrase of nearly every group's claim to a more equal standing in American society has been "equality under the law." Once they are secure in their legal rights, people are in a stronger position to insist that their rights be respected and find it easier to pursue equality in other arenas, such as the economic sector. Americans' claims to legal equality are embodied in a great many laws, a few of which are particularly noteworthy.

Equal Protection: The Fourteenth Amendment

The Fourteenth Amendment, which was ratified in 1868, declares in part that no state shall "deny to any person within its jurisdiction the equal protection of the laws." Through this **equal-protection clause**, the courts have protected groups such as African Americans and women from discrimination by state and local governments.

The Fourteenth Amendment's equal-protection clause does not require government to treat all groups or classes of people the same way in all circumstances. By law, for example, twenty-one-year-olds can drink alcohol but twenty-year-olds cannot. The judiciary allows such inequalities because they are held to be "reasonably" related to a legitimate government interest. In applying this **reasonable-basis test,** the courts require government only to show that a particular law is reasonable. For example, the courts have held that the goal of reducing fatalities from alcohol-related accidents involving young drivers is a valid reason for imposing a twenty-one-year minimum age requirement for the purchase of alcohol.

The reasonable-basis test does not apply, however, to racial or ethnic classifications, particularly when these categories serve to discriminate against minority-group members (see Table 5–1). Any law that treats people differently because of race or ethnicity is subject to the **strict-scrutiny test,** under which such a law is presumed unconstitutional in the absence of an overwhelmingly convincing argument that it is necessary. The strict-scrutiny test has virtually eliminated race and ethnicity as permissible classifications when the effect is to place a hardship on

TABLE 5–1	LEVELS OF COURT REVIEW FOR LAWS THAT TREAT AMERICANS DIFFERENTLY	
Test	**Applies to**	**Standard Used**
Strict scrutiny	Race, ethnicity	Suspect category—assumed unconstitutional in the absence of an overwhelming justification
Intermediate scrutiny	Gender	Almost suspect category—assumed unconstitutional unless the law serves a clearly compelling and justified purpose
Reasonable basis	Other categories (such as age and income)	Not suspect category—assumed constitutional unless no sound rationale for the law can be provided

Although women are excluded by law from having to register for the draft, they are eligible to enlist voluntarily in the U.S. military. Shown here is a U.S. woman soldier controlling the crowd on the streets of Mosul, Iraq. Roughly 2 percent of American military casualties in the Iraq conflict have been women.

members of a minority group. The Supreme Court's position is that race and national origin are **suspect classifications**—in other words, that legal classifications based on race and ethnicity are assumed to have discrimination as their purpose and are presumed unconstitutional.

The strict-scrutiny test emerged after the 1954 *Brown* ruling and became a basis for invalidating laws that discriminated against black people. As other groups, especially women, began to organize and assert their rights in the late 1960s and early 1970s, the Supreme Court gave early signs that it might expand the scope of suspect classifications to include gender. In the end, however, the Court announced in *Craig v. Boren* (1976) that sex classifications were permissible if they served "important governmental objectives" and were "substantially" related to the achievement of those objectives.[34] The Court thus placed sex distinctions in an intermediate (or almost suspect) category, to be scrutinized more closely than some other classifications (for example, income or age level) but, unlike racial classifications, justifiable in some instances. In *Rostker v. Goldberg* (1980), for example, the policy of male-only registration for the military draft was upheld on grounds that the exclusion of women from *involuntary* combat duty serves a legitimate and important purpose.[35]

The inexactness of the **intermediate-scrutiny test** has led some scholars to question its usefulness as a legal principle. Nevertheless, when evaluating claims of sex discrimination, the judiciary applies a stricter level of scrutiny than is required by the reasonable-basis test. Rather than giving government broad leeway to treat men and women differently, the Supreme Court has struck down most of the laws it has recently reviewed that contain sex classifications. A leading case is *United States v. Virginia* (1996), in which the Supreme Court determined that the male-only admissions policy of Virginia Military Institute (VMI), a state-supported college, was unconstitutional. The state had developed an alternative program for women at another college, but the Court concluded that it was no substitute for the unique education and other opportunities that attendance at VMI could provide. (The VMI decision also had the effect of ending the all-male admissions policy of the Citadel, a state-supported military college in South Carolina.)[36]

Equal Access: The Civil Rights Acts of 1964 and 1968

The Fourteenth Amendment applies only to action by government. It does not prohibit discrimination by private parties. As a result, for a long period in the nation's history, owners could legally bar black people from restaurants, hotels, and other accommodations, and employers could freely discriminate in their job practices. Since the 1960s, however, private firms have had much less freedom to discriminate for reasons of race, sex, ethnicity, or religion.

Accommodations and Jobs The Civil Rights Act of 1964, which is based on Congress's power to regulate interstate commerce, entitles all persons to equal access to restaurants, bars, theaters, hotels, gasoline stations, and similar establishments serving the general public. The legislation also bars discrimination in the hiring, promotion, and wages of employees of medium-size and large firms. A few forms of job discrimination are still lawful under the Civil Rights Act. For example, an owner-operator of a small business can discriminate in hiring his or her coworkers, and a religious school can take the religion of a prospective teacher into account.

The Civil Rights Act of 1964 has nearly eliminated the most overt forms of discrimination in the area of public accommodations. Some restaurants and hotels may provide better service to white customers, but outright refusal to serve African Americans or other minority-group members is rare. Such a refusal is a violation of the law and could easily be proved in

POLITICAL CULTURE

Private Discrimination: Liberty or Equality?

The courts have ruled that private organizations are often within their rights in discriminating against individuals because of color, gender, creed, national origin, or other characteristics. The Fifth and Fourteenth Amendments only prohibit discrimination by government bodies.

Jews, Catholics, and blacks are among the groups that historically have been denied membership in private clubs and organizations. The most celebrated recent incident was the decision of the Boy Scouts of America (BSA) to revoke the membership of Scoutmaster James Dale. Dale is gay, and the BSA excludes homosexuals from membership. Dale's suit against the BSA went to the Supreme Court, which ruled in 2000 that the BSA, as a private organization, had the right to deny membership to gays.

Issues of liberty and equality are at the forefront of such cases. Liberty is enhanced when private organizations are free to pick their members. But equality is diminished when people are denied opportunities because of their physical characteristics or lifestyles.

What's your opinion on the Dale–BSA dispute? What general limits, if any, would you impose on the discriminatory acts of private organizations?

many instances. It is harder to prove discrimination in job decisions; accordingly, the act has been less effective in rooting out employment discrimination—a subject that we will discuss in detail later in this chapter.

Housing In 1968, Congress passed civil rights legislation designed to prohibit discrimination in housing. A building owner cannot refuse to sell or rent housing because of a person's race, religion, ethnicity, or sex. An exception is allowed for owners of small multifamily dwellings who reside on the premises.

Despite legal prohibitions on discrimination, housing in America remains highly segregated. Less than a third of all African Americans live in a neighborhood that is mostly white. One reason is that the annual income of most black families is substantially below that of most white families. Another reason is banking practices. At one time, banks contributed to housing segregation by redlining—refusing to grant mortgage loans in certain neighborhoods. This practice drove down the selling *everybody gets loans*

prices of homes in these neighborhoods, which led to an influx of African Americans and an exodus of whites. Redlining is prohibited by the 1968 Civil Rights Act, but many of the segregated neighborhoods that it helped create still exist. Studies indicate that minority status remains a factor in the lending practices of some banks. A report of the U.S. Conference of Mayors indicated that, among applicants with average or slightly higher incomes relative to their community, Hispanics and African Americans were twice as likely as whites to be denied a mortgage.[37]

Equal Ballots: The Voting Rights Act of 1965, as Amended

Free elections are perhaps the foremost symbol of American democracy, yet the right to vote has only recently become a reality for many Americans, particularly African Americans. Although they appeared to have gained that right in 1870 with ratification of the Fifteenth Amendment, southern whites invented a series of devices, including whites-only primaries, poll taxes, and rigged literacy tests, to keep them from registering and voting. For example, almost no votes were cast by African Americans in North Carolina between the years 1920 and 1946.[38]

Barriers to black participation in elections began to crumble in the mid-1940s, when the Supreme Court declared that whites-only primary elections were unconstitutional.[39] Two decades later, the Twenty-fourth Amendment outlawed poll taxes.

The major step toward equal voting rights for African Americans was passage of the Voting Rights Act of 1965, which forbids discrimination in voting and registration. The legislation empowers federal agents to register voters and to oversee participation in elections. The Voting Rights Act, as interpreted by the courts, also prohibits the use of literacy tests as a registration requirement. Although civil rights legislation has seldom had a large and immediate impact on people's behavior, the Voting Rights Act was an exception. In the 1960 presidential election, voter turnout among African Americans was barely 30 percent nationwide. In 1968, three years after passage of the legislation, the turnout rate exceeded 40 percent.

Congress has renewed the Voting Rights Act several times, most recently in 2006. The act includes a provision that compels states and localities to clear with federal officials any electoral change that has the effect, intended or not, of reducing the voting power of a minority group. One way to reduce the power of a group's votes is to spread members of the group across election districts so that their number in any given district is too small to constitute a voting majority. When congressional district boundaries were redrawn after the 1990 census (see Chapter 11), the provision became the basis for the creation of districts that included a majority of Hispanic or African American voters. The result was the election of an unprecedented number of minority-group members to Congress in 1992, when the number of Hispanic and African American representatives jumped from 27 to 63.

However, in three separate cases that were each decided by a 5-4 margin, the Supreme Court ruled that the redistricting of several congressional districts in Texas, North Carolina, and Georgia violated the Fourteenth Amendment because race had been the "dominant" consideration in their creation. The Court held that the redistricting violated the equal-protection rights of white voters and ordered the three states to redraw the districts.[40] In *Easley v. Cromartie* (2001), however, the Court granted states some leeway in creating racially imbalanced districts. At issue was a North Carolina district that had been drawn with the goal of creating a safe Democratic district—resulting in a district with a large proportion of black voters. The Court, which had long allowed partisan redistricting, ruled that if such redistricting incidentally creates a minority-dominated district, as was the case with the North Carolina district in question, the action does not violate the Fourteenth Amendment.[41] But in a 2006 case (*League of United Latin American Voters v. Perry*), the Court held that partisan redistricting that comes at the expense of minority-group members can be unlawful. The case involved Texas's twenty-third congressional district, which had been drawn in a way that deliberately diluted the power of Hispanic voters. In ordering Texas to redraw the district, the Court said: "The troubling blend of politics and race—and the resulting vote dilution of a group that was beginning to [overcome] prior electoral discrimination—cannot be sustained."[42]

EQUALITY OF RESULT

America's disadvantaged groups have made significant progress toward equal rights, particularly during the past few decades. Through acts of Congress and rulings of the Supreme Court, most forms of government-sponsored discrimination—from racially segregated public schools to gender-based pension plans—have been banned.

However, civil rights problems involve deeply rooted conditions, habits, and prejudices and affect whole categories of people. For these reasons, a new civil rights policy rarely produces a sudden and dramatic change in society. Despite their greater equality in law, America's traditionally disadvantaged groups are still substantially unequal in their daily

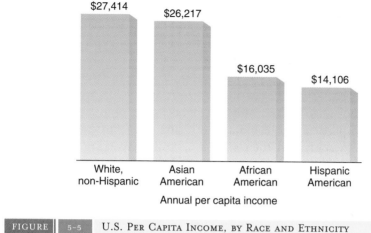

| $27,414 | $26,217 | $16,035 | $14,106 |
| White, non-Hispanic | Asian American | African American | Hispanic American |

Annual per capita income

FIGURE **5-5** U.S. PER CAPITA INCOME, BY RACE AND ETHNICITY

The average income of white Americans is substantially higher than that of most other Americans. *Source: U.S. Bureau of the Census, 2006.*

lives. Consider the issue of income disparity (see Figure 5–5). The average Hispanic or African American's income is less than 60 percent of the average white person's income.

Such disparities reflect **de facto discrimination,** discrimination that is a consequence of social, economic, and cultural biases and conditions. This type of discrimination is different from **de jure discrimination,** which is discrimination based on law, as in the case of the state laws that required black and white children in the South to attend separate public schools in the pre-*Brown* period. De facto discrimination is the more difficult type to root out because it is embedded not in the law but in the structure of society.

Equality of result is the aim of policies intended to reduce de facto discriminatory effects. Such policies are inherently controversial because many Americans believe that government's responsibility extends no further than the removal of legal barriers to equality. This attitude reflects the culture's emphasis on personal *liberty*—the freedom to choose one's associates, employees, neighbors, and classmates. Nevertheless, a few policies—notably affirmative action and busing—have been implemented to achieve equality of result.

Affirmative Action: Workplace Integration

The difficulty of converting newly acquired legal rights into everyday realities is illustrated by the 1964 Civil Rights Act. Although the legislation prohibited discrimination in employment, women and minorities did not suddenly obtain jobs for which they were qualified. Many employers continued to favor white male employees. Other employers adhered to established employment procedures that kept women and minorities at a disadvantage; membership in many union locals, for example, was handed down from father to son. Moreover, the Civil Rights Act did not require employers to prove that their hiring practices were unbiased. Instead, the burden of proof was on the woman or minority-group member who had been denied a particular job. It was costly and often difficult for individuals to prove in court that their sex or race was the reason they had not been hired. In addition, a victory in court helped only the individual in question; these case-by-case settlements did not affect the millions of other women and minorities facing job discrimination.

A broader remedy was obviously required, and the result was the emergence during the late 1960s of affirmative action programs. **Affirmative action** is a deliberate effort to provide full and equal opportunities in employment, education, and other areas for members of traditionally disadvantaged groups. Affirmative action requires corporations, universities, and other organizations to establish programs designed to ensure that all applicants are treated fairly. Affirmative action also places the burden of

"In order to overcome past discrimination, do you favor or oppose affirmative action programs designed to help blacks, women, and other minorities get better jobs and education?"

Oppose 29%
Favor 63%
Don't know 8%

"We should make every possible effort to improve the position of blacks and other minorities, even if it means giving them preferential treatment."

Agree 24%
Disagree 72%
Don't know 4%

FIGURE 5-6 OPINIONS ON AFFIRMATIVE ACTION

Most Americans support affirmative action when it comes to programs that will give women and minorities an equal chance at opportunities but oppose it when it comes to programs that will give them preferential treatment. *Source: Pew Research Center for the People and the Press, May 14, 2003.*

proof on the providers of opportunities, who, to some extent, must be able to demonstrate that any disproportionate granting of opportunities to white males is the result of necessity (such as the nature of the job or the locally available labor pool) and not the result of systematic discrimination against women or minorities.

Few issues in recent decades have sparked more controversy than has affirmative action, reflecting the public's ambivalence about the policy.[43] Most Americans say they favor granting women and minorities equal opportunities, but they also express opposition to programs that would give them preferential treatment (see Figure 5–6).

Affirmative Action in the Law

Most issues that pit individuals against each other in a struggle over society's benefits eventually end up in the courts, and affirmative action is no exception (see Table 5–2). The policy was first tested before the Supreme

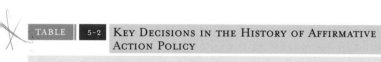

TABLE 5-2 KEY DECISIONS IN THE HISTORY OF AFFIRMATIVE ACTION POLICY

Year	Action
1969	Nixon administration's Department of Labor initiates affirmative action policy
1978	Supreme Court in *Bakke* invalidates rigid quotas for medical school admissions but does not invalidate affirmative action
1980	Supreme Court in *Fullilove* upholds a quota system for minority-owned firms in granting of federal contracts
1980s	Supreme Court in a series of decisions narrows situations in which preferential treatment of minorities will be permitted
1991	In Civil Rights Act of 1991, Congress places burden of proof on business in situations where there is a pattern of white male dominance
1995	Supreme Court in *Adarand* eliminates fixed quotas in the granting of government contracts, reversing the *Fullilove* (1980) precedent
1996	California voters enact Proposition 209, which bans public employment, education, and contracting programs based on race, ethnicity, or sex
2003	Supreme Court in *Gratz v. Bollinger* and *Grutter v. Bollinger* upholds affirmative action but invalidates formula-based (quota-like) programs.

Court in *University of California Regents v. Bakke* (1978). Alan Bakke, a white man, was denied admission to a medical school that, using a race-based quota system, had admitted several minority-group applicants with lower admission test scores. Bakke sued, and the Supreme Court ruled in his favor without invalidating the principle of affirmative action. The Court held that quotas were unconstitutional but said that race could be among the factors taken into account in schools' efforts to create a diverse student body.[44] The *Bakke* ruling was followed by a decision that affirmed the use of quotas in a different context. In *Fullilove v. Klutznick* (1980), the Court upheld a congressional spending bill that required that 10 percent of the funds for building projects be awarded to minority-owned firms.[45]

These rulings strengthened affirmative action as national policy. However, the appointment of more conservative judges to the Supreme Court in the 1980s narrowed the policy's scope. In 1986, for example, the Court ruled that preferential treatment for minorities could be justified only in cases where discrimination had been severe and in ways that did not endanger the employment rights of white workers (limiting, for example, the use of race rather than seniority as the basis for determining which employees would be terminated in the case of job layoffs).[46]

However, the severest blow to advocates of affirmative action was a 1995 decision, *Adarand v. Pena*. The case arose when Adarand Constructors filed suit over a federal contract that had been awarded to a Hispanic-owned company even though Adarand had submitted a lower bid. The Court ruled in Adarand's favor, thereby reversing the *Fullilove* precedent. The Court held that set-aside contracts for minority firms are lawful only when the firms involved have themselves been harmed by discrimination. The Court outlawed rules (such as the 10 percent set-aside of government contracts for minority-owned firms) that give firms an advantage simply because the owners' race is that of a group that has been discriminated against historically. The Court also held that, even in situations where a particular firm has been harmed by discrimination, the remedy must be "narrowly tailored" to the situation—that it must be in proportion to the harm done to the firm.[47]

Adarand marked the end of an era. By holding that affirmative action must address specific acts of discrimination and be designed so as to correct those specific acts, the Court effectively brought a halt to federal contracts that gave preference to applicants on the basis of race or gender. The Court earlier had halted such government contracts at the state and local levels.

Both advocates and opponents of affirmative action wondered whether race- and gender-based college admission programs would be next to be struck down by the Supreme Court. In 2003, in what many observers saw as the most important affirmative action ruling since the *Bakke* decision almost three decades earlier, the Court made its position known. At issue were two University of Michigan affirmative action admission policies: Michigan's point system for undergraduate admission, which granted twenty points (out of a total of 150 possible points) to minority applicants, and its law school admission process, in which race (along with other factors such as work experience and extracurricular activities) was taken into account in admission decisions. The case attracted national attention, including the involvement of major U.S. corporations, which argued that programs such as those at the University of Michigan contributed to their goal of finding well-educated minorities to fill managerial positions.

Opponents of affirmative action hoped that the Court would strike down the Michigan policies, effectively ending the use of race as a factor in college admissions. Indeed, by a 6-3 vote in *Gratz v. Bollinger*, the Supreme Court did strike down Michigan's undergraduate admissions policy because its point system assigned a specific weight to race.[48] However, by a 5-4 vote in *Grutter v. Bollinger*, the Court upheld the law school's program, concluding that it was being applied in a limited and sensible manner and furthered Michigan's "compelling interest in obtaining the educational benefits that flow from a diverse student body." The Court's majority opinion said further that the law school's policy "promotes 'cross-racial understanding,' helps to break down racial stereotypes, and enables [a] better understand[ing of] persons of different races."[49] Thus, affirmative action remains a part of national education policy. Both sides of the issue recognize, however, that the Supreme Court's narrow 5-4 majority in the 2003 case means that the issue has not been fully settled.

Most Americans know that, whatever the future of affirmative action, the issue of equal opportunity cannot be ignored. The nation and its states and communities, as well as its corporations and institutions, have a stake in giving people of all backgrounds a reasonable chance to succeed. Innovative approaches to this challenge have emerged. One example is a Texas policy on college admissions. Recognizing the disparity in the quality of its public schools and other factors that result in lower average scores on standardized tests for minorities, the state established a policy that guarantees admission at a University of Texas institution to any Texas high school student who graduates in the top 10 percent of his or her class. This approach initially faced little opposition even from critics of affirmative action, but opposition has increased as a result of growing enrollment pressure at Texas's flagship universities and the widening perception that students at weaker high schools have an unfair advantage. The reaction to the Texas policy reveals a major reason why issues of education, job, and

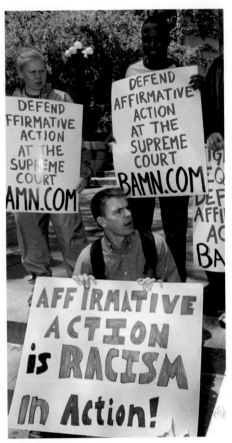

The University of Michigan was the focus of national attention in 2003 as a result of its affirmative action admissions programs. Shown here are demonstrators on both sides of the issue. In its 2003 ruling, the Supreme Court upheld the use of race as a factor in admissions but rejected the use of a "point system" as the method of applying it.

other opportunities are so contentious. Almost every conceivable method of allocating society's benefits—whether through the public sector or the private sector and however fair it might at first appear—inevitably leaves some Americans feeling as if they have been unfairly treated. At that point, if not earlier, the policy invariably becomes a political issue.[50]

Busing: School Integration

The 1954 *Brown* ruling mandated an end to forced segregation of public schools. Government would no longer be permitted to prevent minorities from enrolling in white schools. However, government was not required by the *Brown* decision to compel minority children and white children to attend school together. Fifteen years after *Brown*, because of neighborhood segregation, fewer than 5 percent of America's black children were attending schools that were predominantly white. This situation set the stage for one of the few public policies to force whites into regular contact with blacks: the forced busing of children out of their neighborhoods for the purpose of achieving racial balance in the schools.

In *Swann v. Charlotte-Mecklenburg County Board of Education* (1971), the Supreme Court ruled that the busing of children was an appropriate way to integrate schools that were segregated because past discrimination had contributed to the creation of racially separate neighborhoods.[51] Unlike *Brown*, which affected mainly the South, *Swann* applied also to northern communities where blacks and whites lived separately in part because of discriminatory housing ordinances and real estate practices. *Swann* triggered even larger protests than those that had accompanied the *Brown* decision. Angry and sometimes violent demonstrations lasting weeks took place in Charlotte, Detroit, Boston, and other cities.

Forced busing had mixed results. For a time, it helped reduce the level of segregation in America's schools; at the high point, nearly 40 percent of minority children were attending a school where most of the students were white. Studies found that busing improved the racial attitudes of schoolchildren and improved the performance of minority children on standardized tests without diminishing the performance of their white classmates.[52] However, these achievements came at a high cost. For many children, forced busing meant long hours riding a bus each day to and from school. Moreover, busing contributed to white flight to private schools and to the suburbs. A 1974 Supreme Court decision prohibited busing across school district lines unless those lines had been drawn for the purpose of keeping the races apart.[53] As white students left city schools, it became harder to achieve racial balance through busing and harder as well to gain public support for school spending in urban areas.

In the past fifteen years, the courts have ended most forced busing, saying it was intended as a temporary solution to the problem of segregated schools.[54] Many communities were allowed to devise alternative approaches. Some have increased their spending on neighborhood schools in poorer areas. Others have instituted voluntary busing programs that give minority children a choice among district schools. The most controversial of the newer programs give all students a choice among schools but take race into account when assigning children to them.[55] Children might be denied their first choice if granting it would upset the racial balance. The Supreme Court recently agreed to review two such programs, Louisville's and Seattle's, which were challenged by parents who believe

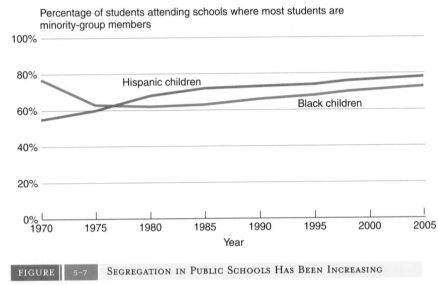

Percentage of students attending schools where most students are minority-group members

| FIGURE | 5-7 | SEGREGATION IN PUBLIC SCHOOLS HAS BEEN INCREASING |

In the past two decades, racial and ethnic segregation in America's public schools has increased. More than two-thirds of black and Hispanic children today attend a school in which most of the students are members of a minority group. An increase in the number of white non-Hispanic students attending private schools and a decrease in race-based busing are factors in the trend. *Source: U.S. Department of Education, 2004.*

that race should have no part in determining their children's school assignments. Regardless of how the Court rules on these programs, the national effect will likely be small. As a result of cutbacks in forced busing, white flight to private and suburban schools, and other factors, the segregation level of America's public schools has been rising steadily since the late 1980s (see Figure 5–7). Today, less than a third of Hispanic and black children attend a school that is predominantly white.

PERSISTENT DISCRIMINATION:
SUPERFICIAL DIFFERENCES,
DEEP DIVISIONS

In 1944, Swedish sociologist Gunnar Myrdal gained fame for his book *An American Dilemma*, whose title referred to deep-rooted racism in a country that idealized equality.[56] Since then, legal obstacles to the mixing of the races have been nearly eliminated, and public opinion has softened significantly. In the early 1940s, a majority of white Americans believed that black children should not be allowed to go to school with white children; today less than 5 percent of white Americans express this belief. There are also visible signs of black progress. In the past two decades, increasing numbers of African Americans have attended college, earned undergraduate degrees, obtained jobs as professionals and managers, and moved into suburban neighborhoods.

Nevertheless, true equality for all Americans remains elusive. The realities of everyday American life are still very different for its white and black citizens. For example, a black child born in the United States has more than twice the chance of dying before reaching his or her first birthday than a white child does. The difference in the infant mortality rates of whites and African Americans reflects differences in their nutrition, medical care, and education—in other words, differences in their access to the most basic resources of a modern society.

The history of equality in America is one of progress and of setbacks and, always, of new challenges. The latest challenge is the treatment of Arab Americans and Muslims in the aftermath of the terrorist attacks of September 11, 2001. Shortly afterward, a radio talk-show host suggested that recent immigrants from the Middle East should be deported, a message eerily reminiscent of what some people once said about Irish Americans and, more recently, Hispanics. Other Americans took the law into their own hands. The Los Angeles Police Department alone recorded more than 150 hate-crime incidents directed against Americans of Middle Eastern origin. Mosques in many U.S. cities were defaced. There was even a bizarre case of malicious misidentification. A Sikh spiritual center in upstate New York was set ablaze by four hooligans because they thought the Sikhs were Arabs who supported Osama bin Laden and his terrorist network. The Sikh spiritual center was named Gobind Sadan, which they thought stood for "go bin Laden."

Although the great majority of Americans have a lot more sense than is displayed by a violent few, many do not necessarily embrace fully the notion that the United States is "one people and one nation." They accept the idea in the abstract but often find it difficult to apply in everyday life. The color of a person's skin or the accent in a person's voice can lead them to respond differently to someone they meet, whether on the street, in a store, on the job, or in the house next door.

Equality is a difficult idea in practice because it requires people to shed preconceived and often deeply embedded notions about how other people think, behave, and feel. Nearly everyone has difficulty seeing beyond superficial differences—whether those differences relate to skin color, national origin, religious preference, sex, or lifestyle—to the shared humanity that unites people of all backgrounds. Myrdal called discrimination "America's curse." He could have broadened the generalization. Discrimination is civilization's curse, as is evident in the scores of ethnic, national, and religious conflicts that have marred human history. But America is a special case because, as Lincoln said in his Gettysburg address, it is a nation founded "on the proposition that all men are created equal." No greater challenge faces America, today as throughout its history, than the challenge of living up to that proposition.

SUMMARY

During the past few decades, the United States has undergone a revolution in the legal status of its traditionally disadvantaged groups, including African Americans, women, Native Americans, Hispanic Americans, and Asian Americans. Such groups are now provided equal protection under the law in areas such as education, employment, and voting. Discrimination by race, sex, and ethnicity has not been eliminated from American life, but it is no longer substantially backed by the force of law.

Traditionally disadvantaged Americans have achieved fuller equality primarily as a result of their struggle for greater rights. The Supreme Court has been an important instrument of change for minority groups. Its ruling in *Brown v. Board of Education* (1954), which declared racial segregation in public schools to be an unconstitutional violation of the Fourteenth Amendment's equal-protection clause, was a major breakthrough in equal rights. Through its busing, affirmative action, and other rulings, the Court also has mandated the active promotion of integration and equal opportunity.

However, because civil rights policy involves general issues of social values and the distribution of society's resources, questions of civil rights are politically explosive. For this reason, legislatures and executives as well as the courts have been deeply involved in such issues, at times siding with established groups and other times backing the claims of underprivileged groups.

In recent decades, affirmative action programs—programs designed to achieve equality of result for African Americans, women, Hispanic Americans, and other disadvantaged groups—have been a civil rights battleground. Affirmative action has had the strong support of civil rights groups and has won the qualified endorsement of the Supreme Court, but it has been opposed by those who claim that it unfairly discriminates against white males. Busing is another issue that has provoked deep divisions within American society, although the era of large-scale forced busing of schoolchildren for the purpose of achieving racial integration is nearly over.

Despite extraordinary gains during recent decades, true equality for all Americans has remained an elusive goal. Tradition, prejudice, and the sheer difficulty of transforming society stand as obstacles to the fuller achievement of America's most challenging ideal—justice for all.

Key Terms

affirmative action (*p. 180*)   equal rights (*p. 152*)
civil rights (*p. 152*)   gender gap (*p. 158*)
de facto discrimination (*p. 179*)   intermediate-scrutiny test (*p. 175*)
de jure discrimination (*p. 179*)   reasonable-basis test (*p. 173*)
equality of result (*p. 179*)   strict-scrutiny test (*p. 173*)
equal-protection clause (*p. 173*)   suspect classifications (*p. 174*)

Suggested Readings

Anderson, Terry H. *The Pursuit of Fairness: A History of Affirmative Action.* New York: Oxford University Press, 2005. A comprehensive look at the affirmative action issue.

Armor, David. *Forced Justice: School Desegregation and the Law.* New York: Oxford University Press, 1996. An evaluation that concludes that the federal courts have overstretched their legal mandate by requiring school integration rather than simply school desegregation.

Chang, Gordon H., ed. *Asian Americans and Politics.* Stanford, Calif.: Stanford University Press, 2001. A broad look at the political engagement of Asian Americans.

Nagel, Joane. *American Indian Ethnic Renewal: Red Power and the Resurgence of Identity and Culture.* New York: Oxford University Press, 1997. Explores the meaning of activism for Native Americans' ethnic identification.

Pinello, Daniel R. *Gay Rights and American Law.* New York: Cambridge University Press, 2003. A careful study of recent appellate-court decisions dealing with gay rights issues.

Reeves, Keith. *Voting Hopes or Fears? White Voters, Black Candidates, and Racial Politics in America.* New York: Oxford University Press, 1997. A critical assessment of race and politics in American society.

Rosen, Ruth. *The World Split Open: How the Modern Women's Movement Changed America.* New York: Viking, 2000. A historian's assessment of the women's rights movement.

Stavans, Ilan. *The Hispanic Condition: Reflections on Culture and Identity in America.* New York: HarperPerennial, 1996. An analysis of the behavioral and cultural differences and similarities among the major Hispanic groups.

Willingham, Alex. *Beyond the Color Line?* New York: Brennan Center for Justice, 2002. A set of articles on race and representation.

LIST OF WEBSITES

http://www.airpi.org/ The website of the American Indian Policy Center, which was established by Native Americans in 1992; includes a political and legal history of Native Americans and examines current issues affecting them.

http://www.naacp.org/ The website of the National Association for the Advancement of Colored People (NAACP); includes historical and current information on the struggle of African Americans for equal rights.

http://www.nclr.org/ The website of the National Council of La Raza (NCLR), an organization dedicated to improving the lives of Hispanics; contains information on public policy, immigration, citizenship, and other subjects.

http://www.rci.rutgers.edu/~cawp The website of the Center for the American Woman and Politics (CAWP) at Rutgers University's Eagleton Institute of Politics.

POLITICS IN THEORY AND PRACTICE

Thinking: What role have political movements played in securing the legal rights of disadvantaged groups? How has the resulting legislation contributed to a furtherance of these groups' rights?

Participating: Think of a disadvantaged group that you would like to assist. It could be one of the federal government's designated groups (such as Hispanics), one of the other groups mentioned in the chapter (such as the disabled), or some other group (such as the homeless). Contact a college, community, national, or international organization that seeks to help this group and volunteer your assistance. (The Internet provides the names of thousands of organizations, such as Habitat for Humanity, that are involved in helping the disadvantaged.)

ADDITIONAL RESOURCES

For quizzes, interactive simulations, games, graphics, and other study tools, visit the book's Online Learning Center at **www.mhhe.com/pattersonwtp7.**

Letter from Birmingham Jail

By Martin Luther King Jr.

Martin Luther King Jr. is the only twentieth-century American to be honored with a national holiday. The civil rights leader was the pivotal figure in the movement to gain legal and political rights for black Americans. The son of a Baptist minister and himself a minister, King used speaking skill and nonviolent protest to galvanize the black community. He was assassinated in Memphis in 1968 as he was preparing to lead a protest march on behalf of the city's sanitation workers.

"Letter from Birmingham Jail" was written in 1963 while King was in the Birmingham, Alabama, city jail. He had been arrested for leading a peaceful protest. While there, he saw a published statement by eight black clergymen questioning his protest activities. They argued that the cause of racial equality was better served by negotiation and delay. King's letter was a reply to their argument.

We know through painful experience that freedom is never voluntarily given by the oppressor; it must be demanded by the oppressed. Frankly, I have yet to engage in a direct-action campaign that was "well timed" in the view of those who have not suffered unduly from the disease of segregation. For years now I have heard the word "Wait!" It rings in the ear of every Negro with piercing familiarity. This "Wait" has almost always meant "Never." We must come to see, with one of our distinguished jurists, that "justice too long delayed is justice denied."

We have waited for more than 340 years for our constitutional and God-given rights. The nations of Asia and Africa are moving with jetlike speed toward gaining political independence, but we still creep at horse-and-buggy pace toward gaining a cup of coffee at a lunch counter. Perhaps it is easy for those who have never felt the stinging dart of segregation to say, "Wait." But when you have seen vicious mobs lynch your mothers and fathers at will and drown your sisters and brothers at whim; when you have seen hate-filled policemen curse, kick and even kill your black brothers and sisters; when you see the vast majority of your twenty million Negro brothers smothering in an airtight cage of poverty in the midst of an affluent society; when you suddenly find your tongue twisted and your speech stammering as you seek to explain to your six-year-old daughter why she can't go to the public amusement park that has just been advertised on television, and see tears welling up in her eyes when she is told that Funtown is closed to colored children, and see ominous clouds of inferiority beginning to form in her little mental sky, and see her beginning to distort her personality by developing an unconscious bitterness toward white people; when you have to concoct an answer for a five-year-old son who is asking: "Daddy, why do white people treat colored people so mean?"; when you take a cross-county drive and find it necessary to sleep night after night in the uncomfortable corners of your automobile because no motel will accept you; when you are humiliated day in and day out by nagging signs reading "white" and "colored"; when your first name becomes "nigger," your middle name becomes "boy" (however old you are) and your last name becomes "John," and your wife and mother are never given the respected title "Mrs."; when you are harried by day and haunted by night by the fact that you are a Negro, living constantly at tiptoe stance, never quite knowing what to expect next, and are plagued with inner fears and outer resentments; when you are forever fighting a degenerating sense of "nobodiness"—then you will understand why we find it difficult to wait. There comes a time when the cup of endurance runs over, and men are no longer willing to be plunged into the abyss of despair. I hope, sirs, you can understand our legitimate and unavoidable impatience.

You express a great deal of anxiety over our willingness to break laws. This is certainly a legitimate concern. Since we so diligently urge people to obey the Supreme Court's decision of 1954 outlawing segregation in the public schools, at first glance it may seem rather paradoxical for us consciously to break laws. One may well ask: "How can you advocate breaking some laws and obeying others?" The answer lies in the fact that there are two types of laws: just and unjust. I would be the first to advocate obeying just laws. One has not only a legal but a moral responsibility to obey just laws. Conversely, one has a moral responsibility to disobey unjust laws. I would agree with St. Augustine that "an unjust law is no law at all."

Now, what is the difference between the two? How does one determine whether a law is just or unjust? A just law is a man-made code that squares with the moral law or the law of God. An unjust law is a code that is out of harmony with the moral law. To put it in the terms of St. Thomas Aquinas: An unjust law is a human law that is not rooted in eternal law and natural law. Any law that uplifts human personality is just. Any law that degrades human personality is unjust. All segregation statutes are unjust because segregation distorts the soul and damages the personality. It gives the segregator a false sense of superiority and the segregated a false sense of inferiority. . . .

Let me give another explanation. A law is unjust if it is inflicted on a minority that, as a result of being denied the right to vote, had no part in enacting or devising the law. Who can say that the legislature of Alabama which set up that state's segregation laws was democratically elected? Throughout Alabama all sorts of devious methods are used to prevent Negroes from becoming registered voters, and there are some counties in which, even though Negroes constitute a majority of the population, not a single Negro is registered. Can any law enacted under such circumstances be considered democratically structured? . . .

I hope you are able to see the distinction I am trying to point out. In no sense do I advocate evading or defying the law, as would the rabid segregationist. That would lead to anarchy. One who breaks an unjust law must do so openly, lovingly, and with a willingness to accept the penalty. I submit that an individual who breaks a law that conscience tells him is unjust, and who willingly accepts the penalty of imprisonment in order to arouse the conscience of the community over its injustice, is in reality expressing the highest respect for law.

Of course, there is nothing new about this kind of civil disobedience. It was evidenced sublimely in the refusal of Shadrach, Meshach and Abednego to obey the laws of Nebuchadnezzar, on the ground that a higher moral law was at stake. It was practiced superbly by the early Christians, who were willing to face hungry lions and the excruciating pain of chopping blocks rather than submit to certain unjust laws of the Roman Empire. To a degree, academic freedom is a reality today because Socrates practiced civil disobedience. In our own nation, the Boston Tea Party represented a massive act of civil disobedience. . . .

Oppressed people cannot remain oppressed forever. The yearning for freedom eventually manifests itself, and that is what has happened to the American Negro. Something within has reminded him of his birthright of freedom, and something without has reminded him that it can be gained. Consciously or unconsciously, he has been caught up by the *Zeitgeist,* and with his black brothers of Africa and his brown and yellow brothers of Asia, South America and the Caribbean, the United States Negro is moving with a sense of great urgency toward the promised land of racial justice. If one recognizes this vital urge that has engulfed the Negro community, one should readily understand why public demonstrations are taking place. The Negro has many pent-up resentments and latent frustrations, and he must release them. So let him march; let him make prayer pilgrimages to the city hall; let him go on freedom rides—and try to understand why he must do so. . . .

. . . Was not Martin Luther an extremist: "Here I stand; I cannot do otherwise, so help me God." And John Bunyan: "I will stay in jail to the end of my days before I make a butchery of my conscience." And Abraham Lincoln: "This nation cannot survive half slave and half free." And Thomas Jefferson: "We hold these truths to be self-evident, that all men are created equal . . ." So the question is not whether we will be extremists, but what kind of extremists we will be. Will we be extremists for hate or for love?

What's Your Opinion?

When—if at all—do you think it is morally proper to disobey the law? Do you think that Martin Luther King Jr. was justified in using civil disobedience to protest laws that barred black Americans from hotels, restaurants, and other public accommodations? Was it the best course of action?

CHAPTER 6

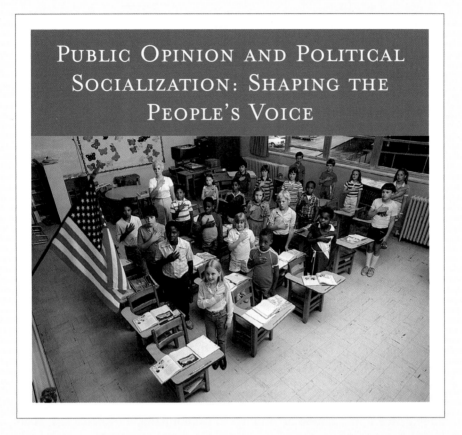

PUBLIC OPINION AND POLITICAL SOCIALIZATION: SHAPING THE PEOPLE'S VOICE

66 To speak with precision of public opinion is a task not unlike coming to grips with the Holy Ghost. **99**

V.O. KEY JR.[1]

As the U.S. troop buildup in the Persian Gulf region continued into 2003, most Americans were unsure of the best course of action. They had been hearing about Saddam Hussein for years and had concluded that he was a brutal tyrant and a terrorist threat. A majority expressed a willingness to support a war in Iraq if President George W. Bush deemed it necessary. But Americans had differing opinions on when and whether war would occur. Some wanted to give United Nations inspectors ample time to investigate Iraq's weapons program before a final decision on war was made. Others preferred to hold off on making the decision for war until the United States could line up international support. Still others supported more immediate action but preferred a bombing campaign to the launching of a ground war that might result in high casualties among U.S. forces.

Nevertheless, once the bombs started dropping on Iraq and U.S. ground troops poured into Iraq from their staging base in Kuwait, Americans strongly supported the action. Polls indicated that roughly 70 percent backed President Bush's decision to use military force against Iraq, with 20 percent opposed and 10 percent undecided.

The Iraq war is a telling example of the influence of public opinion on government: public opinion rarely forces officials to take a particular course of action. If President Bush had decided that the Iraq situation could have been resolved through UN weapons inspectors, public opinion would have supported his decision. A majority of Americans would also have supported the president if he had decided that war made sense only if it had broad international support or was limited to an air war.

Although public opinion has a central place in democratic societies because of a belief that public policy should reflect the will of the people, public opinion is seldom an exact guide to policy. Political leaders ordinarily enjoy leeway in choosing a course of action. Rather than fighting a war against Iraq, for example, President Bush could have decided to concentrate on finishing the war begun earlier in Afghanistan. Concentrations of Al Qaeda and Taliban fighters were still operating in Afghanistan, and terrorist leader Osama bin Laden was still at large. Bush also had the option of a law-enforcement response to the terrorist threat. He could have decided to pump resources into a worldwide police and intelligence effort aimed at finding and eliminating terrorist cells. The September 11, 2001, terrorist attacks on the World Trade Center and the Pentagon had created an expectation among Americans that the Bush administration would act decisively to counter the terrorist threat. But it was largely up to the president and his advisers to decide the precise nature of the response.

This chapter discusses public opinion and its influence on the U.S. political system. A major theme is that public opinion is a powerful yet inexact force in American politics.[2] The policies of the U.S. government cannot be understood apart from public opinion; at the same time, as stated above, public opinion is not a precise determinant of public policy. The main points made in this chapter are these:

★ *Public opinion consists of those views held by ordinary citizens that are openly expressed.* Public officials have many means of gauging public opinion but increasingly have relied on public opinion polls to make this determination.

★ *The process by which individuals acquire their political opinions is called political socialization.* This process begins during childhood, when, through family and school, Americans acquire many of their basic political values and beliefs. Socialization continues into adulthood, during which peers, political institutions and leaders, and the news media are major influences.

★ *Americans' political opinions are shaped by several frames of reference. Four of the most important are ideology, group attachments, partisanship, and political culture.* These frames of reference form the basis of political consensus and conflict among the general public.

★ *Public opinion has an important influence on government but ordinarily does not directly determine what officials will do.* Public opinion works primarily to place limits on the choices made by officials.

THE NATURE OF PUBLIC OPINION

Public opinion is a relatively new concept in the history of political thought. Not until pressures began to mount in the 1700s for representative government was there a need for a term to refer to what ordinary people thought about politics. The first English-speaking philosopher to write at length about public opinion was Jeremy Bentham (1748–1832).[3] Originally an advocate of government by an enlightened elite, Bentham came to believe that the public's views had to be taken into account if leaders were to govern properly.

Public opinion is now a widely used term, but it is a term that is often used inexactly. A common mistake is the assumption that "the public"—meaning the whole citizenry—actually has an opinion on most issues of public policy. In fact, most issues do not attract the attention of even a majority of citizens. Agricultural conservation programs, for example, are of intense interest to some farmers, hunters, and environmentalists but of little interest to most people. This pattern is so pervasive that opinion analysts have described America as having *many* publics.[4]

On numerous issues, there is literally no majority opinion. On some issues, such as agricultural conservation programs, a form of *pluralist* democracy usually prevails. Government responds to the views of particular groups. In other cases, *elitist* opinion prevails. On the question of U.S. relations with Finland, for example, there is little likelihood that ordinary citizens would know or care what the U.S. government does. In such instances, the policy opinions of an elite group of business and policy leaders ordinarily prevail. *Majority* opinion also can be decisive, but its influence normally is confined to a few broad issues that elicit widespread attention and concern, such as war, social security, and employment. This situation may suggest a limited role for popular majorities, but such issues, though few in number, typically have the greatest impact on society as a whole.

Hence, any definition of the term *public opinion* cannot be based on the assumption that all citizens, or even a majority, are actively interested in and hold a preference about all aspects of political life. **Public opinion** can be defined as the politically relevant opinions held by ordinary citizens that they express openly.[5] This expression need not be verbal. It could also take the form, for example, of a protest demonstration or a vote for one candidate rather than another. The crucial point is that a person's private thoughts on an issue become public opinion when they are expressed openly.

How Informed Is Public Opinion?

A practical obstacle to government by public opinion is that people have differing opinions; in responding to one side of an issue, government is compelled to reject other preferences. Public opinion can also be contradictory. Polls indicate, for example, that most Americans would like better schools, health care, and other public services while also favoring a reduction in taxes (see Figure 6–1). Which opinion of the people should govern—their desire for more services or their desire for lower taxes?

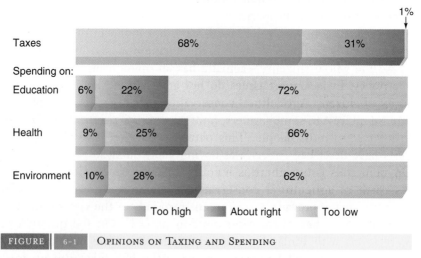

| FIGURE | 6-1 | OPINIONS ON TAXING AND SPENDING |

People's opinions are sometimes contradictory. Americans say, for example, that taxes are too high yet also say that government is spending too little in areas such as health, education, and the environment. *Source: Used by permission of National Opinion Research Center, University of Chicago.*

Dressed in his own clothes and as he requested, the remains (with wax head) of Jeremy Bentham are on display at University College, London. Bentham (1748–1832), who was the first English-speaking theorist to write at length on public opinion, is best known as a founder of utilitarian philosophy. He developed the principle of utility, which holds that action is acceptable if it promotes an increased amount of pleasure and unacceptable if it promotes an increased amount of pain.

Another limitation is that people's opinions, even on issues of great importance, are often misinformed. In the buildup to the U.S. invasion of Iraq in 2003, for example, polls revealed that more than half of the American public wrongly believed that Iraq had close ties to the terrorist network Al Qaeda and that Iraqis were among the nineteen terrorists who had flown airplanes into the World Trade Center and the Pentagon on September 11, 2001. Moreover, despite opposition to the war on the part of most Europeans, Asians, South Americans, and Africans, one-fourth of Americans wrongly believed that world opinion favored the war. Americans who held such views were more supportive of the Iraq war than were other Americans.[6]

Most Americans are not closely attentive to politics and therefore do not possess a lot of factual information. Americans are not unique in this respect, but in some areas they are less informed than citizens of most other Western democracies. In a seven-country survey, Americans ranked next to last (ahead of only Spaniards) in their ability to respond correctly to five factual questions about prominent world leaders and developments.[7] Despite America's leading role in the world, most Americans are less informed about international affairs than are most Europeans.

Even many college-educated Americans lack basic information about public affairs. A survey of Ivy League students found that one-third could not identify the British prime minister, half could not name both U.S. senators from their state, and three-fourths could not identify Abraham Lincoln as the author of the phrase "a government of the people, by the people, and for the people."[8]

Of course, citizens do not always have to be well informed about an issue to have a reasonable opinion about it. Opinions derive largely from people's values and interests.[9] People can have sound opinions on the abortion issue, for example, without a precise knowledge of what courts and lawmakers have done with regard to the issue. Nevertheless, the public's lack of information limits the role public opinion can play in policy formulation. The choice among policy options in some cases requires an understanding of the consequences of the different options. Citizens usually lack this information.

The Measurement of Public Opinion

Woodrow Wilson once said he had spent nearly all his adult life in government and yet had never seen a "government." What Wilson was saying, in effect, was that government is a system of relationships. A government is not a building or a person—it is not tangible in the way that a car or a bottle of soda is. So it is with public opinion. No one has ever seen a "public opinion," and thus it cannot be measured directly. It must be assessed indirectly.

Election returns are a traditional means of assessing public opinion. Journalists and politicians routinely draw conclusions about what citizens are thinking by analyzing how they vote. Letters to the editor in newspapers, e-mail messages to elected officials, and the size of crowds at mass demonstrations are other avenues for assessing public opinion. While all these indicators are useful guides for policymakers, none is a precise indicator of what the broad public is thinking. Elections offer citizens only a yes-no choice between the candidates, and different voters will choose the same candidate for different reasons. As for letter writers and demonstrators, they are nearly always *unrepresentative* of the population as a whole. Fewer than 1 percent of Americans participate each year in a mass demonstration, and fewer than 10 percent write to the president or to a member of Congress. Studies have found that the opinions of letter writers and demonstrators are more extreme than those of most citizens.

Public Opinion Polls   In an earlier day, indicators such as elections and letters to the editor were the only means by which public officials could gauge what the public was thinking. Today, they also rely on opinion polls or surveys, which provide a more systematic method of estimating public sentiment.[10]

In a **public opinion poll**, a relatively few individuals—the **sample**—are interviewed in order to estimate the opinions of a whole **population,** such as the residents of a city or the citizens of a country. If a sufficient number of individuals are chosen at random, their views will tend to be representative—that is, roughly the same as the views held by the population as a whole. *sample # n   pop # N*

How is it possible to measure the thinking of a large population on the basis of a relatively small sample? How can interviews with, say, one thousand Americans provide a reliable estimate of what 300 million

---

★ | **LEADERS**

George Gallup
(1901–84)

George Gallup has been called the father of the public opinion poll. Gallup began his career as a college professor at Drake University after earning a Ph.D. from the University of Iowa. Within a few years, he had taken a job at the New York advertising firm of Young & Rubicam, where he developed pioneering methods for measuring media impact. In 1935, he started a polling firm that sought to distinguish itself by touting "scientific polling"—polls based on systematic sampling. A year later, Gallup's method proved itself in dramatic fashion. The nation's best-known poll of the time, The *Literary Digest* poll, predicted a Republican landslide in the 1936 presidential election. Gallup's poll indicated a landslide for incumbent Democratic President Franklin D. Roosevelt. Roosevelt's victory made Gallup nationally known and gave instant credibility to both his organization and his polling method. Gallup lectured and wrote throughout his career, claiming repeatedly that polls could serve democracy by enabling political leaders to better understand what the public is thinking. Gallup said: "Polling is merely an instrument for gauging public opinion. When a president or any other leader pays attention to poll results, he is, in effect, paying attention to the views of the people. Any other interpretation is nonsense." The Gallup Organization remains the world's best-known survey firm.

are thinking? The answer is found in the laws of probability. Consider the hypothetical example of a huge jar filled with a million marbles, half of them red and half of them blue. If a blindfolded person reaches into the jar, the probability of selecting a marble of a given color is fifty-fifty. And if one thousand marbles are chosen in this random way, it is likely that about half of them will be red and about half will be blue. Opinion sampling works in the same way. If respondents are chosen at random from a population, their opinions will approximate those of the population as a whole.

Random selection is the key to scientific polling, which is based on *probability sampling*—taking a sample in which each individual in the population has a known probability of being chosen at random for inclusion. A scientific poll is different from the surveys found on many Internet sites, whose respondents are selecting themselves for the poll rather than being selected randomly by the pollster. A scientific poll also is different from the "people-in-the-street" interviews that news reporters sometimes conduct. Although a reporter might say that the opinions of those interviewed represent the views of the local population, this claim clearly is faulty. Interviews conducted on a downtown street at the noon hour, for example, will include a disproportionate number of business employees taking their lunch break. Housewives, teachers, and factory workers are among the many groups that would be underrepresented in such a sample.

The science of polling is such that the size of the sample, not the size of the population, is the key to accurate estimates. Although it might be assumed that a much larger sample would be required in order to poll accurately the people of the United States as opposed to the residents of Georgia, the sample requirements are nearly the same. Consider again the example of a huge jar filled with marbles, half of them red and half of them blue. If a thousand marbles were randomly selected, about half would be red and about half would be blue, regardless of whether the jar held 1 million, 10 million, or 100 million marbles. On the other hand, the size of the sample—the number of marbles selected—does matter. If only ten marbles were drawn, it might happen that five would be of each color, but it also would not be unusual for six, seven, or even eight to be of the same color. However, if a thousand marbles were drawn, it would be highly unusual for six hundred of the marbles, much less seven hundred or eight hundred of them, to be of the same color.

The accuracy of a poll is expressed in terms of **sampling error,** the degree to which the sample estimates might differ from what the population actually thinks. The larger the sample, the smaller the sampling error, which usually is expressed as a plus-or-minus percentage. For example, a properly drawn sample of a thousand individuals has a sampling error of roughly plus

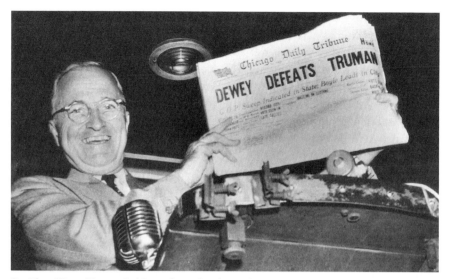

President Harry Truman holds up the early edition *Chicago Tribune* with the headline "Dewey Defeats Truman." The *Tribune* was responding to analysts' predictions that Dewey would win the 1948 election. A Gallup poll a few weeks before the election had shown Dewey with a seemingly insurmountable lead. The Gallup Organization decided that it did not need to conduct another poll closer to the election, a mistake it has not since repeated.

or minus 3 percent. Thus, if 55 percent of a sample of 1,000 respondents say they intend to vote for the Republican presidential candidate, then the probability is high that between 52 percent and 58 percent (55 percent plus or minus 3 percent) of all voters actually plan to vote Republican.

The impressive record of the Gallup poll in predicting the outcome of presidential elections indicates that the theoretical accuracy of polls can be matched in practice. The Gallup Organization has polled voters in every presidential election since 1936 (eighteen elections in all) and has erred badly only once: it stopped polling several weeks before the 1948 election and missed a late voter shift that carried Harry Truman to victory.

Problems with Polls Although pollsters assume that their samples are drawn from a particular population, it is seldom the case that everyone in that population has a chance of becoming part of the sample. Only rarely does a pollster have a list of all individuals in a population from which to draw a sample. An expedient alternative is a sample based on telephone numbers. Pollsters use computers to pick telephone numbers at random and then have interviewers dial those numbers to reach households. Within each sampled household, a respondent is then randomly selected. Because the computer is as likely to pick one telephone number as another and because more than 90 percent of U.S. homes have a telephone, a sample selected in this way is assumed to be representative of the population. Nevertheless, some Americans do not have phones, and many of those who are called either are not home or refuse to participate. These factors reduce the accuracy of telephone polling. In fact, although telephone polls continue to provide precise predictions of elections, pollsters are becoming increasingly worried about the future of such polls. The percentage of Americans who refuse to participate in telephone surveys has increased sharply in recent decades, and the use of cell phones—which are not included in computer-based telephone sampling—has risen significantly.

The accuracy of polling is also diminished when respondents are questioned on a topic they are unfamiliar with or have not thought about. In this case, respondents tend to answer the question, but they have an answer only because the pollster has asked them for one. In such cases, pollsters are measuring what scholars call "nonopinions."

The wording of questions can also affect poll results, particularly with regard to sensitive issues. For example, an NBC News/Wall Street Journal poll found that two-thirds of Americans favor federal funding for research on human embryonic stem cells, whereas a poll conducted for the U.S. Conference of Catholic Bishops found that only a fourth of Americans favor such funding. The wide difference in the two polls is explained by the wording of the question. The NBC News/Wall Street Journal's poll question asked directly about government funding, whereas the Conference of Catholic Bishops' poll question stressed the fact that stem cells are taken from human embryos.[11]

Despite these and other sources of error, the poll or survey is the most relied-upon method of measuring public opinion. More than one hundred organizations are in the business of conducting public opinion polls. Some, like the Gallup Organization, conduct polls that are then released to the news media by syndication. Most large news organizations also have their own in-house polls; one of the most prominent of these is the CBS News/New York Times poll. Some polling firms specialize in conducting surveys for candidates and officeholders.

POLITICAL SOCIALIZATION: HOW AMERICANS LEARN THEIR POLITICS

Analysts have long been interested in how public opinion originates. The learning process by which people acquire their political opinions, beliefs, and values is called **political socialization.** Just as a language, a religion, or an athletic skill is acquired through a learning process, so too are people's political orientations. Americans grow up to believe that free elections are the proper method of choosing leaders. People in some parts of the world are accustomed to other methods, which they find perfectly acceptable.

For most Americans, the socialization process starts in the family with exposure to the political loyalties and opinions of their parents. The schools later contribute to the process, as do the mass media, friends, work associates, and other agents. Political socialization is a lifelong process.

The Process of Political Socialization

The process of political socialization in the United States has several major characteristics. First, although socialization continues throughout life, most people's political outlook is substantially influenced by their childhood learning. That which is learned first is often lodged most firmly in a person's mind. Basic ideas about race, gender, and political affiliation, for example, are often formed uncritically in childhood, much in the way belief in a particular religion—typically the religion of one's parents—is acquired.

 HOW THE UNITED STATES COMPARES

National Pride

Americans are justifiably proud of their nation. It is the oldest continuous democracy in the world, an economic powerhouse, and a diverse yet harmonious society.

What Americans may not recognize, because it is so much a part of everyday life in America, is the degree to which they are bombarded with messages and symbols of their nation's greatness. Political socialization in the United States is not the rigid program of indoctrination that some societies impose on their people. Nevertheless, Americans receive a thorough political education. Their country's values are impressed on them by every medium of communication: newspapers, daily conversations, television, movies, books. After the terrorist attacks of September 11, 2001, these tendencies reached new heights. The NBC television network outfitted its peacock logo with stars and stripes, and computer-generated flags festooned the other networks' broadcasts.

The words and symbols that regularly tell Americans of their country's greatness are important to its unity. In the absence of a common ancestral heritage to bind them, Americans need other methods to instill and reinforce the idea that they are one people.

(continued)

As discussed in Chapter 1, America's political ideals have this effect, as do everyday reminders such as the flying of the flag on homes and private buildings, a practice that is almost uniquely American. (Elsewhere, flags are rarely displayed except on public buildings.)

One indicator of Americans' political socialization is their high level of national pride. Harvard University's Pippa Norris (in Marian Sawer's edited volume *The People's Choice*) constructed an index of national pride based on people's admiration for their country's political, economic, artistic, sporting, scientific, and other achievements. Americans ranked at the top, as shown by the following chart, which is based on Norris's index:

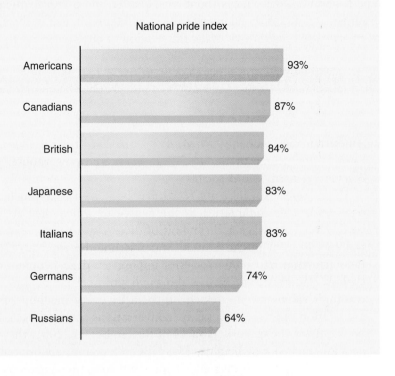

National pride index

Americans	93%
Canadians	87%
British	84%
Japanese	83%
Italians	83%
Germans	74%
Russians	64%

A second characteristic of political socialization is that its effect is cumulative—early learning affects later learning. Individuals have psychological defenses that protect beliefs acquired earlier in life. Many people, for example, remain lifelong Republicans or Democrats even as their personal lives or political conditions change in ways that might logically lead them to identify with the other party. Of course, political change can and does take place. Historically, major shifts in political orientation have occurred around major upheavals and have been concentrated among younger adults, whose beliefs are less firmly rooted than are those of older adults. The **age-cohort tendency** holds that a significant change in the pattern of political socialization is typically concentrated among younger citizens. For example, President Franklin Roosevelt's New Deal, which sought to alleviate the economic hardship of the Great Depression, prompted many younger Republicans, but not many older ones, to shift their loyalty to the Democratic party.

The Agents of Political Socialization

The socialization process takes place through a variety of agents, including family, schools, mass media, peers, and political leaders and events. It is helpful to consider briefly some of these **agents of socialization** and how they affect political learning.

Families The family is a powerful agent of socialization because it has a near-monopoly on the attention of the young child, who places great trust in what a parent says. By the time the child is a teenager and is not likely to listen to any advice a parent might offer, many of the beliefs and values that will stay with the child throughout life are already in place. Many adults are Republicans or Democrats today largely because their parents backed that party. They can give all sorts of reasons for preferring their party to the other, but the reasons come later in life. The loyalty comes first, during childhood. The family also contributes to basic orientations that, while not directly political, have political significance. For example, American families tend to be more egalitarian than families in other nations, and American children often have a voice in family decisions. Basic American values such as equality and individualism have roots in patterns of family interaction.[12]

Schools The school, like the family, affects children's basic political beliefs. Teachers at the elementary level extol the exploits of national heroes such as George Washington, Abraham Lincoln, and Martin Luther King Jr. and praise the country's economic and political systems.[13] Although students in the middle and high school grades receive a more nuanced version of American history, it tends to emphasize the nation's great moments—for example, its decisive role in the two world wars. U.S. schools are probably more instrumental in building support for the nation than are the schools in other democracies. The Pledge of Allegiance, which is recited daily in many U.S. schools, has no equivalent in European countries. Schools also contribute to Americans' sense of social equality. Most American children, regardless of family income, attend public schools and study a fairly standard curriculum. In many countries, schoolchildren are separated at an early age, with some placed in vocational classes while others are slotted in courses that will lead them to attend college.

Mass Media   The mass media are another powerful socializing agent. The themes and images that dominate the media affect people's perceptions of their world. For example, repeated exposure to crime on television can lead people to believe that society itself is more violent than it actually is. Similarly, people's perceptions of political leaders are affected to some extent by how those leaders are represented in the media. When leaders are regularly portrayed as manipulative, for example, people tend to regard them as self-serving.[14]

Peers   Peer groups—friends, neighbors, and coworkers—tend to reinforce what a person already believes. One reason is that most people trust the opinions of their friends and associates. Many individuals also are unwilling to deviate too far from what their peers think. In *The Spiral of Silence*, Elisabeth Noelle-Neumann contends that most individuals are reluctant to express contrary opinions. One effect, she argues, is to make prevailing opinions appear to be more firmly and widely held then they actually are.[15]

Political Institutions and Leaders   Citizens look to political leaders and institutions, particularly the president and political parties, as guides to opinion.[16] In the period immediately after the terrorist attacks on the World Trade Center and the Pentagon on September 11, 2001, many Americans were confused about who the enemy was and what the response should be. That state of mind changed dramatically ten days later after a televised speech by President Bush in which he identified the Al Qaeda and Taliban forces in Afghanistan as the immediate target of what would become a war on terrorism. In polls taken immediately after the speech, nine of every ten Americans said they shared Bush's views.

Churches   Beginning with the Puritans in the seventeenth century, churches have played a substantial role in shaping Americans' social and political opinions. Most Americans say they believe in God, most attend church at least occasionally, and most belong to a religion that includes teachings on the proper form of society. Moreover, most Americans say

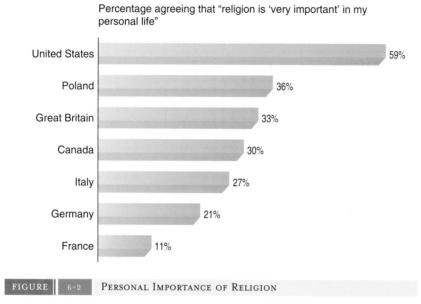

Percentage agreeing that "religion is 'very important' in my personal life"

Country	Percentage
United States	59%
Poland	36%
Great Britain	33%
Canada	30%
Italy	27%
Germany	21%
France	11%

FIGURE 6-2 PERSONAL IMPORTANCE OF RELIGION

Religion is more important to Americans than to Europeans or Canadians.
Source: Pew Research Center for the People and the Press, 2002.

that religion has answers to many of the problems facing today's society. In these and other respects, churches and religion are a more powerful force in the United States than in most other Western countries (see Figure 6–2).

Scholars have not studied the impact of churches on political socialization as closely as they have studied influences such as schools and the media.[17] Nevertheless, churches are a significant source of political attitudes, including those related to society's obligations to children, the poor, and the unborn. (The impact of religion is discussed further in a later section of this chapter.)

FRAMES OF REFERENCE: HOW AMERICANS THINK POLITICALLY

What are the frames of reference that guide the political thinking of Americans? The question is an important one. Shared opinions enable people to find common cause. The opinions of millions of Americans would mean little if everyone's ideas were different, but if enough

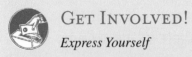
"Get up, stand up: stand up for your rights!" These are the words of one of reggae icon Bob Marley's best-known songs.

American citizens enjoy an impressive array of personal liberties, including the right to speak freely. Yet studies find that many Americans do not voice their opinion when they think it will bring them into conflict with authorities or associates. Social pressure—and in some cases fear of retribution—leads them to stay silent when they hear opposing opinions. Alexis de Tocqueville noted this tendency when he toured America in the 1830s. Tocqueville said that he knew of no country in the world where people were freer to think and speak for themselves. But then he added, "I know of no country in which there is so little independence of mind and real freedom of discussion as in America." Tocqueville attributed the tendency to Americans' embrace of majority opinion. Within that opinion, he said, there is room for disagreement. Outside it, there is social isolation.

Consider, for example, opinions on the Iraq war, which vary sharply across society and yet tend to be similar among people who talk with each other regularly. It is rare for someone who opposes the war but whose acquaintances or work associates support it to express his or her view openly and often. The same is true of someone who supports the war but is surrounded by people who oppose it.

One effect of this tendency is to lead those who hold the majority opinion to believe that others think as they do and that their opinion is therefore the only proper one. The failure of citizens to openly express their opinions also means forgoing the personal liberty that the Constitution provides and that other Americans have sacrificed to preserve at critical moments in the nation's history. Tocqueville identified yet another effect of citizen silence. By failing to speak their minds, citizens empower government to think and speak for them. As Tocqueville wrote:

> It does not break wills, but it softens them, bends them, and directs them; it rarely forces one to act, but it constantly opposes itself to one's acting; it does not destroy, it prevents things from being born; it does not tyrannize, it hinders, compromises, enervates, extinguishes, dazes, and finally reduces [citizens] to being nothing more than a herd of timid and industrious animals of which the government is the shepherd.

Tocqueville may have overstated his case, but the point is a valid one. As a citizen, you have more to lose than to gain by failing to express your opinions. Stand up for what you believe. Stand up for your rights.

people think the same way they might decide to work together to promote their view.

The frames of reference through which Americans think about politics include cultural values, ideology, group attachments, and partisanship.

Cultural Thinking: Common Ideas

As was discussed in Chapter 1, Americans embrace a common set of ideals. Principles such as liberty, equality, and individualism have always meant somewhat different things to Americans but nonetheless are a source of agreement. For example, government programs aimed at redistributing wealth from the rich to the poor are popular among Europeans but are less appealing to Americans, who have a deeper commitment to individualism.

There are limits, of course, to the degree to which Americans' basic beliefs shape their policy opinions. For more than three centuries, African Americans were inferior by law to white Americans, despite the American creed that "all men are created equal." Such inconsistencies speak to the all-too-human capacity to voice one idea and live another. Nevertheless, Americans' political ideals have a powerful influence on their opinions.

Ideological Thinking: The Outlook of Some

Analysts sometimes use words such as *liberal* and *conservative* to describe how ordinary Americans think about politics. These are ideological terms, as are terms such as socialism and communism. An **ideology** is a consistent pattern of political attitudes that stems from a core belief. The core belief of socialism, for example, is that society should ensure that every person's basic economic needs are met. Accordingly, a socialist would support public policies that provide for economic security, such as a government-guaranteed minimum annual income for all families.

America's major ideologies are rooted in beliefs about equality and liberty. The importance that people attach to one or the other of these ideals and the degree to which they think government involvement promotes or impedes it affect their ideological stance. Economic liberals, for example, look to government to create a more equal society than that which results from unregulated markets or untaxed incomes. In contrast, economic conservatives believe that too much government involvement in the economy undermines personal liberty and initiative.

Today, ideological conflict in the United States centers on the scope of government involvement in the economic realm and in the area of social values. In order to measure public attitudes on these two dimensions, pollsters have developed a variety of methods. The Gallup poll employs a two-question method that is widely used:

1. Some people think the government is trying to do too many things that should be left to individuals and businesses. Others think that government should do more to solve our country's problems. Which view is closer to your own?
2. Some people think the government should promote traditional values in our society. Others think that the government should not favor any particular set of values. Which view is closer to your own?

The Gallup poll's two questions are used to categorize Americans into four ideological types. **Liberals** are those who say that government should do more to solve the country's problems and who say that government ought not to support traditional values at the expense of less conventional ones. Thus, for example, a liberal would be inclined to favor an increase in government-provided health care and also to support civil unions for same-sex couples. **Conservatives** are those who think government should be sparing in its programs and who feel government should use its power to uphold traditional values. Thus, a conservative would be likely to oppose an increase in government-provided health care and to oppose civil unions. **Libertarians** are those who are reluctant to use government either as a means of economic redistribution or as a means of favoring particular social values. Thus, a libertarian would prefer that government not get more deeply involved in health-care provision and would be inclined to permit civil unions. **Populists** are those who would use government for both the purpose of economic redistribution and the purpose of guarding traditional values. Thus, a populist would be inclined to support increased health-care spending and to oppose civil unions. (To determine your ideology by this method, see "Political Culture.")

Of these four types, conservatives are the largest group. The proportion of Americans in each category, however, has been found to change as national conditions change. After the economy turned downward in 2000, for example, the number of populists and liberals rose as Americans increasingly looked to government for solutions to their economic problems.[18]

Although ideology is a component of public opinion, its scope can be overstated. Any attempt to neatly categorize Americans by ideology must confront the inconvenient fact that most people want government to solve some problems and want the private sector to address others.

POLITICAL CULTURE
Americans' Ideologies

In the United States, the key dimensions of political conflict center on the extent of government intervention in the economic marketplace and in the maintenance of traditional values. Government intervention in either sphere has implications for liberty—the amount of freedom you should have in deciding on your lifestyle and in making economic choices. Government intervention in the economic sphere can also affect equality—government has been the principal means of providing economic security for those vulnerable to market forces.

You can test your ideology—and thus in a way your conception of liberty and equality—by asking yourself the two measurement questions used in Gallup surveys:

1. Some people think the government is trying to do too many things that should be left to individuals and businesses. Others think that government should do more to solve our country's problems. Which view is closer to your own?

   a. Government is doing too much.

   b. Government should do more.

2. Some people think the government should promote traditional values in our society. Others think that the government should not favor any particular set of values. Which view is closer to your own?

   a. Government should promote traditional values.

   b. Government should not favor particular values.

If you had been a respondent in a poll that asked these questions, you would have been classified as a *conservative* if you agreed with the first statement of each question (1a and 2a); a *liberal* if you agreed with the second statement of each question (1b and 2b); a *libertarian* if you agreed with the first statement of the first question (1a) and the second statement of the second question (2b); and a *populist* if you agreed with the second statement of the first question (1b) and the first statement of the second question (2a).

Is this the label you normally use when describing your political beliefs? If not, do you think it's a more appropriate label? Why or why not?

Many citizens are neither consistently pro-government nor consistently anti-government when it comes to how best to solve the nation's problems.

Moreover, as illustrated by the example of people who favor steep tax cuts while also wanting more spending on government services, some citizens hold incompatible opinions. Thus, by a strict definition of what constitutes a political ideology—a *consistent* pattern of political attitudes—many Americans do not have one. Studies indicate that no more than a third of Americans hold consistent opinions across a broad range of issues.[19]

Although only a minority of Americans can be classified as true ideologues, ideology nonetheless remains a useful way to talk about broad patterns of opinion. Ideological terms help describe the choices Americans make and the conflicts that divide them. Beginning with the New Deal, for example, liberal attitudes—a preference for government action—dominated American politics. Later, as Americans became less trusting of government and more worried about its financial cost, conservative opinions gained strength. Most recently, Americans have been split between those who want government to do less and those who want it to do more. Some observers believe, in fact, that Americans today are wider apart ideologically than at any time in recent decades. (Chapters 8 and 11 will discuss this topic further in the context of splits between Republicans and Democrats.)

Group Thinking: The Outlook of Many

For most citizens, groups are a more important frame of reference than is ideology.[20] Many Americans see politics through the lens of the group or groups that define who they are. Farmers, for example, care a lot more about agricultural issues than do members of other groups. And although farmers are more likely than most other Americans to oppose government benefit programs, they favor farm subsidies. Their ideological opposition to "big government" suddenly disappears when their benefits are at issue.

Because of the country's great size, its settlement by various immigrant groups, and its economic pluralism, Americans are a very diverse people. Later chapters examine group tendencies more fully, but it is useful here to mention a few major group orientations: religion, class, region, race and ethnicity, gender, and age.

Religion   Religious beliefs have always been a source of solidarity among group members and a source of conflict with outsiders. As Catholics and

Religion is a powerful socializing force in American life. Churches, synagogues, mosques, and temples are places where Americans acquire values and beliefs that can affect their opinions about politics. Shown here are Muslim men gathering to pray at a mosque in Garden Grove, California. Traditionally, men and women have prayed in different parts of the mosque. Some U.S. mosques have integrated their prayer services, and a few have allowed women to lead prayer sessions—changes that have been sharply criticized by traditionalists.

Jews came to America in large numbers in the nineteenth and early twentieth centuries, they encountered intense hostility from some Protestants. Today, Catholics, Protestants, and Jews have similar opinions on most policy issues.

Nevertheless, important religious differences remain, although the opposing sides are not always the same. Fundamentalist Protestants and Roman Catholics oppose legalized abortion more strongly than do mainline Protestants and Jews. This split reflects different religious teachings about when human life begins—at conception, or at a later stage in the development of the fetus. Religious doctrine also affects Americans' opinions on poverty programs. Catholics and Jews are more supportive of such programs than are Protestants. An obligation to help the poor is a larger theme in Catholic and Jewish teachings, whereas self-reliance plays a larger role in Protestant thought.

The most powerful religious force in contemporary American politics is the so-called religious right, which consists primarily of individuals who see themselves as born-again Christians and who view the Bible as infallible truth. Their views on issues such as gay rights, abortion, and school prayer differ significantly from those of the population as a whole. A Time/CNN survey found that born-again Christians are a third more likely than other Americans to agree that "the Supreme Court and the Congress have gone too far in keeping religious and moral values like prayer out of our laws, schools, and many areas of our lives."

Class Economic class has less influence on political opinion in the United States than in Europe, but it is nevertheless related to opinions on certain economic issues. For example, lower-income Americans are more supportive of social welfare programs, business regulation, and progressive taxation than are Americans in higher-income categories.

An obstacle to class-based politics in the United States is that people with similar incomes but differing occupations do not share the same opinions. Support for collective bargaining, for example, is substantially higher among factory workers than among small farmers, service workers, and workers in the skilled crafts, even though the average income of members of all these groups is similar. The interplay of class and opinion is examined more closely in Chapter 9, which discusses interest groups.

Region For a long period, region nearly defined American politics. The North and South were divided over the issue of race, which spilled over into issues such as education and welfare policy. Racial progress has diminished the regional divide, as has the relocation of millions of Americans from the Northeast and Midwest to the South and West. The policy beliefs of these newcomers tend to be less conservative than those of people native to these regions. Nevertheless, regional differences are still evident in the areas of social welfare, civil rights, and national defense. Residents of the southern, Rocky Mountain, and Great Plains states have more conservative opinions on these issues than do Americans elsewhere—a reflection of long-standing regional attitudes toward government. The differences are large enough that when analysts talk about "red states" (Republican bastions) and "blue states" (Democratic bastions), they basically are referring to regions. The red states are concentrated in the South, Great Plains, and Rocky Mountains. The blue states are found mostly in the Northeast and northern Midwest and on the West Coast (see "States in the Nation").

Race and Ethnicity As Chapter 5 pointed out, race and ethnicity have a significant influence on opinions. Whites and African Americans, for example, differ on issues of integration: black people more strongly support affirmative action, busing, and other measures designed to promote racial equality and integration. Racial and ethnic groups also differ on economic issues, largely as a result of differences in their economic situations. Law enforcement is another area in which different opinions exist. Opinion polls reveal that blacks are far less likely than whites to trust the police and the judicial system.

Gender   Although male-female differences of opinion are small on most issues, gender does affect opinion in some policy areas. For example, women are somewhat more supportive than men of abortion rights and affirmative action. A Gallup poll found a 63 percent to 53 percent breakdown in support for affirmative action. The difference is even larger on some social welfare issues, such as poverty and education assistance. Compared with men, women have more liberal opinions on these issues, a reflection of their greater economic vulnerability and their traditional responsibility for child care. A *Washington Post*/ABC News poll found, for example, that women were 20 percent more likely than men to favor increased spending for public education.

Women and men also differ in their opinions on the use of military force. In nearly every case, women are less supportive of military action than men are. The terrorist attacks on the World Trade Center and the Pentagon on September 11, 2001, produced an exception to the normal pattern. Men and women were almost equally likely (90 percent and 88 percent, respectively) to favor a military response. But they differed in expected ways when questioned about the Iraq conflict. Women were less likely than men to think that military intervention in Iraq was worthwhile (see Figure 6–3).

Differences such as these contribute to the gender gap discussed in Chapter 5. Women and men do not differ sharply in their political views, but they differ enough to respond somewhat differently to issues, events, and candidates.

Age   Age has always affected opinions, but the gap between young and old is widening. In her book *Young v. Old*, political scientist Susan MacManus notes that the elderly tend to oppose increases in public school funding while supporting increases in social security and Medicare (government-assisted medical care for retirees). MacManus predicts that issues of age will increasingly dominate American politics and that the elderly will have the political clout to prevail. They vote at a much higher rate than do young people, are better organized politically (through groups such as the powerful AARP), and are increasing in number as a result of lengthened life spans (the so-called graying of America).[21]

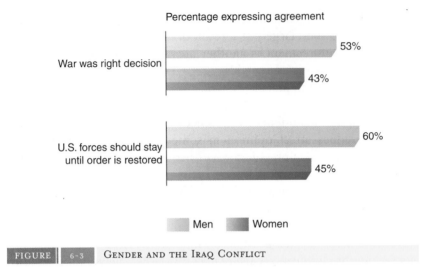

FIGURE 6-3 GENDER AND THE IRAQ CONFLICT

Compared with men, women are somewhat less inclined to support military force as a means of resolving international conflicts. This difference has been evident in polls on support for the Iraq war, as these examples illustrate. *Source:* (In order of questions): *Pew Research Center for the People and the Press, February 2005; ABC News/Washington Post poll, November 2005.*

Crosscutting Cleavages   Although group loyalty can have a powerful impact on people's opinions, this influence is diminished when identification with one group is offset by identification with other groups. In a pluralistic society such as the United States, groups tend to be "crosscutting"—that is, each group includes individuals who also belong to other groups, where they encounter different people and opinions. Crosscutting cleavages encourage individuals to appreciate and understand differences, which leads them toward moderate opinions. By comparison, in societies such as Northern Ireland, where group loyalties are reinforcing rather than crosscutting, opinions are intensified by personal interactions. Catholics and Protestants in Northern Ireland live largely apart from each other, differing not only in their religions but also in their income levels, neighborhoods of residence, ethnicities, and loyalties to the government. The result is widespread mistrust between Northern Ireland's Catholics and Protestants.

Partisan Thinking: The Line That Divides

In the everyday world of politics, no source of opinion more clearly divides Americans than that of their partisanship. Figure 6–4 provides

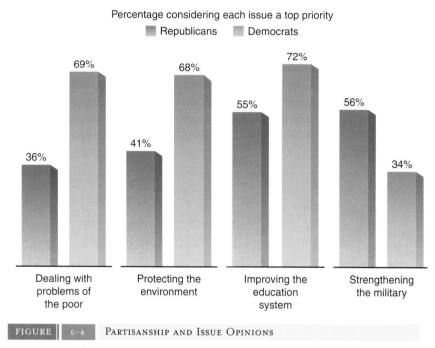

Percentage considering each issue a top priority
▓ Republicans   ▓ Democrats

36% 69%	41% 68%	55% 72%	56% 34%
Dealing with problems of the poor	Protecting the environment	Improving the education system	Strengthening the military

FIGURE 6-4 PARTISANSHIP AND ISSUE OPINIONS

Republicans and Democrats differ significantly in their policy opinions and priorities. *Source: Pew Research Center for the People and the Press, 2006.*

examples, but these show only a few of the differences. On nearly every major political issue, Republicans and Democrats have views that are at least somewhat different. In many cases, such as spending programs for the poor, the differences are substantial.

Party identification refers to a person's ingrained sense of loyalty to a political party. Party identification is not formal membership in a party but rather an emotional attachment to a party—the feeling that "I am a Democrat" or "I am a Republican." About two-thirds of adults call themselves Democrats or Republicans. Of the one-third who prefer the label "Independent," most say they lean toward one party or the other and tend to vote primarily for that party's candidates.

Early studies concluded that party loyalties were highly stable and seldom changed over the course of adult life.[22] Subsequent studies have shown that party loyalties are more fluid than originally believed; they can be influenced by the issues and candidates of the moment.[23] Nevertheless, most adults do not switch their party loyalties easily, and a substantial proportion never waver from their initial commitment to a party, which can often be traced to childhood influences.

Once acquired, partisanship affects how people perceive and interpret events. An example is the differing opinions of Republicans and Democrats about U.S. military intervention in Kosovo in 1999 and in Iraq in 2003. Democrats were more supportive of the first war, while Republicans were more supportive of the second. While differences in the nature and purpose of these wars might partially explain this split, partisanship clearly does. The first of these conflicts was initiated by a Democratic president, Bill Clinton, while the second was begun by a Republican president, George W. Bush.

★ ‖ STATES IN THE NATION

Party Loyalties in the States

The strength of the major parties varies substantially among the states. One indicator of party dominance is the degree to which the party identification of state residents favors one party or the other. In opinion polls, party identification is measured by a question of the following nature: "Generally speaking, do you think of yourself as a Republican, a Democrat, an Independent, or what?" The Gallup Organization, using the results of roughly forty thousand interviews it conducted in 2004, estimated the state-by-state distribution of Republican and Democratic identifiers. For the map below, a state is classified as Republican if Republican identifiers outnumber Democratic identifiers by 7 percentage points or more. It is classified as Democratic if Democratic identifiers have an advantage of 7 percentage points or more. The remaining states are classified as competitive. Republican strength is concentrated in the South and in the Great Plains and Rocky Mountain states by this indicator, while Democratic strength is concentrated in the Northeast and upper Midwest. Other indicators of party strength, such as control of state elective offices, would result in similar categorizations of the states.

Q: Why is the concentration of Republicans particularly high in some states of the South, the Great Plains, and the Rocky Mountains?

A: The South swung Republican after the Democratic party took the lead on civil rights in the 1960s. The Great Plains and Rocky Mountain areas have traditionally been Republican, a reflection in part of the rugged individualism that defined their early settlement and contributed to a preference for small government.

(continued)

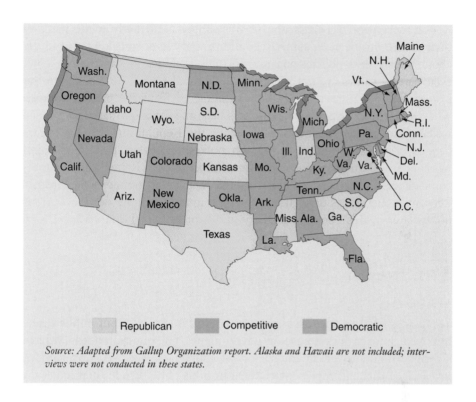

Republican   Competitive   Democratic

Source: Adapted from Gallup Organization report. Alaska and Hawaii are not included; interviews were not conducted in these states.

Senator John McCain (R-Ariz.) stumps in Oregon for the reelection of George W. Bush in 2004. A party maverick on some issues, McCain understood that his support of Bush was necessary if he was to build the Republican support he would need should he run for the presidency himself in 2008. Partisanship is one of the strongest influences on citizens' political opinions.

For most people, partisanship is not simply blind faith in the party of their choice. To be sure, some Republicans and Democrats know very little about their party's policies and unthinkingly embrace its candidates. However, party loyalties are not randomly distributed across the population but instead follow patterns that would be predicted from the parties' policies. The Democratic party, for example, has been the driving force behind social welfare and workers' rights policies, while the Republican party has spearheaded probusiness and tax reduction policies. The fact that most union workers are Democrats and most businesspeople are Republicans is not a coincidence. Their partisanship is rooted in their economic self-interest.[24] This and other issues of partisanship are examined in more detail at various points later in this book, particularly in Chapters 7, 8, 11, and 12.

THE INFLUENCE OF PUBLIC OPINION ON POLICY

Yet unanswered in our discussion is a central question about public opinion: what impact does it have on government? The question does not have a firm or final answer. In any society of appreciable size, self-government takes place through representative institutions. The people themselves do not directly decide issues of policy but instead entrust them to elected and appointed officials. Governing decisions are complex, as are the factors that go into them, including the influence of public opinion.

Some observers claim that officials are relatively insensitive to public opinion—that they are so entrenched in their positions that, however much they claim to serve the people, they actually pay little attention to what ordinary citizens think.[25] This assessment undoubtedly applies to some officials and some issues. However, the most comprehensive study ever conducted on the relationship between public opinion and policy concluded that public opinion does in fact sway government. The study examined fifty years of polls and policy decisions and found that when public opinion on an issue changed, policy usually changed in the direction of the change in public opinion. In the case of major issues, this pattern was particularly evident—in such cases, policy typically aligned with public opinion.[26]

However, a more recent study by Lawrence Jacobs and Robert Shapiro found a widening gap between public opinion and policy, apparently because elected officials of both parties have tilted toward the more extreme positions favored by powerful groups within their respective parties (such as the Christian right within the Republican party and lifestyle liberals within the Democratic party).[27] Jacobs and Shapiro nonetheless

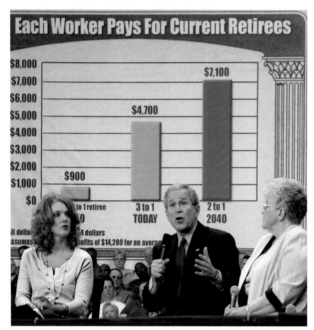

Each Worker Pays For Current Retirees

$8,000
$7,000
$6,000
$5,000 $4,700
$4,000
$3,000
$2,000
$1,000 $900
$0
        to 1 retiree   3 to 1   2 to 1
          0   TODAY   2040
ll dolla   4 dollars
ssumes   efits of $14,200 for an avera

$7,100

In his 2005 State of the Union address, President Bush outlined key provisions of his plan to partially privatize social security. Here he argues for it at a town-hall-style meeting at the University of Notre Dame. A year later, the proposal was dead. Republican lawmakers abandoned it out of fear that it would cost them votes in the 2006 midterm elections.

conclude that officials remain sensitive to public opinion on many issues, particularly those that could become campaign issues. As the midterm congressional elections approached in 2006, for example, a number of congressional Republicans backed away from President Bush's controversial proposal to change the social security program to allow workers to put some of their social security taxes into private investment accounts. These Republicans changed their stance when polls showed declining support for the proposal and for the president.

If elections heighten officials' attention to public opinion, so do particular issues. There are certain actions that officials shy away from for fear of public retribution. Tax hikes are a prime example. Politicians ordinarily will go to great lengths—including borrowing huge amounts of money to shift the problem to future generations—to avoid a major tax increase. Angry taxpayers are officeholders' worst nightmare.

Such examples, however, do not provide an answer to the question of whether public officials are *sufficiently* responsive to public opinion. This question is complicated by the fact that it is partly a normative one—the answer rests on beliefs about the proper relationship between people's opinions and government policies. As discussed in Chapter 2, some theorists hold that representatives should base their policy decisions on what they believe will best serve the people's interests, while others claim that the people themselves are the best judge of their interests and it is the representatives' duty to pay close heed to the people's demands. The question is also complicated by the fact that politics involves attempts to influence public opinion. Citizens' opinions are not fixed. They can be activated, changed, and crystallized through political action. Political leaders invest enormous amounts of money and time in an effort to get citizens to see things their way.

In fact, one of the best indicators of the power of public opinion is the great effort made by political leaders to harness it in support of their goals. In American politics, popular demand for a policy is a powerful argument for that policy. For this reason and others, great effort is made to organize and represent public opinion through elections (Chapter 7), political parties (Chapter 8), interest groups (Chapter 9), the news media (Chapter 10), and political institutions (Chapters 11 through 14).

SUMMARY

Public opinion can be defined as those opinions held by ordinary citizens that they openly express. Public officials have many ways of assessing public opinion, such as the outcomes of elections, but they have increasingly come to rely on public opinion polls. There are many possible sources of error in polls, and surveys sometimes present a misleading portrayal of the public's views. However, a properly conducted poll can be an accurate indication of what the public is thinking and can dissuade political leaders from thinking that the views of the most vocal citizens (such as demonstrators and letter writers) are also the views of the broader public.

The process by which individuals acquire their political opinions is called political socialization. During childhood, the family and schools are important sources of basic political attitudes, such as beliefs about the parties and the nature of the U.S. political and economic systems. Many of the basic orientations that Americans acquire during childhood remain with them in adulthood, but socialization is a continuing process. Major shifts in opinion during adulthood are usually the consequence of changing political conditions; for example, the Great Depression of the 1930s was the catalyst for wholesale changes in Americans' opinions on the government's economic role. Short-term fluctuations in opinion can result from new political issues and problems. Individuals' opinions in these cases are affected by prior beliefs, peers, political leaders, and the news media. Events themselves are also a significant short-term influence on opinions.

The frames of reference that guide Americans' opinions include cultural beliefs, such as individualism, which affect what people will find politically acceptable and desirable. Opinions can also stem from ideology, although most citizens do not have a strong and consistent ideological attachment. In addition, individuals develop opinions as a result of group orientations, notably religion, income level, occupation, region, race, ethnicity, gender, and age. Partisanship is perhaps the major source of political opinions; Republicans and Democrats differ in their voting behavior and views on many policy issues.

Public opinion has a significant influence on government but seldom determines exactly what government will do in a particular instance. Public opinion serves to constrain the policy choices of officials. Some policy actions are beyond the range of possibility because the public will not accept change in existing policy or will not seriously consider policy that seems clearly at odds with basic American values. Evidence indicates that officials are somewhat attentive to public opinion on highly visible and controversial issues of public policy.

KEY TERMS

age-cohort tendency (*p. 203*)
agents of socialization (*p. 203*)
conservatives (*p. 208*)
ideology (*p. 207*)
liberals (*p. 208*)
libertarians (*p. 208*)
party identification (*p. 217*)

political socialization (*p. 200*)
population (*p. 197*)
populists (*p. 208*)
public opinion (*p. 194*)
public opinion poll (*p. 197*)
sample (*p. 197*)
sampling error (*p. 198*)

SUGGESTED READINGS

Alvarez, R. Michael, and John Brehm. *Hard Choices, Easy Answers: Values, Information, and American Public Opinion.* Princeton, N.J.: Princeton University Press, 2002. An analysis that argues that what citizens know about politics is assessed in the context of their values and beliefs.

Asher, Herbert. *Polling and the Public*, 6th ed. Washington, D.C.: Congressional Quarterly Press, 2004. A guide to public opinion poll methods and analysis.

Canes-Wrone, Brandice. *Who Leads Whom? Presidents, Policy, and the Public.* Chicago: University of Chicago Press, 2005. A look at recent presidents and their policies in the context of public opinion.

Green, Donald, Bradley Palmquist, and Eric Schickler. *Partisan Hearts and Minds.* New Haven, Conn.: Yale University Press, 2002. An analysis that concludes partisanship powerfully affects how citizens respond to candidates and issues.

Jacobs, Lawrence, and Robert Shapiro. *Politicians Don't Pander.* Chicago: University of Chicago Press, 2000. An analysis that concludes politicians are not driven by polls.

MacManus, Susan A. *Young v. Old: Generational Combat in the Twenty-first Century.* Boulder, Colo.: Westview Press, 1996. A study of the emerging conflict in the political self-interest of younger and older Americans.

Stimson, James. *Tides of Consent: How Public Opinion Shapes American Politics.* New York: Cambridge University Press, 2004. An analysis of trends in public opinion and their political impact.

Zaller, John R. *The Nature and Origins of Mass Opinion.* New York: Cambridge University Press, 1992. A superb analysis of the nature of public opinion.

LIST OF WEBSITES

http://www.policy.com/ A nonpartisan site that provides a wealth of information about current public policy issues.

http://www.people-press.org/ Website of the Pew Research Center for the People and the Press; includes an abundance of recent polling results, including cross-national comparisons.

http://www.princeton.edu/~abelson/ The Princeton Survey Research Center's site; offers results from surveys conducted by a variety of polling organizations.

http://www.publicagenda.org/ The nonpartisan Public Agenda's site; provides opinions, analyses, and educational materials relevant to current policy issues.

POLITICS IN THEORY AND PRACTICE

Thinking: What factors limit the influence of public opinion on the policy choices of public officials?

Participating: At the website of a polling organization such as the Pew Research Center for the People and the Press (www.people-press.org), examine the poll results on a current policy issue. Study the extent to which opinions differ, if at all, between men and women and between Republicans and Democrats. Would an informal poll of the people you know result in a similar distribution of opinion? Why or why not?

ADDITIONAL RESOURCES

For quizzes, interactive simulations, games, graphics, and other study tools, visit the book's Online Learning Center at **www.mhhe.com/pattersonwtp7.**

The Iraq Syndrome

By John Mueller

Public opinion is a powerful but inexact force in democratic societies. Rarely is it informed enough and loud enough to force political leaders to take a particular course of action. Public opinion serves mainly to place boundaries on policymakers' choices. The Iraq conflict is a case in point, as Ohio State University professor John Mueller notes in this article from Foreign Affairs *(November/December 2005). Years earlier, Mueller conducted studies of public opinion during the Korean and Vietnam Wars, which he uses for comparative purposes in this article.*

American troops have been sent into harm's way many times since 1945, but in only three cases—Korea, Vietnam, and Iraq—have they been drawn into sustained ground combat and suffered more than 300 deaths in action. American public opinion became a key factor in all three wars, and in each one there has been a simple association: as casualties mount, support decreases. Broad enthusiasm at the outset invariably erodes.

The only thing remarkable about the current war in Iraq is how precipitously American public support has dropped off. Casualty for casualty, support has declined far more quickly than it did during either the Korean War or the Vietnam War. And if history is any indication, there is little the Bush administration can do to reverse this decline.

More important, the impact of deteriorating support will not end when the war does. In the wake of the wars in Korea and Vietnam, the American public developed a strong aversion to embarking on such ventures again. A similar sentiment—an "Iraq syndrome"—seems to be developing now, and it will have important consequences for U.S. foreign policy for years after the last American battalion leaves Iraqi soil.

The public gave substantial support to the military ventures in Korea, Vietnam, and Iraq as the troops were sent in. In all cases, support decreased as casualties—whether of draftees, volunteers, or reservists—mounted. In each case, the increase in the number of people who considered the venture to be a mistake was steep during the war's early stages, as reluctant supporters were rather quickly alienated; the erosion slowed as approval was reduced to the harder core. (The dramatic early drop in support for the war in Korea reflected the large number of casualties suffered in the opening phase of that war.)

The most striking thing about the comparison among the three wars is how much more quickly support has eroded in the case of Iraq. By early 2005, when combat deaths were around 1,500, the percentage of respondents who considered the Iraq war a mistake—over half—was about the same as the percentage who considered the war in Vietnam a mistake at the time of the 1968 Tet offensive, when nearly 20,000 soldiers had already died.

This lower tolerance for casualties is largely due to the fact that the American public places far less value on the stakes in Iraq than it did on those in Korea and Vietnam. The main threats Iraq was thought to present to the United States when troops went in—weapons of mass destruction and support for international terrorism—have been, to say the least, discounted. . . .

When one shifts from questions about whether the war was a "mistake" or "worth it" to ones about whether the United States should get out, much the same pattern holds for Korea, Vietnam, and Iraq: relatively steep declines in support for continuing the war in the early stages, slower erosion later. However, it is close to impossible to judge how many people want to get out or stay the course at any given time because so much depends on how the question is worded. For example, there is far more support for "gradual withdrawal" or "beginning to withdraw" than for "withdrawing" or "immediate withdrawal." Thus in August 2005, The Washington Post [poll] found that 54 percent of respondents favored staying and 44 percent favored withdrawing when the options were posed this way: "Do you think the United States should keep its military forces in Iraq until civil order is restored there, even if that means continued U.S. military casualties, or, do you think the United States should withdraw its military forces from Iraq in order to avoid further U.S. military casualties, even if that means civil order is not restored there?" But in the same month, a Harris poll tallied only 36 percent in support of staying and 61 percent in support of withdrawing when it asked, "Do you favor keeping a large number of U.S. troops in Iraq until there is a stable government there or bringing most of our troops home in the next year?" Still, no matter how the questions are phrased, all the polls have logged increases in pro-withdrawal sentiment over the course of the war. . . .

President George W. Bush, like Lyndon Johnson before him, has made countless speeches explaining what the effort in Iraq is about, urging patience, and asserting that progress is being made. But as was also evident during Woodrow Wilson's campaign to sell the League of Nations to the American public, the efficacy of the bully pulpit is much overrated. The prospects for reversing the erosion of support for the war in Iraq are thus limited. The run-ups to the two wars in Iraq are also instructive in this regard: even though both Presidents Bush labored mightily to sell the war effort, the only thing that succeeded in raising the level of enthusiasm was the sight of troops actually heading into action, which triggered a predictable "rally round the flag" effect. . . .

After the war in Vietnam, there was a strong desire among Americans never to do "that" again. And, in fact, there never was "another Vietnam" during the Cold War. Due to this "Vietnam syndrome," Congress hampered the White House's ability to pursue even rather modest anticommunist ventures in Africa and, to a lesser extent, Latin America (though there was bipartisan support for aiding the anti-Soviet jihad in Afghanistan). Meanwhile, the genocide in Cambodia was studiously ignored in part because of fears that paying attention might lead to the conclusion that American troops should be sent over to rectify the disaster; over most of the course of the genocide, the three major networks devoted a total of 29 minutes of their newscasts to a cataclysm in which millions died.

No matter how the war in Iraq turns out, an Iraq syndrome seems likely. A poll in relatively war-approving Alabama earlier this year, for example, asked whether the United States should be prepared to send troops back to Iraq to establish order there in the event a full-scale civil war erupted after a U.S. withdrawal. Only a third of the respondents favored doing so.

Among the casualties of the Iraq syndrome could be the Bush doctrine, unilateralism, preemption, preventive war, and indispensable-nationhood. Indeed, these once-fashionable (and sometimes self-infatuated) concepts are already picking up a patina of quaintness. Specifically, there will likely be growing skepticism about various key notions: that the United States should take unilateral military action to correct situations or overthrow regimes it considers reprehensible but that present no immediate threat to it, that it can and should forcibly bring democracy to other nations not now so blessed, that it has the duty to rid the world of evil, that having by far the largest defense budget in the world is necessary and broadly beneficial, that international cooperation is of only very limited value, and that Europeans and other well-meaning foreigners are naive and decadent wimps. The United States may also become more inclined to seek international cooperation, sometimes even showing signs of humility. . . .

What's Your Opinion?

What conclusions about the relationship between public opinion and public policy do you draw from Mueller's analysis? Do you think recent developments (Mueller's article was written in late 2005) support or contradict his thesis?

CHAPTER 7

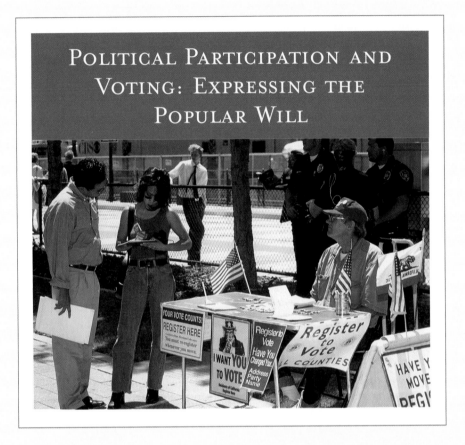

POLITICAL PARTICIPATION AND VOTING: EXPRESSING THE POPULAR WILL

66 We are concerned in public affairs, but immersed in our private ones. 99

WALTER LIPPMANN[1]

At stake in the 2006 midterm election was control of the U.S. House and Senate. Which party would have the leading voice on legislation affecting education, health, welfare, and the environment? Which party would be entrusted with legislative oversight of America's involvement in Iraq? With so much at stake, it might be thought that citizens would have been eager to cast their ballots for the party of their choice. Voter turnout was in fact higher than in the previous midterm election. Nevertheless, tens of millions of American adults did not vote in the 2006 midterm election. Despite a concerted get-out-the-vote campaign by the political parties, news media, and civic groups, the number of people who did not vote was much greater than the number who voted for either party.

Voting is a form of **political participation**—involvement in activities intended to influence public policy and leadership. Political participation also includes activities such as joining community groups, writing to elected officials, and taking part in political protests. Political participation is a hallmark of democratic government, which is based on the idea that ordinary citizens have a right and a duty to involve themselves in public affairs.

Although citizen participation characterizes all democracies, the pattern of participation is somewhat different in the United States, as this chapter will show. The major points made in this chapter are these:

★ *Voter turnout in U.S. elections is low in comparison with that of other democratic nations.* The reasons for this difference include the nature of U.S. election laws, particularly those pertaining to registration requirements and the scheduling of elections.

★ *Active participation in community groups and political organizations is higher in the United States than in other democracies, reflecting the nation's tradition of local government and free association.* Nevertheless, only a minority of Americans can be classified as community or political activists.

★ *Most Americans make a sharp distinction between their personal lives and national life.* This attitude reduces their incentive to participate and contributes to a pattern of participation dominated by citizens of higher income and education.

VOTER PARTICIPATION

At the nation's founding, **suffrage**—the right to vote—was limited to property-owning males. Tom Paine ridiculed this policy in *Common Sense*. Observing that a man whose only item of property was a jackass would lose his right to vote if the jackass died, Paine asked, "Now tell me, which was the voter, the man or the jackass?" It was not until 1840 that all states extended suffrage to propertyless white males, a change made possible by their continued demand for the vote and by the realization on the part of the wealthy that the nation's abundance and openness were natural protections against an assault on property rights by the voting poor.

Women did not secure the vote until 1920, with the ratification of the Nineteenth Amendment. In the 1870s, Susan B. Anthony tried to vote in her hometown of Rochester, New York, asserting that she had a right to do so as a U.S. citizen. She was arrested for "illegal voting" and told that her proper place was in the home. By 1920, men had run out of excuses

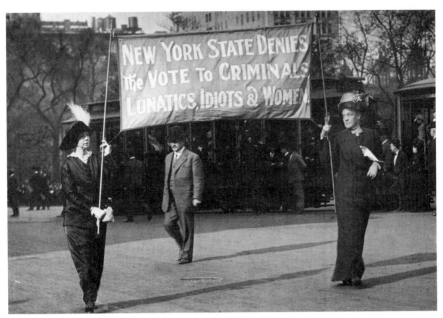

After a hard-fought, decades-long campaign, American women finally won the right to vote in 1920.

Historical Background

for keeping the vote from women. As Senator Wendell Phillips observed: "One of two things is true: either woman is like man—and if she is, then a ballot based on brains belongs to her as well as to him. Or she is different, and then man does not know how to vote for her as she herself does."[2]

African Americans had to wait nearly fifty years longer than women to be granted full suffrage. Blacks seemed to have won the right to vote with passage of the Fifteenth Amendment after the Civil War, but as explained in Chapter 5, they were effectively disenfranchised in the South by a number of electoral barriers, including poll taxes and literacy tests. The poll tax was a fee of several dollars that had to be paid before a person could register to vote. Because most blacks in the South were too poor to pay it, the poll tax effectively barred them from voting. Not until the ratification of the Twenty-fourth Amendment in 1964 was the poll tax outlawed in federal elections. Supreme Court decisions and the Voting Rights Act of 1965 swept away other legal barriers to fuller participation by African Americans.

In 1971, the Twenty-sixth Amendment extended voting rights to include citizens eighteen years of age or older. Previously, nearly all states had restricted voting to those twenty-one years of age or older.

★ | LEADERS

Susan B. Anthony
(1820–1906)

Susan B. Anthony's name is nearly synonymous with women's right to vote—and well it should be. She spent much of her adult life fighting for women's suffrage, even at the risk of arrest. When she was in her twenties, she moved to upstate New York and almost immediately became politically active. Like many of the women who would lead the movement for women's rights, her first crusade was with the temperance movement, which sought to ban the sale of alcohol because of the hardship alcoholism imposed on women and children. She next joined the abolitionist movement, which sought an end to slavery. After the Civil War, she teamed up with an old friend and fellow activist, Elizabeth Cady Stanton, to demand equal pay and voting rights for women. She twice went to the polls in her hometown of Rochester, New York, to assert her right to vote and twice was arrested. By then, Anthony was a national figure who lectured widely on women's suffrage. She died a decade before women gained the right to vote in the United States, but she, as much as any American, made women's suffrage a reality.

Factors in Voter Turnout: The United States in Comparative Perspective

Today nearly any American adult—rich or poor, man or woman, black or white—who is determined to vote can legally and actually do so. Most Americans embrace the symbolism of the vote, saying that they have a duty to vote in elections (see Table 7–1). However, many Americans shirk this duty. Millions choose not to vote regularly, a tendency that sets Americans apart from citizens of most other Western democracies.

Voter turnout is the proportion of adult citizens who actually vote in a given election. Since the 1960s, the voter turnout in presidential elections has averaged about 55 percent (see Figure 7–1). Turnout is even lower in the midterm congressional elections that take place between presidential elections. Midterm election turnout has not reached 50 percent since 1920 and has hovered around the 40 percent mark since 1970.

TABLE 7-1 OPINIONS ON OBLIGATIONS OF CITIZENS			

Americans rank voting as one of the essential obligations of citizenship.

	Essential Obligation	Very Important Obligation	Somewhat Important	Personal Preference
Treating all people equally regardless of race or ethnic background	57%	33%	6%	4%
Voting in elections	53	29	9	9
Working to reduce inequality and injustice	41	42	12	6
Being civil to others with whom we may disagree	35	45	14	6
Keeping fully informed about the news and other public issues	30	42	19	10
Donating blood or organs to help with medical needs	20	37	18	26
Volunteering time to community service	16	42	26	16

Source: Used by permission of the 1996 Survey of American Political Culture, James Davison Hunter and Carol Bowman, Directors, Institute for Advanced Studies in Culture, University of Virginia.

After one midterm election, cartoonist Rigby showed an election clerk eagerly asking a stray cat that had wandered into a polling place, "Are you registered?"[3]

Nonvoting is far more prevalent in the United States than in nearly all other democracies (see "How the United States Compares"). In recent decades, turnout in major national elections has averaged more than 90 percent in Belgium and more than 80 percent in France, Germany,

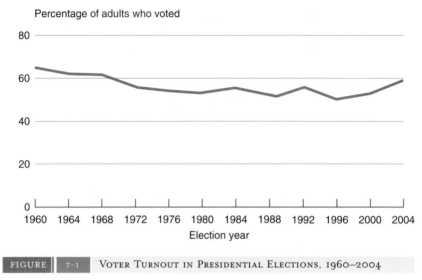

Percentage of adults who voted

 FIGURE 7-1 VOTER TURNOUT IN PRESIDENTIAL ELECTIONS, 1960–2004

After 1960, voter turnout declined steadily. In the past two decades, voter turnout has fluctuated, depending on the issues at stake in a particular election. The 2004 election had a relatively high turnout due to Americans' concern with Iraq and the economy. *Source: U.S. Bureau of the Census. Figures based on percentage of voting-age adults who voted.*

and Denmark.[4] The disparity in turnout between the United States and other nations is not as great as these official voting rates suggest. Some nations calculate turnout solely on the basis of eligible adults, whereas the United States has traditionally based its figures on all adults, including noncitizens and other ineligible groups. Nevertheless, even when such statistical disparities are corrected, turnout in U.S. elections is relatively low.

HOW THE UNITED STATES COMPARES

Voter Turnout

The United States ranks near the bottom among the world's democracies in the percentage of eligible citizens who participate in national elections. One reason for the low voter turnout is that individual Americans are responsible for registering to vote, whereas in

(continued)

most other democracies voters are automatically registered by government officials. In addition, unlike some other democracies, the United States does not encourage voting by holding elections on the weekend or by imposing penalties, such as fines, on those who do not participate.

Another factor affecting voter turnout rate in the United States is the absence of a major labor or socialist party, which would serve to bring lower-income citizens to the polls. America's individualist culture and its electoral system (see Chapter 8) have inhibited the establishment of a major labor or socialist party. In democracies where such parties exist, the turnout difference between upper- and lower-income groups is relatively small. In the United States, however, lower-income persons are much less likely to vote than are higher-income persons.

Country	Approximate Voter Turnout	Automatic Registration?	Social Democrat, Socialist, or Labor Party?	Election Day a Holiday or Weekend Day?
Belgium	90%	Yes	Yes	Yes
Germany	85	Yes	Yes	Yes
Denmark	85	Yes	Yes	No
Italy	80	Yes	Yes	Yes
Austria	80	Yes	Yes	Yes
France	80	No	Yes	Yes
Great Britain	60	Yes	Yes	No
Canada	60	Yes	Yes	No
Japan	60	Yes	Yes	Yes
United States	55	No	No	No

Source: Developed from multiple sources. Turnout percentages are a rough average of national elections during the past two decades.

Contributing to the relatively low turnout in U.S. elections are registration requirements, the frequency of elections, and the lack of clear-cut differences between the political parties.

Registration Requirements   Before Americans are allowed to vote, they must be registered—that is, their names must appear on an official list of eligible voters. **Registration** began around 1900 as a way of preventing voters from casting more than one ballot during an election. Fraudulent voting was a favorite tactic of political party machines in communities where the population was too large for residents to be personally known to poll watchers. However, the extra effort involved in registering placed a burden on honest citizens. Because they could now vote only if they had registered beforehand, those people who forgot or otherwise failed to do so found themselves unable to participate on election day. Turnout in U.S. elections declined steadily after registration was instituted.

Although other democracies also require registration, they place this responsibility on government. In most European nations, public officials have the duty to enroll citizens on registration lists. When someone moves to a new address, for example, the postal service notifies election officials, who update the person's registration. The United States—in keeping with its individualistic culture—is one of the few democracies in which registration is the individual's responsibility. In addition, registration laws have traditionally been established by the state governments, and some states make it difficult for citizens to qualify. Registration periods and locations usually are not highly publicized, and many citizens simply do not know when or where to register.[5] Eligibility can also be a problem. In most states, a citizen must establish legal residency by living in the same place for a minimum period, usually thirty days, before becoming eligible to register. It is estimated that turnout in the United States would be roughly 10 percentage points higher if it had European-style registration.[6]

States with a tradition of lenient registration laws have a higher turnout than most states. Idaho, Maine, Minnesota, New Hampshire, Wisconsin, and Wyoming, which are states that allow people to register at their polling place on election day, have high turnout rates. Those states that have erected the most barriers are in the South, where restrictive registration was originally intended to prevent black people from voting. These historical differences continue to be reflected in state voter turnout (see "States in the Nation").

In 1993, in an effort to increase registration levels nationwide, Congress enacted a voting registration law known as "motor voter." It requires states to permit people to register to vote when applying for a driver's license and when applying for benefits at certain state offices.

Voter Turnout in Presidential Elections

The United States has a low voter turnout relative to most other Western democracies. However, the state-to-state variation is considerable. In a few states, including Minnesota and New Hampshire, nearly seven in ten adults vote in presidential elections. In contrast, there are a few states, including Hawaii and Texas, where barely more than four in ten adults vote.

Q: Why does the South have lower turnout than other regions? Why do states in the Southwest have relatively low turnout rates?

A: Southern states have more poverty and a tradition of more restrictive registration laws (dating to the Jim Crow era of racial segregation). Both factors are associated with lower voting rates. States with large populations of recent immigrants, including the states of the Southwest, also tend to have lower voting rates.

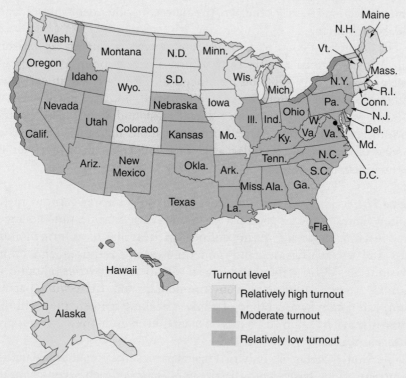

Source: Compiled by author from various sources; based on recent midterm and presidential elections.

231

Registration is not automatic in these situations; the citizen must take the time to fill out an application form. Moreover, the motor voter law does not help citizens who do not drive or do not otherwise have contact with an appropriate state agency. The law has raised registration levels somewhat, but voter turnout has not increased sharply since the law was enacted. Clearly, the registration requirement is only one factor contributing to America's low turnout rate.

Frequency of Elections   The United States holds more elections than any other nation. No other democracy has elections for the lower chamber of its national legislature (the equivalent of the U.S. House of Representatives) as often as every two years, and none schedules elections for chief executive as often as every four years.[7] In addition, elections of state and local officials in the United States are often scheduled separately from national races. Four-fifths of the states elect their governors in non-presidential election years,[8] and 60 percent of U.S. cities hold elections of local officials in odd-numbered years.[9] Finally, the United States uses primary elections to select the party nominees. In other democracies, party leaders pick them.

The high frequency of U.S. elections places a burden on citizens. Americans are asked to vote two to three times as often as Europeans, which increases the likelihood that they will not participate in each election.[10] Moreover, elections in the United States are traditionally held on Tuesday, which means that most adults must find time before or after work to get to the polls. Many European nations hold their elections on Sunday or declare election day a national holiday, making it easier for working people to vote.

Party Differences   A final explanation for lower voter turnout in the United States is the nation's party system. Most European democracies have three or more significant political parties, that have formed along class and social divisions and sometimes along religious and ethnic divisions as well. Labor and social democratic parties abound in Europe, as do middle-class, environmental, and right-wing parties. European voters have a range of choices, making it likely they will find a party that fits their interests, perhaps even one they can support enthusiastically.

The United States has only two major parties, the Republicans and the Democrats. Each has its enthusiastic supporters, yet each party, to get the majority support it needs to win, must have broad support. The major American parties do not completely avoid aligning with certain groups,

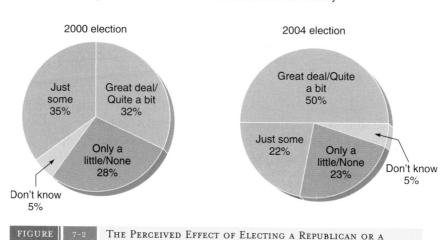

"Importance of outcome . . . to the future of the country"

2000 election

Just some 35%

Great deal/ Quite a bit 32%

Only a little/None 28%

Don't know 5%

2004 election

Great deal/Quite a bit 50%

Just some 22%

Only a little/None 23%

Don't know 5%

FIGURE | 7-2 | THE PERCEIVED EFFECT OF ELECTING A REPUBLICAN OR A DEMOCRATIC PRESIDENT

Many Americans believe that the country will not be greatly affected by whether the Republican or Democratic presidential candidate is elected. However, the proportion holding this belief shrinks when, as in the 2004 campaign, Americans think important issues are at stake in the election. *Source: The Vanishing Voter Project, Shorenstein Center on the Press, Politics and Public Policy, Harvard University. Published by permission of project director.*

but they try to attract a sizable share of votes from nearly all groups in order to gain the 50 percent or more of the vote they need for an election victory. As a consequence, some Americans feel that the parties' candidates are too much alike to represent a real choice, which diminishes their desire to vote.[11]

At times, Americans do see large differences between the parties (see Figure 7–2). In the 2004 presidential election, for example, which was waged against the backdrop of a weak economy and the controversial war in Iraq, Americans thought a lot was at stake in the choice between the Republicans and the Democrats. Four years earlier, however, with the economy strong and the nation not at war, Americans were less convinced that it would make much difference which party won the presidency. Americans voted at a much lower rate in 2000 than they did in 2004. The 2000 election was the more typical one. In most U.S. elections, most adults believe that the outcome will not substantially affect their future or that of the nation. (Chapter 8 has a fuller discussion of the American two-party system and its consequences.)

Why Some Americans Vote and Others Do Not

Even though turnout is lower in the United States than in other major Western democracies, some Americans vote regularly while others seldom or never vote. Among the explanations for these individual differences are civic attitudes, age, and education and income.

Civic Attitudes   Americans differ greatly in their feelings about politics. Some have almost no interest in politics. **Apathy** is the term used to describe a general lack of concern with politics. Just as some people would not attend the Super Bowl if it were free and being played across the street, some Americans would not bother to vote even if a ballot were delivered to their door. Other Americans, however, have a strong sense of **civic duty**—the belief that they are obliged to participate in public affairs.

Apathy and a sense of civic duty are attitudes that are usually acquired during childhood and adolescence as a result of parental influence. When parents vote regularly and take an active interest in politics, their children usually grow up thinking that political participation is important. When parents never vote and show almost no interest in public affairs, their children are likely to be politically apathetic.

Yet a third attitude bears on political participation. **Alienation** is the term that describes a sense of personal powerlessness, the notion that government is unresponsive to or uncaring of citizens like oneself. Politically alienated Americans have low participation rates.[12] Many of them regard voting as a complete waste of time because they are convinced that officials pay no attention to people like them. Alienation can be traced to childhood socialization, but—more so than apathy or civic duty—it has adult roots as well. America's pursuit of the Vietnam War, for example, alienated many young adults. Voter turnout fell in 1968 and in 1972—the two presidential elections in which the Vietnam War was most intensely debated.

Fewer than 10 percent of Americans today are so thoroughly alienated from politics that they have no interest whatsoever in participating. However, most Americans are at least somewhat disenchanted with election politics. For example, they believe that money plays too large a role in determining who gets elected and that candidates routinely make campaign promises they do not intend to keep. Such beliefs ordinarily do not stop people from voting. Nevertheless, a small percentage of Americans are so disgusted with how U.S. campaigns are conducted that they stay home on election day.

Age   When viewers tuned in MTV at various times in the 2004 presidential campaign, they might have thought at first that they had selected

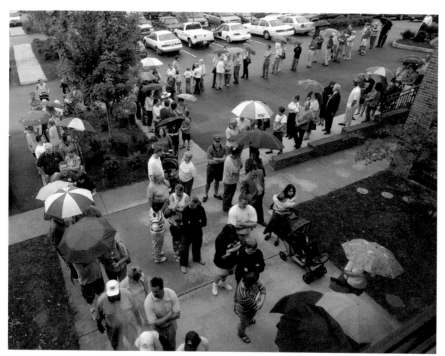

Although Americans have voted in relatively low numbers in recent U.S. elections, the turnout rate increased in 2004 and 2006 in response to the issues and candidates of the moment. Here voters stand in a long line waiting to cast their ballots at a polling place in Fort Mill, South Carolina.

the wrong channel. Rather than a video of their favorite rock star, they saw the presidential candidates urging young people to vote.

The candidates had targeted the audience most in need of a reminder. Young adults are much less likely to vote than are middle-aged citizens. Even senior citizens, despite the infirmities of old age, have a far higher turnout rate than do voters under the age of thirty. Young people are less likely to have the political concern that can accompany lifestyle characteristics such as homeownership, a permanent career, and a family.[13] In fact, citizens under the age of thirty have the lowest voter turnout rate of any major demographic group.

Education and Income Americans at the top levels of education attainment are twice as likely to vote in a presidential election as those at the bottom levels. The same difference describes Americans at the top and bottom income levels (see Figure 7–3). It is no surprise that education and income make a difference in voter participation. Achievement in these

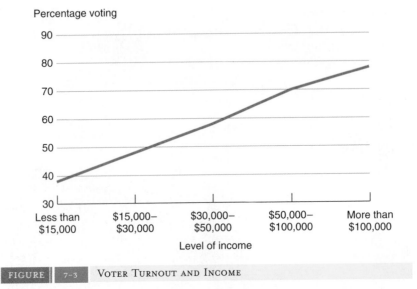

FIGURE   7-3   VOTER TURNOUT AND INCOME

Lower-income Americans are much less likely to vote than are higher-income Americans, which is different from the situation in European democracies, where income level has only a marginal influence on voter turnout level. *Source: U.S. Bureau of the Census, 2006.*

areas contributes to an interest in public affairs and a belief that a person can make a difference politically.[14]

Education and income also affect participation rates in European democracies, but to a lesser degree. Europeans with less education and lower income are encouraged to participate by the presence of class-based organizations and traditions—strong socialist or labor parties, politically oriented trade unions, and class-based political ideologies. The United States does not have, and never has had, a major socialist or labor party. Although the Democratic party by and large represents the working class and the poor, it is more attentive to the middle class, which, because of its size and voting regularity, is the key to victory in U.S. elections. Americans in the bottom third by income are more likely than those in the top third to believe that election outcomes have no appreciable effect on their lives.[15]

CONVENTIONAL FORMS OF PARTICIPATION OTHER THAN VOTING

In one sense, voting is an unrivaled form of citizen participation. Free and open elections are the defining characteristic of democratic government, so voting is regarded as the most basic duty of citizens. Furthermore, most citizens in most democracies vote in elections. No other active form of political participation is so widespread.

In another sense, however, voting is a limited form of involvement. Citizens have the opportunity to vote only at a particular time, and only on the choices listed on the ballot. Other activities, such as working on a campaign or joining a civic group, provide the citizen with a fuller opportunity to participate.

Campaign Activities

Working for a candidate or participating in an election rally requires a lot more time than voting does. Not surprisingly, the proportion of citizens who engage in such activities is relatively small. Fewer than one in twenty adult Americans say they worked for a party or a candidate within the past year.[16]

Nevertheless, campaign participation is higher in the United States than in Europe. A five-country comparative study found that Americans were more likely to contribute money and time to election campaigns than were citizens of Germany, Austria, the Netherlands, and Great Britain.[17] A more recent study of twenty-three countries found that the United States ranked first in terms of citizens' efforts to influence other voters (see Figure 7–4). One reason why Americans are more active in campaigns, even though they vote at a lower rate, is that they have more opportunities to become active.[18] The United States is a federal system with campaigns for national, state, and local offices. A citizen who wants to participate is almost certain to find an opportunity at one level of office or another. Most of the governments in Europe are unitary in form (see Chapter 3), which means that there are fewer elective offices and thus fewer campaigns in which citizens can participate.

Lobbying Group Contributions

As government has extended its reach into more areas of American life, political activity outside the context of elections has increased substantially. Thousands of interest groups now actively lobby government on almost every conceivable policy and program. Lobbying activities once were conducted without much involvement by ordinary citizens, but that is no longer the case. Lobbying groups encourage citizens to place pressure on policymakers and to contribute money to support the groups' activities. Millions of Americans every year play their part. In fact, Americans are more likely than citizens elsewhere to contribute money, usually in the form of annual dues, to lobbying groups. These donations support professionally run organizations that contact government officials and otherwise attempt to influence policy decisions.[19] Examples of such groups are the National Organization for Women, Common Cause, the

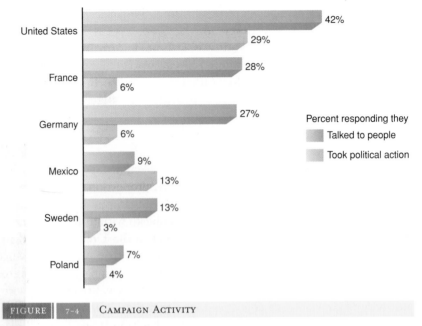

United States 42%
              29%

France   28%
              6%

Germany   27%
              6%

Percent responding they
▓ Talked to people
▓ Took political action

Mexico   9%
              13%

Sweden   13%
              3%

Poland   7%
              4%

FIGURE 7-4 CAMPAIGN ACTIVITY

Although Americans are less likely to vote in elections than citizens elsewhere, they are more likely to engage in other campaign activities, such as trying to influence the vote choice of others. *Source: Surveys by Comparative Studies of Electoral Systems, 2001–4. Reported in Russell J. Dalton, "The Myth of the Disengaged American," CSES Report, October 25, 2005, web release.* Seventeen other countries were included in surveys; none had a higher participation rate than the United States.

Christian Moral Government Fund, the American Association of Retired Persons, and the National Conservative Political Action Committee. Chapter 9 discusses lobbying groups in more detail.

Community Activities

Many Americans participate in public affairs not through campaigns and political parties but through local organizations such as parent-teacher associations, neighborhood groups, business clubs, church-affiliated groups, and hospital auxiliaries. The actual number of citizens who participate actively in a community group is difficult to estimate, but the number is surely in the tens of millions. The United States has a tradition of local participation that goes back to colonial days. Moreover, compared with cities and towns in Europe, localities in the United States have more authority over policy issues, which is an added incentive to participation.

Because of increased mobility and other factors, Americans may be less tied to their local communities than in the past and therefore less involved

Youthful volunteers work to fix up a children's playground. Americans are more likely than citizens of other democracies to take part in voluntary community activities.

in community action. Nevertheless, half of Americans claim that they volunteer time to groups and community causes, compared with 20 percent or less in most European countries. Young adults in America increasingly are engaging in community volunteer work. A 2003 survey of the nation's college students by Harvard University's Institute of Politics found that students were more interested in—and more active in—community volunteering than in election volunteering.

In a widely publicized book titled *Bowling Alone*, Harvard's Robert Putnam claims that America has been undergoing a long-term decline in its **social capital** (the sum of the face-to-face civic interactions among citizens in a society).[20] Putnam attributes the decline to television and other factors that draw people inward and away from participation in civic and political groups. Not all scholars accept Putnam's interpretation of trends in civic involvement (some indicators point toward a rise in certain types of participation), but no one challenges his assumption about the importance of civic participation. It brings people together, gives them an understanding of other points of view, and builds skills that make them more effective citizens.

Attending to the News

Informed participation is a democratic ideal, and news is the means by which most citizens try to keep abreast of public affairs. Although news consumption is an individual activity rather than a form of collective action, it is nonetheless a vital part of democratic citizenship. And it is a form of citizenship that increasingly is practiced by fewer adults.

Americans spend a huge number of hours attending to the media. Next to sleeping and working, media use absorbs the largest share of people's time. However, only a fraction of this use involves news consumption—in fact, news audiences in the United States have been shrinking. Because of cable television, the Internet, computer games, and other forms of newer media, the news faces stiff competition for people's time and attention. Newspapers have lost readers to television news, which in turn has lost viewers to entertainment telecasts. Before cable television became widely available in the 1980s, many television viewers had no media alternative to watching a newscast during the dinner hour. With cable, viewers always have a variety of program choices, and many viewers simply prefer entertainment content to news content. Although the Internet has become a source of news for an increasing number of Americans, most Internet users do not depend on it for news—and some of those who do rarely go beyond the headlines they come across.

Americans fall into three groups of nearly equal size based on their attention to news. About a third of the public follows the news on a daily basis; most of these citizens read the daily paper and also watch television newscasts. Another third follows the news intermittently, scanning a paper's news sections once in a while or catching an occasional newscast or webcast. The final third pays no appreciable attention to news in any form except when an extraordinary event occurs. This last group is the one that is growing in size, and the reason is simple: most young adults do not have much interest in news. News habits usually are formed by early adulthood, and today's young adults show less interest in the news than their predecessors. Fewer than one in five adults under thirty years of age, for example, read a daily newspaper, half the percentage of a few decades ago. Although young adults increasingly cite alternative sources of political information, such as late-night comedy shows, most of these sources contain minimal news. Studies have found that young adults who depend on alternative sources for their news are less informed about public affairs than are other citizens.[21]

Virtual Participation

The prospect of an entire generation of politically inattentive citizens is disturbing to many observers. Yet there is a glimmer of hope—the Internet. It is used more heavily by younger people and is packed with political information and participation possibilities.

It is unclear whether the Internet will actually serve as an entry into the world of politics for large numbers of citizens. Most people use it primarily for entertainment, school assignments, shopping, and personal and workplace communication. Nevertheless, thousands of websites

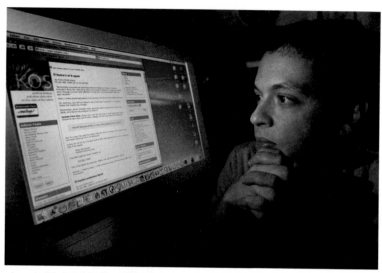

Shown here is Markos Moulitsas Zuniga, who aided in the creation of presidential candidate Howard Dean's "meetups"—supporters connected with one another through the Internet. Zuniga runs a political web log ("blog") called Daily Kos.

feature news or politics. There have been remarkable examples of citizen mobilization through the Internet, none more successful than MoveOn, which claims two million "online activists," many of them young people. Internet use during the 2004 Democratic presidential nominating campaign provided a glimpse into the medium's potential. One-third of Internet users engaged in some form of election-related activity, such as sending or receiving campaign e-mails. A relatively small number—4 percent of Internet users—made use of election-related blogs or chat rooms, but the Internet was for some Americans a significant point of contact with the campaign. Howard Dean's candidacy, though ultimately unsuccessful, caught the imagination of Internet users, and he raised millions of dollars for his campaign through the Internet.

The full impact of the Internet on citizen participation is not likely to become clear until its technological capacity is developed further and another generation of computer-savvy children reaches voting age.[22] Some analysts believe the Internet will usher in an era of unprecedented citizen involvement and influence. Other analysts are less optimistic, noting that the Internet has hundreds of thousands of websites, most of which have little or nothing to do with public affairs. They note further that users have almost complete control of web content. These analysts doubt that citizens will avail themselves of the Internet's political material unless they are otherwise interested in public affairs. (The Internet is discussed further in Chapter 10.)

UNCONVENTIONAL ACTIVISM: SOCIAL MOVEMENTS AND PROTEST POLITICS

During the era of absolute monarchies, the public resorted to protest as a way of expressing dissatisfaction with its rulers. Tax and food riots occurred with some frequency. When democratic governments came into existence, the vote gave citizens a way to express their views in a regular and less disruptive way.

However, voting is double-edged. Although the vote gives citizens a degree of control over government, *the vote also gives government a degree of control over citizens.*[23] Because government officials are freely chosen by the people, they can claim that their policies reflect the will of the people and therefore must be respected and obeyed. The power of the vote is also limited by the choices listed on the ballot. In the American case, citizens who are dissatisfied with both the Republican party and the Democratic party have no realistic way to exercise power through the vote.

Social movements are an alternative form of influence. **Social movements,** or **political movements** as they are sometimes called, refer to broad efforts to achieve change by citizens who feel that government is acting improperly.[24] These efforts are sometimes channeled through conventional forms of participation, such as political lobbying, but citizens can also take to the streets in protest against government. In 2003, as the Bush administration was preparing for war with Iraq, protest demonstrations were held in many U.S. cities, including Washington and San Francisco. Two percent of adult Americans said they participated in an antiwar demonstration. Many of them were young adults. Participants in social movements are younger on average than nonparticipants, a reversal of the pattern for voting.[25]

Social movements do not always succeed, but they sometimes force government into action. For example, the timing and scope of the landmark 1964 Civil Rights Act and 1965 Voting Rights Act can be explained only as a response by Congress to the pressure created by the civil rights movement. Another effective social movement in the 1960s was that of the farm workers, whose protests led to improved conditions for migrant workers.

Political protests have taken on new forms in recent years. Protest was traditionally a desperate act that began, often spontaneously, when a group had lost hope that it could succeed through more conventional methods. Today, however, protest is usually a calculated act—a means of bringing added attention and impetus to a cause.[26] These tactical protests often involve a great deal of planning, including, in some instances, the busing of thousands of people to Washington for a rally staged for television. Civil

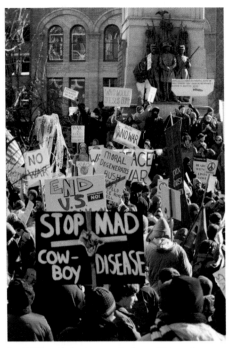

Protesters demonstrate in 2003 against the war in Iraq. Although protest movements are an American tradition, they do not routinely receive strong public support.

rights, environmental, agricultural, and pro- and antiabortion groups are among those that have staged tactical protests in Washington within the past few years.

Protest politics has a long history in America, dating to the Boston Tea Party and earlier. It would be no exaggeration to claim that the United States was founded on a protest movement that sparked a revolution against Britain. Despite this tradition, protest activity is less common in the United States than in many Western democracies (see Figure 7–5). Spain, France, Germany, Sweden, and Mexico are among the countries that have higher rates of participation in political protests.

Public support for protest activity is also relatively low in the United States. For reasons that are not fully clear, Americans often side with the authorities against protesters. The Vietnam War protests, which in limited cases were accompanied by the burning of draft cards, enjoyed only marginal public support outside the circle of protesters. When unarmed student protesters at Kent State University and Jackson State University were shot to death in May 1970 by members of the National Guard, a majority

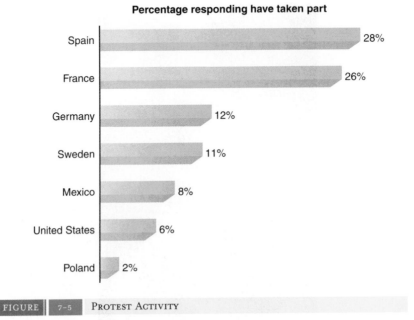

Percentage responding have taken part

Spain	28%
France	26%
Germany	12%
Sweden	11%
Mexico	8%
United States	6%
Poland	2%

FIGURE   7–5   PROTEST ACTIVITY

Despite the significance of protest activity in U.S. history, Americans are less likely to protest than are citizens in many other democracies. *Source: Surveys by Comparative Studies of Electoral Systems, 2001–04. Reported in Russell J. Dalton, "The Myth of the Disengaged American," CSES Report, October 25, 2005, web release.* Of twenty-three countries surveyed, the United States ranked eighteenth in level of protest activity. Only selected countries are included in this figure.

of Americans polled blamed the students, not the guardsmen, for the tragedy.

The public was more accepting of protests against the war in Iraq (see Figure 7–6). Even after the fighting began in 2003, according to an ABC News/*Los Angeles Times* poll, three in every five Americans said they saw the protests as "a sign of a healthy democracy." Still, almost two in five felt that "opponents of the war should not hold antiwar demonstrations"; about half of these said that antiwar demonstrations should be banned. In another poll, about a third of respondents said that protesters were "the kind of people who tend to blame America first."[27]

Nonetheless, there is a basic acceptance of protest activity. Rarely are protesters attacked by those who disagree with their actions, and most Americans display at least some understanding of protest as part of America's tradition of free expression. In that sense, protest is seen as something to be allowed, if not admired.

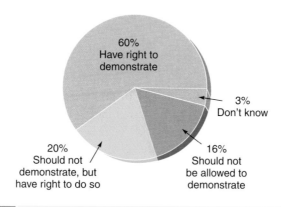

60%
Have right to
demonstrate

3%
Don't know

20%
Should not
demonstrate, but
have right to do so

16%
Should not
be allowed to
demonstrate

FIGURE 7-6 AMERICANS' OPINIONS OF IRAQ WAR PROTESTS

A majority supported the right of antiwar protesters to demonstrate, although some Americans felt they should not be allowed to do so. *Source: ABC News/Washington Post poll, March 23, 2003.*

PARTICIPATION AND THE POTENTIAL FOR INFLUENCE

Although Americans claim that political participation is important, many of them do not practice what they preach. Most citizens show little interest in participation except to vote, and a significant minority cannot even be persuaded that voting is worth their time. However, Americans are not completely apathetic: many millions of them contribute to political causes, and more than a hundred million vote in presidential elections.

Yet sustained political activism does not engage a large proportion of the public. Moreover, many of those who do participate are drawn to politics by a habitual sense of civic duty rather than by an intense concern with current issues. The emphasis that American culture places on individualism tends to diminish interest in political participation. "In the United States, the country of individualism *par excellence*," William Watts and Lloyd Free write, "there is a sharp distinction in people's minds between their own personal lives and national life."[28] Although wars and severe recessions can lead Americans to look to government for help, most people under most conditions expect to solve their own problems. This is not to say that Americans have a disdain for collective action. In their communities particularly, citizens frequently take part in collective efforts to support a local hospital, improve the neighborhood, and the like. But most Americans tend not to see their material well-being as being closely linked to partisan political activity.

GET INVOLVED!

Register and Vote

Some observers take comfort in low-turnout elections. They claim that the country is better off if less interested and less knowledgeable citizens stay home on election day. In a 1997 cover story in *Atlantic Monthly*, Robert Kaplan wrote: "The last thing America needs is more voters—particularly badly educated and alienated ones—with a passion for politics." The gist of this age-old argument is that low turnout protects society from erratic or even dangerous shifts in power. However, America's voters have not acted whimsically. Except for an interlude in the 1780s, when the Articles of Confederation governed the United States, erratic voting has not been a persistent source of political instability.

On the other hand, a low participation rate can be a problem. In general, the smaller the electorate, the less representative it is of the public as a whole. Polls indicate that the outcomes of elections would in some instances have changed if turnout had been substantially higher. And even if greater voter turnout would not have altered the outcomes, campaign platforms have always been tailored to those who vote. As political scientists Steve Rosenstone and Mark Hanson note in *Mobilization, Participation, and Democracy in America* (1993): "The idle go unheard: They do not speak up, define the agenda, frame the issues, or affect the choices leaders make."

Voting can strengthen democracy in other ways, too. When people vote, they are more attentive to politics and are better informed about issues affecting them. As the philosopher John Stuart Mill theorized a century ago, voting also deepens community involvement. Studies indicate that voters participate more frequently in community affairs and are more likely to work with others on community projects. Of course, these associations say more about the type of person who votes than about the effect of voting. But recent evidence, as Harvard University's Robert Putnam notes in *Bowling Alone* (2000), "suggests that voting itself encourages volunteering and other forms of good citizenship."

Voting among young adults in particular has declined. When eighteen-to twenty-one-year-old citizens gained eligibility to vote in the 1972 election, nearly 50 percent of them voted. In 2000, less than 35 percent did so. The hotly contested 2004 election, waged against the backdrop of a soft economy and turmoil in Iraq, produced increased turnout

(continued)

among young adults, although the level was substantially below that of 1972. Unless increased turnout among young voters can be sustained, the overall voting rate will continue to stagnate, because the oldest generation, those who grew up during the Depression and World War II, participate at very high rates.

Changes in registration laws have made it easier for students to vote if they choose to do so. Voting is not a time-consuming task, and the benefits to the individual and society are considerable. Have you registered yet?

This tendency contributes to a class bias in American politics. For one thing, it helps maintain a relatively sharp distinction between that which is properly public (political) and that which is properly private (economic). Americans, as political scientist Robert Lane notes, prefer to see benefits distributed primarily through the economic marketplace rather than through the policies of government.[29] For example, access to medical care in the United States, unlike in Europe where government-provided health care is available to all, is to some degree based on a person's ability to pay for it. Roughly forty-five million Americans do not have access to adequate health care because they cannot afford health insurance.

Lower-income Americans are a relatively weak force in the nation's politics. They are less likely to have the financial resources and communication skills that encourage participation in politics and make it personally rewarding. Among citizens who are most active in politics, three times as many have incomes in the top third as in the bottom third.[30] This difference is much greater than in other Western democracies, where poorer citizens are assisted through automatic voter registration and by the presence of class-based political organizations. The poor in the United States must arrange their own registration and must choose between two political parties that are attuned primarily to middle-class interests.

The low participation rate of lower-income Americans reduces their influence on public policy. Studies indicate that representatives are more responsive to the demands of participants than to those of nonparticipants.[31] Although it must be kept in mind that participants do not always promote only their own interests, it would be a mistake to conclude that large numbers of people regularly support policies that would mainly benefit others. For example, a turning point in the defeat of President Bill Clinton's health care reform proposal, which would have extended health care coverage to nearly all Americans, came when middle-class taxpayers decided that it might increase the cost and reduce the quality of their own medical care. According to *Time*/CNN polls, support for the Clinton plan dropped from 57 percent to 37 percent between September 1993 and July 1994. Although this decline reflected a loss of support among all groups, the drop was particularly severe among middle- and higher-income people who already had health insurance, through either an individual policy or an employment-related group policy.

In sum, the pattern of individual political participation in the United States parallels the distribution of influence that prevails in the private sector. Those who have the most power in the marketplace also have the most power in the political arena. However, the issue of individual participation is only one piece of the larger puzzle of who rules America and for what purposes. Subsequent chapters will supply additional pieces.

SUMMARY

Political participation is involvement in activities designed to influence public policy and leadership. A main issue of democratic government is the question of who participates in politics and how fully they participate.

Voting is the most widespread form of active political participation among Americans. Yet voter turnout is significantly lower in the United States than in other democratic nations. The requirement that Americans must personally register in order to establish their eligibility to vote is one reason for lower turnout among Americans; other democracies place the burden of registration on government officials rather than on the individual citizen. The fact that the United States holds frequent elections also discourages some citizens from voting regularly. Finally, the major American political parties, unlike many of those in Europe, do not clearly represent the interests of opposing economic classes; thus, the policy stakes in American elections are lower. Some Americans do not vote because they think that policy will not change greatly regardless of which party holds power.

Only a minority of citizens engage in the more demanding forms of political activity, such as work on community affairs or on behalf of a candidate during a political campaign. The proportion of Americans who engage in these more demanding forms of activity exceeds the proportion of Europeans who do so. Nevertheless, only about one in every four Americans will take an active part in a political organization at some point in their lives. Most political activists are individuals of higher income and education; they have the skills and material resources to participate effectively and tend to take a greater interest in politics. More than in any other Western democracy, political participation in the United States is related to economic status.

Social movements are broad efforts to achieve change by citizens who feel that government is not properly responsive to their interests. These efforts sometimes take place outside established channels; demonstrations, picket lines, and marches are common means of protest. Protesters are younger and more idealistic on average than are other citizens, but they are a very small proportion of the population. In addition, protest activities do not have a high level of public support, despite the country's tradition of free expression.

Overall, Americans are only moderately involved in politics. While they are concerned with political affairs, they are mostly immersed in their private pursuits, a reflection in part of a cultural belief in individualism. The lower level of participation among low-income citizens has particular significance in that it works to reduce their influence on public policy and leadership.

KEY TERMS

alienation (*p. 234*)
apathy (*p. 234*)
civic duty (*p. 234*)
political participation (*p. 224*)
registration (*p. 230*)

social capital (*p. 239*)
social (political) movements (*p. 242*)
suffrage (*p. 224*)
voter turnout (*p. 226*)

SUGGESTED READINGS

Bimber, Bruce, and Richard Davis. *Campaigning Online: The Internet in U.S. Elections*. New York: Oxford University Press, 2003. A careful study of citizens' use of the Internet in elections.

Burns, Nancy, Kay Lehman Schlozman, and Sidney Verba. *The Private Roots of Public Action: Gender, Equality, and Public Action*. Cambridge, Mass.: Harvard University Press, 2001. An analysis of gender differences in political participation.

Leighley, Jan. *Strength in Numbers: The Political Mobilization of Racial and Ethnic Minorities*. Princeton, N.J.: Princeton University Press, 2001. A study of the factors that motivate blacks and Hispanics to participate.

Patterson, Thomas E. *The Vanishing Voter*. New York: Knopf, 2002. A study of the decline in electoral participation and what might be done to reverse the trend.

Putnam, Robert. *Bowling Alone*. New York: Simon and Schuster, 2000. A provocative analysis of the trend in civic participation.

Schudson, Michael. *The Good Citizen: A History of American Civic Life*. New York: Free Press, 1998. A thoughtful history of civic participation in America.

Skocpol, Theda. *Diminished Democracy: From Membership to Management in American Civic Life*. Norman: University of Oklahoma Press, 2003. An analysis of the trend away from active membership in civic and political organizations.

Zukin, Cliff, Scott Keeter, Molly Andolina, Krista Jenkins, and Michael X. Delli Carpini. *A New Engagement: Political Participation, Civic Life, and the Changing American Citizen*. New York: Oxford University Press, 2006. A comprehensive study that concludes that young adults are finding ways other than election politics to exercise citizenship.

LIST OF WEBSITES

http://www.rockthevote.org/ The website of Rock the Vote, an organization dedicated to helping young people realize and utilize their power to affect the civic and political life of their communities.

http://www.umich.edu/~nes/ The University of Michigan's National Election Studies (NES) site; provides survey data on voting, public opinion, and political participation.

http://www.vanishingvoter.org/ Harvard University's election study site; provides information on voter participation.

http://www.vote-smart.org/ Project Vote Smart site; includes information on Republican and Democratic candidates and officials and also has the latest in election-related news.

POLITICS IN THEORY AND PRACTICE

Thinking: Why does economic class—differences in people's income levels—make such a large difference in the level of political participation in the United States? What are the policy consequences of this difference?

Participating: If you are not currently registered to vote, consider registering. You can obtain a registration form from the election board or clerk in your community of residence. Several websites contain state-by-state registration information. One such site is www.vanishingvoter.org. If you are already registered, consider participating in a registration or voting drive on your campus. Although students typically register and vote at relatively low rates, they will often participate if encouraged by other students to do so.

ADDITIONAL RESOURCES

For quizzes, interactive simulations, games, graphics, and other study tools, visit the book's Online Learning Center at **www.mhhe.com/pattersonwtp7.**

Voter Participation and Electoral Competition

By Thomas E. Patterson

The United States ranks low by comparison with other Western democracies in terms of voter turnout. A number of factors, including differences in registration procedures, account for the difference. One of the most recent developments contributing to lower voter turnout in the United States is declining competition in legislative elections, including those for Congress. This article addresses that issue in the context of the 2006 midterm election. In addition to being the author of this textbook, the writer is the director of The Vanishing Voter Project at Harvard University's Kennedy School of Government. The project seeks to explain Americans' involvement in election politics.

Writing in the 1950s, political observers were optimistic about the future of voter participation. College-educated Americans were half again as likely to vote as those who had not finished high school. With college attendance on the rise, an upward trend appeared inevitable. Moreover, women had been steadily closing the voting gap that had existed ever since they had gained the vote in 1920. Their turnout rate initially was barely more than half that of men; by the 1950s, the gap had narrowed to 10 percentage points. And signs of racial change were clearly evident. It would only be a matter of time before literacy tests, poll taxes, and the other legal barriers suppressing black participation in the South were eliminated.

Yet, turnout did not increase after the 1950s. In fact, it declined. The 2006 midterm election was a partial exception to the long-term trend. Turnout was higher in 2006 than in the midterm election four years earlier. Still, it was markedly below that of the midterm elections of a half century ago, despite all that was at stake when voters went to the polls in 2006. Americans were deeply worried about Iraq and other issues, and the House and Senate were both up for grabs. Would the Republicans hold onto their narrow majorities in both chambers and continue to control the legislative agenda? Or would the Democrats capture one or both houses and bring a new outlook to national policy?

Despite the high stakes, far more adult Americans stayed away from the polls on Election Day than went to the polls. What's going on here? Why does even a critical election like that of 2006 fail to draw a hefty majority to the polls? There is no single or simple answer to that question, but one of the reasons is particular to congressional elections: the decline of competition in U.S. House races. In 2006, according to the Cook Political Report, 80 percent of the House seats were solidly Democratic or Republican before the campaign began. Of the rest, only half were likely to be competitive. In other words, the outcome of the 2006 election would depend on races in about 10 percent of the House districts.

A trio of developments explains this one-sidedness. Four decades ago, Congress decided to increase its staffing in order to better evaluate information coming from the executive branch. Congressional staffs doubled in the 1960s, and then doubled again in the 1970s. By 1980, each House member had a staff of roughly 20 people, far more than were needed for legislative purposes because the staffs of committees, where most of the legislative work is done, had also quadrupled. What House members had actually secured for themselves were personal staffs large enough to run perpetual election campaigns, paid for at taxpayer expense. Combined with free travel, media, mailing, and other perks, House members' staffs gave them a large advantage over election challengers.

House members received another boost when campaign finance reform legislation was enacted in 1974. Although the law closed some loopholes and strengthened disclosure requirements, it relaxed the rules for political action committees (PACs). Within a decade, the number of PACs had increased from 600 to 4,000. PACs discovered that it was risky to bet against House incumbents, as they were already in positions of power and likely to stay there. By the 1990s, PACs were giving House incumbents eight dollars for every dollar they gave to their challengers.

The third and final piece in America's incumbent-protection game fell fully into place after the 2000 census. Traditionally, congressional redistricting after each census has been guided by partisanship. Majorities in state legislatures shape House districts in ways designed to help their party's candidates. State legislatures still act in this way, but they have also increasingly bowed to the reality that incumbents are tough to dislodge. After the 2000 census, state legislatures reconfigured congressional districts to protect incumbents generally, not just those of a particular party. It was not a completely new approach but the scale was

unprecedented, as was the precision with which the boundaries were drawn, thanks to the calculating power of advanced computers. According to the Cook Political Report, the redistricting that took place after the 2000 census created only half as many competitive districts as had been created after the 1990 census.

This situation did not prevent the Democrats from taking control of the House in 2006. Virtually no Democratic incumbent was defeated and Democratic candidates in other districts fared well enough to reverse the total number of Democrats and Republicans in the House, enabling their party to capture the chamber.

However, only fifty or so of the 435 House districts were the site of hotly contested campaigns. Voters in the 300-plus other districts were treated to one-sided contests. In several dozen of these districts, the incumbent ran unopposed. In others, the challenger had so little money that the campaign was barely visible. Even the news media stayed on the sidelines in these districts. Press coverage of congressional elections has been declining anyway, and a one-sided race provides local newspapers and television stations with an excuse to cut the coverage to almost nothing, which they did.

Uncompetitive races diminish the power of the vote. It has been said of incumbent-protection gerrymandering that it enables "candidates to pick the voters" as opposed to allowing the voters to choose the candidates. Incumbents are handed districts that contain so many voters of their party that they could not possibly lose, unless they do something so illegal or scandalous that even their own party's voters find them repugnant—as was the case in 2006 with a couple of incumbents, including Florida's Mark Foley who was caught sending sexually suggestive e-mails to teenage congressional pages.

Uncompetitive races also reduce the incentive to vote. For one thing, there is no closely contested campaign to generate voter interest in the race. Although many voters cast a ballot anyway, the outcome is a foregone conclusion—there is no suspense about which candidate will win and no particular reason for citizens to think that their vote and the vote of others like them could possibly swing the election. Studies indicate that uncompetitive races have a turnout rate that is roughly 5 percent lower than that of competitive races.

Unlike some barriers to voting, incumbent-centered redistricting could easily be fixed. The state of Iowa has taken such a step. Although the Iowa legislature has the final say, it chooses among three plans put forth by a non-partisan legislative agency, which divides the state into congressional districts using four criteria: that districts be as nearly equal in population as possible, that the districts be contiguous as to area, that districts include whole counties and cities, and that districts be compact. Partisanship is not a criterion. As a result, of Iowa's five congressional districts, four are competitive between the parties, a number that exceeds the number of competitive districts in California, which has fifty-three districts, and in New York, which has twenty-nine districts.

Nevertheless, like other steps that could be taken to shift power to the voters and thereby increase the incentive to vote, political elites are not rushing to embrace the Iowa model. They gained power through the current system and evince little interest in changes that would reduce their chances of holding onto it.

What's Your Opinion?

Are there other ways to make congressional elections more competitive? For example, do you favor public funding of campaigns as a way to provide challengers the money they need to run a strong campaign against an incumbent?

CHAPTER 8

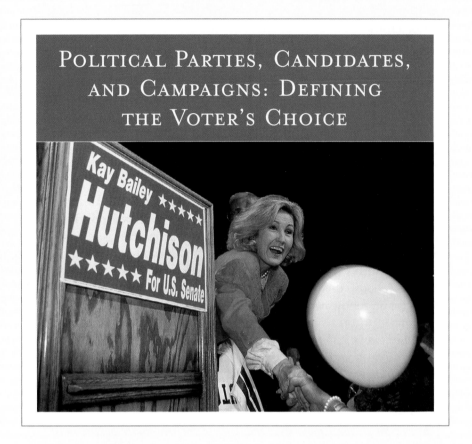

POLITICAL PARTIES, CANDIDATES, AND CAMPAIGNS: DEFINING THE VOTER'S CHOICE

> ❝Political parties created democracy and ... modern democracy is unthinkable save in terms of the parties.❞
>
> E. E. SCHATTSCHNEIDER[1]

Toe-to-toe, they slugged it out in states and districts across the breadth of America, each side saying that it had the answer to America's problems. One side claimed that the fighting in Iraq was a key link in the war on terrorism—that America would be safe only if it took the fight to the enemy. The other side portrayed the Iraq invasion as an ill-conceived venture that had increased the terrorist threat while taking a deep toll on America's soldiers. And Iraq was but one of the issues separating the two sides: among the others were jobs, taxes, education, immigration, health, abortion, budget deficits, and the environment.

The scene of this showdown was the 2006 midterm election. The two sides were the Republican party and the Democratic party, each with a slate of House and Senate candidates that carried its message into cities and towns across America.

A **political party** is an ongoing coalition of interests joined together in an effort to get its candidates for public office elected under a common label.[2] By offering a choice between policies and leaders, parties give voters a chance to influence the direction of government. "It is the competition of [parties] that provides the people with an opportunity to make a choice," political scientist E. E. Schattschneider wrote. "Without this opportunity popular sovereignty amounts to nothing."[3]

This chapter examines political parties and the candidates who run under their banners. U.S. campaigns are **party-centered politics** in the sense that the Republican and Democratic parties compete across the country election after election. Yet campaigns are also **candidate-centered politics** in the sense that individual candidates devise their own strategies, choose their own issues, and form their own campaign organizations. The following points are emphasized in this chapter:

* *Political competition in the United States has centered on two parties, a pattern that is explained by the nature of America's electoral system, political institutions, and political culture.* Minor parties exist in the United States but have been unable to compete successfully for governing power.

* *To win an electoral majority, candidates of the two major parties must appeal to a diverse set of interests; this necessity normally leads them to advocate moderate and somewhat overlapping policies.* Only during periods of stress are America's parties likely to present the electorate with starkly different choices.

* *U.S. party organizations are decentralized and fragmented.* The national organization is a loose collection of state organizations, which in turn are loose associations of autonomous local organizations. This feature of U.S. parties can be traced to federalism and the nation's diversity, which have made it difficult for the parties to act as instruments of national power.

* *The ability of America's party organizations to control nominations and election to office is weak,* which in turn enhances the candidates' role.

* *Candidate-centered campaigns are based on the media and utilize the skills of professional consultants.* Money, strategy, and televised advertising are key components of today's presidential and congressional campaigns.

PARTY COMPETITION AND MAJORITY RULE: THE HISTORY OF U.S. PARTIES

Through their numbers, citizens have the potential for great influence, but that potential cannot be realized unless citizens have the capacity to act together. Parties give them that capacity. When Americans go to the polls, they have a choice between the Republican and Democratic parties. This **party competition** narrows their options to two and in the process enables people with different backgrounds and opinions to unite behind a single alternative. In casting a majority of its votes for one party, the electorate chooses that party's candidates, philosophy, and policies over those of the opposing party.

The history of democratic government is synonymous with the history of parties. When the countries of Eastern Europe gained their freedom more than a decade ago, one of their first steps toward democracy was the legalization of parties. When the United States was founded over two centuries ago, the formation of parties was also a first step toward the building of its democracy. The reason is simple: it is the competition among parties that gives popular majorities a chance to influence how they will be governed.[4] Stated differently, political parties are the instrument that allows the principle of self-government to be realized in practice. If there were no mechanism like the political party to enable citizens to make their voices heard collectively, they would be powerless—each citizen unable to be heard loud enough to get the government's attention.

The First Parties

America's early leaders mistrusted parties. George Washington in his farewell address warned the nation of the "baneful effects" of parties, and James Madison likened parties to special interests. However, Madison's misgivings about parties gradually gave way to a grudging admiration; he recognized that they enabled like-minded people to exercise collective power.

America's parties originated in the rivalry within George Washington's administration between Thomas Jefferson, a supporter of states' rights and small landholders, and Alexander Hamilton, a promoter of strong national government and commercial interests (see Figure 8–1). When Hamilton's ideas prevailed in Congress, Jefferson and his followers formed a political party, the Republicans. By adopting this label, which was associated with popular government, the Jeffersonians sought to portray themselves as the rightful heirs to the American Revolution's legacy of self-government and political equality.

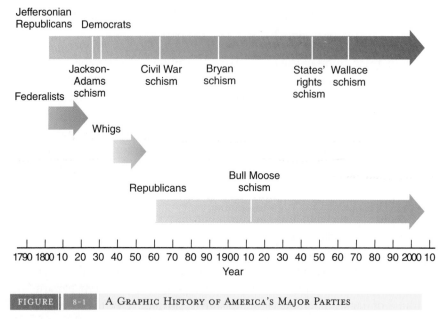

The U.S. party system has been remarkable for its continuity. Competition between two major parties has been a persistent feature of the system.

Hamilton then organized his supporters into a formal party—the Federalists—and in the process created America's first competitive party system. The Federalists took their name from the faction that had supported ratification of the Constitution, thereby implying that they represented America's governing tradition. However, the Federalists' preoccupation with commercial and wealthy interests fueled Jefferson's claim that the Federalists were bent on establishing a government of the rich and well-born. After Jefferson in the election of 1800 defeated John Adams, who had succeeded Washington as president, the Federalists never again controlled the presidency or Congress.

During the so-called Era of Good Feeling, when James Monroe ran unopposed in 1820 for a second presidential term, it appeared as if the political system might operate without parties. Yet by the end of Monroe's second term, policy differences had split the Republicans. The dominant faction, led by Andrew Jackson, retained Jefferson's commitment to the interests of ordinary people. This faction called itself Democratic Republicans, later shortened to Democrats. Thus, the Republican party of Jefferson is the forerunner of today's Democratic party rather than of today's Republican party.

Historical Background

Andrew Jackson and Grassroots Parties

For all its shortcomings, competition between parties is the only system that can regularly mobilize collective influence on behalf of the many who are individually powerless against those few who have extraordinary wealth and status.

This realization led Jackson during the 1820s to develop a **grassroots party.** Whereas Jefferson's party had been well organized only at the leadership level, Jackson sought a party that was built from the bottom up. Jackson's Democratic party consisted of organizations at the local, state, and national levels, with membership open to all eligible voters. These organizations, along with more liberal suffrage laws, contributed to a nearly fourfold rise in voter turnout during the 1830s.[5] At the peak of Jacksonian democracy, Alexis de Tocqueville wrote, "The People reign in the American political world as the Deity does in the universe."[6] Although Tocqueville exaggerated the people's true power, he caught the spirit of popular government that was behind the development of grassroots parties under Andrew Jackson.

In this period, a new opposition party, the Whigs, emerged to challenge the Democrats. The Whigs were a catchall party. Its followers were united not by a coherent philosophy of their own but by their opposition for one reason or another to the policies of the Jacksonian Democrats.

Competition between the Whigs and the Democrats was relatively short-lived. During the 1850s the slavery issue began to tear both parties apart. The Whig party withered, and a northern-based new party, calling itself Republican, arose as the main challenger to the Democrats. In the 1860 presidential election, the Democratic party's northern faction nominated Stephen A. Douglas, who held that the question of whether a new territory would permit slavery was for its voters to decide, while the southern faction nominated John C. Breckinridge, who called for legalized slavery in all territories. The Democratic vote split sharply along regional lines between these two candidates—with the result that the Republican nominee, Abraham Lincoln, who had called for the gradual elimination of slavery, was able to win the presidency with only 40 percent of the popular vote. Lincoln's election prompted the southern states to secede from the Union, which led to the Civil War. For the first and only time in the nation's history, the party system had failed to peaceably resolve Americans' conflicting goals.[7] The issue of slavery proved too explosive to be settled through electoral competition.

Republicans Versus Democrats: Realignments and the Enduring Party System

After the Civil War, the nation settled into the pattern of competition between the Republican and Democratic parties that has lasted through today. The durability of these two parties is due not to their ideological consistency but to their remarkable ability to adapt during periods of crisis. By abandoning at these crucial times their old ways of doing things, the Republican and Democratic parties have repeatedly remade themselves—with new bases of support, new policies, and new public philosophies.

These periods of great political change are known as *realignments*. A **party realignment** involves four basic elements:

1. The disruption of the existing political order because of the emergence of one or more unusually powerful and divisive issues
2. An election contest in which the voters shift their support strongly in favor of one party
3. A major change in policy brought about through the action of the stronger party
4. An enduring change in the party coalitions, which works to the lasting advantage of the dominant party

Realignments are rare. They do not occur simply because one party wrests control of government from the other. They involve deep and lasting changes in the party system that affect not just the most recent election but later ones as well. By this standard, there have been three clear-cut realignments since the 1850s.

The first of these, the Civil War realignment, brought about a thorough change in the party system. The Republicans replaced the Democrats as the nation's majority party. The Republicans dominated the larger and more populous North, while the Democratic party was left with a stronghold in what became known as "the Solid South." During the next three decades, the Republicans held the presidency except for Grover Cleveland's two terms of office and had a majority in Congress for all but four years.

The 1896 election resulted in a second realignment of the Republican-Democratic party system. Three years earlier, an economic panic following a bank collapse had resulted in a severe depression. The Democrat Cleveland was president when the crash happened, and people blamed him and his party. In the aftermath, the Republicans made additional gains in the Northeast and Midwest, solidifying their position as the nation's dominant party. During the four decades between the 1890s realignment and the next one in the 1930s, the Republicans held the presidency except for Woodrow Wilson's two terms and had a majority in Congress for all but six years.

★ | LEADERS

Abraham Lincoln
(1809–65)

Abraham Lincoln had been a member of Congress from Illinois before his election to the presidency in 1860. Homely and gangly, Lincoln is regarded by many as America's greatest president for his principled leadership during the Civil War. Lincoln's accomplishments are all the more remarkable in that, unlike earlier presidents, he came from a humble background. His father was a frontiersman, his mother died when he was ten, and he was largely self-schooled. His greatest legacy is the preservation of the American Union. The Emancipation Proclamation and the Gettysburg Address are two of his other legacies. He was assassinated at Ford's Theater in the nation's capital shortly after the start of his second term as president. Lincoln was the first Republican elected to the presidency, and his successful pursuit of victory in the Civil War led to a party realignment that solidified the GOP's status as the nation's majority party.

The Great Depression of the 1930s triggered yet another realignment of the American party system. The Republican Herbert Hoover was president during the stock market crash of 1929, and many Americans blamed Hoover, his party, and its business allies for the economic catastrophe that followed. The Democrats became the country's majority party. Their political and policy agenda called for an expanded role for the national government. Franklin D. Roosevelt's presidency was characterized by unprecedented policy initiatives in the areas of business regulation and social welfare (see Chapter 3). His election in 1932 began a thirty-six-year period of Democratic presidencies that was interrupted only by Dwight D. Eisenhower's two terms in the 1950s. In this period the Democrats also dominated Congress, losing control only in 1947–48 and 1953–54.

The reason realignments have such a substantial effect on future elections is that they affect voters' *party identification* (see Chapter 6). Young voters in particular tend to identify with the newly ascendant party, and they retain that identity, giving the party a solid base of support for years to come. First-time voters in the 1930s came to identify with the Democratic party by a two-to-one margin, establishing it as the nation's majority party and enabling it to dominate national politics for the next three decades.[8]

Today's Party Alignment and Its Origins

A party realignment inevitably loses strength over time as the issues that gave rise to it decline in importance. By the late 1960s, with the Democratic party divided over the Vietnam War and civil rights, it was apparent that the era of New Deal politics was ending.[9]

The change was most dramatic in the South. The region had been solidly Democratic at all levels since the Civil War, but the Democratic party's leadership on civil rights angered white conservatives.[10] In the 1964 presidential election, five southern states voted Republican, and the South is now a Republican bastion in presidential politics. The Republican party also made gains, though more gradually, in elections for other offices. Today most top officials in the southern states are Republicans.

More slowly and less completely, the northeastern states have become more Democratic. The shift is partly attributable to the growing size of minority populations in the Northeast. But it is also due to the declining influence of the Republican party's moderate wing, which was concentrated in these states. As southern conservatives became Republican in ever larger numbers, the party's stands on social issues such as abortion

The new order begins. Franklin D. Roosevelt rides to his inauguration with outgoing president Herbert Hoover after the realigning election of 1932.

and affirmative action tilted toward the right, reducing the party's appeal among northeastern voters.

Party conflict also extended to federal spending on education, health, and economic security programs. The Democrats, who had started nearly all of these programs, defended them, while Republicans attacked them as being too expensive. Taxing and spending became perennial campaign issues, resulting in a further alignment of liberals against conservatives.

The GOP (short for "Grand Old Party" and another name for the Republican party) gained the most from these changes in party politics. Since 1968, Republicans have held the presidency for twice as many years as the Democrats have. Also, since 1994, the GOP has controlled the House and Senate for more years than the Democrats have. Republicans, after trailing the Democrats for decades, have also narrowed the gap in terms of party identification (see Figure 8–2). In 2004, Democratic identifiers outnumbered Republican identifiers by 2 percentage points in a Gallup poll, the smallest margin ever recorded by that organization. By 2007,

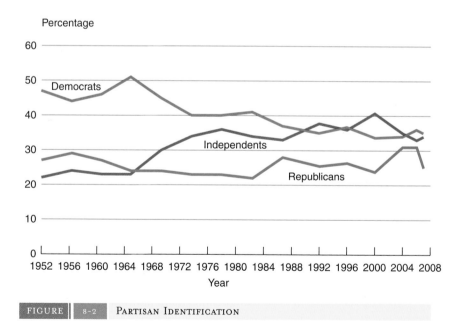

FIGURE 8-2 PARTISAN IDENTIFICATION

After trailing for decades, Republican identifiers nearly achieved parity with Democratic identifiers in 2004 only to fall behind again as Iraq and other issues worked to the Democrats' advantage. Of the roughly one-third of voters who describe themselves as Independents, most also say they "lean" toward one of the two major parties. The leaners divide almost evenly between the two parties. *Source: National Election Studies, 1952–2004; multiple surveys, after 2004.*

however, the Democrats' lead had widened to 10 percentage points, apparently in response to growing discontent with the Bush administration's handling of the conflict in Iraq and other issues.[11]

The slow drift toward the Republican party is not a party realignment in the traditional sense. Rather than occurring abruptly in response to a single disruptive issue, as was the case in the 1860s, 1890s, and 1930s realignments, the change has taken place slowly and somewhat fitfully. As happened in the past two years, Republican support weakened during the mid-1970s. Further, the partisan intensity that marks a full-scale party realignment has at times been missing. The percentage of self-described Independent voters rose sharply during the 1960s and early 1970s, as did the number of voters casting a **split ticket,** that is, casting a ballot on which their vote for different offices is divided between Democratic and Republican candidates. Some analysts described these developments as a *dealignment*—a partial but enduring weakening of partisanship.[12]

Partisanship is not as strong today as in peak periods such as the 1930s, but it has staged a comeback since the 1970s. Conflict between Republican and Democratic officeholders in Washington has intensified since that decade (see Chapters 11 and 12), and the gap in the policy opinions of Republican and Democratic party identifiers has widened (see Chapter 6). In addition, fewer voters today cast a split ticket. When all offices—local, state, and federal—are taken into account, ticket splitting is still relatively common, with about half of all voters casting such a ballot. Ticket splitting among candidates for federal office, however, has declined by nearly half since its peak in the 1970s (see Figure 8–3). Today, fewer than 20 percent of voters back one party's candidate for president and the other party's candidate for the House of Representatives. The fact that more than four of five voters now back the same party's presidential and congressional candidates is a sure sign of robust partisanship.

Analysts are divided in their opinions on where the party system is heading. Some predict a period of Republican dominance as the GOP consolidates its gains.[13] Others foresee a resurgent Democratic party fueled by the increasing voting power of minority groups, particularly blacks and Hispanics.[14] One thing is virtually certain: as they have for over 150 years, Americans will continue to look to the Republican and Democratic parties for political leadership. The enduring strength and appeal of the two major parties is a hallmark of American politics.

Parties and the Vote

The power of party is at no time clearer than when, election after election, Republican and Democratic candidates reap the votes of their party's

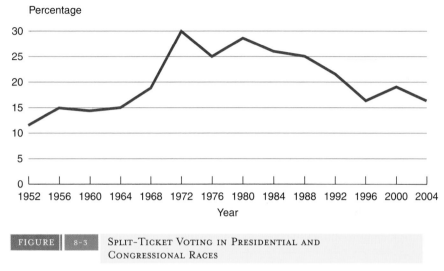

Percentage

FIGURE ║ 8-3   SPLIT-TICKET VOTING IN PRESIDENTIAL AND
CONGRESSIONAL RACES

The level of split-ticket voting, as measured by the percentage who backed one
party's candidate for president and the other party's candidate for the House of
Representatives, has declined in recent elections. The change reflects an increased
level of partisanship among America's voters. *Source: National Election Studies.*

identifiers. In the 2004 presidential election, George W. Bush had the
support of 93 percent of Republican party identifiers, while John Kerry
garnered the votes of 89 percent of self-identified Democrats. Major party
candidates do not always do that well with party loyalists, but it is relatively unusual—in both congressional races and presidential races—for a
party nominee to get less than 80 percent of the partisan vote.

Nevertheless, some voters in every election are swayed by the issues of
the moment. Voters respond to issues both prospectively and retrospectively.
Prospective voting occurs when the voter chooses a candidate on the
basis of what the candidate promises to do if elected. In contrast,
retrospective voting is based on a judgment about past performance—
the situation in which a voter supports the incumbent officeholder or
party when pleased with its performance and opposes it when displeased.
Retrospective voting is the more common form of issue voting. When
things are going poorly with the country, particularly when the economy
is bad, voters are inclined to want a change in leadership. In good economic times, incumbents have less to fear. Studies have found, for example, that a weak economy in 1992 contributed greatly to the defeat of
incumbent President George H. W. Bush and that a strong economy in
1996 underpinned incumbent President Bill Clinton's successful bid for a

second term. The 2004 presidential election was somewhat unusual in that the top issue was not the economy but foreign policy. George W. Bush had a huge edge among voters who believed that the terrorist threat was the nation's top issue, whereas John Kerry had a decisive advantage among those who believed that the U.S. invasion of Iraq was a mistake.[15]

ELECTORAL AND PARTY SYSTEMS

The United States traditionally has had a **two-party system:** Federalists versus Jeffersonian Republicans, Whigs versus Democrats, Republicans versus Democrats. These have not been the only American parties, but they have been the only ones with a realistic chance of acquiring political control. A two-party system, however, is the exception rather than the rule (see "How the United States Compares"). Most democracies have a **multiparty system,** in which three or more parties have the capacity to gain control of government, separately or in coalition. Why the difference? Why are there three or more major parties in most democracies but only two in the United States?

The Single-Member-District System of Election

America's two-party system is due largely to the fact that the nation chooses its officials through plurality voting in **single-member districts.** Each constituency elects a single member to a particular office, such as U.S. senator or representative; the candidate with the most votes (a plurality) in a district wins the office. This system discourages minor parties. Assume, for example, that a minor party received exactly 20 percent of the vote in each of the nation's 435 congressional races. Even though one in five voters nationwide backed the minor party, it would not win any seats in Congress because none of its candidates would have placed first in any of the 435 single-member-district races. The winning candidate in each race would be the major-party candidate who received the larger proportion of the remaining 80 percent of the vote.

By comparison, most European democracies use some form of **proportional representation,** in which seats in the legislature are allocated according to a party's share of the popular vote. This type of electoral system provides smaller parties an incentive to organize and compete for power. In the 2005 German elections, for example, the Green party received 8 percent of the national vote and thereby won 51 seats in the 603-seat Bundestag, the German parliament. If the Greens had been competing under American electoral rules, they would not have won any seats.

HOW THE UNITED STATES COMPARES

Party Systems

For nearly 160 years, electoral competition in the United States has centered on the Republican and Democratic parties. By comparison, most democracies have a multiparty system, in which three or more parties receive substantial support from voters. The difference is significant. In a two-party system, the parties tend to have overlapping coalitions and programs, because each party must appeal to the middle-of-the-road voters who provide the margin of victory. In multiparty systems, particularly those with four or more strong parties, the parties tend to separate themselves as each tries to secure the enduring loyalty of voters who have a particular viewpoint.

Whether a country has a two-party or a multiparty system depends on several factors, but particularly the nature of its electoral system. The United States has a single-member, plurality district system in which only the top vote getter in a district gets elected. This system is biased against smaller parties; even if they have some support in a great many races, they win nothing unless one of their candidates places first in an electoral district. By comparison, proportional representation systems enable smaller parties to compete; each party acquires legislative seats in proportion to its share of the total vote. All the countries in the chart that have four or more parties also have a proportional representation system of election.

Number of Competitive Parties

Two	*Three*	*Four or More*
United States	Canada (at times)	Belgium
	Great Britain	Denmark
		France
		Germany
		Italy
		Netherlands
		Sweden

Politics and Coalitions in the Two-Party System

The overriding goal of a major American party is to gain power by getting its candidates elected to office. Because there are only two major parties, however, the Republicans or Democrats can win consistently only by attracting majority support. In Europe's multiparty systems, a party can hope for a share of power if it has the firm backing of a minority faction. In the United States, if either party confines its support to a narrow segment of society it forfeits its chance of gaining control of government.

Seeking the Center   American parties, Clinton Rossiter said, are "creatures of compromise."[16] The two parties usually take stands that have broad appeal or at least will not alienate significant blocs of voters. Any time a party makes a pronounced shift toward either extreme, the political center is left open for the opposing party. Barry Goldwater, the Republican presidential nominee in 1964, proposed the elimination of mandatory social security and said he might consider the tactical use of small nuclear weapons in wars such as the Vietnam conflict—extreme positions that cost him many votes. Eight years later, the Democratic nominee, George McGovern, took positions on Vietnam and income security that alarmed many voters; like Goldwater, he got buried in one of the greatest landslides in presidential history.

It is impossible to understand the dynamics of the U.S. party system without recognizing that the true balance of power in American elections rests with the moderate voters in the center rather than with those who hold more extreme positions. When congressional Republicans mistook their 1994 election victory as a mandate to trim assistance programs for the elderly, the poor, and children, they alienated many of the moderate voters who had contributed to their 1994 victory. These voters wanted "less" government but not a government that neglected society's most vulnerable citizens. After weak showings in the 1996 and 1998 elections, congressional Republicans shifted course. They unseated Speaker Newt Gingrich, replacing him with a more pragmatic conservative, Dennis Hastert. "We still need to prove that we can be conservative without being mean," was how one Republican member of Congress described the change in strategy.[17] The adjustment reflects a basic truth about U.S. politics: party ideology is acceptable as long as it is tinged with moderation.

Nonetheless, the Republican and Democratic parties do offer somewhat different alternatives and, at times, a clear choice. When Roosevelt was elected president in 1932, Johnson in 1964, and Reagan in 1980, the parties were relatively far apart in their priorities and programs. Roosevelt's New Deal, for example, was an extreme alternative within the American political tradition and caused a decisive split along party lines. A lesson of these periods is that the center of the American political spectrum can be moved. Candidates risk a crushing defeat by straying too far from established ideas during normal times, but they may do so with some chance of success during turbulent times. The terrorist attacks of September 11, 2001, provided President George W. Bush with just such an opportunity. During his first term, Bush pushed major tax cuts through Congress and also sharply increased defense spending while pursuing an aggressive Middle East policy. Democrats contested these changes, but in the face of a unified Republican Congress, they were largely powerless to block them.

The Bush presidency, however, also illustrates the risks of moving away from the political center. The White House strategy, crafted by presidential advisor Karl Rove, was based on issues of concern to the Republicans' conservative base. Rather than reaching out to the center, the strategy combined a policy shift to the right and a massive get-out-the-vote effort to get conservatives to the polls on Election Day. The strategy succeeded in the 2004 election but unraveled as the Iraq conflict and other issues undermined Bush's support. In the 2006 midterm election, Republicans held onto their conservative base but lost the center. Independents and moderates swung heavily toward the Democrats, enabling them to seize control of both houses of Congress.

Party Coalitions The groups and interests that support a party are collectively referred to as the **party coalition.** In multiparty systems, each party is supported by a relatively narrow range of interests. European parties tend to divide along class lines, with the center and right parties drawing most of their votes from the middle and upper classes and the left parties drawing most of theirs from the working class. By comparison, America's two-party system requires each party to accommodate a wide range of interests in order to gain the voting plurality necessary to win elections. The Republican and Democratic coalitions are therefore relatively broad. Each includes a substantial proportion of voters of nearly every ethnic, religious, regional, and economic grouping. Only a few groups are tightly aligned with a party. African Americans are the clearest example; they vote about 85 percent Democratic in national elections.

Although the Republican and Democratic coalitions overlap, they are hardly identical (see Figure 8–4). The party coalitions have been forged primarily through conflict over the federal government's role in solving social and economic problems. Each party has supported government action to promote economic security and social equality, but the Democrats

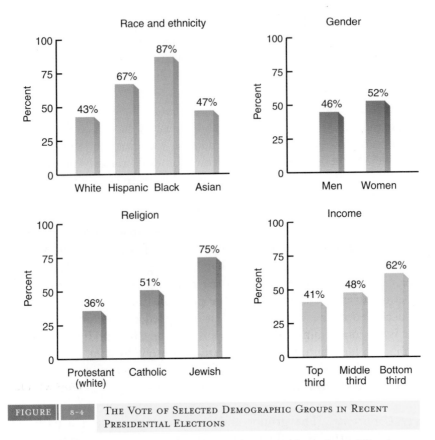

FIGURE   8-4   THE VOTE OF SELECTED DEMOGRAPHIC GROUPS IN RECENT
               PRESIDENTIAL ELECTIONS

Although the Democratic and Republican coalitions overlap substantially, there are important differences, as illustrated by the Democratic party's approximate percentage of the two-party vote among some major demographic groups in the past four elections. *Source: Compiled by author from various sources.*

have favored a higher level of government involvement. Virtually every major assistance program for the poor, the elderly, and low-wage workers since the 1930s has been initiated by the Democrats.

Accordingly, the Democratic coalition draws support disproportionately from society's underdogs—blacks, union members, the poor, city dwellers, Hispanics, Jews, and other "minorities."[18] For a long period, the Democratic party was also the clear choice of the nation's elderly as a result of its support for old-age assistance programs and because the basic political loyalties of the elderly were acquired during the New Deal era, a period favorable to the Democrats. Recently, however, elderly voters have split their vote about evenly between the parties.

The Democratic party's biggest gains recently have been among women, whose voting pattern traditionally was very similar to that of men. Recent elections, however, have revealed a gender gap (see Chapter 6). Women have voted disproportionately for the Democratic party, apparently as a result of its positions on issues such as abortion rights, education spending, employment policies, and gun control. The Democratic party, as a result of its leadership on civil rights issues, has also made gains among gays and lesbians, who are now the party's third most loyal voting bloc (after blacks and Jews).

The Republican coalition consists mainly of white middle-class Protestants. The GOP has historically been the party of tax cuts and business incentives. It has also been more supportive of traditional values, as reflected, for example, in its opposition to abortion and civil unions. Not surprisingly, the GOP is strongest in the suburbs and in regions—such as the South, the Great Plains, and the Rocky Mountains—where traditional values and a desire for lower taxes and less government regulation of economic activity are most pronounced.

The Republican party has made big gains in recent decades among white fundamentalist Christians, who have been drawn to the GOP by its positions on abortion, school prayer, same-sex marriage, and other social issues.[19] In recent presidential elections, the Republican nominee has garnered the votes of roughly three-fourths of fundamentalist Christians.

Minor Parties

Although the U.S. electoral system discourages the formation of third parties, the nation has always had minor parties—more than a thousand over the nation's history.[20] Most have been short-lived, and only a few have had a lasting impact. Only one minor party, the Republican party, has ever achieved majority status.

Minor parties in the United States have formed largely to promote policies that their followers believe are not being adequately represented by either of the two major parties. A major party is always somewhat captive to its past, which is the source of many of its ideas and most of its followers. When conditions change, major parties are often slow to respond, and a minor party can try to capitalize on neglected issues. If the minor party gains a following, one or both major parties typically awaken to the new issues, at which time the minor party usually begins to lose support. Nevertheless, the minor party will have served the purpose of making the major parties more responsive to the public's concerns.

GET INVOLVED!
Take Sides

In high school civics classes, generations of American students have been told to "vote for the person, not the party" or to "vote on the issues, not the party." Commentators sometimes make the same pitch. On the whole, it is pretty bad advice.

To vote for the person is to assume that the individual officeholder wields singular power. But that's not true even in the case of the president. In selecting one presidential candidate over another, Americans are choosing more than the person who will sit behind the desk in the Oval Office. They are also selecting several hundred other executive officers, including the secretary of state, the attorney general of the United States, and the director of the Central Intelligence Agency. The president also nominates all federal judges and justices. The great majority of these individuals, including the judicial officers, will be of the same party as the president.

The election of a senator or a representative is also more than a decision about which individual will occupy a seat in Congress. Rarely does a single member of Congress have a decisive voice in legislation. Congress works through collective action, and power resides with the majority party in each chamber. Dozens of important legislative votes are cast in Congress each term. Typically, most Republican members are on one side of the vote and most Democratic members are on the other side.

Accordingly, a vote based on an issue is usually shortsighted. Once in office, a successful candidate will vote on scores of policy issues, not just the one or two issues that were the cornerstone of the election campaign. And what is the best predictor of how the successful candidate will vote on these issues? In nearly every case, the best predictor is the political party to which the officeholder belongs.

An issue that dominates an election can be overtaken by events and be a secondary issue by the time the winning candidates are sworn into office. Partisanship, on the other hand, tends to endure. Today's Democratic and Republican candidates and officeholders are not all that different in their policy leanings from their partisan counterparts of a decade or two ago.

Many Americans pride themselves on "voting on the issue or the candidate rather than the party." If that's your outlook, give some

(continued)

thought to whether it's the most effective way to make a difference as a voter. If you are a party loyalist already, consider taking your commitment a step further. Party organizations at all levels are looking for volunteers, particularly at election time, when they are engaged in registration, canvassing, and get-out-the-vote efforts.

put together for 1 certain reason (issue)

Single-Issue Parties   Some minor parties form around a single issue of overriding interest to their supporters, such as the present-day Right-to-Life party, which was formed to oppose the legalization of abortion. Some single-issue parties have seen their policy goals enacted into law. The Prohibition party contributed to the ratification in 1919 of the Eighteenth Amendment, which prohibited the manufacture, sale, and transportation of alcoholic beverages (but which was repealed in 1933). Single-issue parties usually disband when their issue either is favorably resolved or fades in importance.[21]

Factional Parties   Although the Republican and Democratic parties are normally adept at managing internal divisions, there have been times when internal conflict has led a faction to break away and form its own party. The most successful of these factional parties at the polls was Theodore Roosevelt's Bull Moose party. In 1908, Roosevelt, after having served eight years as president, declined to seek a third term and hand-picked William Howard Taft for the Republican nomination. When Taft as president showed neither Roosevelt's enthusiasm for a strong presidency nor his commitment to the goals of the Progressive movement, Roosevelt challenged Taft for the 1912 Republican nomination but lost out. Backed by Progressive Republicans, Roosevelt proceeded to form the Bull Moose party (a reference to Roosevelt's claim that he was "as strong as a bull moose"). Roosevelt won 27 percent of the presidential vote to Taft's 25 percent, but the split within Republican ranks enabled the Democratic nominee, Woodrow Wilson, to win the 1912 presidential election.

The States' Rights party in 1948 and George Wallace's American Independent party in 1968 are other examples of strong factional parties. These parties were formed by white southern Democrats angered by northern Democrats' support of civil rights for black Americans.

Deep divisions within a party give rise to factionalism and can lead eventually to a change in its coalition. The conflict over civil rights that began within the Democratic party during the late 1940s continued for the next quarter-century, leading many southern whites to shift their party loyalty to the GOP. *pay taxes · gov. redist, back to who they want*

Ideological Parties   Other minor parties are characterized by their ideological commitment to a broad and radical philosophical position, such as redistribution of economic resources. Modern-day ideological parties include the Citizens party, the Socialist Workers party, and the Libertarian party, each of which operates on the fringes of American politics.

One of the strongest ideological parties in the nation's history was the Populist party. Its candidate in the 1892 presidential election, James B. Weaver, gained 8.5 percent of the national vote and won twenty-two electoral votes in six western states. The party began as an agrarian protest

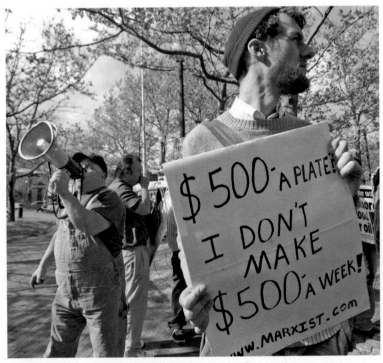

The Republican and Democratic parties have huge advantages over third parties. Major parties can count on the voting loyalty of their party identifiers, have an automatic place on the ballot in every state, have long-standing organizations at all levels of government, and can count on receiving millions of dollars in campaign donations. Minor parties complain particularly about campaign finance laws that work to the advantage of the major parties. Here a protester uses a bullhorn to draw attention to a fund-raiser for Senator Lincoln Chaffee (R-R.I.) hosted by First Lady Laura Bush.

movement in response to an economic depression and the anger of small farmers over low commodity prices, tight credit, and the high rates charged by railroad monopolies to transport farm goods. The Populists' ideological platform called for government ownership of the railroads, a graduated income tax, low tariffs on imports, and elimination of the gold standard.[22]

Until the 2000 election, the Reform party was America's strongest minor party. It was formed by Ross Perot after he ran as an independent and garnered 19 percent of the vote in the 1992 presidential election (second only to Theodore Roosevelt's 27 percent in 1912 among minor-party candidates). Perot's platform was based on middle-class discontent with the major parties' lack of fiscal restraint. Perot ran again in 1996, this time as the Reform party's nominee, and won 8 percent of the vote. When Perot chose not to run in 2000, a fight ensued over the Reform party's nomination, which went to broadcaster Pat Buchanan. His reactionary candidacy attracted only 1 percent of the general-election vote and nearly wrecked the Reform party. Since then, it has been trying without much success to rebuild its base.

The strongest minor party today is the Green party, an ideological party that holds liberal positions on the environment, labor, taxation, social welfare, and other issues. Its 2000 presidential nominee, consumer-rights advocate Ralph Nader, received 3 percent of the national vote. According to polls, Nader (who ran as an Independent in 2004) got most of his support from voters who otherwise would have backed Democrat Al Gore, thus tipping the election to the more conservative Republican nominee, George W. Bush. In 2004,

Historical
Background

the Green party decided to compete in the presidential race, but in a way designed to reduce the chance of tipping the election to the Republicans. The Green party rejected Nader's bid for its 2004 nomination, choosing instead Green-party activist David Cobb, a little-known Texas lawyer.

PARTY ORGANIZATIONS

The Democratic and Republican parties have organizational units at the national, state, and local levels. The main purpose of these **party organizations** is the contesting of elections.

A century ago, party organizations enjoyed almost complete control of nominations and elections. The party organizations still perform all the activities they formerly engaged in. They recruit candidates, raise money, develop policy positions, and canvass for votes. But they do not control these activities as completely as they once did.[23] For the most part, these activities are now directed by the candidates themselves.[24]

The Weakening of Party Organizations

Nomination refers to the selection of the individual who will run as the party's candidate in the general election. Until the early twentieth century, nominees were selected by party organizations. To be nominated, an individual had to be loyal to the party organization, a requirement that included a willingness to share with it the spoils of office—government jobs and contracts. The situation allowed party organizations to attract campaign workers and funds, but it also enabled party leaders to extort money from those seeking political favors. Reform-minded Progressives argued that the power to nominate should rest with ordinary voters rather than with the party leaders (see Chapter 2).

The result was the introduction of the **primary election** (or **direct primary**), which places nomination in the hands of the voters (see Chapters 2 and 12). Primary elections take several forms. Most states conduct closed primaries, in which participation is limited to voters registered or declared at the polls as members of the party whose primary is being held. Other states use open primaries, a form that allows independents and voters of either party to vote in a party's primary, although voters are prohibited by law from participating in both parties' primaries simultaneously. A few states have a third form of primary, known as the blanket primary. These states provide a single primary ballot listing both the Republican and Democratic candidates by office. Each voter can cast only one vote per office but can select a candidate of either party; for instance, a voter might pick a Democratic candidate in the Senate primary and a Republican candidate in the House primary.

Primaries hinder the building of strong party organizations. If primaries did not exist, candidates would have to work through party organizations in order to gain nomination, and they could be denied renomination if they were disloyal to the party's goals. Because of primaries, however, candidates have the option of seeking office on their own, and once elected (with or without the party's help), they can build a personal following that effectively places them beyond the party's direct control.

In the process of taking control of nominations, candidates also acquired control of most campaign money. At the turn of the last century, when party machines were at their peak, most campaign funds passed through the hands of party leaders. Today, most of the money goes to the candidates directly, without first passing through the parties.

Party organizations also lost capacity because of a decline in patronage. When a party won control of government a century ago, it acquired control of public jobs, which were doled out to loyal party workers. However, as government jobs in the early twentieth century shifted from patronage to the merit system (see Chapter 13), the party organizations no longer controlled many of these positions. Today, because of the large size of government, thousands of patronage jobs still exist. These government employees help staff the party organizations (along with volunteers), but most of them are indebted to an individual politician rather than to a party organization. Congressional staff members, for example, are patronage employees, but they owe their jobs and their loyalty to their senator or representative, not to their party.

In Europe, where there are no primary elections, the situation is different. Parties control their nominations, and because of this they also control campaign money and workers. A party's candidates are expected to support the national platform if elected. An officeholder who fails to do so is likely to be denied renomination in the next election.

The Structure and Role of Party Organizations

Although the influence of party organizations has declined, parties are not about to die out. Candidates and activists need an ongoing organization through which they can work together, and the party serves that purpose. Moreover, certain activities, such as get-out-the-vote efforts on election day, affect all of a party's candidates and therefore are more efficiently conducted through the party organization. Indeed, parties have staged a comeback of sorts.[25] National and state party organizations now assist candidates with fund-raising, polling, research, and media production, all essential ingredients of a successful modern campaign.

Structurally, U.S. parties are loose associations of national, state, and local organizations (see Figure 8–5). The national party organizations cannot dictate the decisions made by the state organizations, which in turn do not control the activities of local organizations. However, there is communication between the levels because they all have a stake in the party's success.

Local Party Organizations   In a sense, U.S. parties are organized from the bottom up, not the top down. Of the roughly five hundred thousand elective offices in the United States, fewer than five hundred are contested statewide and only two—the presidency and vice presidency—are contested nationally. All the rest are local offices; not surprisingly, at least 95 percent of party activists work within local organizations.

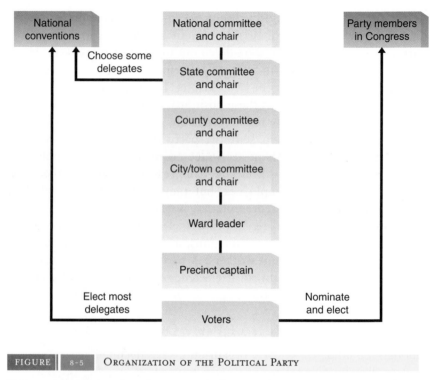

U.S. parties today are loosely structured alliances of national, state, and local organizations.

It is difficult to generalize about local parties because they vary greatly in their structure and activities. Today only a few local party organizations, including the Democratic organizations in Albany, Philadelphia, and Chicago, bear even a faint resemblance to the fabled old-time party machines that, in return for jobs and even welfare services, were able to control the vote on election day. In many urban areas, and in most suburbs and towns, the party organizations today do not have enough activists to allow them to do organizing work outside the campaign period. During campaigns, to the extent their resources allow, they conduct registration drives, send mailings or hand out leaflets, and help get out the vote. These activities are not insignificant. Most local campaigns are not well funded, and the party's efforts can tip the balance in a close race.

Local party organizations tend to concentrate on elections that coincide with local boundaries, such as races for mayor, city council, state legislature, and county offices. They also take part in congressional,

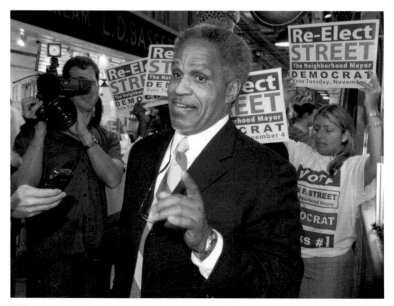

Philadelphia mayor John Street won a second term of office in 2003. A veteran of Philadelphia politics, he previously served as head of the Philadelphia City Council. Philadelphia is one of the few cities—Chicago is another—where a semblance of the old-time party machine is still found.

statewide, and presidential contests, but in these instances their role typically is secondary to that of the candidates' personal campaign organizations, which will be discussed later in this chapter.

State Party Organizations   At the state level, each party is headed by a central committee made up of members of local party organizations and local and state officeholders. State central committees do not meet regularly and provide only general policy guidance for the state organizations. Day-to-day operations are directed by a chairperson, who is a full-time, paid employee of the state party. The central committee appoints the chairperson, but it often accepts the choice of the party's leading politician, usually the governor or a U.S. senator.

The state party organizations engage in activities, such as fund-raising and voter registration, that can improve their candidates' chances of success. State party organizations concentrate on statewide races, including those for governor and U.S. senator,[26] and also focus on races for the state legislature. They play a smaller role in campaigns for national or local offices, and in most states they do not endorse candidates in statewide primary contests.

MEDIA AND POLITICS

Rush Limbaugh, The GOP's "Electronic Precinct Captain"

In 1967, the teenage son of a judge and radio station owner did his first radio show under the name Rusty Sharp. After dropping out of Southeast Missouri State University, he went to Pittsburgh and took another radio job, this time as a disc jockey under the name Jeff Christie. Today that individual, under his real name, hosts America's biggest political talk radio program—*The Rush Limbaugh Show*.

Broadcasting deregulation in the late 1980s enabled Limbaugh to build an audience for his mix of news headlines and stinging attacks on Democrats. Earlier, a station that aired Limbaugh's show would have had to balance its views with a program expressing opposing views. With deregulation, station owners could schedule talk shows of their choosing. Limbaugh's program was picked up by hundreds of stations nationwide, and its audience grew to more than twenty million listeners a week. His syndicated half-hour television show (produced by Republican campaign consultant Roger Ailes, who went on to head Fox News) was less successful; it folded in 1996 after a four-year run.

The Clintons are Limbaugh's favorite target. As a candidate and as president, Bill Clinton was variously characterized by Limbaugh as a draft-dodger, a womanizer, and a wimp. When Clinton accused Limbaugh of polluting the public debate, Limbaugh shot back: "Oh, dissent and disagreement are not good for the United States of America. We're *so sorry*, Mr. President." Hillary Clinton became his prime target after beginning her own career in elective politics in 2000. At one point, Limbaugh ridiculed the Clintons' then teen-aged daughter, Chelsea, calling her an ugly child, but he backed off when his listeners complained.

Limbaugh's audience dwarfs that of any, and all, of the liberal talk shows. In the top twenty-five radio markets, Limbaugh's show in 2006 had more listeners, in all age groups, than did the Al Franken, Ed Schultz, and Jerry Springer shows combined. Limbaugh took particular satisfaction in outdrawing Franken. In 1996, after Limbaugh published his best-seller *See, I Told You So*, Franken wrote a best-seller titled *Rush Limbaugh Is a Big Fat Idiot and Other Observations*. (After

(continued)

publication of Franken's book, Limbaugh went on a year-long diet, announcing at the end that he had shed 100 pounds, a third of his starting weight.)

Limbaugh's finest hour came in the 1994 midterm elections when the Republicans, for the first time in four decades, won control of the Senate and the House of Representatives. Limbaugh's attacks on President Clinton and his praise for the Republicans' "Contract with America" were regarded as decisive contributions. "Operation Restore Democracy" was Limbaugh's label for his months-long radio campaign to get GOP candidates elected. Conservatives turned out to vote in unusually high numbers, prompting journalists to label Limbaugh the Republicans' "electronic precinct captain."

National Party Organizations   The national party organizations are structured much like those at the state level: they have a national committee and a national party chairperson. The national headquarters for the Republican and Democratic parties are located in Washington, D.C. Although in theory the national parties are run by their committees, neither the Democratic National Committee (DNC) nor the Republican National Committee (RNC) has great power. The RNC (with more than 150 members) and the DNC (with more than 300 members) are too cumbersome to act as deliberative bodies. They meet only periodically, and their power is largely confined to setting organizational policy, such as determining the site of the party's presidential nominating convention and the rules governing the selection of convention delegates. They have no power to pick nominees or to dictate candidates' policy positions.

The national party's day-to-day operations are directed by a national chairperson chosen by the national committee, although the committee defers to the president's choice when the party controls the White House. The national chairperson directs a large staff operation that seeks to build the party's base and promote its presidential and congressional candidates. The RNC and DNC, among other things, run training programs for candidates and their staffs, raise money, seek media coverage of party positions and activities, conduct issue and group research, and send field representatives to help state and local parties with their operations.

This model of the national party was created in the 1970s when Republican leaders concluded that an expanded and modernized national organization could contribute to the party's electoral success. The DNC

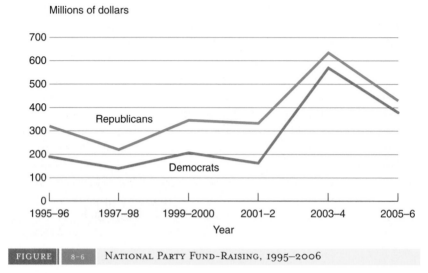

Millions of dollars

FIGURE 8-6 NATIONAL PARTY FUND-RAISING, 1995–2006

Over the years, the Republican party has raised significantly more money than the Democratic party has. The figures include fund-raising by the DNC, RNC, DCCC, NRCC, DSCC, and NRSC. Soft-money fund-raising and disbursements to state parties are not included. *Source: Federal Elections Commission.* The 2005–2006 data are based on projections from an incomplete cycle.

has a similar organization, but it is less substantial than that of the RNC. Modern campaigns, as David Adamany notes, are based on "cash," and Democrats are relatively cash-poor.[27] In every recent election cycle, the Republican national party has outspent its Democratic counterpart (see Figure 8–6).

The Parties and Money   The parties' major role in campaigns is the raising and spending of money. The RNC and the DNC are major sources of campaign funds, as are the party campaign committees in the House and the Senate. These include the Democratic Congressional Campaign Committee (DCCC), the National Republican Congressional Committee (NRCC), the Democratic Senatorial Campaign Committee (DSCC), and the National Republican Senatorial Committee (NRSC).

In addition to providing funds, these campaign committees increasingly have sought to persuade individuals who would make strong candidates to run for Congress. Nevertheless, the party committees have more of a **service relationship** than a power relationship with their party's candidates. Because the party nominees are chosen through primaries and because many potential candidates already have a power base at the local or state level, the national committees are unable to handpick the party's nominees. Accordingly, the party organizations tend to back whoever wins the party primary. If the candidate then wins the general election, the party organization at least has helped deny the office to the opposing party.

A party can legally give $10,000 directly to a House candidate and $37,500 to a Senate candidate. This funding, along with the money a candidate receives from individual contributors ($2,000 maximum per contributor) and interest groups ($5,000 maximum per group), is termed **hard money**; it goes directly to the candidate and can be spent as he or she chooses.

Limits on party contributions were established when the campaign finance laws were reformed in the 1970s in response to the Watergate scandal. However, a loophole in the laws was exposed when a court ruling allowed the parties to raise and spend unlimited campaign funds provided the funds were not channeled directly to a party's candidates. Thus, whereas a wealthy contributor could legally give a candidate only a limited amount, that same contributor could give an unlimited amount to the candidate's party. These contributions were termed **soft money** in that a party could not hand it over directly to a candidate. But the party could use these contributions to support party activities, such as voter registration efforts, get-out-the-vote drives, and party-centered televised ads, that could indirectly benefit its candidates. In some cases, the line between the use of hard and soft money was hard to distinguish. In 1996, for example, the Democratic party ran a $100 million ad campaign that did not directly urge voters to support Clinton but did include pictures of him and references to his accomplishments as president.

In 2002, Congress closed the loophole through enactment of the Bipartisan Campaign Reform Act (BCRA), which prohibits the national parties from raising or spending soft money. BCRA also bans the state parties from spending soft money in support of candidates for federal office. The Supreme Court upheld these restrictions in a 2003 decision,[28] but a new loophole soon surfaced. The ban on soft money does not fully apply to so-called "527 groups." (Section 527 of the Internal Revenue Code defines the rules governing not-for-profit political groups.). Much of the money that before enactment of the new law would have been contributed to a party organization now finds its way into the hands of 527 groups. Although they are prohibited from attacking a candidate directly, these groups can legally engage in issue advocacy. This has

In 2005, the Democratic party chose Howard Dean as its national party chair. Most party chairs are not widely known, but Dean was familiar to voters as a result of his strong bid for the 2004 Democratic presidential nomination. The Democrats picked Dean to be their chair in hopes that he could boost their fund-raising and grassroots efforts.

enabled them to mount thinly veiled candidate attacks. During the 2004 presidential election, 527 groups spent more than $100 million. One such group, America Coming Together, spent $15 million—including $5 million provided by financier George Soros—on attacking the Bush administration's economic and Iraq policies. In short, BCRA has been only partially successful in regulating the flow of soft money in campaigns. Just as water always runs downhill, money always finds its way into election politics.

THE CANDIDATE-CENTERED CAMPAIGN

Although competition between the Republican and Democratic parties provides the backdrop to today's campaigns, the campaigns themselves are largely controlled by the candidates, particularly in congressional, statewide, and presidential races. Each candidate has a personal organization, created especially for the campaign and disbanded once it is over. The candidates are entrepreneurs who play what political consultant Joe Napolitan called "the election game."[29] The game begins with money—lots of it.

★ ‖ STATES IN THE NATION

Public Funding of State Elections

About half the states have public funding of election campaigns. Some of them give the money to political parties, which allocate it to candidates or spend it on party activities such as get-out-the-vote efforts. Other states give funds directly to candidates, although this funding typically is limited to candidates for designated offices, such as governor.

Q: What might explain the fact that there is no clear-cut regional pattern to the public funding of state elections?

A: Public funding of elections is relatively new, so additional states may adopt it in the next decade or two, at which time a regional tendency could emerge. (If your state does not have public funding, do you think it is likely to adopt it anytime soon? Why?)

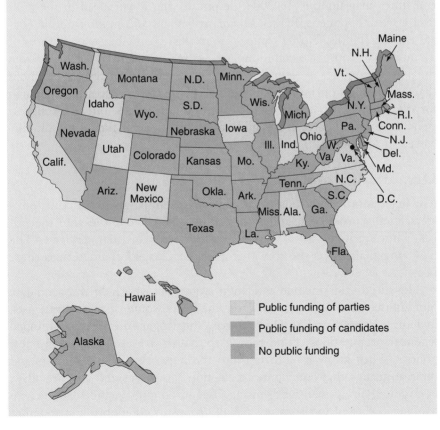

Public funding of parties

Public funding of candidates

No public funding

Campaign Funds: The Money Chase

Campaigns for high office are expensive, and the costs keep rising. In 1980, about $250 million was spent on all Senate and House campaigns combined. The figure had jumped to $425 million by 1990. In 2006, the figure topped $2 billion ($2,000 million), roughly ten times the 1980 level. As might be expected, incumbents have a distinct advantage in fund-raising. They have contributor lists from past campaigns and have the policy influence that donors seek. House and Senate incumbents outspend their challengers by more than two to one.[30]

Because of the high cost of campaigns, candidates spend much of their time raising funds, which come primarily from individual contributors, interest groups (through PACs, discussed in Chapter 9), and political parties. The money chase is relentless.[31] A U.S. senator must raise $20,000 a week on average throughout the entire six-year term in order to raise the minimum $6 million it takes to run a competitive Senate campaign in many states. A Senate campaign in a large state can cost several times that amount. In 2004, despite having a wide lead in the polls over a weak opponent, Barack Obama still spent $10 million on his Senate race in Illinois. House campaigns are less costly, but expenditures of $1 million or more are commonplace. As for presidential elections, even the nominating race is expensive. In 2004, Senator John Kerry spent more than $50 million during the competitive phase of his successful campaign for the Democratic nomination. (In presidential races, but not congressional ones, candidates are eligible to receive federal funds, a topic discussed in Chapter 12.)

Organization and Strategy: Hired Guns

The key operatives in today's campaigns are campaign consultants, pollsters, media producers, and fund-raising and get-out-the-vote specialists. They are **hired guns** who charge hefty fees for their services. "The new king-makers" is the way writer David Chagall characterizes these pros.[32]

The hired guns include campaign strategists who help the candidate plot and execute a game plan. Over the years, some of these strategists, including James Carville, Dick Morris, and Roger Ailes, have developed legendary reputations. Fund-raising specialists are also part of the new politics. They know how to tap into the networks of large donors and interest groups that contribute to election campaigns and also are adept at targeted, direct-mail fund-raising. The hired guns include experts who conduct polls and focus groups (small groups of voters brought together to discuss at length their thoughts on the candidates and issues). Polls and focus groups enable candidates to identify issues and messages that will resonate with voters.[33] Media consultants are another staple of the modern campaign. These experts are adept at producing televised political ads and creating "photo-ops" and other staged events that attract news coverage.

The hired guns of the modern campaign are skilled at **packaging** a candidate—highlighting those aspects of the candidate's partisanship, policy positions, personal background, and personality that are thought to be most attractive to voters. Packaging is not new to politics. Andrew Jackson's self-portrayal in the nineteenth century as "the champion of the people" is an image any modern candidate can appreciate. What is new is the need to fit the image to the requirements of a world of sound bites, 30-second ads, and televised debates and to do it in a persuasive way. In the old days, it was sometimes enough for candidates to drive home the point that they were Republicans or Democrats, playing on the tendency of voters to choose a candidate on the basis of party. Party appeals are still critically important, but today's voters also want to know about a candidate's personality and policy positions.

Hired consultants have been a driving force behind yet another characteristic of modern campaigns—the tearing down of one's opponent. In a sense, negative campaigning is as old as American politics. Thomas Jefferson was the subject of a whispering campaign about his sexual life, and Abraham Lincoln was characterized by opponents as "a baboon" for his hairy, gangly look and his backwoods roots. But today's version of attack politics is unprecedented in its scale, scope, and sophistication. Professional strategists have concluded that they can win more votes by diminishing the opponent than by building up their candidate. In the past three decades, negative televised ads have increased threefold to the point where they now constitute the large share of political ads.[34] Most campaigns nowadays have a nasty edge, and the attacks are sometimes outright vicious. In 2002, for example, incumbent Senator Max Cleland lost his bid for reelection when his lead in the polls withered in the face of blistering attacks on his patriotism, including an ad that showed his face alternately with the faces of Saddam Hussein and Osama bin Laden. Cleland's patriotism would seem above reproach; he lost both legs and an arm in combat in Vietnam. Yet his opponent seized on Cleland's vote against a Senate bill creating the Department of Homeland Security because it did not include the normal protections for civil service employees. The ad ignored Cleland's objection to the bill, portraying him instead as "soft" on terrorism.

Voter Contacts: A Pitched Battle

Today's campaigns for high office have no historical parallel in their length and penetration. Candidates start their active campaigning much earlier—often a year in advance of election day—than in times past. The modern campaign is relentless, with voters being bombarded with messages that arrive by air, by land, and over the Web.

Air Wars   The major battleground of the modern campaign is the mass media, particularly television. Television emerged in the 1960s as the major medium of presidential and congressional politics and has remained the dominant medium ever since.

Candidates spend heavily on televised political advertising, which enables them to communicate directly—and on their own terms—with voters.[35] The production and the airing of political ads account for half or more of the expenditures in presidential campaigns and in most congressional races. Indeed, televised ads are the main reason for the high cost of U.S. campaigns. In most democracies, televised campaigning takes place through parties, which receive free air time to make their pitch. Many democracies even prohibit the purchase of televised advertising time by candidates (see Table 8–1).

Air wars is the term that political scientist Darrell West applies to candidates' use of televised ads. Candidates increasingly play off each other's

---

TABLE 8-1   TELEVISION CAMPAIGN PRACTICES IN SELECTED DEMOCRACIES

In many democracies, free television time is provided to political parties, and candidates are not allowed to buy advertising time. The United States provides no free time to parties and allows candidates to purchase air time. Television debates are also a feature of many U.S. campaigns.

Country	Paid TV Ads Allowed?	Unrestricted Free TV Time Provided?	TV Debates Held?
Canada	Yes	Yes	Yes
France	No	Yes	Yes
Germany	Yes	Yes	Yes
Great Britain	No	Yes	No
Italy	No	Yes	Yes
Netherlands	No	No	Yes
United States	Yes	No	Yes

ads, seeking to gain the strategic advantage.[36] Modern production techniques enable well-funded candidates to get new ads on the air within a few hours' time, which allows them to rebut attacks and exploit fast-breaking developments, a tactic known as *rapid response.*

Candidates also use the press to get their message across, although the amount of news coverage they can expect varies widely by location and office. Many House candidates are nearly ignored by their local news media. The New York City media market, for example, includes more than a score of House districts in New York, New Jersey, Pennsylvania, and Connecticut, and candidates in these districts get little or no coverage from the New York media. The presidential campaign, in contrast, gets daily coverage from both national and local media. Between these extremes are Senate races, which always get some news coverage and, if hotly contested, may get heavy coverage.

Debates are also part of the modern media campaign. Debates often attract large and attentive audiences but can be risky encounters, because they give viewers a chance to compare the candidates directly. A weak or bumbling performance can hurt a candidate. Some analysts believe, for example, that Al Gore's performance in the first of the 2000 general election debates, when he grimaced and sighed loudly when George W. Bush was talking, cost him the election. Gore had been slightly ahead in the opinion polls but lost his lead immediately after the debate.

Ground Wars   Candidates' first priority in a close election is "swing voters"—those voters who conceivably could be persuaded to vote for either side. As election day nears, however, candidates concentrate on getting their supporters to the polls.

The get-out-the-vote effort traditionally has been borne by the parties and other organizations, such as labor unions. Although these groups remain the cornerstone of the effort, the candidates are also involved, and increasingly so. As partisanship has intensified in recent years, candidates have found it more difficult to persuade voters to switch sides. It has therefore become important for them to get as many of their supporters as possible to the polls on election day. Some campaign money that formerly would have been spent on televised advertising is now channeled into voter turnout efforts. In the final phase of the 2006 congressional elections, millions of potential voters were contacted by phone or in person by the Republican and Democratic campaigns.

Web Wars   New communication technology usually makes its way into campaign politics, and the Internet is no exception. Each of the nine candidates for the 2004 Democratic presidential nomination, for example, had a website dedicated to providing information, generating public support, attracting volunteers, and raising money. Howard Dean's website was by far the most successful. Through it, Dean raised more than $20 million and developed a nationwide network of a half-million supporters.

Although television is still the principal medium of election politics, some analysts believe that the Internet may eventually overtake it. E-mail is cheaper than television advertising (and both cheaper and faster than traditional mail). Because it is a targeted medium, the Internet could become the channel through which candidates reach particular voting groups. But the Internet also has some disadvantages relative to television. The most important is that the individual user has greater control over Internet messages. With television, when a political ad appears during a favorite program, most viewers will watch it. An unsolicited message on the Internet is more easily ignored or deleted. Future candidates may conclude that the Internet is the preferred medium for fund-raising and interacting with die-hard supporters and that television is the best medium for achieving public recognition and reaching less-interested voters.

PARTIES, CANDIDATES, AND THE PUBLIC'S INFLUENCE

Candidate-centered campaigns have some distinct advantages. First, they can infuse new blood into electoral politics. Candidate recruitment is normally a slow process in party-centered systems. Would-be officeholders pay their dues by working in the party and, in the process, tend to adopt the outlook of those already there. By comparison, a candidate-centered system is more open and provides opportunities for total newcomers to gain office quickly. John Edwards is a case in point. Edwards had never run for public office when, in 1997, he called a Democratic political consultant to say that he was thinking about running for the Senate. The consultant assumed that Edwards, a little-known trial lawyer, had the North Carolina state senate in mind. Edwards shocked him by saying that he was eyeing the upcoming 1998 U.S. Senate race. Edwards proceeded to gain the Democratic Senate nomination and then poured millions of his own money into a successful general-election campaign against incumbent Republican Senator Lauch Faircloth. In 2003, Edwards decided against seeking a second term in the Senate and entered the race for the 2004 Democratic presidential nomination. Though Edwards lost that bid, he ran so strongly in the primaries that the winner, John Kerry, picked him as his vice presidential running mate.

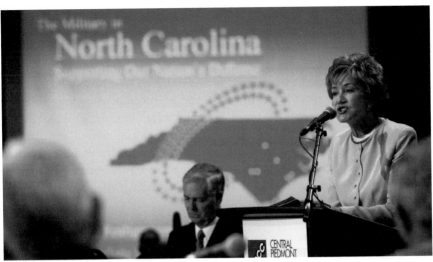

Senator Elizabeth Dole (R-N.C.) chaired the National Republican Senatorial Committee (NRSC) for the 2006 midterm election period. The chair serves a two-year term and helps Republican Senate candidates get the funds and other support they need to run successful campaigns. Dole helped GOP candidates in 2006 raise tens of millions of dollars in campaign funds. The NRSC was established in 1916, shortly after the U.S. Constitution was amended to provide for the direct popular election of senators. The Democrats have an equivalent committee, the Democratic Senatorial Campaign Committee (DSCC).

Candidate-centered campaigns also lend flexibility to electoral politics. When political conditions and issues change, self-directed candidates quickly adjust, bringing new ideas into the political arena. Strong party organizations are rigid by comparison. Until the early 1990s, for example, the British Labour party was controlled by old-line activists who refused to concede that changes in the British economy called for changes in the party's trade unionist and economic policies. The result was a series of humiliating defeats at the hands of the Conservative party that ended only after Tony Blair and other proponents of "New Labour" successfully recast the party's image.

Also, candidate-centered campaigns encourage national officeholders to be responsive to local interests. In building personal followings among their state and district constituents, members of Congress respond to local needs. Nearly every significant domestic program enacted by Congress is adjusted to accommodate the interests of states and localities that otherwise would be hurt by the policy. Members of Congress are not obliged to support the legislative position of their party's majority, and they often extract favors for their constituents as the price of their support. Where strong national parties exist, national interests take precedence over local concerns. In both France and Britain, for example, the pleas of representatives of underdeveloped regions have often gone unheeded by their party's majority.

In other respects, however, candidate-centered campaigns have some distinct disadvantages. Often they degenerate into mud-slinging contests, and they are fertile ground for powerful special interest groups, which contribute much of the money that underwrites candidates' campaigns. Many groups give large sums of money to incumbents of both parties, which enables them to insulate themselves from an election's outcome: whether the Republicans win or the Democrats win, these contributors are assured of having friends in high places.

Candidate-centered campaigns also weaken accountability by making it easier for officeholders to deny personal responsibility for government's actions. If national policy goes awry, an incumbent can always say that he or she is only one vote out of many and that the real problem resides with the president or with "others" in Congress. The problem of accountability in the U.S. system is illustrated by the several trillion dollars that have been added to the national debt since 2000 because of Republican officeholders' insistence on steep tax cuts and huge increases in military spending and Democratic officeholders' refusal to accept cuts in domestic spending programs. "Running on empty" is how former cabinet secretary Peter Peterson describes the huge debt being passed along to future generations of Americans that has enabled today's members of Congress to keep their constituents happy enough to vote them back into office.[37] The problem of accountability is also illustrated by surveys that have asked Americans about their confidence in Congress. Although most citizens do not have a high opinion of Congress as a whole, most citizens also say that they have confidence in their local representative in Congress. This paradoxical attitude prevails in so many districts that the net result in most elections is a Congress whose membership is not greatly changed from the previous one (see Chapter 11). In contrast, party-centered campaigns are characterized by collective accountability. When problems occur, voters tend to hold the majority party responsible and invariably vote many of its members out of office.

In sum, candidate-centered campaigns strengthen the relationship between the voters and their individual representative while at the same time weakening the relationship between the full electorate and their representative institutions. Whether this arrangement serves the public's interest is debatable. Nevertheless, it is clear that Americans do not favor party-centered politics. Parties survived the shift to candidate-centered campaigns and will persist, but their organizational heyday has passed. (Congressional and presidential campaigns are discussed further in Chapters 11 and 12, respectively.)

Summary

Political parties serve to link the public with its elected leaders. In the United States, this linkage is provided by the two-party system; only the Republican and Democratic parties have any chance of winning control of government. The fact that the United States has only two major parties is explained by several factors: an electoral system—characterized by single-member districts—that makes it difficult for third parties to compete for power; each party's willingness to accept differing political views; and a political culture that stresses compromise and negotiation rather than ideological rigidity.

Because the United States has only two major parties, each of which seeks to gain majority support, their candidates normally tend to avoid controversial or extreme political positions. Sometimes, particularly during times of crisis, Democratic and Republican candidates do offer sharply contrasting policy alternatives. Ordinarily, however, Republican and Democratic candidates pursue moderate and somewhat overlapping policy objectives. Each party can count on its party loyalists, but U.S. elections can hinge on swing voters. These voters respond to the issues of the moment either prospectively, basing their vote on what the candidates promise to do if elected, or retrospectively, basing their vote on their satisfaction or dissatisfaction with what the party in power has already done.

America's parties are decentralized, fragmented organizations. The national party organization does not control the policies and activities of the state organizations, and these in turn do not control the local organizations. Traditionally the local organizations have controlled most of the party's work force because most elections are contested at the local level. Local parties, however, vary markedly in their vitality. Whatever their level, America's party organizations are relatively weak. They lack control over nominations and elections. Candidates can bypass the party organization and win nomination through primary elections. Individual candidates also control most of the organizational structure and money necessary to win elections. The state and national party organizations have recently expanded their capacity to provide candidates with modern campaign services. Nevertheless, party organizations at all levels have few ways of controlling the candidates who run under their banners. They assist candidates with campaign technology, workers, and funds, but they cannot compel candidates' loyalty to organizational goals.

American political campaigns, particularly those for higher office, are candidate centered. Most candidates are self-starters who become adept at "the election game." They spend much of their time raising campaign funds, and they build their personal organizations around hired guns: pollsters, media producers, fund-raisers, and election consultants. Strategy and image making are key components of the modern campaign, as is televised political advertising, which accounts for half or more of all spending in presidential and congressional races.

The advantages of candidate-centered politics include a responsiveness to new leadership, new ideas, and local concerns. Yet this form of politics can result in campaigns that are personality-driven, depend on powerful interest groups, and blur responsibility for what government has done.

KEY TERMS

air wars (*p. 284*)
candidate-centered politics (*p. 252*)
grassroots party (*p. 255*)
hard money (*p. 279*)
hired guns (*p. 282*)
money chase (*p. 282*)
multiparty system (*p. 262*)
nomination (*p. 272*)
packaging (of a candidate) (*p. 283*)
party-centered politics (*p. 252*)
party coalition (*p. 265*)
party competition (*p. 253*)
party organizations (*p. 271*)

party realignment (*p. 256*)
political party (*p. 252*)
primary election (direct primary)
   (*p. 272*)
proportional representation (*p. 262*)
prospective voting (*p. 261*)
retrospective voting (*p. 261*)
service relationship (*p. 278*)
single-member districts (*p. 262*)
soft money (*p. 279*)
split ticket (*p. 260*)
two-party system (*p. 262*)

SUGGESTED READINGS

Aldrich, John H. *Why Parties? The Origin and Transformation of Political Parties in America*. Chicago: University of Chicago Press, 1995. An insightful analysis of what parties are and how they emerge and develop.

Flanigan, William H., and Nancy H. Zingale. *Political Behavior of the American Electorate*, 11th ed. Washington, D.C.: Congressional Quarterly Press, 2005. An overview of Americans' electoral behavior.

Greenberg, Stanley B. *The Two Americas: Our Current Political Deadlock and How to Break It*. New York: Thomas Dunne Books, 2004. An assessment of party politics in today's America.

Lijphardt, Arend. *Electoral Systems and Party Systems: A Study of Twenty-Seven Democracies, 1945–1990*. New York: Oxford University Press, 1994. A comprehensive study of the relationship between electoral systems and party systems.

Patterson, Kelly D. *Political Parties and the Maintenance of Liberal Democracy.* New York: Columbia University Press, 1996. A systematic look at the effects of political parties on American government and politics.

Sifreg, Micah L. *Spoiling for a Fight: Third-Party Politics in America.* New York: Routledge, 2003. An analysis of America's third parties and their impact on the two-party system.

Stonecash, Jeffrey. *Class and Party in American Politics.* Boulder, Colo.: Westview Press, 2001. An insightful analysis that argues that class is still very much a part of America's party politics.

West, Darrell M. *Air Wars: Television Advertising in Election Campaigns, 1952–2000,* 4th ed. Washington, D.C.: Congressional Quarterly Press, 2005. A thorough study of the role of televised advertising in election campaigns.

LIST OF WEBSITES

http://www.democrats.org/ The Democratic National Committee's site; provides information on the party's platform, candidates, officials, and organization.

http://www.greenparties.org/ The Green party's website; contains information on the party's philosophy and policy goals.

http://www.rnc.org/ The Website of the Republican National Committee; offers information on Republican leaders, policy positions, and organizations.

http://www.jamescarvillesoffice.com/ The website of James Carville, one of the nation's top campaign consultants.

POLITICS IN THEORY AND PRACTICE

Thinking: Why are elections conducted so differently in the United States than they are in European democracies? Why are U.S. campaigns so much longer, more expensive, and more candidate-centered?

Participating: Consider becoming a campaign volunteer. The opportunities are numerous. Candidates at every level from the presidency on down seek volunteers to assist in organizing, canvassing, fund-raising, and other campaign activities. As a college student, you have communication and knowledge skills that would be valuable to a campaign. You might be pleasantly surprised by the level of responsibility you are given.

ADDITIONAL RESOURCES

For quizzes, interactive simulations, games, graphics, and other study tools, visit the book's Online Learning Center at **www.mhhe.com/pattersonwtp7.**

GOP Has Lock on South, and Democrats Can't Find Key

By Ronald Brownstein

In recent decades, America's political party system has undergone a slow and partial realignment that has substantially altered the political landscape. The clearest case is the American South. Once staunchly Democratic, it has become solidly Republican. In a December 15, 2004, article, Los Angeles Times *national political correspondent Ronald Brownstein concluded on the basis of voting returns from the 2004 presidential election that the Democratic party has little prospect of reversing the situation. Following is an abbreviated version of his article.*

The generation-long political retreat of Democrats across the South is disintegrating into a rout.

President Bush dominated the South so completely in last month's presidential election that he carried nearly 85% of all the counties across the region—and more than 90% of counties where whites are a majority of the population, according to a *Times* analysis of election results and census data.

The *Times'* analysis which provides the most detailed picture yet of the vote in Southern communities, shows that Bush's victory was even more comprehensive than his sweep of the region's 13 states would suggest.

His overwhelming performance left Sen. John F. Kerry clinging to a few scattered islands of support in a region that until the 1960s provided the foundation of the Democratic coalition in presidential politics. Kerry won fewer Southern counties than any Democratic nominee since the Depression except Walter F. Mondale in 1984 and George S. McGovern in 1972, according to data assembled by the *Times* and Polidata, a firm that specializes in political statistics.

In Southern counties without a substantial number of African American or Latino voters, Bush virtually obliterated Kerry. Across the 11 states of the old Confederacy, plus Kentucky and Oklahoma, whites constitute a majority of the population in 1,154 counties. Kerry won 90 of them. By contrast, Bill Clinton won 510 white-majority counties in the South eight years ago.

"We are out of business in the South," said J. W. Brannen, the Democratic Party chairman in Russell County, Ala., the only white-majority county in the state that Kerry carried.

The results underscore the enormity of the challenge facing Democrats as they try to rebuild their Southern support. Most ominously for them, the patterns suggest that under Bush, the GOP is solidifying its hold not just on Southern white conservatives but white moderates as well, a trend also apparent in exit polls of Southern voters on election day. "As the older white moderates leave the scene, they are being replaced with younger moderates more willing to vote Republican," said Merle Black, a political scientist at Atlanta's Emory University and the author of several books on Southern politics.

Compounding the Democratic dilemma is the growing tendency of Southern whites who vote Republican for president to support GOP candidates down the ballot. In 1984, Ronald Reagan won slightly more counties across the South than Bush did this year; but after Reagan's landslide, Republicans held 12 of the 26 U.S. Senate seats in the region. After Bush helped the GOP win six open Southern Senate seats last month, Republicans now hold 22 of the 26 Senate seats in the 13 states.

That is the most either party has controlled in the region since Democrats also won 22 in 1964—ironically, the election in which the white backlash against the Civil Rights Act allowed the GOP to make its first inroads into the South.

Forty years later, under a Southern Republican president, the South has become an electoral fortress for the GOP. Outside the South, Democrats hold more House and Senate seats and won many more electoral college votes than the GOP last month. But the GOP's advantage in the region has been large enough to overcome those deficits and create Republican majorities in both chambers of Congress and the electoral college. And the magnitude of November's Republican sweep last month suggests the GOP advantage across the region is expanding.

"I don't think that for 50 years we're going to be a Republican section of the country," said former Democratic National Committee Co-Chairman Donald L. Fowler of South Carolina. "I really believe we have the potential to turn a lot of this around in a decade. But it will take constructive, directed, consistent work to do it. It's just not going to happen by itself. We're in too big a hole."

Politically, the South includes 13 states: Alabama, Arkansas, Florida, Georgia, Kentucky, Louisiana, Mississippi, North Carolina, Oklahoma, South Carolina, Tennessee, Texas and Virginia. Together they cast 168 electoral college votes, more than three-fifths of the 270 required for election.

Many political analysts see Bush's commanding performance across the region—

and Republican gains in other elections during his presidency—as the fourth wave in the GOP's Southern ascendance.

The GOP, which was founded in the 1850s as a Northern party opposed to the expansion of slavery, won very few Southern states in presidential races for a full century after the Civil War. Democrat Franklin D. Roosevelt won every Southern state in all four of his presidential campaigns.

Republican President Dwight D. Eisenhower had some Southern success in the 1950s. But the GOP planted its first lasting roots in the region amid the white backlash against the passage of the Civil Rights and Voting Rights acts under Democratic President Lyndon B. Johnson in the mid-1960s.

Opposition to the new civil rights laws, and to such follow-on initiatives as affirmative action and school busing for racial integration, powered the first wave of GOP gains in the South. But the party expanded its appeal by courting Southern whites with conservative messages on such nonracial issues as taxes, national defense and moral values. That second advance reached a crescendo during Ronald Reagan's two elections. "Reagan's presidency was the turning point in the evolution of a competitive, two-party electorate in the South," Black and his brother, Earl Black, wrote in their 2002 book, *The Rise of Southern Republicans.*

For the next decade, Democrats remained competitive enough for Southerner Bill Clinton to capture five Southern states in 1992. But the disenchantment over Clinton's chaotic first two years fueled a third wave of GOP Southern gains. In their midterm landslide of 1994, Republicans for the first time captured the majority of House and Senate seats from the South. As Clinton pursued a more centrist course after 1994, Democrats stanched their congressional losses in the South and even regained some governorships. In 1996, Clinton again won five Southern states.

But under Bush, the GOP is on the march again. In the Senate, Republicans have increased the number of seats they hold in the 13 Southern states from 18 before Bush took office to 22. (The GOP has now won the last 10 open-seat Senate races in the South.) In the House, Republicans have stretched their advantage in the Southern states from 27 seats before Bush took office to 40 today. "This is a cumulative process that has gained critical momentum in the past four years," said Karl Rove, Bush's chief political advisor.

Analyzing the results at the county level illustrates Bush's dominance vividly. In 2000, Bush won 1,047 counties across the South and held then-Vice President Al Gore to 294, according to Polidata. This year, Bush won 1,124 counties and held Kerry to 216, according to Polidata figures based on preliminary election results.(The South had one fewer county this year than in 2000 because two jurisdictions merged in Virginia.)

Those numbers represent a catastrophic decline for the Democrats since the 1990s, when Clinton won more than 650 counties in each of his presidential victories. Bush has become the first candidate since Franklin D. Roosevelt in 1940 and 1944 to carry more than 1,000 Southern counties twice.

What's Your Opinion?

Do you believe, as does South Carolina's Fowler, that Democrats can "turn a lot of this around in a decade"? Or do you think he's being wildly optimistic about the Democratic party's prospects in the South? Why?

CHAPTER 9

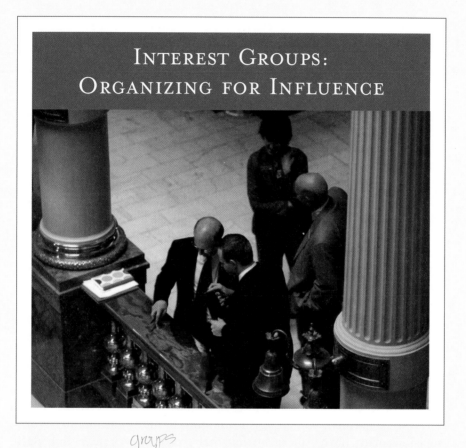

INTEREST GROUPS:
ORGANIZING FOR INFLUENCE

groups

66 The flaw in the pluralist heaven is that the heavenly chorus sings with a
strong upper-class bias. 99

E. E. SCHATTSCHNEIDER[1]

Senior-citizen groups launched their attack within hours of President
Bush's 2005 State of the Union address. Bush had specified for the first
time key components of his social security reform plan: workers would be
able to funnel a third of their social security taxes into private individual
investment accounts, and benefits on the remaining two-thirds would be
scaled back; current retirees and workers 55 years of age or older would
be exempt from benefit reductions. Bush claimed that his plan would save
social security from going "bankrupt" in 2042, the year when benefit pay-
outs are scheduled to exceed incoming revenues if no changes are made
in the system.

Led by the American Association of Retired Persons (AARP), the sen-
iors' lobby assailed the plan and orchestrated a campaign involving tens

of thousands of angry calls, letters, telegrams, and faxes from retirees to their congressional representatives. AARP poured nearly $10 million into newspaper advertisements—"If we feel like gambling, we'll play the slots"—attacking Bush's proposal to partially privatize social security. Seniors' groups found an ally in congressional Democrats. Senate minority leader Harry Reid (D-Nev.) called Bush's plan "social security roulette." "Democrats are all for giving Americans more of a say and more choices when it comes to their retirement savings," Reid declared. "But that doesn't mean taking Social Security's guarantee and gambling with it. And that's coming from a senator who represents Las Vegas." Within days, opinion polls showed declining support for Bush's plan. Over the next several months, public support for his proposal continued to fall, and by summer all but a few Republican diehards had given up on Bush's plan.

The campaign against Bush's social security initiative suggests why interest groups are both admired and feared. On one hand, groups have a legitimate right to express their views on public policy issues. It is entirely appropriate for senior citizens or other groups—whether farmers, consumers, business firms, or college students—to promote their interests through collective action. In fact, the *pluralist* theory of American politics (see Chapter 1) holds that society's interests are most effectively represented through group action.

On the other hand, groups can wield too much power. If a group gets its way at an unreasonable cost to the rest of society, the public interest is harmed. When Bush announced his intention to reform social security, most Americans felt that a change was necessary. Bush did not help his cause by proposing a change—the creation of private retirement accounts—that was more closely aligned with his belief in the marketplace than with his stated goal of protecting social security from bankruptcy. Economists calculated that Bush's plan might actually cost more money than it would save. Nevertheless, the time seemed ripe for a fruitful debate on the future of social security. Did AARP and its group allies, in pursuit of their own agenda, needlessly derail that debate?

Opinions might differ as to the answer to this question, but there is no doubt that groups have considerable influence over public policy. Indeed, most observers believe that group influence is increasing. The situation has been described as the rise of **single-issue politics**: separate groups are organized around nearly every conceivable policy issue, with each group pressing its demands to the utmost.

An **interest group**—also called a "faction," "pressure group," or "special interest"—has two characteristics: an organized membership and the pursuit of policy goals that stem from its members' shared interest. Thus, a bridge club or an amateur softball team is not an interest group because it does not seek to influence the political process. Organizations such as the Association of Wheat Growers, Common Cause, the National Organization for Women, the World Wildlife Fund, and the National Rifle Association are interest groups because each is an organized entity and each seeks to further its members' interests through political action.

Interest groups are similar to political parties in certain respects, but the two types of organizations differ in important ways. Major political parties address a broad range of issues so as to appeal to diverse blocs of voters. Parties exist to contest elections. They change their policy positions as the voters' preferences change; for the party, winning is almost everything. Interest groups, in contrast, focus on specific issues of direct concern to their members; farm groups, for example, concentrate on agricultural policy. A group may involve itself in elections, but its purpose is to influence public policy in its area of interest.

This chapter examines the degree to which various interests in American society are represented by organized groups, the process by which interest groups exert influence, and the costs and benefits of group politics with respect to the public good. The main points made in the chapter are these:

* *Although nearly all interests in American society are organized to some degree, those associated with economic activity, particularly business enterprises, are by far the most thoroughly organized.* Their advantage rests on their superior financial resources and on the fact that they offer potential members private goods (such as wages and jobs).

* *Groups that do not have economic activity as their primary function often have organizational problems.* These groups pursue public or collective goods (such as a safer environment) that are available even to individuals who are not group members, so individuals may choose not to pay the costs of membership.

* *Lobbying and electioneering are the traditional means by which groups communicate with and influence political leaders.* Recent developments, including grassroots lobbying and PACs, have heightened interest groups' influence.

* *The interest-group system overrepresents business interests and higher-income groups and fosters policies that serve a group's interest more than the public interest.* Thus, although groups are an essential part of the policy process, they also distort that process.

HOW THE UNITED STATES COMPARES

Groups: "A Nation of Joiners"

"A nation of joiners" is how the Frenchman Alexis de Tocqueville described the United States during his visit to this country in the 1830s. Tocqueville was stunned by the group and community activity he saw, suggesting that Europeans would find it hard to comprehend. "The political activity that pervades the United States," said Tocqueville, "must be seen to be understood."

Today, Americans still are more actively involved in groups and community causes than are Europeans. Some observers, including Robert Putnam, believe that group activity in the United States is in decline (*Bowling Alone*, 2000). Even if that is true, Americans are more engaged in groups than citizens elsewhere. Among the reasons are the nation's tradition of free association, the prominence of religion, and the open nature of American society.

Another reason is the structure of the U.S. political system. Because of federalism and the separation of powers, the American system offers numerous points at which groups can try to influence public policy. If unsuccessful with legislators, groups can turn to executives or to the courts. If thwarted at the national level, groups can turn to state and local governments. By comparison, the governments of most other democratic nations are not organized in ways that facilitate group access and influence. France's unitary government, for example, concentrates power at the national level.

Such differences are reflected in citizens' participation rates. Americans are more likely to belong to groups than are the French, Italians, British, or Germans, as the accompanying figures from the World Values Survey indicate.

	No group	1–3 groups	4 or more groups
United States	18%	63%	19%
Germany	33%	60%	7%
Great Britain	46%	45%	9%
Italy	59%	40%	←1%
France	61%	35%	4%

Percentage belonging to: ■ No group ■ 1–3 groups ■ 4 or more groups

The Interest-Group System

In the 1830s, the Frenchman Alexis de Tocqueville wrote that the "principle of association" was nowhere more evident than in America.[2] The country's tradition of free association has always made it easy for Americans to join together for political purposes, and their diversity has given them reason to pursue their separate interests (see "How the United States Compares"). Nevertheless, the nation's various interests are not equally well organized. Organizations develop when people with shared interests have the opportunity and the incentive to join together. Some individuals have the skills, money, contacts, or time to participate effectively in group politics. Others do not. Moreover, some groups are inherently more attractive to potential members than others and thus find it easier to organize. Groups also differ in their financial resources and thus in their capacity for political action.

Therefore, a first consideration in regard to group politics in America is the issue of how thoroughly various interests are organized. Interests that are highly organized stand a good chance of having their views heard by policymakers. Poorly organized interests run the risk of being ignored.

Economic Groups

No interests are more fully or effectively organized than those that have economic activity as their primary purpose. An indication of their advantage is the fact that Washington lobbyists who represent economic groups outnumber those of all other groups by more than two to one.

Corporations, labor unions, farm groups, and professional associations, among others, exist primarily for economic purposes: to make profits, provide jobs, improve pay, or protect an occupation. For the sake of discussion, we will call such organizations **economic groups,** although it is important to recognize that their political goals can include policies that transcend the narrow economic interests of their members. Although the AFL-CIO, for example, concentrates on labor policies, it also takes positions on other foreign and domestic issues.

An Organizational Edge   One reason for the abundance of economic groups is their access to financial resources. Political activity does not come cheap. If a group is to make its views known, it normally must have a headquarters, an expert staff, and communication facilities. Economic groups can obtain the requisite money and expertise from their economic activities. Corporations have the greatest built-in advantage. They do not have to charge membership dues or conduct fund-raisers to support their lobbying. Their political money comes from their business income.

Some economic groups do depend on dues for their support but can offer prospective members a powerful incentive to join: **private (individual) goods,** or the benefits that a group can grant directly to the individual member. For example, workers in the state of Michigan cannot hold automobile assembly jobs unless they belong to the United Auto Workers (UAW). The UAW has a **material incentive**—the economic lure of a high-paying job—to attract potential members.

The predominance of economic interests was predicted in *Federalist* No. 10, in which James Madison declared that property is "the most common and durable source of factions." Stated differently, nothing seems to matter quite so much to people as their economic self-interest.

Types of Economic Groups   Most economic groups are of four general types: business groups, labor groups, agricultural groups, and professional groups.

Business Groups   More than half of all groups formally registered to lobby Congress are business organizations. Virtually all large corporations and many smaller ones are politically active. They concentrate their activities on policies that touch directly on business interests, such as tax, tariff, and regulatory decisions.

Business firms are also represented through associations such as the U.S. Chamber of Commerce, which includes nearly three million businesses of all sizes. Other business associations, such as the American Petroleum Institute, are confined to a single trade or industry. Because each trade association represents a single industry, it can promote the interests of member corporations even when these interests conflict with those of business generally. Thus, while the Chamber of Commerce promotes a global free-trade policy, some trade associations seek protective tariffs because their member firms want barriers against foreign competition.

Business interests have the advantage of what economist Mancur Olson calls "the size factor."[3] It might be thought that in a democracy groups with large numbers of members would nearly always prevail over small groups when their interests conflict. However, as Olson points out, small groups are ordinarily more cohesive, and if they also have other advantages, such as lots of money, their interests can frequently win out over those of large groups. Business groups in a particular industry typically are few in number and recognize the significance of working together to influence government. Consumers, in contrast, number in the tens of millions, but most do not see any benefit in paying money to consumer groups that would advocate on their behalf. In 2005, these differences came together in ways that hurt consumers while helping the Big Three U.S. automakers

This 1873 lithograph illustrates the benefits of membership in the National Grange, an agricultural interest group.

(Chrysler, Ford, and General Motors). At issue was comprehensive legislation designed to address the nation's energy needs. With help from their friends in Congress and with an assist from a government agency that delayed issuing a report showing that little progress had been made since the 1980s in increasing the average gas mileage of automobiles, U.S. automakers worked together to keep a mandated increase in gas mileage out of the legislation. In the process, each automaker saved tens of millions of dollars they would have had to spend to design and manufacture more fuel-efficient vehicles. Their gain came at an unknown cost to new car buyers, whose autos are less fuel efficient than they could have been.

Labor Groups Since the 1930s, organized labor has been politically active on a large scale. Its goal has been to promote policies that benefit workers in general and union members in particular. Although there are some major independent unions, such as the United Mine Workers and the Teamsters, the dominant labor group is the AFL-CIO, which has its

national headquarters in Washington, D.C. The AFL-CIO has nine million members in its roughly fifty affiliated unions, which include the
International Brotherhood of Electrical Workers, the Sheet Metal Workers, and the Communications Workers of America.

At one time, about a third of the U.S. work force was unionized, but
today only about one in eight workers belongs to a union. Skilled and
unskilled laborers have historically been the core of organized labor, but
their numbers are decreasing while the numbers of professionals, technicians, and service workers are increasing. Professionals have shown little
interest in union organization, perhaps because they identify with management or consider themselves economically secure. Service workers and
technicians are also difficult for unions to organize because they work
closely with managers and, often, in small offices.

Nevertheless, unions have made inroads in their efforts to organize service and public employees. Teachers, postal workers, police, firefighters, and
social workers are among the public employee groups that have become
increasingly unionized. Today, the nation's largest unions are those that
represent service and public employees rather than skilled and unskilled
laborers (see Table 9–1).

Agricultural Groups   Farm organizations represent another large economic lobby. The American Farm Bureau Federation is the largest of
the farm groups, with more than four million members. The National

TABLE	9-1	THE LARGEST LABOR UNIONS, 1950 AND TODAY

The largest labor unions today represent service and public employees; fifty years ago, the largest unions represented skilled and unskilled workers.

1950	2000
1. United Auto Workers	1. National Education Association
2. United Steel Workers	2. International Brotherhood of Teamsters
3. International Brotherhood of Teamsters	3. United Food and Commercial Workers International
4. United Brotherhood of Carpenters & Joiners	4. American Federation of State, County, & Municipal Employees
5. International Association of Machinists	5. Service Employees International

Source: U.S. Department of Labor.

Farmers Union, the National Grange, and the National Farmers Organization are smaller farm lobbies. Agricultural groups do not always
agree on policy issues. For instance, the Farm Bureau sides with
agribusiness and owners of large farms, while the Farmers Union promotes the interests of smaller "family" farms.

There are also numerous specialty farm associations, including the
Association of Wheat Growers, the American Soybean Association, and
Associated Milk Producers. Each association acts as a separate lobby to
try to secure policies beneficial to its members' specific interest.

Professional Groups   Most professions have lobbying associations. Among
the most powerful of these groups is the American Medical Association
(AMA), which, with nearly three hundred thousand members, represents
about half the nation's physicians. The AMA has consistently opposed any
government policy that would limit physicians' autonomy. Other professional groups include the American Bar Association (ABA) and the American Association of University Professors (AAUP), each of which
maintains a lobbying office in Washington.

Citizens' Groups

Although economic interests are the best-organized groups, they do not
have a monopoly on group activity. There are a great number and variety of other organized interests, which are referred to collectively as
citizens' groups (or **noneconomic groups**). The members of groups in
this category are drawn together not by the promise of direct economic
gain but by **purposive incentives**—opportunities to promote a cause in
which they believe.[4] Whether a group's purpose is to protect the environment, return prayer to the public schools, or feed the poor at home
or abroad, there are citizens who are willing to participate simply because
they believe the cause is a worthy one.[5]

Compared to economic groups, citizens' groups have a harder time
acquiring the resources necessary for organization. These groups do not
generate profits or fees as a result of economic activity. Moreover, the incentives they offer prospective members are not exclusive. As opposed to the
private or individual goods provided by many economic groups, most
noneconomic groups offer **collective goods** (or **public goods**) as an incentive for membership. Collective goods are, by definition, benefits that belong
to all; they cannot be granted or withheld on an individual basis. The air
people breathe and the national forests people visit are examples of collective goods. They are available to one and all, those who pay dues to a clean-
air group or a wilderness group as well as those who do not.

The Internet has made it easier for citizens' groups to organize and increase their membership. One of the most successful examples is MoveOn. It was founded by a small group of
liberal activists, including Wes Boyd and Joan Blades, shown here standing outside their home
in California.

The Free-Rider Problem The shared characteristic of collective goods
creates what is called the **free-rider problem:** individuals can receive the
good even when they do not contribute to the group's effort. Take the case
of National Public Radio (NPR). Although NPR's programs are funded
primarily through listeners' donations, those who do not contribute can
hear the programs. The noncontributors are free riders: they receive the
benefit without paying for it. About 90 percent of regular listeners to NPR
do not contribute to their local station.

As economist Mancur Olson noted, it is not rational, in a purely economic sense, for individuals to contribute to a group when they can obtain
its benefit for free.[6] Moreover, the dues paid by any single member are
too small to affect the group's success one way or another. Why pay dues
to an environmental group when any improvements in the air, water, or
wildlife from its lobbying efforts are available to everyone and when one's
individual contribution is too small to make a real difference? Although
many people do join such groups anyway, the free-rider problem is a reason why citizens' groups are less fully organized than economic groups.

Citizens' groups try to surmount the free-rider problem by creating
individual benefits, akin to those offered by economic groups, to make
membership more attractive. Organizational newsletters and social activities are among the individual benefits that some citizens' groups offer as
an incentive to membership. Computer-assisted direct mail has also

helped citizens' groups attract members. Group organizers buy mailing lists and flood the mails with computer-typed "personal" letters asking recipients to pay a small annual membership fee. For some individuals, a fee of $25 to $50 annually represents no great sacrifice and offers the satisfaction of supporting a cause in which they believe. Until the computer era, citizens' groups had great difficulty identifying and contacting potential members, which is a reason why the number of such groups was so much smaller in the past than today.

The Internet has also been a boon to citizens' groups. Nearly every such group of any size has its own website and e-mail list. MoveOn is an example of the Internet's organizing capacity. MoveOn was started by a handful of liberal activists working out of a garage. By 2004, they had created an Internet network that linked hundreds of thousands of citizens who could be mobilized in support of liberal candidates and causes. MoveOn raised more than $3 million in 2006 for Democratic congressional candidates while also launching a massive get-out-the-vote effort in the election's closing days.

On the whole, however, the organizational advantages rest with economic groups. They have an edge on citizens' groups in nearly every respect—money, solidarity, and control (see Table 9–2).

TABLE 9-2 ADVANTAGES AND DISADVANTAGES HELD BY ECONOMIC AND CITIZENS' GROUPS

Compared with economic groups, citizens' groups have fewer advantages and more disadvantages.

Economic Groups	Citizens' Groups
Advantages	*Advantages*
Economic activity provides the organization with the resources necessary for political action.	Members are likely to support leaders' political efforts because they joined the group in order to influence policy.
Individuals are encouraged to join the group because of economic benefits they individually receive (e.g., wages).	*Disadvantages*
Disadvantages	The group has to raise funds, especially for its political activities.
Persons within the group may not support leaders' political efforts because they did not join the group for political reasons.	Potential members may choose not to join the group because they get collective benefits even if they do not join (the free-rider problem).

GET INVOLVED!
Join Up

When the Frenchman Alexis de Tocqueville came to the United States in the 1830s, he marveled at the abundance of civic and political groups and concluded that they were the underlying strength of American democracy. Little has happened in the nearly two centuries since to change this conclusion. Recent research, in fact, confirms it. In his pioneering *Making Democracy Work* (1993), Harvard University's Robert Putnam found that the more abundant a society's voluntary associations are, the more likely it is that the society's institutions will act in the public interest. Putnam uses the term *civic community* to describe a society in which voluntary associations flourish.

Democratic theorists such as Rousseau, Jefferson, Mill, and Dewey argued that communities should be constructed in ways that encourage the individual to participate as fully as possible in civic affairs. The theorists' assumption was that citizens "invest" in a community when they are an integral part of it. The theorists also assumed that participation expands the individual's vision, giving him or her the capacity, in Rousseau's words, for "seeing things in general." Said differently, civic participation enables individuals to surmount a narrowly self-interested view of what is best for society.

Putnam argues that America has undergone a long-term decline in its *social capital* (the sum of its civic relationships). In *Bowling Alone* (2000), Putnam presents evidence that indicates Americans are now less involved in community groups and other forms of social interaction. He attributes the change to television and other factors that produce social isolation. Not all scholars agree with Putnam's view of the trend (some indicators point to a rise in certain types of group membership), but no one has challenged his assumption about the importance of maintaining high levels of civic participation. The relationships fostered by this participation are a foundation of democratic life. And no democratic theorist has suggested that there can be "too much" civic participation. The higher the level of participation, the firmer the democratic base.

Citizens *should* participate in voluntary groups. By doing so, they contribute to improvements in their community, whether it be a college campus, a town, a state, or the nation. Moreover, the relationships that develop among people as a result of civic participation enable individuals to better understand the opinions and values of others. Consider joining a volunteer group. Groups of all kinds would welcome your membership.

Types of Citizens' Groups   Most citizens' groups are of three general types: public-interest groups, single-issue groups, and ideological groups.

Public-Interest Groups   Public-interest groups are those that claim to represent the broad interests of society as a whole. Despite their label, public-interest groups are not led by people elected by the public at large, and the issues they target are ones of their own choosing, not the public's. Moreover, people often disagree on what constitutes "the public interest," which raises the issue of whether any particular viewpoint can truly be said to represent that interest. Nevertheless, there is a basis for distinguishing the so-called public-interest groups from economic groups: the latter seek direct material benefits for their members, while the former seek benefits that are less tangible and more broadly shared. For example, the National Association of Manufacturers, an economic group, seeks policies favorable to large corporations, while the League of Women Voters, a public-interest group, seeks policies—such as simplified voter registration—that can benefit the public in general.

More than half of the currently active public-interest groups were established after 1960. One such organization is Common Cause, which has more than two hundred thousand members and describes itself as "a national citizens' lobby"; it concentrates on political reform in areas such as campaign finance.

Single-Issue Groups   A single-issue group is organized to influence policy in just one area. Notable current examples are the National Rifle Association and the various right-to-life and pro-choice groups that have formed around the issue of abortion. The number of single-issue groups has risen sharply in the past three decades, and these groups now pressure government on almost every conceivable issue, from nuclear arms to day care centers to drug abuse.

Environmental groups are sometimes classified as public-interest groups, but they may also be considered single-issue organizations in that most of them seek to influence public policy in a specific area, such as pollution reduction, wilderness preservation, or wildlife protection. The Sierra Club, one of the oldest environmental groups, was formed in the 1890s to promote the preservation of scenic areas. Also prominent are the National Audubon Society, the Wilderness Society, the Environmental Defense Fund, Greenpeace U.S.A., and the Izaak Walton League. Since 1960, membership in environmental groups has more than tripled as a result of the public's increased concern about the quality of the environment.[7]

Ideological Groups   Single-issue groups have an issue-specific policy agenda. In contrast, ideological groups have a broader agenda that derives from a philosophical or moral position. An example is the Christian Coalition of America, which was organized to restore "Christian values" to American life and politics. The group has addressed a wide range of issues, including school prayer, abortion, and television programming. Ideological groups on both the left and the right have increased substantially in number since the 1960s.

Groups such as the National Organization for Women (NOW) and the National Association for the Advancement of Colored People (NAACP) can also be classified generally as ideological groups. Although they represent particular demographic groups, they do so across a wide range of issues. For example, NOW addresses issues that range from jobs to reproduction to political representation.

A Special Category of Interest Group: Governments

While the vast majority of organized interests in the United States represent private concerns, a growing number of interest groups represent governments, both foreign and subnational.

The U.S. federal government makes policies that directly affect the economic development, political stability, and security of nations throughout the world. Arms sales, foreign aid, immigration, and import restrictions and other trade practices have a great impact on foreign nations. For this reason, most foreign nations supplement the political efforts made through their embassies with the services of paid lobbyists in Washington.[8] However, foreign governments are prohibited from engaging in certain lobbying activities, including contributions to U.S. election campaigns.

States, cities, and other governmental units within the United States also lobby heavily. Most major cities and two-thirds of the states have at least one Washington lobbyist. Lobbying also occurs through groups such as the Council of State Governments, the National Governors Conference, the National Association of Counties, the National League of Cities, and the U.S. Conference of Mayors. These organizations sometimes play a large role in policy debates. For example, as Congress was preparing in 2006 to renew and amend the antiterrorism legislation that had gone into effect in 2001, the National Governors Conference and the U.S. Conference of Mayors lobbied to ensure that the changes reflected state and local concerns.

Pat Robertson
(1930–)

No one has done more in recent decades to make religion a powerful force in American politics than Pat Robertson. Through his Christian Coalition of America, formed in the late 1980s, Robertson has mobilized conservative Christians in support of a religion-based policy agenda. The Christian Coalition's website contains the phrase "America's leading grassroots organization protecting our Godly heritage." Robertson ran for public office himself in 1988, when he challenged for the Republican presidential nomination. He astonished opponents and pundits alike by placing second (ahead of George H. W. Bush but behind Robert Dole) in the Iowa caucuses, the first contest of the campaign. Although his presidential candidacy eventually faltered, Robertson's campaign inspired thousands of conservative Christians to become politically active, and many of them continued to work in Republican politics after the 1988 election.

As a young man, Robertson had planned a law career, but he failed his bar exam shortly after earning a law degree from Yale University. He underwent a religious conversion and decided to participate in ministry rather than retake the bar exam. A Southern Baptist, Robertson developed an active ministry and became involved in broadcasting. In 1960, he bought a small television station and established the Christian Broadcasting Network, which eventually grew into a worldwide organization. Robertson's own television program, *The 700 Club*, airs regularly on the network. This program has enabled Robertson to continue to promote conservative causes, although his on-the-air remarks sometimes have backfired. In 2005, Robertson suggested that the United States should consider assassinating Venezuelan president Hugo Chavez, saying it would be a lot cheaper than going to war over Venezuela's oil. Robertson later apologized for the statement.

INSIDE LOBBYING: SEEKING INFLUENCE THROUGH OFFICIAL CONTACTS

Modern government provides a supportive environment for interest groups. First, modern government is involved in so many issues—business regulation, income maintenance, urban renewal, cancer research, and energy development, to name only a few—that hardly any interest in society could fail to benefit significantly from having influence over federal policies or programs. Second, modern government is oriented toward action. Officials are inclined to respond to problems rather than let problems linger. For example, when forest fires in California, Arizona, and other western states destroyed property worth millions in 2006, Washington granted immediate assistance to residents who had incurred losses and cleanup costs.

Groups seek government's support through **lobbying**, a term that refers broadly to efforts by groups to influence public policy through contact with public officials. Lobbying is big business in America. A section of the nation's capital, known as K Street, is populated almost entirely by lobbying firms. There are more than twenty thousand Washington lobbyists, and official records indicate that more than $1 billion is spent on lobbying each year. The actual amount is higher, but no one is quite sure how much. Lobbying is regulated by the Lobbying Disclosure Act of 1995, which defines who must register as a lobbyist and what lobbying activities and expenditures must be reported. However, the act had weak provisions that allowed members of Congress to accept substantial gifts from lobbyists, including lavish trips. This situation contributed to the Abramoff lobbying scandal that rocked Washington in 2006 and led House Republican leader Tom DeLay to resign his seat. After Democrats took control of the House and Senate in 2007, they enacted reforms that, among other things, ban members of Congress from accepting trips, gifts, and meals from lobbyists.

Interest groups rely on two main lobbying strategies, which have been labeled "inside lobbying" and "outside lobbying."[9] Each strategy involves communication with public officials, but the strategies differ in what is communicated and who does the communicating. This section discusses **inside lobbying,** which is based on group efforts to develop and maintain close ("inside") contacts with policymakers. (Outside lobbying is described in the next section.)

Acquiring Access to Officials

Inside lobbying is designed to give a group direct access to officials in order to influence their decisions. Access is not the same as influence, which is the capacity to affect policy decisions. But access is a critical first step in the influence process.[10] The importance of access is evident, for example, in the high salaries that former members of Congress can command when they become lobbyists. Former congressional members are prohibited for two years from lobbying Congress, but thereafter they are free to do so. They usually represent groups with which they had close ties while they were in office. Unlike other lobbyists, they have the right, as former legislators, to go directly onto the floor of the House or the Senate to speak with current members.

Lobbying once depended significantly on tangible inducements, sometimes including indirect or even outright bribes. This old form of lobbying survives, but modern lobbying generally involves subtler and more sophisticated methods than providing money or personal favors to officials. It focuses on supplying officials with information and indications of group strength that will persuade them to adopt the group's perspective.[11]

For the most part, inside lobbying is directed at policymakers who are inclined to support the group rather than at those who have opposed it in the past. This tendency reflects both the difficulty of persuading opponents to change long-held views and the advantage of having trusted allies who will work actively to promote the group's policy positions. Thus, union lobbyists work mainly with pro-labor officeholders, just as corporate lobbyists work mainly with policymakers who support business interests.

Money is the basic ingredient of inside lobbying efforts. The American Petroleum Institute, for example, with its abundant financial resources, can afford a downtown Washington office staffed by lobbyists, petroleum experts, and public relations specialists who help the oil companies maintain access to and influence with legislative and executive leaders. Many groups spend upward of $1 million annually on lobbying. The American Hospital Association (AHA), for example, spent $19 million on lobbying in 2005. Other groups get by on much less, but it is difficult to lobby effectively on a small budget. Given the costs of maintaining a Washington lobby, the domination by corporations and trade associations is understandable. These groups have the money to retain high-priced lobbyists, while many other interests do not.

The targets of inside lobbying are officials of all three government branches—legislative, executive, and judicial.

Lobbying Congress   The benefits of a close relationship with members of Congress are substantial. With support in Congress, a group can obtain the legislative help it needs to achieve its policy goals. By the same token, members of Congress gain from working closely with lobbyists. The volume of legislation facing Congress is heavy, and members rely on trusted lobbyists to identify bills that deserve their attention and support. When Republican lawmakers took control of Congress in 1995, they invited corporate lobbyists to participate directly in drafting legislation affecting business. Congressional Democrats complained loudly, but Republicans

Lobbying in the United States rests on access, information, persuasion, and mutual support. Occasionally, lobbying is a shadier business in which favors are granted that skirt the laws governing lobbying. In 2005, news broke that a prominent Washington lobbyist, Jack Abramoff, had engaged in possibly illegal deals with a number of legislative and executive officials. It did not help Abramoff's case that he had lavished expensive trips on some officials. Controversy surrounding his relationship with Abramoff prompted House majority leader Tom DeLay to resign his congressional seat. Abramoff is shown here leaving federal court in Washington in 2006.

said they were merely getting help from those who best understood business's needs and accused Democrats of having engaged in the same practice with organized labor when they were in power.

Lobbyists' effectiveness with members of Congress depends in part on their reputation for fair play. Lobbyists are expected to play it straight. Said one congressman: "If any [lobbyist] gives me false or misleading information, that's it—I'll never see him again."[12] Arm-twisting is another unacceptable practice. During the debate over the North American Free Trade Agreement in 1993, the AFL-CIO threatened retaliation against congressional Democrats who supported the legislation. The backlash from these Democrats was so intense that the union backed down on its threat. The safe lobbying strategy is the aboveboard approach: provide information, rely on longtime allies among members of Congress, and push steadily but not too aggressively for legislative goals.

Lobbying Executive Agencies   As the scope of the federal government has expanded, lobbying of the executive branch has increased in importance.

Bureaucrats make key administrative decisions and develop policy initiatives that the legislative branch later makes into law. By working closely with executive agencies, groups can influence policy decisions at the implementation and initiation stages. In return, groups assist agencies by providing support when their programs and budgets are renewed by Congress and the president.

Nowhere is the link between groups and the bureaucracy more evident than in the regulatory agencies that oversee the nation's business sectors. For example, the Federal Communications Commission (FCC), which regulates the nation's broadcasters, uses information provided by broadcast organizations to decide many of the policies governing their activities. The FCC is sometimes cited as an example of agency capture. The capture theory suggests that regulatory agencies pass through a series of phases that constitute a life cycle. Early in an agency's existence, it regulates an industry on the public's behalf, but as the agency matures, its vigor declines until at best it protects the status quo and at worst it falls captive to the very industry it is supposed to regulate. In the mid-1990s, the FCC concluded that television broadcasters should be granted use of the new digital channels without charge. Some members of Congress and numerous citizens' groups had urged that the new channels be auctioned off to the highest bidders, a procedure that would have netted taxpayers billions of dollars.

Research indicates that the capture theory describes only some agencies—and then only some of the time. Agencies selectively cooperate with or oppose interest groups, depending on which strategy better suits agency purposes. Agency officials are aware that they can lose support in Congress, which controls agency funding and program authorization, if they show too much favoritism toward an interest group.[13]

Lobbying the Courts   Court rulings in areas such as education and civil rights have made interest groups recognize that the judiciary too can help them reach their goals.[14] Interest groups have several judicial lobbying options, including efforts to influence the selection of federal judges. Right-to-life groups have pressured Republican administrations to make opposition to abortion a prerequisite for nomination to the federal bench. Democratic administrations have in turn faced pressure from pro-choice groups in their judicial nominations.

Groups also rely on lawsuits in their efforts to influence the courts. For some organizations, such as the American Civil Liberties Union (ACLU), legal action is the primary means of influencing policy. The ACLU often takes on unpopular causes, such as the free speech rights of fringe groups.

Such causes have little chance of success in legislative bodies but may prevail in a courtroom.

As interest groups increasingly resort to legal action, they often find themselves facing one another in court. Environmental litigation groups such as the Environmental Defense Fund have frequently sued oil, timber, and mining corporations.

Webs of Influence: Groups in the Policy Process

To get a fuller picture of how inside lobbying works, it is helpful to consider two policy processes—iron triangles and issue networks—in which many groups are enmeshed.

Iron Triangles An **iron triangle** consists of a small and informal but relatively stable set of bureaucrats, legislators, and lobbyists who seek to develop policies beneficial to a particular interest. The three "corners" of one such triangle are the Department of Agriculture (bureaucrats), the agriculture committees of Congress (legislators), and farm groups such as the Associated Milk Producers and the Association of Wheat Growers (lobbyists). Together they determine many of the policies affecting farmers. Of course, the support of other players, including the president and a majority in Congress, is needed to enact programs helpful to farmers. However, these players often defer to the policy views of the agricultural triangle. Its members are intimately familiar with the policy needs of farmers.

A group in an iron triangle has an inside track to those legislators and bureaucrats who are in the strongest position to help its cause. And because it has something of value to offer each of them, the relationships tend to be ironclad. The group provides lobbying support for the agency's funding and programs and makes campaign contributions to its congressional allies. Agricultural groups, for example, contribute millions of dollars to congressional candidates in each election. Most of this money is given to incumbents, and most of these contributions go to the campaigns of members of the House and Senate agriculture committees. Figure 9–1 summarizes the benefits that flow to each member of an iron triangle.

Issue Networks Iron triangles represent the pattern of influence in only certain policy areas and are less common now than in the past. A more frequent pattern of influence today is the **issue network**, an informal grouping of officials, lobbyists, and policy specialists (the "network") who are brought together temporarily by their shared interest in a particular policy problem (the "issue").

Issue networks are a result of the increasing complexity of policy problems. Participants must have specialized knowledge of the issue at

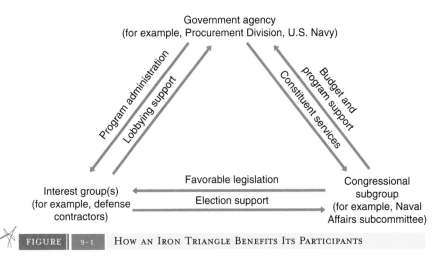

Government agency
(for example, Procurement Division, U.S. Navy)

Program administration
Lobbying support
Constituent services
Budget and program support

Interest group(s)
(for example, defense contractors)

Favorable legislation
Election support

Congressional subgroup
(for example, Naval Affairs subcommittee)

FIGURE   9-1   HOW AN IRON TRIANGLE BENEFITS ITS PARTICIPANTS

An iron triangle works to the advantage of each of its participants: an interest group, a congressional subgroup, and a government agency.

hand in order to participate effectively. Thus, unlike iron triangles, where a participant's position is everything, an issue network is built around specialized interests and information. On any given issue, the participants might come from a variety of executive agencies, congressional committees, interest groups, and institutions such as universities or think tanks. Compared to iron triangles, issue networks are less stable. As the issue develops, new participants may join the debate and old ones drop out. Once the issue is resolved, the network disbands.[15]

An example of an issue network is the set of participants who would come together over the issue of whether a large tract of old forest should be opened to logging. A few decades ago, that issue would have been settled in an iron triangle consisting of the timber companies, the U.S. Forest Service, and relevant members of the House and Senate agriculture committees. But as forestlands have diminished and environmental concerns have grown, such issues can no longer be contained within the cozy confines of an iron triangle. Today, an issue network would form that included logging interests, the U.S. Forest Service, House and Senate agriculture committee members, research scientists, and representatives of environmental groups, the housing industry, and animal-rights groups. Unlike the old iron triangle, which was confined to like-minded interests, this issue network would include opposing interests (for example, the loggers and the environmentalists). And unlike an iron triangle, the issue network would dissolve once the issue that brought the parties together was resolved.

Issue networks, then, differ substantially from iron triangles. In an iron triangle, a common interest brings the participants together in a stable, long-lasting, and mutually beneficial relationship. In an issue network, an immediate issue brings the participants together in a temporary network that is based on their ability to address the issue in a sophisticated way and where they play out their separate interests before disbanding once the issue is settled.

Despite these differences, iron triangles and issue networks do have one thing in common: they are arenas in which organized groups operate. The interests of the general public may be taken into account in these webs of influence, but the interests of the participating groups are paramount.

OUTSIDE LOBBYING: SEEKING INFLUENCE THROUGH PUBLIC PRESSURE

Although an interest group may rely solely on inside lobbying, this approach is not likely to be successful unless the group can demonstrate convincingly that its concerns reflect those of a vital constituency. Accordingly, groups make use of constituency connections when it is advantageous for them to do so. They engage in **outside lobbying**, which involves bringing public ("outside") pressure to bear on policymakers (see Table 9–3).[16]

| TABLE 9-3 | TACTICS USED IN INSIDE AND OUTSIDE LOBBYING STRATEGIES |

Inside and outside lobbying are based on different tactics.

Inside Lobbying	Outside Lobbying
Developing contacts with legislators and executives	Encouraging group members to write, phone, or e-mail their representatives in Congress
Providing information and policy proposals to key officials	Seeking favorable coverage by news media
Forming coalitions with other groups	Encouraging members to support particular candidates in elections
	Targeting group resources on key election races
	Making PAC contributions to candidates

Constituency Advocacy: Grassroots Lobbying

One form of outside pressure is **grassroots lobbying**—that is, pressure designed to convince government officials that a group's policy position has popular support.

No group illustrates grassroots lobbying better than AARP (American Association of Retired Persons). With more than thirty million members and a staff of sixteen hundred, AARP is a powerful lobby on retirement issues such as social security and Medicare. When major legislation affecting retirees is pending, AARP swings into action. Congress receives more mail from members of AARP than it does from members of any other group. AARP's support was critical to passage in 2003 of a controversial prescription drug program for the elderly. Until AARP's last-minute endorsement, the program appeared to be headed for a narrow defeat in Congress.

As with other forms of lobbying, the precise impact of grassroots campaigns is often difficult to assess. Some members of Congress downplay its influence, but all congressional offices monitor letters, phone calls, and e-mails as a way of tracking constituents' opinions.

Electoral Action: Votes and PAC Money

An "outside" strategy can also include election campaigns. "Reward your friends and punish your enemies" is a political adage that loosely describes how interest groups view elections. The possibility of electoral opposition from a powerful group can keep an officeholder from openly obstructing the group's goals. For example, opposition from the three-million-member National Rifle Association is a major reason why the United States has lagged behind other Western societies in its handgun control laws, despite polls that show most Americans favor such laws.

Interest groups gain influence by contributing money to candidates' campaigns. As one lobbyist said, "Talking to politicians is fine, but with a little money they hear you better."[17] Members of Congress sometimes get into hot water by listening to lobbyists while also receiving favors from them. When it was alleged in 2005 that lobbyist Jack Abramoff had cheated some of his clients while also lavishing trips and money on members of Congress in return for favorable legislation, it sent a shock wave through Washington. Several members of Congress quickly returned campaign donations they had received from Abramoff in the hope that doing so would insulate them from the corruption scandal. A casualty of the Abramoff affair was Representative Tom DeLay (R-Texas), who lost his post as House majority leader and resigned his seat in

Outside lobbying involves the use of media publicity and other tactics to generate constituent pressure on policymakers. Shown here are actor Michael J. Fox and Senator Orrin Hatch (R-Utah) at an event staged to persuade Congress to enact legislation expanding federal support for stem cell research. Congress passed the legislation, but it was vetoed by President George W. Bush.

Congress after his close relationship with Abramoff became known. Abramoff had funneled hundreds of thousands of dollars to DeLay for political purposes, some of it of questionable legality.

A group's election contributions are funneled through its **political action committee (PAC).** A group cannot give organizational funds (such as corporate profits or union dues) to candidates, but through its PAC a group can solicit and donate voluntary contributions from members or employees. A PAC is legally limited in the amount it can contribute to a candidate running for federal office. The ceiling is $10,000 per candidate—$5,000 in the primary campaign and $5,000 in the general election campaign. There is no legal limit on the number of candidates a PAC can support. (These financial limits do not apply to candidates for state and local office. Their campaigns are regulated by state laws, and many states allow PACs to make unlimited campaign contributions.)

There are more than four thousand PACs, and PAC contributions account for roughly a third of total contributions to congressional campaigns. Their role is less significant in presidential campaigns, which are

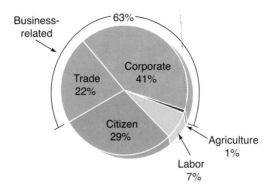

FIGURE 9-2 PERCENTAGE OF PACs BY CATEGORY

Most PACs represent business. Corporate and trade association PACs make up more than three-fifths of the total number. *Source: Federal Election Commission, 2006.*

larger in scale and publicly funded in part and therefore are less dependent on PAC contributions.

More than 40 percent of all PACs are associated with corporations (see Figure 9–2). Examples include the Ford Motor Company Civic Action Fund, the Sun Oil Company Political Action Committee (Sunpac), and the Coca-Cola PAC. The next largest group of PACs consists of those linked to citizens' groups (that is, public-interest, single-issue, and ideological groups), such as the liberal People for the American Way and the conservative National Conservative Political Action Committee (NCPAC). Ranking third are PACs tied to trade and professional associations, such as AMPAC (American Medical Association) and R-PAC (National Association of Realtors). Labor unions, once the major source of group contributions, now rank fourth.

PACs contribute roughly eight times as much money to incumbents as to their challengers. PACs are well aware of the fact that incumbents are likely to win and thus to remain in a position to make policy. One PAC director, expressing a common view, said, "We always stick with the incumbent when we agree with them both."[18] The tendency of PACs to back incumbents has to some extent blurred long-standing partisan divisions in campaign funding. Business interests are especially pragmatic. Although they tend to favor Republican candidates, they are reluctant to anger Democratic incumbents. The result is that Democratic incumbents, particularly in House races, have received substantial support over the years from business-related PACs.[19] Other PACs, of course, are less pragmatic. The Christian Moral Government Fund, for example, backs only

★ ‖ STATES IN THE NATION

Limits on PAC Contributions

Elections of state officials (such as governors and state legislators) are regulated by state law rather than by federal law. In some states, there is no law limiting how much money PACs can contribute to a candidate. Of the states that limit PAC contributions, only New York and Nevada allow contributions in excess of $10,000.

Q: Why might states located to the west of the Mississippi River (which runs down the eastern borders of Minnesota, Iowa, Missouri, Arkansas, and Louisiana) place fewer limits on PAC contributions than other states?

A: A possible explanation is that the political cultures of the westernmost states, as a result of their frontier heritage, are less accepting of government regulation of any kind.

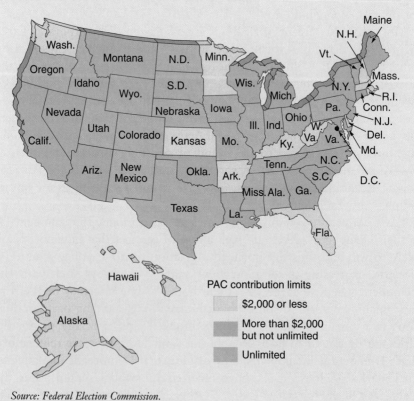

PAC contribution limits

$2,000 or less

More than $2,000 but not unlimited

Unlimited

Source: Federal Election Commission.

candidates who take conservative stands on issues such as school prayer and abortion. Another example is EMILY's List (*"early money is like yeast, it makes the dough rise"*). It supports only liberal women candidates.

The influence of PACs has been the subject of intense debate. Because PACs raise their money from contributions by small donors, advocates see them as a better system of campaign finance than one based on wealthy donors. On the other hand, critics complain that PACs give interest groups far too much influence with members of Congress.[20]

Although members of Congress deny they are unduly influenced by PACs, there is no question that PACS give interest groups a level of access to lawmakers that ordinary citizens do not have. Nevertheless, Congress is unlikely in the foreseeable future to pass legislation that would outlaw PACs. The fact is, most members of Congress are unwilling to eliminate a source of campaign funds that helps them to get reelected.

THE GROUP SYSTEM: INDISPENSABLE BUT BIASED

As noted in the chapter's introduction, pluralist theory holds that organized groups are a source of sound governance. On one level, this claim is beyond dispute. Without groups to carry their message, most of society's interests would find it difficult to get government's attention and support. Yet the issue of representation is also a question of whether all interests in society are fairly represented through the group system, and here the pluralist argument is less compelling.

The Contribution of Groups to Self-Government: Pluralism

Group activity is an essential part of self-government. An obstacle to popular sovereignty is the difficulty that public officials have in trying to discover what the people want from government. To discern their wishes, lawmakers consult public opinion polls, meet with constituents, and assess election results. Lobbying activities are also a clue to what people are seeking. Moreover, government does not exist simply to serve majority interests. The fact that most people are not retirees or labor union members or farmers or college students or Hispanics does not mean that the concerns of such "minorities" are unworthy of attention. And what better instrument exists for promoting their interests than organizations formed by them?

Some pluralists even question the usefulness of terms such as *the common good* and *the collective interest*. If people disagree on society's goals and

priorities, as they always do, how can it be said that people have a
"common" or "collective" interest? As an alternative, pluralists contend
that, because society has so many interests, the common good ultimately
is best served by a process that serves these many interests. Thus, if manufacturing interests prevail on one issue, environmentalists on another,
farmers on a third, minorities on a fourth, and so on until many interests
are served, the collective interest of society will have been promoted.

Finally, interest groups often take up issues that are neglected by the
political parties. Party leaders typically shy away from issues, such as
affirmative action and abortion, on which the party's voters disagree. Such
issues would get less notice if not for the groups that promote them. And
when groups succeed in drawing attention to these issues, the parties are
nearly compelled to address them as well. In this sense, as political scientist Jack Walker noted, the party and group systems "are complemen-
tary and together constitute a more responsive and adaptive system than
either would be if they somehow operated on their own."[21]

Flaws in Pluralism: Interest-Group Liberalism and Economic Bias

Although pluralist theory includes some compelling arguments, it also has
some questionable aspects. Political scientist Theodore Lowi argues that
there is no concept of society's collective interest in a system that gives
special interests the ability to determine the policies affecting them.[22] The
basis of decision in such cases is not majority (collective) rule but minority
(special-interest) rule.

It is seldom safe to assume that what most people would favor is what
a special-interest group wants. Consider the case of the federal law that
required auto dealers to list the known defects of used cars on window
stickers. The law was repealed after an extensive lobbying campaign
financed by contributions of more than $1 million by the National Asso-
ciation of Automobile Dealers to the reelection campaigns of members of
Congress.

Lowi uses the term **interest-group liberalism** to describe the tendency of officials to support the policy demands of the interest group or
groups that have a special stake in a policy. Interest-group liberalism constitutes a partial abandonment by government of its responsibility to
determine the policies by which society is governed. In practical terms,
groups have as much or more say than government over the policies
affecting them. One of the adverse effects is a weakening of majority rule;
rather than policymaking by the majority acting through its elected representatives, interest-group liberalism involves policymaking by narrow

The Houston headquarters of the now-bankrupt Enron Corporation. Until its collapse due to illegal business practices, Enron was one of the nation's largest corporations and one of the most powerful lobbying groups in Washington. Enron used its insider contacts to play a major role in the comprehensive energy bill that the Bush administration proposed to Congress. The bill was laden with favorable provisions for energy companies like Enron.

segments of society acting on their own behalf. Another adverse effect is an inefficient use of society's resources: groups get what they want, whether or not their priorities match those of society as a whole.

Another flaw in the pluralist argument resides in its claim that the group system is representative. Pluralists recognize that better-organized interests have more influence but argue that the group process is relatively open and that few interests are at a serious disadvantage. These claims contain an element of truth, but they are far from the complete truth.

As this chapter has pointed out, organization is a political resource that is distributed unequally across society. Economic interests, particularly corporations, are the most highly organized, and some analysts argue that group politics works chiefly to the advantage of business. Of course, economic groups do not dominate everything, nor do they operate unchecked. Many of the public interest groups formed since the 1960s were deliberately created as a check against the influence of corporate lobbies. Environmental groups are an example. Although some of them like the Sierra Club have been in existence for the better part of a century or longer, many of them are more recent in origin and work to shield the environment from threats posed by business activity. Activist government has also brought the group system into closer balance; the government's poverty programs have spawned groups that act to protect these programs. Nevertheless, nearly two-thirds of all lobbying groups in Washington are business-related. The interest-group system is biased toward America's economically oriented groups, particularly its corporations.

The group system is also slanted toward the interests of upper-middle-class Americans. Studies indicate that individuals of higher socioeconomic status are disproportionately represented among group members and even more so among group leaders. Affluent Americans have the money, communication skills, and savvy to participate effectively in special-interest politics. The poor, minorities, women, and the young are greatly underrepresented in the group system. A lack of organization does not ensure an interest's failure, just as the existence of organization does not guarantee success. However, organized interests are obviously in a better position to promote their views.

The business and class bias of the group system is especially significant because the most highly organized interests are, in a sense, those least in need of political clout. Corporations and affluent citizens already control the largest share of society's resources. The group system magnifies their power.

A Madisonian Dilemma

James Madison recognized the dilemma inherent in group activity. Although he worried that interest groups would have too much political control, he argued in *Federalist* No. 10 that a free society is obliged to permit the advocacy of self-interest. Unless people can promote the separate opinions that stem from differences in their needs, values, and possessions, they do not have liberty.

Ironically, Madison's constitutional solution to the problem of factions has become part of the problem. The American system of checks and balances, with a separation of powers at its core, was designed primarily to prevent a majority faction from trampling on the interests of smaller groups. Indeed, throughout the nation's history, majorities have been frustrated in their efforts to exercise power by America's elaborate system of divided government, which makes it relatively easy for a determined minority to block action by the majority.

This same system, however, makes it relatively easy for minority factions—or, as they are called today, special-interest groups—to gain government support. If they can get the backing of even a small number of well-placed policymakers, as in the case of iron triangles, they are likely to get many of the benefits they seek. Because of the system's division of power, they have numerous points at which to exert influence. Often, they need only to find an ally in one place, whether that be a congressional committee or an executive agency or a federal court, to get at least some of what they seek. And once they obtain a government benefit, it is likely to persist. Benefits are hard to eliminate because concerted action by the executive branch and both houses of Congress is usually required. If a group has strong support in even a single institution, it usually can fend off attempts to terminate its benefits. Such support ordinarily is easy to acquire, because the group has resources—information, money, and votes—that officeholders want. (Chapters 11 and 13 discuss further the issue of interest-group power.)

SUMMARY

A political interest group is composed of a set of individuals organized to promote a shared political concern. Most interest groups owe their existence to factors other than politics. These groups form for economic reasons, such as the pursuit of profit, and maintain themselves by making profits (in the case of corporations) or by providing their members with private goods, such as jobs and wages. Economic groups include corporations, trade associations, labor unions, farm organizations, and professional associations. Collectively, economic groups are by far the largest set of organized interests. The group system tends to favor interests that are already economically and socially advantaged.

Citizens' groups do not have the same organizational advantages as economic groups. They depend on voluntary contributions from potential members, who may lack interest and resources or who recognize that they will get the collective good from a group's activity even if they do not participate (the free-rider problem). Citizens' groups include public-interest, single-issue, and ideological groups. Their numbers have increased dramatically since the 1960s despite their organizational problems.

Organized interests seek influence largely by lobbying public officials and contributing to election campaigns. Using an inside strategy, lobbyists develop direct contacts with legislators, government bureaucrats, and members of the judiciary in order to persuade them to accept the group's perspective on policy. Groups also use an outside strategy, seeking to mobilize public support for their goals. This strategy relies in part on grassroots lobbying—encouraging group members and the public to communicate their policy views to officials. Outside lobbying also includes efforts to elect officeholders who will support group aims. Through political action committees (PACs), organized groups now provide nearly a third of all contributions received by congressional candidates.

The policies that emerge from the group system bring benefits to many of society's interests, and in some instances these benefits also serve the collective interest. But when groups can essentially dictate policies, the common good is not served. The majority's interest is subordinated to group (minority) interests. In most instances, the minority consists of individuals who already enjoy a substantial share of society's benefits.

KEY TERMS

citizens' (noneconomic) groups (*p. 301*)
collective (public) goods (*p. 301*)
economic groups (*p. 296*)
free-rider problem (*p. 302*)
grassroots lobbying (*p. 315*)
inside lobbying (*p. 308*)
interest group (*p. 294*)
interest-group liberalism (*p. 320*)
iron triangle (*p. 312*)

issue network (*p. 312*)
lobbying (*p. 308*)
material incentive (*p. 298*)
outside lobbying (*p. 314*)
political action committee (PAC)
   (*p. 316*)
private (individual) goods (*p. 298*)
purposive incentive (*p. 301*)
single-issue politics (*p. 294*)

SUGGESTED READINGS

Berry, Jeffrey M. *The New Liberalism: The Rising Power of Citizen Groups.* Washington, D.C.: Brookings Institution Press, 2000. An exploration of the influence that citizen groups exercise.

Browne, William P. *Cultivating Congress: Constituents, Issues, and Interests in Agriculture Policymaking.* Lawrence: University Press of Kansas, 1995. An analysis of the limits of "iron triangles" as a description of congressional policymaking.

Grossman, Gene M., and Elhanan Helpman. *Interest Groups and Trade Policy.* Princeton, N.J.: Princeton University Press, 2002. An examination of the impact of groups' campaign and lobbying activities on trade policy.

Herrnson, Paul S., Ronald G. Shaiko, and Clyde Wilcox, eds. *The Interest Group Connection: Electioneering, Lobbying, and Policymaking in Washington,* 2nd ed. Washington, D.C.: CQ Press, 2004. Essays and commentaries on groups and officials and the linkages between them.

Lowery, David, and Holly Brasher. *Organized Interests and American Government.* New York: McGraw-Hill, 2004. An overview of interest-group politics.

Lowi, Theodore J. *The End of Liberalism*, 2d ed. New York: Norton, 1979. A thorough critique of interest groups' influence on American politics.

Olson, Mancur, Jr. *The Logic of Collective Action*, rev. ed. Cambridge, Mass.: Harvard University Press, 1971. A pioneering analysis of why some interests are more fully and easily organized than others.

Rozell, Mark J., and Clyde Wilcox. *Interest Groups in American Campaigns*. Washington, D.C.: Congressional Quarterly Press, 1999. An assessment of the election role of interest groups.

LIST OF WEBSITES

http://www.fec./gov/ The Federal Election Commission site; offers information on elections, voting, campaign finance, parties, and PACs, as well as a citizens' guide to campaign contributions.

http://www./pirg.org/ The Public Interest Research Group (PIRG) site; PIRG has chapters on many college campuses, and its site provides state-by-state policy and other information.

http://www.sierraclub.org/ The Sierra Club, one of the oldest environmental protection interest groups, promotes conservation; its website provides information on its activities.

http://www.townhall.com/ The website of the American Conservative Union (ACU); includes policy and political information and a lively chat room.

POLITICS IN THEORY AND PRACTICE

Thinking: Why are there so many more organized interests in the United States than elsewhere? Why are so many of these groups organized around economic interests—particularly business interests?

Participating: Consider contributing to a citizens' interest group. Such groups depend on members' donations for operating funds. Citizens' groups cover the political spectrum from right to left and touch on nearly every conceivable public issue. You will not have difficulty locating a group through the Internet that has policy goals consistent with your beliefs and values.

ADDITIONAL RESOURCES

For quizzes, interactive simulations, games, graphics, and other study tools, visit the book's Online Learning Center at **www.mhhe.com/pattersonwtp7.**

The Lobbying Game Today

Jonathan D. Salant

Lobbying is a natural part of the political process but nowhere is it more prominent than in the United States. More than twenty thousand lobbyists work in Washington, D.C., spending upward of $2 billion annually to impress their views on federal officials. In this 2006 article, which was published in the journal of the Carl Albert Congressional Research and Studies Center at the University of Oklahoma, Jonathan Salant, a reporter with Bloomberg News, describes congressional lobbying and the influence patterns resulting from it.

Capitol Hill lobbyists have traditionally served as a source of information for law-makers and their staffs. In recent years, they have become an important source of campaign contributions as well as a coveted place for officials to land once their terms have expired.

The traditional role of lobbyist has been to advocate, letting a lawmaker or staff member know how a proposal would affect the corporation or interest group employing him or her. A good lobbyist supplies unbiased details that the lawmaker can use in deciding whether to support or oppose the particular provision. . . .

In recent years, newspapers have reported that lobbyists have gone beyond advocating a particular position to helping draft the leg-islation itself. Representative Rahm Emanuel (D-Ill.), the chairman of the Democratic Congressional Campaign Committee, has decried what he calls the "blurring of the line between lobbying and writing legislation."

Lobbying is big business in Washington, its growth mirroring the increase in the federal budget. Between 1999 and 2005, the amount of money spent on lobbying by companies, trade associations and other interest groups grew to $2.4 billion from $1.5 billion, a 60 percent increase, accord-ing to PoliticalMoneyLine, an independent group that tracks lobbying, During the same period, the federal budget rose to $2.5 trillion from $1.7 trilion, a 47 percent boost, according to the Congressional Budget Office.

"The size and scope of government is just staggering," said John Feehery, a for-mer spokesman for House Speaker Dennis Hastert (R-Ill.), and now executive vice president of the Motion Picture Association of America. "If you want to get your share, you need a lobbyist. That's how you do it. As long as there's more money there's going to be a need for people in Washington to be hired to get it."

What do companies get for that money? Bloomberg News examined the 20 largest publicly traded federal contractors using data from the Federal Contracts Database, PoliticalMoneyLine, and Dwight L. Morris and Associates (which analyzes Fedral Election Commission filings). The idea was to see how much companies spent to influence lawmakers versus how much they received in federal contracts.

The nation's largest federal contactor, Lockheed Martin Corp., received $39.8 billion in federal contracts in 2003-04; During the same period, the company spent $15.8 million on lobbying expenses and campaign donations. The ratio of con-tracts to expenditures was $2,517 to $1.

"It's an investment strategy," former House Appropriations Committee Democratic spokesman David Sirora said. "We shouldn't blame companies for spending a lot of money on lobbying because it's an investment strategy. We should blame those lawmakers who we the public empower to spend our dollars for selling off that power in exchange for campaign cash. That's the problem."

Lawmakers say they approve government spending on the merits, not on who's doing the lobbying. "For every one [project] that we will agree to, you'll find two or three we do not agree to," said Representative C.W. (Bill) Young (R-Fla.), the chairman of the House Appropriations defense subcommittee. "I don't deal with the lobbyist. What I tell the lobbyist to do is bring in the CEO or the project manager so I can deal directly with the people involved."

When they're not trying to influence lawmakers, lobbyists are helping them raise money. Lobbyists serve as treasurers of campaign committees or political action committee for almost 80 lawmakers, according to the Center for Public Integrity, a watchdog group. They also host fundraisers for lawmakers; in one week in April, while House committees drafted lobbying legislation, there were at least four fundraisers sponsored by lobbyists.

Republican lobbyist Jack Abramoff (who pleaded guilty in January to conspiring to corrupt public officials), his associates, and Indian tribal clients contributed $1.4 million to 171 lawmakers between 2001 and 2004, two-thirds to Republicans. During his time at the lobbying firm of Greenberg Traurig LLP, the firm's political action committee donations rose form $183,851 in 2000 to $360,185.

Overall, campaign donations from lobbyists rose to $18.5 million in 2006 from $7.5 million in 1996. Federal Election Commission records show.

"Because campaign donations are the way that lobbyists believe they can get access, the campaign fianance system keeps rolling along untouched," said Rogan Kersh, a political science professor (now scrving as associate dean at New York University) who teaches courses on lobbying. "Members of Congress are terrified they're going to be knocked off by a challenger. The lobbyists fuel the process and give money to those already in office". . . .

Lobbyists also play prominent roles in obtaining earmarks—local projects inserted into legislation—for clients.

The number of earmarks has increased from 4,126 in 1994, the last year the Democrats controlled both houses of Congress, to 15,569 in 2006, according to the Congressional Research Service.

At least 46 former House Appropriations Committee aides registered as lobbyists after leaving their congressional jobs since 1998, according to records compiled by the Center for Public Integrity. That compared with 36 for the House Ways and Means Committee and 34 for the House Energy and Commerce panel.

One lobbying firm that has hired former appropriations staff members is PMA Group of Arlington, Virginia, whose founder, Paul Magliocchetti, and six other employees once worked for the committee. The firm got 66 special projects worth $119 million for its clients inserted into defense spending legislation for the fiscal year that began Oct. 1, according to Taxpayers for Common Sense, an advocacy group that favors less government spending.

The Washington-based firm Van Scoyoc Associates Inc. employed three former appropriations staff members and got 18 special projects worth $66 million in the defense measure, according to Taxpayers for Common Sense records.

"The revolving door allows these lobbyists to exploit the relationships they have with lawmakers that can hand out billions and billions of dollars," said Alex Knott, political editor for the Center for Public Integrity.

Stu Van Scoyoe, president of the firm that bears his name, said former congressional aides give his clients the technical knowledge they need, such as the proper format for a funding request, and can anticipate objections and address them to prevent an allocation from being rejected.

"The appropriations staffers tend to be very much into the details, very much green eyeshades type of people," Van Scoyoc said. "Having people who are currently knowledgeable in programs and in the details of programs is always an advantage."

Former top-level staff members can lawfully lobby their former committee after a one-year waiting period. Lower-level staff members can lobby immediately after leaving their congressional job.

One lawmaker who writes spending legislation said former appropriations aides have an advantage in securing funds because they know the process.

"Obviously, they're more knowledgeable because of their experience, but they don't have any undue influence," said Representative Harold Rogers, a Kentucky Republican who chairs the appropriations homeland security subcommittee. "If you know your subject, you're usually more successful."

The Appropriations Committee's top two staff members had left the congressional payroll and worked as lobbyists before joining staff of panel Chairman Jerry Lewis of California. Committee staff director Frank Cushing left the panel in 2003 to lobby for defense contractors, and rejoined it in 2005.

Jeffrey Shockey initially worked for Lewis from 1991 to 1999, and later worked for a lobbying firm in which Lewis's longtime friend, former Republican Representative Bill Lowery of California, is a partner. Shockey became deputy director of the Appropriations Committee staff in 2005.

Appropriations Committee spokesman John Scofield said Cushing and Shockey returned to the Appropriations Committee because they wanted to work for Lewis. "These guys gave up good situations and high-paying jobs to do public service," Scofield said.

The House this year passed new rules to identify the lawmakers who request catmarks. The rules expire at the end of the year.

That was the only ethics reform passed. When Congress considered stronger legislation, some lobbyists began lobbying against the measure.

"No matter how well-intentioned a reform effort may be, it will be meaningless to the American people if we first don't begin by talking about enforcement of the current rules," said Paul Miller, president of the American League of Lobbyists, in testimony to the Senate Homeland Security and Government Affairs Committee in January.

On Election Day 2006, three House Republicans with ties to Reppublican lobbyist Jack Abramoff, who pleaded guilty to conspiring to corrupting public officials, lost their reelection campaigns. Three seats vacated by Republicans who resigned because of ethical problems also fell to the Democrats. A CNN exit poll found 42 percent of voters saying ethics were an "extremely important" factor in their vote.

What's Your Opinion?

What limits, if any, would you place on lobbying? Would you change, for example, "the revolving door" restrictions governing lobbying by individuals that have worked in Congress? Do you think such changes would substantially or only slightly diminish the influence of lobbyists?

CHAPTER 10

THE NEWS MEDIA:
COMMUNICATING POLITICAL
IMAGES

“The press in America . . . determines what people will think and talk about—an
authority that in other nations is reserved for tyrants, priests, parties, and
mandarins.”

THEODORE H. WHITE[1]

The news from Iraq was horrific. Day after day, the headlines told of
suicide bombings, roadside explosions, kidnappings, and beheadings.
Almost no day passed without a U.S. soldier being reported killed, and no
day passed without reports of Iraqi civilians being killed. More than two
thousand Iraqis a month were dying in the conflict, and U.S. troops were
being killed and maimed at a rate of more than one hundred a month.

Yet the situation in Iraq was not all blood and violence. Iraqi soldiers
and police were being trained and equipped, schools were being built and

opened, roadways were being fixed, and basic services were being restored. The United States was spending billions of dollars a month on the rebuilding of Iraq, a point that Bush administration officials made repeatedly at press briefings. Nevertheless, the news from Iraq only occasionally addressed the reconstruction effort and instead focused on the fighting and dying.

Although the news has been compared to a mirror held up to society, it is a highly selective portrayal of reality. The **news** is mainly an account of obtruding events, particularly those that are *timely* (new or unfolding developments rather than old or static ones), *dramatic* (striking developments rather than commonplace ones), and *compelling* (developments that arouse people's emotions).[2] These tendencies have their origin in a number of factors, not the least of which is that the news organizations seek to make a profit, which leads them to prefer news stories that will attract and hold an audience. Thus, compared with the fighting in Iraq, the reconstruction effort was less newsworthy. As a gradual process, it did not lend itself to vivid storytelling in the way the fighting did. The fighting was also the easier story for journalists to tell because it fit with the news audience's conception of war—war is about killing, not rebuilding.

News organizations and journalists are referred to collectively as the **press** or the **news media.** The press includes broadcast networks (such as ABC and NPR), cable networks (such as CNN and Fox), newspapers (such as the *Chicago Tribune* and *Dallas Morning News*), news magazines (such as *Time* and *Newsweek*), and Internet sites that provide news and commentary (such as Instapundit and the Drudge Report). The U.S. news system has been undergoing substantial changes. For decades, it was virtually controlled by local daily newspapers and broadcast television. Though still the dominant players, during the past quarter-century these news outlets have lost much of their audience and influence to cable news, talk radio, and the Internet, a point that will be addressed in detail later in the chapter.

The news media hold a privileged position in the United States. In many democracies, the press operates under substantial legal constraints. In Great Britain, for example, the news media are barred from reporting on subjects that have been designated "official secrets" by the government, and tough libel laws inhibit the media from publishing weakly substantiated claims that could damage a person's reputation. U.S. libel laws, on the other hand, favor the press (see Chapter 4). It is almost impossible for a public official to meet the U.S. legal standard for a libel judgment: that a news organization was both false in its accusations and

After Saddam Hussein's regime in Iraq was toppled, the United States began the task of reconstructing Iraq's oil operations, schools, hospitals, roads, and other facilities. The reconstruction was of secondary interest to the news media. The fighting in Iraq was the main story.

knowingly or recklessly careless in its effort to reach the truth. The American press is also free to cover politics in nearly any way it chooses. The press is protected from government interference by the First Amendment, which the Supreme Court has interpreted as a broad grant of immunity (see Chapter 4). The government is prohibited, for example, from blocking the publication of national-security information unless the government can prove to a court that its release would pose a serious danger to the United States.

The American press has another advantage: an ongoing daily relationship with the public. Like the political party and the interest group, the press is a political intermediary in the sense that it links citizens with their government. Yet the press alone has daily contact with a broad cross section of the American people.

This chapter examines the news media's role in the American political system. The chapter will argue that the press is a key intermediary between Americans and their leaders but also that the press is a different kind of intermediary than either the political party or the interest group.[3] News organizations, unlike political parties or interest groups, generally do not aim to represent particular interests. While news organizations do claim, with some justification, to serve the public interest by keeping people informed about public affairs, their news coverage is driven as much by a need to tell stories that will get people's attention as it is by the goal of keeping people informed. The news media need an audience in order to sell advertising, which finances their operations. News coverage therefore tends to focus on sensational events that will catch and hold people's attention rather than on ordinary developments that can be far more important in people's lives. This chapter explores this and other aspects of the press and its coverage of the news. The main ideas presented in the chapter are these:

★ *The American press initially was tied to the nation's political party system (the partisan press) but gradually developed an independent position (the objective press).* In the process, the news shifted from a political orientation, which emphasizes political values and ideas, to a journalistic orientation, which stresses newsworthy information and events.

★ *In recent years, traditional news organizations have faced increased competition for people's attention. Cable and the Internet have contributed to a fragmenting of the news audience and, to a lesser extent, to the rise of opinionated journalism.*

★ *In fulfilling their responsibility to the public, the news media play several roles: the signaling role (the press brings relevant events and problems into public view), the common-carrier role (the press serves as a channel through which leaders and citizens can communicate), the watchdog role (the press scrutinizes official behavior for evidence of deceitful, careless, or corrupt acts), and the representative role (the press promotes particular interests and values).* The American press is better equipped to handle the first three of these roles than the last one.

HISTORICAL DEVELOPMENT: FROM PARTISANSHIP TO OBJECTIVE JOURNALISM

Democracy thrives on a free flow of information. Communication enables a free people to keep in touch with one another and with officials, a fact not lost on America's early leaders. Alexander Hamilton persuaded John Fenno to start a newspaper, the *Gazette of the United States*, in order to publicize the policies of George Washington's administration. In return,

Hamilton, as secretary of the treasury, granted Treasury Department printing contracts to Fenno's newspaper. Hamilton's political adversary, Thomas Jefferson, dismissed the *Gazette*'s reporting as "pure Toryism" and convinced Philip Freneau to start the *National Gazette* as an opposition paper. Jefferson, who was secretary of state, gave Freneau the authority to print State Department documents.

Early newspapers were printed on flat presses, a process that limited production and kept the cost of each copy beyond the reach of ordinary citizens—many of whom were illiterate anyway. Leading papers such as the *Gazette of the United States* had fewer than fifteen hundred subscribers and could not have survived without party support. Not surprisingly, the "news" they printed was a form of party propaganda.[4] In this era of the **partisan press,** publishers openly backed one party or the other.[5] *politics*

Technological innovation in the early decades of the 1800s helped bring about the gradual decline of the partisan newspaper. Invention of the telegraph provided editors with timely information on events outside the local area, which led them to substitute news stories for opinion commentary.[6] Creation of the hand-cranked rotary press was equally important because it enabled publishers to print their newspapers more cheaply and quickly. The *New York Sun* was the first paper to pass on the benefit of higher-speed printing to subscribers by reducing the price of a daily copy from six cents to a penny. The *Sun*'s circulation rose to one thousand to ten thousand in less than a year.[7] Increased circulation meant increased advertising revenue, which freed newspapers from their dependence on government printing contracts.

By the late nineteenth century, helped along by the invention of newsprint and power-driven presses, many American newspapers were printing fifty thousand or more copies a day, and their large circulations enabled them to charge high prices for advertising. The period marked the height of newspapers' power and the low point in their sense of public responsibility. A new style of reporting—"yellow journalism"—had emerged as a way of boosting circulation.[8] It was "a shrieking, gaudy, sensation-loving, devil-may-care kind of journalism which lured the reader by any possible means."[9] A circulation battle between William Randolph Hearst's *New York Journal* and Joseph Pulitzer's *New York World* is believed to have contributed to the outbreak of the Spanish-American War through sensational (and largely inaccurate) reports on the cruelty of Spanish rule in Cuba. A young Frederic Remington (who later became a noted painter and sculptor), working as a news artist for Hearst, planned to return home because Cuba appeared calm and safe, but Hearst cabled back: "Please remain. You furnish the pictures and I'll furnish the war."[10]

Yellow journalism was characterized by its sensationalism. William Randolph Hearst's *New York Journal* whipped up public support for a war in Cuba against Spain through inflammatory reporting on the sinking of the battleship *Maine* in Havana Harbor in 1898.

The excesses of yellow journalism led some publishers to consider ways of reporting the news more responsibly. One step was to separate the newspaper's advertising department from its news department, thus reducing the influence of advertisers on news content. A second development was a new model of reporting called **objective journalism,** which was based on the reporting of "facts" rather than opinions and was "fair" in that it presented both sides of partisan debate.[11]

A chief advocate of this new form of journalism was Adolph Ochs of the *New York Times*. Ochs bought the *Times* in 1896, when its circulation was 9,000; four years later, its readership had grown to 82,000. Ochs told his reporters that he "wanted as little partisanship as possible . . . as few judgments as possible."[12] The *Times* gradually acquired a reputation as the country's best newspaper. Objective reporting was also promoted through newly formed journalism schools. Among the first of these professional schools were those at Columbia University and the University of Missouri.

THE POLITICS OF AMERICA'S NEWS MEDIA

Objective journalism is still the defining norm of American reporting. But it does not dictate what news organizations and journalists must do, nor does it govern all news media equally. As the following discussion will show, its influence varies.

Newspapers

The United States has roughly fifteen hundred daily newspapers. Although most of them side with one political party or the other on their editorial and opinion pages, it usually is difficult to tell from their news pages which party they back editorially. In their news coverage, they tend to highlight the same national stories each day, and if a high-ranking public official is caught in a scandal or makes a policy mistake, they will play it up—whether that official is a Republican or a Democrat. As developments in Iraq soured, President George W. Bush received reams of bad press in nearly all U.S. newspapers. During low periods of his presidency, Bill Clinton received the same rough treatment from reporters.

Even the editorial and opinion pages of most American newspapers are not completely one-sided. They usually include among their regular columnists at least one columnist who has an opposing opinion. Since the early 1970s, for example, the *New York Times* has always had at least one conservative columnist—William Safire, a Nixon speechwriter, was the first—to serve as a counterbalance to its liberal columnists.

Of course, America's newspapers differ in their reporting styles. Some thrive on sensationalism. The top story on the front page of the staid *Denver Post*, for example, normally will compete for readers' attention with a half dozen other front-page stories. That same story in the tabloid *Rocky Mountain News* might be splashed across the entire front page. Differences in approach, however, do not disguise the fact that most news organizations, regardless of their editorial position, tell their various audiences the same top stories each day. U.S. newspapers do not report a Republican version of the news and an opposing Democratic version.

The evenhandedness of America's newspapers is buttressed by their dependence on wire services.[13] Most U.S. newspapers lack the resources to gather substantial amounts of news outside their own localities and depend for their national coverage on the wire services, particularly the Associated Press (AP). The AP has three hundred full-time reporters stationed throughout the country and the world to gather news stories, which are relayed to subscribing newspapers. More than 95 percent of the nation's dailies (as well as most broadcast stations) are serviced by AP, which, because it serves the full range of American newspapers, studiously avoids partisanship.

A few U.S. newspapers—including the *New York Times, Wall Street Journal, Los Angeles Times, Washington Post,* and *Chicago Tribune*—have large enough reporting staffs to generate their own national coverage. Although these papers usually cover the same top stories in pretty much the same way each day, they diverge in their feature, follow-up, and investigative reporting. This is where their partisan leanings become evident. For example, the *New York Times* devotes more news space to America's social problems than does the editorially conservative *Wall Street Journal.* For its part, the *Journal* devotes more space to the problems of corporate America than does the *Times.* Nevertheless, differences of this kind are a far cry from the robust partisanship that characterized nineteenth-century American newspapers and is still found today in some European newspapers (see "How the United States Compares").

Broadcast News

Until the early twentieth century, the print media were the only form of mass communication. Within a few decades, however, hundreds of radio stations were broadcasting throughout the nation. Broadcasting was the first truly *national* mass medium. Newspapers had local readerships, whereas radio could reach millions of Americans across the country simultaneously.

Television followed radio, and by the late 1950s more than 90 percent of American homes had a television set. However, television newscasts of the 1950s were brief, lasting no more than fifteen minutes, and relied on news gathered by other organizations, particularly the Associated Press and other wire services. In the early 1960s, the three commercial networks—CBS, NBC, and ABC—expanded their evening newscasts to thirty minutes, and their audience ratings increased. Simultaneously, they increased the size of their news divisions, and television soon became the leading medium of national politics.

Today, television provides a twenty-four-hour forum of political news and information. The creation of the Cable News Network (CNN) and C-SPAN in the late 1970s brought Americans round-the-clock public-affairs coverage. Television talk shows, such as *The O'Reilly Factor* and *Larry King Live,* have broadened the range of choices available to politically interested viewers. A parallel development is the emergence of radio talk shows. Nearly a sixth of the American public claim to listen regularly to politically oriented radio talk shows, most of which have a conservative slant. The best known of the radio talk show hosts is Rush Limbaugh, whose blistering attacks on Democratic politicians and policies have gained him a devoted following among conservative listeners.

Radio Talk Shows   Partisan programs like Rush Limbaugh's talk show were virtually nonexistent until two decades ago. In 1934, Congress passed the Communications Act, which regulated broadcasting and created the Federal Communications Commission (FCC) to oversee the regulation. Broadcasters are required to be licensed by the federal government, and, because the number of available broadcasting frequencies is limited, those few individuals who are awarded a broadcasting license are expected to serve the public interest in addition to their own. Section 315 of the Communications Act, for example, imposes on broadcasters an "equal time" restriction, which means that they cannot sell or give air time to a political candidate without offering to sell or give an equal amount of air time to other candidates running for the same office. (Election debates are an exception; broadcasters can televise them even if participation is limited to the Republican and Democratic nominees, excluding third-party candidates.)

Until the late 1980s, broadcasters also were bound by the Fairness Doctrine, which required their news programming to treat fairly all sides of the debate on controversial public issues. In practice, this meant that the objective-reporting model practiced voluntarily by the newspapers was also the model that broadcasters by law were required to practice. The Fairness Doctrine was rescinded in the late 1980s on grounds that cable television, which is not subject to broadcasting regulation because it does not use public airways, had expanded the number of television news channels available to viewers.

Broadcasters no longer were required to balance their public affairs programming by airing a liberal talk show to balance a conservative one. Freed from this constraint, a number of local radio stations switched from playing music to airing political talk shows. They soon discovered that talk radio appealed mostly to conservative listeners. Limbaugh was among the conservative talk show hosts who quickly gained a wide following. Limbaugh's show alone was being heard by as many as twenty million listeners a week by the early 1990s. The only radio competitor with comparable audience numbers was National Public Radio (NPR), with a mix of news and talk shows. NPR's reporting model is nonpartisan; it balances the time given to Republican and Democratic leaders. NPR's talk shows, however, typically address topics with greater appeal to liberal listeners, who make up a disproportionate share of its audience.

Television Network News   Television production is vastly more expensive than radio production, which limits the ability of local television stations to produce anything other than local news. As a consequence, broadcast production of televised national and international news is dominated by the three leading networks—ABC, CBS, and NBC. For news of the nation and the world, America's nearly nine hundred local television stations depend on video transmissions fed to them by these three broadcast networks.

In their heyday, the ABC, CBS, and NBC nightly national newscasts were the envy of the news industry. Each evening at the dinner hour, these newscasts attracted 80 percent of television viewers. They now attract about 40 percent of viewers—more than twenty million people each night. Viewers are divided somewhat evenly between the three networks; thus, even today each network has a daily audience much larger than that of any other U.S. news organization.

The three networks attract audiences of roughly equal size in part because their newscasts are similar in content. Ten minutes of these half-hour newscasts are taken up by advertising. With so little time for news, the day's top stories tend to dominate the coverage of all three networks. In addition, network correspondents cover the same beats, rely on the same sources, and employ the same reporting techniques. Long practice at television reporting leads network correspondents to develop a common understanding of what makes a good story.[14] After filming a congressional hearing, for example, network correspondents are likely to agree on what was most newsworthy about it—often a testy exchange

 HOW THE UNITED STATES COMPARES

Partisan Neutrality as a News Value

In the nineteenth century, the United States had a partisan press. Journalists were partisan actors, and news was a blend of reporting and advocacy. Facts and opinions were freely intermixed in news stories. This type of reporting gradually gave way to a model of journalism that emphasizes the "facts" and covers the two major parties more or less equally. American journalists today are fairly evenhanded in their daily news reporting. For example, a political scandal, whether it involves a Democrat or a Republican, is a big story for any major U.S. news organization.

(continued)

European news organizations are less committed to political neutrality. Many European newspapers are aligned with a party, and although they focus on events, their coverage has a partisan component. In Great Britain, for example, the *Daily Telegraph* often serves as a voice of the Conservative party, while the *Guardian* favors the Liberals. Broadcasters in most European countries are politically neutral by law and practice, but there are exceptions, as in the case of French and Italian broadcasters.

The difference between the U.S. and European media is evident in a five-country survey that asked reporters whether they thought journalists should remain neutral in reporting on political parties. Compared with their counterparts in Great Britain, Germany, Sweden, and Italy, U.S. journalists were more likely to believe in partisan neutrality.

Source: Thomas E. Patterson, Media and Democracy Project, in progress. Reprinted by permission of the author.

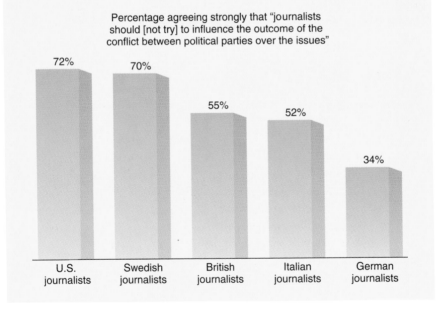

Percentage agreeing strongly that "journalists should [not try] to influence the outcome of the conflict between political parties over the issues"

U.S. journalists	Swedish journalists	British journalists	Italian journalists	German journalists
72%	70%	55%	52%	34%

between a witness and one of the committee members. Similarly, the live "stand-ups" that the networks' White House correspondents do each evening from the lawn outside the Oval Office are nearly indistinguishable. Rarely are they much more than a review of the day's major development at the White House.

Franklin D. Roosevelt was the first president to make effective use of the radio to communicate directly with the American people. He broadcast a series of fireside chats that reached millions of listeners across the country. By the 1950s, television was overtaking radio as a political medium.

Despite the emphasis on top stories, the networks frequently are accused of partisan bias—usually by conservatives. In a best-selling book, former network correspondent Bernard Goldberg accused the networks of having a liberal agenda.[15] Such allegations are not completely baseless. Until recently, for example, the concerns of evangelical Christians were rarely a subject of broadcast news except in the context of divisive issues such as creationism and abortion. Also, most broadcast news journalists, like most journalists generally, lean Democratic in their personal beliefs.[16]

However, content analysis studies have not revealed a large or consistent liberal bias on the evening newscasts. In fact, the television-age president who was found to have received the most negative coverage was Democrat Bill Clinton. The Center for Media and Public Affairs found that Clinton's negative coverage exceeded his positive coverage in every quarter of every year of his two-term presidency—a dubious record unmatched by any president before or since.[17] Instead of a partisan bias, scholars have highlighted a different tendency, namely, the networks' preference for the negative. Michael Robinson concluded that broadcast journalists have a "negativist, contentious" outlook on politics.[18] The networks' preference for "bad news" can be seen, for example, in their coverage of presidential candidates. Virtually every nominee since the 1980s—Democratic and Republican nominees alike—has received mostly negative coverage during the course of the campaign. In any given election, one nominee gets more favorable coverage than the other, but not by much and not with any partisan regularity. Compared to his Democratic rivals, George W. Bush received more favorable coverage during the 2000 presidential campaign but less favorable coverage during the 2004 campaign.[19]

Objective journalism dictates that the opposing parties be treated equally, not that they be treated well. No rule of journalism limits criticism, and the networks take it to the extreme. Network coverage of the Democratic-controlled Congress of 1993–94 was nearly 70 percent negative, deriding the legislature as a "do-nothing" Congress. When Republicans had control of Congress in 1995–96, network coverage again was nearly 70 percent negative. That particular Congress was criticized for trying to do too much.[20] Such evidence suggests that the consistent bias of the networks is not liberal as opposed to conservative but rather a pronounced tendency to report what might be wrong with politics and politicians as opposed to what might be right.

The networks' unbridled negativity helps explain why they are widely perceived as biased. Research has found that negative news is perceived differently by those who support and those who oppose the official being criticized. Opponents tend to see the criticism as valid, while supporters tend to see it as slanted. This reaction is heightened when people see the attack on television as opposed to reading about it.[21] It is not surprising, then, that Democrats during the Clinton presidency tended to think the networks favored the Republicans while Republicans during the two Bush presidencies tended to think the networks favored the Democrats. Such findings do not mean that the networks are unbiased, but they do indicate that much of the perceived bias is in the eye of the beholder.

Cable Television

Because cable television is transmitted by wire rather than over the airwaves, it was not governed by the Fairness Doctrine. Thus, cable news organizations have always been free to cover politics in a manner of their choosing. Nevertheless, when media mogul Ted Turner started CNN in 1980, he chose to abide by the Fairness Doctrine, instructing his correspondents to pursue a path of partisan neutrality. He sought to make his mark by delivering the news around the clock and through live, on-the-scene coverage. Turner's marketing idea worked. CNN's audience and reputation ballooned whenever a major event occurred. In 1991, for example, Americans were riveted to CNN's live coverage from Baghdad as the first American bombs of the Persian Gulf War began falling on that city.

When billionaire media owner Rupert Murdoch started Fox News in 1996, he had a different marketing model in mind. Murdoch hired a Republican consultant, Roger Ailes, to run Fox News and instructed him to devise a format that would appeal to political conservatives. Ailes hired a number of conservative talk show hosts, including Bill O'Reilly, and developed a news division that—though it concentrates on top stories—reports on them through a conservative lens. During the period of the 2004 presidential debates, for example, Fox did not ignore the post-debate polls that indicated most Americans thought John Kerry had outdebated George W. Bush. However, according to a study by the Project for Excellence in Journalism, Fox News did fewer debate stories than the other networks and was the only network during the debate period to cover Bush more favorably than Kerry.[22]

Murdoch's market strategy has paid off. Fox News is today the most highly rated cable news network, a position it has held for more than five years. The Fox News audience at a given time averages about one million viewers, compared with CNN's seven hundred thousand viewers. Moreover, as Murdoch anticipated, Fox's audience is heavily Republican (see Figure 10-1). Compared to Democrats, Republicans are more than twice as likely to be regular viewers of Fox News. CNN's audience, which was rather evenly balanced between Republicans and Democrats until Fox News came along, now has a disproportionate number of Democrats, largely because of the exodus of Republican viewers to Fox. The third-rated cable news network, MSNBC, is closer to CNN than to Fox News both in its audience and in its news practices.

Traditional journalists are critical of Fox News, claiming that partisanship should play no part in political reporting. Their view, while defensible from a professional perspective, has no basis in law, in audience preference, or in history. Objective reporting is based on a professional code, not a legal one. Moreover, judging by Fox's success in attracting Republicans, some Americans prefer news that has a partisan slant. Finally, Fox News is part of an age-old journalism tradition, though not the one dominant at the moment in the United States. Partisan journalism once was the mainstay of the American press and still is widely practiced in Europe. It also is found with some frequency on the Internet, the medium to which we turn next.

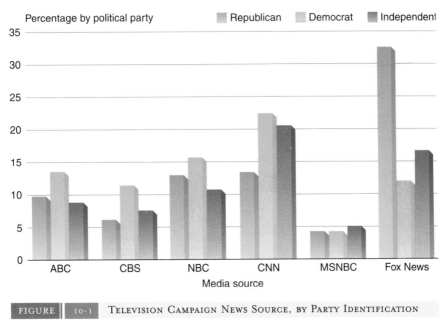

Percentage by political party   ■ Republican   ■ Democrat   ■ Independent

FIGURE 10-1 TELEVISION CAMPAIGN NEWS SOURCE, BY PARTY IDENTIFICATION

As indicated by a poll of where people got most of their news about the 2004 presidential election campaign, Fox News is far and away the preferred choice of Republican voters. *Source: Pew Research Center for the People and the Press report, September 16, 2004.*

The Internet

Although the First Amendment protects each individual's right to press freedom, in practice the right has been reserved for a tiny few. Journalist A. J. Liebling wrote that freedom of the press belongs to those with the money to own a broadcast station or newspaper.[23] Even a small broadcast station or daily newspaper costs millions to buy; larger ones are worth hundreds of millions.

Access to the Internet is no substitute for owning a newspaper or a television station, but it does provide ordinary citizens with an opportunity to exercise their free-press rights. By creating a website, any citizen can post news and information about public affairs, harangue officials, argue for public policies, and mobilize the support of others. The Internet has lowered the barriers to public communication to a level not seen since colonial days, when pamphlets, some of them handwritten, were the primary medium of politics. The Internet also has been a boon to political organizers. During the 2004 presidential campaign, for example, Vermont governor Howard Dean used his opposition to the Iraq war and the power

The Internet has opened up the media system, allowing citizens, groups, and leaders to communicate more directly and powerfully than was possible during the not-so-distant era when news organizations almost totally controlled the instruments of mass communication. Shown here is a web page of Rock the Vote, an organization dedicated to helping young adults register and vote.

of the Internet to vault from relative obscurity to a strong early presence in the race for the Democratic presidential nomination. Dean's campaign raised more than $50 million, mostly through Internet contributions averaging less than $100. The Internet was also the medium for one of the most successful citizen-led efforts in history—a global movement that succeeded in getting nearly one hundred countries to sign an international treaty banning the use of land mines. Its organizer, Jody Williams, was awarded the Nobel Peace Prize.

When it comes to news, however, the Internet's significance is more difficult to assess. Because the entry cost is low, literally thousands of websites regularly post and examine news. However, Internet news is characterized by what analysts call "the long tail." When news-based websites are arrayed by the number of visitors to each site, there are a few heavily visited sites on one end and many lightly visited sites on the other—"the long tail." As it happens, most heavily visited sites are sites offered by the traditional media, including CNN.com, nytimes.com, and MSNBC.com. In addition, most of the other heavily visited sites, such as Google News, simply republish news gathered and reported first by the established media. In other

★ LEADERS

Jody Williams
(1950–   )

In 1992, Jody Williams launched a global Internet campaign that aimed to get countries around the world to ban the use of antipersonnel land mines. Each year, more than ten thousand civilians—mostly peasant farmers and children—are killed when they accidentally detonate an abandoned land mine while working or playing in areas that once were war zones. Working out of her home, Williams relentlessly sought allies in her effort to convince countries not to place additional antipersonnel mines and to remove those already in place. Williams gained a key supporter when the Canadian government joined the effort. In 1997, she achieved her goal when an international treaty banning antipersonnel mines was signed in Ottawa, Canada, by scores of countries. For her efforts, she received the Nobel Peace Prize, which was awarded jointly to her and to the International Campaign to Ban Landmines (ICBL), a coalition of nongovernmental organizations (NGOs) that she headed. Since then, Williams has tried to convince nonsignatory countries, including the United States, to sign the treaty. Before dedicating herself to land-mine eradication, Williams worked for a decade on humanitarian issues affecting Central America, including medical and food relief.

words, most Americans who turn to the Internet for news are seeing news generated by the same sources they otherwise rely on.

Of course, a news outlet's influence is not measured merely by the size of its audience. For example, the *New York Times*, with a daily circulation of roughly one million readers, has rightly been called "the bulletin board" for the network evening newscasts, with their combined audience of twenty-five million viewers. When network executives gather in the morning to plan the evening newscast, one of the first things they do is review the stories in that day's *New York Times*. In a similar vein, Internet-based news outlets have broken some important stories, most famously the Drudge Report's revelation of President Clinton's affair with White House intern Monica Lewinsky.

MEDIA AND POLITICS

Are Bloggers Today's Pamphleteers?

At the time of the writing of the Constitution, the news as we know it today did not exist. A major newspaper printed at most a few hundred copies of each issue, and there were no full-time reporters. Often, the newspaper owner did everything, from covering local events to hand-printing the copies. Most of what newspapers printed was not even news by today's standards, consisting mainly of ship manifests and government notices. Not until the 1830s, when the invention of the hand-cranked rotary press made it possible to print newspapers at low cost, was the first full-time reporter hired—and he was brought over from England by a New York newspaper to write sensational stories about street crime.

At the time of the nation's founding, the most influential writers were pamphleteers, not journalists. Thousands of pamphlets urging a break with Britain appeared in the decade before the American Revolution. Their authors usually published anonymously to hide their identity from British authorities. Thomas Paine, the most influential pamphleteer of the age, was no exception. When his pamphlet *Common Sense*, which sold over a hundred thousand copies, first appeared, it had no name on it. "We have the power to begin the world over again," wrote Paine, who also penned the famous line "These are the times that try men's souls." Paine would later go to France to foment revolution there, at one point landing in jail for his writings.

Are bloggers today's equivalent of revolutionary America's pamphleteers? Like the pamphleteers, bloggers are not regular journalists and engage in advocacy rather than straightforward reporting. They are a product of the Internet and of the opportunity created by the traditional media's reluctance (with a few exceptions, such as Fox News) to take stands on controversial issues. The bloggers themselves are a diverse lot. Some write from a conservative perspective, others from a liberal perspective. Some are careful in their use of facts, others are careless or deceptive. A few have a substantial audience, but most have only a small one. What they, like the colonal-era pamphleteers, have in common is a commitment to promoting a point of view.

The Drudge Report was started in 1995 by Matt Drudge and for a time was the most popular Internet-specific news site. Its visitors now number fewer than those of several other websites, including Instapundit, Daily Kos, and Boing Boing. Known as "blogs" (for "web logs"), such sites often more closely resemble political talk radio than news pages or newscasts in that they freely mix news and opinion. Unlike most successful talk radio programs, however, most successful blogs have a liberal bias. (The Drudge Report is an exception.) Liberal blogs tend to be less narrowly partisan than conservative talk shows. In their criticism of the war in Iraq, for example, liberal blogs are nearly as scathing in their denunciation of Democratic leaders who support the war as they are of the Bush administration's pursuit of the war.

Many liberal and conservative blogs have one thing in common, however—a lack of respect for the mainstream press, which they accuse of everything from bias to irrelevance. Many traditional journalists have a similarly low opinion of blogs, saying that because they do little original reporting, they should be regarded as nothing more than places where opinions are aired.

The Internet is in its early years as a news medium, so it is hazardous to guess whether initial tendencies will continue. With Americans increasingly looking to the Internet for information, including news, it is safe to say that the Internet's importance will continue to grow. Another prediction also seems safe: economics will drive much of what happens on the Internet, just as it helped shape the development of older media. News is expensive to produce, and reputations take time to develop. That explains why traditional media have been successful in attracting visitors to their websites. A major question is whether relative newcomers to the news business will be able to overcome the huge head start that the established media have on the Internet because they are known brands with a substantial capacity for original reporting.

THE NEWS MEDIA AS LINK: ROLES THE PRESS CAN AND CANNOT PERFORM WELL

When the objective model of reporting came to dominate American news coverage, the relationship between the press and the public was fundamentally altered. The nineteenth-century partisan press gave its readers clear-cut cues as to how to evaluate political issues and leaders. In the presidential election campaign of 1896, the *San Francisco Call* devoted 1,075 column-inches of photographs to the Republican ticket of McKinley-Hobart and only 11 inches to the Democrats, Bryan and Sewell.[24] Many

European newspapers still function in this way, guiding their readers by applying partisan or ideological values to current events. The *Daily Telegraph*, for example, is an unofficial but fiercely loyal mouthpiece of Britain's Conservative party.

The modern American press operates by a different standard. Partisanship is accepted on talk shows and editorial pages but is discouraged in news reporting. Journalists are expected to concentrate on describing and explaining events and developments. The media thus are very different from political parties and interest groups, the other major links between the public and its leaders. Parties and groups exist to promote political positions. The media are driven by the search for interesting and important stories.

This distinction provides a basis for determining what roles the media can and cannot be expected to fulfill. The press is adept at fulfilling those public responsibilities that are compatible with journalistic values: the signaling role, the common-carrier role, and the watchdog role. The media are less successful in their attempts to perform a fourth and more politically oriented role: public representative.

The Signaling Role

As journalists see it, their responsibilities include a **signaling role.** They seek to alert the public to important developments as soon as possible after they happen—a state visit to Washington by a foreign leader, a bill that has just been passed by Congress, a change in the nation's unemployment level, a terrorist bombing in a foreign capital.

The U.S. media are well equipped to play a signaling role (also known as a signaler role). They are poised to converge on any major news event anywhere in the nation and nearly anywhere in the world. For instance, as the United States prepared to attack Iraq in 2003, hundreds of U.S. journalists descended on that part of the world. Many of them were "embedded" in U.S. combat units. When the attack began, they traveled into battle with the troops. Their news stories kept Americans abreast of the war and the subsequent struggle to form a stable government in Iraq.

The media are particularly well suited to signal developments from Washington. More than half of all national news coverage emanates from the nation's capital, most of it from the White House and Congress. Altogether, more than ten thousand people in Washington work in the news business. The key players are the leading correspondents of the television networks and the major newspapers, the heads of the Washington news bureaus, and a few top editors.

The press, in its capacity as signaler, has the power to focus the public's attention. The term **agenda setting** has been used to describe the media's

★ STATES IN THE NATION

In the News, or Out?

Most of the news that reaches Americans no matter where they live originates with a handful of news outlets, such as NBC News. This coverage, however, concentrates on events in a few places. The map shows the relative frequency with which each of the fifty states was mentioned on NBC News during a recent one-year period.

Q: Why do some states get more coverage than other states?

A: The heavily covered states are the more populous ones, which increases the likelihood that a newsworthy event will occur. In NBC's case, coverage is also heavier in states where one of its news bureaus is located. NBC has bureaus in New York, Washington, Los Angeles, Dallas, Atlanta, Chicago, and Boston.

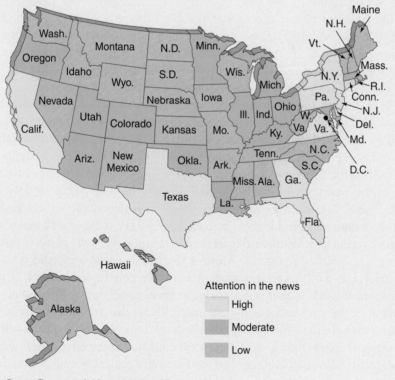

Source: Data compiled by author from Nexis.

ability to influence what is on people's minds.[25] By covering the same events, problems, issues, and leaders—simply by giving them space or time in the news—the media place them on the public agenda. The press, as Bernard Cohen notes, "may not be successful much of the time in telling people what to think, but it is stunningly successful in telling them what to think about."[26] This influence is most obvious in situations such as the U.S. war in Iraq, a development that continues to occupy Americans' attention.

The Common-Carrier Role

The press also plays a **common-carrier role** in that it provides political leaders a channel through which to communicate with the public. The importance of this role to officials and citizens alike is obvious. Citizens cannot very well support or oppose a leader's plans and actions if they do not know about them, and leaders need news coverage if they are to get the public's attention. Indeed, national news is mainly about the actions of political leaders and institutions, as reflected in the hundreds of reporters who station themselves regularly at the Capitol and the White House.

Officials try to get the most favorable news coverage they can. For example, the White House Press Office and the White House Office of Communications try to shape information in a way favorable to the president. Sometimes they succeed in placing their spin (that is, the president's interpretation) on the media's coverage of events.

Even though the president and Congress can expect wide coverage, the press increasingly places its own spin on stories out of Washington. Because of their increased celebrity status, a heightened skepticism of politicians after Vietnam and Watergate, and a greater need to draw the audience's attention, journalists have become accustomed not only to covering what newsmakers say but to having their own say as well. In fact, the news today—at least on television—is as much journalist-centered as it is newsmaker-centered. For every minute the presidential candidates spoke on the network newscasts during recent presidential campaigns, for example, the journalists covering them spoke for six minutes.[27] Most of the time a candidate could be seen on television with his mouth moving, his voice could not be heard; it was the journalist's voice that was audible. At these times, it was the journalist's version of the day's events—not the candidate's—that the viewing audience was hearing. In the 1960s, a candidate's sound bite (the length of time within a television story that a candidate speaks without interruption) was more than forty seconds on average.[28] In recent campaigns, the average sound bite has been less than ten seconds, barely enough time for the candidate to utter a long sentence (see Figure 10–2).

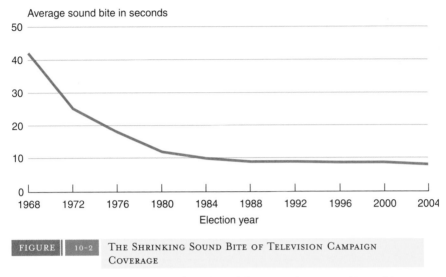

Average sound bite in seconds

FIGURE | 10-2 | THE SHRINKING SOUND BITE OF TELEVISION CAMPAIGN COVERAGE

The average length of time presidential candidates are shown speaking without interruption on broadcast television newscasts has declined sharply in recent elections. *Source: Adapted from Daniel C. Hallin, "Sound Bite News: Television Coverage of Elections 1968–1988."* Journal of Communication *42 (Spring 1992): 6.* The 1992–2004 data are from the Center for Media and Public Affairs.

The Watchdog Role

Traditionally, the American press has accepted responsibility for protecting the public from deceitful, careless, incompetent, and corrupt officials. In this **watchdog role,** the press stands ready to expose any official who violates accepted legal, ethical, or performance standards.

The press was acting in its watchdog role in 2004 when it reported the abuse of prisoners by U.S. soldiers in Iraq. Graphic photos of naked Iraqi prisoners forced into humiliating sexual poses and acts shocked the nation and the world. Allegations of abuse in U.S. military prisons in Iraq had been circulating for months, but publication of the photos brought the issue into the open. High-ranking U.S. officials, including Secretary of Defense Donald Rumsfeld, had learned of the photos months earlier but had not shared their discovery with President Bush or Congress. After the photos were aired on television and published in newspapers, Congress launched hearings to discover why U.S. troops had violated laws governing the treatment of war prisoners and who should be held responsible.

Acting in its watchdog role, the press in recent decades has vigorously pursued allegations of official wrongdoing. The Watergate scandal is the most renowned example. Led by the *Washington Post,* the press uncovered evidence that high-ranking officials in the Nixon administration had lied about their role in the burglary of the Democratic National Committee's headquarters and the subsequent cover-up. President Richard Nixon was forced to resign, as was his attorney general, John Mitchell. The press also exposed illegal government activity (the Iran-Contra connection) during the Reagan presidency; illicit personal behavior (the Monica Lewinsky scandal) during the Clinton presidency; and unauthorized wiretapping (the NSA flap) during the George W. Bush presidency. These examples indicate that the press, as watchdog, is a vital part of the American system of checks on those who hold positions of power.

There is an inherent tension between the watchdog role and the common-carrier role. The watchdog role demands that the journalist maintain a skeptical view of government and keep it at a distance. The common-carrier role requires the journalist to maintain close ties with government officials. In the period before Watergate, the common-carrier role was clearly the dominant orientation. It perhaps still is, but journalists have become increasingly critical of political leaders and institutions.

The press's watchdog role is especially controversial when issues of national security are involved. In 1970, the *New York Times* published the so-called Pentagon Papers—classified documents that revealed the government had deceived the public by claiming that the war in Vietnam was going well when in fact it knew the war was going badly. The Nixon administration tried to block the publication but was overruled by the Supreme Court (see Chapter 4). After the *Times* published the story, the Nixon administration had the option of charging the *Times* with transmitting classified information but decided that to do so would only compound an embarrassing situation. The *Times* found itself enmeshed in a similar controversy in late 2005 when it revealed that President George W. Bush, without judicial authorization, had ordered National Security Agency (NSA) wiretapping of communication originating in the United States and connecting to parties overseas. The Bush White House claimed that the story reported in the *Times* had damaged the U.S. government's ability to discover in advance whether terrorist groups were planning attacks on the United States. However, the story put the White House on the defensive because of a 1978 law that expressly prohibits the type of surveillance the NSA was conducting unless authorized by a judge. Even some congressional Republicans considered the Bush wiretaps illegal.

The *Times* had less support in 2006 when it revealed that President Bush had ordered the secret monitoring of international banking transactions as a means of detecting the flow of money to terrorist organizations. This surveillance program appeared to be within the law, and the White House

U.S. journalists covering the war in Iraq. The top correspondents were from the major networks, the wire services, and leading newspapers such as the *New York Times*. These news organizations supply most of the national and international news that Americans receive.

immediately struck back. Bush called the revelation "disgraceful." He said, "We're at war with a bunch of people who want to hurt the United States of America, and for people to leak that program, and for a newspaper to publish it, does great harm to the United States of America." Vice President Dick Cheney added, "Some of the press, in particular the *New York Times*, have made the job of defending against further terrorist attacks more difficult by insisting on publishing detailed information about vital national security programs." Congressman Peter King called the action of the *Times* "treasonous." House Republicans, backed by seventeen Democrats, passed a nonbinding congressional resolution saying that the revelation "may have placed the lives of Americans in danger."

The *Times* called its decision to publish the banking story "a close call," explaining that it chose to reveal the secret program because it possibly was connected to other programs that were unlawful. It was an argument that resonated with other news organizations. Journalists subscribe to the view that the American people are best served when the press errs on the side of making public what the government is doing, even if doing so opens the press to attack from those in power. As CNN correspondent Bob Franken put it, "We historically are not supposed to be popular, and it's almost our role to be the bearer of bad news."[29]

The Public-Representative Role

Traditionally, the **public-representative role**—that of spokesperson for and advocate of the public—has belonged to political leaders, political institutions, and political organizations. Today, however, many reporters believe they also have a mandate to represent the public. "[Our] chief duty," said a prominent newscaster, "is to put before the nation its unfinished business."[30]

Although the press has to some degree always acted as a stand-in for the people, the desire of journalists to play the role of public advocate increased significantly after the 1960s. As journalists' status rose, they became more assertive, a tendency sharpened by the trend toward interpretive reporting. Vietnam and Watergate also contributed to the change by convincing many journalists that their judgments were superior to those of political leaders. James Reston of the *New York Times* said of Vietnam, "Maybe the historians will agree that the reporters and cameras were decisive in the end. They brought the issue of the war to the people, before the Congress and the courts, and forced the withdrawal of American power from Vietnam."[31]

Nevertheless, there are at least two basic reasons for concluding that journalists are not nearly as well suited as political leaders to the role of public representative. First, the news media are not subject to the level of public accountability required of a public representative. Political institutions are made responsible to the public by a formal mechanism of accountability—elections. The vote gives officeholders a reason to act in the majority's interest, and it offers citizens an opportunity to boot from office anyone they feel has failed them. Thousands of elected officials have lost their jobs this way. The public has no comparable hold over the press. Journalists are neither chosen by nor removable by the people.

A second obstacle to journalists' attempts to play the role of public representative is that representation requires a point of view. Politics is essentially the mobilization of bias—that is, it involves the representation of particular values and interests. Political parties and interest groups, as explained in Chapters 8 and 9, exist to represent particular interests in society. But what political interests do the media represent? A few news outlets, such as Fox News, consciously promote a point of view, but the vast majority do not. As a television executive once said, journalists cover news "from nobody's point of view."[32] What he was saying, in effect, was that journalists do not consistently represent the political concerns of any segment of society. They respond to news opportunities, not to political interests. Above all, they prize good stories.[33]

The 2004 criminal trials of Michael Jackson, Kobe Bryant, Scott Peterson, and Martha Stewart are prime examples. These trials, and the hoopla surrounding them, received far more news coverage in 2004 than

Whenever a high-ranking official becomes enmeshed in an uncomfortable episode, a media feeding frenzy erupts that momentarily disrupts the ordinary flow of life in Washington. One such episode was the accidental shooting of a hunting companion by Vice President Dick Cheney. For a week, it was the nation's top story, eclipsing even what was happening in Iraq. Shown here is attorney Harry Wittington meeting with members of the press outside the Corpus Christi hospital where he was taken after being shot accidentally by Cheney.

did health care, unemployment, drug abuse, education, and every other domestic policy problem.

Underlying the press's obsession with the dramatic story is its quest for profits. The bottom line, rather than the public interest, increasingly drives news coverage. Audience competition has intensified with the spread of cable and satellite television, and the news has become increasingly sensational. During the 2004 campaign, as the public was expressing concern over Iraq and the economy, the press spent weeks on end rehashing events of thirty years earlier: whether George W. Bush had fulfilled his National Guard duties and whether the heroic portrayal of John Kerry's Vietnam service was fully accurate.

Even when the media cover policy developments, the reporting can be distorted by the quest for higher ratings. The U.S. invasion of Iraq in March of 2003, for example, was accompanied by audience-pleasing reports from the battlefield, while other important aspects were underplayed, including reactions elsewhere in the world to the invasion. This balance affected perceptions of the war. Many Americans wrongly believed, for example, that the U.S. invasion had the support of most other countries.[34]

The relentless search for attention-getting stories weakens the press's ability to provide citizens with a clear understanding of what is broadly at issue in politics. Journalist Walter Lippmann put it plainly when he said:

> The press is no substitute for [political] institutions. It is like the beam of a searchlight that moves restlessly about, bringing one episode and then another out of darkness into vision. Men cannot do the work of the world by this light alone. They cannot govern society by episodes, incidents, and interruptions.[35]

ORGANIZING THE PUBLIC IN THE MEDIA AGE

Lippmann's point was not that news organizations are somehow inferior to political organizations but that each has a different role and responsibility in society. Democracy cannot function properly unless the news media effectively carry out their signaling, common-carrier, and watchdog roles. Citizens must have access to timely and uncensored news about public affairs. However, the media cannot also be expected to do the job of political institutions.

As previous chapters have emphasized, the challenge of democracy lies in organizing the public so that people can act together effectively. The news media merely appear to meet this challenge. The fact that millions of people each day receive the same news about their government does not mold them into an organized community. The news creates a pseudo-community: citizens who feel they are part of a functioning whole until they try to act on their news awareness. The futility of media-centered democracy was dramatized in the movie *Network* when its central character, a television anchorman, became enraged at the nation's political leadership and urged his viewers to go to their windows and yell "I'm mad as hell and I'm not going to take it anymore!" Citizens heeded his instructions, but the main effect was to raise the network's ratings. It was not clear what officials in Washington were expected to do about several million people leaning out their windows and shouting a vague slogan. The film vividly illustrated the fact that the news can raise public consciousness as a prelude to action but cannot itself organize the public to take action, a task for which political parties and interest groups are much better suited.

Whether the press in the future will be in a better or a worse position to order and direct public opinion is unclear. By some indicators, the American media are in trouble. Newspaper circulations are declining, as are television news audiences. As their profits have shrunk, news organizations have cut back on their news budgets and hyped their coverage—actions that reduce the quality of news. At the same time, however, cable television and the Internet have increased the number of news outlets, including some—such as blogs and Fox News—that mix politics more openly with news. An uncertain factor in the equation is the public's appetite for news, whatever its form. Today's young adults show less interest in news than did their predecessors, a disturbing development regardless of one's preferred news model — objective or partisan. If citizens cannot be prompted to follow public affairs, the nation one day will face the larger challenge of how to maintain self-government among citizens who know little to nothing about the policy problems and choices they face.

SUMMARY

In the nation's first century, the press was allied closely with the political parties and helped the parties mobilize public opinion. Gradually the press freed itself from this partisan relationship and developed a form of reporting, known as objective journalism, that emphasizes the fair and accurate reporting of newsworthy developments. The foundation of modern American news rests on the presentation and evaluation of significant events, not on the advocacy of partisan ideas. The nation's news organizations do not differ greatly in their reporting; broadcast stations and newspapers throughout the country emphasize many of the same events, issues, and personalities, following the lead of the major broadcast networks, a few elite newspapers, and the wire services. This pattern, however, is not characteristic of bloggers or radio and television talk show hosts. Many of them pursue partisan agendas and thus differ in what they emphasize and how they interpret events and political developments.

The press performs four basic roles in a free society. First, in their signaling role, journalists communicate information to the public about events and problems that they consider important, relevant, and therefore newsworthy. Second, the press serves as a common carrier in that it provides political leaders with a channel for addressing the public. Third, the press acts as a public protector, or watchdog, by exposing deceitful, careless, or corrupt officials. The American media can and, to a significant degree, do perform these roles adequately.

The press is less well suited, however, to the fourth role it plays, that of public representative. This role requires a consistent political viewpoint and public accountability, neither of which the press possesses. The media are not a substitute for effective political institutions. The press's strength lies ultimately in its capacity to inform the public, not in its attempt to serve as the public's representative.

KEY TERMS

agenda setting (*p. 346*)
common-carrier role (*p. 348*)
news (*p. 328*)
objective journalism (*p. 332*)
partisan press (*p. 331*)

press (news media) (*p. 328*)
public-representative role (*p. 351*)
signaling role (*p. 346*)
watchdog role (*p. 349*)

SUGGESTED READINGS

Bagdikian, Ben H. *The New Media Monopoly*. Boston: Beacon Press, 2004. An examination of the growing power of the press, including tendencies toward monopolies of ownership and news production.

Baum, Matthew. *Soft News Goes to War*. Princeton, N.J.: Princeton University Press, 2003. A study of the impact of soft-news coverage of war.

Hamilton, James T. *All the News That's Fit to Sell*. Princeton, N.J.: Princeton University Press, 2004. A careful study of the economic influences on news content.

Kovach, Bill, and Tom Rosenstiel. *The Elements of Journalism*. New York: Three Rivers Press, 2001. An insightful look at the values of American journalism.

Maltese, John Anthony. *Spin Control: The White House Office of Communications and the Management of Presidential News*. Chapel Hill: University of North Carolina Press, 1994. An assessment of how presidents attempt to manage news coverage.

Overholser, Geneva, and Kathleen Hall Jamieson. *The Press*. New York: Oxford University Press, 2005. A comprehensive survey of U.S. journalism and news.

Patterson, Thomas E. *Out of Order*. New York: Vintage Books, 1994. An analysis of how election news coverage has changed in recent decades.

Sparrow, Bartholomew H. *Uncertain Guardians*. Baltimore, Md.: Johns Hopkins University Press, 1999. A systematic assessment of the news media's political role and tendencies.

LIST OF WEBSITES

http://www.cmpa.com/ The website for the Center for Media and Public Affairs (CMPA), a nonpartisan organization that analyzes news coverage on a continuing basis, provides analyses of news content that are useful to anyone interested in the media's political coverage.

http://www.drudgereport.com/ The website through which Matt Drudge (the Drudge Report) has challenged the traditional media's control of the news.

http://www.fcc.gov/ The Federal Communications Commission (FCC) website, which provides information on broadcasting regulation and current issues.

http://www.newslink.org/ Provides access to more than a thousand news organizations, including most U.S. daily newspapers.

POLITICS IN THEORY AND PRACTICE

Thinking: Why does almost every U.S. news outlet, despite having the freedom to say nearly anything it wants, cover virtually the same national stories in virtually the same way as other news organizations?

Participating: If you are like most citizens, news consumption is the politically related activity that takes up most of your time. And, if you are like most citizens, you will spend this time without thinking critically about what you are seeing and hearing. The next time you watch a television newscast or read a newspaper, pay attention to how a story is constructed. Is it framed in terms of conflict? Does it sensationalize the material? Is it framed critically—that is, does it present a negative view of a development, institution, or leader? How else might the same factual information have been presented? Do significant items of information or points of view seem to be missing from the story?

ADDITIONAL RESOURCES

For quizzes, interactive simulations, games, graphics, and other study tools, visit the book's Online Learning Center at **www.mhhe.com/pattersonwtp7.**

To Publish, or Not to Publish?

By Alex Jones

In late 2005 and again in 2006, the New York Times *released stories telling of secret U.S. surveillance programs that were part of the war on terrorism. Two programs exposed by the* Times *possibly were outside the law, while the third program seemed within the law. Should the* Times *have revealed any of the classified programs, particularly the third one? The question goes to the heart of the role of the free press in a democratic society. Is a democracy better served by a press that aggressively exposes the actions of government, or is it better served by a press that follows the government's judgment about what the American people should or should not know? This question is addressed in this essay by Alex Jones, director of the Joan Shorenstein Center on the Press, Politics, and Public Policy at Harvard University's Kennedy School of Government. He argues that the press serves the public interest when it errs on the side of openness. (A revised and abbreviated version of this essay was developed in collaboration with four communication school deans— Geoffrey Cowan of the University of Southern California, John Lavine of Northwestern University, Nicholas Lemann of Columbia University, and Orville Schell of the University of California, Berkeley—and published jointly in their names in 2006.)*

Most Americans want their government to be held accountable, which is the *raison d'etre* of watchdog journalism. At the same time, they do not want the press to disclose their government's vital secrets.

Since 9/11, serious news organizations have wrestled with the enduring problem of performing the press's vital watchdog role while also honoring citizenship responsibilities. The issue is once again front and center because of June 23rd articles, published by the *New York Times, Los Angeles Times* and *Wall Street Journal,* describing the government's efforts to track terrorist financing information. The *New York Times* has attracted most of the outrage because it took the lead in investigating the system.

For citizens, the dilemma comes down to choosing between the risk that would result from disclosure and the parallel risk of being kept in the dark, as the government often prefers. As the director of a center charged with imparting the values of responsible journalism to the next generation of reporters and editors, I favor disclosure when there are not very strong reasons for withholding information.

It is appropriate that Americans should be concerned when news organizations publish information that the President of the United States and others in authority have strongly urged not be published. No sane citizen would wish for the media to provide terrorists with information that would be likely to endanger American lives.

President Bush has denounced the *Times* in exceptionally harsh language, and on June 29 the House of Representatives formally condemned the paper. Some critics of the *Times* have termed its actions as treasonous and called for criminal charges under the Espionage Act. One conservative commentator told the *San Francisco Chronicle* that she would happily send Bill Keller, the paper's executive editor, to the gas chamber.

Keller has characterized the decision to publish the information as a "close call," which makes this an especially important moment to examine the proper balance between the press's watchdog role and its obligation to keep legitimate secrets whose exposure would badly damage the national interest.

The public has repeatedly expressed its support for the press's watchdog role, while also excoriating the media for bias and other faults. In a 2004 survey by the University of Missouri, 83 percent of respondents agreed with the statement that "it is important for journalists to press for access to information about our government, even when officials would like to keep it quiet." In the same poll, about the same number of people said that they see "social or political bias in news coverage." Clearly, the public wants the press to keep a sharp lookout, but wants the job performed responsibly. We share this sentiment.

Walking the line between its watchdog and its citizenship roles requires the press to exercise an independent judgment, and at times to defy the government. In the case of the stories about financial data under question, the government's main concern seemed to be that hitherto cooperative banks might stop cooperating if the *Times* disclosed the existence of their financial tracking system. So far that has apparently not happened. For many Amer-

icans, however, the possibility of damage to terrorist surveillance should have been sufficient justification for the *Times* to remain silent. Why, they ask, should the press take such a chance?

There are situations in which that chance should not be taken. For instance, we agree with Porter Goss, the former director of the Central Intelligence Agency, that it was wrong for the *Washington Times* in 1998 to disclose that the C.I.A. was listening in on Osama bin Laden's satellite phone. We think it equally clear that Robert Novak's column should not have unmasked Valerie Plame as a covert C.I.A. agent.

Yet, as a general rule, we believe that if it is a close call, and there is no good reason to believe that the story will put American lives at risk, the press should publish because far more damage will be done to a democratic society by keeping important information away from the American people than by leveling with them.

In our society, there is inevitable tension between liberty and security, but the two are interdependent. A knowledgeable public strengthens security in most circumstances, and makes government accountable. Similarly, excessive secrecy undermines security by treating real secrets and faux secrets the same, thus diluting a sense of urgency when information truly needs protecting. We know from our history that the government often claims to be concerned about national security when its actual concern is that disclosure will prove politically or personally embarrassing. The documents that came to be known as the Pentagon Papers in 1971 told how Presidents Eisenhower, Kennedy, and Johnson had all misled the American people regarding our role in Vietnam. Many of the documents were classified to keep their contents out of the public's view for political reasons.

The nation's founders adopted the First Amendment for the express purpose of making it more difficult for government to shield itself from the kind of careful, if often unwelcome, scrutiny that a democracy requires. For the same reason, Congress passed the Freedom of Information Act, and many states enacted Sunshine Laws to forestall government's tendency to prefer acting behind closed doors.

In the wake of 9/11, national security understandably became the top priority, and a new climate of caution regarding information was a sensible response to a sophisticated terrorist foe. President Bush's response was to declare a "war on terror" and has since claimed almost limitless powers that he views as inherently granted the president in time of war by the Constitution. Such extraordinary presidential power, in the context of what seems likely to be a permanent state of war, is unprecedented. The wise men who forged our nation created checks and balances and spoke passionately about the need for a free and independent press out of fear that too much power in any one branch of government would be dangerous.

The Bush administration has been excessively aggressive in restricting access to information on grounds of national security. There is an unmistakable pattern of limiting what Americans may reasonably know. For example, earlier this year historians complained that intelligence agencies were removing previously declassified historical documents from libraries and archives on the grounds of national security. Some of these papers dated from as far back as the Korean War; many had already been cited multiple times in books.

In general, the Bush Administration has sought to conduct much if not most of the war on terror in secret, and it has been able to do so with little oversight from Congress, which would normally be a key check on power. When the press has played such an oversight role, it has often been harshly criticized. For instance, a few months ago President Bush denounced the *Times* for revealing the National Security Agency's program of monitoring international telephone calls by Americans without first getting warrants, as a law passed by Congress required. In that case, the president rebuked the *Times* for revealing a classified secret. For most observers, however, the most important secret that was revealed, was that the president had ignored Congressional accountability and the statutory process that had been established.

The F.B.I. was summoned to conduct an aggressive effort to discover the source of the information. The F.B.I. even conducted a probe into the papers of columnist Jack Anderson after his death, which prompted a rebuke from the Senate Judiciary Committee and a number of journalists are under subpoena in cases where their sources are being sought. There is concern that journalists' phone records are going to be made available to the government, again on the basis of national security concerns.

A proper balance between disclosure and secrecy is in the nation's interest, but that balance has tilted in a direction that threatens to weaken watchdog reporting at a time when it is badly needed.

Despite the rhetoric of their fiercest critics, most news organizations—and most journalists—take secrets very seriously. Indeed, in a number of cases since 9/11, the *Times* has forgone publication of information at the request of the Bush Administration. In the case of the article on domestic eavesdropping, the *Times* held the story for a year before publishing it only after it felt that the issues raised were of great importance.

We believe that the extraordinary power of the presidency at this moment in history mandates more scrutiny by the public rather than less. Yet, Attorney General Alberto R. Gonzales has said publicly that he would consider prosecuting journalists for publishing classified information. Such an action would be devastating to the right of citizens to know what their government is doing in their name. The drumbeat for such extreme action appears to be an effort to intimidate and cow the press from probing dark corners.

We subscribe to the vision of Carl C. Magee, a crusading journalist whose Albuquerque, N.M., newspaper infuriated another president in the 1920s with revelations in the Teapot Dome scandal. Forced to close his paper after being driven into bankruptcy, Magee emerged two months later with another newspaper. Emblazoned on the front page was a new motto, borrowed from Dante: Give Light and the People Will Find Their Way."

What's Your Opinion?

Do you share Alex Jones's view of press responsibility when it comes to issues of national security? Is the nation best served by a press that leans toward revealing what officials would like to keep hidden from the public? Under what conditions do you think it might be inappropriate for the press to publish information about classified government programs?

CHAPTER 11

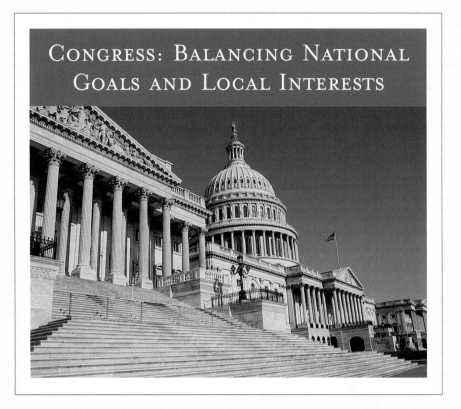

CONGRESS: BALANCING NATIONAL
GOALS AND LOCAL INTERESTS

❝There are two Congresses. . . . The tight-knit complex world of Capitol Hill
is a long way from [the member's district], in perspective and outlook as
well as in miles.❞

ROGER DAVIDSON AND WALTER OLESZEK[1]

In September 2005, Congress faced the question of how to come up with the billions of dollars that would be required to rebuild New Orleans and the other Gulf Coast communities devastated by hurricane Katrina.

One option was to trim the $286 billion transportation bill enacted by Congress a little more than a month earlier. It included hundreds of pork-barrel projects that members of Congress had secured for their home states and districts. One such project was a bridge that came to be known as "the bridge to nowhere." Nearly the length of San Francisco's Golden Gate Bridge, it would link the town of Ketchikan, Alaska (population 9,000), to Gravina Island (population 50). Its inclusion in the transportation bill was due to the power of its sponsor, Representative Don Young (R-Alaska), who chaired the House Transportation and Infrastructure

Committee—the committee that oversaw the legislation. Congressman Young's project was only the most conspicuous example. Virtually every member of Congress, in both the House and the Senate, had put something into the transportation bill that served constituent interests.

When commentators proposed that the projects be canceled and the money spent instead on Katrina relief, the response from Congress was a deafening no. Almost no member stepped forward to say that his or her pet project should be shelved. When a reporter asked Representative Young whether he would be willing to cancel the Ketchikan-Gravina bridge, he replied: "They can kiss my ear! That's the dumbest thing I've ever heard." Young later relented, but the money for the bridge, rather than being spent in the Gulf Coast area was redirected to Alaska transportation officials for use on other state projects.

The story of Katrina and the 2005 transportation bill illustrates the dual nature of Congress. It is both a lawmaking institution for the country and a representative assembly for states and districts.[2] Members of Congress have a duty to serve both the interests of their constituencies and the interests of the nation as a whole. The nation's needs sometimes take precedence, but not always. Senators and representatives depend for reelection on the voters back home and seldom miss an opportunity to serve their constituents' interests.[3]

The Framers of the Constitution established Congress as the leading branch of the national government. Congress is the first institution defined in the Constitution. Moreover, Article I does not simply give to Congress the lawmaking powers of government. It grants this power to Congress and Congress alone: "All legislative powers herein granted shall be invested in a Congress, which shall consist of a Senate and House of Representatives." Congress also is granted the authority to decide the form and function of the executive departments and the lower courts. No executive agency or lower court can exist except as authorized by Congress.

The positioning of Congress as first among equals in a system of divided powers reflects the Framers' trust in representative institutions. Congress was to be the branch of government where the interests of the people (through the House of Representatives) and the interests of the states (through the Senate) would find their fullest expression. This model was a rejection of the European monarchical model of executive supremacy. The Framers had an innate mistrust of political power, however, and were not about to give Congress free rein. They therefore granted the president and the courts significant checks on legislative power. Yet the government's lawmaking and representation functions, which together are the signature functions of a republic, were granted to Congress.

The Framers' vision of how the federal branches would operate has not fully withstood the test of time, as this chapter and subsequent chapters on the presidency and the judiciary will show. Nevertheless, an accounting of U.S. political institutions rightfully starts with Congress. This chapter examines that institution, beginning with congressional elections and organization and concluding with congressional policymaking. The points emphasized in the chapter are these:

★ *Congressional elections tend to have a strong local orientation and to favor incumbents.* Congressional office provides incumbents with substantial resources (free publicity, staff, and legislative influence) that give them (particularly House members) a major advantage in election campaigns. However, incumbency also has some liabilities that contribute to turnover in congressional membership.

★ *Leadership in Congress is provided by party leaders, including the Speaker of the House and the Senate majority leader.* Party leaders are in a more powerful position today than a few decades ago because the party caucuses have become more cohesive.

★ *The work of Congress is done mainly through its committees and subcommittees, each of which has its separate leadership and policy jurisdiction.* The committee system of Congress allows a broad sharing of power and leadership, which serves the power and reelection needs of Congress's members but fragments the institution.

★ *Congress lacks the direction and organization required to provide consistent leadership on major national policies, but it is well organized to handle policies of relatively narrow scope.* At times, Congress takes the lead on broad national issues, but ordinarily it does not do so.

★ *Congress's policymaking role is based on three major functions: lawmaking, representation, and oversight.* remember

CONGRESS AS A CAREER: ELECTION TO CONGRESS

In the nation's first century, service in Congress was not a career for most of its members. Before 1900, at least a third of the seats in Congress changed hands at each election. Most members left voluntarily. Because travel was slow, service in the nation's capital meant spending months away from one's family. Moreover, the national government was not the center of power that it is today; many politicians preferred to serve in state capitals.

Newt Gingrich and three hundred Republican congressional candidates stand in front of the Capitol in 1994 to dramatize their Contract with America. The Senate meets in the wing on the left, and the House meets in the wing on the right. The offices of the House and Senate party leaders—Speaker, vice president, majority and minority leaders, and majority and minority whips—are located in the Capitol. Other members of Congress have their offices in nearby buildings.

The modern Congress is a different kind of institution. Most of its members are professional politicians, and a seat in the U.S. Senate or House is as high as most of them can expect to rise in politics. The pay (about $165,000 a year) is reasonably good, and the prestige of their office is substantial, particularly if they serve in the Senate. A lengthy career in Congress is the goal of most of its members.

The chances of sustaining a career in Congress are good. Getting elected to Congress is difficult, but staying there is relatively easy. In recent decades, roughly 95 percent of House incumbents and about 90 percent of Senate incumbents seeking another term have been reelected (see Figure 11–1). These figures slightly overestimate incumbents' success rate. A few incumbents each term retire from Congress rather than face a challenger they fear will beat them. On balance, however, incumbents have a commanding edge over their opponents. Most of them, particularly those in the House, win reelection by a margin of 20 percentage points or higher.

U.S. House of
Representatives

Reelected 96%

Defeated 4%

U.S. Senate

Reelected 87%

Defeated 13%

FIGURE 11-1 RECENT REELECTION RATES OF HOUSE AND SENATE INCUMBENTS

Congressional incumbents have a very good chance of winning another term, as indicated by the approximate reelection rates of U.S. representatives and senators who sought reelection during the five congressional elections from 1998 to 2006.

Using Incumbency to Stay in Congress

One reason incumbents run so strongly is that many congressional districts and some states are so lopsidedly Democratic or Republican that candidates of the stronger party seldom lose. In Utah and Kansas, for example, residents who identify themselves as Republicans outnumber by a wide margin residents who identify themselves as Democrats. Massachusetts and California are examples of states where the Democrats hold a commanding majority. However, whether their constituency is lopsided or competitive, incumbents have several built-in advantages over their challengers.

The Service Strategy: Taking Care of Constituents   An incumbent promotes his or her reelection prospects by catering to the **constituency:** the body of citizens eligible to vote in the incumbent's state or district. Members of Congress pay attention to constituency opinions when choosing positions on legislation, and they work hard to get their share of **pork-barrel projects** (a term referring to legislation that funds a special project for a particular locale, such as a new highway or hospital). They also respond to their constituents' individual needs, a practice known as the **service strategy.** Whether a constituent is seeking information about a government program, expressing an opinion about pending legislation, or looking for help in obtaining a federal benefit, the representative's staff is ready to assist.

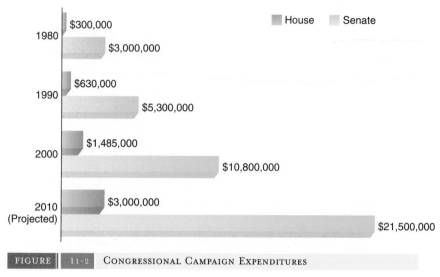

| | House | Senate |

1980 $300,000
      $3,000,000

1990 $630,000
      $5,300,000

2000 $1,485,000
      $10,800,000

2010
(Projected) $3,000,000
             $21,500,000

FIGURE   11-2   CONGRESSIONAL CAMPAIGN EXPENDITURES

The cost of running for congressional office has risen sharply as campaign tech-niques—television advertising, opinion polling, and so on—have become more elabo-rate and sophisticated. The increase in spending can be seen from a comparison of the approximate median spending level by both candidates per House or Senate seat at ten-year intervals, beginning in 1980. The cost has about doubled each decade, which is the basis for the 2010 projection. *Source: Federal Election Commission.*

Congressional staffers spend most of their time not on legislative mat-ters but on constituency service and public relations—efforts that pay off on election day.[4] Each House member receives an office allowance of roughly $800,000 a year with which to hire no more than eighteen per-manent staff members.[5] Senators receive allowances that range between about two and four million dollars a year, depending on the population of the state they represent. Smaller-state senators tend to have staffs of around thirty people, while larger-state senators have staffs of close to fifty.[6] Each member of Congress is also permitted several free mailings annually to constituent households, a privilege known as the frank. These mailings, along with press releases and other public relations efforts, help incumbents build name recognition and constituent support—major advantages in their reelection campaigns.

Campaign Fund-Raising: Raking in the Money   Incumbents also have a decided advantage when it comes to raising campaign funds. Con-gressional elections are expensive because of the high cost of polling, televised advertising, and other modern techniques (see Figure 11–2). Today a successful House campaign in a competitive district costs more

boring

| | Challengers | Incumbents |

| 29% | 30% | 21% | 18% | 19% | 21% | 11% | 14% | 11% | 18% | 12% | 13% | 12% | 9% | 12% |

| 71% | 70% | 79% | 82% | 81% | 79% | 89% | 86% | 89% | 82% | 88% | 87% | 88% | 91% | 88% |

1978 1980 1982 1984 1986 1988 1990 1992 1994 1996 1998 2000 2002 2004 2006
Year

FIGURE 11-3 ALLOCATION OF PAC CONTRIBUTIONS BETWEEN INCUMBENTS AND CHALLENGERS IN CONGRESSIONAL RACES THAT INCLUDED AN INCUMBENT, 1978–2006.

In allocating campaign contributions, PACs favor incumbent members of Congress over their challengers by a wide margin. *Source: Federal Election Commission. Figures for 2006 based on preliminary data.*

than a million dollars. The price of victory in competitive Senate races is much higher, ranging from several million dollars in small states to $20 million or more in larger states. Rarely do incumbents say they had trouble raising enough money to conduct an effective campaign. Challengers, however, usually say their fund-raising fell far short of what they needed.[7] However, although challengers still trail incumbents, they find it easier to attract funds when they have a chance of winning. In the 2006 midterm election, with political conditions working in their favor, Democratic challengers had a much easier time raising money than they did in the 2002 midterm elections, when the issues favored the Republicans.

Incumbents' past campaigns and constituent service enable them to develop mailing lists of potential contributors. Individual contributions, most of which are $100 or less, account for about 60 percent of all funds raised by congressional candidates and are obtained mainly through fund-raising events and direct-mail solicitation. Incumbents also have an edge with political action committees, or PACs, which are the fund-raising arm of interest groups (see Chapter 9). Most PACs are reluctant to oppose an incumbent unless it is clear that the candidate is vulnerable. More than 85 percent of PAC contributions in recent elections have been given to incumbents; their challengers received less than 15 percent (see Figure 11-3). "Anytime you go against an incumbent, you take a minute and think long and hard about what your rationale is," said Desiree Anderson, director of the Realtors PAC.[8] (A race without an incumbent—called an **open-seat election**—usually brings out a strong candidate from each party and involves heavy spending, especially when the parties are closely matched in the state or district.)

Redistricting: Favorable Boundaries for House Incumbents House members, but not senators, have a final advantage in winning reelection. Because incumbents are hard to unseat, they are always a force to be reckoned with, a fact that is blatantly apparent during redistricting. Every ten years, after each population census, the 435 seats in the House of Representatives are reallocated among the states in proportion to their population. This process is called **reapportionment.** States that have gained population since the last census may acquire additional House seats, while those that have lost population may lose seats. New York and Illinois were among the states that lost one or more House seats as a result of the 2000 census; Arizona and Washington were among the states that gained one or more seats. (The Senate is not affected by population change, because each state has two senators regardless of its size.)

The responsibility for redrawing House election districts after a reapportionment—a process called **redistricting**—rests with the state governments. States are required by law to make their districts as nearly equal in population as possible. There are many ways, however, to divide a state into districts of nearly equal size, and the party in power in the state legislature will draw the new district boundaries in ways that favor candidates of its party—a process called **gerrymandering.** The party's incumbents will be given districts packed with enough of the party's voters to ensure their reelection. What of the other party's incumbents? The safest tactic in this case is to place them in districts with overwhelming numbers of voters of their own party, assuring them of an easy victory but also reducing the number of voters of that party in other districts and placing that party at a disadvantage in these races.

For a small number of House incumbents, redistricting threatens their reelection. When a state loses a congressional seat or seats, there may be fewer seats than there are incumbents who plan to seek another term. In this case, incumbents can end up running against each other. Moreover, the party in control of the state legislature might conclude that a particular incumbent of the opposing party can be beaten and will redraw the boundaries of the incumbent's district to the incumbent's disadvantage. Turnover in House seats typically is higher in the first election after redistricting than in subsequent elections. The newly redrawn districts include some voters who are

When Massachusetts was redistricted in 1812, Governor Elbridge Gerry had the lines of one district redrawn in order to ensure that a candidate of his party would be elected. Cartoonist Elkanah Tinsdale, noting that the strangely shaped district resembled a salamander, called it a "Gerry-mander."

unfamiliar with the incumbent, diminishing one advantage incumbents ordinarily enjoy over their challengers. By and large, however, incumbents do not suffer greatly from redistricting, and the great majority of them wind up in districts that virtually assure their reelection. After the 2000 census, no more than 50 of the 435 House districts were competitive in the sense that they had a relatively close balance of Republican and Democratic voters. The rest were either heavily Republican or heavily Democratic. In the 2002 midterm election, the first election after the 2000 census, four incumbents lost their seats by virtue of losing a primary to another incumbent, and eight incumbents lost in the general election. Most of the other incumbents breezed to victory, many of them running unopposed and many winning 65 percent or more of the vote.

Pitfalls of Incumbency

Incumbency is not without its risks. In addition to the outside possibility that a House member will be placed in an unfavorable district as a result of reapportionment, potential pitfalls for Senate and House members alike include disruptive issues, personal misconduct, and variation in voter turnout.

Disruptive Issues Most elections are not waged in the context of disruptive issues, but when they are, incumbents are at greater risk. When voters are angry about existing political conditions, they are more likely to believe that those in power should be tossed out of office. In the 1994 midterm elections, when the public was upset over the economy and Democratic president Bill Clinton's leadership, more than 10 percent of congressional incumbents—more than twice the usual percentage and virtually all of them Democrats—were defeated. The 2006 midterm election, which was waged in the context of Republican President George W. Bush's leadership of an unpopular war in Iraq, also saw the defeat of more than twice the usual number of incumbents; this time, virtually all of them were Republicans. A prominent victim was Pennsylvania Senator Rick Santorum, who as chair of the Republican Senate Conference was the third-ranking member of the Republican Senate leadership. Easily reelected six years earlier, Santorum was soundly defeated by Bob Casey, Pennsylvania's state treasurer.

Personal Misconduct   Members of Congress can also fall prey to scandal. Life in Washington can be fast paced, glamorous, and expensive, and some members of Congress get caught up in influence peddling, sex scandals, and other forms of misconduct. Roughly a fourth of House incumbents who lost their bid for reelection in the past two decades were shadowed by ethical questions. "The first thing to being reelected is to stay away from scandal, even minor scandal," says political scientist John Hibbing.[9] Even top congressional leaders are not immune to the effects of scandal, as illustrated by the experience of former House majority leader Tom DeLay. Accused of questionable fund-raising and deal making, DeLay in 2005 stepped down from his leadership post. Nonetheless, he planned to seek reelection and won his district's contested 2006 Republican primary. However, as charges of influence peddling continued to swirl around him and as his support in the district plummeted, DeLay resigned his House seat, choosing to not even serve out the remainder of his term. Another House Republican, Florida's Mark Foley, also resigned in 2006. He was discovered to have sent sexually explicit email messages to underage congressional interns. The Foley scandal was particularly damaging to his party because it occurred within weeks of the November election, placing the GOP on the defensive at an inopportune time.

Turnout Variation: The Midterm Election Problem   Typically, the party holding the presidency loses seats in the midterm congressional elections, particularly in the House of Representatives. In only four of the last twenty-five midterm elections (including those in 1998 and 2004) has the president's party gained seats. The 2006 midterm election, when the Republicans lost seats, fit the typical pattern.

The tendency is attributable partly to the drop-off in turnout that accompanies a midterm election. The electorate in a presidential election is substantially larger than the midterm electorate. People who vote only in the presidential election tend to have weaker party affiliation and to be more responsive to the issues of the moment. These issues are likely to favor one party, which contributes to the success not only of its presidential candidate but also of its congressional candidates. In the midterm election, those who turn out tend to vote along party lines. Accordingly, the congressional candidates of the president's party do not get the boost they enjoyed in the previous election, and House seats are lost as a result.[10] The pattern also can be explained by the tendency of voters to view national politics through their opinion of the president's performance. Presidents usually lose popularity after taking office as a result of tough policy choices or the emergence of new problems. As the president's support declines, so does the voters' inclination to support congressional candidates from the president's party.[11]

Strong Challengers: A Particular Problem for Senators   Incumbents are also vulnerable to strong challengers. Senators are particularly likely to face formidable opponents: after the presidency, the Senate is the highest rung of the political ladder. Governors and House members are frequent challengers for Senate seats, and they have the electoral base, reputation, and experience to compete effectively. Moreover, the U.S. Senate lures wealthy challengers. Maria Cantwell spent $10 million of her own money to defeat Senator Slade Gorton in the state of Washington's Senate race in 2000. Cantwell made her fortune as an executive with RealNetworks, a high-tech company. Running again in 2006, Cantwell found herself in a tight race, partly because her opponent, Mike McGavick, was himself a millionaire executive.

House incumbents have less reason to fear strong challengers. A House seat often is not attractive enough to induce prominent local politicians, such as mayors or state legislators, to risk their political careers in a challenge to an incumbent.[12] This situation leaves the field open to weak opponents with little or no government or political experience. However, the dynamic changes somewhat when the electorate is angry and wants a change in leadership. Then the party not in power has an easier time convincing potentially strong challengers to run. In 1994, when the political mood favored the Republicans, the GOP fielded a relatively strong slate of challengers, which contributed to its success in unseating Democratic incumbents. In 2006, the parties' roles were reversed. The Democrats were able to field a relatively strong group of challengers and thereby gain congressional seats.

★ LEADERS

John McCain
(1936–   )

There have always been a few members of Congress who have stood out in the public's mind. Arizona Senator John McCain is one of those members today. McCain comes from a Navy family. His grandfather and his father both attained the rank of admiral, and McCain followed them into the Navy. Although his career got off to a rocky start—McCain placed near the bottom of his Naval Academy class and crashed his jet into the sea while in training—he served with distinction in Vietnam before his jet was shot down over North Vietnam. After more than five years of imprisonment, McCain was released along with other American POWs and resumed his naval career. He retired in 1980, but his retirement was short-lived. In 1982, he ran successfully for a seat in the U.S. House and four years later won the Senate seat being vacated by the retiring Barry Goldwater, the Republicans' 1964 presidential nominee.

McCain soon gained a reputation as a maverick, backing his party on national defense and abortion but breaking with it frequently over tax and spending policy. In 2000, he campaigned for the Republican presidential nomination. Although he won New Hampshire's opening primary, McCain lacked the financial and organizational support to defeat George W. Bush. In 2004, he was offered the second spot on the Democratic ticket by John Kerry, a close Senate colleague, but chose instead to work for Bush's reelection. McCain makes no secret of his desire to become president and is positioned for a run in 2008. McCain's reputation as a straight-talker has gained him a devoted following. In 2005, to the chagrin of many Republicans, he pressured the Bush administration to accept legislation that would ban the use of torture by U.S. personnel. Exposés of the torture of prisoners held in U.S. custody had outraged McCain, and he rejected the White House's claim that it was not bound by the Geneva Conventions in its handling of terrorist suspects. Drawing on his experiences as a POW, during which he himself was tortured, McCain said that America must uphold a higher standard than that of its enemies.

Safe Incumbency and Representation

Although incumbents can and do lose their reelection bids, they normally win easily. An effect is to reduce Congress's responsiveness to political change. Research indicates that incumbents tend to hold relatively stable policy positions during their time in office.[13] Thus, because few congressional seats normally change hands during an election, Congress normally does not change its direction all that much from election to election. Even when people are dissatisfied with national conditions, congressional elections sometimes produce only a small turnover in congressional membership.

Safe incumbency weakens the public's influence on Congress. Democracy depends on periodic shifts in power between the parties to bring public policy into closer alignment with public opinion. In European democracies, incumbents tend to win or lose depending on their political party's popularity, which can change markedly from one election to the next; shifts in popularity can produce huge shifts in the number of legislative seats controlled by the various parties. In the United States, incumbents often are able to overcome an adverse political climate through constituency service and other advantages of their office. In 1980, for example, the U.S. economy was mired in double-digit inflation and unemployment. A similar situation in a European democracy would result in huge losses for the party in power. In the 1980 U.S. election, however, the Democratic party held onto its majority in the House of Representatives, largely because most Democratic incumbents had enough cushion to win despite the public mood.

It is worth noting that national legislators in other democracies do not have the large personal staffs or the travel and publicity budgets that members of Congress have. Nor do national legislators elsewhere enjoy the inside track to campaign funding that members of Congress enjoy.

Who Are the Winners in Congressional Elections?

The Constitution places only a few restrictions on who can be elected to Congress. House members must be at least twenty-five years of age and have been a citizen for at least seven years. For senators, the age and citizenship requirements are thirty years and nine years, respectively. Senators and representatives alike must be residents of the state from which they are elected.

But if the formal restrictions are minimal, the informal limits are substantial. Members of Congress are in no way a microcosm of the people they are elected to serve. For example, although lawyers constitute less than 1 percent of the population, they make up a third of Congress.

Attorneys enter politics in large numbers in part because of the central place of law in government and also because seeking elective office is a good way—even if a candidate loses—to build up a law practice. Along with lawyers, professionals such as business executives, educators, bankers, and journalists account for more than 90 percent of congressional membership.[14] Blue-collar workers, clerical employees, and homemakers are seldom elected to Congress. Farmers and ranchers are not as rare; a fair number of House members from rural districts have agricultural backgrounds. Finally, members of Congress are disproportionately white and male. Minority-group members and women each account for less than 15 percent of the Congress (see Chapter 5). This proportion, however, is twice that of a decade ago.

Safe incumbency is a major obstacle to the election to Congress of more women and minorities.[15] In open-seat races in which they have run, they have won about half the time. However, they have been no more successful than other challengers in dislodging congressional incumbents. In elections to state and local office, where incumbency is less important, women and minority candidates have made greater inroads (see "States in the Nation").

CONGRESSIONAL LEADERSHIP

The way Congress functions is related to the way its members win election. Because each of them has an independent power base in their state or district, they have substantial independence within the institution they serve. The Speaker of the House and other top leaders in Congress are crucial to its operation, but unlike their counterparts in European legislatures, they cannot force their members to follow their lead. There is an inherent tension in Congress between the institution's need for strong leadership at the top and the individual members' need to exercise power on behalf of their constituents and to protect their reelection prospects. The result is an institution in which the power of the top leaders rests on the willingness of other members to back them.

Party Leadership in Congress

The House and Senate are organized along party lines. When members of Congress are sworn in at the start of a new two-year session, they automatically are members of either the Republican or the Democratic **party caucus** in their chamber. Through the caucuses, the Democrats and Republicans in each chamber meet periodically to plan strategy and discuss their differences in the process of settling on the party's

★ ‖ STATES IN THE NATION

Women in the State Legislatures

More than one in five state legislators are women, a four-fold increase since 1970. The state of Maryland, with more than 35 percent, has the highest proportion of women legislators. South Carolina, with fewer than 10 percent, has the lowest.

Q: Why do the northeastern and western regions have the most women legislators?

A: The northeastern and western regions have a higher proportion of college-educated women in the work force than do other regions. College-educated women are more likely to run for public office and to actively support those who do run.

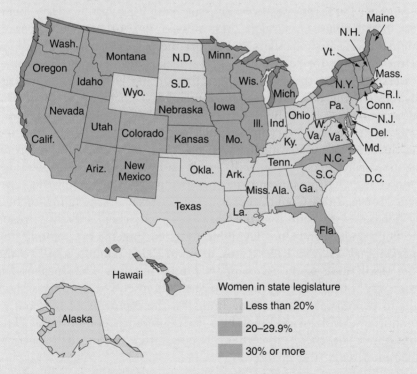

Women in state legislature

Less than 20%

20–29.9%

30% or more

Source: Created from data gathered by the Center for the American Woman and Politics (CAWP). National Information Bank on Women in Public Office. Eagleton Institute of Politics, Rutgers University, 2006.

legislative program. The caucuses also select the **party leaders** who represent the party's interests in the chamber and give direction to the party's goals.

The House Leadership   The main party leaders in the House are the Speaker, majority leader, majority whip, minority leader, and minority whip. The Constitution provides only for the post of Speaker. The Constitution further provides that the Speaker is to be elected by the members of the House. In practice, this means that the Speaker will be a member of the majority party, because it has enough votes to elect one of its own to the post. Thus, when the Democrats took control of the House after the 2006 election, Nancy Pelosi, the Democrats' leader in the chamber, replaced Republican Dennis Hastert as Speaker. (Table 11–1 shows the party composition in Congress during the past two decades.)

The Speaker is sometimes said to be the second most powerful official in Washington, after the president. The Speaker is active in developing the party's positions on issues and in persuading party members in the House to support these positions.[16] Although the Speaker cannot force party members to support the party's program, they look to the Speaker for leadership. The Speaker also has certain formal powers, including the right to speak first during House debate on legislation and the power to recognize members—that is, give them permission to speak from the floor. Because the House places a time limit on floor debate, not everyone has a chance to speak on a given bill, and the Speaker can sometimes influence legislation simply by exercising the power to decide who will speak and when. The Speaker also chooses the chairperson and the majority-party members of the powerful House Rules Committee, which controls the scheduling of bills for debate. Legislation that the Speaker wants passed is likely to reach the floor under conditions favorable to its enactment; for example, the Speaker may ask the Rules Committee to delay sending a bill to the floor until there is enough support for its passage. The Speaker has other ways of influencing the work of the House. The Speaker assigns bills to committees, places time limits on the reporting of bills out of committees, and assigns members to conference committees. (The importance of these powers over committee action will become apparent later in this chapter.)

The Speaker is assisted by the House majority leader and the House majority whip, who also are chosen by the majority party's members. The majority leader acts as the party's floor leader, organizing the debate on bills and working to line up legislative support. The whip has the job of

TABLE 11–1	Number of Democrats and Republicans in the House of Representatives and Senate, 1987–2008										
	87–88	89–90	91–92	93–94	95–96	97–98	99–00	01–02	03–04	05–06	07–08
House											
Democrats	258*	262*	268*	259	205*	207*	212*	213	208	203	233*
Republicans	177	173	167	176	230	228	223	222	227	232	202
Senate											
Democrats	54*	55*	56*	56	46*	45*	45*	51*	49	45	51*
Republicans	46	45	44	44	54	55	55	49	51	55	49

*Chamber not controlled by the president's party. Independents are included in the total for the party with which they caucused.

informing party members when critical votes are scheduled. As voting is getting under way on the House floor, the whip sometimes will stand at a location that is easily seen by party members and let them know where the leadership stands on the bill by giving them a thumbs-up or thumbs-down signal.

The minority party has its own leaders in the House. The House minority leader heads the party's caucus and its policy committee and plays the leading role in developing the party's legislative positions. The minority leader is assisted by a minority whip.

The Senate Leadership   In the Senate, the most important party leadership position is that of the majority leader, who heads the majority-party caucus. The majority leader's role is much like that of the Speaker of the House in that the Senate majority leader formulates the majority party's legislative agenda and encourages party members to support it. Like the Speaker, the Senate majority leader chairs the party's policy committee and acts as the party's voice in the chamber. The majority leader is assisted by the majority whip, who sees to it that members know when important votes are scheduled and ensures that the party's strongest advocates on a legislative measure are present for the debate. The Senate also has a minority leader and a minority whip, whose roles are comparable to those performed by their counterparts in the House.

Unlike the Speaker of the House, the Senate majority leader is not the chamber's presiding officer. The Constitution assigns this responsibility to the vice president of the United States. However, because the vice president is allowed to vote in the Senate only to break a tie, the vice president normally is not in the Senate chamber unless support for a bill is so closely divided that a tie vote appears possible. The Senate has a president pro tempore, who, in the absence of the vice president, has the right to preside over the Senate. President pro tempore is largely an honorary position that by tradition is usually held by the majority party's senior member. The presiding official has limited power, because each senator has the right to speak at any length on bills under consideration.

The Senate's tradition of unlimited debate stems mainly from its small size (only 100 members, compared with the House's 435 members). Senators like to view themselves as the equals of all others in their chamber and thus are reluctant to take orders from their leadership. For these reasons, the Senate majority leader's position is weaker than that of the House Speaker.

HOW THE UNITED STATES COMPARES

Legislative Leadership and Authority

The U.S. House and Senate are separate and coequal chambers, each with its own leadership and rules. This type of legislative structure is not found in most democracies. Many democracies, for example, have a single legislative chamber, which is apportioned by population. If the United States had an equivalent legislature, it would consist only of the House of Representatives.

Even most of the democracies that have a bicameral (two-chamber) legislature organize it differently from how the U.S. Congress is organized. The U.S. Senate is apportioned strictly by geography: there are two senators from each state. Germany is among the democracies that have a chamber organized along geographical lines, but Germany's upper house (the Bundesrat) differs from the U.S. Senate. Each of the German states (known as Länder) has at least three representatives in the Bundesrat, but the more populous states have more than three representatives.

Moreover, in most bicameral legislatures, one legislative chamber has substantially less power than the other. In the British Parliament, for example, the House of Lords is far weaker than the House of Commons; the House of Lords can delay legislation in some instances but cannot kill it. In the German Parliament, the Bundesrat has a voice on constitutional policy issues but not on most national policy issues, and its vote can in some cases be overridden by the population-based chamber (the Bundestag). In the United States, the Senate and House are equal in their legislative powers; without their joint agreement, a law cannot be enacted.

The U.S. Congress is fragmented in other ways as well: it has elected leaders with limited formal powers, a network of relatively independent and powerful committees, and members who are free to follow or ignore other members of their party. It is not uncommon for a fourth or more of a party's legislators to vote against their party's position on important legislative issues. In contrast, European legislatures have a centralized power structure: top leaders have substantial authority, the committees are weak, and the parties are unified. European legislators are expected to support their party unless granted permission to vote otherwise on a particular bill. Legislative leadership is much easier to exercise in

(continued)

Europe's hierarchical parliaments than in America's "stratarchical" Congress.

Country	Form of Legislature
Canada	One house dominant
France	One house dominant
Germany	One house dominant (except on certain issues)
Great Britain	One house dominant
Israel	One house only
Japan	One house dominant
Mexico	Two equal houses
Sweden	One house only
United States	Two equal houses

The Power of Party Leaders   The power of Senate and House party leaders rests substantially on the trust placed in them by the members of their party. They do not have the strong formal powers of parliamentary leaders (see "How the United States Compares"), but they are expected to lead. If they are skilled at promoting ideas and building coalitions, they can exercise considerable power. By the same token, their power can evaporate if they make a mistake that hurts their party. In 2002, Republican Senate leader Trent Lott of Mississippi resigned his post after he placed his party at the center of an unwanted controversy by publicly praising the South's segregated past.

Party leaders are in a more powerful position today than they were a few decades ago as a result of shifts in the composition of the congressional parties. The GOP once had a substantial progressive faction within it, but this faction has been eclipsed by its conservative wing. At the same time, the Democratic party's conservative wing, represented by its southern lawmakers, has withered. As congressional Republicans have become more like each other and less like congressional Democrats, each group has found it easier to band together and stand against the opposing party. Accordingly, the party leaders through the party caucus have found it easier to bring their party's members together on legislative issues.

The party leadership has also been strengthened by the high cost of election campaigns. Party leaders acquire loyalty from their members by making fund-raising appearances on behalf of vulnerable candidates and by organizing large-scale fund-raising efforts that benefit all party members. Party leaders also are positioned to steer pork-barrel money to party loyalists.

Party leaders' of influence is limited, however. Most party members are secure in their reelection prospects and thus have some leeway in accepting

★ | LEADERS

Nancy Pelosi
(1940–)

Democrat Nancy Pelosi, House Democratic leader since 2002, is the first woman in U.S. history to lead a major political party in Congress. Pelosi comes from a politically active family. Her father was in the House of Representatives and later served five terms as Baltimore's mayor. A brother subsequently served as that city's mayor as well. A graduate of Trinity College in Washington, D.C., she moved west with her husband, a native of San Francisco. She was first elected to Congress in 1987 from a liberal northern California district in a special election to fill the vacancy created by the death of the incumbent. Once in Congress, she quickly made a reputation for herself as a serious, tenacious legislator. As a member of the House Appropriations Committee, she became a leading advocate of improving the nation's health-care policies. She was serving on the House Permanent Select Committee on Intelligence when the terrorist attacks of September 11, 2001, occurred. In this position, she was a key congressional player in efforts to strengthen the country's intelligence agencies. She was elected House minority leader when Missouri's Dick Gephardt, who had held the post for eight years, voluntarily stepped down. Representative Pelosi became Speaker when the Democrats took control of the House after the 2006 election.

party leadership. Also, members of Congress have their own policy goals, which do not always accord with those of the party leadership. Moreover, some members have close ties to the special interests that back their campaigns and feel an obligation to help them out, an outlook not shared in every instance by the party leadership. Some members of Congress, particularly those in the Senate, have personal ambitions—such as a desire to become president or to attain national recognition—that can put them at odds with party leaders or cause them to compete with the leadership for media attention.

Nevertheless, skilled party leaders can wield considerable power. Members of a party have their separate interests but they also have reason to hang together. By acting as a bloc, they increase their chances of getting legislation they want and of stopping the opposing party from achieving its goals. If party leaders succeed in devising positions that enable their party members to work as one, the party's chances of success increase markedly. Party leaders need to be mindful that they are "agents" of their members. Their job is not to pursue their personal legislative agenda but to identify positions that will unite their members. And by taking on this task, they will free the members from having to do it, enabling them to devote more time to pursuits that will further their individual goals.[17]

Recent party leaders have been fairly adept at managing their party's caucus, primarily because party members are increasingly like-minded. Congress today has fewer liberal Republicans and fewer conservative Democrats. Moreover, those who are somewhat outside the party mainstream usually have more in common with the other members of their party than with members of the opposing party. Finally, those who are further removed from the party mainstream must conform to it to a large degree if they want to enjoy the perks of office, as Senator Arlen Specter (R-Penn.) discovered after the 2004 election. Specter was in line to become chair of the powerful Senate Judiciary Committee when he publicly cautioned against appointing judges that would overturn *Roe v. Wade*, a goal of many Republicans. As a condition of granting him the position of chair, the GOP's Senate caucus forced Specter to agree that he would not use the position to block antiabortion judicial nominees. A more systematic indicator of heightened party leadership and discipline in Congress is the pattern of *roll-call votes* (votes on which each member's vote is officially recorded, as opposed to voice votes, where the members simply say "aye" or "nay" in unison and the presiding officer indicates which side prevails without tallying individual members' positions). Over the past three decades, party-line voting on

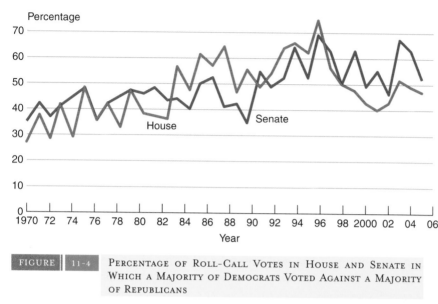

PERCENTAGE OF ROLL-CALL VOTES IN HOUSE AND SENATE IN WHICH A MAJORITY OF DEMOCRATS VOTED AGAINST A MAJORITY OF REPUBLICANS

Democrats and Republicans in Congress are often on opposite sides of issues; party-line voting has been relatively high since the 1980s. *Source: Congressional Quarterly Weekly, various dates.*

roll calls has increased considerably (see Figure 11–4). In the 1970s, roll-call votes generally did not pit most Republicans against most Democrats. More recently, most roll-call votes have divided along party lines.

Committee Chairs: The Seniority Principle

Party leaders are not the only important leaders in Congress. Most of the work of Congress takes place in the meetings of its thirty-five standing (permanent) committees and their numerous subcommittees, each of which is headed by a chairperson. A committee chair schedules committee meetings, determines the order in which committee bills are considered, presides over committee discussions, directs the committee's majority staff, and can choose to lead the debate when a committee bill reaches the floor of the chamber for a vote by the full membership.

Committee chairs are always members of the majority party, and they usually have the most **seniority** (the most consecutive years of service on a particular committee). Seniority is based strictly on time served on a committee, not on time spent in Congress. If a member switches committees, the years spent on the first committee do not count toward seniority on the second one.

The seniority system has advantages: it reduces the number of power struggles that would occur if the chairs were decided each time by open competition, it provides experienced and knowledgeable committee leadership, and it enables members to look forward to the reward of a position as chair after years of service on the same committee.

However, a strict seniority system can place committee chairs beyond any control by the House and Senate's elected leaders. To counter this problem, Senate and House Republicans, but not Democrats, place term limits on committee chairs. After a set number of years, a chair must relinquish the post, which then usually goes to the next most senior GOP committee member.

Congressional organization and leadership extend into subcommittees, smaller units within each committee formed to conduct specific aspects of the committee's business. Altogether there are about two hundred subcommittees in the House and Senate, each with a chairperson who decides its order of business, presides over its meetings, and coordinates its staff. In both chambers, a subcommittee chair is often the most senior member on the panel, but seniority is not as important in these appointments as it is in the designation of committee chairs.

Oligarchy or Democracy: Which Principle Should Govern?

In 1995, House Republicans gave committee chairs the power to select the chairs of their subcommittees and granted them authority to appoint all majority-party staff members, including those who work for the subcommittees. Each committee chair was to use this power to promote within their committees the Republican party's overall policy goals. The changes reversed House reforms of the 1970s that gave subcommittees and their chairs greater autonomy in order to spread power more widely among House members.

The opposing ideas embodied in the 1970s and 1995 reforms have played themselves out many times in the history of Congress. The institution is at once a place for conducting the nation's business and a venue for promoting constituency interests. At times, the power of top party leaders has been strengthened. At other times, the power of rank-and-file members has been enlarged. At all times, there has been an attempt to achieve a workable balance of the two. The result is an institution very different from European parliaments, where power is always concentrated at the top (an arrangement reflected even in the name for rank-and-file members: "backbenchers"). The distinguishing feature of congressional power is its division among the membership, with provision for added power—sometimes more and sometimes less—at the top.

The Committee System

As indicated earlier, most of the work in Congress is conducted through **standing committees,** permanent committees with responsibility for a particular area of public policy. At present there are twenty standing committees in the House and sixteen in the Senate (see Table 11–2). Both the House and the Senate, for example, have a standing committee that handles foreign policy issues. Other important standing committees are those that deal with agriculture, commerce, the interior (natural resources and public lands), defense, government spending, labor, the judiciary, and taxation. House committees, which average about thirty-five to forty members each, are about twice the size of Senate committees. Each standing committee has legislative authority in that it can draft and

TABLE 11-2 The Standing Committees of Congress

House of Representatives	Senate
Agriculture	Agriculture, Nutrition, and Forestry
Appropriations	
Armed Services	Appropriations
Budget	Armed Services
Education and the Workforce	Banking, Housing, and Urban Affairs
Energy and Commerce	
Financial Services	Budget
Government Reform	Commerce, Science, and Transportation
Homeland Security	
House Administration	Energy and Natural Resources
International Relations	Environment and Public Works
Judiciary	Finance
Resources	Foreign Relations
Rules	Health, Education, Labor, and Pensions
Science	
Small Business	Homeland Security and Governmental Affairs
Standards of Official Conduct	Judiciary
Transportation and Infrastructure	Rules and Administration
Veterans' Affairs	Small Business and Entrepreneurship
Ways and Means	Veterans' Affairs

rewrite proposed legislation and can recommend to the full chamber the passage or defeat of the legislation it considers.

Each standing committee in Congress has its own staff. Unlike the members' personal staffs, which concentrate on constituency relations, the committee staffs perform an almost entirely legislative function. They help draft legislation, organize hearings, and participate in altering bills within the committee.

In addition to its standing committees, Congress also has a number of *select committees*, which are created to perform specific tasks. An example is the Senate Select Committee on Intelligence, which oversees the work of intelligence agencies, such as the CIA. Congress also has *joint committees*, composed of members of both houses, that perform advisory functions. The Joint Committee on the Library, for example, oversees the Library of Congress, which is the largest library in the world. Finally, Congress has **conference committees**, which are joint committees formed temporarily to work out differences in House and Senate versions of a particular bill. The role of conference committees is discussed more fully later in the chapter.

Congress could not possibly handle its workload without the help of its committee system. About ten thousand bills are introduced during each two-year session of Congress. The sheer volume of legislation would paralyze the institution if it did not have a division of labor. Yet the very existence of committees and subcommittees helps fragment Congress: each of these units is relatively secure in its power, jurisdiction, and membership.

Committee Membership

Each committee includes Republicans and Democrats, but the majority party holds the majority of seats. The ratio of Democrats to Republicans on each committee is roughly the same as the ratio in the full House or Senate, but there is no fixed rule on this matter, and the majority party decides what the ratio will be (mindful that at the next election it could become the chamber's minority party). Members of the House typically serve on only two committees. Senators often serve on four, although they can sit on only two major committees, such as Foreign Relations and Finance.

Each standing committee has a fixed number of members, and a committee must have a vacancy before a new member can be appointed. Most vacancies occur after an election as a result of the retirement or defeat of committee members. Each party has a special committee in each chamber that decides who will fill committee vacancies. Several factors influence these decisions, including the preferences of the legislators themselves. Most newly elected members of Congress ask for and receive assignment to a committee on which they can serve their constituents' interests and at the same time enhance their reelection prospects. For example, when Barack Obama was elected to the Senate in 2004 from Illinois, a state that depends heavily on transportation and other public works, he asked for and received an appointment on the Senate Environment and Public Works Committee that oversees these policy areas.

Members of Congress also prefer membership on one of the more prominent committees, such as Foreign Relations or Finance in the Senate and Appropriations or Ways and Means in the House. A seat on these committees is coveted because they deal with vital issues, such as taxation and international affairs. Factors such as members' work habits, party loyalty, and length of congressional service weigh heavily in the determination of appointments to these prestigious committees.[18]

Subcommittee assignments are handled differently. The members of each party on a committee decide who among them will serve on each of its subcommittees. The members' preferences and seniority, as well as the interests of their constituencies, are key influences on subcommittee assignments.

Committee Jurisdiction

The 1946 Legislative Reorganization Act requires that each bill introduced in Congress be referred to the proper committee. An agricultural bill introduced in the Senate must be assigned to the Senate Agriculture Committee, a bill dealing with foreign affairs must be sent to the Senate Foreign Relations Committee, and so on. This requirement is a major source of each committee's power. Even if its members are known to oppose certain types of legislation, bills clearly within its **jurisdiction**— the policy area in which it is authorized to act—must be sent to it for deliberation.

However, policy problems are increasingly complex, and jurisdiction accordingly has become an increasingly contentious issue, particularly with regard to major bills. Which House committee, for example, should handle a major bill addressing the role of financial institutions in global trade? The Financial Services Committee? The Commerce Committee? The International Relations Committee? All committees seek legislative influence and each is jealous of its jurisdiction, so bills that overlap committee boundaries provoke "turf wars."[19] Party leaders can take advantage of these situations by shuttling a bill to the committee that is most likely to handle it in the way they would like. But because party leaders depend on the committee chairs for support, they cannot regularly ignore a committee that has a strong claim to a bill. At times, party leaders have responded by dividing up a bill, handing over some of its provisions to one committee and other provisions to a second committee.

House and Senate subcommittees also have defined jurisdictions. The House International Relations Committee, for instance, has seven subcommittees: Europe and Emerging Threats; Middle East and Central Asia; Asia and the Pacific; Western Hemisphere; Africa, Global Human Rights, and International Operations; International Terrorism and Nonproliferation; and Oversight and Investigations. Each subcommittee has about a dozen members, and these few individuals do most of the work and have the major voice in the disposition of most bills in their policy area.

HOW A BILL BECOMES LAW

Parties, party leaders, and committees are critical actors in the legislative process. Their roles and influence, however, vary with the nature of the legislation under consideration.

Committee Hearings and Decisions

The formal process by which bills become law is shown in Figure 11–5. A **bill** is a proposed legislative act. Many bills are prepared by executive agencies, interest groups, or other outside parties, but members of Congress also draft bills, and only they can formally submit a bill for consideration by their chamber. Once a bill is introduced by a member of the House or Senate, it is given a number and a title and is then sent to the appropriate committee, which assigns it to one of its subcommittees. Less than 10 percent of the bills that committees consider reach the floor for a vote; the others are "killed" when committees decide that they do not warrant further consideration and table them. The full House or Senate can overrule committee decisions, but this rarely occurs.

The fact that committees kill more than 90 percent of the bills submitted in Congress does not mean that committees exercise 90 percent of the power in Congress. A committee rarely decides fully the fate of legislation that is important to the majority party or its leadership. Most bills die in committee because they are of little interest to anyone other than a few members of Congress or are so poorly conceived

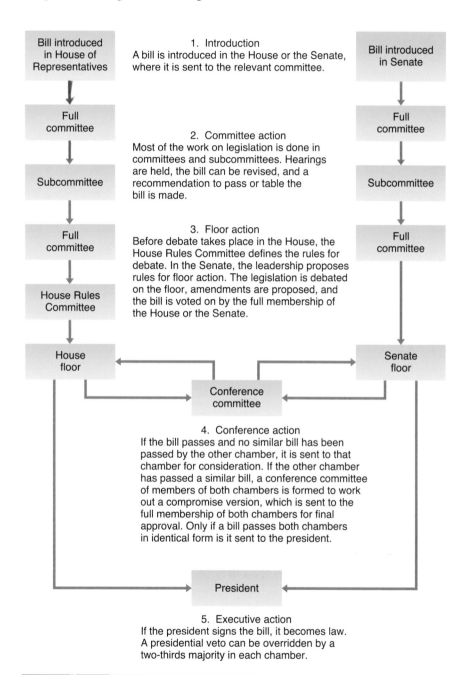

Bill introduced in House of Representatives

Full committee

Subcommittee

Full committee

House Rules Committee

House floor

Bill introduced in Senate

Full committee

Subcommittee

Full committee

Senate floor

Conference committee

President

1. Introduction
A bill is introduced in the House or the Senate, where it is sent to the relevant committee.

2. Committee action
Most of the work on legislation is done in committees and subcommittees. Hearings are held, the bill can be revised, and a recommendation to pass or table the bill is made.

3. Floor action
Before debate takes place in the House, the House Rules Committee defines the rules for debate. In the Senate, the leadership proposes rules for floor action. The legislation is debated on the floor, amendments are proposed, and the bill is voted on by the full membership of the House or the Senate.

4. Conference action
If the bill passes and no similar bill has been passed by the other chamber, it is sent to that chamber for consideration. If the other chamber has passed a similar bill, a conference committee of members of both chambers is formed to work out a compromise version, which is sent to the full membership of both chambers for final approval. Only if a bill passes both chambers in identical form is it sent to the president.

5. Executive action
If the president signs the bill, it becomes law. A presidential veto can be overridden by a two-thirds majority in each chamber.

FIGURE 11-5 HOW A BILL BECOMES LAW

Although the legislative process can be short-circuited in many ways, this diagram describes the steps that may be required for a bill to become law.

that they lack merit. Some bills are not even supported by the members who introduce them. A member may submit a bill to appease a powerful constituent group and then quietly inform the committee to ignore it.

If a bill seems to have merit, the subcommittee will schedule hearings on it. The subcommittee invites testimony on the proposed legislation from lobbyists, administrators, and experts. After the hearings, if the subcommittee still feels that the legislation is warranted, members recommend the bill to the full committee, which can hold additional hearings. In the House, both the full committee and a subcommittee can "mark up," or revise, a bill. In the Senate, markup usually is reserved for the full committee.

From Committee to the Floor

If a majority of the committee vote to recommend passage of the bill, it is referred to the full chamber for action. In the House, the Rules Committee has the power to determine when the bill will be voted on, how long the debate on the bill will last, and whether the bill will receive a "closed rule" (no amendments will be permitted), an "open rule" (members can propose amendments relevant to any of the bill's sections), or something in between (for example, only certain sections of the bill will be subject to amendment). The Rules Committee has this scheduling power because the House is too large to operate effectively without strict rules for the handling of legislation by the full chamber. The rules are also a means by which the majority party controls legislation. House Democrats employed closed rules to prevent Republicans from proposing amendments to major bills, a tactic House Republicans said they would forgo when they took control in 1995. Once in control, however, the Republicans applied closed rules to a number of major bills. The tactic was too effective to ignore.

On most House bills, only a small number of legislators are granted the opportunity to speak on the floor. In most cases, the decision as to who will speak is delegated to the bill's chief sponsor and one of the bill's leading opponents. Typically, both of these House members are members of the committee that handled the bill.

The Senate also has a rules committee, but it has much less power than in the House. In the Senate, the majority leader, usually in consultation with the minority leaders, schedules bills. All Senate bills are subject to unlimited debate unless a three-fifths majority of the full Senate votes for **cloture,** which limits debate to thirty hours. Cloture is a way of defeating a Senate **filibuster,** which is a procedural tactic whereby a

Former House majority leader Tom DeLay (R-Texas) speaking to reporters. DeLay was known as the "hammer" for his ability to round up the votes necessary to drive home Republican-sponsored legislation. In 2006, months after quitting his House leadership post following accusations of wrongdoing, DeLay resigned his House seat.

minority of senators prevent a bill from coming to a vote by holding the floor and talking until other senators give in and the bill is withdrawn from consideration. In late 2005, Senate Democrats used the filibuster to block a vote on renewal of the USA Patriot Act, saying that they would allow it to come to a vote only if Republicans agreed to add protections for privacy rights. Three months later, Senate Democrats got the changes they wanted, and the bill passed by an overwhelming majority.

The Senate also differs from the House in that its members can propose any amendment to any bill. Unlike House amendments, those in the Senate do not have to be germane to a bill's content. For example, a senator may propose an antiabortion amendment to a bill dealing with defense expenditures. Such an amendment is called a **rider,** and riders are frequently introduced.

Leadership and Floor Action

Committee action is usually decisive on bills that address small issues. If a majority of committee members favor such a bill, it normally is passed

GET INVOLVED!
Become an Insider

Each year, thousands of college students serve as interns in Congress or state legislatures. Many internships are unpaid, but students can receive college credit for the experience.

Internships provide an opportunity to see the political process first-hand. For most citizens, politics is a secondhand world seen largely through the window on that world provided by the news media. An internship offers an opportunity to see how institutions work on a daily basis from the inside. Internships are not always a great adventure. Many legislative interns envision themselves contributing ideas and research that might influence public policy only to find that they are answering letters, developing mailing lists, or duplicating materials. Nevertheless, few interns conclude that their experience has been a waste of time. Most find it rewarding and, ultimately, memorable.

Many executive agencies at the federal and state levels also accept interns, and some have well-organized internship programs. The Department of State has one of the best internship programs, but it is in heavy demand and has an early application deadline. The internships offered by executive agencies typically are more challenging than those provided by legislative offices. Legislators dedicate a lot of their staff time to constituency service, whereas agencies concentrate on the administration of policies and programs. On the other hand, legislative offices are usually more spirited, and interns in these offices are more likely to strike up friendships with other interns in the same office or in nearby offices.

Information about internships can be obtained from the American Political Science Association (www.apsa.org). In addition, there are organizations in Washington that arrange internships in Congress and the executive agencies. These organizations frequently charge a fee for their services, so you might want to contact a legislative office or executive agency directly. It is important to make your request as early as possible in the college year, because some internship programs have deadlines and nearly all offices receive more requests than they can accommodate. You could also check with the student services office at your college or university. Some of these offices have information on internship programs and can be of assistance.

by the full chamber, often without amendment. In a sense, the full chamber merely votes to confirm or modify decisions made previously by committees and subcommittees. Of course, these units do not operate in a vacuum. In making its decisions, a committee takes into account the fact that its action can be reversed by the full chamber, just as a subcommittee recognizes that the full committee can overrule its decision.[20] Partisanship also serves as a check on committee action. When a committee's vote is sharply divided along party lines, other members may conclude that they need to look more closely at the bill before deciding whether to vote for it.

On major bills, the party leaders are the key players. They will have worked closely with the committee during its deliberations and may assume leadership of the bill when it clears the committee. (In the case of "minor" bills, leadership during floor debate normally is provided by committee members.)

The majority party's leaders (particularly in the House) have increasingly set the legislative agenda and defined the debate on major bills.[21] They shape the bills' broad outlines and set the boundaries of the floor debate. In these efforts, they depend on the support of their party's members. To obtain it, they consult their members informally and through the party caucus. **Party discipline**—the willingness of a party's House or Senate members to act as a unified group—is increasingly important in congressional action and is the key to party leaders' ability to shape major legislation. (The role of parties in Congress is discussed further in the section on Congress's representation function.)

Conference Committees and the President

For a bill to pass, it must have the support of a simple majority (50 percent plus one) of the House or Senate members voting on it. To become law, however, a bill must be passed in identical form by both the House and the Senate. About 10 percent of all bills that pass both chambers—the proportion is larger for major bills—differ in important respects in their House and Senate versions. These bills are referred to conference committees to resolve the differences. Each conference committee is formed temporarily for the sole purpose of handling a particular bill; its members are usually appointed from the House and Senate standing committees that drafted the bill. The conference committee's job is to develop a compromise version, which then goes back to the House and Senate floors for a vote. There it can be passed, defeated, or returned to conference, but not amended.

A bill that is passed in identical form by the House and the Senate is not yet a law. The president also plays a role. If the president signs the bill, it becomes **law.** If the president exercises the **veto,** the bill is sent back to Congress with the president's reasons for rejecting it. Congress can override a veto by a two-thirds vote of each chamber; the bill then becomes law.

If the president fails to sign a bill within ten days (Sundays excepted) and Congress is still in session, the bill automatically becomes law anyway. If the president fails to sign within ten days and Congress has concluded its term, the bill does not become law. This last situation, called a pocket veto, forces Congress in its next term to start over from the beginning: the bill again must pass both chambers and again is subject to presidential veto.

CONGRESS'S POLICYMAKING ROLE

The Framers of the Constitution expected that Congress, as the embodiment of representative government, would be the institution to which the people would look for policy leadership. During most of the nineteenth century, Congress enjoyed that stature. Aside from a few strong leaders such as Jackson and Lincoln, presidents did not play a major legislative role (see Chapter 12). However, as national and international forces combined to place greater leadership and policy demands on the federal government, the president became a vital part of the national legislative process. Today Congress and the president substantially share the legislative effort, although their roles differ greatly.[22]

Congress's policymaking role revolves around its three major functions: lawmaking, representation, and oversight (see Table 11–3). In practice, the three functions overlap, but they are conceptually distinct.

The Lawmaking Function of Congress

Under the Constitution, Congress is granted the **lawmaking function:** the authority to make the laws necessary to carry out the powers granted to the national government. The constitutional powers of Congress are substantial; they include the power to tax, to spend, to regulate commerce, and to declare war. However, whether Congress takes the lead in the making of laws depends heavily on the type of policy at issue.

Broad Issues: Fragmentation as a Limit on Congress's Role   Congress is structured in a way that can make agreement on large issues difficult to obtain. Congress is not one house but two, each with its own authority

TABLE 11-3	THE MAJOR FUNCTIONS OF CONGRESS
Function	**Basis and Activity**
Lawmaking	Through its constitutional grant to enact law, Congress makes the laws authorizing federal programs and appropriating the funds necessary to carry them out.
Representation	Through its elected constitutional officers—U.S. senators and representatives—Congress represents the interests of constituents and the nation in its deliberations and in its lawmaking.
Oversight	Through its constitutional responsibility to see that the executive branch carries out the laws faithfully and spends appropriations properly, Congress oversees and sometimes investigates executive action.

and constituency base. Neither the House nor the Senate can enact legislation without the other's approval, and the two chambers are hardly two versions of the same thing. California and North Dakota have exactly the same representation in the Senate, but in the House, which is apportioned by population, California has fifty-three seats compared to North Dakota's one.

Congress also includes a lot of people: 100 members of the Senate and 435 members of the House. They come from different constituencies and represent different and sometimes opposing interests, which leads to disagreements. Nearly every member of Congress, for example, supports the principle of global free trade. Yet when it comes to specific trade provisions members often disagree. Foreign competition means different things to manufacturers who produce automobiles, computer chips, or underwear; it means different things to farmers who produce corn, sugar, or grapes; and it means different things to firms that deal in international finance, home insurance, or student loans. And because it means different things to different people in different parts of the country, members of Congress who represent these areas have conflicting views on when free trade makes sense.

For such reasons, Congress often has difficulty taking the lead on broad issues of national policy. A legislative institution can easily lead on such issues only if it grants this authority to its top leader—but Congress does not have such a leader. The House has its separate leaders, as does the Senate. Moreover, although the rise in party discipline in Congress has strengthened the role of the chambers' leaders, House and Senate members of the same party still are free to go their separate ways if they so choose. As a result, Congress sometimes struggles when it is faced with the task of developing a comprehensive policy response to broad national issues. Few recent controversies illustrate this more clearly than does immigration reform. In 2006, House Republicans, in part because elections in their districts seldom hinge on the Hispanic vote, held firm to their opposition to a guest worker program. Senate Republicans were more concerned about alienating Hispanic voters, who in some parts of the country have enough votes to tip the balance in a statewide race. Enough Senate Republicans sided with their Democratic colleagues in support of a guest worker program to force a deadlock with the House.

As an institution, the presidency is better suited to the task of providing leadership on major national issues. First, whereas Congress's authority is divided, the presidency's authority is not. Executive power is vested constitutionally in the hands of a single individual—the president. Unlike congressional leaders, who must negotiate with their members when taking a stand on legislation, the president does not have to consult with other executive officials when taking a position. Second, whereas members of Congress tend to see issues mainly from the perspective of their state or district, the president tends to see them from a national perspective.

Presidential leadership means that Congress normally will pay attention to White House proposals, not that it will adopt them. Congress typically accepts a presidential initiative only as a starting point in its deliberations. It may reject the proposal outright—particularly when the president is from the opposing party—but any such proposal provides Congress with a tangible bill to focus on. If the proposal is at all close to what a congressional majority would regard as acceptable, Congress will use it as a baseline from which to make changes that will bring it in line with the thinking of a congressional majority. (The legislative roles of Congress and the president are discussed further in Chapter 12.)

In its lawmaking activities, Congress has the support of three congressional agencies. One is the Congressional Budget Office (CBO), which was created as part of the Budget Impoundment and Control Act of 1974. Its two hundred fifty employees provide Congress with general economic projections, overall estimates of government expenditures and revenues, and specific estimates of the costs of proposed programs. (The budgetary process is described more fully in later chapters.)

A second congressional agency is the Government Accountability Office (GAO). With three thousand employees, the GAO is the largest congressional agency. Formed in 1921, it has primary responsibility for overseeing executive agencies' spending of money that has been appropriated by Congress. The programs that the executive agencies administer are authorized and funded by Congress. The GAO's responsibility is to ensure that executive agencies operate in the manner prescribed by Congress.

The third and oldest congressional agency is the Congressional Research Service (CRS). It has a staff of one thousand employees and operates as a nonpartisan reference agency. It conducts research and responds to information requests from congressional committees and members.

Congress in the Lead: Fragmentation as a Policymaking Strength
Congress occasionally does take the lead on large issues. Except during Roosevelt's New Deal, Congress has been a chief source of major labor legislation. Environmental legislation, federal aid to education, and urban development are other areas in which Congress has played an initiating role.[23] The "First One-Hundred Hours Agenda" that Democrats pursued after they took control of the House of Representatives in 2007 is yet another example of congressional policy leadership. The legislative initiative included the passage of bills relating to lobbying reform, the minimum wage, deficit reduction, college loans, and stem-cell research. Nevertheless, Congress does not routinely develop

Members of Congress are keenly sensitive to local opinion on issues of personal interest to their constituents. Representatives from urban areas are more supportive of gun control than are those from rural areas, where sport hunting is widespread.

broad policy programs and carry them through to passage. "Congress remains organized," James Sundquist notes, "to deal with narrow problems but not with broad ones."[24]

As it happens, the great majority of the hundreds of bills that Congress considers each session deal with narrow issues. The leading role in the disposition of these bills falls not on the president but on Congress and, in most cases, on the relatively small number of its members that sit on the committee responsible for the bill. The same fragmentation that makes it difficult for Congress to take the lead on broad issues makes it easy for Congress to tackle scores of narrow issues simultaneously. Most of the legislation passed by Congress is "distributive"—that is, it distributes benefits to a particular group while spreading the costs across the taxpaying public. Veterans' benefits are one example.

Such legislation, because it directly benefits a constituent group, is a type of policy that members of Congress like to support. It is also a type of policy that Congress, through its committee system, is organizationally best suited to handle. Most committees parallel a major constituent interest, such as agriculture, commerce, labor, or veterans.

The Representation Function of Congress

In the process of making laws, the members of Congress represent various interests within American society, giving them a voice in the national legislature. The proper approach to the **representation function** has been debated since the nation's founding. A recurrent issue has been whether the main concern of a representative should be the interests of the nation as a whole or those of his or her own constituency. These interests overlap to some degree but rarely coincide exactly. Policies that are of benefit to the full society are not always equally advantageous to particular localities and can even cause harm to some constituencies.

Representation of States and Districts   The choice between national and local interests is not a simple one, even for a legislator who is inclined toward either orientation. To be fully effective, members of Congress must be reelected time and again, a necessity that compels them to pay attention to local demands. Yet, as part of the nation's legislative body, no member can easily put aside his or her judgment as to the nation's needs. In making the choice, most members of Congress, on narrow issues at least, tend toward a local orientation. Opposition to gun control legislation, for example, has always been much higher among members of Congress representing rural areas where hunting weapons are part of the fabric of everyday life.

Local representation also occurs through the committee system. Although studies indicate that the views of committee members are not radically different from the views of the full House or Senate member-ship,[25] senators and representatives typically sit on committees and sub-committees with policy jurisdictions that coincide with their constituents' interests. For example, farm-state legislators dominate the membership of the House and Senate Agriculture Committees, and westerners dominate the Interior Committees (which deal with federal lands and natural resources, most of which are concentrated in the West). Committees are also the site of most of the congressional **logrolling,** the practice of trad-ing one's vote with another member's so that both get what they want. It is not uncommon, for example, for Agriculture Committee members from livestock-producing states of the North to trade votes with committee members from the South, where crops such as cotton, tobacco, and peanuts are grown.

Nevertheless, representation of constituency interests has its limits. A representative's constituents have little interest in most issues that come before Congress. Whether the government should appropriate a few mil-lion dollars in foreign aid for Bolivia is not the sort of issue that local constituent groups are likely to know or care about. Moreover, members of Congress often have no choice but to go against the wishes of a sig-nificant portion of their constituency. The interests of workers and employers in a district or state, for example, can differ considerably.

Of course, constituent groups are not the only groups that get legisla-tors' support. The nation's capital is filled with powerful lobbies that con-tribute funds to congressional campaigns. These lobbying groups sometimes have as much influence with a member of Congress as do interest groups in the member's home district or state.

Representation of the Nation Through Parties   When a clear-cut and vital national interest is at stake, members of Congress can be expected to respond to that interest. The difficulty of using the common good as a routine basis for thinking about representation, however, is that Americans often disagree on what constitutes the common good and what govern-ment should do to further it.

Most Americans believe, for example, that the nation's education sys-tem requires strengthening. The test scores of American school children on standardized reading, math, and science examinations are significantly below those of children in many other industrial democracies. This situ-ation creates pressure for political action. But what action is necessary and desirable? Does more money have to be funneled into public schools, and, if so, which level of government—federal, state, or local—should provide it? Or does the problem rest with teachers? Should they be subject to higher certification and performance standards? Or is the problem a lack of competition for excellence? Should schools be required to compete for students and the tax dollars they represent? Should private schools be part of any such competition, or would their participation wreck the public school system? There is no general agreement on such issues. The quality of America's schools is of vital national interest, and quality schools would serve the common good. But the means to that end are the subject of endless dispute.

In Congress, debates over national goals occur primarily along party lines. Republicans and Democrats have different perspectives on national issues because their parties differ philosophically and politically. In the end-of-the-year budget negotiations in 1998 and 1999, for example, Republicans and Democrats were deadlocked on the issue of new funding to hire thousands of public school teachers. The initiative had come from President Clinton and was supported by congressional Democrats. But it was opposed by congressional Republicans, who objected to spending federal (as opposed to state and local) funds for that purpose and who also objected to the proposed placement of the new teachers (most of whom would be placed in overcrowded schools, most of which are in Democratic constituencies). Democrats and Republicans alike agreed that more teachers were needed, but they disagreed on how that goal should be reached. In the end, through concessions in other areas, Clinton and the congressional Democrats obtained federal funding for new teachers, but it was obtained through an intensely partisan process.

Partisanship also affects the president's relationship with Congress. Presidents serve as legislative leaders not so much for the whole Congress as for members of their own party. Opposition and support for presidential initiatives usually divide along party lines. Accordingly, the president's legislative success typically has depended on which party controls Congress (see Chapter 12).

In short, any accounting of representation in Congress that minimizes the influence of party is faulty. If constituency interests drive the thinking of many members of Congress, so do partisan values. In fact, constituent and partisan influences are often difficult to separate in practice. In the case of conflicting interests within their constituencies, members of Congress naturally side with those that align with their party. When local business and labor groups take opposing sides on issues before Congress, for example, Republican members tend to back business's position, while Democratic members tend to line up with labor.

The Oversight Function of Congress

Although Congress enacts the nation's laws and appropriates the money to implement them, the administration of these laws is entrusted to the executive branch. Congress has the responsibility to see that the executive branch carries out the laws faithfully and spends the money properly, a supervisory activity referred to as the **oversight function** of Congress.[26]

Oversight is carried out largely through the committee system of Congress and is facilitated by the parallel structure of the committees and the executive bureaucracy: the House International Relations Committee and Senate Foreign Relations Committee oversee the work of the State Department, the House and Senate Agriculture Committees monitor the Department of Agriculture, and so on. The Legislative Reorganization Act of 1970 spells out each committee's responsibility for overseeing its parallel agency:

> Each standing committee shall review and study, on a continuing basis, the application, administration, and execution of those laws, or parts of laws, the subject matter of which is within the jurisdiction of that committee.

Most federal programs must have their funding renewed every year, a requirement that gives Congress leverage in its ongoing oversight function. If an agency has acted improperly, Congress may reduce the agency's appropriation or tighten the restrictions on the way its funds can be spent. A major difficulty is that the House and Senate Appropriations Committees must review nearly the entire federal budget, a task that limits the amount of attention they can give any particular program.

Oversight is a challenging task. If congressional committees were to try to monitor all the federal bureaucracy's activities, they would have no time to do anything else. Although Congress is required by law to maintain "continuous watchfulness" over programs, oversight normally is not pursued aggressively unless members of Congress are annoyed with an agency, have discovered that a legislative authorization is being grossly abused, or are reviewing a program for possible major changes.

The biggest obstacle to effective oversight is the sheer magnitude of the task. With its hundreds of agencies and thousands of programs, the bureaucracy is beyond comprehensive scrutiny. Even some of Congress's most publicized oversight activities are relatively trivial when viewed against the extensive scope of the bureaucracy. For example, congressional investigations into the Defense Department's purchase of small hardware items, such as wrenches and hammers, at many times their market value do not begin

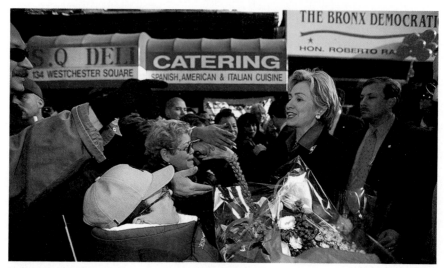

U.S. Senator Hillary Clinton is the only first lady to seek elective office. She moved to New York to compete in the state's 2000 Senate race, which she won. She ran for reelection in 2006 amid widespread speculation that she would seek the presidency in 2008. Clinton is shown here campaigning on the streets of New York City.

to address the issue of whether the country is overspending on the military. Overpriced hand tools represent pocket change in a defense budget of hundreds of billions of dollars. The real oversight question is whether the defense budget as a whole provides cost-effective national security. It is a question that Congress has neither the capacity nor the determination to investigate fully.

When an agency is suspected of serious abuses, a committee is likely to hold hearings. Except in cases involving *executive privilege* (the right to withhold confidential information affecting national security), executive-branch officials must testify at these hearings if asked to do so. If they refuse, they can be cited for contempt of Congress, a criminal offense. Congress's investigative power is not listed in the Constitution, but the judiciary has not challenged that power, and Congress has used it extensively.

Congress's zeal for oversight increases substantially when the White House is the target, particularly if the presidency is in the hands of the other party. Republican-controlled committees scheduled numerous hearings to grill President Bill Clinton's appointees on allegations of presidential wrongdoing and, in the case of the Lewinsky scandal, even sought to remove the president from office. Republican-controlled committees were less inclined to schedule hearings in response to allegations of wrongdoing by the Bush administration. When hearings were held, such as the 2006 hearings on the issue of National Security Agency (NSA) wiretapping without judicial permission, their scope and testimony were tightly controlled. Republicans were determined not to stage hearings that day after day would produce headlines damaging to the Bush presidency. However, when Republicans lost control of Congress after the 2006 election, they were powerless to prevent congressional Democrats from holding such hearings. Democrats mimicked the strategy congressional Republicans had used earlier against Clinton—scheduling hearings as a means of embarrassing President Bush and his party.

CONGRESS: TOO MUCH PLURALISM?

Congress is an institution divided between service to the nation and service to the separate constituencies within it. Its members have responsibility for the nation's laws, yet for reelection they depend on the voters of their states and districts and are highly responsive to constituency interests. This latter focus is facilitated by the committee system, which is organized around particular interests. Agriculture, labor, education, banking, and commerce are among the interests represented through this system. It is hard to conceive of a national legislature structured to respond to special interests more closely than is the Congress of the United States.

Pluralists admire this feature of Congress. They argue that the United States has a majoritarian institution in the presidency and that Congress is a place where a *diversity* of interests is represented. Critics of this view say that Congress sometimes is so responsive to particular interests that it neglects the overall national interest. This criticism is blunted from time to time by a strong majoritarian impulse in Congress. The current period is one of those moments. The high level of party discipline in recent years, coupled with a widening ideological gap between the parties, has placed Congress at the center of many national policy debates.

Yet Congress cannot easily be an institution that is highly responsive both to diverse interests and to the national interest. These interests often conflict, as the rise and fall of former Speaker Newt Gingrich illustrate. He sought to make the Republican congressional majority into the driving force in American national politics, but he was ousted from his position when the conflicts generated by his uncompromising pursuit of conservative policy goals weakened the GOP's support in the states and districts, threatening the reelection chances of Republican incumbents. This inherent tension between Congress's national role and its local base has been replayed many times in U.S. history. In a real sense, the strengths of Congress are also its weaknesses. Those features of congressional election and organization that make Congress responsive to separate constituencies are often the very ones that make it difficult for Congress to act as a strong instrument of a national majority. The perennial challenge for members of Congress is to find a workable balance between what Roger Davidson and Walter Oleszek call the "two Congresses": one embodied by the Capitol in Washington and the other embodied by the members' separate districts and states.[27]

SUMMARY

Members of Congress, once elected, are likely to be reelected. Members of Congress can use their office to publicize themselves, pursue a service strategy of responding to the needs of individual constituents, and secure pork-barrel projects for their states or districts. House members gain a greater advantage from these activities than do senators, whose larger constituencies make it harder for them to build close personal relations with voters and whose office is more likely to attract strong challengers. Incumbency does have some disadvantages. Members of Congress must take positions on controversial issues, may blunder into political scandal or indiscretion, must deal with changes in the electorate, or may face strong challengers; any of these conditions can reduce members' reelection chances. By and large, however, the advantages of incumbency far outweigh the disadvantages. Incumbents' advantages extend into their reelection campaigns: their influential positions in Congress make it easier for them to raise campaign funds from PACs and individual contributors.

Congress is a fragmented institution. It has no single leader; rather, the House and Senate have separate leaders, neither of whom can presume to speak for the other chamber. The principal party leaders of Congress are the Speaker of the House and the Senate majority leader. They share leadership power with committee and subcommittee chairpersons, who have influence on the policy decisions of their committee or subcommittee.

It is in the committees that most of the day-to-day work of Congress is conducted. Each standing committee of the House or the Senate has jurisdiction over congressional policy in a particular area (such as agriculture or foreign relations), as does each of its subcommittees. In most cases, the full House and Senate accept committee recommendations about the passage of bills, although amendments to bills are quite common and committees are careful to take other members of Congress into account when making legislative decisions. Congress is a legislative system in which influence is widely dispersed, an arrangement that suits the power and reelection needs of its individual members. However, partisanship is a strong and binding force in Congress. It is the basis on which party leaders are able to build support for major legislative initiatives. On this type of legislation, party leaders and caucuses, rather than committees, are the central actors.

The major function of Congress is to enact legislation. Yet the role it plays in developing legislation depends on the type of policy involved. Because of its divided chambers and committee structure, as well as the concern of its members with state and district interests, Congress, through its party leaders and caucuses, only occasionally takes the lead on broad national issues; Congress instead typically looks to the president for this leadership. Nevertheless, presidential initiatives are passed by Congress only if they meet its members' expectations and usually only after a lengthy process of compromise and negotiation. Congress is more adept at handling legislation that deals with problems of narrow interest. Legislation of this sort is decided mainly in congressional committees, where interested legislators, bureaucrats, and groups concentrate their efforts on issues of mutual concern.

A second function of Congress is the representation of various interests. Members of Congress are highly sensitive to the state or district they depend on for reelection. They do respond to overriding national interests, but for most of them local concerns generally come first. National or local representation often operates through party representation, particularly on issues that divide the Democratic and Republican parties and their constituent groups.

Congress's third function is oversight, the supervision and investigation of the way the bureaucracy is implementing legislatively mandated programs. Although oversight is a difficult process, it is an important means of legislative control over the actions of the executive branch.

KEY TERMS

bill (*p. 386*)
cloture (*p. 388*)
conference committees (*p. 384*)
constituency (*p. 363*)

filibuster (*p. 388*)
gerrymandering (*p. 366*)
jurisdiction (of a congressional
  committee) (*p. 385*)

Suggested Readings

Dwyre, Diana, and Victoria Farrar-Myers. *Legislative Labyrinth: Congress and Campaign Finance Reform.* Washington, D.C.: Congressional Quarterly Press, 2001. An inside look at the mix of Congress and campaign money.

Herrnson, Paul S. *Congressional Elections: Campaigning at Home and in Washington,* 4th ed. Washington, D.C.: Congressional Quarterly Press, 2003. A study that argues that members of Congress run two campaigns, one at home and one in Washington.

Hibbing, John R., and Elizabeth Theiss-Morse. *Congress as Public Enemy: Public Attitudes Toward American Political Institutions.* New York: Cambridge University Press, 1995. An analysis through survey and focus group data of Americans' attitudes toward Congress.

Jacobson, Gary C. *The Politics of Congressional Elections,* 6th ed. New York: Longman, 2003. An overview of the congressional election process and its impact on policy and representation.

Quirk, Paul J., and Sarah A. Binder, eds. *The Legislative Branch.* New York: Oxford University Press, 2005. A comprehensive set of essays on Congress by many of the best congressional scholars.

Sidlow, Edward. *Challenging the Incumbent: An Underdog's Undertaking.* Washington, D.C.: Congressional Quarterly Press, 2003. A fascinating case study of the difficulties faced by those who dare to challenge an incumbent.

Sinclair, Barbara. *Unorthodox Lawmaking: New Legislative Processes in the U.S. Congress,* 2nd ed. Washington, D.C.: Congressional Quarterly Press, 2000. A detailed analysis of the American legislative process.

List of Websites

http://www.usafmc.org/default.asp?pagenumber=8 The website of the
  United States Association of Former Members of Congress, which has a
  "Congress to Campus" program that on request brings former congressional
  members to campuses for talks.

http://thomas.loc.gov/ The Library of Congress site, named after Thomas Jefferson; provides information about the congressional process, including the status of pending legislation.

http://www.house.gov/ The U.S. House of Representatives' website; has information on party leaders, pending legislation, and committee hearings, as well as links to each House member's office and website.

http://www.senate.gov/ The U.S. Senate's website, which is similar to that of the House and provides links to each senator's website.

POLITICS IN THEORY AND PRACTICE

Thinking: How does the structure of Congress (for example, its two chambers and its committee system) affect its policymaking role?

Participating: Consider writing to your U.S. representative or one of your U.S. senators to express your view on a public policy issue currently before Congress. You can find the names and addresses of your members of Congress at www.ushouse.gov and www.ussenate.gov. These sites will also indicate the congressional committees on which your members sit.

ADDITIONAL RESOURCES

For quizzes, interactive simulations, games, graphics, and other study tools, visit the book's Online Learning Center at **www.mhhe.com/pattersonwtp7.**

Running for Congress, Staying in Congress

By Paul S. Herrnson

In this essay, University of Maryland Professor Paul Herrnson discusses the nature of congressional campaigns and the decisive role incumbency plays in their outcome. Once elected, members of Congress use the resources of their office to solidify their hold on that office. An effect is a warping of both the electoral process and the legislative process.

In order to win a congressional election or even to be remotely competitive, candidates must compete in two campaigns: one for votes and one for resources. The campaign for votes is the campaign that generally comes to mind when people think about congressional elections. It requires a candidate to assemble an organization and to use that organization to target key groups of voters, select a message they will find compelling, communicate that message, and get supporters to the polls on election day.

The other campaign, which is based largely in Washington, D.C., requires candidates to convince the party operatives, interest group officials, political consultants, and journalists who play leading roles in the nation's political community that their races will be competitive and worthy of support. Gaining the backing of these various individuals is a critical step in attracting the money and campaign services that are available in the nation's capital and in other wealthy urban centers. These resources enable the candidate to run a credible campaign back home. Without them, most congressional candidates would lose their bids for election. . . .

Candidates, not political parties, are the major focus of congressional campaigns, and candidates, not parties, bear the ultimate responsibility for election outcomes. These characteristics of congressional elections are striking when viewed from a comparative perspective. In most democracies, political parties are the principal contestants in elections, and campaigns focus on national issues, ideology, and party programs and accomplishments. In the United States, parties do not run congressional campaigns nor do they become the major focus of elections. Instead, candidates run their own campaigns, and parties contribute money or election services to some of them. Parties also may advertise or mobilize voters on behalf of candidates. A comparison of the terminology commonly used to describe elections in the United States with that used in Great Britain more than hints at the differences. In the United States, candidates are said to *run* for Congress, and they do so with or without party help. In Britain, by contrast, candidates are said to *stand* for election to Parliament, and their party runs most of the campaign. The difference in terminology only slightly oversimplifies reality.

Unlike candidates for national legislatures in most other democracies, U.S. congressional candidates are self-selected rather than recruited by party organizations. They must win the right to run under their party's label through a participatory primary, caucus, or convention, or by scaring off all opposition.

. . . Although they talk about the competition and are, indeed, wary of it, congressional incumbents, particularly House members, operate in a political setting that works largely to their benefit. . . . [I]ncumbents enjoy significant levels of name recognition and voter support, are able to assemble superior campaign organizations, and can draw on their experience in office to speak knowledgeably about issues and claim credit for the federally financed programs and improvements in their state or district. Incumbents also tend to get favorable treatment from the media. Moreover, most can rely on loyal followers from previous campaigns for continued backing: supporters at home tend to vote repeatedly for incumbents, and supporters in Washington and the nation's other wealthy cities routinely provide incumbents with campaign money.

Things look different from the typical challenger's vantage point. Most challengers, particularly those with some political experience, recognize that most of the cards are stacked against an individual who sets out to take on an incumbent. Little in the setting in which most congressional campaigns take place favors the challenger. Most challengers lack the public visibility, money, and campaign experience to wage a strong campaign. Moreover, because those who work in and help finance campaigns recognize the strong odds against challengers, they usually see little benefit in helping them. As a result, high incumbent success rates have become a self-fulfilling prophecy. Senate reelection rates ranged from 55 percent to almost 97 percent between 1950 and 2002. Between 1982 and 2002 almost 4 percent of all Senate incumbents had no major-party opponent, and just over half of those involved in contested races won by 60 percent or more of the two-party vote. Only 16 percent of all senators seeking reelection in

2000 and 2002 were defeated. Between 1950 and 2002, House incumbents enjoyed an overall reelection rate of better than 93 percent; the 2000 and 2002 elections returned to Congress roughly 98 percent and 96 percent, respectively, of those who sought to keep their jobs. Even during the tidal wave that swept away thirty-four Democrats in the House in the 1994 elections, just over 90 percent of all House incumbents who sought to remain in office did so. With some important exceptions, most experienced politicians wait until an incumbent retires, runs for another office, or dies before running for office. Thus, many House seats fail to attract meaningful competition. . . .

Many explanations exist for the relative lack of competition in House elections. Some districts are so dominated by one party that few individuals of the other party are willing to commit their time, energy, or money to running for office. In many cases, the tradition of one-party dominance is so strong that virtually all the talented, politically ambitious individuals living in the area join the dominant party. When an incumbent in these districts faces a strong challenge, it usually takes place in the primary, and the winner is all but guaranteed success in the general election.

Uncompetitive House districts are often the product of the redistricting process. In states where one party controls both the governorship and the state legislature, partisan gerrymandering is often used to maximize the number of House seats the dominant party can win. In states where each party controls at least some portion of the state government, compromises are frequently made to design districts that protect congressional incumbents. Party officials and political consultants armed with computers, election returns, and demographic statistics can "pack" and "crack" voting blocs in order to promote either of these goals. The result is that large numbers of congressional districts are designed to be uncompetitive. In 2002, for example, only three of California's fifty-three House elections were decided by a margin of less than twenty points, and one of those seats might not have been competitive if scandal-plagued Gary Condit had not lost the Democratic primary. States that use nonpartisan commissions, which often ignore incumbency, tend to produce more competitive House races. In contrast to the situation in California, four of Iowa's five House seats were decided by fewer than fifteen points.

The desire of incumbents to retain their seats has changed Congress in ways that help discourage electoral competition. Most of those who are elected to Congress quickly understand that they will probably never hold a higher office because there are too few of such offices to go around. Like most people, they do everything in their power to hold on to their jobs. Congress has adapted to the career aspirations of its members by providing them with resources that can be used to increase their odds of reelection. Free mailings, WATS lines, Internet web sites, district offices, and subsidized travel help members gain visibility among their constituents. Federal "pork-barrel" projects also help incumbents win the support of voters. Congressional aides help members write speeches, respond to constituent mail, resolve problems that constituents have with executive branch agencies, and follow the comings and goings in their bosses' districts. These perquisites of office give incumbents tremendous advantages over challengers. They also discourage experienced politicians who could put forth a competitive challenge from taking on an entrenched incumbent.

The dynamics of campaign finance have similar effects. Incumbents have tremendous fundraising advantages over challengers, especially among PACs and wealthy individual donors. Many incumbents build up large war chests to discourage potential challengers from running against them. With the exception of millionaires and celebrities, challengers who decide to contest a race against a member of the House or Senate typically find they are unable to raise the funds needed to mount a viable campaign.

What's Your Opinion?

As a citizen, are you troubled by a congressional election system in which incumbents have an overwhelming edge over challengers? What are the advantages and disadvantages of this arrangement? What steps, if any, would you take to reduce incumbents' electoral advantage?

CHAPTER 12

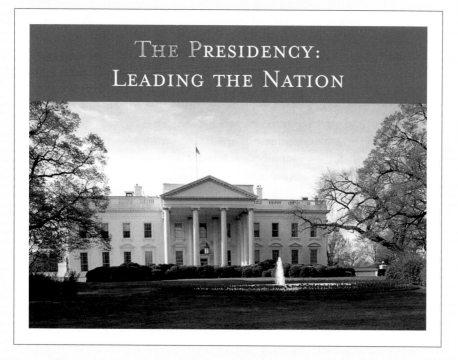

THE PRESIDENCY:
LEADING THE NATION

> **"** [The president's] is the only voice in national affairs. Let him once win the admiration and confidence of the people, and no other single voice will easily overpower him. **"**
>
> WOODROW WILSON[1]

George W. Bush was sinking in the polls. The economy was weakening, and the newly elected president was being criticized for not doing enough to reverse the downturn. Bush was also getting heat for the defection of Senator James Jeffords of Vermont, which cost Republicans control of the Senate. The news media had given him the honeymoon period traditionally accorded a new president, but they were now turning on him.

Everything changed on September 11, 2001. After the terrorist attacks on the World Trade Center and the Pentagon, Americans rallied around their president. Bush vowed that America would not rest until the terrorists were brought to justice and the international network of which they were a part was destroyed. His presidential approval rating reached 96 percent, the highest level ever recorded. Not even Franklin Roosevelt and Harry Truman had received approval ratings that high during the Second World War. During the next two years, buoyed by public support,

Bush led the nation into wars in Afghanistan and Iraq as part of his "war on terrorism."

By 2005, everything had changed again for President Bush. The U.S. invasion of Iraq was followed by problems the Bush administration had not anticipated. Continued attacks on U.S. forces, a failure to find weapons of mass destruction, abuse of Iraqi prisoners by U.S. soldiers, and the escalating financial cost of Iraq's reconstruction were eroding his public support. Bush was able to win reelection in 2004, but his victory was by the smallest margin for an incumbent since Harry Truman's victory in 1948. Bush's reelection gave him a boost in the opinion polls, but it was short-lived. By early 2005, his approval rating was dropping again, and it eventually fell below 40 percent.

The Bush story is but one in the saga of the ups and downs of the modern presidency. Lyndon Johnson's and Richard Nixon's dogged pursuit of the Vietnam War led to talk of "the imperial presidency," an office so powerful that constitutional checks and balances were no longer an effective constraint on it. Within a few years, because of the undermining effects of Watergate and of changing international conditions during the Ford and Carter presidencies, the watchword became "the imperiled presidency," an office too weak to meet the nation's demands for executive leadership. Ronald Reagan's policy successes before 1986 renewed talk heard in the Roosevelt and Kennedy years of "a heroic presidency," an office that is the inspirational center of American politics. After the Iran-Contra scandal in 1986, Reagan was more often called a lame duck. The first George Bush's handling of the Gulf crisis—leading the nation in 1991 into a major war and emerging from it with a stratospheric public approval rating—bolstered the heroic conception of the office. A year later, Bush was on his way to being removed from office by the voters. Bill Clinton overcame a fitful start to his presidency to become the first Democrat since Franklin D. Roosevelt in the 1930s to win reelection. As Clinton was launching an aggressive second-term policy agenda, however, he got entangled in an affair with a White House intern, Monica Lewinsky, that led to his impeachment by the House of Representatives and weakened his claim to national leadership.

No other political institution has been subject to such varying characterizations as the modern presidency. One reason is that the formal powers of the office are somewhat limited and thus presidential power changes with national conditions, political circumstances, and the personal capacity of the office's occupant.[2] The American presidency is always a central office in that its occupant is a focus of national attention. Yet the presidency is not an inherently powerful office, in the sense that presidents routinely get what they want. Presidential power is conditional. It depends on the president's

President George W. Bush gestures as he responds to reporters' questions in 2006 as part of a White House effort to revive public support for his presidency. In 2001, his presidential approval rating soared above 90 percent. By 2006, it had fallen below 40 percent and was hurting his ability to lead Congress and the public.

own abilities but even more on circumstances—on whether the situation demands strong leadership and whether the political support for that leadership exists. When conditions are favorable, the president will look powerful. When conditions are adverse, the president will appear vulnerable.

This chapter examines the roots of presidential power, the presidential selection process, the staffing of the presidency, and the factors associated with the success and failure of presidential leadership. The main ideas of this chapter are these:

★ *Public expectations, national crises, and changing national and world conditions have required the presidency to become a strong office.* Underlying this development is the public support the president acquires from being the only nationally elected official.

★ *The modern presidential election campaign is a marathon affair in which self-selected candidates must plan for a strong start in the nominating contests and center their general-election strategies on media, issues, and a baseline of support.* The lengthy campaign process heightens the public's sense that the presidency is at the center of the U.S. political system.

★ *The modern presidency could not operate without a large staff of assistants, experts, and high-level managers, but the sheer size of this staff makes it impossible for the president to exercise complete control over it.*

★ *The president's election by national vote and position as sole chief executive ensure that others will listen to the president's ideas; but to lead effectively, the president must have the help of other officials and, to get their help, must respond to their interests as they respond to the president's.*

★ *Presidential influence on national policy is highly variable.* Whether presidents succeed or fail in getting their policies enacted depends heavily on the force of circumstance, the stage of their presidency, partisan support in Congress, and the foreign or domestic nature of the policy issue.

FOUNDATIONS OF THE MODERN PRESIDENCY

The writers of the Constitution knew what they wanted from a president—national leadership, statesmanship in foreign affairs, command in time of war or insurgency, enforcement of the laws—but they could devise only general phrases to describe the president's constitutional authority. Compared with Article I, which enumerates Congress's specific powers, Article II of the Constitution contains relatively general statements on the president's powers.[3]

Over the course of American history, each of the president's constitutional powers has been extended in practice beyond the Framers' intention. For example, the Constitution grants the president command of the nation's military, but only Congress can declare war. In *Federalist* No. 69, Alexander Hamilton wrote that a surprise attack on the United States was the only justification for war by presidential action. Nevertheless, the nation's presidents have sent troops into military action abroad more than two hundred times. Of the more than a dozen wars included in that figure, only five were declared by Congress.[4] All of America's most recent wars—the Korean, Vietnam, Persian Gulf, Balkans, Afghanistan, and Iraq conflicts—have been undeclared.

The Constitution also empowers the president to act as diplomatic leader with the authority to appoint ambassadors and to negotiate treaties with other countries, subject to approval by a two-thirds vote of the Senate. The Framers anticipated that Congress would define the nation's foreign policy objectives, while the president would oversee their implementation. However, the president has become the principal architect of U.S. foreign policy and has even acquired the power to make treaty-like arrangements with other nations, in the form of executive agreements. In 1937, the Supreme Court ruled that such agreements, signed and approved only by the president, have the same legal status as treaties, although Congress can cancel executive agreements with which it disagrees.[5] Since World War II, presidents have negotiated more than ten thousand executive agreements, compared to fewer than one thousand treaties ratified by the Senate.[6]

The Constitution also vests "executive power" in the president. This power includes the responsibility to execute the laws faithfully and to appoint major administrators, such as heads of the various departments of the executive branch. In *Federalist* No. 76, Hamilton indicated that the president's real authority as chief executive was to be found in this appointive capacity. Presidents have indeed exercised substantial power through their appointments, but they have found their administrative authority—the power to execute the laws—to be of even greater value, because it enables them to determine how laws will be interpreted and applied. President Ronald Reagan used his executive power to *prohibit* the use of federal funds by family-planning clinics that offered abortion counseling. President Bill Clinton exerted the same power to *permit* the use of federal funds for this purpose. The same act of Congress was the basis for each of these actions. The act authorizes the use of federal funds for family-planning services, but it neither requires nor prohibits their use for abortion counseling, enabling the president to decide this issue.

Finally, the Constitution provides the president with legislative authority, including use of the veto and the opportunity to recommend proposals to Congress. The Framers expected this authority to be used in a limited way. George Washington acted as the Framers anticipated: he proposed only three legislative measures and vetoed only two acts of Congress. Modern presidents have assumed a more active legislative role. They regularly submit proposals to Congress, and most of them have not hesitated to veto legislation they find disagreeable.

The presidency is a more powerful office than the Framers envisioned, for many reasons. But two features of the office in particular—*national election* and *singular authority*—have enabled presidents to make use of changing demands on government to claim the position of leader of the American people. It is a claim that no other elected official can routinely make, and it is a key to understanding the role and power of the president.

Asserting a Claim to National Leadership

The first president to forcefully assert a claim to popular leadership was Andrew Jackson, who had been swept into office in 1828 on a tide of public support that broke the hold of the upper classes on the presidency. Jackson used his popular backing to challenge Congress's claim to national policy leadership, contending that he was "the people's tribune."

Historical Background

However, Jackson's view was not shared by most of his successors during the nineteenth century, because national conditions did not routinely call for strong presidential leadership. The prevailing conception was the **Whig theory,** which held that the presidency was a limited or constrained office whose occupant was confined to the exercise of expressly granted constitutional authority. The president had no implicit powers for dealing with national problems but was primarily an administrator, charged with carrying out the will of Congress. "My duty," said President James Buchanan, a Whig adherent, "is to execute the laws . . . and not my individual opinions."[7]

Theodore Roosevelt rejected the Whig tradition upon taking office in 1901. He attacked the business trusts, pursued an aggressive foreign policy, and pressured Congress to adopt progressive domestic policies. Roosevelt embraced the **stewardship theory,** which calls for an assertive presidency that is confined only at points specifically prohibited by law. As "steward of the people," Roosevelt said, he was permitted "to do anything that the needs of the Nation demanded unless such action was forbidden by the Constitution or by the laws."[8]

Roosevelt's image of a strong presidency was shared by Woodrow Wilson, but his other immediate successors reverted to the Whig notion of the limited presidency.[9] Herbert Hoover's restrained conception of the presidency prevented him from acting decisively during the devastation of the Great Depression. Hoover said that he lacked the constitutional authority to establish public relief programs for jobless Americans. However, Hoover's successor, Franklin D. Roosevelt, shared the stewardship theory of his distant cousin Theodore Roosevelt, and FDR's New Deal signaled the end of the limited presidency. As FDR's successor, Harry Truman, wrote in his memoirs: "The power of the President should be used in the interest of the people and in order to do that the President must use whatever power the Constitution does not expressly deny him."[10]

George Washington
(1732–99)

George Washington, the nation's first president and its greatest in the minds of some historians, was born into a Virginia planter family. As a child, he excelled as a horseman, a skill that along with family connections earned him an officer's commission. He was involved in the first major skirmish of the French and Indian War. His daring and bravery under fire—two horses were shot out from under him as he rallied troops who had fled in the face of the enemy—made him a national hero. When the American colonies a decade later declared their independence from Britain, he was the natural choice to lead the Continental Army. Throughout the six-year Revolutionary War, Washington avoided pitched battles, knowing that his poorly equipped soldiers were no match for British regulars. Finally, in 1781, his forces trapped the British army at Yorktown and with the help of French naval vessels scored a decisive victory that ended the war. Some of his countrymen thought Washington should be named king, but he dismissed the idea, saying America would instead be a new type of nation. He retired to his Mount Vernon plantation, only to grow increasingly worried by the growing discord among the states and the inability of Congress to govern effectively.

In 1787, Washington presided over the Philadelphia convention that drafted a constitution that became the basis for a stronger central government. Following ratification of the Constitution, Washington was elected president by unanimous vote of the Electoral College. He recognized that his presidency would define future ones. In a letter to James Madison, Washington wrote, "It is devoutly wished on my part that these precedents may be fixed on true principles." Washington pushed for a strong national government, believing that it could keep the nation from devolving into sectional rivalries. He also kept the United States out of foreign affairs, believing the new country was too weak militarily to play such a role. Washington could have been elected to a third term, but he stepped down after two terms, stating that the

(continued)

presidency was a citizen's office, not a monarchal one. It was a precedent that all presidents adhered to until Franklin Roosevelt ran for and won a third term in 1940 at a time when the country was confronting the twin threats of economic depression and war. Roosevelt's presidency prompted Congress to initiate the Twenty-Second Amendment to the Constitution, which limits a president to two terms in office.

Today the presidency is an inherently strong office.[11] The modern presidency becomes a more substantial office in the hands of a confident individual like George W. Bush, but even a less assertive person like Jimmy Carter is expected to act forcefully. This expectation not only is the legacy of former strong presidents but also stems from changes that have occurred in the federal government's national and international policy responsibilities.

The Need for Presidential Leadership of an Activist Government

During most of the nineteenth century (the Civil War being the notable exception), the United States did not need a strong president. The federal government's policymaking role was small, as was its bureaucracy. Moreover, the nation's major issues were of a sectional nature (especially the North-South split over slavery) and thus were suited to action by Congress, which represented state interests. The U.S. government's role in world affairs was also small. As these conditions changed, however, the presidency also changed.

Foreign Policy Leadership The president has always been the nation's foreign policy leader, but the role was initially a rather undemanding one. The United States avoided entanglement in the turbulent affairs of Europe and was preoccupied with westward expansion. By the end of the nineteenth century, however, the nation was seeking a world market for its goods. President Theodore Roosevelt advocated an American economic empire and looked south toward Latin America and west toward Hawaii, the Philippines, and China for new markets (the "Open Door" policy). However, the United States' tradition of isolationism remained a powerful influence on national policy. The United States fought in World War I but immediately thereafter demobilized its armed forces. Over President Woodrow Wilson's objections, Congress then voted against the entry of the United States into the League of Nations.

Harry S Truman's presidency was characterized by bold foreign policy initiatives. He authorized the use of nuclear weapons against Japan in 1945, created the Marshall Plan as the basis for the economic reconstruction of postwar Europe, and sent U.S. troops to fight in Korea in 1950. Truman is shown here greeting British Prime Minister Winston Churchill at a Washington airport in early 1952.

World War II fundamentally changed the nation's international role and the president's role in foreign policy. In 1945, the United States emerged as a global superpower, a giant in world trade, and the recognized leader of the noncommunist world. The United States today has a military presence in nearly every part of the globe and an unprecedented interest in trade balances, energy supplies, and other international issues affecting the nation.

The effect of these developments on America's political institutions has been one-sided. Because of the president's constitutional authority as chief diplomat and military commander and the special demands of foreign policy leadership, the president, not Congress, has taken the lead in addressing the nation's increased responsibilities in the world. Foreign policy requires singleness of purpose and, at times, fast action. Congress—a large, divided, and unwieldy institution—is poorly suited to such a response. In contrast, the president, as sole head of the executive branch, can act quickly and speak authoritatively for the nation as a whole in its relations with other nations.

This capacity has rarely been more evident than after the terrorist attacks of September 11, 2001. The initiative in the war on terrorism rested squarely with the White House. President Bush decided on the

U.S. response to the attacks and took the lead in obtaining international support for U.S. military, intelligence, and diplomatic initiatives. Congress backed these actions enthusiastically. The joint resolution that endorsed Bush's decision to attack the Taliban government in Afghanistan passed unanimously in the Senate and with only a single dissenting vote in the House. In reality, however, Congress had little choice but to support whatever policies Bush chose. Americans wanted decisive action and were looking to the president, not to Congress, for leadership.

In other situations, of course, Congress is less compliant. In recent decades, it has contested presidential positions on issues such as global trade and international human rights. Nevertheless, the president is clearly the leading voice in U.S. foreign policy. (The changing shape of the world and its implications for presidential power and leadership are discussed more fully later in the chapter.)

Domestic Policy Leadership The change in the president's domestic leadership role has also been substantial. Throughout most of the nineteenth century Congress jealously guarded its constitutional powers, making it clear that it was in charge of domestic policy. James Bryce wrote in the 1880s that Congress paid no more attention to the president's views on legislation than it did to the editorial positions of newspaper publishers.[12]

Historical Background

By the early twentieth century, however, the national government was taking on regulatory and policy responsibilities imposed by the nation's transition from an agrarian to an industrial society, and the executive branch was growing ever larger. In 1921, Congress conceded that it lacked the centralized authority to coordinate the growing national budget and enacted the Budget and Accounting Act, which provided for an executive budget. Federal departments and agencies would no longer submit their annual budget requests directly to Congress. Instead, the president would develop the various agencies' requests into a comprehensive budgetary proposal, which then would be submitted to Congress as a starting point for its deliberations.

During the Great Depression of the 1930s, Franklin D. Roosevelt's New Deal responded to the public's demand for economic relief with a broad program that required a level of policy planning and coordination beyond the capacity of Congress. In addition to public works projects and social welfare programs, the New Deal made the government a partner in nearly every aspect of the nation's economy. If economic regulation was to work, unified and continuous policy leadership was needed, which only the president could routinely provide.

Presidential authority has continued to grow since Roosevelt's time. In response to pressures from the public, the national government's role in areas such as education, health, welfare, safety, and protection of the environment has expanded greatly, which in turn has created additional demands for presidential leadership.[13] Big government, with its emphasis on comprehensive planning and program coordination, has favored executive authority at the expense of legislative authority. All democracies have seen a shift in power from their legislature to their executive. In Britain, for example, the prime minister has taken on responsibilities that once belonged to the cabinet or to Parliament.

CHOOSING THE PRESIDENT

As the president's policy and leadership responsibilities changed during the nation's history, so did the process of electing presidents. The changes do not parallel each other exactly, but they are related both politically and philosophically. As the presidency drew ever closer to the people, their role in selecting the president grew ever more important.[14] The United States in its history has had four systems of presidential selection, each more "democratic" than its predecessor (see Table 12–1).

The delegates to the 1787 constitutional convention feared that popular election of the president would make the office too powerful and so devised an electoral vote system (the so-called Electoral College). The president was to be chosen by electors picked by the states, with each

Historical Background

state entitled to one elector for each of its members of Congress (House and Senate combined). This system was changed after the 1828 election of Andrew Jackson, who believed the people's will had been denied four years earlier when he received the most popular votes but failed to gain an electoral majority. Jackson was unable to persuade Congress to support a constitutional amendment that would have eliminated the Electoral College, but he did obtain the next-best alternative: he persuaded the states to link their electoral votes to the popular vote. Under Jackson's reform, which is still in effect today, each party in a state has a separate slate of electors who gain the right to cast a state's electoral votes if their party's candidate places first in the state's popular voting. Thus, the popular vote for the candidates directly affects their electoral vote, and one candidate is likely to win both forms of the presidential vote. Since Jackson's time, only Rutherford B. Hayes (in 1876), Benjamin Harrison (in 1888), and George W. Bush (in 2000) have won the presidency after having lost the popular vote.

TABLE 12-1 THE FOUR SYSTEMS OF PRESIDENTIAL SELECTION		
Selection System	**Period**	**Features**
1. Original	1788–1828	Party nominees are chosen in congressional caucuses.
		Electoral College members act somewhat independently in their presidential voting.
2. Party convention	1832–1900	Party nominees are chosen in national party conventions by delegates selected by state and local party organizations.
		Electoral College members cast their ballots for the popular-vote winner in their respective states.
3. Party convention, primary	1904–68	As in system 2, except that a *minority* of national convention delegates are chosen through primary elections (the majority still being chosen by party organizations).
4. Party primary, open caucus	1972–present	As in system 2, except that a *majority* of national convention delegates are chosen through primary elections.

Jackson also championed the national convention as a means of nominating the party's presidential candidate (before this time, nominations were made by party caucuses in Congress and in state legislatures). The parties' strength was at the grass roots, among the people, and Jackson saw the convention process as a means of bringing the citizenry and the presidency closer together. Since Jackson's time, presidential nominees have been formally chosen at national party conventions. Each state party sends delegates to the national convention, and these delegates select the party's nominee.

Jackson's system of presidential nomination remained fully intact until the early twentieth century, when the Progressives devised the primary election as a means of curbing the power of the party bosses (see Chapter 2). State party leaders had taken control of the nominating process by handpicking their states' convention delegates. The Progressives sought to give voters the power to select the delegates. Such a process is called an *indirect primary*, because the voters are not choosing the nominees directly (as they do in House and Senate races) but rather are choosing delegates who in turn select the nominees.

However, the Progressives were unable to persuade most states to adopt presidential primaries, which meant that party leaders continued to control enough delegates to pick the parties' nominees. That arrangement lasted until 1968, when Democratic party leaders ignored the strength of anti–Vietnam War sentiment as expressed in the primaries and nominated Vice President Hubert Humphrey, who had not entered a single primary and was closely identified with the Johnson administration's Vietnam policy. After Humphrey narrowly lost the 1968 general election to Richard Nixon, reform-minded Democrats forced changes in the nominating process. The new rules gave rank-and-file party voters more control by requiring states to choose their delegates through either primary elections or **open party caucuses** (meetings open to any registered party voter who wants to attend). Although the Democrats initiated the change, the Republicans were also affected by it. Most states that adopted a presidential primary in order to comply with the Democrats' new rules also required Republicans to select their convention delegates through a primary.

Today it is the voters in state primaries and open caucuses who play the decisive role in the selection of the Democratic and Republican presidential nominees.[15] A state's delegates are awarded to candidates in accordance with how well they do in the state's primary or caucus. Thus, to win the majority of national convention delegates necessary for nomination, a candidate must place first in a lot of states and do at least reasonably well in most of the rest. (About forty states choose their delegates through a primary election; the others use the caucus system.)

In sum, the presidential election system has changed from an elite-dominated process to one based on voter support. This model has strengthened the presidency by providing the office with the reserve of power that popular election confers on democratic leadership.

The Primary Elections

The fact that voters pick the party nominees has opened the nominating races to any politician with the energy and resources to run a major national campaign. Nominating campaigns, except those in which an incumbent president is seeking reelection, typically attract a half-dozen contenders. The 2004 Democratic race drew an even larger number—nine candidates.

In early 2007, almost two years before Americans would choose their next president, nearly two dozen presidential hopefuls were positioning themselves for a possible run by raising funds, sounding out party leaders, visiting key states, and seeking media attention. The list of hopefuls was so long that not even seasoned pundits could rattle off all the names. Among the possible contenders on the Democratic side were Wesley Clark, Joe Biden, Hillary Clinton, Christopher Dodd, John Edwards, Russ Feingold, Al Gore, Dennis Kucinich, Barack Obama, Bill Richardson, and Tom Vilsack. Among those mentioned as possible Republican candidates were Sam Brownback, Jim Gilmore, Newt Gingrich, Rudy Giuliani, Chuck Hagel, Mike Huckabee, John McCain, George Pataki, Mitt Romney and Tom Tancredo.

Candidates have no choice but to start early and campaign hard. A key to success in the nominating campaign is **momentum**—a strong showing in the early contests that leads to a buildup of public support in subsequent ones. Nobody has time for an also-ran—not the press, not donors, not the voters. No candidate in recent decades has had a slow start in the first few contests and then picked up enough steam to come anywhere near winning nomination. All the advantages rest with the fast starters, who get more attention from the press, more money from contributors, and more consideration from voters. Not surprisingly, presidential contenders strive to do well in the early contests, particularly the first caucuses in Iowa and the first primary in New Hampshire.

Money, always a critical factor in elections, has become increasingly important in the last three decades because states have moved their primaries and caucuses to the early weeks of the nominating period in order to increase their influence on the outcome. To compete effectively in so many contests over such a short period, candidates need money—lots of it. A candidate can be in only one place at a time, so the campaign must be carried to other voters through costly televised political advertising. Observers estimate it takes at least $40 million to run a strong nominating campaign, and possibly a lot more than that for a candidate who does not have substantial name recognition and public support before the campaign begins. In every nominating race but one from 1984 to 2004, the winner was the candidate who had raised the most money before the start of the primaries. (The exception was the 2004 race, when Howard Dean was the top Democratic fund-raiser in advance of the Iowa caucuses.)

Candidates in primary elections receive federal funding if they meet the eligibility criteria. The Federal Election Campaign Act of 1974 (as amended in 1979) provides for federal matching funds. Under the program, the government matches the first $250 of each private donation received by a primary election candidate, provided the candidate raises at

Every Four Years

No event over the years has lured more young people into politics than has the presidential campaign. It is to American politics what the Super Bowl is to professional football or what the World Series is to professional baseball. On election day, the number of voters who go to the polls is nearly 50 percent greater than in a midterm election. A presidential election is also an occasion for more active political participation. There is no exact tally of the number of Americans who contribute time or money to a presidential campaign, but it is in the millions.

The points of entry for a campaign volunteer are many and start early. Residents of Iowa, Nevada, South Carolina, and New Hampshire—the states with the first nominating contests—get the first shot at helping candidates of their choice. From there, the campaign unfolds state by state, although the nominating race usually is over in March, when it reaches the point at which one candidate's lead is so substantial that the other contenders drop out. (Information on the presidential nominating contests, including the date for the contest in your state, can be found online at http://www.thegreenpapers.com/P08.)

After the nominating races end, months remain in the presidential campaign, and there is still much to do. Volunteers are needed to staff phone banks, knock on doors, and do the many other things that comprise a presidential campaign. Sending e-mail messages to family and friends promoting one's candidate is another way to get involved. And for those with little or no spare time, a small monetary donation to the candidate of choice is always an option. Consider getting involved. Millions of other Americans in one way or another will be taking part in the presidential campaign.

least $5,000 in individual contributions of up to $250 in at least twenty states. This provision is designed to restrict matching funds to candidates who can show they have a reasonable amount of public support. In addition, any candidate who receives matching funds must agree to limit expenditures for the nominating phase to a set amount overall (roughly $50 million in 2008) and in particular states (the 2008 limits in Iowa and New Hampshire, for example, are roughly $1.4 million and $800,000, respectively). The limits are adjusted upward each election year to account for inflation. Taxpayers fund the matching program by checking a box on their income-tax return allocating $3 of their taxes to it.

Until the 2000 election, when George Bush declined matching funds so that he could raise unrestricted amounts of money for his nominating campaign, candidates had routinely accepted matching funds, which meant they were willing to abide by the spending limit. In 2004, Bush again turned down matching funds, raising more than $200 million for a nominating campaign in which he faced no Republican opponent. He spent the money to improve his standing with the voters—a perfectly legal tactic as long as the candidate spends the money before the party's summertime nominating convention. On the Democratic side in 2004, Kerry and Dean chose not to accept matching funds, which enabled them to outspend their Democratic rivals in Iowa, New Hampshire, and other early contests.

As candidates have increasingly declined public funding, there have been calls to raise the allowable spending limit under public financing, perhaps to as high as $100 million. Otherwise, observers say, the only candidates who will accept matching funds will be those with no chance of victory. This development would defeat the purpose of public funding, which is to free candidates from the obligations that come from accepting large sums of money from private groups and individuals.

The National Party Conventions

The summertime national party conventions mark the end of the nominating campaign. In an earlier era, the convention was where the nomination was actually decided. State party delegations would come together at their convention to bargain and choose among potential nominees. Since 1972, when the delegate-selection process was changed, the leading candidate in every case has acquired enough delegates in the primaries to lock up the nomination before the convention begins. Nevertheless, the convention is a major event. It brings together the delegates elected in the state caucuses and primaries, who then approve a party platform and formally nominate the party's presidential and vice presidential candidates.

By tradition, the choice of the vice presidential nominee rests with the presidential nominee. In 2004, Kerry alone decided upon John Edwards as his running mate. Critics say the vice presidential nomination should be decided in open competition, because the vice president could become president someday (see Table 12–2). The chief argument for the existing method is that the president needs a trusted and like-minded vice president.

TABLE	12-2	THE PATH TO THE WHITE HOUSE

President	Years in Office	Highest Previous Office	Second-Highest Office
Theodore Roosevelt	1901–8	Vice president*	Governor
William Howard Taft	1909–12	Secretary of war	Federal judge
Woodrow Wilson	1913–20	Governor	None
Warren G. Harding	1921–24	U.S. senator	Lieutenant governor
Calvin Coolidge	1925–28	Vice president*	Governor
Herbert Hoover	1929–32	Secretary of commerce	War relief administrator
Franklin D. Roosevelt	1933–45	Governor	Assistant secretary of Navy
Harry S Truman	1945–52	Vice president*	U.S. senator
Dwight D. Eisenhower	1953–60	None (Army general)	None
John F. Kennedy	1961–63	U.S. senator	U.S. representative
Lyndon Johnson	1963–68	Vice president*	U.S. senator
Richard Nixon	1969–74	Vice president	U.S. senator
Gerald Ford	1974–76	Vice president*	U.S. representative
Jimmy Carter	1977–80	Governor	State senator
Ronald Reagan	1981–88	Governor	None
George Bush	1989–92	Vice president	Director, CIA
Bill Clinton	1993–2000	Governor	State attorney general
George W. Bush	2001–	Governor	None

*Became president on death or resignation of incumbent.

The Campaign for Election

The winner in the November general election is certain to be either the Republican or the Democratic candidate. Two-thirds of the nation's voters identify with the Republican or Democratic party, and most Independents lean toward one or the other of them. As a result, the major-party presidential nominees have a built-in source of votes. Even Democrat George McGovern, who had the lowest level of party support in the past half-century, was backed in 1972 by 60 percent of his party's identifiers. The level of party support for a major-party nominee can be quite high. In 2004, Bush was backed by 93 percent of Republicans, while Kerry was supported by 89 percent of Democrats.

Because the Democratic and Republican nominees have this huge advantage, a third-party candidate has no realistic hope of victory. Even Ross Perot, who in 1992 ran the most successful third-party campaign in nearly a century, was able to garner only a fifth of the vote. On the other hand, third-party candidates have sometimes caused problems for a major party by siphoning votes away from its nominee. In 2000 and again in 2004, third-party candidate Ralph Nader drew the bulk of his support from voters who indicated they otherwise would have backed the Democratic nominee.

Election Strategy The candidates' strategies in the general election are shaped by many considerations, including the constitutional provision that each state shall have electoral votes equal in number to its representation in Congress. Each state thus gets two electoral votes for its Senate representation and a varying number of electoral votes depending on its House representation. Altogether, there are 538 electoral votes (including 3 for the District of Columbia, even though it has no voting representatives in Congress). To win the presidency, a candidate must receive at least 270 votes, an electoral majority. (If no candidate receives a majority, the election is decided in the House of Representatives. No president since John Quincy Adams in 1824 has been elected in this way. The procedure is defined by the Constitution's Twelfth Amendment, which is reprinted in the appendixes.)

The importance of the electoral votes is magnified by the existence of the **unit rule:** all the states except Maine and Nebraska grant all their electoral votes as a unit to the candidate who wins the state's popular vote. For this reason, candidates are concerned with winning the most populous states, such as California (with 55 electoral votes), Texas (34), New York (31), Florida (27), Pennsylvania (21), Illinois (21), Ohio (20), Michigan (17), and Georgia, New Jersey, and North Carolina (15 each).

Even more so than a state's size, however, the closeness of the vote in a state dictates how much attention it will get from the candidates. Because of the unit rule, a state that is lopsidedly Democratic or Republican will be ignored. Its electoral votes are already locked up. Thus, the fall campaign becomes a fight over the toss-up states or, as they have come to be called, the battleground states. In 2004, only one-third of the states—many of them in a band that stretched west from Pennsylvania through Iowa and Minnesota—were seen by the Bush and Kerry campaigns as states that realistically could be won by either candidate. The two candidates spent nearly all their money and time in the battleground states during the closing months of the campaign. Other states might just as well have been located in Canada for the attention they received from the candidates.

At campaign's end, electoral votes and not popular votes determine the winner (see "States in the Nation"). In 2000, Bush was elected with 271 electoral votes, two more than required, even though he received 550,000 fewer popular votes than Al Gore. Bush was the first president since Harrison in 1888 to win the presidency despite losing the popular vote. In 2004, Bush won with 286 electoral votes. His popular margin exceeded 3 million votes, but he would have lost if Kerry had attracted 150,000 more votes in Ohio, which would have earned him Ohio's 20 electoral votes—enough for an electoral college victory.

Media and Money   The modern presidential campaign is a media campaign. At one time, candidates relied heavily on party organization and rallies to carry their messages to the voters, but now they rely on the media, particularly television. Candidates strive to produce the pithy ten-second sound bites that the television networks prefer to highlight on the evening newscasts. They also rely on the power of the "new media," making frequent appearances on programs such as *Larry King Live* and creating their own Internet websites.

The television campaign includes political advertising. Televised commercials are by far the most expensive part of presidential campaigns, accounting for about half the candidates' general election expenditures.

Television is also the forum for the major confrontation of the fall campaign: the presidential debates. The first televised debate took place in 1960 between Kennedy and Nixon, and an estimated one hundred million people saw at least one of their four debates.[16] Televised debates resumed in 1976 and have become a fixture of presidential campaigns. Debates can influence voters' assessments of the candidates. In 2004, George W. Bush's weak performance in the debates—polls indicate that viewers felt John Kerry won all three encounters—hurt his candidacy. Before the first debate, the polls showed Bush with a clear lead. By the last debate, the race was nearly a dead heat.

The Republican and Democratic nominees are each eligible for federal funding of their general election campaigns even if, as in Kerry's and

Electoral Votes in the 2004 Election

There are a total of 538 electoral votes, and a candidate must receive a majority to win the presidency. In 2004, George W. Bush was elected to a second term with 286 electoral votes—sixteen more than required. If John Kerry had gathered roughly 150,000 more popular votes in Ohio, he would have had an electoral vote majority and become president, even though he trailed Bush by 3.5 million popular votes nationwide. Because electoral votes are allocated on a state-by-state basis, the loser of the national popular vote can gain an electoral-vote victory. In 2000, Bush trailed Democratic nominee Al Gore by half a million popular votes nationwide but became president by virtue of a 537-vote popular margin in Florida. Bush was the first president since Benjamin Harrison in 1888 to win the presidency while losing the national popular vote.

States can determine for themselves how their electors will be chosen. Today, all states except two (Maine and Nebraska, which give one electoral vote to the winner of each congressional district and two electoral votes to the statewide winner) give all of their electoral votes to the popular-vote winner in the state.

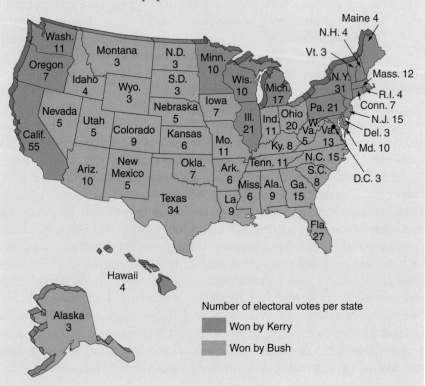

Number of electoral votes per state

▇ Won by Kerry

▇ Won by Bush

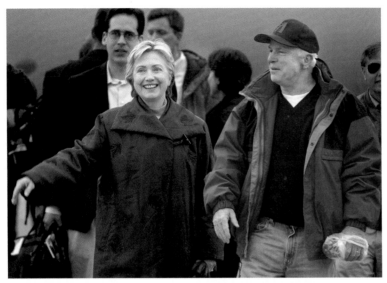

The modern presidential campaign is a marathon event that formally lasts nearly a year and speculatively is always under way. Two years before the 2008 election, nearly two dozen presidential hopefuls—about half Republican and half Democratic—were traveling around the country trying to gather enough support to make a run for their party's nomination. Pundits picked Senator Hillary Clinton on the Democratic side and Senator John McCain on the Republican side as two of the early favorites for nomination. Clinton and McCain are shown here while visiting Norway as part of a Senate delegation studying global environmental issues.

Bush's case in 2004, they did not accept it during the primaries. The amount for the general election was set at $20 million in 1975 and has been adjusted for inflation in succeeding elections. The figure for the major-party nominees in 2008 is more than $80 million. The only string attached to this money is that candidates who accept it can spend no additional funds on their campaigns (although each party is allowed to spend some money—in 2008, roughly $5 million—on behalf of its nominee).

Candidates can choose not to accept public funds, in which case the amount they spend is limited only by their ability to raise money privately. However, all major-party nominees since 1976 have accepted public funding in the general election. Other candidates for the presidency qualify for a proportional amount of federal funding if they receive at least 5 percent of the vote and do not spend more than $50,000 of their own money on the campaign. In 1992, Perot spent over $60 million of his own money and thus was ineligible for federal funding. He accepted $29 million in federal funding in 1996, receiving about half as much as the major-party nominees because his 1992 vote total was roughly half that averaged by the two major-party candidates.

The Winners   The Constitution specifies only that the president must be at least thirty-five years old, a natural-born U.S. citizen, and a U.S. resident for at least fourteen years. Yet the holding of high public office is nearly a prerequisite for gaining the presidency. Except for four army generals, all presidents to date have served previously as vice presidents, members of Congress, state governors, or top federal executives.

All presidents have been white and male, but it is likely only a matter of time before the nation has its first minority-group president or its first woman president. Until the early 1950s, a majority of Americans polled said they would not vote for a woman for president. Today, fewer than 10 percent hold this view. A similar change of opinion preceded John Kennedy's election to the presidency in 1960. Kennedy was the nation's first Catholic president and only the second Catholic to receive a major party's nomination.

STAFFING THE PRESIDENCY

When Americans go to the polls on election day, they have in mind the choice between two individuals, the Democratic and the Republican presidential nominees. In effect, however, they are choosing a lot more than a single executive leader. They are also picking a secretary of state, the director of the FBI, the chair of the Federal Reserve Board, and a host of other executives. Each of these is a presidential appointee.

Presidential Appointees

A president's ability to make executive appointments is a significant source of power. For one thing, modern policymaking rests on a deep understanding of policy issues and also on knowing how to successfully guide proposals through policy channels. Many presidential appointees have these skills. Further, the president cannot be in a hundred different places at once—but the president's appointees can be. They extend the president's influence into the huge federal bureaucracy by overseeing those agencies they are appointed to head. Not surprisingly, the president seeks to appoint individuals who are members of the same political party and are committed to the Administration's policy goals.

The Executive Office of the President   The key staff organization is the Executive Office of the President (EOP), created by Congress in 1939 to provide the president with the staff necessary to coordinate the activities of the executive branch.[17] The EOP has since become the command center of the presidency. Its configuration is determined by the president,

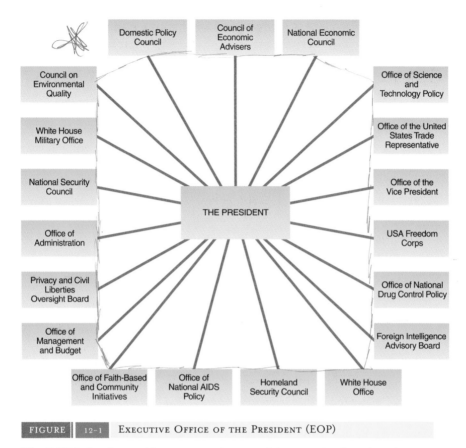

FIGURE   **12-1**   EXECUTIVE OFFICE OF THE PRESIDENT (EOP)

The EOP helps the president manage the rest of the executive branch and promotes the president's policy and political goals. *Source: White House, 2007.*

and it currently consists of the Office of the Vice President and eighteen other organizations (see Figure 12–1). These include the White House Office (WHO), which consists of the president's closest personal advisers; the Office of Management and Budget (OMB), which consists of experts who formulate and administer the federal budget; and the National Security Council (NSC), which advises the president on foreign and military affairs.

The Vice President   The Constitution assigns all executive authority to the president and none to the vice president. Earlier presidents often refused to delegate significant duties to their vice presidents, which diminished the office's appeal. Nomination to the vice presidency was refused by many leading politicians, including Daniel Webster and Henry Clay.

Said Webster, "I do not propose to be buried until I am really dead."[18] Recent presidents, however, have assigned important duties to their vice presidents. George W. Bush, for example, chose Dick Cheney as his running mate in part because of Cheney's experience as White House chief of staff and secretary of defense during previous Republican administrations. Cheney played such a large role in setting the policies of the Bush administration, including the decision to invade Iraq, that seasoned Washington observers questioned whether he had too much influence, a claim that would have baffled Daniel Webster. The vice president is supported by an administrative staff (the Office of the Vice President) of a dozen people, including a domestic policy adviser and a national security policy adviser.

The White House Office   Of the EOP's eighteen other organizations, the White House Office serves the president most directly and personally. The units within the WHO include the Communications Office, the Office of the Press Secretary, the Office of the Counsel to the President, and the Office of Legislative Affairs. As these names suggest, the WHO consists of the president's personal assistants, including close personal advisers, press agents, legislative and group liaison aides, and special assistants for domestic and international policy. They work in the White House, and the president can hire and fire them at will. The personal assistants do much of the legwork for the president and serve as a main source of advice. Most of them are skilled at developing political strategy and communicating with the public, Congress, state and local governments, key groups, and the news media. Because of their proximity to the president, they are among the most powerful individuals in Washington.

Policy Experts   The president is also served by the policy experts in the EOP's other organizations. These include economists, legal analysts, national security specialists, and others. The president is advised on economic issues, for example, by the National Economic Council (NEC). The NEC gathers information to develop indicators of the economy's strength and applies economic theories to various policy alternatives. Modern policymaking cannot be conducted in the absence of such expert knowledge and advice.

The President's Cabinet   The heads of the fifteen executive departments, such as the Department of Defense and the Department of Agriculture, constitute the president's **cabinet.** They are appointed by the president, subject to confirmation by the Senate. Although the cabinet once served as the president's main advisory group, it has not played this role since Herbert Hoover's administration. As national issues have become increasingly complex, the cabinet has become outmoded as a policymaking forum: department heads are likely to be well informed only about issues in their respective policy areas.[19] Cabinet meetings are no longer a forum for deciding policy. Nevertheless, cabinet members, as individuals who head major departments, are important figures in any administration. The president chooses them for their prominence in politics, business, government, or the professions.[20] The office of secretary of state is generally regarded as the most prestigious of the cabinet posts.

Other Presidential Appointees In addition to cabinet secretaries, the president appoints the heads and top deputies of federal agencies and commissions. Altogether, the president appoints a few thousand executive officials. However, most of these appointees are selected at the agency level or are part-time workers. This still leaves nearly seven hundred full-time appointees who serve the president more or less directly, a much larger number than are appointed by the chief executive of any other democracy.[21]

The Problem of Control

Although the president's appointees are a valuable asset, they also pose a problem: because they are so numerous, the president has difficulty controlling them. President Truman had a wall chart in the Oval Office listing more than one hundred officials who reported directly to him; he often told visitors, "I cannot even see all of these men, let alone actually study what they are doing."[22] Since Truman's time, the number of bureaucratic agencies has more than doubled, compounding the problem of presidential control over subordinates.[23]

The problem of presidential control is most severe in the case of appointees who work outside the White House, in the departments and agencies. The loyalty of agency heads and cabinet secretaries often is split between a desire to promote the president's goals and an interest in boosting themselves or the agencies they lead. In late 2002, Harvey Pitt, appointed by President Bush to chair the Securities and Exchange Commission (SEC), resigned amid charges that he had not aggressively pursued corporate accounting irregularities. The Enron, WorldCom, and other corporate scandals had put regulatory action in the spotlight, and Pitt's apparent favoritism toward accounting firms, which he had represented as a lawyer before his appointment to the SEC, was an embarrassment to the Bush administration.

The Constitution assigns no executive authority to the vice president, whose role is determined by the president. Recent vice presidents have been assigned major policy responsibilities. Earlier vice presidents played a smaller role. Vice President Dick Cheney, pictured here with President George W. Bush, is reputedly the most powerful vice president in history.

Lower-level appointees within the departments and agencies pose a different type of problem. The president rarely, if ever, sees them, and they typically are political novices (most have fewer than two years of government experience) and are not very knowledgeable about policy. These appointees are often "captured" by the agency in which they work because they depend on the agency's career bureaucrats for advice. (Chapter 13 examines further the relationship between presidential appointees and career bureaucrats.)

In sum, the modern presidential office is a double-edged sword. Presidents today have greater responsibilities than their predecessors, and this increase in responsibilities expands their opportunities to exert power. At the same time, the range of these responsibilities is so broad that presidents must rely on staffers who may or may not act in the president's best interests. The modern president's recurring problem is to find some way of making sure that appointees serve the interests of the presidency above all others. (The subject of presidential control of the executive branch is discussed further in Chapter 13.)

FACTORS IN PRESIDENTIAL LEADERSHIP

The president operates within a system of separate institutions that share power (see "How the United States Compares"). Significant presidential action normally depends on the approval of Congress, the cooperation of the bureaucracy, and sometimes the acceptance of the judiciary. Because other officials have their own priorities, presidents do not always get their way. Congress in particular—more than the courts or the bureaucracy—holds the key to presidential success. Without congressional authorization and funding, most presidential proposals are nothing but ideas, empty of action.

Whether a president's initiatives succeed or fail depends substantially on several factors, including the force of circumstance, the stage of the president's term, the nature of the particular issue, the president's support in Congress, and the level of public support for the president's leadership. The remainder of this chapter examines each of these factors.

The Force of Circumstance

During his first months in office and in the midst of the Great Depression, Franklin D. Roosevelt accomplished the most sweeping changes in domestic policy in the nation's history. Congress moved quickly to pass nearly every New Deal initiative he proposed. In 1964 and 1965, Lyndon Johnson pushed landmark civil rights and social welfare legislation through Congress on the strength of the civil rights movement, the legacy of the assassinated President Kennedy, and large Democratic majorities in the House and Senate. When Ronald Reagan assumed the presidency in 1981, high unemployment and inflation had greatly weakened the national economy and created a mood for significant change, enabling Reagan to persuade Congress to support some of the most substantial taxing and spending changes in history.

From such presidencies has come the popular impression that presidents single-handedly decide national policy. However, each of these periods of presidential dominance was marked by a special set of circumstances: a decisive election victory that gave added force to the president's leadership, a compelling national problem that convinced Congress and the public that bold presidential action was needed, and a president who was mindful of what was expected and who vigorously advocated policies consistent with those expectations.

When conditions are favorable, the power of the presidency is remarkable. The problem for most presidents is that conditions normally are not conducive to strong leadership. Political scientist Erwin Hargrove

Systems of Executive Policy Leadership

The United States instituted a presidential system in 1789 as part of its constitutional checks and balances. This form of executive leadership was copied in Latin America but not in Europe. European democracies adopted parliamentary systems, in which executive leadership is provided by a prime minister, who is a member of the legislature. In recent years, some European prime ministers have campaigned and governed as if they were a singular authority rather than the head of a collective institution. France in the 1960s created a separate chief executive office but retained its parliamentary form of legislature.

The policy leadership of a president can differ substantially from that of a prime minister. As the singular head of an independent branch of government, a president does not have to share executive authority but nevertheless depends on the legislative branch for support. By comparison, a prime minister shares executive leadership with a cabinet, but once agreement within the cabinet is reached, he or she is almost assured of the legislative support necessary to carry out policy initiatives.

Presidential System	*Presidential/ Parliamentary System*	*Parliamentary System*
Mexico	Finland	Australia
United States	France	Belgium
Venezuela		Canada
		Germany
		Great Britain
		Israel
		Italy
		Japan
		Netherlands
		Sweden

suggests that presidential influence depends largely on circumstance.[24] Some presidents serve in periods when resources are scarce or when important problems are surfacing in American society but have not yet become critical. Such a situation, Hargrove contends, works against the president's efforts to accomplish significant policy change. In 1994, reflecting on the constraints of budget deficits and other factors beyond his control, President Clinton said he had no choice but "to play the hand that history had dealt" him.

The Stage of the President's Term

If conditions conducive to great accomplishments occur infrequently, it is nonetheless the case that nearly every president has favorable moments. Such moments often come during the first months in office. Most newly elected presidents enjoy a **honeymoon period** during which Congress, the press, and the public anticipate initiatives from the Oval Office and are more predisposed than usual to support these initiatives.

Not surprisingly, presidents have put forth more new programs in their first year in office than in any subsequent year. James Pfiffner uses the term *strategic presidency* to refer to a president's need to move quickly on priority items in order to take advantage of the policy momentum gained from the election.[25] Later in their terms, presidents tend to be less successful in presenting initiatives and getting them enacted. They may run out of good ideas, get caught up in scandal, or exhaust their political resources; the momentum of their election is gone and sources of opposition have emerged. Even highly successful presidents like Johnson and Reagan tended to have weak records in their final years. Franklin Roosevelt began his presidency with a remarkable period of achievement—the celebrated "Hundred Days"—but during his last six years in office, few of his major domestic proposals were enacted.

An irony of the presidency, then, is that presidents are usually most powerful when they are least knowledgeable—during their first months in office. These months can, as a result, be times of risk as well as times of opportunity. An example is the Bay of Pigs fiasco during the first year of John Kennedy's presidency, in which a U.S.-backed invasion force of anticommunist Cubans was easily defeated by Fidel Castro's army.

The Nature of the Issue: Foreign or Domestic

In the 1960s, political scientist Aaron Wildavsky wrote that although the nation has only one president, it has two presidencies: one domestic and one foreign.[26] Wildavsky was referring to Congress's greater tendency to defer to presidential leadership on foreign policy issues than on domestic policy issues. He had in mind the broad leeway Congress had granted Truman, Eisenhower, Kennedy, and Johnson in their foreign policies. Wildavsky's thesis is now regarded as a somewhat time-bound conception of presidential influence. Today, many of the same factors that affect a president's domestic policy success, such as the partisan composition of Congress, also affect foreign policy success.

Nevertheless, presidents still have somewhat of an advantage when the issue is foreign policy, because they have more authority to act on their own and are more likely to receive support from Congress.[27] The clash between powerful interest groups that occurs over many domestic issues is less prevalent in the foreign policy area. Additionally, the president is recognized by other nations as America's voice in world affairs, and members of Congress sometimes will defer to the president in order to maintain America's credibility abroad. In some cases, Congress effectively has no choice but to accept presidential authority. When President Bush ordered 20,000 additional U.S. combat troops into Iraq in early 2007, many in Congress questioned the policy, as did a majority of Americans in opinion polls. Yet, because Bush was acting within his constitutional authority as commander-in-chief of the armed services, Congress could not block the troop deployment. "It won't stop us," was Vice President Cheney's response to complaints from Congress.

Presidents also have leverage in foreign and defense policy because of their special relationship with the defense, diplomatic, and intelligence agencies, sometimes called "presidential agencies." Other agencies that are responsive to the president are sometimes even more receptive to Congress; the Department of Agriculture, for example, often is more concerned with having the support of farm-state senators and representatives than with having the president's backing. The defense, diplomatic, and intelligence agencies, however, are different in that their missions are closely tied to the president's constitutional authority as commander-in-chief and chief diplomat. In the buildup to the Iraq war, for example, the defense and intelligence agencies operated in ways that promoted President Bush's stand on the need to confront Saddam Hussein militarily. Only later did Congress discover that the intelligence information it was provided, as well as the assessments it was given by the Defense Department on the level of military force required to invade and pacify Iraq, had been tailored to suit President Bush's plans.

Relations with Congress

Although the presidency is not nearly as powerful as most Americans assume, presidents' ability to influence the agenda of national debate is

POLITICAL CULTURE
Executive Power and Liberty

When the Constitution was written, fear of executive power was widespread. The American Revolution had been fought to overthrow the punitive policies of the British king, who was far less tyrannical than most monarchs of the period.

The Framers, worried that a too-powerful executive would threaten Americans' hard-won liberty, placed executive power within a system of divided power. Each branch would act as a check on the others. The Framers also chose an indirect method of electing the president, fearing that direct popular election would make it too easy for the president to harness the power of popular majorities in pursuit of policies destructive of the rights and interests of minorities.

American history can be read as a refutation of the Framers' concerns. Presidents often have been in the forefront of efforts to expand Americans' liberty. Thomas Jefferson, Abraham Lincoln, and Lyndon Johnson are among the presidents whose names are linked to such efforts. Johnson's leadership, for example, was instrumental in passage of the 1964 Civil Rights Act and the 1965 Voting Rights Act.

On the other hand, U.S. history also contains examples of presidents who have used their power to shrink personal liberty. During the Wilson administration, for example, antiwar dissenters were harassed and more than two thousand jailed for actions such as the distribution of antiwar leaflets. During Franklin Roosevelt's administration, Japanese Americans were uprooted from their West Coast homes and placed in internment camps. During the Nixon administration, antiwar activists were spied upon by the FBI, had their tax returns audited by the IRS, and had their homes and offices burglarized by White House hirelings. In each case, the president argued that a larger issue of liberty—the nation's survival—was at stake and that intrusions on individual liberty were an unfortunate but necessary consequence of the threat. By and large, public opinion supported these presidential actions, although in Nixon's case it eventually turned against the president.

How do you read American history on the issue of executive power and liberty? Where do you think the balance between personal liberty and national security should be struck? What is your opinion of

(continued)

executive action in the context of the war on terrorism? Do you think actions such as expanded wiretapping and detention are necessary if America is to counter the threat of terrorist groups? Or do you think these executive actions constitute an unwarranted intrusion on personal liberty?

unrivaled, reflecting their unique claim to represent the whole country. Whenever the president directs attention to a particular issue, members of Congress take notice. But will they take action? The answer is sometimes yes and sometimes no, depending in part on whether the president takes their concerns into account.

important

Seeking Cooperation from Congress As the center of national attention, presidents can start to believe that their ideas should prevail over those of Congress. This reasoning invariably gets any president into trouble. Jimmy Carter had not held national office before he was elected president in 1976 and thus had no clear understanding of how Washington operates.[28] Soon after taking office, Carter deleted from his budget nineteen public works projects that he believed were a waste of taxpayers' money, ignoring the determination of members of Congress to obtain federally funded projects for their constituents. Carter's action set the tone for a conflict-ridden relationship with Congress.

In order to get the help of members of Congress, the president must respond to their interests as they respond to those of the president.[29] The most basic fact about presidential leadership is that it takes place in the context of a system of divided powers. Although the president gets most of the attention, Congress has most of the constitutional authority in the American system. The powers of the presidential office are by themselves insufficient to sustain the president in a strong position.

Even the president's most direct legislative tool, the veto, has limits. Congress can seldom muster the two-thirds majority in each chamber required to override a presidential veto, so the threat of a veto can make Congress bend to the president's demands. Yet, as presidential scholar Richard Neustadt argues, the veto is as much a sign of presidential weakness as it is a sign of strength, because it comes into play only when Congress refuses to go along with the president's ideas.[30] The first veto cast by George W. Bush is a case in point. Bush had been on track to join Thomas Jefferson as the only two-term president never to veto a bill. In 2006, however, Bush vetoed a bill that would have expanded federal support for embryonic stem cell research. He had announced his opposition to such research early in his presidency and was successful for a time in getting congressional Republicans to back him. As Bush's popularity plummeted in 2005, however, congressional Republicans separated themselves from the president out of concern for their reelection chances. Enough Republicans defected on the stem-cell bill to get it through Congress, setting the stage for Bush's veto.

Congress is a constituency that all presidents must serve if they expect to have its support. Neustadt concludes that presidential power, at base, is "the power to persuade."[31] Like any singular notion of presidential power, Neustadt's has limitations. Presidents at times have the power to command and to threaten. They can also appeal directly to the American people as a means of pressuring Congress. But Congress can never be taken for granted. Theodore Roosevelt expressed the wish that he could "be the president and Congress, too," if only for a day, so that he would have the power to enact as well as to propose laws.

Benefiting from Partisan Support in Congress For most presidents, the next best thing to being "Congress, too" is to have a Congress filled with members of their own party. The sources of division within Congress are many. Legislators from urban and rural areas, wealthier and poorer constituencies, and different regions of the country often have very different views of the national interest. To obtain majority support in Congress, the president must find ways to overcome these differences.

No source of unity is more important to presidential success than partisanship. Presidents are more likely to succeed when their own party controls Congress (see Figure 12–2). Between 1954 and 1992, each Republican president—Eisenhower, Nixon, Ford, Reagan, and Bush—had to contend with a Democratic majority in one or both houses of Congress. Congress passed a smaller percentage of the initiatives supported by each of these presidents than those supported by any Democratic president of the period—Kennedy, Johnson, or Carter. In his first two years in office, backed by Democratic majorities in the House and Senate, more than 85 percent of the bills Clinton supported were enacted into law. After Republicans took control of Congress in 1995, Clinton's legislative success rate sank below 40 percent, a dramatic illustration of the way presidential power is affected by whether the president's party controls Congress.

Colliding with Congress On rare occasions, presidents have pursued their goals so zealously that Congress has been compelled to take steps to curb their use of power.

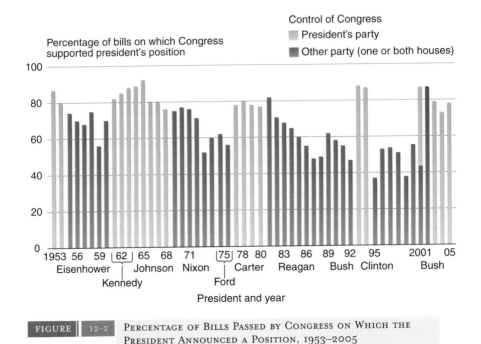

FIGURE 12-2 PERCENTAGE OF BILLS PASSED BY CONGRESS ON WHICH THE PRESIDENT ANNOUNCED A POSITION, 1953–2005

In most years, presidents have been supported by Congress on a majority of policy issues on which they have taken a stand. Presidents fare better when their party controls Congress. *Source: Congressional Quarterly Weekly Report, various dates. Used by permission.*

The ultimate sanction of Congress is its constitutional power to impeach and remove the president from office. The House of Representatives decides by majority vote whether the president should be impeached (placed on trial), and the Senate conducts the trial and then votes on the president's case, with a two-thirds vote required for removal from office. In 1868, Andrew Johnson came within one Senate vote of being removed from office for his opposition to Congress's harsh Reconstruction policies after the Civil War. In 1974, Richard Nixon's resignation halted congressional proceedings on the Watergate affair that almost certainly would have ended in his impeachment and removal from office.

The specter of impeachment arose again in 1998 when the House of Representatives by a vote of 258 to 176 authorized an investigation of President Clinton's conduct. He was accused of lying under oath about his relationship with intern Monica Lewinsky and of obstructing justice by trying to conceal the affair. The gravity of the allegations was leavened by the circumstances. The charges had grown out of an extramarital affair rather than a gross abuse of executive power and were tied to a controversial five-year, $40 million investigation by independent counsel Kenneth Starr. For its part, the public was ambivalent about the whole issue. Most Americans disapproved of Clinton's behavior but did not think it constituted "treason, bribery, or other high crimes and misdemeanors," the Constitution's basis for impeachment and removal from office. Not surprisingly, congressional Republicans and Democrats differed sharply on the impeachment issue. At all formal stages of the process—the House vote to authorize an inquiry, the House vote on the articles of impeachment, and the Senate vote on whether to remove the president—the vote was divided largely along party lines. In the end, Clinton was acquitted by the Senate, but his legacy will forever be tarnished by his impeachment by the House.

The gravity of an impeachment action makes it an unsuitable basis for curbing presidential power except in rare instances. More often, Congress has responded legislatively to what it views as unwarranted assertions of executive power. An example is the Budget Impoundment and Control Act of 1974, which prohibits a president from indefinitely withholding funds that have been appropriated by Congress. The legislation was enacted in response to President Nixon's practice of withholding funds from programs he disliked.

A similar controversy erupted in 2006 when it was revealed that President Bush had used so-called signing statements to challenge the constitutionality of more than seven hundred bills. These statements, appended to a bill when the president signs it, are meant to indicate that the president does not necessarily intend to abide by particular provisions of a law. Although Bush was not the first president to use signing statements, he had attached them to more bills than all his predecessors combined—and had done so in secrecy. Even congressional Republicans expressed concern about the practice. At Senate Judiciary Committee hearings, Senator Arlen Specter (R-Penn.), chair of the committee, argued: "There's a real issue here as to whether the president may, in effect, cherry-pick the provisions he likes, excluding the provisions he doesn't like. . . . The president has the option under the Constitution to veto or not." Not unexpectedly, Senate Democrats had harsher words for the president. Senator Russ Feingold (D-Wisc.) said: "[The executive has] assigned itself the sole responsibility for deciding which laws it will comply with, and in the process has taken upon itself the powers of all three branches of government."[32]

Congress's most significant historical effort to curb presidential power is the War Powers Act. During the Vietnam War, Presidents Johnson and Nixon repeatedly misled Congress, supplying it with intelligence estimates that painted a falsely optimistic picture of the military situation. Believing the war was being won, Congress regularly provided the money to keep it going. However, congressional support changed abruptly in 1971 with publication in the *New York Times* of classified documents (the so-called Pentagon Papers) that revealed the Vietnam situation to be much worse than portrayed by Johnson and Nixon.

To prevent future presidential wars, Congress in 1973 passed the War Powers Act. Nixon vetoed the measure, but Congress overrode his veto. The act does not prohibit the president from sending troops into combat, but it does require the president to notify Congress of the reason for committing combat troops within forty-eight hours of their deployment. The Act also specifies that hostilities must end within sixty days unless Congress extends the period; gives the president an additional thirty days to withdraw the troops from hostile territory, although Congress can shorten this period; and requires the president to consult with Congress whenever feasible before sending troops into a hostile situation.

Every president since Nixon has claimed that the War Powers Act infringes on his constitutional power as commander in chief, and each has refused to accept it fully. Nevertheless, the Act is a potentially significant constraint on the president's war-making powers.

Thus, the effect of executive efforts to circumvent congressional authority has heightened congressional opposition. Even if presidents gain in the short run by acting on their own, they undermine their capacity to lead in the long run if they fail to keep in mind that Congress is a coequal branch of the American governing system.

Public Support

Every recent president has had the public's confidence at the start of his term of office. When asked in polls whether they "approve or disapprove of how the president is doing his job," a majority of Americans have expressed approval during the first months of the president's term. Sooner or later, however, all **presidential approval ratings** have slipped below this high point, and several recent presidents have left office with a rating below 50 percent (see Table 12–3).

Public support affects a president's ability to achieve policy goals. Presidential power rests in part on a claim to national leadership, and the legitimacy of that claim is roughly proportional to the president's public support. With public backing, the president's leadership cannot easily be dismissed by other Washington officials. If the president's public support sinks, officials are less inclined to accept presidential leadership.

| TABLE | 12-3 | PERCENTAGE OF PUBLIC EXPRESSING APPROVAL OF PRESIDENT'S PERFORMANCE |

Presidential approval ratings generally are higher at the beginning of the term than at the end.

President	Years in Office	Average During Presidency	First-Year Average	Final-Year Average
Harry Truman	1945–52	41%	63%	35%
Dwight Eisenhower	1953–60	64	74	62
John Kennedy	1961–63	70	76	62
Lyndon Johnson	1963–68	55	78	40
Richard Nixon	1969–74	49	63	24
Gerald Ford	1974–76	46	75	48
Jimmy Carter	1977–80	47	68	46
Ronald Reagan	1981–88	53	58	57
George H. W. Bush	1989–92	61	65	40
Bill Clinton	1993–2000	57	50	60
George W. Bush	2001–	—	68	—

Source: Averages compiled from Gallup polls.

Congress's response to George W. Bush's leadership illustrates the pattern. In the early years of his presidency, Bush got from Congress nearly everything he asked for—a reason why five years elapsed before he cast his first veto. As his popularity declined, however, congressional inaction on his major proposals became almost the rule. Among the casualties were major components of Bush's social security, energy, and immigration reform proposals.

Events and Issues The public's support for the president is affected by national and international conditions. Threats from abroad tend to produce a patriotic "rally 'round the flag" reaction that initially creates widespread support for the president. Every foreign policy crisis in the past four decades has followed this pattern. Americans were deeply divided in 2003 over the wisdom of war with Iraq, but when the fighting began, President Bush's approval rating immediately increased.

Ongoing crises, however, can erode a president's support if they are not resolved successfully. George W. Bush's approval rating rose above 70 percent with the attack on Iraq in 2003 but then fell steadily as months passed and U.S. casualties mounted. By 2006, his approval rating was less than 40 percent and his party suffered a huge defeat in that year's midterm election.

Historically, the economy has had the greatest influence on presidents' public support. Economic downswings reduce the public's confidence in the president.[33] Ford, Carter, and the first President Bush lost their reelection bids when their popularity plummeted after the economy swooned. In contrast, Clinton's popularity rose in 1995 and 1996 as the economy strengthened, contributing to his reelection in 1996. In 2004, an improving economy contributed to George W. Bush's reelection. Of course, the irony is that presidents do not actually have that much control over the economy. If they did, the economy would always be strong.

The Televised Presidency A major advantage that presidents enjoy in their efforts to nurture public support is their access to the media, particularly television. Only the president can expect the television networks to provide free air time on occasion, and in terms of the amount of news coverage, the president and top presidential advisers receive half again as much coverage as all members of Congress combined.

Political scientist Samuel Kernell calls it "going public" when the president bypasses inside bargaining with Congress and promotes "himself and his policies by appealing to the American public for support."[34] Such appeals are at least as old as Theodore Roosevelt's use of the presidency as a "bully pulpit," but they have increased substantially in recent years. As the president's role has moved from administrative leader to policy advocate and agenda setter, public support has become increasingly important to presidential success. Television has made it easier for presidents to go public with their programs. Ronald Reagan was called "the Great Communicator" in part because of his ability to use television to generate public support for his initiatives.

On the other hand, the press is adept at putting its own spin on events and tends to play up adverse developments. For example, although presidents get some credit in the press when the economy is doing well, they get mounds of negative coverage when the economy is doing poorly. Scandal is the biggest threat to a president's ability to influence news coverage. When the whiff of a possible scandal is detected, a media "feeding frenzy" ensues, and power shifts from the White House to the press and the president's political opponents. In 2004, for example, informed sources claimed that the Bush administration had targeted Iraq long before it ordered an invasion of that country. Secretary of Defense Donald

White House press secretary Tony Snow briefs reporters in the cramped space of the White House briefing room. Effective communication is an essential part of the modern presidency.

Rumsfeld reportedly wanted to bomb Iraq immediately after the terrorist attacks of September 11, 2001, even though there was no evidence linking Iraq to the attacks. Rumsfeld was quoted by a White House insider as saying "There aren't any good targets in Afghanistan and there are lots of good targets in Iraq." The allegations were front-page news for days on end and placed the Bush administration on the defensive.

The Illusion of Presidential Government   Presidents have no choice but to try to counter negative press coverage with their own version of events. President George W. Bush did exactly that by scheduling blocks of interviews with journalists from local and regional news outlets to say that the real story of the Iraq effort—the success story of reopened schools, restored oil production, and renewed hope for the Iraqi people—was not being told by the Washington press corps. Bush accused national reporters of focusing only on the death and destruction in Iraq.

Such efforts can carry a president only so far, however. No president can fully control his communicated image, and national conditions ultimately have the largest impact on a president's public support. No amount of public relations can disguise adverse developments at home or abroad. Indeed, presidents run a risk by building up their images through public relations. By thrusting themselves into the limelight, presidents contribute to the public's belief that the president is in charge of the national government, a perception political scientist Hugh Heclo calls "the illusion of presidential government."[35] If they are as powerful as they project themselves to be, they will be held responsible for policy failures as well as policy successes.

Because the public expects so much from its presidents, they get too much credit when things go well and too much blame when things go badly. Therein lies an irony of the presidential office. More than from any constitutional grant, more than from any statute, and more than from any crisis, presidential power derives from the president's position as the sole official who can claim to represent the entire American public. Yet because presidential power rests on a popular base, it erodes when public support declines. The irony is that the presidential office typically grows weaker as problems mount. Just when the country most needs effective leadership, strong leadership often is hardest to achieve.[36]

SUMMARY

The presidency has become a much stronger office than the Framers envisioned. The Constitution grants the president substantial military, diplomatic, legislative, and executive powers, and in each case the president's authority has increased measurably over the nation's history. Underlying this change is the president's position as the one leader chosen by the whole nation and as the sole head of the executive branch. These features of the office have enabled presidents to claim broad authority in response to the increased demands placed on the federal government by changing world and national conditions.

During the course of American history, the presidential selection process has been altered in ways intended to make it more responsive to the preferences of ordinary people. Today, the electorate has a vote not only in the general election, but also in the selection of party nominees. To gain nomination, a presidential hopeful must gain the support of the electorate in state primaries and open caucuses. Once nominated, the candidates receive federal funds for their general election campaigns, which today are based on televised appeals.

Although the campaign tends to personalize the presidency, the responsibilities of the modern presidency far exceed any president's personal capacities. To meet their obligations, presidents have surrounded themselves with large staffs of advisers, policy experts, and managers. These staff members enable the president to extend control over the executive branch while at the same time providing the information necessary for policymaking. All recent presidents have discovered, however, that their control of staff resources is incomplete and that some things others do on their behalf can work against what they are trying to accomplish.

As sole chief executive and the nation's top elected leader, presidents can always expect that their policy and leadership efforts will receive attention. However, other institutions, particularly Congress, have the authority to make presidential leadership effective. No president has come close to winning approval of all the programs he has placed before Congress, and the presidents' records of success have varied considerably. The factors in a president's success include whether national conditions that require strong leadership from the White House are present and whether the president's party has a majority in Congress.

To hold onto an effective leadership position, the president depends on the backing of the American people. Recent presidents have made extensive use of the media to build support for their programs, yet they have had difficulty maintaining that support throughout their terms of office. A major reason is that the public expects far more from its presidents than they can deliver.

exec

KEY TERMS

cabinet (*p. 430*)
honeymoon period (*p. 435*)
momentum (in campaigns) (*p. 420*)
open party caucuses (*p. 419*)

presidential approval ratings (*p. 442*)
stewardship theory (*p. 412*)
unit rule (*p. 424*)
Whig theory (*p. 412*)

SUGGESTED READINGS

Cohen, Jeffrey, and David Nice. *The Presidency.* New York: McGraw-Hill, 2002. A comprehensive overview of the presidency.

Eisinger, Robert M. *The Evolution of Presidential Polling.* New York: Cambridge University Press, 2003. A close look at the use of opinion polls by the White House and how their use has changed since Franklin Roosevelt.

Entman, Robert M. *Projections of Power: Framing News, Public Opinion, and U.S. Foreign Policy.* Chicago: University of Chicago Press, 2003. An assessment of the president's power to set the news agenda.

Jackson, John S., and William J. Crotty. *The Politics of Presidential Selection.* New York: Longman, 2001. A careful look at the presidential election process by two of its best analysts.

Milkis, Sidney, and Michael Nelson. *The American Presidency: Origins and Development, 1776–2002*, 4th ed. Washington, D.C.: Congressional Quarterly Press, 2003. A thoughtful assessment of the factors and conditions that have molded the presidential office.

Neustadt, Richard E. *Presidential Power and the Modern Presidents: The Politics of Leadership from Roosevelt to Reagan*. New York: Free Press, 1990. The classic analysis of the limitations on presidential power.

Pika, Joseph A., and John Anthony Maltese. *The Politics of the Presidency*, 6th ed. Washington, D.C.: Congressional Quarterly Press, 2004. An insightful look at the leadership skills demanded of presidents.

Schlesinger, Arthur M., Jr. *The Imperial Presidency*. Boston: Mariner Books, 2004. An assessment of the modern presidency by a Pulitzer Prize–winning historian.

LIST OF WEBSITES

http://www.ibiblio.org/lia/president A site with general information on specific presidents and links to the presidential libraries.

http://www.ipl.org/ref/POTUS Profiles of the nation's presidents, their cabinet officers, and key events during their time in office.

http://www.usa.gov/Agencies/Federal/Executive.shtml Information on the presidency and the Executive Office of the President as well as links to key executive agencies and organizations.

http://www.whitehouse.gov/ The White House's home page; includes an e-mail guest book and information on the president, the vice president, and current White House activities.

POLITICS IN THEORY AND PRACTICE

Thinking: Why is presidential power "conditional"—that is, why is it affected so substantially by circumstance, the makeup of Congress, and popular support? (The separation of powers should be part of your answer.)

Participating: Consider writing a letter or sending an e-mail to the president or a top presidential appointee that expresses your opinion on an issue that is currently the object of executive action. You can inform yourself about the Administration's policy or stance on the issue through the website of the White House (www.whitehouse.gov) or of the agency in question (for example, the State Department's site is www.state.gov).

ADDITIONAL RESOURCES

For quizzes, interactive simulations, games, graphics, and other study tools, visit the book's Online Learning Center at **www.mhhe.com/pattersonwtp7**.

Presidential Power

By Richard Cheney

When George W. Bush took office in 2001, his vice president, Dick Cheney, helped persuade him to take a forceful view of the presidency. Cheney believed that Congress had encroached on the powers of the president, particularly in the realm of national security but also in the areas of executive secrecy and administrative discretion. Cheney's view prevailed. The White House claimed broad authority in its pursuit of the war on terrorism and the handling of enemy combatants, on several occasions refusing to provide Congress with executive memos dealing with policy decisions. President Bush also made extensive use of "signing statements," which indicated points at which he thought legislation passed by Congress infringed on executive authority. Vice President Cheney's fullest public statement on the question of presidential power came during a December 2005 press conference that he held on Air Force Two (the vice president's plane) while traveling with reporters to the Middle East. Following is a transcript of that press conference.

REPORTER: Sir, if I could ask you to step back for a moment, there has been a lot written and talked about recently about executive power, the power of the presidency. You have a really interesting perspective on this having served in the Ford White House, which arguably was the point at which presidential power had reached its absolute nadir. And I'm curious how that experience has shaped your view of presidential powers. . . .

CHENEY: Yes, I do have the view that over the years there had been an erosion of presidential power and authority that [is] reflected in a number of developments [including] the War Powers Act, which many people believe is unconstitutional. It's never really been tested. We sort of have an understanding when we commit force that the U.S., the government, the executive branch will notify the Congress, but making it clear we're not doing it [in response to] the War Powers Act, in fact. It has never been tested. It will be tested at some point. I am one of those who believe that was an infringement upon the authority of the President. The [Impoundment] and Control Act, back in the '70s, passed during the Ford administration that limited the President's authority to impound funds, a series of things [like] Watergate—a lot of the things around Watergate and Vietnam, both, in the '70s—served to erode the authority, I think, the President needs to be effective especially in a national security area. If you want reference to an obscure text, go look at the minority views that were filed with the Iran-Contra Committee; the Iran Contra Report in about 1987. Nobody has ever read them, but part of the argument in Iran Contra was whether or not the President had the authority to do what was done in the Reagan years. And those of us in the minority wrote minority views, but they were actually authored by a guy working for me, for my staff, that I think are very good in laying out a robust view of the President's prerogatives with respect to the conduct of especially foreign policy and national security matters. It will give you a much broader perspective. I served in the Congress for 10 years. I've got enormous regard for the other body, [Article] I of the Constitution, but I do believe that, especially in the day and age we live in, the nature of the threats we face, it was true during the Cold War, as well as I think what is true now, the President of the United States needs to have his constitutional powers unimpaired, if you will, in terms of the conduct of national security policy. That's my personal view.

In other areas, in the perspective looking at issues that come up during this administration, one of those was the Energy Task Force. My belief is that the President is entitled to and needs to have unfiltered advice in formulating policy, that he ought to be able to seek the opinion of anybody he wants to, and that he should not have to reveal, for example, to a member of Congress who he talked to that morning. That issue was litigated all the way up to the Supreme Court, and we won—ultimately referred back to the D.C. Circuit where we got a unanimous opinion supporting our position. So when you're asking about my view of the presidency, yes, I believe in a strong, robust executive authority. And I think the world we live in demands it. And to some extent, that we have an obligation as an administration to pass on the offices we hold to our successors in as good a shape as we found them.

REPORTER: Do you think the pendulum is in the right place now?

CHENEY: I do think it's swung back. If you look at it from a historical standpoint, the presidency in the late 1800s was a relatively weak organization, a relatively weak institution. I describe Teddy Roosevelt as a strong President—to some extent, maybe Woodrow Wilson. F.D.R. really established a sense of the modern presidency during the Depression and World War II. And of course, World War II changed circumstances so that instead of demobilizing at the end of the war, we maintained robust military forces afterwards because of the Cold War. Circumstances change. I think you're right, probably the end of the next administration, you had the nadir of the modern presidency in terms of authority and legitimacy, then a number of limitations that were imposed in the aftermath of Vietnam and Watergate. But I do think that to some extent now, we've been able to restore the legitimate authority of the presidency.

REPORTER: Do you think the NSA thing [secret wiretaps of conversations that were not authorized by a judge] will reignite that debate then? . . .

CHENEY: It's important that you be clear that we're talking about individuals who are al Qaeda or have an association with al Qaeda, who we have reason to believe are part of that terrorist network. There are two requirements, and that's one of them. It's not just random conversations. If you're calling Aunt Sadie in Paris, we're probably not really interested. . . .

REPORTER: But aren't you concerned that because of that, this place where you are right now, where you feel comfortable in terms of presidential power could swing the other way, that there could be a backlash, and then Congress would impose even more restrictions on the executive branch?

CHENEY: No, I think when the American people look at this, they will understand and appreciate what we're doing and why we're doing it. It's not an accident that we haven't been hit in four years. There's a temptation for people to sit around and say, well, gee, that was just a one-off affair, they didn't really mean it. Bottom line is we've been very active and very aggressive defending the nation and using the tools at our disposal to do that. That ranges from everything to going into Afghanistan and closing down the terrorist camps, rounding up al Qaeda wherever we can find them in the world, to an active robust intelligence program, putting out rewards, the capture of bad guys, and the Patriot Act. . . .

Either we're serious about fighting the war on terror or we're not. Either we believe that there are individuals out there doing everything they can to try to launch more attacks, to try to get ever deadlier weapons to use against, or we don't. The President and I believe very deeply that there's a hell of a threat, that it's there for anybody who wants to look at it. And that our obligation and responsibility given our job is to do everything in our power to defeat the terrorists. And that's exactly what we're doing.

But if there's anything improper or inappropriate in that, my guess is that the vast majority of the American people support that, support what we're doing. They believe we ought to be doing it, and so if there's a backlash pending, I think the backlash is going to be against those who are suggesting somehow that we shouldn't take these steps in order to protect the country.

What's Your Opinion?

Do you share Vice President Cheney's view of presidential power? Should the president have nearly unlimited discretion, relative to Congress and the courts, to deal with threats to national security?

CHAPTER 13

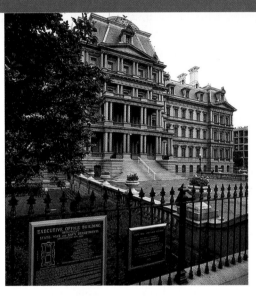

THE FEDERAL BUREAUCRACY:
ADMINISTERING THE GOVERNMENT

❝ [No] industrial society could manage the daily operations of its public affairs
without bureaucratic organizations in which officials play a major policymaking
role. **❞** *administrative*
laws

NORMAN THOMAS[1]

Early on the morning of September 7, 1993, a truck pulled up to the
south lawn of the White House and unloaded pallets stacked with federal
regulations. The display was the backdrop for a presidential speech
announcing the completion of the National Performance Review or, as it
is commonly called, NPR. The federal regulations piled atop the pallets
symbolized bureaucratic red tape, and NPR was the Clinton administration's initiative to make government more responsive.

The origins of the National Performance Review were plain enough.
For years, the federal bureaucracy had been derided as being too big, too
expensive, and too intrusive. These charges gained strength as federal
budget deficits increased and the public became increasingly dissatisfied
with the performance of the government in Washington. Reform attempts

in the 1970s and 1980s had not stemmed the tide of federal deficits or markedly improved the bureaucracy's performance. Clinton campaigned on the issue of "reinventing government" and acted swiftly on the promise. Vice President–elect Al Gore was placed in charge of the National Performance Review. He assembled more than two hundred career bureaucrats, who knew firsthand how the bureaucracy operated, and organized them into "reinventing teams." NPR's report included 384 specific recommendations grouped into four broad imperatives: reducing red tape, putting customers first, empowering administrators, and cutting government back to basic services.[2]

NPR was the most recent in a lengthy list of major twentieth-century efforts to remake the federal bureaucracy. NPR was different in its particulars, but its claim to improve administration while saving money was consistent with the claims of earlier reform panels, including the Brownlow, Hoover, and Volcker commissions.[3] Like those efforts, NPR addressed an enduring issue of American politics: the bureaucracy's efficiency, responsiveness, and accountability.

Modern government would be impossible without a large bureaucracy. It is the government's enormous administrative capacity that makes it possible for the United States to have ambitious programs such as space exploration, social security, interstate highways, and universal postal service. Yet the bureaucracy also poses special problems. Even those who work in federal agencies agree that the bureaucracy can be unresponsive, wasteful, and self-serving.

This chapter examines both the need for bureaucracy and the problems associated with it. The chapter describes the bureaucracy's responsibilities, organizational structure, and management practices and explains the "politics" of the bureaucracy. The three constitutional branches of government impose a degree of accountability on the bureaucracy, but its sheer size and fragmented nature confound efforts to control it completely. The main points discussed in this chapter are these:

- *Bureaucracy is an inevitable consequence of complexity and scale.* Modern government could not function without a large bureaucracy. Through authority, specialization, and rules, bureaucracy provides a means of managing thousands of tasks and employees.
- *The bureaucracy is expected simultaneously to respond to the direction of partisan officials and to administer programs fairly and competently.* These conflicting demands are addressed through a combination of personnel management systems—the patronage, merit, and executive leadership systems.

As one of thousands of services provided by the federal bureaucracy, the National Hurricane Service monitors hurricane activity and provides early warning to affected coastal areas.

★ *Bureaucrats naturally take an "agency point of view." They seek to pro-mote their agency's programs and power.* They do this through their expert knowledge, support from clientele groups, and backing by Congress or the president.

★ *Although agencies are subject to oversight by the president, Congress, and the judiciary, bureaucrats are able to exercise power in their own right.*

FEDERAL ADMINISTRATION: FORM, PERSONNEL, AND ACTIVITIES

For many Americans, the word *bureaucracy* brings to mind waste, mindless rules, and rigidity. This image is not unfounded, but it is one-sided. Bureaucracy is also an efficient and effective method of organization. Although Americans tend to equate bureaucracy with the federal government, bureaucracy is found wherever there is a need to manage large numbers of people and tasks. All large-scale, task-oriented organizations—public and private—are bureaucratic in form.[4] General Motors is a bureaucracy, as is every university. The state governments are also every bit as "bureaucratic" as the federal government (see "States in the Nation").

In formal terms, **bureaucracy** is a system of organization and control that is based on three principles: hierarchical authority, job specialization, and formalized rules. **Hierarchical authority** refers to a chain of command whereby the officials and units at the top of a bureaucracy have authority

The Size of State Bureaucracies

Although the federal bureaucracy is often criticized as being "too big," it is actually smaller on a per capita basis than even the smallest state bureaucracy. There is 0.91 federal employee for every 100 Americans. Illinois, with 1.04 state employees for every 100 residents, has the smallest state bureaucracy on a per capita basis. Hawaii has the largest—4.48 state employees per 100 residents.

Q: What do the states with larger per capita bureaucracies have in common?

A: In general, the least populous states, especially those that are larger geographically, have larger bureaucracies on a per capita basis. This pattern reflects the fact that a state, whatever its population, has basic functions (such as highway maintenance and policing) that it must perform.

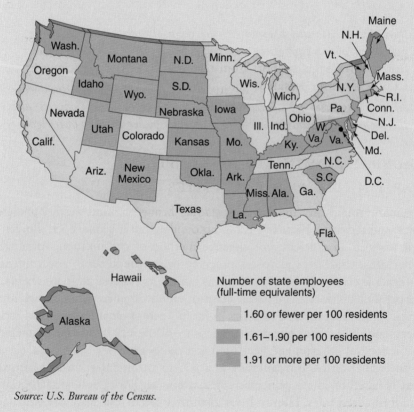

Number of state employees
(full-time equivalents)

▢ 1.60 or fewer per 100 residents

▢ 1.61–1.90 per 100 residents

▢ 1.91 or more per 100 residents

Source: U.S. Bureau of the Census.

over those in the middle, who in turn control those at the bottom. In a system of **job specialization,** the responsibilities of each job position are explicitly defined, and there is a precise division of labor within the organization. **Formalized rules** are the standardized procedures and established regulations by which a bureaucracy conducts its operations.

These features are the reason why bureaucracy, as a form of organization, is the most efficient means of getting people to work together on tasks of great magnitude. Hierarchy speeds action by reducing conflict over the power to make decisions: those higher in the organization have authority over those below them. Specialization yields efficiency because each individual is required to concentrate on a particular job: workers acquire specialized skills and knowledge. Formalized rules enable workers to make quick and consistent judgments because decisions are based on preestablished rules rather than on a case-by-case basis.

These organizational characteristics are also the source of bureaucracy's pathologies. Administrators perform not as whole persons but as parts of an organizational entity. Their behavior is governed by position, specialty, and rule. At its worst, bureaucracy grinds on, heedless of the interests of its members or their clients. Fixed rules become an end unto themselves, as anyone who has applied for a driver's license or a student loan knows all too well.

If bureaucracy is an indispensable condition of large-scale organization, gross bureaucratic inefficiency and unresponsiveness are not. At least that is the assumption underlying efforts to strengthen the administration of government, a topic examined later in this chapter.

The Federal Bureaucracy in Americans' Daily Lives

The U.S. federal bureaucracy has roughly 2.5 million employees, who have the responsibility for administering thousands of programs. The president and Congress get far more attention in the news, but it is the bureaucracy that has the more immediate impact on Americans' daily lives. The federal bureaucracy performs a wide range of functions; for example, it delivers the daily mail, maintains the national forests, administers social security, enforces environmental protection laws, develops the country's defense systems, provides foodstuffs for school lunch programs, and regulates the stock markets.

Types of Administrative Organizations

The U.S. federal bureaucracy is organized along policy lines. One agency handles veterans' affairs, another specializes in education, a third is responsible for agriculture, and so on. No two units are exactly alike.

secretary *organizes*

cabinet *each one*

new *agencies* *start*

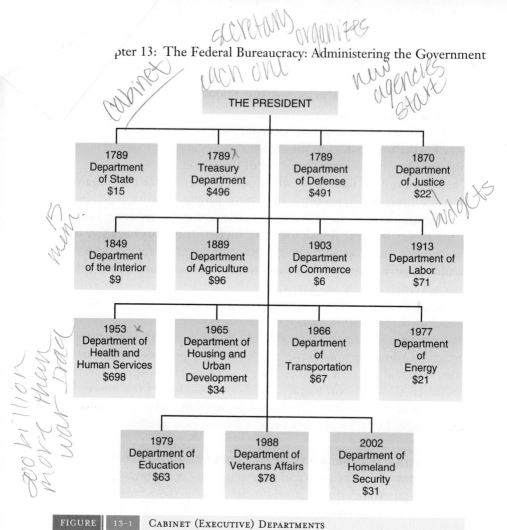

15 mem.

budgets

200 billion more than war Dad

FIGURE 13-1 CABINET (EXECUTIVE) DEPARTMENTS

Each executive department is responsible for a general policy area and is headed by a secretary or, in the case of Justice, the attorney general, who serves as a member of the president's cabinet. Shown are each department's year of origin (above the title) and annual budget in billions of dollars (below the title). (The Office of the Attorney General was created in 1789 and became the Department of Justice in 1870.)
Source: White House Office of Management and Budget, FY2007.

Nevertheless, most of them take one of five general forms: cabinet department, independent agency, regulatory agency, government corporation, or presidential commission.

Cabinet Departments The major administrative units are the fifteen **cabinet (or executive) departments** (see Figure 13–1). Except for the Department of Justice, which is led by the attorney general, the head of each department is its secretary (for example, the secretary of defense), who also serves as a member of the president's cabinet.

Cabinet departments vary greatly in their visibility, size, and importance. The Department of State, one of the oldest and most prestigious departments, is also one of the smallest, with approximately twenty-five thousand employees. The Department of Defense has the largest work force, with more than six hundred thousand civilian employees (apart from the more than 1.4 million uniformed active service members). The Department of Health and Human Services has the largest budget; its activities account for more than a fourth of all federal spending, much of it in the form of social security benefits. The Department of Homeland Security is the newest department, dating from 2002.

Each cabinet department has responsibility for a general policy area, such as defense or law enforcement. This responsibility is carried out by semiautonomous operating units that typically carry the label "bureau," "agency," "division," or "service." The Department of Justice, for example, has thirteen such operating units, including the Federal Bureau of Investigation (FBI), the Civil Rights Division, the Tax Division, and the Drug Enforcement Administration (DEA). In short, the Department of Justice is itself a large bureaucracy.

Independent Agencies **Independent agencies** resemble the cabinet departments, but most of them have a narrower area of responsibility. They include organizations such as the Central Intelligence Agency (CIA) and the National Aeronautics and Space Administration (NASA). The heads of these agencies are appointed by and report to the president but are not members of the cabinet. In general, the independent agencies exist apart from cabinet departments because their placement within a department would pose symbolic or practical policy problems. NASA, for example, could conceivably be located in the Department of Defense, but such positioning would suggest that the space program exists solely for military purposes and not also for civilian purposes such as space exploration and satellite communication.

Regulatory Agencies **Regulatory agencies** are created when Congress recognizes the importance of close and continuous regulation of an economic activity. Because such regulation requires more time and expertise than Congress can provide, the responsibility is delegated to a regulatory agency. The Securities and Exchange Commission (SEC), which oversees the stock and bond markets, is a regulatory agency. So is the Environmental Protection Agency (EPA), which monitors and prevents industrial

TABLE 13-1	SELECTED U.S. REGULATORY AGENCIES, INDEPENDENT AGENCIES, GOVERNMENT CORPORATIONS, AND PRESIDENTIAL COMMISSIONS
Central Intelligence Agency	National Foundation on the Arts and the Humanities
Commission on Civil Rights	
Consumer Product Safety Commission	National Labor Relations Board
Environmental Protection Agency	National Railroad Passenger Corporation (Amtrak)
Equal Employment Opportunity Commission	National Science Foundation
Export-Import Bank of the United States	National Transportation Safety Board
Farm Credit Administration	Nuclear Regulatory Commission
Federal Communications Commission	Occupational Safety and Health Review Commission
Federal Deposit Insurance Corporation	Office of Personnel Management
	Peace Corps
Federal Election Commission	Securities and Exchange Commission
Federal Maritime Commission	
Federal Reserve System, Board of Governors	Selective Service System
	Small Business Administration
Federal Trade Commission	U.S. Arms Control and Disarmament Agency
General Services Administration	
National Aeronautics and Space Administration	U.S. Information Agency
	U.S. International Trade Commission
National Archives and Records Administration	U.S. Postal Service

Source: *The U.S. Government Manual.*

pollution. Table 13–1 lists some of the regulatory agencies and other non-cabinet units of the federal bureaucracy.

Beyond their executive functions, regulatory agencies have legislative and judicial functions. They issue regulations and judge whether individuals or organizations have complied with them. The SEC, for example, can impose fines and other penalties on business firms that violate regulations pertaining to the trading of stocks and bonds.

Some regulatory agencies, particularly the older ones (such as the SEC), are "independent" by virtue of their relative freedom from on-going political control. They are headed by a commission of several members who are appointed by the president and confirmed by Congress but who are not subject to removal by the president. Commissioners serve for a fixed number of years, a legal stipulation intended to free them and thereby their agencies from political interference. The newer regulatory agencies (such as the EPA) lack such autonomy. They are headed by a presidential appointee who can be removed at the president's discretion.

Government Corporations   **Government corporations** are similar to private corporations in that they charge clients for their services and are governed by a board of directors. However, government corporations receive federal funding to help defray operating expenses, and their directors are appointed by the president with Senate approval. The largest government corporation is the U.S. Postal Service, with roughly seven hundred thousand employees. Other government corporations include the Federal Deposit Insurance Corporation (FDIC), which insures savings accounts against bank failures, and the National Railroad Passenger Corporation (Amtrak), which provides passenger rail service.

Presidential Commissions   **Presidential commissions** provide advice to the president. Some of them are permanent bodies; examples are the Commission on Civil Rights and the Commission on Fine Arts. Other presidential commissions are temporary and disband after making recommendations on specific issues. An example is the President's Commission to Strengthen Social Security, which was established by President Bush in 2001 to study possible ways of reforming social security.

Federal Employment

The roughly 2.5 million civilian employees of the federal government include professionals who bring their expertise to the problems involved in governing a large and complex society, service workers who perform such tasks as the typing of correspondence and the delivery of mail, and middle and top managers who supervise the work of the various federal agencies.

More than 90 percent of federal employees are hired by merit criteria, which include educational attainment (in the case, for example, of lawyers and engineers), employment experience, and performance on competitive tests (such as the civil service and foreign service examinations). The merit system is intended to protect the public from inept or biased administrative practices that could result if partisanship were the employment criterion.

Federal employees are underpaid in comparison with their counterparts in the private sector. The large majority of federal employees have a GS (Graded Service) job ranking. The rankings range from GS-1 (the lowest rank) to GS-18 (the highest). College graduates who enter the federal service usually start at the GS-5 level, which provides a salary of about $30,000 for a beginning employee. With a master's degree, employees begin at level GS-9 with a salary of $45,000. Federal employees' salaries increase with rank and length of service. Public employees receive substantial fringe benefits, including full health insurance, secure retirement plans, and generous vacation time and sick leave.

Public service has its drawbacks. Federal employees can form labor unions, but their unions by law have limited authority: the government maintains full control of job assignments, compensation, and promotion. Moreover, the Taft-Hartley Act of 1947 prohibits strikes by federal employees and permits the firing of striking workers. When federal air traffic controllers went on strike anyway in 1981, they were fired by President Reagan. There are also limits on the partisan activities of civil servants. The Hatch Act of 1939 prohibited them from holding key positions in election campaigns. In 1993, Congress relaxed this prohibition but retained it for certain high-ranking career bureaucrats.

Government employment is overseen by two independent agencies. The Merit Service Protection Board handles appeals of career civil servants who have been fired or who face other disciplinary action. The Office of Personnel Management supervises the hiring and classification of federal employees.

The Federal Bureaucracy's Policy Responsibilities

The Constitution mentions executive departments but does not grant them any powers. Their authority derives from grants of power to the three constitutional branches: Congress, the president, and the courts. Nevertheless, the bureaucracy is far more than an administrative extension of the three branches. It never merely follows orders.

The primary function of administrative agencies is **policy implementation,** that is, carrying out decisions made by Congress, the president, and the courts. Although implementation is sometimes described as "mere administration," it is a creative activity. In the course of their work, administrators come up with policy ideas that are then brought to the attention of the president or members of Congress. Administrative agencies also make policy in the process of determining how to implement congressional, presidential, and judicial decisions. The Telecommunications Act of 1996, for example, had as its stated goal "to promote competition and reduce regulation in order to secure lower prices and higher quality services for American telecommunication consumers and encourage the rapid deployment of new telecommunications technologies." Although the act

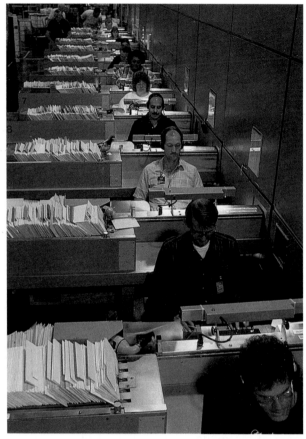

The U.S. Postal Service is one of the most efficient in the world, delivering hundreds of millions of pieces of mail each day, inexpensively and without undue delay. Yet, like many other government agencies, it is often criticized for its inefficiency and ineptness.

included specific provisions, its implementation was determined in large part by the Federal Communications Commission (FCC). The FCC decided, for example, that regional telephone companies (the Bell companies) had to open their networks to AT&T and other competitors at wholesale rates far below what they were charging their retail customers. The purpose was to enable AT&T and other carriers to compete with the Bell companies for local phone customers; in other words, the FCC was responding to its legislative mandate "to promote competition." But it was the FCC, not Congress, that determined the wholesale rates and many of the interconnection rules. This development of policy—through *rulemaking* that determines how laws will work in practice—is perhaps the chief way administrative agencies exercise real power.[5]

Agencies also are charged with the delivery of services—carrying the mail, processing welfare applications, approving government loans, and the like. Such activities are governed by rules, and in most instances the rules determine what gets done. But some services allow agency employees enough discretion that laws end up being applied arbitrarily, a situation that Michael Lipsky describes as "street-level bureaucracy."[6] For example, FBI agents more diligently pursue organized crime than they do white-collar crime, even though the laws do not say that white-collar crime should somehow be pursued less aggressively.

In sum, administrators exercise discretion in carrying out their responsibilities. They initiate policy, develop it, evaluate it, apply it, and determine whether others are complying with it. The bureaucracy does not simply administer policy: it also *makes policy.*

DEVELOPMENT OF THE FEDERAL BUREAUCRACY: POLITICS AND ADMINISTRATION

Agencies are responsible for programs that serve society, yet each agency was created and is maintained in response to partisan interests. Each agency thus confronts two simultaneous but incompatible demands: that it administer programs fairly and competently and that it respond to partisan demands.

Historically, this conflict has worked itself out in ways that have made the organization of the modern bureaucracy a blend of the political and the administrative. This dual line of development is reflected in the mix of management systems that characterizes the bureaucracy today—the *patronage, merit,* and *executive leadership* systems.

Small Government and the Patronage System

The federal bureaucracy originally was small (three thousand employees in 1800, for instance). The federal government's role was confined mainly to defense and foreign affairs, currency and interstate commerce, and the delivery of the mail. The nation's first six presidents, from George Washington through John Quincy Adams, believed that only distinguished men should be entrusted with the management of the national government. Nearly all top presidential appointees were men of education and political experience, and many of them were members of socially prominent families. They often remained in their jobs year after year.

The nation's seventh president, Andrew Jackson, did not share his predecessors' admiration for the social elite. In Jackson's view, government would be more responsive to the public if it were administered by ordinary people of good sense.[7] Jackson also believed that top administrators should remain in office only for short periods to ensure a steady influx of fresh ideas. *# of ppl get their job*

Jackson's version of the **patronage system** was popular with the public, *baddy* but critics labeled it a **spoils system**—a device for placing political cronies in government office as a reward for partisan support. Although Jackson was motivated as much by a concern for responsive government as by his desire to reward loyal partisans, later presidents were often more interested in giving the spoils of victory to friends and supporters. Jackson's successors extended patronage to all levels of administration.

Growth in Government and the Merit System

Historical
Background

Because the government of the early nineteenth century was relatively small and limited in scope, it could be managed by employees who had little or no administrative training or experience. As the century advanced, however, the nature of the country changed rapidly, and the bureaucracy changed along with it. The Industrial Revolution brought with it massive economic shifts, which prompted groups to look to government for assistance. Farmers were among these groups, and in 1889 Congress created the Department of Agriculture. Business and labor interests also pressed their claims, and in 1903 Congress established the Department of Commerce and Labor to "promote the mutual interest" of the nation's firms and workers. (The separate interests of business and labor proved stronger than their shared concerns, and thus in 1913 Labor became a separate department.)

By 1930, federal employment had reached six hundred thousand, a sixfold increase over the level of the 1880s (see Figure 13–2). During the 1930s, as a result of President Franklin Roosevelt's New Deal, the federal work force again expanded, climbing to 1.2 million. Public demand for relief from the economic hardship and uncertainty of the Great Depression led to the formation of economic and social welfare agencies such as the Securities and Exchange Commission and the Social Security Board. An effect was to give the federal government an ongoing role in promoting Americans' economic well-being.

A large and active government requires skilled and experienced personnel. In 1883, Congress passed the Pendleton Act, which established a **merit** (or **civil service**) **system** whereby certain federal employees were hired through competitive examinations or by virtue of having special

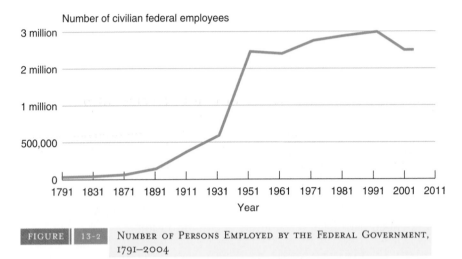

Number of civilian federal employees

FIGURE   13-2   NUMBER OF PERSONS EMPLOYED BY THE FEDERAL GOVERNMENT, 1791–2004

The federal bureaucracy grew slowly until the 1930s, when an explosive growth began in programs that required ongoing administration by the federal government. *Source: U.S. Office of Personnel Management, 2004.*

qualifications, such as an advanced degree in a particular field. The transition to a career civil service was gradual. Only 10 percent of federal positions in 1885 were filled on the basis of merit. But the pace accelerated when the Progressives (see Chapter 2) championed the merit system as a way of eliminating partisan graft and corruption in the administration of government. By 1920, as the Progressive era was concluding, more than 70 percent of federal employees were merit appointees. Since 1950, the proportion of merit employees has never dipped below 80 percent.[8]

The administrative objective of the merit system is **neutral competence.**[9] A merit-based bureaucracy is "competent" in the sense that employees are hired and retained on the basis of their skills, and it is "neutral" in the sense that employees are not partisan appointees and thus are expected to do their work on behalf of everyone, not just those who support the incumbent president.

Although the merit system contributes to the impartial and proficient administration of government programs, it has its own sources of bias and inefficiency. Career bureaucrats tend to place their agency's interests ahead of those of other agencies and typically oppose substantial efforts to trim their agency's activities. They are not partisans in the sense of Democratic or Republican politics, but they are partisans when it comes to protecting their own positions and agencies, as explained more fully later in the chapter.

Big Government and the Executive Leadership System

As problems with the merit system surfaced after the early years of the twentieth century, reformers looked to a strengthened presidency—an **executive leadership system**—as a means of coordinating the bureaucracy's activities to increase its efficiency and responsiveness.[10] The president was to provide the general leadership that would overcome agency boundaries. As Chapter 12 describes, Congress in 1939 provided the president with some of the tools needed for improved coordination of the bureaucracy. The Office of Management and Budget (OMB) was created to give the president the authority to coordinate the annual budgetary process. Agencies would be required to prepare their budget proposals under the direction of the president, who would then submit the overall budget to Congress for its approval and modification. The president was also authorized to develop the Executive Office of the President, which oversees the agencies' activities on the president's behalf.

Like the merit and patronage systems, the executive leadership system has brought problems as well as improvements to the administration of government. In practice, the executive leadership concept can give the president too much leverage over the bureaucracy and thereby weaken Congress's ability to act as a check on presidential power. A case in point is the intelligence estimates the Bush administration gave Congress while seeking a congressional resolution authorizing a military attack on Iraq. The Bush administration claimed that the CIA had evidence that Iraq's Saddam Hussein was accumulating weapons of mass destruction (WMDs) that threatened the security of the United States. Bush also used this argument in the effort to generate public and international support for the war. In his 2003 State of the Union address, President Bush said, "The dictator of Iraq is not disarming. To the contrary, he is deceiving." In a speech to the United Nations, Secretary of State Colin Powell claimed, "The facts on Iraq's behavior demonstrate . . . that Saddam Hussein and his regime are concealing their efforts to produce more weapons of mass destruction."

Yet the facts proved different. In testimony before Congress in 2004, the chief U.S. weapons inspector in Iraq, David Kay, said that his team had failed to uncover evidence of an Iraq weapons program on the scale claimed by the Bush administration. This and other revelations produced heated debate over who was to blame for the faulty claim. Did the blame rest largely with the White House, which had pressured the intelligence agencies to make the strongest case possible for war with Iraq, or did the blame rest largely with the intelligence agencies themselves? Many

TABLE 13-2	STRENGTHS AND WEAKNESSES OF MAJOR SYSTEMS FOR MANAGING THE BUREAUCRACY	
System	**Strengths**	**Weaknesses**
Patronage	Makes the bureaucracy more responsive to election outcomes by allowing the president to appoint some executive officials.	Gives executive authority to individuals chosen for their partisan loyalty rather than for their administrative or policy expertise; can favor interests that supported the president's election.
Merit	Provides for *competent* administration in that employees are hired on the basis of ability and allowed to remain on the job and thereby become proficient, and provides for *neutral* administration in that civil servants are not partisan appointees and are expected to work in an evenhanded way.	Can result in fragmented, unresponsive administration because career bureaucrats are secure in their jobs and tend to place the interests of their particular agency ahead of those of other agencies or the nation's interests as a whole.
Executive leadership	Provides for presidential leadership of the bureaucracy in order to make it more responsive and to coordinate and direct it (left alone, the bureaucracy tends toward fragmentation).	Can upset the balance between executive and legislative power and can make the president's priorities, not fairness or effective management, the basis for administrative action.

observers blamed both, concluding that the White House had overstated its case and that the intelligence agencies had been too eager to tell the White House what it wanted to hear.

Thus, the executive leadership system, like the patronage and merit systems, is not foolproof. It can make bureaucratic agencies overly dependent on the presidency, thereby distorting their activities and reducing congressional checks on executive power. Nevertheless, the executive leadership system is a necessary part of an overall strategy for the effective handling of the bureaucracy. At its best, the system imposes principles of effective management—such as eliminating wasteful duplication—on the work of government agencies.

The federal bureaucracy today embodies aspects of all three systems—patronage, merit, and executive leadership—a situation that reflects the tensions inherent in governmental administration. The bureaucracy is expected to carry out programs fairly and competently (the merit system), but it is also expected to respond to political forces (the patronage system) and to operate efficiently (the executive management system). Table 13–2 summarizes the strengths and weaknesses of each of these administrative systems.

THE BUREAUCRACY'S POWER IMPERATIVE

A common misperception is that the president, as the chief executive, has the sole claim on the bureaucracy's loyalty. In fact, each of the elected institutions has reason to claim ownership: the president as chief executive and Congress as the source of the bureaucracy's programs and funding. One presidential appointee asked a congressional committee whether it had any problem with his plans to reduce one of his agency's programs. The committee chairman replied, "No, you have the problem, because if you touch that bureau I'll cut your job out of the budget."[11]

The U.S. system of separate institutions sharing power results in a natural tendency for each institution to guard its turf. In addition, the president and members of Congress differ in their constituencies and thus in the interests to which they are most responsive. For example, although the agricultural sector is just one of many concerns of the president, it is of vital interest to senators and representatives from farm states. Finally, because the president and Congress are elected separately, the White House and one or both houses of Congress may be in the hands of opposing parties. Since 1968, this source of executive-legislative conflict has been as much the rule as the exception.

If agencies are to operate successfully in this system, they must seek support where they can find it—if not from the president, then from Congress. In other words, agencies have no choice but to play politics.[12] Any agency that sits by idly while other agencies fight for their programs is certain to lose out.

The Agency Point of View

Administrators tend to look out for their agency's interests, a perspective that is called the **agency point of view.** This perspective comes naturally to most high-ranking civil servants. More than 80 percent of all top bureaucrats reach their high-level positions by rising through the ranks of the same agency.[13] As one top administrator said when testifying before the House Appropriations Committee, "Mr. Chairman, you would not think it proper for me to be in charge of this work and not be enthusiastic about it . . . would you? I have been in it for thirty years, and I believe in it."[14] Studies confirm that bureaucrats believe in the importance of their agency's work. One study found that social welfare administrators are three times as likely as other civil servants to believe that social welfare programs should be a high policy priority.[15]

Professionalism also cements agency loyalties. High-level administrative positions have increasingly been filled by scientists, engineers, lawyers, educators, physicians, and other professionals. Most of them take jobs in an agency whose mission they support, as in the case of the aeronautical engineers who work for NASA.

Sources of Bureaucratic Power

In promoting their agency's interests, bureaucrats rely on their specialized knowledge, the support of interests that benefit from the programs they run, and the backing of the president and Congress.

The Power of Expertise Most of the policy problems that the federal government confronts do not lend themselves to simple solutions. Whether the issue is space travel or hunger in America, expert knowledge is essential to the development of effective public policy. Much of this expertise is held by bureaucrats. They spend their careers working in a particular policy area, and many of them have had scientific, technical, or other specialized training.[16]

By comparison, elected officials are generalists. To some degree, members of Congress do specialize through their committee work, but they rarely have the time or the inclination to acquire a commanding knowledge of a particular issue. The president's understanding of policy issues is even more general. Not surprisingly, the president and members of Congress rely on the bureaucracy for policy advice and guidance.

All agencies acquire some power through their careerists' expertise. No matter how simple a policy issue may appear at first, it invariably involves more complexity than meets the eye. A recognition that the United States has a trade deficit with China, for example, can be the premise for policy change, but this recognition does not begin to address basic issues such as the form the new policy might take, its probable cost and effectiveness, and its links to other issues, such as America's

HOW THE UNITED STATES COMPARES

Educational Backgrounds of Bureaucrats

To staff its bureaucracy, the U.S. government tends to hire persons with specialized educations to hold specialized jobs. This approach heightens the tendency of bureaucrats to take the agency point of view. By comparison, Great Britain tends to recruit its bureaucrats from the arts and humanities, on the assumption that general aptitude is the best qualification for detached professionalism. The continental European democracies also emphasize detached professionalism, but in the context of the supposedly impartial application of rules. As a consequence, high-ranking civil servants in Europe tend to have legal educations. The college majors of senior civil servants in the United States and other democracies reflect these tendencies.

College Major of Senior Civil Servants	Norway	Germany	Great Britain	Italy	Belgium	United States
Natural science/ engineering	8%	8%	26%	10%	20%	32%
Social science/ humanities/ business	38	18	52	37	40	50
Law	38	63	3	53	35	18
Other	16	11	19	—	5	—
	100%	100%	100%	100%	100%	100%

Adapted from The Politics of Bureaucracy, *5th ed. By B. Guy Peters. Copyright © 2001 by Routledge. Printed by permission of Thomsen Publishing Services.*

standing in Asia. Among the officials most likely to understand these issues are the career bureaucrats in the Commerce Department and the Federal Trade Commission.

The Power of Clientele Groups   Most agencies have **clientele groups,** special interests that benefit directly from an agency's programs. Clientele

The popular children's program *Sesame Street* is produced through the Corporation for Public Broadcasting, a government agency that gains leverage in budgetary deliberations from its public support. Singer Garth Brooks is shown here with two muppets during his appearance on *Sesame Street.*

groups assist agencies by placing pressure on Congress and the president to support those programs from which they benefit.[17] For example, when House Speaker Newt Gingrich threatened in 1995 to "zero out" funding for the Corporation for Public Broadcasting, audience members and groups such as the Children's Television Workshop wrote, called, faxed, and cajoled members of Congress, saying that programs like *Sesame Street* and *All Things Considered* were irreplaceable. Within a few weeks, Gingrich had retreated from his position, saying that a complete cessation of funding was not what he had in mind.

In general, agencies both assist and are assisted by the clientele groups that depend on the programs they administer.[18] Many agencies were created for the purpose of promoting particular interests in society. For example, the Department of Agriculture's career bureaucrats are dependable allies of farm interests year after year. The same cannot be said of the president, Congress as a whole, or either political party, all of whom must balance farmers' demands against those of other interests.

The Power of Friends in High Places   Although members of Congress and the president sometimes appear to be at war with the bureaucracy, they need it as much as it needs them. An agency's resources—its programs, expertise, and group support—can assist elected officials in their efforts to achieve their goals. When President George W. Bush in 2001 announced plans for a war on terrorism, he needed the help of careerists in the Central Intelligence Agency and the Department of Defense to make his efforts successful. At a time when other agencies were feeling the pinch of a tight federal budget, these agencies received substantial new funding.

Bureaucrats also seek favorable relations with members of Congress. Congressional support is vital because agencies' funding and programs are established through legislation. Agencies that offer benefits to major constituency interests are particularly likely to have close ties to Congress. In some policy areas, more or less permanent alliances—iron triangles—form among agencies, clientele groups, and congressional subcommittees. In other policy areas, temporary issue networks form among bureaucrats, lobbyists, and members of Congress. As explained in Chapters 9 and 11, these alliances are a means by which an agency can gain support from key legislators and groups.

BUREAUCRATIC ACCOUNTABILITY

Even though most Americans say that they have a favorable impression of their most recent personal experience with the bureaucracy (as, say, when a senior citizen applies for social security), they have an unfavorable impression of the bureaucracy as a whole. They see the programs of government bureaucracies as wasteful and inefficient. This view is somewhat unfair. In areas such as health care and retirement insurance, government bureaucracies are actually more efficient than private organizations. In other areas, efficiency is an inappropriate standard for government programs. The most efficient way to administer government loans to college students, for example, would be to give money to the first students who apply and then close down the program when the money runs out. However, college loan programs, like many other government programs, operate on the principles of fairness and need, which require that each application be judged on its merits.

Studies indicate that the U.S. bureaucracy compares favorably to government bureaucracies elsewhere. "Some national bureaucracies," writes Charles Goodsell, "may be roughly the same [as the U.S. bureaucracy] in quality of overall performance, but they are few in number."[19] Of course, not all U.S. agencies have strong performance records. The Immigration and Naturalization Service (INS) is one agency that has been chronically mismanaged. Yet the performance of many U.S. agencies is superior to that of their counterparts in other industrialized democracies. The U.S. postal service, for example, has an on-time and low-cost record that few postal services can match.

Nevertheless, it is easy to see why most Americans hold a relatively unfavorable opinion of the federal bureaucracy. Americans have traditionally mistrusted political power, and the bureaucracy is the symbol of "big government." It is also a convenient target for politicians who claim that "Washington bureaucrats" are wasting taxpayer money. (The irony is that the bureaucracy has no power to create programs or authorize spending; these decisions are made by Congress and the president.) It is no surprise that Americans have qualms about the federal bureaucracy and want it to be more closely supervised.

Adapting the requirements of the bureaucracy to those of democracy is challenging. Bureaucracy is the antithesis of democracy. Bureaucrats are unelected and hold office indefinitely, and they make decisions based on fixed rules rather than on debate and deliberation. This situation raises the question of **bureaucratic accountability**—the degree to which bureaucrats are held accountable for the power they exercise. Bureaucratic accountability occurs primarily through oversight by the president, Congress, and the courts.[20]

Accountability Through the Presidency

The president can only broadly influence, not directly control, the bureaucracy. "We can outlast any president" is a maxim of bureaucratic politics. Each agency has its clientele and its congressional supporters as well as statutory authority for its existence and activities. No president can unilaterally eliminate an agency or its funding and programs. Nor can the president be indifferent to the opinions of career civil servants—not without losing their support and expertise in developing and implementing presidential policy objectives.

To encourage the bureaucracy to act responsibly, the president can apply management tools that have developed out of the "executive leadership" concept discussed earlier in this chapter. These tools include reorganization, presidential appointments, and the executive budget.

Reorganization   The bureaucracy's extreme fragmentation—its hundreds of separate agencies—makes presidential coordination of its activities difficult. Agencies pursue independent and even contradictory paths, resulting in an undetermined amount of waste and duplication of effort. For example, more than one hundred governmental units are responsible for different pieces of federal education policy.

All recent presidents have tried to streamline the bureaucracy and make it more accountable.[21] Such changes seldom greatly improve things, but they can produce marginal gains.[22] For George W. Bush, the challenge came after the terrorist attacks on the World Trade Center and the Pentagon. Breakdowns in the FBI and CIA had undermined whatever chance there might have been to prevent the attacks. These agencies had neither shared nor vigorously pursued the intelligence information they had gathered. Bush concluded, and Congress agreed, that a reorganization of the FBI and CIA, as well as the creation of the Department of Homeland Security (DHS), was necessary. Nevertheless, neither the White House nor Congress was under the illusion that this reorganization would fully correct the coordination problems plaguing the agencies accountable for responding to external and internal threats to Americans' safety.

Indeed, DHS failed miserably in its first big test after the reorganization. That test came not from terrorists but from Hurricane Katrina, which slammed into the Gulf Coast in 2005, killing hundreds of Americans and displacing tens of thousands. One of DHS's agencies, the Federal Emergency Management Agency (FEMA), has responsibility for coordinating disaster response efforts, and its response by all accounts was disorganized and inadequate. At times, FEMA appeared to know less than the news media about what was happening in the Gulf area. Its communication and transportation systems broke down, resulting in long delays in providing relief assistance. FEMA's director, Michael Brown, did not even keep his boss, DHS secretary Michael Chertoff, informed of his actions, telling Congress months later that doing so would have been "a waste of time" because DHS did not have the needed resources. Brown was fired two weeks into the relief effort, and some observers felt that Chertoff's job was saved only to avoid the appearance that the entire department was in disarray.

Presidential Appointments   Although there is almost no direct confrontation with a bureaucrat that a president cannot win, the president does not have time to deal personally with every troublesome careerist or to make sure that the bureaucracy has complied with every presidential order. The president relies on political appointees in federal agencies to ensure that directives are followed.

The power of presidential appointees is greater in those agencies where wide latitude exists in the making of decisions. Although the Social Security Administration (SSA) has a huge budget and makes monthly payments to more than forty million Americans, the eligibility of recipients

Herbert Hoover
(1874–1964)

Herbert Hoover was president when the Wall Street crash of 1929 propelled the United States into the Great Depression. Convinced that the free market would correct itself and bring a recovery, Hoover stood by as Americans lost their jobs and their homes. In 1932, he was voted out of office. While Hoover is not regarded as a great president, he is perhaps the finest bureaucrat America has produced. In China during the Boxer Rebellion, he used the engineering skills he had been taught at Stanford University to build barricades that protected his work crew from marauding gangs. When World War I broke out, he was in London and was asked to head a relief effort to help ten million food-starved Belgians. Although Belgium was sandwiched between the British and German armies, Hoover's organizing skills enabled him to dispatch the food, trucks, and ships needed to get the job done. When the United States entered the war in 1917, Hoover became U.S. Food Administrator, charged with supplying food to the U.S. military and its allies without starving the American public in the process. Hoover developed a campaign—"Food Will Win the War"— that asked Americans to eat less. "Meatless Mondays" was one part of it. Domestic food consumption declined by a sixth, enabling the United States to triple its shipments abroad. After the war, Hoover headed the American Relief Organization, the main supplier of food for more than three hundred million people in nearly two dozen countries. Hoover's food packets were the origin of CARE packages.

When Warren Harding was elected president in 1920, Hoover was appointed to head the Commerce Department, which took on the task of eliminating waste and duplication in industry—for example, by standardizing the size of nuts, bolts, and other manufacturing parts. He brought statistical analysis into the department, arguing that policy decisions should be based on precise information, not guesswork. In 1927, Hoover oversaw the nation's response to a devastating Mississippi River flood. A year later, Hoover was elected to the presidency. After his White House years, Hoover stayed active in public life. Presidents Roosevelt and Truman placed him in charge of food and famine relief efforts during and after World War II. In the 1950s, at the request of President Eisenhower, he chaired the first and second Hoover Commissions, which proposed ways to improve the federal bureaucracy.

is determined by relatively fixed rules. The head of the SSA does not have the option, say, of granting a retiree an extra $100 a month because the retiree is facing financial hardship. In contrast, most regulatory agencies have broad discretion over regulatory policy, and the heads of these agencies have wide latitude in their decisions. For example, President Reagan's appointee to chair the Federal Trade Commission (FTC), James Miller III, was a strong-willed economist who shared Reagan's belief that consumer protection policy had gone too far and was adversely affecting business interests. In Miller's first year as head of the FTC, the commission dropped one-fourth of its pending cases against business firms.[23] Overall, enforcement actions declined by about 50 percent during Miller's tenure compared with the previous period.

However, as noted in Chapter 12, there are limits to what a president can accomplish through appointments. High-level presidential appointees number in the hundreds, and their turnover rate is high: the average appointee remains in the Administration for less than two years before moving on to other employment.[24] No president can keep track of all appointees, much less instruct them in detail on all intended policies. Moreover, many presidential appointees have little knowledge of the agencies they head, which makes it difficult for them to exercise control. FEMA's fired director, Michael Brown, was appointed to head the agency because of his political connections. He had little management experience and virtually no disaster relief experience before taking up his post at FEMA.

The Executive Budget   Faced with the difficulty of controlling the bureaucracy, presidents have come to rely heavily on their personal bureaucracy, the Executive Office of the President (EOP).

In terms of presidential management, the key unit within the EOP is the Office of Management and Budget (OMB). Funding, programs, and regulations are the mainstays of every agency, and the OMB has substantial influence on each of these areas. No agency can issue a major regulation without the OMB's verification that the regulation's benefits outweigh its costs, and no agency can propose legislation to Congress without the OMB's approval. However, the OMB's greatest influence over agencies derives from its budgetary role. At the start of the annual budget cycle, the OMB assigns each agency a budget limit in accord with the president's directives. The agency's tentative allocation requests are sent back to the OMB, which then conducts a final review of all requests before sending the full budget to Congress in the president's name (see Table 13–3).

TABLE 13-3 THE BUDGETARY PROCESS

Bureaucratic agencies are funded through a process that assigns significant roles to the president and Congress, as well as to the agencies themselves. The annual federal budget allocates the hundreds of billions of dollars that support federal agencies and programs. This table gives a simplified step-by-step summary of the process.

1. In the calendar year preceding enactment of the budget, the Office of Management and Budget (OMB) instructs each agency to prepare its budget request within guidelines established by the White House.

2. Agencies work out their budget proposals in line with White House guidelines and their own goals. Once completed, agency proposals are sent to the OMB for review and adjustment to fit the president's goals.

3. In January, the president submits the adjusted budget to Congress.

4. The president's budget is reviewed by the Congressional Budget Office (CBO) and is referred to the House and Senate budget and appropriations committees. The budget committees in each chamber then set expenditure ceilings in particular areas, which are voted upon by the members of Congress. Once set (usually in April), the budget ceilings establish temporary limits within which the appropriations committees must act.

5. Through subcommittee hearings, the House and Senate appropriations committees meet with agency heads and adjust the president's budgetary recommendations to fit congressional goals. Once the appropriations committees have completed their work, the proposals are submitted to the full House and Senate for a vote. Differences in the House and Senate versions are reconciled in conference committee.

6. The legislation is sent to the president for approval or veto. Before this point, the White House and Congress will have engaged in intense negotiations to resolve differences in their priorities. If the White House is satisfied with the outcome of the bargaining, the president can be expected to sign the legislation.

7. The new budget takes effect October 1, unless Congress has not completed its work by then or the president exercises the veto. If agreement has not been reached by this date, temporary funding (authorized by Congress and approved by the president) is required to keep the government in operation until a permanent budget can be enacted. If temporary funding is not provided, a shutdown of nonessential government services occurs.

In most cases, an agency's overall budget does not change much from year to year, indicating that a significant portion of the bureaucracy's activities persist regardless of who sits in the White House or Congress. It must be noted, however, that the bulk of federal spending is for programs such as social security that, although enacted in the past, enjoy the continuing support of the president, Congress, and the public.

Accountability Through Congress

Congress has powerful means of influencing the bureaucracy. All agencies depend on Congress for their existence, authority, programs, and funding.

The most substantial control that Congress exerts on the bureaucracy is through its power to authorize and fund programs. Without authorization and funding, a program simply does not exist, regardless of the priority an agency claims it deserves. Congress can also void an administrative decision through legislation that instructs the agency to follow a different course of action. However, Congress lacks the time and expertise to work out complex policies down to the last detail.[25] The government would grind to a halt if Congress tried to define fully how federal programs will be designed and run.

Congress also exerts some control through its oversight function, which involves monitoring the bureaucracy's work to ensure its compliance with legislative intent.[26] However, as noted in Chapter 11, oversight is a difficult and relatively unrewarding task, and members of Congress ordinarily place less emphasis on oversight than on their other major duties. Only when an agency has clearly stepped out of line is Congress likely to take decisive corrective action by holding hearings to ask tough questions and to warn of legislative punishment.

Because oversight is burdensome, Congress has shifted much of the responsibility to the Government Accountability Office (GAO). The GAO's primary function once was to keep track of the funds spent within the bureaucracy; it now also monitors whether policies are being implemented as Congress intended. The Congressional Budget Office (CBO) also carries out oversight studies. When the GAO or CBO uncovers a major problem with an agency's handling of a program, it notifies Congress, which can then take remedial action.

Bureaucrats generally are kept in check by an awareness that misbehavior can trigger a response from Congress. Nevertheless, oversight cannot correct mistakes or abuses that have already occurred. Recognizing this limit on oversight, Congress has devised ways to constrain the bureaucracy *before* it acts. The simplest method is to draft laws that contain very specific provisions that limit bureaucrats' options in implementing policy. Another restrictive device is the **sunset law,** which establishes a specific date when a law will expire unless it is reenacted by Congress. Advocates of sunset laws see them as a means to counter the bureaucracy's reluctance to give up programs that have outlived their usefulness. Because members of Congress usually want the programs they create to last far into the future, however, most legislation does not include a sunset provision.

Accountability Through the Courts

The judiciary's influence on agencies is less direct than that of the elected branches, but the courts too can and do act to ensure the bureaucracy's compliance with Congress's directives. Legally, the bureaucracy derives its authority from acts of Congress, and an injured party can bring suit against an agency on the grounds that it has failed to carry out a law properly. Judges can then order an agency to change its application of the law.[27]

However, the courts have tended to support administrators if their actions seem at all consistent with the laws they are administering. The Supreme Court has held that agencies can apply any reasonable interpretation of statutes unless Congress has specifically stated something to the contrary and that agencies in many instances have wide discretion in deciding whether to enforce statutes.[28] These positions reflect the need for flexibility in administration. The bureaucracy and the courts would both grind to a halt if judges regularly second-guessed bureaucrats' decisions. The judiciary promotes bureaucratic accountability primarily by encouraging administrators to act responsibly in their dealings with the public and by protecting individuals from the bureaucracy's worst abuses. In 1999, for example, a federal court approved a settlement in favor of African American farmers who demonstrated that the Department of Agriculture had systematically favored white farmers in granting federal farm loans.[29]

Accountability Within the Bureaucracy Itself

A recognition of the difficulty of ensuring adequate accountability of the bureaucracy through the presidency, Congress, and the courts has led to the development of mechanisms of accountability within the bureaucracy itself. Two measures, whistle-blowing and demographic representativeness, are particularly noteworthy.

Turning In Someone

Whistle-Blowing   Although the bureaucratic corruption that is rampant in some countries is relatively uncommon in the United States, a certain amount of waste, fraud, and abuse is inevitable in a bureaucracy as big as that of the federal government. **Whistle-blowing,** the act of reporting instances of official mismanagement, is a potentially effective internal check. To encourage whistle-blowers to come forward with their information, Congress enacted the Whistle Blower Protection Act to protect them against retaliation. Federal law also provides whistle-blowers with financial rewards in some cases.

Nevertheless, whistle-blowing is not for the faint-hearted. Many federal employees are reluctant to report instances of mismanagement because they fear retaliation. Their superiors might claim that they are malcontents or find subtle ways to punish them. Even their fellow employees are unlikely to think highly of "tattletales."

Accordingly, whistle-blowing sometimes does not occur until an employee has left an agency or quit government service entirely. A case in point is Richard Clarke, the former chief terrorist adviser in the Bush administration. In 2004, Clarke accused President Bush and other top White House officials of downplaying the terrorist threat and being preoccupied with Iraq in the period leading up to the September 11, 2001, terrorist attacks. "I believe the Bush administration in the first eight months considered terrorism an important issue, but not an urgent issue," Clarke told the 9/11 Commission, a bipartisan commission formed by Congress to

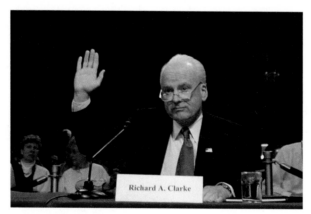

Whistle-blower Richard Clarke testifies about Bush administration antiterrorism policies in the months before the September 11, 2001, attacks on the World Trade Center and the Pentagon. In high-profile appearances before Congress and the 9/11 Commission, Clarke accused the Bush administration, in which he had served as the top terrorist adviser, of ignoring warnings of a possible large-scale terrorist attack on the United States.

investigate the attacks. The White House countered with accusations that Clarke was exaggerating his claims in order to boost sales of his recently published book. Vice President Dick Cheney claimed that Clarke "wasn't in the loop" and could not possibly have known what was going on in the Bush administration's inner circle. The White House slowed its attack on Clarke only after documents surfaced supporting some of his allegations. In a pre-9/11 memo prepared for Bush's national security advisor Condoleezza Rice, Clarke had expressed alarm at the slow pace of the Administration's antiterrorism planning, saying "Imagine a day after hundreds of Americans lay dead at home or abroad after a terrorist attack."[30]

Demographic Representativeness   Although the bureaucracy is an unrepresentative institution in the sense that its officials are not elected by the people, it can be representative in the demographic sense. If bureaucrats were a demographic microcosm of the general public, they presumably would treat the various groups and interests in society more fairly.[31]

At present, the bureaucracy is not demographically representative at its top levels (see Table 13–4). Roughly 60 percent of managerial and

TABLE 13-4 FEDERAL JOB RANKINGS (GS) OF VARIOUS DEMOGRAPHIC GROUPS						
Women and minority group members are underrepresented in the top jobs of the federal bureaucracy but their representation has been increasing						
	Women's Share		Blacks' Share		Hispanics' Share	
Grade Level*	1982	2002	1982	2002	1982	2002
GS 13–15 (highest ranks)	5%	32%	5%	10%	2%	4%
GS 9–12	20	46	10	16	4	7
GS 5–8	60	67	19	26	4	9
GS 1–4 (lowest ranks)	78	69	23	28	5	8

*In general, the higher-numbered grades are managerial and professional positions, and the lower-numbered grades are clerical and manual labor positions.
Source: Office of Personnel Management, 2006.

professional positions are held by white males. However, the employment status of women and, to a lesser extent, minorities has improved in recent decades, and top officials in the bureaucracy include a greater proportion of women and minorities than is found in Congress or the judiciary. Moreover, if all employees are considered, the federal bureaucracy comes reasonably close to being representative of the nation's population.[32]

Demographic representativeness is only a partial answer to the problem of bureaucratic accountability. A fully representative civil service would still be required to play agency politics. The careerists in, say, defense agencies and welfare agencies are similar in their demographic backgrounds, but they differ markedly in their opinions about policy. Each group believes that the goals of its agency should take priority. The inevitability of an agency point of view is the most significant of all political facts about the U.S. federal bureaucracy.

Reinventing Government?

In *Reinventing Government*, David Osborne and Ted Gaebler argue that the bureaucracy of today was created in response to earlier problems, particularly those spawned by the Industrial Revolution and a rampant spoils system. They claim that the information age requires a different kind of administrative structure, one that is leaner and more responsive. Osborne and Gaebler argue that government should set program standards but should not necessarily take on all program responsibilities. If, for example, a private firm can furnish meals to soldiers at U.S. army posts at a lower cost than the military can provide them, it should be contracted to provide the meals. Osborne and Gaebler also say that administrative judgments should be made at the lowest bureaucratic level feasible. If, for example, Department of Agriculture field agents have the required knowledge to make a certain type of decision, they should be empowered to make it rather than being required to get permission from superiors. Finally, Osborne and Gaebler argue that the bureaucracy should focus on outputs (results) rather than inputs (dollars spent). Federal loans to college students, for example, should be judged by how many students stay in college as a result of these loans rather than by how much money they receive.[33]

These ideas informed the Clinton administration's National Performance Review (described in this chapter's introduction). Even though the Bush administration decided not to continue the initiative, NPR's impact is felt through laws and administrative practices established during its tenure. An example is a law that requires agencies to systematically

🎙 ▏ MEDIA AND POLITICS

National Public Radio and the Corporation for Public Broadcasting

The Corporation for Public Broadcasting (CPB), established by Congress in 1967, is a nonprofit corporation rather than a government agency. Congress provides an annual appropriation to CPB, but most of its funds come from contributions by audience members, corporate sponsors, and foundations. Like a government agency, the CPB is directed by political appointees. Members of the CPB governing board are appointed to six-year terms by the president, subject to confirmation by the Senate. Unlike agency heads, however, the CPB governors do not direct day-to-day operations.

Public broadcasting got off to a slow start in the United States. Unlike the case in Europe, where public broadcasting networks (such as Britain's BBC) were created at the start of the radio age, the U.S. government initially handed control of broadcasting to commercial networks such as NBC and CBS. By the time Congress decided in the 1960s that public broadcasting was needed, the commercial networks were so powerful that they convinced Congress to assign it second-class status. Public broadcasting was poorly funded and was denied access to the most powerful broadcast frequencies. Most television sets in the 1960s had tuners that could not dial in the stations that aired public broadcast programs. Not surprisingly, public broadcasting faltered at the beginning and still operates in the shadow of commercial broadcasting.

Nevertheless, public broadcasting does have a success story— National Public Radio (NPR). During the past two decades, NPR's audience has quadrupled. Each week, more than 20 million Americans listen to NPR, many of them on a regular basis. NPR's growth is in stark contrast to the situation for commercial newscasts during the same period. The combined audience of the ABC, CBS, and NBC evening newscasts today is half that of the early 1980s.

NPR has built its audience through a strategy that is opposite that of the commercial networks. As the news audiences of these networks declined in the face of widening competition from cable television, the networks "softened" their newscasts, boosting entertainment content in the hope of luring viewers away from cable

(continued)

programs. Former Federal Communication Commission chairman Newton Minow derided the change as "pretty close to tabloid." NPR, in contrast, has held to the notion that news is news and not also entertainment. Although NPR carries features, they typically are tied to news developments. Studies indicate that NPR's audience is more politically interested and informed than any other broadcast news audience. Many of its listeners are refugees from the broadcast network news they used to watch but now find lacking in substance. Informative news is not the sole reason for NPR's success, however. Americans spend more time in their cars commuting to and from work, and radio listening has increased overall for this reason. Nevertheless, NPR has shown that there is still a market in America for serious broadcast news.

measure their performance by standards such as efficiency, responsiveness, and outcomes.

Some analysts question whether government bureaucracy can or even should be reinvented. They have asked, for example, whether the principles of decentralized management and market-oriented programs are as sound as their advocates claim. A reason for hierarchy is to ensure that decisions made at the bottom of the bureaucracy are faithful to the laws enacted by Congress. Free to act on their own, lower-level administrators, as they did under the spoils system, might favor certain people and interests over others.[34] There is also the issue of the identity of the "customers" in a market-oriented administration.[35] Who are the Security and Exchange Commission's customers—firms, brokerage houses, or shareholders? Won't some agencies inevitably favor their more powerful customers at the expense of their less powerful ones?

Furthermore, there are practical limits on how much the federal bureaucracy can be trimmed. While some activities can be delegated to states and localities and others can be privatized, most of Washington's programs cannot be reassigned. National defense, social security, and Medicare are but three examples, and they alone account for well over half of all federal spending. In addition, the outsourcing of tasks to private contractors does not necessarily result in smaller government or reduced waste. Many contracts are a better deal for the private firms awarded them than for taxpayers. In one case, the GAO found that a contractor was charging the government $86 per sheet for plywood that normally sold for $14 per sheet. Nor does outsourcing necessarily result in better performance. When the space shuttle *Columbia* disintegrated upon reentry in 2003, some analysts suggested that the tragedy was rooted in NASA's decision to assign many of the shuttle program's safety checks to private contractors in order to cut costs.

Thus, although the current debate over the functioning of the federal bureaucracy is unique in its specific elements, it involves long-standing issues. How can the federal government be made more efficient and yet accomplish all that Americans expect of it? How can it be made more responsive and yet act fairly? How can it be made more creative and yet be held accountable? As history makes clear, there are no easy or final answers to these questions. *paychecks to paybills*

SUMMARY

Bureaucracy is a method of organizing people and work, based on the principles of hierarchical authority, job specialization, and formalized rules. As a form of organization, bureaucracy is the most efficient means of getting people to work together on tasks of great magnitude and complexity. It is also a form of organization that is prone to waste and rigidity, which is why efforts are always being made to "reinvent" it.

The United States could not be governed without a large federal bureaucracy. The day-to-day work of the federal government, from mail delivery to provision of social security to international diplomacy, is done by the bureaucracy. Federal employees work in roughly four hundred major agencies, including cabinet departments, independent agencies, regulatory agencies, government corporations, and presidential commissions. Yet the bureaucracy is more than simply an administrative giant. Administrators exercise considerable discretion in their policy decisions. In the process of implementing policy, they make important policy and political choices.

Each agency of the federal government was created in response to political demands on national officials. Because of its origins in political demands, the administration of government is necessarily political. An inherent conflict results from two simultaneous but incompatible demands on the bureaucracy: that it respond to the preferences of partisan officials and that it administer programs fairly and competently. This tension is evident in the three concurrent personnel management systems under which the bureaucracy operates: patronage, merit, and executive leadership.

Administrators are actively engaged in politics and policymaking. The fragmentation of power and the pluralism of the American political system result in a policy process that is continually subject to conflict and contention. There is no clear policy or leadership mandate in the American system, and hence government agencies must compete for the power required to administer their programs effectively. Accordingly, civil servants tend to have an agency point of view: they seek to advance their agency's programs and to repel attempts by others to weaken their position. In promoting their agency, civil servants rely on their policy expertise, the backing of their clientele groups, and the support of the president and Congress.

Administrators are not elected by the people they serve, yet they wield substantial independent power. Because of this, the bureaucracy's accountability is a central issue. The major checks on the bureaucracy are provided by the president, Congress, and the courts. The president has some power to reorganize the bureaucracy and the authority to appoint the political head of each agency. The president also has management tools (such as the executive budget) that can be used to limit administrators' discretion. Congress has influence on bureaucratic agencies through its authorization and funding powers and through various devices (including sunset laws and oversight hearings) that hold administrators accountable for their actions. The judiciary's role in ensuring the bureaucracy's accountability is smaller than that of the elected branches, but the courts do have the authority to force agencies to act in accordance with legislative intent, established procedures, and constitutionally guaranteed rights.

Nevertheless, administrators are not fully accountable. They exercise substantial independent power, a situation not easily reconciled with democratic values. Because of this, and also because of the desire to make the bureaucracy more efficient, there have been numerous efforts over time to reform the bureaucracy. The most recent such effort includes contracting out the work of government to private firms. Like all such efforts, this latest reinvention has solved some problems while creating new ones—an indication of the immensity of the challenge.

Key Terms

agency point of view (*p. 465*)
bureaucracy (*p. 451*)
bureaucratic accountability (*p. 470*)
cabinet (executive) departments
  (*p. 454*)
clientele groups (*p. 467*)

demographic representativeness
  (*p. 479*)
executive leadership system (*p. 463*)
formalized rules (*p. 453*)
government corporations (*p. 457*)
hierarchical authority (*p. 451*)

independent agencies (*p. 455*)

job specialization (*p. 453*)

merit (civil service) system (*p. 461*)

neutral competence (*p. 462*)

patronage system (*p. 461*)

policy implementation (*p. 458*)

presidential commissions (*p. 457*)

regulatory agencies (*p. 455*)

spoils system (*p. 461*)

sunset law (*p. 476*)

whistle-blowing (*p. 477*)

SUGGESTED READINGS

Aberbach, Joel D., and Bert A. Rockman. *In the Web of Politics: Two Decades of the U.S. Federal Executive.* Washington, D.C.: Brookings Institution, 2000. An evaluation of the federal bureaucracy and its evolving nature.

Du Gay, Paul. *The Values of Bureaucracy.* New York: Oxford University Press, 2005. An insightful analysis of how bureaucracies work and the values they embody.

Gormley, William T. Jr., and Steven J. Balla. *Bureaucracy and Democracy: Accountability and Performance.* Washington, D.C.: Congressional Quarterly Press, 2003. A close look at the effort to hold agencies accountable.

Kerwin, Cornelius M. *Rulemaking: How Government Agencies Write Law and Make Policy,* 3d ed. Washington, D.C.: Congressional Quarterly Press, 2003. An analysis of rulemaking in the federal bureaucracy.

Meier, Kenneth J., and Laurence J. O'Toole Jr. *Bureaucracy in a Democratic State.* Baltimore, Md.: Johns Hopkins University Press, 2006. A careful assessment of the relationship between bureaucracy and democracy.

Osborne, David, and Ted Gaebler. *Reinventing Government: How the Entrepreneurial Spirit Is Transforming the Public Sector.* New York: Addison-Wesley, 1992. The book that Washington policymakers in the 1990s regarded as the guide to transforming the bureaucracy.

Page, Edward C., and Bill Jenkins. *Policy Bureaucracy: Government with a Cast of Thousands.* New York: Oxford University Press, 2005. An assessment of the bureaucracy as a policymaking institution.

Sagini, Meshack M. *Organizational Behavior: The Challenges of the New Millennium.* Lanham, Md.: University Press of America, 2001. A comprehensive assessment of bureaucratic structures and behaviors.

LIST OF WEBSITES

http://www.census.gov/ Website of the Census Bureau; the bureau is the best source of statistical information on Americans and the government agencies that administer programs affecting them.

http://www.whistleblower.org/ The Government Accountability Project's website; this project is designed to protect and encourage whistle-blowers by providing information and support to federal employees.

http://www.whitehouse.gov/government/cabinet.html Lists the cabinet secretaries and provides links to each cabinet-level department.

POLITICS IN THEORY AND PRACTICE

Thinking: What are the major sources of bureaucrats' power? What mechanisms for controlling that power are available to the president and Congress?

Participating: If you are considering a semester or summer internship, you might want to look into working for a federal, state, or local agency. Compared with legislative interns, executive interns are more likely to get paid and to be given significant duties. (Many legislative interns spend the bulk of their time answering phones or responding to mail.) Internship information can often be obtained through an agency's website. You should apply as early as possible; some agencies have application deadlines.

ADDITIONAL RESOURCES

For quizzes, interactive simulations, games, graphics, and other study tools, visit the book's Online Learning Center at **www.mhhe.com/pattersonwtp7.**

Hurricane Katrina: A Nation Unprepared

By Senate Committee on Homeland
Security and Governmental Affairs

As a form of organization,
bureaucracy is unrivaled in its
capacity to undertake large-scale
operations. Yet it is a relatively
inflexible form of organization that
can falter when circumstances
require a quick and adaptive
response. By all accounts, the
American bureaucracy failed when
hurricane Katrina hit the Gulf
Coast states in 2005. The following
selection is from a Senate
committee's assessment of local,
state, and federal response to that
catastrophic event. It is a story of
poor planning, poor communication,
poor coordination, poor execution,
and poor leadership. The problem
was not solely a bureaucratic one.
It was also the result of political
failure and of the unprecedented
scale of one of the worst natural
disasters in modern U.S. history.
Nevertheless, the human and
property loss was much larger than
it would have been had the
bureaucratic response at all levels
been more effective.

Hurricane Katrina was an extraordinary act
of nature that spawned a human tragedy. It
was the most destructive natural disaster in
American history, laying waste to 90,000
square miles of land, an area the size of the
United Kingdom. In Mississippi, the storm
surge obliterated coastal communities and
left thousands destitute. New Orleans was
overwhelmed by flooding. All told, more
than 1,500 people died. Along the Gulf
Coast, tens of thousands suffered without
basic essentials for almost a week.

But the suffering that continued in the
days and weeks after the storm passed did
not happen in a vacuum; instead, it continued longer than it should have because of—
and was in some cases exacerbated by—the
failure of government at all levels to plan,
prepare for and respond aggressively to the
storm. These failures were not just conspicuous; they were pervasive. . . .

While authorities recognized the need to
begin search-and-rescue missions even
before the hurricane winds fully subsided,
other aspects of the response were hindered
by a failure to quickly recognize the dimensions of the disaster. These problems were
particularly acute at the federal level. The
Homeland Security Operations Center
(HSOC)—charged with providing reliable
information to decision makers including
the Secretary and the President—failed to
create a system to identify and acquire all
available, relevant information, and as a
result situational awareness was deeply
flawed. With local and state resources
immediately overwhelmed, rapid federal
mobilization of resources was critical. Yet
reliable information on such vital developments as the levee failures, the extent of
flooding, and the presence of thousands of
people in need of life-sustaining assistance

at the New Orleans Convention Center did not reach the White House, Secretary Chertoff, or other key officials for hours, and in some cases more than a day. [Michael] Brown [head of the Federal Emergency Management Agency (FEMA)], then in Louisiana, contributed to the problem by refusing to communicate with Secretary Chertoff, opting instead to pass information directly to White House staff. Moreover, even though senior DHS [Department of Homeland Security] officials did receive on the day of landfall numerous reports that should have led to an understanding of the increasingly dire situation in New Orleans, many indicated they were not aware of the crisis until sometime Tuesday morning.

DHS was slow to recognize the scope of the disaster or that FEMA had become overwhelmed. On the day after landfall, DHS officials were still struggling to determine the "ground truth" about the extent of the flooding despite the many reports it had received about the catastrophe; key officials did not grasp the need to act on the less-than-complete information that is to be expected in a disaster. DHS leaders did not become fully engaged in recovery efforts until Thursday, when in Deputy Secretary Michael Jackson's words, they "tried to kick it up a notch"; after that, they did provide significant leadership within DHS (and FEMA) as well as coordination across the federal government. But this effort should have begun sooner. . . .

Overwhelmed by Katrina, the city and state [had] turned to FEMA for help. On Monday, [Louisiana] Governor [Kathleen] Blanco asked Brown for buses, and Brown assured the state the same day that 500 buses were en route to assist in the evacuation of New Orleans and would arrive within hours. In spite of Brown's assurances and the state's continued requests over the course of the next two days, FEMA did not direct the U.S. Department of Transportation to send buses until very early on Wednesday, two days after landfall,

and the buses did not begin to arrive at all until Wednesday evening and not in significant numbers until Thursday. Concerned over FEMA's delay in providing buses—and handicapped by the Louisiana Department of Transportation and Development's utter failure to make any preparation to carry out its lead role for evacuation under the state's emergency plan—Governor Blanco directed members of her office to begin locating buses on Tuesday and approved an effort to commandeer school buses for evacuation on Wednesday. But these efforts were too little, too late. Tens of thousands of people were forced to wait in unspeakably horrible conditions until as late as Saturday to be evacuated. . . .

Problems with obtaining, communicating and managing information plagued many other aspects of the response as well. FEMA lacked the tools to track the status of shipments, interfering with the management of supplying food, water, ice and other vital commodities to those in need across the Gulf Coast. So too did the incompatibility of the electronic systems used by federal and state authorities to manage requests for assistance, which made it necessary to transfer requests from the state system to the federal system manually.

Supplies of commodities were especially problematic. Federal shipments to Mississippi did not reach adequate levels until 10 days after landfall. The reasons for this are unclear, but FEMA's inadequate "surge capacity"—the ability to quickly ramp up the volume of shipments—is a likely cause. In both Mississippi and Louisiana, there were additional problems in getting the supplies the "last mile" to individuals in need. Both states planned to make supplies available for pickup at designated distribution points, but neither anticipated the problems people would face in reaching those points, due to impassable roads or other issues. And in Louisiana, the National Guard was not equipped to assume this task. One of Louisiana's greatest shortages was portable toilets, which were requested for the Superdome but never arrived there, as more than 20,000 people were forced to reside inside the Superdome without working plumbing for nearly a week. . . .

By Tuesday afternoon, the New Orleans Superdome had become overcrowded, leading officials to turn additional refugees away. Mayor [Ray] Nagin then decided to open the Morial Convention Center as a second refuge of last resort inside the city, but did not supply it with food or water. Moreover, he communicated his decision to open the Convention Center to state and federal officials poorly, if at all. That failure, in addition to the delay of shipments due to security concerns and DHS's own independent lack of awareness of the situation, contributed to the paucity of food, water, security, or medical care at the Convention Center, as a population of approximately 19,000 gathered there. Those vital commodities and services did not arrive until Friday, when the Louisiana National Guard, assisted by National Guard units from five other states, brought in relief supplies provided by FEMA, established law and order, and then evacuated the Convention Center on Saturday within eight hours. . . .

Federal law-enforcement assistance was too slow in coming, in large part because the two federal Departments charged under the NRP [National Response Plan] with providing such assistance—DHS and the Department of Justice (DOJ)—had done almost no pre-storm planning. In fact, they failed to determine even well into the post-landfall period which of the two departments would assume the lead for federal law enforcement. . . . As a result, later in the week, as federal law-enforcement officers did arrive, some were distracted by a pointless "turf war" between DHS and DOJ over which agency was in the lead. In the end, federal assistance was crucial, but should have arrived much sooner.

What's Your Opinion?

From the information provided here, what do you think was the major source of the failure of government to respond adequately to Katrina: was it mostly a bureaucratic failure, mostly a political failure, or mostly a consequence of the scale of the problem? Are there large lessons about the nature of bureaucracy that you would derive from the Katrina response, recognizing that Katrina was a rare occurrence as opposed to a routine event?

CHAPTER 14

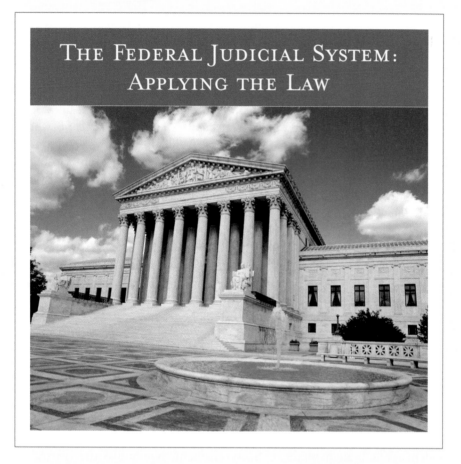

THE FEDERAL JUDICIAL SYSTEM:
APPLYING THE LAW

66It is emphatically the province and duty of the judicial department to say what
the law is. Those who apply the rule to particular cases, must of necessity
expound and interpret that rule. If two laws conflict with each other, the courts
must decide on the operation of each.99

JOHN MARSHALL[1]

Through its ruling in *Bush v. Gore*, the U.S. Supreme Court effectively
ended the 2000 presidential election. At issue was whether the "undervotes"
in Florida—ballots on which counting machines had detected no vote for
president—would be tabulated by hand. Florida's top court had ordered a
statewide manual recount, but the U.S. Supreme Court by a narrow 5-4
margin had issued a rare emergency order halting the action. Three days
later, the Supreme Court's majority delivered its ruling, saying that the
manual recount violated the Constitution's equal-protection clause.
Florida's high court had said that officials should base the hand count on

the "intent of the voter." The Supreme Court held that this standard gave county officials in Florida too much leeway and violated the right of citizens to have their votes counted fairly and equally.

The ruling brought charges that the Supreme Court had acted politically rather than on any strict interpretation of the law. In issuing a halt to the recount, the Court had divided sharply along ideological lines. The majority consisted of its most conservative members, all of whom were Republican appointees: Chief Justice William Rehnquist and associate justices Sandra Day O'Connor, Anthony Kennedy, Antonin Scalia, and Clarence Thomas. In a dissenting opinion, Justice John Paul Stevens said, "Preventing the recount from being completed will inevitably cast a doubt upon the legitimacy of the election." Stevens argued that the Supreme Court's majority had ignored "the basic principle, inherent in our Constitution and our democracy, that every legal vote should be counted."[2]

Bush v. Gore illustrates three key points about court decisions. First, the judiciary is an extremely important policymaking body. Some of its rulings are as consequential as a law of Congress or an executive order of the president. Second, the judiciary has considerable discretion in its rulings. The *Bush v. Gore* ruling was not based on any literal reading of the law: the justices invoked their individual interpretations of the law. Third, the judiciary is a political as well as legal institution. The *Bush v. Gore* case was a product of contending political forces, was developed through a political process, had political content, and was decided by political appointees.

This chapter describes the federal judiciary and the work of its judges and justices. Like the executive and legislative branches, the judiciary is an independent branch of the U.S. government, but unlike the two other branches, its top officials are not elected by the people. The judiciary is not a democratic institution, and its role is different from and, in some areas, more contentious than the roles of the executive and legislative branches. This chapter explores this issue in the process of discussing the following main points:

★ *The federal judiciary includes the Supreme Court of the United States, which functions mainly as an appellate court; courts of appeals, which hear appeals; and district courts, which hold trials.* Each state has a court system of its own, which for the most part is independent of supervision by the federal courts.

★ *Judicial decisions are constrained by applicable constitutional law, statutory and administrative law, and precedent.* Nevertheless, political factors have a major influence on judicial appointments and decisions; judges are political officials as well as legal ones.

★ *The judiciary has become an increasingly powerful policymaking body in recent decades, raising the question of the judiciary's proper role in a democracy.* The philosophies of judicial restraint and judicial activism provide different answers to this question.

THE FEDERAL JUDICIAL SYSTEM

The Constitution establishes the judiciary as a separate and independent branch of the federal government. The Constitution provides for the Supreme Court of the United States but gives Congress the power to determine the number and types of lower federal courts.

Federal judges are nominated and appointed to office by the president, subject to confirmation by a majority vote in the Senate. Unlike the case for the president, senators, and representatives, the Constitution places no age, residency, or citizenship requirements on federal judicial officers. Nor does the Constitution require judges to have legal training, though by tradition they do. Once seated on the bench, as specified in the Constitution, they "hold their offices during good behavior." This has meant, in effect, that federal judges serve until they die or voluntarily retire. No Supreme Court justice and only a handful of lower-court judges have been removed through impeachment and conviction by Congress, the method of early removal provided for by the Constitution.

The Supreme Court of the United States

The Supreme Court of the United States is the nation's highest court. The chief justice of the United States presides over the Supreme Court and, like the eight associate justices, is nominated by the president and is subject to Senate confirmation. The chief justice has the same voting power as the other justices but usually has exercised additional influence because of the position's leadership role.

The Constitution grants the Supreme Court both original and appellate jurisdiction. A court's **jurisdiction** is its authority to hear cases of a particular type. **Original jurisdiction** is the authority to be the first court to hear a case. The Supreme Court's original jurisdiction includes legal disputes involving foreign diplomats and cases in which the opposing parties are state governments. The Court in its history has convened as a court of original jurisdiction only a few hundred times and has rarely done so in recent decades.

The Supreme Court does its most important work as an appellate court. **Appellate jurisdiction** is the authority to review cases that have already been heard in lower courts and are appealed to a higher court by the losing party;

these higher courts are called appeals courts or appellate courts. The Supreme Court's appellate jurisdiction extends to cases arising under the Constitution, federal law and regulations, and treaties. The Court also hears appeals involving legal controversies that cross state or national boundaries. Appellate courts, including the Supreme Court, do not retry cases; rather, they determine whether a trial court acted in accord with applicable law.

Selecting and Deciding Cases   The primary function of the judiciary is to interpret the law in such a way that rules made in the past (for example, the Constitution or legislation) can be applied reasonably in the present. This function gives the courts—all courts—a role in policymaking. Antitrust legislation, for example, is designed to prevent uncompetitive business practices, but like all such legislation, it is not self-enforcing. It is up to the courts to decide whether and how the laws apply to the case at hand.

As the nation's highest court, the Supreme Court is particularly important in establishing legal precedents that guide lower courts. A **precedent** is a judicial decision that serves as a rule for settling subsequent cases of a similar nature. Lower courts are expected to follow precedent—that is, to resolve cases of a like nature in ways consistent with upper-court rulings. However, for reasons that will be explained later in this chapter, they do not always do so.

The Supreme Court's ability to set legal precedent is strengthened by its nearly complete discretion in choosing the cases it will hear. Nearly all cases that reach the Supreme Court do so through a **writ of certiorari**, in which the losing party in a lower-court case explains in writing why its case should be heard by the Court. Four of the nine justices must agree to accept a particular case before it is granted a writ. Each year roughly seven thousand parties apply for certiorari, but the Court accepts only about a hundred cases for a full hearing and signed ruling. The Court issues another fifty or so per curiam ("by the court") decisions each year. Typically, these decisions are very brief, are issued without a hearing, and are a response to relatively noncontroversial issues. They are issued in the name of the full Court rather than signed by the particular justices who wrote the opinion.

The Court is most likely to grant certiorari when the U.S. government through the **solicitor general** (the high-ranking Justice Department official who serves as the government's lawyer in Supreme Court cases) requests it.[3] The solicitor general tracks cases in which the federal government is a party. When the government loses a case in a lower court, the solicitor general decides whether to appeal it to the Supreme Court. Such cases often make up half or more of the cases the Court hears in a term.

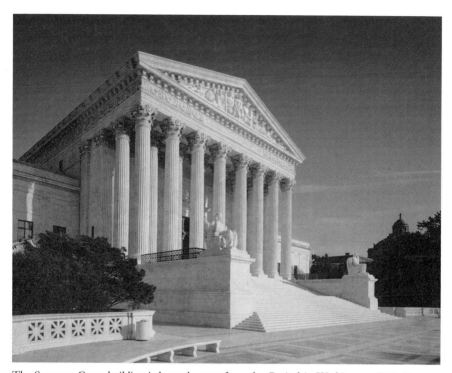

The Supreme Court building is located across from the Capitol in Washington, D.C. Sixteen marble columns support the pediment. Two bronze doors, each weighing more than six tons, lead into the building. The courtroom, the justices' offices, and the conference room are on the first floor. Administrative staff offices and the Court's records and reference materials occupy the other floors.

The Court seldom accepts a routine case, even if the justices believe that a lower court has made a mistake. The Supreme Court's job is not to correct the errors of other courts but to resolve substantial legal issues. This vague criterion essentially means that a case must center on an issue of significance not merely to the parties involved but to the nation. As a result, most cases heard by the Court raise major constitutional issues, affect the lives of many Americans, address issues that are being decided inconsistently by the lower courts, or involve rulings that conflict with a previous Supreme Court decision.[4] When the Court does accept a case, chances are that most of the justices disagree with the lower court's ruling. About three-fourths of the Supreme Court's decisions have reversed the judgments of lower courts.[5]

Once the Supreme Court accepts a case, it sets a date on which the attorneys for the two sides will present their oral arguments. Strict time limits, usually thirty minutes per side, are imposed on these presentations.

However, the oral arguments are less important than the lengthy written **brief** submitted earlier by each side, which contains the side's complete argument.

The oral session is also far less important than the **judicial conference** that follows, which is attended only by the nine justices and in which they discuss and vote on the case. The conference's proceedings are kept strictly confidential. This secrecy allows the justices to speak freely about a case and to change their minds as the discussion unfolds.[6]

Issuing Decisions and Opinions   After a case has been decided on in conference, the Court prepares and issues its ruling, which consists of a decision and one or more opinions. The **decision** indicates which party the Court supports and by how large a margin. The **opinion** explains the reasons behind the decision. The opinion is the most important part of a Supreme Court ruling because it contains the justices' legal reasoning. For example, in the landmark *Brown v. Board of Education of Topeka* (1954) opinion, the Court held that government-sponsored school segregation was unconstitutional because it violated the Fourteenth Amendment provision that guarantees equal protection under the law to all citizens. This opinion became the legal basis by which communities throughout the southern states were ordered by lower courts to end their policy of segregating public school students by race.

When a majority of the justices agree on the legal basis of a decision, the result is a **majority opinion** (see Table 14–1). In some cases there is no majority opinion because a majority of the justices agree on the decision but cannot agree on the legal basis for it. The result in such cases is a **plurality opinion,** which presents the view held by most of the justices who side with the winning party. Another type of opinion is a **concurring opinion,** a separate view written by a justice who votes with the majority but disagrees with their reasoning.

Justices on the losing side can write a **dissenting opinion** to explain their reasons for disagreeing with the majority position. Sometimes these dissenting arguments become the foundation of subsequent decisions. In a 1942 dissenting opinion, Justice Hugo Black wrote that defendants in state felony trials should have legal counsel even if they could not afford to pay for it. Two decades later, in *Gideon v. Wainwright* (1963), the Court adopted Justice Black's position.[7]

When part of the majority, the chief justice decides which justice will write the majority opinion. Otherwise, the senior justice in the majority determines the author. Chief justices have often given themselves the task of writing the majority opinion in important cases. John Marshall did so

| TABLE 14-1 | TYPES OF SUPREME COURT OPINIONS |

Supreme Court opinions vary by type, depending on how many justices agree with the opinion and whether the opinion is on the winning or losing side of the decision.

Per curiam: Unsigned decision of the Court that states the facts of the case and the Court's ruling.

Majority opinion: A written opinion of the majority of the Court's justices stating the reasoning underlying their decision on a case.

Plurality opinion: A written opinion that in the absence of a majority opinion presents the reasoning of most of the justices who side with the winning party.

Concurring opinion: A written opinion of one or more justices who support the majority position but disagree with the majority's reasoning on a case. This opinion expresses the reasoning of the concurring justices.

Dissenting opinion: A written opinion of one or more justices who disagree with the majority's decision and opinion. This opinion provides the reasoning underlying the dissent.

often; *Marbury v. Madison* (1802) and *McCulloch v. Maryland* (1819) were among the opinions he wrote. The justice who writes the Court's majority opinion has the responsibility to express accurately the majority's reasoning. The vote on a case is not considered final until the opinion is written and agreed upon, so plenty of give-and-take can occur during the writing stage.

Other Federal Courts

There are more than one hundred federal courts but only one Supreme Court, and its position at the top of the judicial system gives the Supreme Court unparalleled importance. It is a mistake, however, to conclude that the Supreme Court is the only court that matters. Judge Jerome Frank once wrote of the "upper-court myth," which is the view that appellate courts, and in particular the Supreme Court, are the only truly significant judicial arena and that lower courts just dutifully follow the rulings handed down by courts at the appellate level.[8] The reality is very different, as the following discussion explains.

U.S. District Courts   The lowest federal courts are the district courts (see Figure 14–1). There are more than ninety federal district courts altogether—at least one in every state and as many as four in some states. District court

FIGURE 14-1   THE FEDERAL JUDICIAL SYSTEM

This simplified diagram shows the relationships among the various levels of federal courts and between state and federal courts. The losing party in a case can appeal a lower-court decision to the court at the next-highest level, as the arrows indicate. Cases normally can be moved from state courts to U.S. courts only if a federal constitutional issue is involved.

judges, who number about seven hundred in all, are appointed by the president with the consent of the Senate. Federal cases usually originate in district courts, which are trial courts where the parties argue their sides. District courts are the only courts in the federal system in which juries hear testimony. Most cases at this level are presented before a single judge.

Lower federal courts unquestionably rely on and follow Supreme Court decisions in their own rulings. The Supreme Court reiterated this requirement in a 1982 case, *Hutto v. Davis:* "Unless we wish anarchy to prevail within the federal judicial system, a precedent of this Court must be followed by the lower federal courts no matter how misguided the judges of those courts may think it to be."[9]

However, the idea that lower courts are guided strictly by Supreme Court rulings is part of the upper-court myth. District court judges might misunderstand the Supreme Court's position and deviate from it for that reason. In addition, the facts of a case before a district court are seldom identical to those of a case settled by the Supreme Court. In such instances, the lower-court judge must decide whether a different legal judgment is appropriate. Finally, it is not unusual for the Supreme Court to issue a general ruling that gives lower courts some flexibility in deciding similar cases that come before them. Trial court judges then have a creative role in judicial decision making that rivals that of appellate court judges.

Most federal cases end with the district court's decision; the losing party does not appeal the decision to a higher court. This fact is another indication of the highly significant role of district court judges.

U.S. Courts of Appeals When cases are appealed from district courts, they go to a federal court of appeals. These appellate courts are the second level of the federal court system. Courts of appeals do not use juries. Ordinarily, no new evidence is submitted in an appealed case; rather, appellate courts base their decisions on a review of lower-court records. Appellate judges act as supervisors in the legal system, reviewing trial court decisions and correcting what they consider to be legal errors. Facts (i.e., the circumstances of a case) found by district courts are ordinarily presumed to be correct.

The United States has thirteen courts of appeals, each of which serves a "circuit" comprised of between three and nine states, except for the circuit that serves the District of Columbia only and the U.S. Court of Appeals for the Federal Circuit, which specializes in appeals involving patents and international trade (see Figure 14–2). Between four and twenty-six judges sit on each court of appeals, but each case usually is heard by a panel of three judges. On rare occasions, all the judges of a court of appeals sit as a body (*en banc*) in order to resolve difficult controversies, typically ones that have resulted in conflicting decisions within the same circuit. Each circuit is monitored by a Supreme Court justice, who normally takes the lead in reviewing appeals originating in that circuit.

Courts of appeals offer the only real hope of reversal for many appellants, because the Supreme Court hears so few cases. The Supreme Court reviews less than 1 percent of the cases heard by federal appeals courts.

Special U.S. Courts In addition to the Supreme Court, the courts of appeals, and the district courts, the federal judiciary includes a few specialty courts. Among them are the U.S. Claims Court, which hears cases in which the U.S. government is being sued for damages; the U.S. Court of International Trade, which handles cases involving appeals of U.S. Customs Office rulings; and the U.S. Court of Military Appeals, which hears appeals of military courts-martial. Some federal agencies and commissions also have judicial powers (for example, the issuing of fines), and their decisions can be appealed to a federal court of appeals.

The State Courts

The American states are separate governments within the U.S. political system. The Tenth Amendment protects each state in its sovereignty, and each state has its own court system. Like the federal courts, state

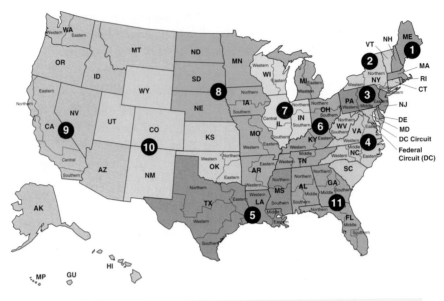

FIGURE 14-2 GEOGRAPHIC BOUNDARIES OF U.S. COURTS OF APPEALS

The United States has thirteen courts of appeals, each of which serves a "circuit." Eleven of these circuit courts serve anywhere from three to nine states, as the map shows. The other two are located in the District of Columbia: the Court of Appeals for the District of Columbia and the Court of Appeals for the Federal Circuit, which specializes in appeals involving patents and international trade. Within each circuit are federal trial courts, most of which are district courts. Each state has at least one district court within its boundaries. Larger states like California (which has four district courts, as can be seen on the map) have more than one. *Source: Administrative Office of the U.S. Courts.*

court systems have trial courts at the bottom level and appellate courts at the top.

Each state decides for itself the structure of its courts and the method of judicial appointment. In some states judges are appointed by the governor, but in most states judgeships are *elective offices.* The most common form involves competitive elections of either a partisan or a nonpartisan nature. Other states appoint their judges. Some of them use a system called the *merit plan* (also called the "Missouri Plan" because Missouri was the first state to use it) under which the governor appoints a judge from a short list of acceptable candidates provided by a judicial selection commission. The judge selected must then periodically be reviewed by the voters, who, rather than choosing between the judge and an opponent, simply decide by a "yes" or "no" vote whether the judge should be allowed to stay in office (see "States in the Nation").

★ STATES IN THE NATION

Principal Methods of Selecting State Judges

The states use a variety of methods for selecting the judges on their highest court, including the merit plan, election, and political appointment. The states that appoint judges grant this power to the governor, except in Virginia, Connecticut, and South Carolina, where the legislature makes the choice.

Q: What might explain why several states in the middle of the nation use the merit plan for selecting judges?

A: The merit plan originated in the state of Missouri. Innovations in one state sometimes spread to adjacent states that have similar political cultures.

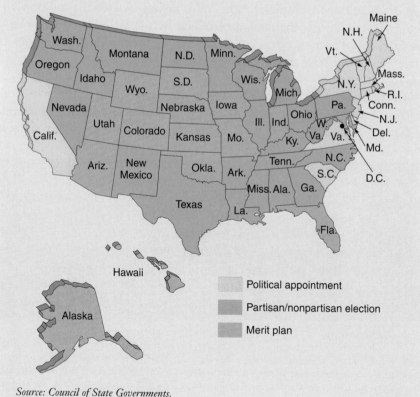

Source: Council of State Governments.

Besides the upper-court myth, there exists a "federal court myth," which holds that the federal judiciary is the most significant part of the judicial system and that state courts play a subordinate role. This view also is inaccurate. More than 95 percent of the nation's legal cases are decided in state courts. Most crimes (from shoplifting to murder) and most civil controversies (such as divorces and business disputes) are defined by state or local law. Moreover, nearly all cases that originate in state courts end there. The federal courts don't come into the picture because the case does not include a federal issue.

In state criminal cases, after a person has been convicted and after all avenues of appeal in the state court system have been exhausted, the defendant can seek a writ of habeas corpus from a federal district court on grounds that constitutional rights were violated—as, for example, in a claim that local police failed to inform the suspect of the right to remain silent (see Chapter 4). If the federal court accepts such an appeal, it ordinarily confines itself to the federal aspects of the matter, such as whether the defendant's constitutional rights were in fact violated. In addition, the federal court accepts the facts determined by the state court unless such findings are clearly in error. In short, legal and factual determinations of state courts can bind the federal courts—a clear contradiction of the federal court myth.

However, issues traditionally within the jurisdiction of the states can become federal issues through the rulings of federal courts. In its *Lawrence v. Texas* decision in 2003, for example, the Supreme Court invalidated

Texas solicitor general Ted Cruz presents a case before the Supreme Court of Texas. It is one of two high courts in the state and has the final say in civil and juvenile cases. The other high court is the Court of Criminal Appeals, which hears appeals of criminal cases. Each court has nine judges, elected to staggered six-year terms. More than 95 percent of the nation's legal cases are decided entirely by state courts, a refutation of the federal court myth, which wrongly holds that the federal courts are all that matter in the end. The United States has a federal system of government, and the division of power between the national and state governments affects the courts as well as other governing institutions.

state laws that made it illegal for consenting adults of the same sex to engage in private sexual relations.[10] Earlier, the Court had held that states had the authority to decide for themselves whether to prohibit such acts.[11]

FEDERAL COURT APPOINTEES

The quiet dignity of the courtroom and the lack of fanfare with which a court delivers its decisions give the impression that the judiciary is as far removed from the world of politics as a governmental institution can possibly be. In reality, federal judges and justices are political officials who exercise the authority of a separate and powerful branch of government. All federal jurists bring their political views with them to the courtroom and have regular opportunities to promote their political beliefs through the cases they decide. Not surprisingly, the process by which federal judges are appointed is a partisan one.

The Selection of Supreme Court Justices and Federal Judges

The formal method for appointments to the Supreme Court and to the lower federal courts is the same: the president nominates, and the Senate confirms or rejects. Beyond that basic similarity, however, lie significant differences.

Supreme Court Nominees A Supreme Court appointment is a major opportunity for a president.[12] Most justices retain their positions for many years, enabling presidents to influence judicial policy through their appointments long after they have left office. The careers of some Supreme Court justices provide dramatic testimony to the enduring effects of judicial appointments. Franklin D. Roosevelt appointed William O. Douglas to the Supreme Court in 1939, and for thirty years after Roosevelt's death in 1945, Douglas remained a strong liberal influence on the Court.

Presidents invariably seek nominees who share their political philosophy, but they also must take into account a nominee's acceptability to others. Every nominee is closely scrutinized by the legal community, interested groups, and the media; must undergo an extensive background check by the FBI; and then must gain the approval of a Senate majority. Within the Senate, the key body is the Judiciary Committee, whose members have responsibility for conducting hearings on judicial nominees and recommending their confirmation or rejection by the full Senate.

Nearly 20 percent of presidential nominees to the Supreme Court have been rejected by the Senate on grounds of judicial qualification, political views, personal ethics, or partisanship. Most of these rejections occurred

The justices of the U.S. Supreme Court pose for a photo. From left, they are Anthony Kennedy, Stephen Breyer, John Paul Stevens, Clarence Thomas, Chief Justice John Roberts, Ruth Bader Ginsburg, Antonin Scalia, Samuel Alito, David Souter.

before 1900, and partisan politics was the main reason. Today a nominee with strong professional and ethical credentials is less likely to be blocked for partisan reasons alone. An exception was Robert Bork, whose 1987 nomination by President Reagan was rejected primarily because of intense opposition to his judicial philosophy on the part of Senate Democrats.

On the other hand, nominees can expect confirmation if they have personal integrity and a solid legal record and also show during Senate confirmation hearings the temperament and reasoning expected of a Supreme Court justice. The nomination of John Roberts in 2005 to be chief justice is a case in point. He faced tough questioning during Senate hearings, but nothing startlingly new or disturbing came out, and he was confirmed by a 78-22 vote. Senate hearings held a few months later on the nomination of Samuel Alito, whose past record raised more issues than did that of Roberts, went less smoothly, but he nonetheless was confirmed by a 58-42 vote.

Lower-Court Nominees The president normally delegates to the deputy attorney general the task of screening potential nominees for lower-court judgeships. **Senatorial courtesy** is also a consideration in these appointments; this tradition, which dates back to the 1840s, holds that a senator from the state in which a vacancy has arisen should be given a say in the nomination if the senator is of the same party as the president.[13] If not consulted, the senator involved can request that confirmation be denied, and other senators will normally grant the request as a "courtesy" to their colleague.

Although the president does not become as personally involved in selecting lower-court nominees as in naming potential Supreme Court justices, lower-court appointments are collectively a significant factor in the impact of a president's Administration. Recent presidents have appointed on average more than one hundred judges during a four-year term of office.

Justices and Judges as Political Officials

Presidents generally manage to appoint jurists who have a similar political philosophy. Although Supreme Court justices are free to make their own decisions, their legal positions usually can be predicted from their prior work. A study by judicial scholar Robert Scigliano found that about three of every four appointees have behaved on the Supreme Court approximately as presidents could have expected.[14] Of course, a president has no guarantee that a nominee will fulfill his hopes. Justices Earl Warren and William Brennan proved to be more liberal than President Dwight D. Eisenhower had anticipated. Asked whether he had made any mistakes as president, Eisenhower replied, "Yes, two, and they are both sitting on the Supreme Court."[15]

The Role of Partisanship   In nearly every instance, presidents choose members of their own party as Supreme Court nominees. Partisanship is also decisive in nominations to lower-court judgeships. More than 90 percent of recent district and appeals court nominees have been members of the president's own party.[16]

This fact should not be interpreted to mean that federal judges and justices engage in blatant partisanship while on the bench. They are officers of a separate branch and prize their judicial independence. All Republican appointees do not vote the same way on cases, nor do all Democratic appointees. Nevertheless, partisanship influences judicial decisions. A study of the voting records of appellate court judges, for example, found that Democratic appointees are more likely than Republican appointees to side with parties that claim their civil rights or civil liberties have been violated.[17]

Other Characteristics of Judicial Appointees   In recent years, increasing numbers of federal justices and judges have had prior judicial experience; the assumption is that such individuals are best qualified for appointment

| TABLE 14-2 | JUSTICES OF THE SUPREME COURT, 2006 |

All recent appointees held an appellate court position before being nominated to the Supreme Court.

Justice	Year of Appointment	Nominating President	Position Before Appointment
John Paul Stevens	1975	Ford	Judge, U.S. Court of Appeals
Antonin Scalia	1986	Reagan	Judge, U.S. Court of Appeals
Anthony Kennedy	1988	Reagan	Judge, U.S. Court of Appeals
David Souter	1990	G.H.W. Bush	Judge, U.S. Court of Appeals
Clarence Thomas	1991	G.H.W. Bush	Judge, U.S. Court of Appeals
Ruth Bader Ginsburg	1993	Clinton	Judge, U.S. Court of Appeals
Stephen Breyer	1994	Clinton	Judge, U.S. Court of Appeals
John Roberts, Jr.*	2005	G. W. Bush	Judge, U.S. Court of Appeals
Samuel Alito, Jr.	2006	G. W. Bush	Judge, U.S. Court of Appeals

*Chief Justice.

to the federal bench. Most recent appellate court appointees have been district or state judges or have worked in the office of the attorney general.[18] Elective office (particularly a seat in the U.S. Senate) was once a common route to the Supreme Court,[19] but recent justices have typically held an appellate court judgeship before their appointment (see Table 14–2).

White males are greatly overrepresented on the federal bench, just as they dominate in Congress and at the top levels of the executive branch. However, the number of women and minority-group members appointed to federal judgeships has increased significantly in recent decades. The number of such appointees has varied according to which party controls the presidency. Women and minority-group members are key constituencies of the Democratic party; not surprisingly, Democratic presidents have appointed more judges from these groups than have Republican presidents (see Figure 14–3). Of President Bill Clinton's

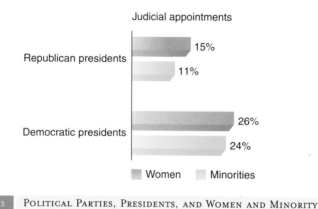

Judicial appointments

Republican presidents
15%
11%

Democratic presidents
26%
24%

■ Women   ■ Minorities

FIGURE 14-3 POLITICAL PARTIES, PRESIDENTS, AND WOMEN AND MINORITY JUDICIAL APPOINTEES

Reflecting differences in their parties' coalitions, recent Republican and Democratic presidents have quite different records in terms of the percentage of their judicial appointees who have been women or minority-group members. *Source: Various sources. Data based on appointees of Presidents Carter, Reagan, G.H.W. Bush, Clinton, and G. W. Bush.*

appointees, for example, 30 percent were women and 25 percent were members of racial or ethnic minority groups. For President George W. Bush, the figures are 21 percent and 19 percent, respectively.

The Supreme Court is less demographically representative than are the lower courts. Of the nine current justices, only one (Ruth Bader Ginsburg) is a woman, and only one (Clarence Thomas) is a minority-group member. The historical pattern is even more one-sided. Until 1916, when Louis D. Brandeis was appointed to the Court, no Jewish justice had ever served. At least one Catholic, but at most times only one, has sat on the Court almost continuously for nearly a century. Thurgood Marshall in 1967 was the first black justice, and Sandra Day O'Connor in 1981 was the first woman justice. Antonin Scalia in 1986 was the Court's first justice of Italian descent. No person of Hispanic or Asian descent has ever been a member of the Supreme Court.

THE NATURE OF JUDICIAL DECISION MAKING

Federal judges and justices are political officials—they constitute one of three coequal branches of the national government. Yet, unlike members of Congress or the president, judges make their decisions within the context of a legal process. As a consequence, their discretionary power is less than that of elected officials. Article III of the Constitution bars a federal court from issuing a decision except in response to an actual case presented to it. As federal judge David Bazelon noted, a judge "can't wake up one morning and simply decide to give a helpful little push to a school system, a mental hospital, or the local housing agency."[20]

Judicial decisions are also restricted in scope. Technically, a court ruling is binding only on the parties involved. Its broader impact depends on the willingness of others to follow its lead. For example, if a court should decide that a school is bound by law to spend more on programs for the learning-disabled, the ruling would extend to other schools in the same situation only if those schools voluntarily responded or were forced by subsequent court action to do so. By comparison, if Congress were to pass legislation granting funds for programs for the learning-disabled, all eligible schools would receive the funding.

Another major restriction on the courts is the law itself. Although a president or Congress can make almost any decision that is politically acceptable, the judiciary must justify its decisions in terms of existing provisions of the law. When asked by a friend to "do justice," Justice Oliver Wendell Holmes Jr. said that the law, rather than his inclination, was his guide.[21] In applying the law, judges engage in a creative legal process that requires them to identify the facts of the case, determine and sometimes formulate the relevant legal principles or rules, and then apply these to the case at hand.

The Constraints of the Facts

A basic distinction in any legal case is between "the facts" and "the laws." The **facts** of a case, as determined by trial courts, are the relevant circumstances of a legal dispute or offense. In the case of a person accused of murder, for example, key facts would include evidence about the murder and whether the rights of the accused were respected by police in the course of their investigation. The facts of a case are crucial because they determine which law or laws apply to the case. A murder case cannot be used as an occasion to pronounce judgment on freedom of religion, for example.

The Constraints of the Law

In deciding cases, the judiciary is also constrained by existing **laws.** To use an obvious comparison, the laws that apply to a case of alleged murder differ from those that apply to a case of alleged shoplifting. A judge must treat a murder case as a murder case, applying to it the laws that define murder and the penalties that can be imposed when someone is found guilty of that crime.

Laws fall into three broad categories: civil, criminal, and procedural. Civil law governs relations between private parties. Marriage, divorce, business contracts, and property ownership are examples of relations covered by civil law. In all states but Massachusetts, for example, civil law limits marriage to a man and a woman; same-sex couples in these states are prohibited by law from marrying. In this example, civil law defines the basis for a legally binding contract. Civil law also applies to disputes between private parties. The courts ordinarily do not get involved in such disputes unless the parties themselves cannot resolve their differences. For example, a dispute in which a homeowner alleges that an insurance company has failed to pay a policy claim could end up in court if the homeowner and the insurance company cannot settle it themselves. The losing party in a civil suit might be ordered to pay or otherwise compensate the other party but would not face jail time unless he or she refuses to comply with a court order—a possible punishable offense.

Criminal law deals with acts that the government defines as illegal and that can result in a fine, imprisonment, or other punishment. Murder, assault, shoplifting, and drunk driving are examples of acts covered by criminal law. The government is always a party to a criminal law case; the other party is the individual alleged to have broken the law.

Procedural law refers to rules that govern the legal process. In some cases, these rules apply to government. For example, police are obliged to inform suspects of their right to an attorney and to remain silent. In other cases, the rules apply to private parties. For example, in some states a homeowner cannot take an insurance company to court over a policy claim without first having that claim heard—and possibly resolved—by an arbitration board.

Three sources of law constrain the courts: the Constitution, legislative statutes (and the administrative regulations derived from them), and precedents established by previous court rulings (see Table 14–3).

The Constitution and Its Interpretation   The Constitution of the United States is the nation's highest law, and judges and justices are sworn to uphold it. When a case raises a constitutional issue, a court has the duty to apply the Constitution to the case. For example, the Constitution prohibits the states from printing their own currency. If a state decided that it would do so anyway, a federal judge would be obligated to rule against the practice.

Nevertheless, constitutional provisions are open to interpretation in some cases. For example, the Fourth Amendment of the Constitution

TABLE 14-3	SOURCES OF LAW THAT CONSTRAIN THE DECISIONS OF THE FEDERAL JUDICIARY

Federal judges make their decisions in the context of law, which limits their discretion. The Constitution, statutes, and precedents are major constraints on the judiciary.

U.S. Constitution: The federal courts are bound by the provisions of the U.S. Constitution. The sparseness of its wording, however, requires the Constitution to be applied in the light of present circumstances. Thus, judges are accorded some degree of discretion in their constitutional judgments.

Statutory law: The federal courts are constrained by statutes and by administrative regulations derived from the provisions of statutes. Most laws, however, are somewhat vague in their provisions and often have unanticipated applications. As a result, judges have some freedom in deciding cases based on statutes.

Precedent: Federal courts tend to follow precedent (or stare decisis), which is a legal principle developed through earlier court decisions. Because times change and not all cases have a clear precedent, judges have some discretion in their evaluation of the way earlier cases apply to a current case.

protects individuals against "unreasonable searches and seizures," but the meaning of "unreasonable" is not specified. Judges must decide upon its meaning in particular situations. Take, for example, the question of whether wiretapping, which was not invented until 150 years after ratification of the Fourth Amendment, is included in the prohibition on unreasonable searches and seizures. Reasoning that the Fourth Amendment was intended to protect individuals from government snooping into their private lives, judges have ruled that indiscriminate wiretapping is unconstitutional.

Statutes and Administrative Laws, and Their Interpretation The vast majority of court cases involve issues of statutory and administrative law rather than constitutional law. Statutory law is law enacted by a legislative body, such as Congress. Administrative law is derived from statutory law but is set by government agencies rather than by legislatures. Administrative law consists of the rules and regulations that agencies develop in the process of implementing and enforcing statutes.

All federal courts are bound by federal statutes (laws passed by Congress) and by federal administrative regulations, as well as by treaties.

When hearing a case involving statutory law or administrative regulation, judges must work within the limits of the applicable law or regulation. A company that is charged with violating an air-pollution law, for example, will be judged within the context of that law—what it permits and what it prohibits, and the penalties that apply if the company is found to have broken the law.

When hearing such a case, judges will often try to determine whether the meaning of the statute or regulation can be determined by common sense (the "plain meaning rule"). The question for the judge is what the law or regulation was intended to safeguard (such as clean air). The law or regulation in most cases is clear enough that when the facts of the case are considered, the decision is fairly predictable. Not all cases, however, are clear-cut in their facts or in the applicable law or laws. Where, for example, do college admissions programs that take race into account cross the line from legal to illegal by placing too much weight on race? In such instances, courts have no choice but to exercise their judgment.

Legal Precedents (Previous Rulings) and Their Interpretation   The U.S. legal system developed from the English common-law tradition, which includes the principle that a court's decision on a case should be consistent with previous judicial rulings. This principle, known as precedent, reflects the philosophy of stare decisis (Latin for "to stand by things that have been settled"). Precedent holds that principles of law, once established, should be applied in subsequent similar cases. Judges and justices often cite past rulings as justification for their decisions in the cases before them.

Precedent is important because it gives predictability to the application of law. Government has an obligation to make clear what its laws are and how they are being applied. If courts routinely ignored how similar cases had been decided in the past, they would create confusion and uncertainty about what is lawful and what is not. A business firm that is seeking to comply with environmental protection laws, for example, can develop company policies that will keep the company safely within the law if court decisions in this area are consistent. If courts routinely ignored precedent, a firm could unintentionally engage in an activity that a court might conclude was unlawful.

POLITICAL INFLUENCES ON JUDICIAL DECISIONS

Although judicial rulings are constrained by existing laws, judges nearly always have some degree of discretion in their decisions.[22] The Constitution is a sparsely worded document and must be adapted to new and changing situations. The judiciary also has no choice at times but to apply its own judgment to statutory law. Congress often cannot anticipate or reach agreement on all the specific applications of a legislative act and therefore uses general language to state the act's purpose. It is left to the judiciary to decide what this language means in the context of a specific case arising under the act. Precedent is even less precise as a guide to decisions. Precedent must be considered in the context of the changes that have occurred since it was established. In the words of Justice Oliver Wendell Holmes Jr., precedent must be judged against the "felt necessities of the time."

The Supreme Court's ruling in a 1998 case (*Faragher v. City of Boca Raton*) involving sexual harassment in the workplace illustrates the ambiguity that can occur in existing law. The Court developed its ruling in the context of the antidiscrimination provisions of the Civil Rights Act of 1964. However, the act itself contains no description of, or even reference to, job-related sexual harassment. Nevertheless, the act does prohibit workplace discrimination, and the Court was unwilling to dismiss sexual harassment as an irrelevant form of job-related discrimination. In judging the case, the Court had to determine for itself which actions in the workplace are instances of harassment and which are not. In this sense, the Court was "making" law; it was deciding how legislation enacted by Congress applied to behavior that Congress had not specifically addressed when it wrote the legislation.[23]

In sum, judges have leeway in their decisions. As a consequence, their rulings reflect not only legal influences but also political ones. Political influences can come from both outside and inside the judicial system.

Outside Influences on Court Decisions

The courts can and do make unpopular choices, but in the long run judicial decisions must be seen as fair if they are to be obeyed. In other words, the judiciary cannot ignore the expectations of the general public, interest groups, and elected representatives.

Public Opinion and Interest Groups   Judges are responsive to public opinion, although much less so than are elected officials. In some cases, for example, the Supreme Court has tailored its rulings in an effort to gain public support or reduce public resistance. In the *Brown* case, the justices, recognizing that school desegregation would be an explosive issue in the South, required only that desegregation take place "with all deliberate speed" rather than immediately or on a fixed timetable. The Supreme Court typically has stayed close enough to public opinion to avoid massive public resistance to its decisions.[24]

The Supreme Court's power is never more evident than when its strikes down a law passed by Congress or a state legislature on grounds that it violates the Constitution. Over the years, the Court has invalidated a number of state laws that have sought to promote religion in public schools. The Court considers the issue of religion in the schools to be an issue of individual rights rather than of majority rule.

The courts also respond to interest groups, primarily through rulings in the lawsuits filed by them. Some groups rely on lawsuits as their primary political strategy because their issues are more likely to be decided favorably in a court than through an elected institution. An example is the American Civil Liberties Union (ACLU), which has filed hundreds of lawsuits over the years on issues of individual rights. In 2006, for example, the ACLU filed suit against the Bush administration over its wiretapping of individuals' phone and e-mail messages without obtaining a court order, claiming such action to be a violation of the First and Fourth Amendments. A group can also try to influence the courts by filing an amicus curiae ("friend of the court") brief in which it presents its views on a case in which it is not one of the parties directly involved (see Chapter 9). Groups' influence on the courts has increased in recent decades as a result of both a sharp rise in group activity and the use of more sophisticated judicial strategies. Groups carefully select the cases they pursue, choosing those with the greatest chance of success. They also carefully pick the courts in which they file, because some judges are more sympathetic than others to their particular issue.

Congress and the President Groups and the general public also make an impact on the judiciary indirectly, through their elected representatives. Both Congress and the president have powerful means of influencing the federal judiciary.

Congress is constitutionally empowered to establish the Supreme Court's size and appellate jurisdiction and can rewrite legislation that it feels the judiciary has misinterpreted. Although Congress seldom threatens the judiciary directly, its members often express displeasure with judicial action. In a 1998 Senate speech, the chair of the Judiciary Committee, Orrin Hatch (R-Utah), lashed out at judges who he claimed were "making laws instead of interpreting the law."[25] Hatch argued that judges should be "strict constructionists." (*Strict constructionism* holds that a judicial officer should apply a narrow interpretation of the law, whereas *loose constructionism* holds that a judicial officer can apply an expansive interpretation.)

The president too has ways of influencing the judiciary. The president is responsible for enforcing court decisions and has some influence over the issues that come before the courts. Under President Ronald Reagan, for instance, the Justice Department pushed lawsuits that challenged the legality of affirmative action. Judicial appointments also provide the president with opportunities to influence the judiciary's direction. When Democrat Bill Clinton took office in 1993, more than a hundred federal judgeships were vacant. The first President Bush had expected to win reelection and had not moved quickly to fill vacancies as they arose. As it became apparent that he might lose the election, the Democrat-controlled Congress delayed action on his appointments. This enabled Clinton to fill many of the positions with loyal Democrats. The tables were turned in 2001. Senate Republicans had slowed action on Clinton nominees, enabling George W. Bush to appoint Republicans to existing vacancies when he took office.

In recent decades, the judicial appointment process has been unusually contentious, reflecting both the growing partisanship in Congress (see Chapter 11) and the widening range of issues (everything from abortion to the environment) being fought out in the courts. Nevertheless, the influence of elected officials on the judiciary is never total. Judges prize their independence. The fact that they are not popularly elected and hold their appointments indefinitely allows them to resist undue pressure from the elected branches of government. In 2004, for example, the Supreme Court rejected the Bush administration's claim that U.S. citizens charged with terrorism can be jailed indefinitely without a judicial hearing (see Chapter 4).

GET INVOLVED!
Sit When Called

The right to a jury trial is one of the oldest features of the American political experience, dating back to the colonial period. Jury trials offer the average citizen a rare opportunity to be part of the governing structure. Yet Americans increasingly shirk jury duty. When summoned, many people find all sorts of reasons why they should be excused from serving on a jury. In some areas of the country, the avoidance rate exceeds 50 percent. Some citizens even give up their right to vote because they know that jurors in their area are selected from names on voter registration lists.

There are reasons, however, to look upon jury duty as an opportunity and not just a responsibility. Studies indicate that citizens come away from the jury experience with a fuller appreciation of the justice system. Jurors acquire an understanding of the serious responsibility handed to them when asked to decide on someone's guilt or innocence. The legal standard in American courts—"guilty beyond a reasonable doubt"—is a solemn one. No wonder jurors in difficult cases often take hours or even days to reach a verdict. The fairness of the jury system, however, requires full participation by the community. Studies show that jurors' life experiences can affect the decisions they reach. If everyone on a jury has the same background and it is different from the defendant's, the odds of a wrongful verdict increase. "A jury of one's peers" should mean just that—a jury of individuals who, collectively, represent the range of diverse groups in the community.

A test that can be applied to any political arrangement is whether a person is willing to abide by it without knowing his or her role in that arrangement. If you are called to serve, you should answer the call. You would want nothing less from others if you or one of your friends or family members were the person on trial.

Inside Influences: The Justices' Own Political Beliefs

Although the judiciary symbolizes John Adams's characterization of the U.S. political system as "a government of laws, and not of men," judicial rulings are affected by the political beliefs of the men and women who sit on the courts.[26] Decisions of the Supreme Court often divide along political lines. In more than two-thirds of recent nonunanimous Supreme Court decisions, for example, justices Antonin Scalia and Clarence Thomas, each of whom was a Republican appointee, were opposed by justices Stephen Breyer and Ruth Bader Ginsburg, the two Democratic appointees on the Court.[27]

Arguably, partisanship was never more evident than in the Supreme Court's *Bush v. Gore* (2000) decision.[28] The five justices in the majority were the same justices who in previous decisions had upheld states' rights and had opposed new applications of the Fourteenth Amendment's equal protection clause. Yet they used the equal-protection clause to block the statewide manual recount that had been ordered by Florida's high court because no uniform standard for counting the ballots existed. When the Court issued a rare stay order to stop the recount, Justice Antonin Scalia claimed that it was justified because the recount could cast doubt on the legitimacy of Bush's victory even though Bush had not yet been elected. Some observers suggested that if Bush had been trailing in the Florida vote, the Court's majority would have allowed the recount to continue. Justice John Paul Stevens, who thought the Florida high court had acted properly in ordering a manual count, accused the Court's majority of

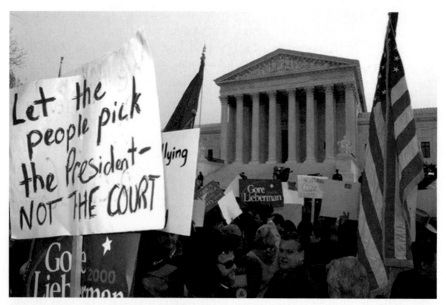

Demonstrators rally outside the U.S. Supreme Court building during hearings on the *Bush v. Gore* case that effectively brought the 2000 presidential election to an end. At times, the policy rulings of the judiciary are as significant as the decisions of the president or Congress.

devising a ruling based on their partisan desires rather than on the law. Stevens noted that different standards for casting and counting ballots are used throughout the country, even within the same state.[29]

Most Supreme Court justices do not change their views greatly during their tenure. As a result, major shifts in the Supreme Court's positions usually occur when its membership changes. Such shifts are related to political changes. When the Court in the 1980s watered down the criminal justice rulings of the 1960s, for instance, it was largely because the more recently appointed justices, like the presidents who had nominated them, believed that government should have more leeway in its efforts to fight crime.

JUDICIAL POWER AND DEMOCRATIC GOVERNMENT

The issue of judicial power is heightened by the fact that federal judges are not elected. The principle of self-government asserts that lawmaking majorities have the power to decide society's policies. Because the United States has a constitutional system that places checks on the will of the majority, there is obviously an important role in the system for an institution such as the judiciary to play (see Table 14–4). Yet court decisions often reflect the political philosophy of the judges, who constitute a tiny political elite that wields significant power.[30] A critical question is how far unelected judges ought to go in substituting their policy judgments for those of the legislative and executive officials who are elected by the people.

The judiciary's power is most evident when it declares executive or legislative action to be unconstitutional. The power of the courts to make such determinations, called **judicial review,** was first asserted in the landmark *Marbury v. Madison* case of 1803, when the Supreme Court rebuked both the president and Congress (see Chapter 2). Without judicial review, the federal courts would be unable to restrain an elected official or institution that has gone out of control.

Yet judicial review places the judgment of the courts above that of elected officials when interpretation of the Constitution is at issue, creating the possibility of conflict between the courts and the elected branches. The imposing nature of judicial review has led the courts to apply it judiciously, but the Supreme Court alone has invoked it in more than a thousand cases. Only a small percentage of these cases have involved action by Congress or the president, an indication that the Supreme Court normally prefers to avoid showdowns with the other

TABLE 14-4 SIGNIFICANT SUPREME COURT CASES	
Included are a few of the most significant cases decided by the U.S. Supreme Court.	
Case	**Ruling**
Marbury v. Madison (1803)	Established principle of judicial review (Chapter 2)
McCulloch v. Maryland (1819)	Strengthened national power over states (Chapter 3)
Dred Scott v. Sanford (1857)	Decided that slaves were property and not citizens (Chapter 3)
Plessy v. Ferguson (1896)	Established the "separate but equal" doctrine (Chapter 5)
Gitlow v. New York (1925)	Protected free expression from state action through Fourteenth Amendment (Chapter 4)
Brown v. Board of Education of Topeka (1954)	Abolished the "separate but equal" doctrine and banned segregation in public schools (Chapter 5)
Gideon v. Wainwright (1963)	Decided that states must provide an attorney for poor defendants accused of committing felonies (Chapter 4)
Roe v. Wade (1973)	Decided that women have full freedom to choose abortion during the first three months of pregnancy under the right of privacy (Chapter 4)
Bush v. Gore (2000)	Decided that a hand count of disputed Florida ballots would violate equal protection, thereby deciding the 2000 election in George W. Bush's favor (Chapter 12)

branches of the federal government. The state and local governments are an entirely different matter. More than 90 percent of rulings involving judicial review have been directed at states and localities. A prime example is the 1954 *Brown v. Board of Education* decision, which employed the Fourteenth Amendment to invalidate state laws that prevented black children from attending the same local public schools as white children.

The Debate over the Proper Role of the Judiciary

The question of judicial power centers on the basic issue of **legitimacy**—the proper authority of the judiciary in a political system based in part on the principle of majority rule. The judiciary's policymaking significance and discretion have been sources of controversy throughout the country's history, but the controversies have seldom been livelier than during recent decades.

The judiciary at times has acted almost legislatively by defining broad social policies, such as abortion, busing, affirmative action, church-state relations, and prison reform. During the 1990s, for example, the prison systems in forty-two states were operating under federal court orders that mandated improvements in health care or overcrowding. Through such actions the judiciary has restricted the policymaking authority of the states, has narrowed legislative discretion, and has made judicial action an effective political strategy for certain interests.[31]

The judiciary has become more extensively involved in policymaking for many of the same reasons that Congress and the president have been thrust into new policy areas and become more deeply involved in old ones. Social and economic changes have required government to play a larger role in society, and this development has generated a seemingly endless series of new legal controversies. Environmental pollution, for example, was not a major issue until the 1960s; since then, it has been the subject of numerous court cases.

Judicial action raises an important question: How far should the judiciary go in asserting its authority when that authority conflicts with or goes beyond the action of elected institutions? There are two schools of thought on this question: judicial activism and judicial restraint. Although these terms are somewhat imprecise and not fully consistent, they provide a lens through which to examine the judiciary's proper role.[32]

Judicial Restraint Versus Judicial Activism   The doctrine of **judicial restraint** holds that judges should work closely within the wording of the law, be respectful of precedent, and generally defer to decisions made by legislatures. The restraint doctrine holds that in nearly all cases public issues should be decided by elected lawmakers and not by appointed judges. The role of judges is to determine how the Constitution, statutes, and precedents apply to specific cases rather than to find new meanings that create new law or substantially modify existing law.

Advocates of judicial restraint say that when judges substitute their views for those of elected institutions, they undermine the fundamental principle of self-government—the right of the majority, through its elected representatives, to decide the policies by which they will be governed.[33] Advocates also claim that restraint serves to maintain public confidence in the judiciary, thereby increasing the likelihood of **compliance** with its decisions, that is, whether people will respect and obey court rulings.[34] Advocates of judicial restraint acknowledge that established law is not precise enough to provide exact answers to every question raised by every case and that judges therefore must exercise some degree of discretion. They also acknowledge that in some instances judges have little choice but to override the decisions of elected institutions, as in cases where lawmakers have overstepped their constitutional authority. Nevertheless, the judicial restraint philosophy broadly holds that the role of judges is to review the law, not make the law.

Contrasting the judicial restraint doctrine is the doctrine of **judicial activism,** which holds that judges should actively interpret the Constitution, statutes, and precedents in light of established principles when the elected branches ignore or trample on these principles. Although advocates of judicial activism acknowledge the importance of precedent and majority rule, they claim that the courts should not be wholly subservient to past rulings or to the decisions of elected officials when core principles are at issue.

Advocates of judicial activism argue that law is not simply a narrow reading of the exact words in a statute or constitution but must take into account the larger meaning of the words. What is it that a constitutional provision is designed to protect or that a statute is intended to promote? Judicial activism proponents argue that judges should be especially vigilant on questions of constitutional rights and the democratic process. They claim that the judiciary must prevent majorities, acting through lawmakers, from violating the legitimate rights of the minority or rigging the political process in ways that deprive certain classes of citizens of a meaningful voice. They view the Constitution as designed chiefly to protect individuals from unresponsive or repressive government, a goal that can be accomplished only by a judiciary willing to act when lawmaking majorities perpetrate or fail to correct injustice.[35]

A classic example of the conflict between the opposing judicial philosophies of restraint and activism was the malapportionment issue. Until the 1960s, the legislative districts in many states varied greatly in the number of voters they encompassed. Rural legislators controlled the state legislatures, and as the urban population grew they refused to adjust election districts to increase the number of urban districts. Each such district accordingly was packed with voters, while each rural district had relatively few. By this means, rural areas maintained control of state legislatures and used that control to enact policies disadvantageous to

I was sentenced to The State Penitentiary by The Circuit Court of Bay County, State of Florida. The present proceeding was commenced on a petition for a Writ of Habeus Corpus To The Supreme Court of The State of Florida to vacate The sentence, on the grounds that I was made to stand Trial without The aid of counsel, and, at all times of my incarseretion. The said Court refused To appoint counsel and therefore deprived me of Due process of law, and violate my rights in The Bill of Rights and the constitution of The United States.

5th day of Jan 1962 Petitioner

Notary Public

Gideon's Letter to the Supreme Court
John F. Davis, Clerk, Supreme Court of the United States

The handwritten letter that Clarence Gideon (insert) sent to the Supreme Court in 1962. The letter led eventually to the *Gideon* decision in which the Court held that states must provide poor defendants with legal counsel (see Chapter 4). Seen by many people at the time as judicial activism, the ruling is now fully accepted.

the cities. Legal challenges to this situation initially were denied under the philosophy of judicial restraint. Redistricting was regarded as a "political" issue, not a legal one, properly decided by legislatures rather than courts. In *Colegrove v. Green* (1946), the Supreme Court rejected a malapportionment claim; in a classic statement of judicial restraint, Justice Felix Frankfurter wrote, "Courts ought not to enter this political thicket."[36] Nearly two decades later, the Supreme Court changed its stand. In *Baker v. Carr* (1962), the Court by a 6-2 vote took an activist position, holding that state legislative districts must be apportioned on the principle of "one person, one vote." The Court's majority said that any other apportionment system violated the equal protection clause of the Fourteenth Amendment. Justice William Brennan wrote for the majority: "The political question doctrine, a tool for maintenance of governmental order, will not be so applied as to promote only disorder." Justice John Harlan, in a dissent that was joined by Justice Frankfurter, argued for judicial restraint: "I can find nothing in the Equal Protection Clause or elsewhere in the Federal Constitution which expressly or impliedly supports the view that state legislatures must be so structured as to reflect with approximate equality the voice of every voter. . . . Its acceptance would require us to turn our backs on the regard which this Court has always shown for the judgment of state legislatures and courts on matters of basically local concern."[37]

HOW THE UNITED STATES COMPARES

Judicial Power

U.S. courts are highly political compared to the courts of most other democracies. First, U.S. courts operate within a common-law tradition, in which judge-made law becomes (through precedent) a part of the legal code. Many democracies have a civil-law tradition, in which nearly all law is defined by legislative statutes. Second, because U.S. courts operate in a constitutional system of divided powers, they are required to rule on conflicts between state and nation or between the executive and the legislative branches, which thrusts the judiciary into the middle of political conflicts. It should not be surprising, then, that federal judges and justices are appointed through an overtly political process in which partisan views and activities are major considerations. Many federal judges, particularly at the district level, have no significant prior judicial experience. In fact, the United States is one of the few countries that does not mandate formal training for judges.

The pattern is different in most European democracies, where judgeships tend to be career positions. Individuals are appointed to the judiciary at an early age and then work their way up the judicial ladder largely on the basis of seniority. Partisan politics does not play a large role in appointment and promotion. By tradition, European judges see their job as the strict interpretation of statutes, not the creative application of them.

The power of U.S. courts is nowhere more evident than in the exercise of judicial review—the voiding of a legislative or executive action on the grounds that it violates the Constitution. Judicial review had its origins in European experience and thought, but it was first formally applied in the United States when, in *Marbury v. Madison* (1803), the Supreme Court declared an act of Congress unconstitutional. Some democracies, including Great Britain, still do not allow broad-scale judicial review, but most democracies now provide for it.

In the so-called American system of judicial review, all judges can evaluate the applicability of constitutional law to particular cases and can declare ordinary law invalid when it conflicts with constitutional law. By comparison, the so-called Austrian system restricts

(continued)

judicial review to a special constitutional court. Judges in other courts cannot declare a law void on the grounds that it is unconstitutional: they must apply ordinary law as it is written. In the Austrian system, moreover, constitutional decisions can be made in response to requests for judicial review by elected officials when they are considering legislation. In the American case, judges can act only within the framework of actual legal cases; thus, their rulings are made only after laws have been enacted.

Restraint Versus Activism in Practice Just as presidential and congressional politics in recent years have become more intensely partisan (see Chapters 11 and 12), so too has the judiciary. Judicial appointments and rulings have been increasingly contentious, and judicial restraint and activism have become part of the vocabulary of these fights. Republicans, who have controlled the U.S. Senate for most of the past decade, have demanded that judicial appointees adhere to the principle of judicial restraint. A leading Republican member of the Senate Judiciary Committee, Orren Hatch of Utah, has said repeatedly that judges should not legislate from the bench and that "activist judges" should step down from the bench and run for public office if they are intent on promoting their policy views.

However, judicial restraint does not precisely describe the legal rulings of Republican appointees, just as judicial activism does not precisely describe those of Democratic appointees. Supreme Court justices appointed by both parties have variously tended toward restraint or activism at different points in history and on different issues. The Republican-dominated Supreme Court in the period between the Civil War and the Great Depression was an activist judiciary, striking down most state and congressional legislation aimed at economic regulation (see Chapter 3). It did not defer to laws passed by elected representatives. By the same token, the Democratic-dominated Supreme Court in the period after World War II was also an activist judiciary, expanding the civil rights of black Americans (see Chapter 5) and the civil liberties of the criminally accused (see Chapter 4). It vigorously asserted its authority against that of local and state elected officials.

Even today, it is difficult on the basis of their partisan backgrounds to neatly assign judges and justices to the activist or restraint category. A study of Supreme Court decisions found that, as measured by a willingness to invalidate acts of Congress, all recent Supreme Court justices have been activists to some degree. Republican appointees have been just as likely as Democratic appointees to reject laws enacted by Congress—in other words, to place their judgments ahead of those of the people's elected representatives.[38] The Republican-dominated Supreme Court has struck down more acts of Congress in the past decade than were invalidated during the entire previous half-century. Although Chief Justice William Rehnquist has often been described as a proponent of judicial restraint, the Court he led until his death in 2005 had an agenda that, if not entirely activist, was not entirely restrained. Rehnquist led a federalist revolution, with the goal of increasing state sovereignty and diminishing Congress's power to enact laws binding on state governments (see Chapter 3). It could be argued that the Rehnquist Court was establishing a balance of federal-state power more consistent with the original intent of the Constitution than was the balance that emerged from the New Deal; in this sense, the Court could be seen as having acted with restraint.[39] On the other hand, the Rehnquist Court was repudiating precedent and laws of Congress—actions consistent with judicial activism. Walter Dellinger, a former U.S. Solicitor General, said of the Rehnquist court: "[It] doesn't defer to government at any level. [It] is confident it can come up with the right decisions, and it believes it is constitutionally charged with doing so."[40]

One reason why justices' decisions do not neatly align with specific judicial philosophies is that disputes that reach the Supreme Court are anything but clear-cut. If they were, they would have been settled in the lower federal courts. Also, the justices are political appointees and have political leanings. Studies indicate that, in cases that reasonably could be decided for either side, justices tend toward the side that suits their political ideology.[41] On the liberal side, this leads to the active promotion of social justice for the disadvantaged; on the conservative side, it leads to the protection of property claims and the upholding of preferred forms of authority, such as state government.

Thus, all justices are activists in the sense that they are willing to pit their judgment against the judgment of elected officials. The law as expressed through the Constitution, statutes, and precedent is not precise enough to provide an automatic answer to every court case. Judges and justices must exercise their judgment when the text of the law is inexact. And all judges and justices are restrained in the sense that their decisions must be rooted in the law. Judges cannot simply make any decision they might choose but rather are confined by the facts of the case and the laws that might reasonably be applied to it.

Nonetheless, judges and justices vary in the degree to which they are willing to contest the judgment of elected officials as well as in the degree to which they are willing to depart from the wording of the law. These differences do, on some issues, coincide with judges' and justices' partisan

John Marshall
(1755–1835)

John Marshall served thirty-four years as chief justice of the Supreme Court, the longest tenure in that position in U.S. history. Marshall had served for a time as John Adams's secretary of state and in the House of Representatives before being appointed chief justice by Adams. Before Marshall's tenure, the Supreme Court was perceived as a feeble branch of the federal government. Marshall changed that notion. An ardent nationalist who saw himself as a guardian of federal authority, Marshall steered the Court through a series of decisions that established it as a powerful institution and helped lay the foundation for a strong Union. The Supreme Court's ruling in *McCulloch v. Maryland* (1819) affirmed the claims that national law was supreme over conflicting state law and that the federal government's powers were not narrowly constrained by the Constitution.

Despite philosophical differences with the presidents who succeeded Adams, Marshall dominated the Court throughout his long tenure, persuading newly appointed justices to back him on key constitutional issues. Marshall saw himself as a framer of the Constitution, acting as the ongoing architect of the work begun in Philadelphia during the summer of 1787. Although Marshall was a distant cousin of Thomas Jefferson, the two men were bitter opponents. Marshall's first landmark decision, *Marbury v. Madison* (1803), which established the principle of judicial review, was a rebuke to President Jefferson's executive authority. Their ongoing dispute peaked in 1807 at the trial of Aaron Burr, who was justly accused of treason by the Jefferson administration. Marshall presided over the trial and acquitted Burr, ruling that the word of a single eyewitness was insufficient grounds for conviction.

backgrounds. In *Vieth v. Jubelirer* (2004), for example, the Supreme Court was split over a case that had some similarities to the *Baker v. Carr* case of forty years earlier. At issue was whether partisan gerrymandering, in which state legislatures stack election districts with voters of one party when they redraw election district boundaries after a census, is a violation of the voters' right to equal protection under the Fourteenth Amendment. The Court's three most conservative justices, all of them Republican appointees, were joined by the more moderate Justice Sandra Day O'Connor in concluding that the partisan gerrymandering issue is for the legislatures, not the courts, to decide. The Court's four most liberal justices, two of them Democratic appointees, said that the Court should be open to ruling on such cases. The deciding vote was cast by Justice Anthony Kennedy, a relative moderate, who wrote that in some future case—but not in this particular one—the abuse of redistricting power might be so extreme as to warrant judicial involvement.[42]

Over its history, the Supreme Court has had many great (as well as many mediocre) justices who have been proponents of each philosophy. Chief Justice John Marshall was an activist who used the Court to enlarge the judiciary's power and to promote the national government (see Chapters 2 and 3). Judicial review—the most substantial form of judicial power—is not explicitly granted by the Constitution but was claimed through Marshall's opinion in *Marbury v. Madison*. Associate Justice Oliver Wendell Holmes Jr. was Marshall's philosophical opposite, favoring judicial restraint. In the court opinions he wrote, as well as in his other writings, Holmes spoke of the need for the judiciary to work within the tight confines of the law: "My job is to play the game according to the rules."[43] But he too left an indelible mark on jurisprudence, particularly in the area of free expression (see Chapter 4). Looking back on history, an observer could conclude that the nation has been well served by the fact that its judges and justices have not all been advocates of judicial restraint or advocates of judicial activism—both the nation and the judiciary are stronger for having had jurists of each persuasion.

The Judiciary's Proper Role: A Question of Competing Values

The dispute between advocates of judicial activism and advocates of judicial restraint is a philosophical one that involves opposing values. The debate is important because it addresses the normative question of what role the judiciary ought to play in American democracy. Should unelected judges involve themselves deeply in policy by adopting a broad conception of their power, or should they grant wide discretion to elective institutions? Should judges defer to precedent, or should they be willing to change course, even at the risk of sending the law down uncharted paths? These questions cannot be answered simply on the basis of whether one personally agrees or disagrees with a particular judicial decision. The answer necessarily depends on a value judgment about the role the judiciary should play in a governing system based on the often-conflicting concepts of majority rule and individual rights.

The United States is a constitutional democracy that recognizes both the power of the majority to rule and the claim of the minority to protection of its rights. The judiciary was not established as the nation's moral conscience and does not have a monopoly on the issue of minority interests and rights. Yet the judiciary was established as a coequal branch of government charged with the responsibility of protecting individual rights and minority interests. In short, the constitutional question of how far the courts should be allowed to go in substituting their judgment for that of elected institutions and established law is open to interpretation. The trade-off is significant on all issues: minority rights versus majority rule, states' rights versus federal power, legislative authority versus judicial authority.

Summary

At the lowest level of the federal judicial system are the district courts, where most federal cases begin. Above them are the federal courts of appeals, which review cases appealed from the lower courts. The U.S. Supreme Court is the nation's highest court. Each state has its own court system, consisting of trial courts at the bottom and one or two appellate levels at the top. Cases originating in state courts ordinarily cannot be appealed to the federal courts unless a federal issue is involved, and then the federal courts can choose to rule only on the federal aspects of the case. Federal judges at all levels are nominated by the president, and if confirmed by the Senate they are appointed by the president to the office. Once on the federal bench, they serve until they die, retire, or are removed by impeachment and conviction.

The Supreme Court is unquestionably the most important court in the country. The legal principles it establishes are binding on lower courts, and its capacity to define the law is enhanced by the control it exercises over the cases it hears. However, it is inaccurate to assume that lower courts are inconsequential (the upper-court myth). Lower courts have considerable discretion, and the great majority of their decisions are not reviewed by a higher court. It is also inaccurate to assume that federal courts are far more significant than state courts (the federal court myth).

The courts have less discretionary authority than elected institutions do. The judiciary's positions are constrained by the facts of a case and by the laws as defined through the Constitution, statutes and government regulations, and legal precedent. Yet existing legal guidelines are seldom so precise that judges have no choice in their decisions. As a result, political influences have a strong impact on the judiciary. It responds to national conditions, public opinion, interest groups, and elected officials, particularly the president and members of Congress. Another political influence on the judiciary is the personal beliefs of judges, who have individual preferences that are evident in the way they decide issues that come before the courts. Not surprisingly, partisan politics plays a significant role in judicial appointments.

In recent decades, the Supreme Court has issued broad rulings on individual rights, some of which have required governments to take positive action on behalf of minority interests. As the Court has crossed into areas traditionally left to lawmaking majorities, the legitimacy of its policies has been questioned. Advocates of judicial restraint claim that the justices' personal values are inadequate justification for exceeding the proper judicial role; they argue that the Constitution entrusts broad issues of the public good to elective institutions and that judicial activism ultimately undermines public respect for the judiciary. Judicial activists counter that the courts were established as an independent branch and should not hesitate to promote new principles when they see a need, even if this action brings them into conflict with elected officials.

KEY TERMS

appellate jurisdiction (*p. 489*)

brief (*p. 492*)

civil law (*p. 505*)

compliance (*p. 516*)

concurring opinion (*p. 492*)

criminal law (*p. 505*)

decision (*p. 492*)

dissenting opinion (*p. 492*)

facts (of a court case) (*p. 504*)

judicial activism (*p. 516*)

judicial conference (*p. 492*)

judicial restraint (*p. 515*)

judicial review (*p. 513*)

jurisdiction (of a court) (*p. 489*)

laws (of a court case) (*p. 504*)

legitimacy (of judicial power) (*p. 515*)

majority opinion (*p. 492*)

opinion (of a court) (*p. 492*)

original jurisdiction (*p. 489*)

plurality opinion (*p. 492*)

precedent (*p. 490*)

procedural law (*p. 505*)

senatorial courtesy (*p. 500*)

solicitor general (*p. 490*)

writ of certiorari (*p. 490*)

SUGGESTED READINGS

Carp, Robert, and Ronald Stidham. *The Federal Courts*, 4th ed. Washington, D.C.: Congressional Quarterly Press, 2001. An overview of the federal judiciary system.

Davis, Richard. *Electing Justices: Fixing the Supreme Court Nomination Process.* New York: Oxford University Press, 2005. An examination of the now contentious process through which Supreme Court justices are nominated and confirmed.

Gillman, Howard. *Votes That Counted: How the Court Decided the 2000 Presidential Election.* Chicago: University of Chicago Press, 2001. An accounting of the *Bush v. Gore* ruling.

Hansford, Thomas G., and James F. Spriggs II. *The Politics of Precedent on the Supreme Court.* Princeton, N.J.: Princeton University Press, 2006. An examination of how the Court interprets precedent to suit new situations and goals.

McGuire, Kevin T. *Understanding the Supreme Court: Cases and Controversies.* New York: McGraw-Hill, 2002. An overview of Supreme Court decisions and approaches to legal disputes.

O'Brien, David M. *Storm Center: The Supreme Court in American Politics*, 7th ed. New York: Norton, 2005. A thorough assessment of the Supreme Court.

Sandler, Ross, and David Schoenbrod. *Democracy by Decree: What Happens When Courts Run Government.* New Haven, Conn.: Yale University Press, 2003. A critical evaluation of the courts' growing policy role.

Seidman, Louis Michael. *Our Unsettled Constitution.* New Haven, Conn.: Yale University Press, 2002. A defense of constitutionalism and judicial review.

LIST OF WEBSITES

http://www.courttv.com/cases A website that allows you to take the facts of actual court cases, examine the law and the arguments, and then decide each case for yourself.

http://www.fjc.gov/ The home page of the Federal Judicial Center, an agency created by Congress to conduct research and provide education on the federal judicial system.

http://www.lib.umich.edu/govdocs/fedjudi.html A University of Michigan web page that provides detailed information on the federal judicial system.

http://www.rominger.com/supreme.htm A vast site that provides links to the Supreme Court, pending cases, the state court systems, and other subjects.

POLITICS IN THEORY AND PRACTICE

Thinking: Which philosophy—judicial restraint or judicial activism—comes closer to your own thinking about the proper role of the courts? Does your support for restraint or activism depend on whether a judicial decision conforms to your own preference on the issue in question?

Participating: The right to a fair and open trial decided by a jury is one of the oldest hallmarks of the American justice system. If you have never done so, you might want to attend a trial at your local courthouse to see how the process works. If you live in or near Washington, D.C., or a state capital, you might choose instead to observe a session of a supreme court. Such courts are appellate courts, so there is no jury, but you are more likely to hear arguments on cases of broad significance.

ADDITIONAL RESOURCES

For quizzes, interactive simulations, games, graphics, and other study tools, visit the book's Online Learning Center at **www.mhhe.com/pattersonwtp7.**

Judicial Interpretation

By William J. Brennan Jr.

*As a legal institution, the Supreme
Court operates within the framework of laws. But how fully binding
on the Court is the law? In a speech
delivered at Georgetown University,
the late Justice William Brennan
discussed this issue in the context of
the Constitution's provisions. Brennan
explained the difficulty of discerning
the Framers' intentions, beginning
with the fact that they frequently
disagreed among themselves on the
meaning of particular constitutional
provisions. He argued that the
Constitution cannot mean whatever
a momentary majority wants it to
mean and claimed that some of its
principles (such as checks and
balances) are unmistakable. Nevertheless, he embraced the view that
the Constitution was meant to be a
flexible document that can and must
be adapted to meet America's
changing needs. Brennan served on
the Supreme Court for three
decades.*

The Constitution is fundamentally a public
text—the monumental charter of a government and a people—and a Justice of the
Supreme Court must apply it to resolve
public controversies. For, from our beginning, a most important consequence of the
constitutionally created separation of powers has been the American habit, extraordinary to other democracies, of casting social,
economic, philosophical and political questions in the form of lawsuits, in an attempt
to secure ultimate resolution by the
Supreme Court.... Not infrequently, these
are the issues upon which contemporary
society is most deeply divided. They arouse
our deepest emotions. The main burden of
my twenty-nine terms on the Supreme
Court has thus been to wrestle with the
Constitution in this heightened public context, to draw meaning from the text in order
to resolve public controversies.

Two other aspects of my relation to this
text warrant mention First, constitutional
interpretation for a federal judge is, for the
most part, obligatory. When litigants
approach the bar of court to adjudicate a
constitutional dispute, they may justifiably
demand an answer. Judges cannot avoid a
definitive interpretation because they feel
unable to, or would prefer not to, penetrate
to the full meaning of the Constitution's
provisions. Unlike literary critics, judges
cannot merely savor the tensions or revel in
the ambiguities inhering in the text—judges
must resolve them.

Second, consequences flow from a
Justice's interpretation in a direct and
immediate way. A judicial decision respecting the incompatibility of Jim Crow with a
constitutional guarantee of equality is not
simply a contemplative exercise in defining
the shape of a just society. It is an order—
supported by the full coercive power of the
state—that the present society change in a
fundamental aspect.... More than the litigants may be affected. The course of vital
social, economic and political currents may
be directed.

These ... defining characteristics of my
relation to the constitutional text—its public
nature, obligatory character, and consequen-
tialist aspect—cannot help but influence the

way I read that text. When Justices interpret the Constitution they speak for their community, not for themselves alone. The act of interpretation must be undertaken with full consciousness that it is, in a very real sense, the community's interpretation that is sought. Justices are not platonic guardians appointed to wield authority according to their personal moral predilections. Precisely because coercive force must attend any judicial decision to countermand the will of a contemporary majority, the Justices must render constitutional interpretations that are received as legitimate. The source of legitimacy is, of course, a wellspring of controversy in legal and political circles. At the core of the debate is what the late Yale Law School Professor Alexander Bickel labeled "the countermajoritarian difficulty." Our commitment to self-governance in a representative democracy must be reconciled with vesting in electorally unaccountable Justices the power to invalidate the expressed desires of representative bodies on the ground of inconsistency with higher law. . . .

There are those who find legitimacy in fidelity to what they call "the intentions of the Framers." In its most doctrinaire incarnation, this view demands that Justices discern exactly what the Framers thought about the question under consideration and simply follow that intention in resolving the case before them. It is a view that feigns self-effacing deference to the specific judgments of those who forged our original social compact. But in truth it is little more than arrogance cloaked as humility. It is arrogant to pretend that from our vantage we can gauge accurately the intent of the Framers on application of principle to specific, contemporary questions. All too often, sources of potential enlightenment such as records of the ratification debates provide sparse or ambiguous evidence of the original intention. Typically, all that can be gleaned is that the Framers themselves did not agree about the application or meaning

of particular constitutional provisions, and hid their differences in cloaks of generality. Indeed, it is far from clear whose intention is relevant—that of the drafters, the congressional disputants, or the ratifiers in the states—or even whether the idea of an original intention is a coherent way of thinking about a jointly drafted document drawing its authority from a general assent of the states. And apart from the problematic nature of the sources, our distance of two centuries cannot but work as a prism refracting all we perceive. One cannot help but speculate that the chorus of lamentations calling for interpretation faithful to "original intention"—and proposing nullification of interpretations that fail this quick litmus test—must inevitably come from persons who have no familiarity with the historical record. . . .

Another, perhaps more sophisticated, response to the potential power of judicial interpretation stresses democratic theory: because ours is a government of the people's elected representatives, substantive value choices should by and large be left to them. This view emphasizes not the transcendent historical authority of the Framers but the predominant contemporary authority of the elected branches of government. . . .

The view that all matters of substantive policy should be resolved through the majoritarian process has appeal under some circumstances, but I think it ultimately will not do. Unabashed enshrinement of majority would permit the imposition of a social caste system or wholesale confiscation of property so long as a majority of the authorized legislative body, fairly elected, approved. Our Constitution could not abide such a situation. It is the very purpose of a Constitution—and particularly of the Bill of Rights—to declare certain values transcendent, beyond the reach of temporary political majorities. The majoritarian process cannot be expected to rectify claims of minority right that arise as a response to the outcomes of that very majoritarian process. . . .

Faith in democracy is one thing, blind faith quite another. Those who drafted our Constitution understood the difference. One cannot read the text without admitting that it embodies substantive value choices; it places certain values beyond the power of any legislature. Obvious are the separation of powers; the privilege of the Writ of Habeas Corpus; prohibition of Bills of Attainder and *ex post facto* laws; prohibition of cruel and unusual punishments; the requirement of just compensation for official taking of property; the prohibition of laws tending to establish religion or enjoining the free exercise of religion; and, since the Civil War, the banishment of slavery and official race discrimination. With respect to at least such principles, we simply have not constituted ourselves as strict utilitarians. While the Constitution may be amended, such amendments require an immense effort by the People as a whole.

To remain faithful to the content of the Constitution, therefore, an approach to interpreting the text must account for the existence of these substantive value choices, and must accept the ambiguity inherent in the effort to apply them to modern circumstances. . . .

We current Justices read the Constitution in the only way that we can: as Twentieth Century Americans. We look to the history of the time of framing and to the intervening history of interpretation. But the ultimate question must be, what do the words of the text mean in our time? For the genius of the Constitution rests not in any static meaning it might have had in a world that is dead and gone, but in the adaptability of its great principles to cope with current problems and current needs.

Source: From William J. Brennan, Jr., *"Judicial Interpretation."* Address to the Text and Teaching Symposium, Georgetown University, October 12, 1985.

What's Your Opinion?

Justice Brennan's view of constitutional interpretation emphasizes the principles embedded in the Constitution and a need to apply these principles to contemporary problems. Do you agree with this view? Why or why not?

CHAPTER 15

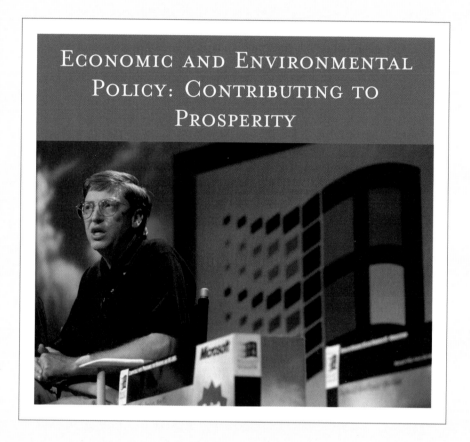

ECONOMIC AND ENVIRONMENTAL
POLICY: CONTRIBUTING TO
PROSPERITY

66 We the people of the United States, in order to . . . insure domestic
tranquility . . . 99

PREAMBLE, U.S. CONSTITUTION

The stock market was downright scary. The Dow Jones and Nasdaq indexes had dropped steadily for two years, knocking trillions of dollars off the value of stocks. Stocks that sold on the technology-heavy Nasdaq index were particularly hard hit. By 2003, it had fallen 75 percent—a steeper decline over the same length of time than had occurred at the onset of the Great Depression. Was history about to repeat itself? Was the U.S. economy in danger of collapse?

In fact, Wall Street and the rest of America reacted rather calmly to the market downturn. Institutional and individual investors were unhappy with the drop in the value of their stocks, but they did not panic. Among the reasons was the existence of substantial government programs designed to stabilize and stimulate the U.S. economy. When the Great

Depression struck, no such programs existed. Moreover, the response to the 1929–31 drop in stock prices made matters worse: businesses cut back on production, investors fled the stock market, depositors withdrew their bank savings, and consumers slowed their spending. All these actions accelerated the downward spiral. In 2003, however, government programs were in place to protect depositors' savings, slow the drop in stock prices, and steady the economy through adjustments in interest rates and spending programs. By 2004, the economy was already showing signs of strengthening.

This chapter examines economic policy. As was discussed in Chapter 1, public policy is a decision by government to follow a course of action designed to produce a particular result. Economic policy centers on the promotion and regulation of economic interests and, through fiscal and monetary actions, on economic growth and stability. Directly or indirectly, the federal government is a party to almost every economic transaction in which Americans engage. Although the private decisions of firms and individuals are the main force in the American economic system, these decisions are influenced by government policy. Washington seeks to maintain high productivity, employment, and purchasing power; regulates business practices that otherwise would harm the environment or result in economic inefficiencies and inequities; and promotes economic interests. The main ideas presented in this chapter are these:

★ *Through regulation, the U.S. government imposes restraints on business activity that are designed to promote economic efficiency and equity.* This regulation is often the cause of political conflict, which is both ideological and group-centered.

★ *Through regulatory and conservation policies, the U.S. government seeks to protect and preserve the environment from the effects of business firms and consumers.*

★ *Through promotion, the U.S. government helps private interests achieve their economic goals.* Business in particular benefits from the government's promotional efforts, which take place largely in the context of group politics.

★ *Through its taxing and spending decisions (fiscal policy), the U.S. government seeks to maintain a level of economic supply and demand that will keep the economy prosperous.* The condition of the economy is generally the leading issue in American electoral politics and has a major influence on each party's success.

★ *Through its money-supply decisions (monetary policy), the U.S.*
government—through the Fed—seeks to maintain a level of inflation con-
sistent with sustained, controllable economic growth.

THE PUBLIC POLICY PROCESS

Government action in the economic sector is part of the **public policy
process**—the political interactions that lead to the emergence and resolution of public policy issues. Before examining U.S. economic policy, we
will first describe the process through which public policy is developed.

Political scientists have identified six stages that make up the policy
process (see Figure 15–1). The first two stages—problem recognition and
problem transformation—refer to the emergence of issues. The last four
stages—policy formulation, policy adoption, policy implementation, and
policy evaluation—refer to the resolution of issues.

Emergence of Policy Issues

Policy problems stem from conditions of society—the employment rate,
the quality of schools, the security of the nation, the safety of the streets,
and so on. Yet only certain conditions are seen as problems of a *public*
nature. Even conditions that are life-threatening can intensify for years
without being thought of as anything but a personal problem. Obesity is
an example. Americans did not suddenly wake up one day to discover that
they had gained dozens of pounds during the course of a night's sleep.
Yet they had slowly become heavier until obesity was seen as a leading

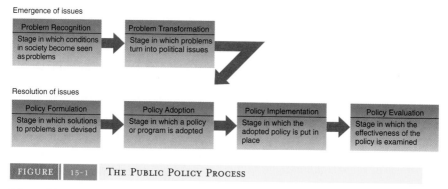

FIGURE 15-1   THE PUBLIC POLICY PROCESS

The public policy process refers to the political interactions that lead to the
emergence and resolution of public policy issues. The process includes six stages,
although not every issue goes through all stages or necessarily goes through them
in the exact order in which they are shown here.

cause of poor health. Only recently have Americans begun to think of obesity as a public policy problem.

In some cases *problem recognition* happens suddenly, as in the case of the terrorist attacks of September 11, 2001. In one shocking moment, hatred of the United States by extremist elements abroad—a condition—erupted into a threat to America's long-term security—a policy problem. Yet ordinarily it takes time for people to realize that a problem requires attention. During World War II, Americans of all races fought together against the Nazis and their racist ideology. When the war ended, however, white Americans at first acted as if nothing in their own society needed correcting. Black Americans knew better. They were still by law shuttled off to separate and inferior public schools and denied entry to white hospitals, restaurants, and theaters. The contradiction was simply too obvious to be ignored. Within a decade, America had begun to dismantle its system of government-imposed racial segregation.

Problem transformation, the second stage in the policy process, is where policy problems are turned into political issues. Not all problems make the transition. In many American neighborhoods, residents are resigned to unsightly streets and yards. They might complain about the unpleasant conditions, but that is as far as it goes. Leadership is a vital part of this stage in the policy process. Leadership sometimes can transform even a small problem into a leading issue. Although the estate tax has been a fact of dying ever since the Progressive era, it bothered only the very rich until the 1990s, when conservative groups made it an issue. They even relabeled it, believing that Americans would more readily oppose a "death tax." Through public forums, media appearances, and op-ed pieces, they sought to change how Americans thought about the inheritance tax. Their campaign was remarkably successful. In a 2006 NBC News/Wall Street Journal poll, more than twice as many respondents said they would support a candidate who favored repeal of the estate tax as said they would oppose such a candidate.

Special interests do not always seek to publicize their issue. Political scientist E. E. Schattschneider noted that the "scope of conflict" affects the outcome of issues.[1] As a conflict widens, an ever larger number of interests join the fight, forcing concessions from those interests already involved in it. Accordingly, if a group can manage to limit the scope of conflict—that is, to keep an issue to itself—it improves its chances of getting what it wants. Iron triangles are this type of arrangement (see Chapter 9). Through close, ongoing relationships with relevant executive agencies and congressional committees, well-placed interest groups are able to exert considerable influence over issues affecting them.

Striking janitors parade in Beverly Hills, California. Citizen action has the potential to influence several stages of the policy process. A protest march typically would be part of the problem transformation stage—the point at which problems turn into issues.

Interest groups are not the only actors that help set the issue agenda. Members of Congress, political parties, and the news media also do so. The media, for example, have the power to focus public attention. By highlighting a problem day after day, the media can lead people to decide that something needs to be done about it. No agenda setter, however, has more influence than does the president. Even a single presidential pronouncement sometimes will trigger a policy response. The AIDS crisis in Africa was far from Americans' minds until January 28, 2003. That evening, in his State of the Union address, President George W. Bush declared that Africa's problem could no longer be ignored. Within months, Congress had appropriated $1.4 billion to fight AIDS in Africa.

Resolution of Policy Issues

An occasional policy proposal is so straightforward that almost anyone could draft it. As the 2006 midterm elections approached, congressional Republicans revived an old issue—flag burning—as a means of energizing their conservative base. Their proposed constitutional amendment, which came within a single Senate vote of passage, contained just seventeen words: "The Congress shall have power to prohibit the physical desecration of the flag of the United States."

Most policy proposals, however, are as intricate as the problems they address. Because of the complexity of modern society, almost no problem exists in isolation. Problems invariably are connected to other problems. Consider, for example, the question of whether government price supports for corn should be increased in order to ease the problems of corn farmers.

Although a subsidy clearly would help corn growers, other interests might or might not be helped by it. How would a subsidy impact consumers, farmers' decisions about which crops to plant, ethanol production, and the federal deficit? How might such a subsidy affect foreign policy? Other countries have corn growers who compete in the world market with America's farmers. If U.S. growers are provided a subsidy, they can sell their corn at a lower price, giving them an advantage over other sellers in the world market. Faced with that prospect, foreign governments might decide to subsidize their own corn growers, possibly triggering a trade war. As farfetched as this example might seem, it approximates what happened in 2006 at the international round of trade talks. After five years of negotiation among scores of countries, the talks collapsed—partly because the United States refused to reduce its hefty farm subsidies.

The complexity of modern policymaking has created an entire industry—that of policy analysts. Thousands of scholars, consultants, and policy specialists are engaged in *policy formulation*. Most economic policy, for example, is designed by trained economists. Their ideas do not always work, but the success rate is far higher than that of economic proposals set forth by noneconomists.

Politicians also formulate policy. While they lack the analytic tools of the policy specialists, they have their own strengths. Above all, they have a sense of what other politicians will support. The best-crafted policy proposal in the world is worthless if lawmakers will not vote for it. When President Lyndon Johnson decided in 1965 to tackle the issue of public health, some of his advisers wanted him to propose to Congress a government-paid universal health care system like those of Europe. Knowing that Congress would not enact such a program, Johnson opted for a medical-care amendment to the social security act. The result was Medicare, which today serves the medical needs of nearly forty million American retirees.

Policies on the scale of the Medicare program are rare. *Policy adoption* in the United States occurs within a system of divided powers that is a barrier to enactment of ambitious programs. To become law, a bill must receive majority support in the House and in the Senate and be signed by the president. Unless there is solid support in each institution for substantial change, a bill is unlikely to succeed. A Senate filibuster by itself sometimes is enough to deter further action. Because of the obstacles they face, most policies enacted by Congress are modest in scope. As political scientist Aaron Wildavsky noted, incremental policies—those that depart only slightly from existing policies—are the characteristic output of the U.S. policy process.[2]

Political scientist John Kingdon found that major policy breakthroughs tend to occur only when several stages of the policy process converge.[3] When a problem is compelling, when political leaders are ready to tackle it, and when policy analysts think they have an answer to it, decisive action can result. Kingdon's analysis describes the circumstances that led in 2001 to enactment of President Bush's ambitious tax cut plan. At the time, the economy needed a boost, Republicans were empowered by their victory in the presidential election, and GOP policy analysts had amassed an array of tax-cutting proposals. Bush got nearly everything he asked for, including a reduction of the capital-gains tax by nearly half.

After policy is adopted, *policy implementation* occurs. Responsibility for implementation rests mostly with bureaucrats and judges. Bureaucrats are charged with administering the law, and judges are responsible for applying it in specific cases. As was explained in Chapters 13 and 14, administrators and judges often have considerable latitude in carrying out the law.

Bureaucrats and judges often take the blame when implementation goes astray. Frequently, however, the problem rests with the lawmakers. Federal bureaucrats had the unenviable task in 2006 of implementing a prescription drug benefit for the elderly that was based on poorly drafted legislation. It contained so many exceptions, thresholds, and exclusions that many senior citizens were baffled by the options. When they asked for help, they often found that there was none to be had. Congress had neglected to appropriate enough money to staff the program fully. At one point during implementation, fewer than half as many retirees were enrolled in the program as had been projected to be enrolled by that time.

During *policy evaluation*, the final stage of the policy process, the basic question is whether a program is working as intended. Sometimes the question can be answered in specific terms, such as whether the construction of a new stretch of federal highway is on time and within budget. Many policies, however, are hard to evaluate. An example is foreign economic aid. Economic development in poor countries is subject to so many factors that it is difficult to assess the effect of assistance grants. In such cases, policy evaluation usually centers on how well the program is being administered—for example, whether the money is being channeled to the right places or instead is finding its way into the pockets of corrupt officials.

Policy evaluation is a substantial part of the policy process. Nearly every government agency has an evaluation unit. In addition, broad oversight is provided by agencies such as the Government Accountability Office (GAO) within Congress and the Office of Management and Budget within the executive branch (see Chapters 11–13). The GAO alone has a budget of nearly $500 million.

On occasion, the public has the final say in policy evaluation. Some programs have been terminated because of public opposition. In 1989, for example, Congress rescinded a law, passed less than a year earlier, intended to protect Medicare recipients from the financial ruin of catastrophic illness. Retirees afflicted with such illness would pay only the first $1,000 in medical costs; the federal government would pay the rest. In formulating the policy, Congress decided to require all Medicare recipients to pay an insurance premium to help defray program costs. The outcry from seniors was deafening. They liked the benefit but were dead set against paying the premium. When Dan Rostenkowsky (D-Ill.), chair of the House committee that drafted the legislation, was leaving a meeting in Chicago at which he had tried to explain the logic of the program, irate senior citizens followed him to his car, beating it with their canes and yelling "Rottenkowski" at him. Feeling trapped, Rostenkowsky broke through the crowd and raced down the street on foot.[4]

In summary, the public policy process is a set of stages through which problems pass on their way to some sort of resolution. In practice, the stages sometimes merge or reverse their order. Policy formulation, for example, sometimes goes hand in hand with problem transformation. Interested parties might conclude that they can strengthen their case by offering a solution at the same time they are highlighting the problem. Nevertheless, the stages are analytically distinct. The problem recognition stage is when conditions in society become seen as public problems, the problem transformation stage is when these problems turn into political issues, the policy formulation stage is when solutions to problems are devised, the policy adoption stage is when a solution is settled upon in the form of a policy or program, the policy implementation stage is when the adopted policy is put into place, and the policy evaluation stage is when the effectiveness of the policy is examined.

We turn now to a particular area of policy—the economy. The discussion starts with regulatory policy and concludes with an explanation of government efforts to maintain a stable economy.

Government as Regulator of the Economy

An **economy** is a system of production and consumption of goods and services that are allocated through exchange. When a shopper chooses groceries at a store and pays money for them, that transaction is one of the millions of economic exchanges that make up the economy. In *The Wealth of Nations* (1776), Adam Smith presented the case for the **laissez-faire**

doctrine, which holds that private individuals and firms should be left alone to make their own production and distribution decisions. Smith reasoned that when there is a demand for a good (that is, when people are willing and able to buy a good), private entrepreneurs will respond by producing the good and distributing it to those places where demand exists. Smith argued that the desire for profit is the "invisible hand" that guides the system of demand and supply toward the greatest benefit for all.

Smith acknowledged that the doctrine of laissez-faire capitalism has limits. Certain areas of the economy, such as roadways, are natural monopolies and are better run by government than by private firms. In addition, by regulating banking, currency, and contracts, government can give stability to private transactions. Otherwise, Smith argued, the economy is best left in private hands.

For a period in the twentieth century, an alternative way of thinking about the economy, Marxism, held sway in the Communist bloc countries, although their economies were not precisely what Karl Marx intended. In *Das Kapital* (*Capital,* 1867), Marx argued that a free-market system is exploitative because producers, through their control of markets, can compel workers to labor at a wage below the value they add to production. Marx proposed a collective economy in which workers own the means of production. In the former Soviet Union and its satellite countries, even though the economy was collectivized, ordinary workers had little say in its operation. The Soviet model collapsed because it proved to be an inefficient method for allocating capital and labor and for coordinating the supply of goods with the demand for them.

Today, free-market systems dominate the world economy, although they are not the laissez-faire systems that Smith envisioned. All economies assign a substantial role to government. However, the level of government involvement varies widely. In the partially socialized economies of the Scandinavian countries, the government owns some industry (for example, the airline and energy companies) and redistributes wealth through relatively steep progressive taxes and through the broad provision of welfare services, such as government-provided health care for all. In these economies, business and labor are closely regulated by government, but the free market determines most supply-and-demand decisions. The U.S. economy is also a "mixed" system in that it contains elements of both public and private control. Indeed, the U.S. government owns some industry (for example, the Tennessee Valley Authority, which produces electricity) and provides some welfare services (for example, its Medicare and Medicaid programs that furnish health care for the elderly and the

| TABLE 15-1 | THE MAIN OBJECTIVES OF REGULATORY POLICY |

The government intervenes in the economy to promote efficiency and equity.

Objective	Definition	Representative Actions by Government
Efficiency	Fulfillment of as many of society's needs as possible at the cost of as few of its resources as possible. The greater the output for a given input, the more efficient the process.	Preventing restraint of trade; requiring producers to pay the costs of damage to the environment; reducing restrictions on business that cannot be justified on a cost-benefit basis.
Equity	When the outcome of an economic transaction is fair to each party.	Requiring firms to bargain in good faith with labor; protecting consumers in their purchases; protecting workers' safety and health.

poor, respectively). Compared to the partially socialized Scandinavian countries, however, the U.S. economy tilts more toward the free-market end of the continuum than toward the government-control end. Even by comparison with most democracies, the United States relies more heavily on the free market than on government to make its production, distribution, and consumption decisions.

Nevertheless, the U.S. government plays a substantial economic role through the **regulation** of privately owned businesses. U.S. firms are not free to act as they please but rather must operate within production and distribution rules set by federal regulations. Regulatory policy is generally intended to promote either economic *efficiency* or *equity* (see Table 15–1).

Efficiency Through Government Intervention

Economic efficiency results when firms fulfill as many of society's needs as possible while using as few of its resources as possible.[5] **Efficiency** refers to the relationship of inputs (the labor and material that go into making a product or service) to outputs (the product or service itself). The greater the output for a given input, the more efficient the production process.

Preventing Restraint of Trade   Adam Smith and other classical economists argued that the free market is the optimal means of achieving efficiency. Producers will try to use as few resources as possible in order to keep their prices low enough to attract customers. To compete, less efficient producers then will either have to find a way to cut their production costs or be forced out of business. However, the assumption that the market always determines price is flawed. The same profit motive that drives producers to keep prices low can drive them to seek a monopoly on a good or to conspire with other producers to fix its price. If they succeed in their effort to restrain trade, consumers who want or need a particular good are forced to buy it at the price being charged. A monopoly does not have to worry about efficiency because it has no competitors.

Restraint of trade was prevalent in the United States in the late nineteenth century when large trusts came to dominate many areas of the economy, including the oil, steel, railroad, and sugar markets. Railroad companies, for example, had no competition on short routes and charged such high rates that many farmers went broke because they could not afford to ship their crops to markets. In 1887, Congress took its first step toward regulating the trusts by enacting the Interstate Commerce Act. The legislation created the Interstate Commerce Commission (ICC), which was charged with regulating railroad practices and fares.

Business competition today is regulated by a wide range of federal agencies, including the Federal Trade Commission (FTC), the Food and Drug Administration (FDA), and the Antitrust Division of the Justice Department. The goal of regulatory activity is to protect consumers while preserving the market incentives that create a dynamic economy. In some cases, the government has prohibited mergers in order to increase competition. In 1999, for example, the Federal Communications Commission (FCC) voided a proposed merger of Bell Atlantic and GTE, ruling that the merger would reduce competition and could result in increased prices for phone customers.

In most cases, however, the government tolerates mergers on the assumption that larger firms can take advantage of economies of scale, thereby operating more efficiently and passing on the lower costs to consumers. The government is particularly inclined to accept concentrated ownership in industries—such as the oil industry—with capital costs so high that small firms find it difficult to operate, much less compete.[6] Government acceptance of corporate giants also reflects the realization that market competition no longer is simply an issue of competition among domestic firms. U.S. automakers, for example, compete for customers not only with one another but with Asian and European auto manufacturers. Indeed, the best-selling car in America over the past decade is a Japanese model, the Toyota Camry.

The U.S. government's general policy toward corporate giants that act in restraint of trade has been to penalize them financially. In 1993, for example, a number of air carriers (including American, Delta, United, Northwest, and US Air) were found to have engaged in price fixing and were ordered to award hundreds of millions of dollars in certificates to travelers who could prove they had flown on these carriers during the period in question. More than four million individuals, organizations, and businesses filed claims.

Making Business Pay for Indirect Costs   Economic inefficiencies can result not only from restraint of trade but from the failure of businesses or consumers to pay the full costs of resources used in production. Consider companies whose industrial wastes seep into nearby lakes and rivers. The price of these companies' products does not reflect the resulting water pollution, and hence customers do not pay all the costs that society has incurred in the making of the products. Economists label these unpaid costs **externalities.**

Until the 1960s, the federal government did not require firms to pay such costs. The impetus to begin doing so came not only from lawmakers but also from the scientific community and environmental groups. The Clean Air Act of 1963 and the Water Quality Act of 1965 required industry to install antipollution devices to keep the discharge of air and water pollutants within specified limits. In 1970, Congress created the Environmental Protection Agency (EPA) to monitor firms and ensure their compliance with federal regulations governing air and water quality and the disposal of toxic wastes. (Environmental policy is discussed more fully later in the chapter.)

Overregulation   Although government regulation is intended to increase economic efficiency, it can have the opposite effect by raising the cost of doing business. Firms have to expend work hours to monitor and implement government regulations, which in some instances (for example, pollution control) also require companies to buy and install expensive equipment. These costs are efficient to the degree that they produce commensurate benefits. Yet if government places excessive regulatory burdens on firms, they waste resources in the process of complying. The result is higher-priced goods that are more expensive for consumers and less competitive in the domestic and global markets (see "How the United States Compares").

Global Economic Competitiveness

The United States ranked second only to Finland in the World Economic Forum's 2005 economic growth competitiveness survey. The World Economic Forum (WEF) is a private economic research organization based in Switzerland.

To determine its rankings, the WEF takes into account factors such as a nation's corporate management, finance, institutional openness, government regulation, public infrastructure, science and technology, and labor. The United States ranks particularly high on its technology, management, and finance. A weakness is its labor practices. U.S. workers enjoy fewer protections and benefits (such as health care coverage) than do their counterparts in many other industrialized societies.

The United States has been at or near the top of the WEF's rankings for a number of years. It has ranked substantially higher than some of its major economic rivals, such as Germany and Japan. These countries rank lower because their management, regulation, and finance systems are comparatively rigid, reducing their ability to respond flexibly to the global marketplace.

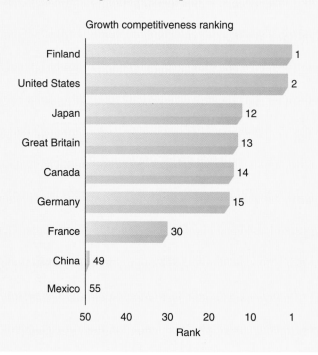

Growth competitiveness ranking

Overregulation can also be costly to governments. An example is a provision of the Safe Drinking Water Act that required communities to reduce contaminants in their water supply from the current level, whatever that level happened to be. In most communities, the effect was to improve the quality of the water supply. But in Anchorage, Alaska, the result was an absurd remedy. The city's water supply was already so clean that officials had to ask local fish-processing plants to dump their wastes into the sewer system so that Anchorage would have impurities to remove from its water.[7]

Situations of this kind led to regulatory reform.[8] In 1995, Congress enacted legislation to tighten the regulatory process by requiring cost-benefit analysis and risk assessment (determining the severity of the problem) to be taken into account in certain regulatory decisions.

Deregulation   Another response to regulatory excess is the policy of **deregulation**—the rescinding of regulations already in force for the purpose of improving efficiency. This process began in 1977 with passage of the Airlines Deregulation Act, which eliminated government-set airfares and, in some instances, government-mandated air routes. The change had the intended effect: airfares declined, and competition between airlines increased on most routes. Congress followed airline deregulation with partial deregulation of the trucking, banking, energy, and communications industries, among others.

Reductions in regulation, however, can be carried too far.[9] Underregulation can result in harmful business practices. The profit motive can lead firms and their executives to manipulate the market illegally. Companies are more likely to try unlawful schemes when weak regulation leads them to believe they can escape detection. Such was the case with top executives of the Enron Corporation. They employed illegal maneuvers that falsely inflated the firm's earnings, which drove up the price of its stock. Only after the schemes failed and the firm went bankrupt were the deceptions exposed. It was too late to help the stockholders who lost billions of dollars and the low-level Enron employees who lost their jobs as well as their company-based retirement savings.

The Enron scandal demonstrates that the issue of business regulation is not a simple question of whether or not to regulate. On one hand, too much regulation can burden firms with bureaucratic red tape, costly implementation procedures, and limited options. On the other hand, too little regulation can give firms the leeway to exploit the public unfairly or recklessly. Either too little or too much regulation can result in economic inefficiency. The challenge for policymakers is to strike the proper balance between regulatory measures and free-market mechanisms.

The collapse of Enron Corporation, which had been America's seventh-largest firm, cost investors and Enron employees (through the loss of retirement accounts) billions of dollars. The debacle brought calls for closer government regulation of corporations, accounting firms, and pension plans. Shown here is Enron founder Kenneth Lay as he leaves the courthouse during his 2006 trial for fraud and conspiracy. Lay was convicted but died of a heart attack while awaiting sentencing.

Equity Through Government Intervention

The government intervenes in the economy to bring equity as well as efficiency to the marketplace. **Equity** occurs when an economic transaction is fair to each party.[10] Equity is judged by *outcomes*—whether they are reasonable and mutually acceptable to the parties involved. A transaction can be considered fair if each party enters into it freely and is not unknowingly at a disadvantage (for example, if the seller knows a product is defective, equity requires that the buyer also know of the defect).

An early equity measure was the creation of the Food and Drug Administration (FDA) in 1907. Because consumers often are unable to tell whether foods and drugs are safe to use, the FDA works to keep adulterated foods

and dangerous or ineffective drugs off the market. In the 1930s, financial reforms were among the equity measures enacted under the New Deal. The Securities and Exchange Act of 1934 and the Banking Act of 1934 were designed in part to protect

Historical
Background

investors and savers from dishonest or imprudent brokers and bankers. The New Deal also provided greater equity for organized labor, which previously had been in a weak position in its dealings with management. The Fair Labor Standards Act of 1938, for example, established minimum wages, maximum working hours, and constraints on the use of child labor.

The 1960s and 1970s produced the greatest number of equity reforms. Ten federal agencies, including the Consumer Product Safety Commission, were established to protect consumers, workers, and the public from harmful effects of business activity. Among the products declared to be unsafe in the 1960s and 1970s were the insecticide DDT, cigarettes, and leaded gasoline. The benefits have been substantial. Lead, for example, can cause brain damage in children. Since regulation went into effect, the average level of lead in children's blood has decreased by 75 percent.[11]

The Politics of Regulatory Policy

Economic regulation has come in waves, as changes in national conditions have produced intermittent bursts of social consciousness. The first wave came during the Progressive Era, when reformers sought to stop the unfair business practices of the new monopolies. The second wave came during the Great Depression, when reformers sought to stimulate economic recovery through regulatory policies that were designed as much to save business as to restrain it.

Although business fought the Progressive and New Deal reforms, long-term opposition was lessened by the fact that most of the resulting regulation applied to a particular industry rather than to firms of all types. This pattern makes it possible for a regulated industry to gain influence with those officials responsible for regulating it. By cultivating close ties to the FCC, for example, the broadcast networks have managed to obtain policies that protect their near monopoly on broadcasting and give them high and sustained profits.[12] Although not all industries have as much leverage with their regulators as broadcasting has, it is generally true that industries have not been greatly hampered by the older form of regulation and in many cases have benefited from it.

The third wave of regulatory reform, in the 1960s and 1970s, differed from the Progressive and New Deal phases in both its form and its politics. This third wave has been called the era of "new social regulation" because of the social goals it addressed in its three major policy areas: environmental protection, consumer protection, and worker safety.

Most of the regulatory agencies established during the third wave have broader mandates than those created earlier. They have responsibility not for a single industry but for firms of all types, and their policy scope covers a wide range of activities. The Environmental Protection Agency (EPA), for example, is charged with regulating environmental pollution of almost any kind by almost any firm. Unlike the older agencies that are run by a commission whose members serve for fixed terms, some of the newer agencies, including the EPA, are headed by a single director who is appointed by the president with Senate approval and is subject to immediate removal by the president.

Because newer agencies such as the EPA have a wide-ranging clientele, no one firm or industry can easily influence agency policy to a great extent. There is also strong group competition within some of the newer regulatory spheres. For example, business lobbies must compete with environmental groups such as the Sierra Club and Greenpeace for influence with the EPA.[13] The firms regulated by the older agencies, in contrast, face no powerful competition in their lobbying activities. Broadcasters, for example, are largely unopposed in their efforts to influence the FCC. Although television viewers and radio listeners have a stake in FCC decisions, they are not well enough organized to petition it effectively.

GOVERNMENT AS PROTECTOR OF THE ENVIRONMENT

Few changes in public opinion and policy during recent decades have been as dramatic as those relating to the environment. Most Americans today recycle some of their garbage, and roughly two-thirds say they are either an active environmentalist or sympathetic to environmental concerns. In the 1960s, few Americans sorted their trash, and few could have answered a polling question that asked them whether they were an "environmentalist." The term was not commonly used, and most people would not have understood its meaning.

The publication in 1962 of Rachel Carson's *The Silent Spring* helped launch the environmental movement.[14] Written at a time when the author was dying of breast cancer, *Silent Spring* revealed the threat of harmful pesticides such as DDT and challenged the notion that scientific breakthroughs were an unqualified benefit to society. Carson's appearance at a Senate hearing contributed to legislative action that produced the 1963 Clean Air Act and the 1965 Water Quality Act. They were the first major federal laws designed to protect the nation's air, water, and ground from pollution. Today, environmental protection extends to nearly two hundred harmful forms of emission.

★ ‖ LEADERS

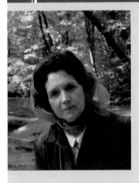

Rachel Carson
(1907–64)

Born on a farm near Pittsburgh, Rachel Carson had hoped to become a writer but switched to biology as an undergraduate and went on to earn a master's degree in zoology at Johns Hopkins University. She then started work on a doctorate, but the untimely death of her father and the need to take care of her mother ended this pursuit. In 1936, while working part-time at the U.S. Bureau of Fisheries (later the U.S. Fish and Wildlife Services), she learned of a full-time position that was opening up and decided to take the civil service exam, a rare ambition at the time for a woman. Carson outscored all the men who took the exam with her and was given the position.

In her job, Carson worked on scientific journals, but she wanted to reach a wider audience. She astonished even herself when *Atlantic Monthly* accepted an article she had submitted. The article's publication led to a book contract with Simon and Schuster, but the resulting book sold hardly any copies. Undeterred, she continued to publish articles in popular magazines, and her second book, *The Sea Around Us*, won the 1952 National Book Award. But it was *The Silent Spring*, published in 1962, that brought her lasting fame. Even before the book was released, chemical companies were threatening lawsuits and conducting a public relations campaign that portrayed her as unstable and lacking in scientific expertise. Even the Department of Agriculture came out against her, labeling as false the book's charge that the insecticide DDT was a carcinogen and was destroying natural diversity. *The Silent Spring* was a huge best-seller, however, and led to invitations for Carson to testify before Congress. Her book and her widely publicized congressional testimony contributed to passage of the first federal safe air and water legislation. At the height of her fame, Carson was fatally stricken with breast cancer. In 1981, she was posthumously awarded the Presidential Medal of Freedom, the nation's highest civilian award.

Conservationism: The Older Wave

Although government policy aimed at reducing pollution is relatively new, the government has been involved in land conservation for more than a century.[15] The first national park was created at Yellowstone in 1872 and, like the later ones, was established to preserve the nation's natural heritage for generations to come. The national park system serves more than one hundred million visitors each year and includes a total of eighty million acres, an area larger than every state except Alaska, Texas, California, and Montana.

The national parks are run by the National Park Service, an agency within the Department of Interior. Another agency, the U.S. Forest Service, located within the Department of Agriculture, manages the national forests, which cover an area more than twice the size of the national parks. They too have been preserved in part to protect America's natural heritage.

However, the nation's parks and forests are subject to a "dual use" policy. They are nature preserves and recreation areas, but they are also rich in natural resources—minerals, trees, and grazing lands. The federal government sells permits to ranchers, timber companies, and mining firms that give them the right to take some of these resources, a policy that can

The federal government's environmental efforts include programs designed to conserve nature through the protection of forests and other natural assets. Shown here is a scene from Yellowstone National Park.

place their interests in conflict with those of conservationists. A case in point is Alaska's Arctic National Wildlife Refuge. The refuge is home to numerous species, including caribou and moose, but it also contains oil and natural gas. Oil companies have long wanted to drill in this wilderness area, while environmental groups have sought to prohibit drilling. Over the past few decades, the Arctic National Wildlife Refuge has periodically been the focus of intense political debate and lobbying. President Clinton threatened to veto any bill that would open the area to drilling. President Bush, in contrast, proposed that the area be opened to drilling as part of his program to increase the nation's energy supplies.

As the debate over Alaska's Arctic National Wildlife Refuge reveals, conservation is more than an issue of protecting nature's unspoiled beauty. Also involved is the protection of species that need their natural habitat to survive. Some species, such as the deer and the raccoon, adapt easily to human encroachment. Others are threatened by it. These species are covered by the Endangered Species Act (ESA) of 1973, which directs federal agencies to protect threatened and endangered species and authorizes programs to preserve natural habitats. Hundreds of mammals, birds, fishes, insects, and plants are currently on ESA's protected list.

Disputes have arisen between ESA administrators and those individuals and firms that depend on natural resources for their jobs and profits. The northern spotted owl, which inhabits the forests of Oregon and Washington, was at the center of one such controversy. The spotted owl nests in old-growth trees that are prized by the logging industry. Federal administrators, citing ESA, banned logging in the owl's habitat. The ensuing legal battle ended with a compromise—logging was permitted in some old-growth timber areas and prohibited in others. Although this outcome left neither side fully satisfied, it is typical of how most such disputes are settled. More recently, federal officials have emphasized cooperative relationships with private parties, making them eligible for grants if they act to protect threatened or endangered species. In 2006, for example, a Wyoming group, Trout Unlimited, was awarded a $120,000 grant to dredge a creek that is traveled by a rare species of trout on its way to its traditional spawning area.

Environmentalism: The Newer Wave

The pivotal decade in the federal government's realization that Americans needed protection from the harmful effects of air, water, and ground pollutants was the 1960s. The period was capped by the first Earth Day. Held in the spring of 1970, it was the brainchild of Senator Gaylord Nelson

Get Involved!

Do Your Part

The environment is a policy area where individual citizens can make a difference by reducing the amount of the natural resources they use and the pollution they cause. In the United States, the largest polluter is the personal automobile. Car owners understandably are unwilling to sell their vehicles and rely entirely on public transportation. However, taking some simple steps can reduce the environmental impact of owning a car. By accelerating and driving more slowly, you will burn significantly less fuel, reducing the stress on your pocketbook as well as on the environment. Choosing a fuel-efficient car, keeping your car properly tuned, walking rather than driving short distances to stores, and living closer to work or school are other ways to cut gas consumption.

At home, the simplest steps are to turn off lights as you leave the room and to set the thermostat lower than usual during cold periods and higher than usual during hot periods. Smaller but meaningful savings can be achieved through simple things such as using low-flow shower heads and replacing incandescent bulbs with fluorescent lights, which require less energy and last longer.

Even a change in eating habits will make a difference. Frozen convenience foods are wasteful of energy. They are cooked, frozen, and then cooked again—not to mention the resources used up in their packaging. Fresh foods are more nutritious and less wasteful. Also, if you prefer bottled water to tap water, consider using a water filter system instead. Nearly the entire cost of bottled water is due to the plastic container, which is a nonbiodegradable petroleum product.

The recycling of paper, plastics, and bottles also conserves natural resources. However, the recycling process itself uses energy. By cutting back on your use of recyclables and by recycling those you do use, you will contribute twice to a better environment.

You can find additional environmentally friendly tips on the Internet. Most have the added benefit of saving you money because you'll be using fewer natural resources in your daily life.

(D-Wis.), who had devoted nearly ten years to finding ways to increase public interest in environmental issues. With Earth Day, Nelson succeeded to a degree not even he could have imagined: ten thousand grade schools and high schools, two thousand colleges, and one thousand communities participated in the event, which included public rallies and environmental cleanup efforts. Earth Day has been held every year since 1970 and is now a worldwide event.

Environmental Protection   The year 1970 also marked the creation of the Environmental Protection Agency. Within a few months, the EPA was issuing new regulations at such a rapid pace that business firms had difficulty keeping track of all the mandates, much less complying fully with them. Corporations eventually found an ally in President Gerald Ford, who in a 1975 speech claimed that business regulation was costing $150 billion annually, or $2,000 for every American family.[16] Although Ford's estimate exceeded that of economic analysts, his point was not lost on policymakers or the public. The economy was in a slump, and the costs of complying with the new regulations were slowing an economic recovery. Polls indicated a decline in public support for regulatory action.

Since then, environmental protection policy has not greatly expanded, but neither has it greatly contracted. The emphasis has been on administering and amending the laws put into effect in the 1960s and 1970s. Nevertheless, the EPA has a broad mandate to protect America's air and water. In a 2001 decision, for example, the Supreme Court ruled unanimously that the EPA is to consider only public health and not industry costs in setting air quality standards.[17]

Environmental regulation has led to dramatic improvements in air and water quality. Pollution levels today are far below their levels of the 1960s, when yellowish-gray fog ("smog") hung over cities like Los Angeles and New York and when bodies of water like the Potomac River and Lake Erie were open sewers. In the past four decades, toxic waste emissions have been cut by half, hundreds of polluted lakes and rivers have been revitalized, energy efficiency has increased, food supplies have been made safer, and urban air pollution has decreased by more than 60 percent.[18]

Progress has been slower in cleaning up badly contaminated toxic-waste sites. Such sites can contaminate area water supplies and become a health hazard. Abnormally high cancer rates have been noted in the vicinity of some of these sites. In the 1980s, Congress established the so-called Superfund program to rid toxic-waste sites of their contaminants. However, the cleanup process has been slow and contentious. Firms that caused the pollution are liable for some of the cleanup costs, but many of these firms are no longer in business, have since been purchased

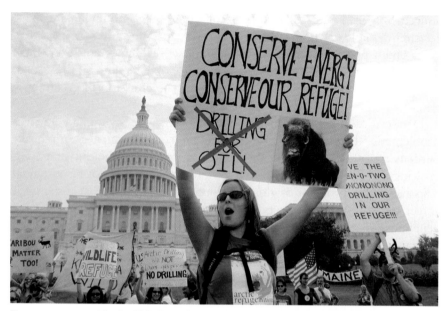

Demonstrators outside the U.S. Capitol in Washington urge Congress to keep the Arctic National Wildlife Refuge off-limits to oil drilling. The dispute over the wildlife refuge reflects the intense conflict that can ensue when environmental interests clash with energy concerns.

by other companies, or lack the money to comply. Firms that can afford to pay have often chosen instead to fight the issue in court, further delaying the cleanup. To date, only about half the sites targeted by the Superfund program as posing serious hazards have been cleaned up.

Global Warming and Energy Policy No environmental issue has received more attention recently than has global warming. The scientific community has been warning for more than a decade that carbon emissions are creating a "greenhouse effect" (the trapping of heat in the atmosphere). The result has been a rise in the earth's temperatures and in ocean levels, as a result of melting of the polar ice caps. Until recently, many politicians dismissed the evidence, claiming that "more research was needed." Today, few politicians doubt the existence of global warming.

However, politicians disagree sharply on what should be done about it. Global warming can be slowed only by carbon-emission reductions that in some cases require costly technological innovations and would dampen economic growth. So far in the United States, the pro-growth side has had the upper hand. The United States is the single largest source of worldwide carbon emissions, and U.S. policymakers have resisted demands at home and from abroad for substantial new restrictions on air pollution. In 2002, for example, President George W. Bush declared that the United States would not participate in the Kyoto agreement, a multinational effort to reduce the emission of greenhouse gases.

Even critics of Bush's action acknowledge that the Kyoto agreement is problematic. It imposes light burdens on some countries and heavy burdens on others, including the United States. Nevertheless, support is growing among Republican and Democratic leaders alike for a substantial response to the problem of global warming. The form of that response is as yet unclear. Virtually every possibility has drawbacks. Wind-powered generators increasingly are used, but they do not produce enough electricity even to keep up with new demand. Nuclear power plants generate large amounts of electricity, but they are the costliest source of energy and are thought by many to be unsafe. Hydrogen fuel cells show promise, but the technology is not anywhere near the point where it could help meet the nations' energy needs.

Energy conservation through a steep hike in the gasoline tax would be a short-term answer, but America's consumers are unlikely to embrace it and officeholders would risk their political careers by voting for it. The price of gasoline is already a hot issue because of the rise in the world price of oil. Instability in the Middle East and increased demand for oil in China and India helped push oil prices in 2006 above seventy-five dollars a barrel—five times the price of oil a few years earlier. As the price of oil rose, so did the price of gasoline: it topped three dollars a gallon, far more than Americans were accustomed to paying.

In addition to its impact on oil prices, worldwide economic growth is accelerating the rate at which carbon emissions are being spewed into the atmosphere, exacerbating the problem of global warming. In the years ahead, Americans increasingly will have to make trade-offs among environmental protection, energy costs, and economic growth. To a degree, they are already prepared to make them. Polls indicate that a majority of Americans would support further environmental regulation even if slower economic growth and some job loss resulted. However, in part because of their greater resistance to government regulation and to taxes (including the gasoline tax), Americans are less willing to make the necessary trade-offs than are Canadians, the Japanese, or Western Europeans (see Figure 15–2).

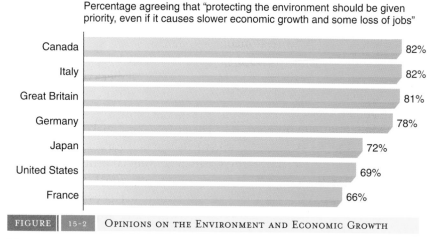

Percentage agreeing that "protecting the environment should be given priority, even if it causes slower economic growth and some loss of jobs"

Country	Percentage
Canada	82%
Italy	82%
Great Britain	81%
Germany	78%
Japan	72%
United States	69%
France	66%

FIGURE 15-2 OPINIONS ON THE ENVIRONMENT AND ECONOMIC GROWTH

Majorities in industrialized democracies support environmental protection, even if it means somewhat slower economic growth. However, Americans are somewhat less likely than citizens elsewhere to accept this trade-off. *Source: Pew Research Center for the People and the Press, Global Attitudes Survey, 2002.*

GOVERNMENT AS PROMOTER OF ECONOMIC INTERESTS

The U.S. government has always made important contributions to the nation's economy. Congress in 1789 gave a boost to the nation's shipping industry by placing a tariff on imported goods carried by foreign ships. Since that first favor, the U.S. government has provided thousands of direct benefits to economic interests. The following sections provide brief examples of a few of these benefits.

Promoting Business

American business is not opposed to government regulation as such. Corporations object only to regulatory policies that hurt their interests. At various times and in different ways, as in the case of the FCC and broadcasters, some regulatory agencies have promoted the interests of the very industries they are supposed to regulate in the public interest.

Providing loans and tax breaks is another way that government promotes business. Firms receive loan guarantees, direct loans, tax credits for capital investments, and tax deductions for capital depreciation. Over the past forty years, the burden of federal taxation has shifted dramatically from corporations to individuals. A few decades ago, the revenues raised from taxes on corporate income were roughly the same as the revenues raised from taxes on individual income. Today, individual taxpayers carry the heavier burden by a five-to-one ratio. Some analysts do not regard the change as particularly significant, arguing that higher corporate taxes would be passed along to the public anyway in the form of higher prices for goods and services.

The most significant contribution that government makes to business is the traditional services it provides, such as education, transportation, and defense. Colleges and universities, which are funded primarily by governments, furnish business with most of its professional and technical work force and with much of the basic research that goes into product development. The nation's roadways, waterways, and airports are other public-sector contributions without which business could not operate. In short, America's business has no bigger booster than government.

Promoting Labor

Laissez-faire thinking dominated government's approach to labor well into the twentieth century. The governing principle, developed by the courts a century earlier, held that workers had limited rights of collective action. Union activity was regarded as interference with the natural supply of labor and the free setting of wages. Government's hostility toward labor was evident, for example, in the use of police and soldiers during the late 1800s to break up strikes.

The 1930s brought major changes. The key legislation was the National Labor Relations Act of 1935, which guaranteed workers the right to bargain collectively and prohibited business from discriminating against union employees and from unreasonably interfering with union activities. Government has also aided labor over the years by legislating minimum wages and maximum work hours, unemployment benefits, safer and more healthful working conditions, and nondiscriminatory hiring practices. Although government support for labor extends beyond these examples, it is not nearly as extensive as its assistance to business. America's culture of individualism has resulted in public policies that are less favorable to labor than are policies in European countries.

Promoting Agriculture

Until well into the twentieth century, most Americans still lived on farms and in small rural communities. Agriculture was America's dominant business and was assisted by the government's land policies. The Homestead

Act of 1862, for example, opened government-owned lands to settlement, creating spectacular "land rushes" by offering 160 acres of government land free to each family that staked a claim, built a house, and farmed the land for five years.

Farm programs today provide assistance to both small farmers and large commercial enterprises (agribusinesses) and cost the federal government billions of dollars annually. A major goal of this spending is to eliminate some of the risks associated with farming. Weather, world markets, and other factors can radically affect crop and livestock prices, and federal programs are designed to protect farmers from adverse developments.

Experience has shown that the agricultural sector benefits from government intervention. In 1996, Congress passed legislation that trimmed long-standing crop subsidy and crop allocation programs. The goal was to let the free market largely determine the prices farmers would get for their crops and to let farmers themselves decide on the crops they would plant. The result was a depressed farm economy—prices fell sharply because of the surplus production of particular crops. In 2002, Congress abandoned the free-market approach. Crop subsidies were increased and expanded to include more crops, and quotas were established for the planting of particular crops. The 2002 Farm Bill put farmers in line for hundreds of billions of dollars in government assistance in future years. At present, federal subsidies account for more than a third of net farm income.

FISCAL POLICY: GOVERNMENT AS MANAGER OF THE ECONOMY, I

Until the 1930s, the U.S. government adhered to the prevailing free-market theory and made no attempt to regulate the economy as a whole. The economy, which was regarded as largely self-regulating, was fairly prosperous, but it collapsed periodically, resulting in widespread unemployment.

The greatest economic collapse in the nation's history—the Great Depression of the 1930s—finally brought an end to traditional economics. Franklin D. Roosevelt's government spending and job programs, designed to stimulate the economy and put Americans back to work, heralded the change. Although Roosevelt's use of government policy as an economic stimulus was highly controversial, today it is accepted practice. Government is expected to pursue policies that will foster economic growth and stability.

TABLE 15-2 FISCAL POLICY: A SUMMARY	
Taxing and spending levels can be adjusted in order to affect economic conditions.	
Problem	**Fiscal Policy Actions**
Low productivity and high unemployment	Demand side: increase spending Supply side: cut business taxes
Excess production and high inflation	Decrease spending Increase taxes

Taxing and Spending Policy

The government's efforts to maintain a thriving economy are made mainly through its taxing and spending decisions, which together are referred to as its **fiscal policy** (see Table 15–2).

The annual federal budget is the basis of fiscal policy. Thousands of pages in length, the budget allocates federal expenditures among government programs and identifies the revenues—taxes, social insurance receipts, and borrowed funds—that will be used to pay for these programs (see Figure 15–3). From one perspective, the budget is the national government's allocation of costs and benefits. Every federal program benefits

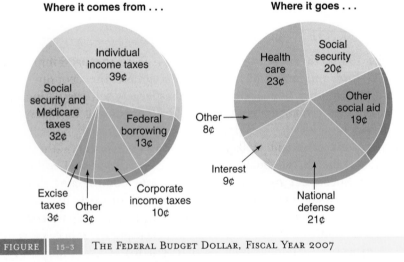

Where it comes from . . .

Individual income taxes 39¢

Social security and Medicare taxes 32¢

Federal borrowing 13¢

Excise taxes 3¢

Other 3¢

Corporate income taxes 10¢

Where it goes . . .

Health care 23¢

Social security 20¢

Other social aid 19¢

Other 8¢

Interest 9¢

National defense 21¢

FIGURE 15-3 THE FEDERAL BUDGET DOLLAR, FISCAL YEAR 2007

Source: Office of Management and Budget.

some interest, whether it be farmers who get price supports, defense firms that obtain military contracts, or retirees who receive monthly social security checks. From another standpoint, that of fiscal policy, the budget is a device for stimulating or dampening economic growth. Through changes in overall levels of spending and taxing, government can help keep the economy running smoothly.

Fiscal policy has origins in the economic theories of John Maynard Keynes. In *The General Theory of Employment, Interest, and Money* (1936), Keynes noted that employers naturally become cautious during a depression and cut back on production and on the number of workers. Challenging the traditional idea that government should also cut back during depressions, Keynes claimed that severe economic downturns can be shortened only by increased government spending. Keynes said that government should engage in **deficit spending**—spending more than it gets from taxes, which can be accomplished through the borrowing and printing of money. By placing additional money in the hands of consumers, government can stimulate spending, which in turn will stimulate production and create jobs, thereby promoting an economic recovery.[19]

According to Keynesian theory, the level of the government's response should be commensurate with the severity of the problem. During an **economic depression**—an exceptionally steep and sustained downturn in the economy—the government should engage in massive new spending programs to hasten the recovery. During an **economic recession,** which is a less severe downturn, government spending should also be increased but by a smaller amount.

Demand-Side Stimulation   Keynes's theory focused on government's efforts to stimulate consumer spending. This **demand-side economics** emphasizes the consumer "demand" component of the supply-demand equation. When the economy is sluggish, the government can increase its spending, thus placing more money in consumers' hands. With additional money to spend, consumers buy more goods and services. This increased demand, in turn, stimulates businesses to produce more goods and hire more workers. In this way, government spending contributes to economic recovery.

Although increased spending is a tool that government can employ during a severe economic crisis, it is not a sensible response to every economic dip. Its application is affected by government's overall financial situation. In the early 1990s, for example, the U.S. economy was in its longest downturn since World War II, but policymakers chose not to boost federal spending temporarily as a means of blunting the recession.

The reason was simple enough. During the previous two decades, there had been a **budget deficit**—each year, the federal government had spent more than it had received in tax and other revenues. The result was a huge **national debt**, which is the total cumulative amount that the U.S. government owes to creditors. By the early 1990s, the national debt had reached $4 trillion, and an enormous sum of money was required each year just to pay the interest on it. Interest payments were roughly the total of all federal income taxes paid by Americans living west of the Mississippi River. This ongoing drain on the government's resources made it politically difficult for policymakers to increase government spending in order to stimulate the economy.

The situation changed dramatically in the late 1990s. In 1998, for the first time since 1969, the U.S. government had a **balanced budget**—revenues were equal to government expenditures. Thereafter, there was a **budget surplus**—the federal government received more in tax and other revenues than it spent. The surplus was attributable to a surging U.S. economy that was in the midst of its longest period of sustained growth in the country's history. With more people working and with the stock market climbing, tax revenues had increased and government welfare expenditures had declined. The rosy budget picture also reflected the fiscal discipline of the Clinton administration and the Republican Congress, which had slowed the growth in federal spending.

The turnaround was short-lived. A slowdown in the economy, steep tax cuts, and a sharp increase in defense spending contributed by 2002 to a budget shortfall. Deficits are now projected to persist for years to come (see Figure 15–4). The severity of the deficit is a constraint on policymakers' ability to apply demand-side measures as a means of boosting the economy. Even though a large tax cut or a major spending increase would contribute to economic growth, it would also increase the deficit.

The impact of demand-side fiscal policy, however, cannot be measured only by its effect during economic downturns. Although the United States has had recessionary periods since the 1930s, none of these downturns has come anywhere near the severity of the Great Depression. One reason is that government spending is now at permanently high levels. Each month, for example, roughly forty million Americans receive a social security check from the government. In turn, they spend it on food, clothing, housing, entertainment, and other goods and services. They pump billions of dollars each month into the U.S. economy, which creates jobs and income for millions of other Americans. And social security is only one—albeit the largest—of numerous federal spending programs. Every day, the federal government spends about $4 billion, more than the

Annual federal budget deficit/surplus
(in billions of dollars)

THE FEDERAL BUDGET DEFICIT/SURPLUS

The federal government ran a budget deficit until 1998, at which time a surplus that was expected to last for years emerged. In 2001, however, the surplus quickly disappeared as a result of an economic downturn, costs associated with the war on terrorism, and a cut in federal taxes. *Source: Office of Management and Budget, 2006.*

typical large corporation pumps into the economy during an entire year. The U.S. economy thus has a constant demand-side stimulus: government spending on an ongoing and massive scale.

Supply-Side Stimulation   A fiscal policy alternative to demand-side stimulation is **supply-side economics,** which emphasizes the business (supply) component of the supply-demand equation. Supply-side theory was a cornerstone of President Reagan's economic program. He believed that economic growth could occur as easily from stimulation of the business sector as from stimulation of consumer demand. "Reaganomics" included substantial tax breaks for businesses and upper-income individuals.[20]

The Reagan administration overestimated the stimulus effect of its tax-cuts policy. It had estimated that the increased tax revenues from increased business activity would soon offset the loss of revenue from reduced tax rates. However, the loss in tax revenues was much greater than the gain in revenues from the economic growth that followed. As a result, the tax cuts contributed to a growing budget deficit. Despite this discouraging result, Reagan's supply-side measures contributed to the economic growth in the United States during the 1990s. The Reagan tax cuts allowed business firms to spend more on capital investments and enabled higher-income Americans to place more money into the stock markets, providing additional funds for business investment.

Supply-side theory was also the basis of President George W. Bush's economic program. Although his Economic Growth and Tax Reconciliation Act of 2001 included a demand-side component (an immediate cash rebate to taxpayers), supply-side measures were its signature: sharp cuts in the tax rate on individuals, with most of the gains going to high-income taxpayers, and a reduction in the **capital-gains tax,** the tax that individuals pay on gains in capital investments such as property and stocks. A reduction in the capital-gains tax increases the incentive for individuals to invest their money in capital markets. In turn, firms use this money to expand their operations and markets. The subsequent job creation and increased supply of goods can stimulate consumer demand and contribute to economic growth.

When Bush's tax bill was enacted in 2001, he had agreed—in order to get the congressional support necessary for its passage—to a phase-in of the individual and capital-gains tax cuts. In 2003, he went back to Congress and asked for a speeded-up timetable as a means of boosting the economy. Bush got what he requested. The capital-gains tax rate, which had been 28 percent in 2001, fell to 15 percent, as did the tax rate for dividend income. Meanwhile, the highest marginal rate assessed on individual income fell to 35 percent, down from 39 percent in 2001. The larger share of the tax savings resulting from Bush's policies went to high-income taxpayers—precisely those people who, according to supply-side economics, are the key to economic growth.

However, as indicated previously, the Bush tax cuts, combined with large increases in defense spending, drove the U.S. budget deficit to record highs, threatening to cancel any long-term contribution the tax cuts might make to economic growth.[21] During congressional testimony in 2005, outgoing Federal Reserve chairman Alan Greenspan warned that the budget deficits were "unsustainable" and posed a severe threat to the continued health of the U.S. economy. The Fed chairman said he would prefer to see the deficit reduced through spending cuts rather than increased taxes, but he argued that both should occur. Deficit reduction, said Greenspan, must be "the overriding principle." (Bush's tax cuts are discussed further in Chapter 16.)

Controlling Inflation High unemployment and low productivity are only two of the economic problems that government is called on to solve. Another is **inflation,** an increase in the average level of prices of goods and services. Before the late 1960s, inflation was a minor problem: prices rose by less than 4 percent annually. But inflation rose sharply during the last years of the Vietnam War and remained high throughout the 1970s, reaching a postwar record rate of 13 percent in 1979. Since then, the annual inflation rate has averaged about 4 percent, and concern about inflation has lessened significantly.

To fight inflation, government can apply remedies exactly the opposite of those used to fight unemployment and low productivity. Inflation normally occurs when jobs are plentiful and people have extra money to spend. Demand is high in such periods, and prices go up. By cutting spending or raising personal income taxes, government takes money from consumers, thus reducing demand and dampening prices. (The main policy tool for addressing inflation is monetary policy, which is discussed later in the chapter.)

The Process and Politics of Fiscal Policy

The president and Congress jointly determine fiscal policy, mainly through the annual budgetary process. The Constitution grants Congress the power to tax and spend, but the president, as chief executive, plays a major role in shaping the budget (see Chapter 12). In reality, the budgetary process involves give-and-take between Congress and the president as each tries to exert influence over the final budget.[22]

The Budgetary Process   The budgetary process is an elaborate one, as could be expected when billions of dollars in federal spending are at issue. From beginning to end, the process lasts a year and a half (see Figure 15–5). The process begins in the executive branch when the president, in consultation with the Office of Management and Budget (OMB), establishes general budget guidelines. The OMB is part of the Executive Office of the President (see Chapter 12) and takes its directives from the president. Hundreds of agencies and thousands of programs are covered by the budget, and the OMB uses the president's directives to issue instructions that will guide each agency's budget preparations. For example, each agency is assigned a budget ceiling within which it must work.

The agencies receive these instructions in the spring and then work through the summer to develop a detailed agency budget, taking into account their existing programs and any new proposals. These agency budgets then go to the OMB in September for a full review that invariably includes further consultation with each agency. The agency budgets are then finalized and combined into the full budget. Throughout, the OMB stays in touch with the White House to ensure that the budget items conform to the president's objectives.

The agencies naturally tend to want more money, whereas the OMB has the job of matching the budget to the president's priorities. In fact,

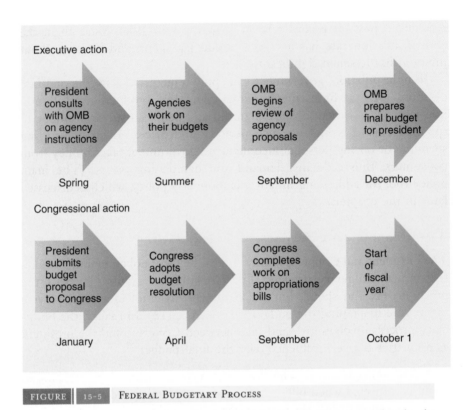

FIGURE   15-5   FEDERAL BUDGETARY PROCESS

The budget begins with the president's instructions to the agencies and ends when Congress enacts the budget. The entire process spans about eighteen months.

however, the president does not have any real say over most of the budget, about two-thirds of which involves mandatory spending. This spending is authorized by current law, and the government must allocate and spend the money unless the law itself is rescinded, an unlikely occurrence. Examples are social security and Medicare, which provide benefits to the elderly. The president does not have the authority to suspend or reduce these programs. Interest on the national debt is also part of the budget, and here too the president has no real option. The federal government is obligated to pay interest on the money it has borrowed.

The OMB focuses on the one-third of the budget that involves discretionary spending, which includes areas such as defense, foreign aid, education, national parks, space exploration, public broadcasting, and highways. In reality, even a large part of this spending is not truly discretionary. No president would even consider slashing defense spending to almost nothing or closing the national parks, and even modest cuts in a discretionary program may encounter resistance in Congress.

The president, then, works on the margins of the budget, trying to push it in directions that are consistent with administration goals. The effort in many policy areas consists of a modest increase or decrease in spending compared with the previous year. There are always a few areas, however, where the president will attempt a more dramatic adjustment. In each of his budgets, for example, President Bush asked for large increases in defense spending to assist in the war on terrorism and to pay for the Iraq war and reconstruction.

In January, the president transmits the full budget to Congress. This budget is just a proposal, because Congress alone has the constitutional power to appropriate funds. In reviewing the president's proposed budget, Congress relies heavily on the Congressional Budget Office (CBO), which, as discussed in Chapter 11, is the congressional equivalent of the OMB. If the CBO believes that an agency has misjudged the amount of money needed to meet its legislatively required programs, it will bring this information to the attention of the appropriate committees of Congress. Similarly, if the CBO concludes that the OMB has miscalculated how much the government can be expected to receive in taxes and other revenues, committees will be notified of the discrepancy.

The key congressional committees in the budgetary process are the budget committees and the appropriations committees. The House and Senate Budget Committees are responsible for drafting a "budget resolution," which includes guidelines on total spending, total revenues, and allocations between the mandatory and discretionary spending categories. These guidelines then go to the full House and Senate for approval. The budget ceilings that are part of the resolution place a tentative limit on how much money will be allocated for each spending area.

The House Appropriations Committee through its subcommittees then takes on the primary task of reviewing the budget items, a review that includes hearings with each federal agency. There are ten such subcommittees, each of which has responsibility for a substantive area, such as defense or agriculture. Agency budgets invariably are changed at this stage. A subcommittee may cut an agency's budget because it believes that the agency's work is not a priority or that the agency has asked for more funds than it needs. Or the subcommittee may decide to increase an agency's budget beyond what the president has requested. The subcommittees' recommendations are then submitted to the House Appropriations Committee for final review and submission to the full House for a vote. The Senate Appropriations Committee and its subcommittees

★ ‖ STATES IN THE NATION

Federal Taxing and Spending: Winners and Losers

Fiscal policy (the federal government's taxing and spending policies) varies in its effect on the states. The residents of some states pay a lot more in federal taxes than they receive in benefits. The biggest loser is New Jersey, whose taxpayers get back in federal spending in their state only $0.62 for every dollar they pay in federal taxes. Connecticut taxpayers ($0.65 for every dollar) are the next-biggest losers. In contrast, the residents of some states get back more from federal spending programs than they contribute in taxes. The biggest winners are New Mexico and North Dakota, whose taxpayers get back $2.37 and $2.07, respectively, in federal spending in their states for every dollar they pay in federal taxes.

Q: Why are most of the "losers" in the northeastern section of the country?

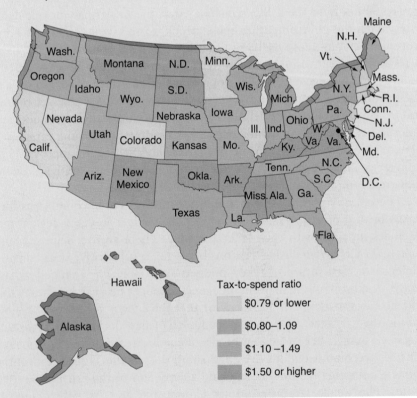

Tax-to-spend ratio

- $0.79 or lower
- $0.80–1.09
- $1.10–1.49
- $1.50 or higher

A: The federal taxes that originate in a state reflect its wealth, and the northeastern states are generally the wealthier ones. Because they are wealthier, they also get less federal assistance for programs designed to help lower-income people and areas. Finally, most federal lands and military installations—sources of federal money—lie outside the northeastern region.

conduct a similar review, but the Senate is a smaller body and its review of agency requests is normally less thorough. To some degree, the Senate committee and its subcommittees serve as a "court of appeals" for agencies that have had their budget requests reduced by the House.

During Congress's work on the budget, the president's recommendations undergo varying degrees of change. The priorities of a majority in Congress are never exactly those of the president, even when they are members of the same party. When they are members of opposite parties, their priorities may differ greatly.

After the work of the appropriations committees has been completed and is approved by the full House and Senate, differences in the Senate and House versions of the appropriations bill are reconciled in conference committee (see Chapter 11). The legislation is then sent to the president for approval or veto. The threat of a presidential veto often is enough to persuade Congress to accept many of the president's recommendations. In the end, the budget inevitably reflects both presidential and congressional priorities. Neither branch ever gets everything it wants, but each branch always gets some of what it wants.

Once the budget has been passed by both the House and the Senate and is signed by the president, it takes effect on October 1, the starting date of the federal government's fiscal year. If agreement on the budget has not been reached by October 1, temporary funding is required in order to maintain government operations. In late 1995, President Clinton and the Republican Congress deadlocked on budgetary issues to such an extent that they could not even agree on temporary funding. Their standoff twice forced a brief shutdown of nonessential government activities.

Partisan Differences Partisan politics is a component of fiscal policy. The Democratic coalition has traditionally included the majority of lower-income and working-class Americans. Accordingly, the party's leaders are sensitive to rising unemployment because blue-collar workers are often the first and most deeply affected. Democrats in Washington have usually responded to a sluggish economy with increased government spending (demand-side fiscal policy), which offers direct help to the unemployed and stimulates consumption. Virtually every increase in federal unemployment benefits during the past fifty years, for example, has been initiated by Democratic officeholders.

Republican leaders are more likely to see an economic downturn through the eyes of business firms. Republicans in Washington typically have sought ways to stimulate business activity as a means of economic recovery. Thus, in most cases, Republicans have resisted large increases in government spending (with the exception of defense spending) as a response to a sluggish economy. Such spending requires government to borrow money, which leads to upward pressure on interest rates. This pressure in turn raises business costs, because firms must pay higher interest rates for the money they borrow.

Tax policy also has partisan dimensions. Democratic policymakers have typically sought tax policies that help working-class and lower-middle-class Americans. Democrats have favored a **graduated** (or progressive) **personal income tax,** in which the tax rate goes up substantially as income rises. Republicans have preferred to keep taxes on upper incomes at a relatively low level, contending that this policy encourages the savings and investment that foster economic growth (supply-side fiscal policy). These differences were evident, for example, in the battle over the Economic Growth and Tax Relief Reconciliation Act of 2001. Proposed by President Bush, the legislation contained the largest tax cut since 1981. The chief beneficiaries were upper-income taxpayers. In both the Senate and the House of Representatives, the bill had the overwhelming support of Republicans and very little support from Democrats. In the Senate, for example, about 90 percent of Republicans voted for it, whereas about 80 percent of Democrats voted against it.[23] (Tax policy is discussed further in Chapter 16.)

MONETARY POLICY: GOVERNMENT AS MANAGER OF ECONOMY, II

Fiscal policy is not the only instrument of economic management available to government; another is **monetary policy,** which is based on manipulation of the amount of money in circulation (see Table 15–3). Monetarists such as economist Milton Friedman hold that control of the money supply is the key to sustaining a healthy economy. Friedman was not convinced that government spending of the type advocated by Keynes

TABLE 15-3 MONETARY POLICY: A SUMMARY OF THE FED'S ROLE	
The money supply can be adjusted in order to affect economic conditions.	
Problem	**Monetary Policy Actions by Federal Reserve**
Low productivity and high unemployment (require an increase in the money supply)	Decrease interest rate on loans to member banks Decrease cash reserve that member banks must deposit in Federal Reserve System
Excess productivity and high inflation (require a decrease in the money supply)	Increase interest rate on loans to member banks Increase cash reserve that member banks must deposit in Federal Reserve System

was beneficial and argued instead for a marketplace mechanism, letting the money supply drive demand and production decisions. Too much money in circulation contributes to inflation because too many dollars are chasing too few goods, which drives up prices. Too little money in circulation results in a slowing economy and rising unemployment, because consumers lack the ready cash and easy credit required to push up spending levels. Monetary policy involves increasing the money supply to boost the economy and decreasing the supply to slow it down.

The Fed

Control over the money supply rests not with the president or Congress but with the Federal Reserve System (known as "the Fed"). Created by the Federal Reserve Act of 1913, the Fed has a board of governors whose seven members serve for fourteen years, except for the chair and vice chair, who serve for four years. All members are appointed by the president, subject to Senate approval. The Fed regulates all national banks and those state banks that meet certain standards and choose to become members of the Federal Reserve System.

The Fed decides how much money to add to or subtract from the economy, seeking a balance that will permit steady growth without causing an unacceptable level of inflation. One way the Fed affects the money supply is by raising or lowering the cash reserve that member banks are required to deposit with the Federal Reserve. This reserve is a proportion of each member's total deposits. By increasing the reserve rate, the Fed takes money from member banks and thereby takes it out of circulation. When the Fed lowers the reserve rate, banks have more money available to loan to consumers and investors.

A second and more visible way the Fed affects the money supply is by lowering or raising the interest rate that member banks are charged when they borrow from the Federal Reserve. When the Fed raises the interest rate, banks also tend to raise the rate they charge for new loans, which discourages borrowing and thus reduces the amount of money entering the economy. Conversely, by lowering the interest rate, the Fed encourages firms and individuals to borrow from banks, which increases the money supply.

The Fed's interest-rate adjustments are often front-page news because they are a signal of the strength of the economy and thus affect the decisions of consumers and firms. As the economy accelerated in 2004, for example, the Fed began a series of adjustments that by 2006 had raised the interest rate by more than four percentage points. As the rate increased, home buying and refinancing slowed, as did other loan activity, including credit card borrowing. As demand weakened, so did the threat of inflation that accompanies periods of economic growth.

Economists debate the relative effectiveness of monetary policy and fiscal policy, but monetary policy has one obvious advantage: it can be implemented more quickly than fiscal policy. The Fed can adjust interest and reserve rates on short notice, thus providing the economy with a psychological boost to go along with the financial effect of a change in the money

University of Chicago economist Milton Friedman became the leading proponent of monetary policy as a tool for managing the economy. Friedman was named "Economist of the Century" by *Time* magazine.

supply. In contrast, changes in fiscal policy usually take much longer to implement. Congress is normally a slow-acting institution, and new taxing and spending programs ordinarily require a substantial preparation period before they can be put into effect. Moreover, Republicans and Democrats are often divided over which fiscal policy tool to use—taxing or spending—and may not be able to reach agreement on how to respond to a faltering economy.

The Politics of the Fed

The greater flexibility of monetary policy has positioned the Fed as the institution with primary policy responsibility for keeping the U.S. economy on a steady course. The Fed's power can easily be exaggerated. The U.S. economy is subject to a lot of influences, of which the money supply is only one. Nevertheless, the Fed is a vital component of U.S. economic policy.[24]

The power of the Fed raises important questions. One is the issue of representation: whose interests does the Fed serve, those of the public as a whole or those of the banking sector? The Fed is not a wholly impartial body. Although it makes decisions in the context of economic theories and projections, it is "the bankers' bank" and as such is protective of monied interests. The Fed typically is more concerned with rising inflation, which erodes the value of money, than with rising unemployment, which has its greatest impact on people at the bottom of the economic ladder. The Fed tends to hike interest rates when signs of rising inflation appear. Higher rates have the effect of slowing inflation, but they also slow job and income growth.

A related issue is one of accountability: should the Fed, an unelected body, have so much power? Though appointed by the president, members of the Federal Reserve Board are not subject to removal. They serve for fixed terms and are relatively insulated from political pressures, including the changes that take place through elections. Of course, the Fed, as a banking institution, has a vested interest in a healthy economy (too much inflation erodes banks' returns on loans; too much unemployment decreases demand for loans) and thus operates within its own system of checks and balances. Nevertheless, the restraints on the Fed are much weaker than those on popularly elected institutions. The Fed is a preeminent example of elitist politics at work.

At the time the Fed was created in 1913, economists had not yet "invented" the theory of monetary policy, and the Fed had no role in the management of the nation's economy. If the Fed were being created today, it would likely have a different structure, although there is general agreement among policymakers that some degree of independence is desirable.

Congress at some future point may decide that an overly independent Fed can no longer be tolerated and may bring monetary policy more closely under the control of elected institutions. Whether this happens will likely hinge on the Fed's willingness to exercise power sparingly and in the broad interests of society.

Regardless, the Fed is part of the new way of thinking about the federal government and the economy that emerged during the Great Depression of the 1930s. Until then, the federal government's economic role was largely confined to the provision of a limited number of public services, such as the postal service and the currency. Roosevelt's New Deal permanently changed policymakers' thinking. Through economic management and regulatory activities, the government would have an ongoing influence on the economy, contributing to its stability and efficiency.

The results nearly speak for themselves. In the roughly three-quarters of a century that the U.S. government has played a significant policy role, the American economy has prospered. The economic depressions that periodically wreaked havoc with firms and workers have disappeared. The cycle of economic ups and downs has remained but the cycle no longer consists of booms and busts, a testimony to the soundness of economic theory and of its use by policymakers. History has shown that the economy can be managed and regulated through government action, and that the nation is better off because of it.

Economic theory does not always give policymakers the answers they need. In the late 1970s, an unusual combination of circumstances created an economic condition that came to be known as "stagflation." Inflation, as was noted earlier in the chapter, was at a postwar high. Ordinarily, when inflation is high, so is economic growth. The late 1970s was a stark exception—the economy was stagnant. Economists had no theory to apply. Actions that would normally be taken to stimulate the economy would worsen the inflation problem. Actions that would normally be taken to bring down inflation would worsen the stagnation problem. Policymakers were stymied and had little choice but to let the economy work itself out, which it eventually did.

Nevertheless, economic theories have given U.S. policymakers a set of powerful tools for addressing problems such as jobs, productivity, and inflation. Most Americans appear to have little understanding of this fact. Many citizens continue to believe that the economy would work better if the government's economic role was curtailed. Moreover, most citizens are largely unaware of how federal economic policy works. A Harris poll found that, whereas Americans are relatively savvy consumers, only one in eight has a reasonable understanding of government's contribution to a sound economy. But even if they are not aware of it, Americans are indebted to the economists who devised the theories and to the federal policymakers who have had the skill to apply the theories effectively. (The economic policies of the federal government in the areas of social welfare and national security are discussed in the next two chapters.)

SUMMARY

Although private enterprise is the main force in the American economic system, the federal government plays a significant role through its policies to regulate, promote, and stimulate the economy.

Regulatory policy is designed to achieve efficiency and equity, which require government to intervene, for example, to maintain competitive trade practices (an efficiency goal) and to protect vulnerable parties in economic transactions (an equity goal). Many of the regulatory decisions of the federal government, particularly those of older agencies (such as the Federal Communication Commission), are made largely in the context of group politics. Business lobbies have an especially strong influence on the regulatory policies that affect them. In general, newer regulatory agencies (such as the Environmental Protection Agency) have policy responsibilities that are broader in scope and apply to a larger number of firms than those of the older agencies. As a result, the policy decisions of newer agencies are more often made in the context of party politics. Republican administrations are less vigorous in their regulation of business than are Democratic administrations.

Business is the major beneficiary of the federal government's efforts to promote economic interests. A large number of programs, including those that provide loans and research grants, are designed to assist businesses, which are also protected from failure through measures such as tariffs and favorable tax laws. Labor, for its part, obtains government assistance through laws concerning matters such as worker safety, the minimum wage, and collective bargaining. Yet America's individualistic culture tends to put labor at a disadvantage, keeping it less powerful than business in its dealings with the government. Agriculture is another economic sector that depends substantially on government's help, particularly in the form of income stabilization programs such as those that provide crop subsidies and price supports.

The U.S. government pursues policies that are designed to protect and conserve the environment. A few decades ago, the environment was not a policy priority. Today, there are many programs in this area, and the public has become an active participant in efforts to conserve resources and prevent exploitation of the environment.

Through its fiscal and monetary policies, Washington attempts to maintain a strong and stable economy—one characterized by high productivity, high employment, and low inflation. Fiscal policy is based on government decisions in regard to spending and taxing, which are aimed at either stimulating a weak economy or dampening an overheated (inflationary) economy. Fiscal policy is worked out through Congress and the president and consequently is responsive to political pressures. However, because it is difficult to raise taxes or cut programs, the government's ability to apply fiscal policy as an economic remedy is limited. Monetary policy is based on the money supply and works through the Federal Reserve System, which is headed by a board whose members hold office for fixed terms. The Fed is a relatively independent body, a fact that has given rise to questions as to whether it should have such a large role in influencing national economic policy.

KEY TERMS

balanced budget (*p. 556*)
budget deficit (*p. 556*)
budget surplus (*p. 556*)
capital-gains tax (*p. 558*)
deficit spending (*p. 555*)
demand-side economics (*p. 555*)
deregulation (*p. 540*)
economic depression (*p. 555*)
economic recession (*p. 555*)
economy (*p. 534*)
efficiency (*p. 536*)
equity (in relation to economic
  policy) (*p. 541*)

externalities (*p. 538*)
fiscal policy (*p. 554*)
graduated personal income
  tax (*p. 564*)
inflation (*p. 558*)
laissez-faire doctrine (*p. 534*)
monetary policy (*p. 564*)
national debt (*p. 556*)
public policy process (*p. 529*)
regulation (*p. 536*)
supply-side economics (*p. 557*)

SUGGESTED READINGS

Duncan, Richard. *The Dollar Crisis: Causes, Consequences, Cures,* rev. ed. New York: John Wiley & Sons, 2005. A look at the problem of budget and trade deficits.

Keith, Robert, and Allen Schick. *The Federal Budget Process.* Hauppauge, N.Y.: Now Science Publishers, 2003. An explanation of the federal budgetary process.

Lindbloom, Charles E. *The Market System: What It Is, How It Works, and What to Make of It.* New Haven, Conn.: Yale University Press, 2001. A clear analysis of the advantages and disadvantages of the market system.

Mayer, Martin. *FED: The Inside Story of How the World's Most Powerful Financial Institution Drives the Markets.* New York: Free Press, 2001. A look at the Fed's impact on the economy and politics.

McChesney, Robert. *The Problem of the Media.* New York: Monthly Review Press, 2004. A scathing critique of media regulation.

Rosenbaum, Walter A. *Environmental Politics and Policy,* 6th ed. Washington, D.C.: Congressional Quarterly Press, 2004. A comprehensive examination of the politics of environmental policy.

Shaiko, Ronald G. *Voices and Echoes for the Environment.* New York: Columbia University Press, 1999. The representation and communication of environmental groups.

Sheingate, Adam D. *The Rise of the Agricultural Welfare State.* Princeton, N.J.: Princeton University Press, 2003. A penetrating analysis of farm policy in the United States, France, and Japan.

LIST OF WEBSITES

http://www.federalreserve.gov/default.htm The Federal Reserve System website; describes the Fed, provides information about its current activities, and has links to some of the Fed's national and international information sources.

http://www.epa.gov/ The Environmental Protection Agency (EPA) website; has information on environmental policy and regulations, EPA projects, and related subjects.

http://www.ftc.gov/ The website of the Federal Trade Commission, one of the older regulatory agencies; describes the range of the FTC's activities.

http://www.whitehouse.gov/OMB The home page of the Office of Management and Budget; contains a summary of the annual federal budget and describes the OMB's operations and responsibilities.

POLITICS IN THEORY AND PRACTICE

Thinking: What are the tools of fiscal policy and monetary policy? What are the advantages and disadvantages of each of these two approaches to managing the economy?

Participating: There are membership groups that address problems in almost every conceivable area of the environment: conservation groups such as the Sierra Club, litigant groups such as the Environmental Defense Fund, sporting groups such as Ducks Unlimited, and so on. Consider joining a group that touches on your particular interest in nature. On the Internet, if you enter "group" and your particular interest in the search line, you should be able to locate a compatible group. Review the group's activities to see whether it's the right one for you.

ADDITIONAL RESOURCES

For quizzes, interactive simulations, games, graphics, and other study tools, visit the book's Online Learning Center at **www.mhhe.com/pattersonwtp7**.

Global Warming

By Al Gore

In 2006, an unlikely subject became a box-office hit. On its opening weekend, it had the highest average box-office take per screening of any documentary film in history. The movie was An Inconvenient Truth *narrated by Al Gore, the former vice president and presidential nominee. For several years previously, Gore had been presenting a slide show on global warming to audiences around the country, trying to raise public awareness of the problem. Following is an excerpt of what Gore said during a presentation at New York City's Beacon Theater on January 15, 2004. The event was sponsored by MoveOn, a liberal organization that relies on the Internet to mobilize its followers.*

[T]he vast majority of the most respected environmental scientists from all over the world have sounded a clear and urgent alarm. The international community—including the United States—began a massive effort several years ago to assemble the most accurate scientific assessment of the growing evidence that the earth's environment is sustaining severe and potentially irreparable damage from the unprecedented accumulation of pollution in the global atmosphere. In essence, these scientists are telling the people of every nation that global warming caused by human activities is becoming a serious threat to our common future. I am also troubled that the Bush/Cheney Administration does not seem to hear the warnings of the scientific community in the same way that most of us do.

Here is what we are talking about: Even though the earth is of such vast size, the most vulnerable part of the global environment is the atmosphere—because it is surprisingly thin—as the late Carl Sagan used to say: like a coat of varnish on a globe. I don't think there is any longer a credible basis for doubting that the earth's atmosphere is heating up because of global warming. So the evidence is overwhelming and undeniable. Global Warming is real. It is happening already and the anticipated consequences are unacceptable. But it is important to understand that this crisis is actually just a symptom of a deeper underlying cause.

Yet in spite of the clear evidence available all around us, there are many who still do not believe that Global Warming is a problem at all. And it's no wonder: because they are the targets of a massive and well-organized campaign of disinformation lavishly funded by polluters who are determined to prevent any action to reduce the greenhouse gas emissions that cause global warming, out of a fear that their profits might be affected if they had to stop dumping so much pollution into the atmosphere.

And wealthy right-wing ideologues have joined with the most cynical and irresponsible companies in the oil, coal and mining industries to contribute large sums of money to finance pseudo-scientific front groups that specialize in sowing confusion in the public's mind about global warming. They issue one misleading "report" after another, pretending that there is significant disagreement in the legitimate scientific community in areas where there is actually a broad-based consensus. The techniques they use were pioneered years earlier by the tobacco industry in its long campaign to create uncertainty in the public's mind about the health risks caused by tobacco smoke. Indeed, some of the very same scientific camp-followers who took money from the tobacco companies during that effort are now taking money from coal and oil companies in return for their willingness to say that global warming is not real.

In a candid memo about political strategy for Republican leaders, pollster Frank Luntz expressed concern that voters might punish candidates who supported more pollution, but offered advice on the key tactic for defusing the issue. The Bush Administration has gone far beyond Luntz' recommendations, however, and has explored new frontiers in cynicism by time and time again actually appointing the principal lobbyists and lawyers for the biggest polluters to be in charge of administering the laws that their clients are charged with violating. Some of these appointees have continued to work very closely with the outside pseudoscientific front groups even though they are now on the public payroll.

Two Attorneys General have now publicly accused officials in the Bush White House Council on Environmental Quality of conspiring with one of the outside groups to encourage the filing of a lawsuit as part of a shared strategy to undermine the possibility of government action of Global Warming. Vice President Cheney's infamous "Energy Task Force" advised lobbyists for polluters early in the new administration that there would be no action by the Bush White House on Global Warming and then asked for their help in designing a totally meaningless "voluntary" program. . . .

The problem is that our world is now confronting a five-alarm fire that calls for bold moral and political leadership from the United States of America. With such leadership, there is no doubt that we could solve the problem of global warming. After all, we brought down communism, won wars in the Pacific and Europe simultaneously, enacted the Marshall Plan, found a cure for polio and put men on the moon. When we set our sights on a visionary goal and are unified in pursuing it, there is very little we cannot accomplish. . . .

Instead of spending enormous sums of money on an unimaginative and retread effort to make a tiny portion of the Moon habitable for a handful of people, we should focus instead on a massive effort to ensure that the Earth is habitable for future generations. If we make that choice, the U.S. can strengthen our economy with a new generation of advanced technologies, create millions of good new jobs, and inspire the world with a bold and moral vision of humankind's future.

We are now at a true fork in the road. And in order to take the right path, we must choose the right values and adopt the right perspective. My friend the late Carl Sagan, whose idea it was to take this picture of the Earth, said this: "Look again at that dot. That's here. That's home. That's us. On it everyone you love, everyone you know. Everyone you ever heard of, every human being who ever WAS lived out their lives. The aggregate of our joy and suffering, thousands of confident religions, ideologies and economic doctrines, every hunter and forager, every hero and coward, every creator and destroyer of civilization, every king and peasant, every young couple in love, every mother and father, hopeful child inventor and explorer, every teacher of morals, every corrupt politician, every "superstar," every "supreme leader," every saint and sinner in the history of our species lived there—on a mote of dust suspended in a sunbeam.

"The Earth is a very small stage in a vast cosmic arena. Think of the rivers of blood spilled by all those generals and emperors, so that, in glory and triumph, they could become the momentary masters of a fraction of a dot. Think of the endless cruelties visited by the inhabitants of one corner of this pixel on the scarcely distinguishable inhabitants of some other corner, how frequent their misunderstandings, how eager they are to kill one another, how fervent their hatreds. Our posturings, our imagined self-importance, the delusion that we have some privileged position in the Universe, are challenged by this point of pale light. . . .

"The Earth is the only world known so far to harbor life. There is nowhere else, at least in the near future, to which our species could migrate. Visit, yes. Settle, not yet. Like it or not, for the moment the Earth is where we make our stand. There is perhaps no better demonstration of the folly of human conceits than this distant image of our tiny world. To me, it underscores our responsibility to deal more kindly with one another, and to preserve and cherish the pale blue dot, the only home we've ever known."

What's Your Opinion?

Do you share former Vice President Gore's concern with global warming? Do you share his interpretation of the scientific evidence and of the Bush administration's position on the issue? What do you think is the appropriate trade-off between environmental protection and economic growth, given that any substantial effort to reduce global warming would involve policies that would slow economic growth somewhat in the near term?

CHAPTER 16

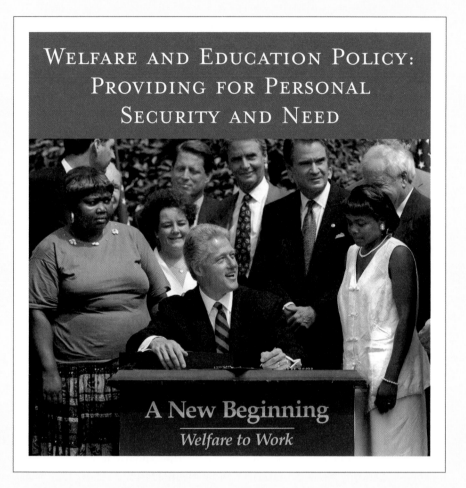

WELFARE AND EDUCATION POLICY:
PROVIDING FOR PERSONAL
SECURITY AND NEED

A New Beginning
Welfare to Work

"We the people of the United States, in order to . . . promote the general welfare . . ."

PREAMBLE, U.S. CONSTITUTION

As the Welfare Reform Act came up for renewal in 2002, there was cause for both hope and fear. The original legislation had been a stunning success. In the latter part of the 1990s, the number of people on the welfare rolls had been cut almost in half. In only three states—Hawaii, Rhode Island, and New Mexico—was the drop less than 20 percent (see "States in the Nation"). The trend defied what had been called welfare policy's "reverse gravity" law: welfare rolls that went up but never came down. Two factors accounted for the change. One was the booming national economy. As more Americans found jobs, the demand for welfare decreased. The second factor was the 1996 Welfare Reform Act, which shortened the length of eligibility and required that able-bodied recipients find work or risk loss of benefits.

The situation in 2002 was starkly different. Those welfare recipients who had found work were the ones easiest to place in jobs. Many of those still unemployed lacked the education, skill, or temperament to find and hold a job. Moreover, the economy had weakened, and welfare rolls were starting to rise while government revenues were declining. "At the beginning of welfare reform, we had the happy circumstance of a booming economy, low unemployment, falling welfare caseloads, and the states having the money to give more help to the poor, especially the working poor," said Sharon Parrott of the Center on Budget and Policy Priorities. "Now, everything is going the other way. Caseloads are rising, the value of the federal block grant is down, and state budgets are in catastrophic shape."[1]

The 2002 debate in Congress reflected these new realities. Yet it also brought out old partisan differences. Congressional Republicans wanted to increase pressure on the states to move more people off welfare and into work; they also argued for strict adherence to the eligibility rules, tight controls on federal spending, and increased work hours for welfare recipients. Congressional Democrats sought more funding for day care, education, and job-training programs; they also wanted to give the states more latitude in their administration of the welfare program. The differences were substantial enough to create a months-long deadlock between the Republican-controlled House and the Democratic-controlled Senate. "By stalling on . . . welfare reform," said Bill Thomas (R-Calif.) of the House Committee on Ways and Means, "the Senate is shaping their legacy—inaction." Senate majority leader Tom Daschle (D-S. Dak.) was unbending, vowing to hold out until the Republicans agreed to "strong child care provisions."[2]

Social welfare policy is an area in which opposing philosophies of government collide. Some people, like Senator Daschle, believe the government should provide substantial assistance to those Americans who are less equipped to compete effectively in the marketplace. Others, like Representative Thomas, believe that welfare payments, except to those who are indisputedly unfit to work, discourage personal effort and create welfare dependency.

Another source of conflict over welfare policy is the country's federal system of government. Welfare was traditionally a responsibility of state and local governments. Only since the 1930s has the federal government also played a major role. Some welfare programs are jointly run by the federal and state governments. They are funded at different levels from

The Declining Number of Families on Welfare

The welfare rolls in the United States peaked in March 1994. After that, the number of American families on welfare dropped precipitously, which analysts attributed to both the surge in the U.S. economy and the 1996 welfare reform bill that instituted new work rules. Between 1994 and 2002, welfare cases fell by 57 percent. The biggest drop (89 percent) was in Wisconsin. The smallest (7 percent) was in Hawaii. The decline in each state during this period is shown in the map below.

Q: What might explain the state-to-state variation in the decline in the welfare rolls?

A: States that had weaker economies in the early 1990s had bigger drops in their welfare rolls in the latter part of the 1990s. These states had more laid-off workers on welfare and, as the economy strengthened, many of these unemployed workers found jobs.

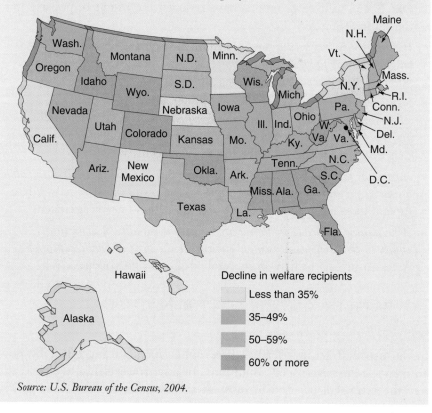

Decline in welfare recipients

- Less than 35%
- 35–49%
- 50–59%
- 60% or more

Source: U.S. Bureau of the Census, 2004.

one state to the next but operate within federal guidelines and are partly funded by Washington. The strictness of federal guidelines and the amount that the federal government should spend on these programs are contentious issues.

This chapter examines the social problems that federal welfare programs are designed to alleviate and describes how these programs operate. It also addresses public education policies. This chapter seeks to provide an informed basis for understanding issues of social welfare and education and to show why disagreements in these areas are so substantial. These issues involve hard choices that inevitably require trade-offs between federal and state power and between the values of individual self-reliance and egalitarian compassion. The main points of the chapter are these:

★ *Poverty is a large and persistent problem in America, deeply affecting about one in seven Americans, including many of the country's most vulnerable—children, female-headed families, and minority-group members.* Social welfare programs have reduced the extent of poverty in the United States.

★ *Welfare policy has been a partisan issue, with Democrats taking the lead on government programs to alleviate economic insecurity and Republicans acting to slow down or reverse these initiatives.*

★ *Social welfare programs are designed to reward and foster self-reliance or, when this is not possible, to provide benefits only to those individuals who are truly in need.* U.S. welfare policy is not based on the assumption that every citizen has a right to material security.

★ *Americans favor social insurance programs (such as social security) over public assistance programs (such as food stamps).* As a result, most social welfare expenditures are not targeted toward the nation's neediest citizens.

★ *A prevailing principle in the United States is equality of opportunity, which in terms of policy is most evident in the area of public education.* America invests heavily in its public schools and colleges.

POVERTY IN AMERICA: THE NATURE OF THE PROBLEM

In the broadest sense, social welfare policy includes any effort by government to improve social conditions. In a narrower sense, which is the way the term will be used in most of this chapter, social welfare policy refers to government programs that help individuals meet basic human needs, including food, clothing, and shelter.

The Poor: Who and How Many?

Americans' social welfare needs are substantial. Although Americans are far better off economically than most of the world's peoples, poverty is a significant and persistent problem in the United States. The government defines the **poverty line** as the annual cost of a thrifty food budget for an urban family of four, multiplied by three to include the cost of housing, clothes, and other necessities. Families whose incomes fall below that line are officially considered poor. In 2007, the poverty line was set at an annual income of roughly $20,000 for a family of four. One in eight Americans—roughly thirty-five million people, including more than ten million children—lives below the poverty line. If they could all join hands, they would form a line stretching from New York to Los Angeles and back again.

America's poor include individuals of all ages, races, religions, and regions, but poverty is concentrated among certain groups. Children are one of the largest groups of poor Americans. One in every five children lives in poverty. Most poor children live in single-parent families, usually with the mother. In fact, as can be seen from Figure 16–1, a high proportion of Americans residing in families headed by divorced, separated, or unmarried women live below the poverty line. These families are at a disadvantage because most women earn less than men for comparable work, especially in nonprofessional fields. Women without higher education or special skills often cannot find jobs that pay significantly more than the child care expenses they incur if they work outside the home.

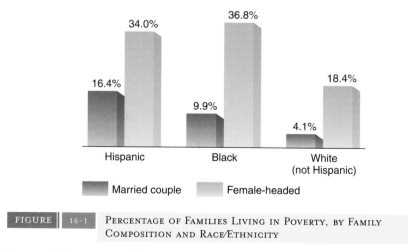

FIGURE | 16-1 | PERCENTAGE OF FAMILIES LIVING IN POVERTY, BY FAMILY COMPOSITION AND RACE/ETHNICITY

Poverty is far more prevalent among female-headed households and African American and Hispanic households. *Source: U.S. Bureau of the Census, 2006.*

Single-parent, female-headed families are roughly five times as likely as two-income families to fall below the poverty line, a situation referred to as "the feminization of poverty."

Poverty is widespread among minority-group members. Compared with whites, twice as many African Americans and Hispanics live below the poverty line. Poverty is also geographically concentrated. Although poverty is often portrayed as an urban problem, it is somewhat more prevalent in rural areas. About one in seven rural residents—compared with one in nine urban residents—lives in a family with income below the poverty line. The urban figure is misleading, however, in that poverty is very high in some inner-city areas. Suburbs have a lower rate. Because suburbanites are more removed from it, many of them have no sense of the impoverished condition of what Michael Harrington called "the other America."[3]

The "invisibility" of poverty in America is evident in polls that show that most Americans greatly underestimate the number of poor in their country. Certainly nothing in the daily lives of many Americans or in what they see on television would lead them to think that poverty rates are uncommonly high. Yet the United States has the highest level of poverty among the advanced industrialized nations, and its rate of child poverty is more than twice the average rate of the other countries (see "How the United States Compares").

 HOW THE UNITED STATES COMPARES

Children Living in Poverty

The United States has the highest child poverty rate among industrialized nations. One in five American children lives in poverty; in most other industrialized nations, the number is fewer than one in ten. These numbers are from the United Nation's Children's Fund, which defines as being in poverty any household with an income less than half that of the median household.

The United States ranks at the top in part because its income is less evenly distributed. As a consequence, the United States has the highest percentage of both rich and poor children in the industrialized world. In addition, the United States spends less on government assistance for the poor. Without government help, for example, the child poverty rates in the United States and France

(continued)

would be about equal—25 percent. Through its governmental programs, France has reduced the rate to just over 7 percent. Through
its welfare programs, the United States has cut the rate only slightly.

Child poverty in the United States is made worse by the relatively
large number of single-parent families, although Sweden, which has a
similarly large number of such families, has one of the world's lowest
rates of child poverty.

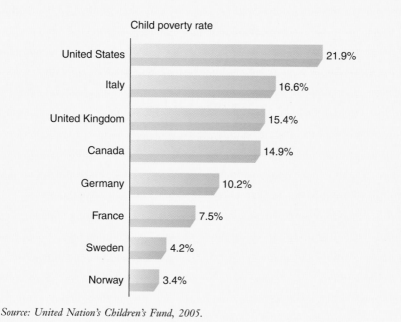

Child poverty rate

United States — 21.9%
Italy — 16.6%
United Kingdom — 15.4%
Canada — 14.9%
Germany — 10.2%
France — 7.5%
Sweden — 4.2%
Norway — 3.4%

Source: United Nation's Children's Fund, 2005.

Living in Poverty: By Choice or Chance?

Many Americans hold to the idea that poverty is largely a matter of
choice—that most low-income Americans are unwilling to make the effort
to hold a responsible job and get ahead in life. In his book *Losing Ground,*
Charles Murray argues that America has a permanent underclass of
unproductive citizens who prefer to live on welfare and whose children
receive little educational encouragement at home and grow up to be copies
of their parents.[4] There are, indeed, many such people in America. They
number in the millions. They are the toughest challenge for policymakers
because almost nothing about their lives equips them to escape from
poverty and its attendant ills.

Yet most poor Americans are in their situation as a result of circumstance rather than choice. After reviewing the extensive research on the causes of poverty and examining data that tracked individuals over periods of time, economists Signe-Mary McKernan and Caroline Ratcliffe concluded that most of the poor are poor only for a while and then for reasons largely beyond individual control—such as a job layoff or desertion by the father—rather than because they prefer not to work.[5] When the U.S. economy goes into a tailspin, the impact devastates many families. The U.S. Department of Labor reported that three million jobs were lost in the manufacturing sector alone during the recessionary period that began in 2000.

It is also true that a full-time job does not guarantee that a family will rise above the poverty line. A family of four with one employed adult who works forty hours a week at six dollars an hour (roughly the minimum wage) has an annual income of about $12,000, which is well below the poverty line. Millions of Americans—mostly household workers, service workers, unskilled laborers, and farm workers—are in this position. The U.S. Bureau of Labor Statistics estimates that roughly 10 percent of full-time workers do not earn enough to lift their family above the poverty line.[6]

THE POLITICS AND POLICIES OF SOCIAL WELFARE

Historical
Background

At one time in the nation's history, the federal government was not involved in social welfare policy. Poverty and other welfare problems were deemed to fall within the powers reserved to the states by the Tenth Amendment and to be adequately addressed by them, even though they did not offer substantial welfare services. Individuals were expected to fend for themselves, and those unable to do so were usually supported by relatives and friends. This approach reflected the idea of **negative government,** which holds that government governs best by staying out of people's lives, giving them as much freedom as possible to determine their own pursuits and encouraging them to become self-reliant.

The Great Depression changed that outlook. The unemployment level reached 25 percent, and many of those with jobs were working for pennies. Americans looked to the federal government for help. Franklin D. Roosevelt's New Deal brought economic relief in the form of public jobs and assistance programs and changed opinions about the federal government's welfare role.[7] This new attitude reflected a faith in **positive government,** the idea that government intervention is necessary in order to enhance personal liberty and security when individuals are buffeted by economic and social forces beyond their control.

★ | LEADERS

Franklin D. Roosevelt
(1882–1945)

Franklin D. Roosevelt won the presidency in 1932 during the depths of the Great Depression. FDR's job programs put Americans back to work, and his social programs met their immediate and long-term economic needs. His greatest domestic policy legacy is the Social Security Act of 1935, which for nearly eight decades has been the foundation of elderly Americans' financial security. Roosevelt's New Deal also changed Americans' conception of government—it could be an instrument for protecting citizens against economic adversity. A distant cousin of President Theodore Roosevelt, FDR had a passion for politics even as a youth. After graduating from Harvard and Columbia Law School, he won a seat in the New York State Senate. During World War I, he served as assistant secretary of the Navy, and in 1920, when he was still in his thirties, he was chosen as the Democratic party's vice-presidential nominee. A year later, he contracted polio and lost full use of his legs, a fact that he kept largely hidden from the public. He fought to regain his health and was elected governor of New York before winning election to the presidency. In 1940, Roosevelt broke with tradition and announced that he would seek a third presidential term. Against the backdrop of war in Europe and continuing economic problems at home, he won the election—though by a narrower margin than in his two previous campaigns. Roosevelt was in office when the Japanese attacked Pearl Harbor, and he oversaw the mobilization of the greatest military power the world had yet known. America's industrial might and its armed forces were critical weapons in the Allies' defeat of the Axis powers. FDR won a fourth term in 1944 but died in office of a cerebral hemorrhage as the war was concluding.

Not all Americans of the 1930s embraced the new philosophy. Most Republican leaders and loyalists clung to traditional ideas about self-reliance and free markets. Democrats spearheaded the change. The key vote in the House of Representatives on the Social Security Act of

1935, for example, had 85 percent of Democrats voting in favor of it and 99 percent of Republicans voting against it.[8]

Republicans gradually came to accept the idea that the federal government has a role in social welfare but argued that the role should be kept as small as practicable. Thus, in the 1960s, Republican opposition to President Lyndon Johnson's Great Society was substantial. His programs included federal initiatives in health care, education, public housing, nutrition, and other areas traditionally dominated by state and local governments. More than 70 percent of congressional Republicans voted against the 1965 Medicare and Medicaid programs, which provide government-paid medical assistance for the elderly and the poor. In contrast, the 1996 Welfare Reform Act, which was designed to cut welfare rolls and costs, had the overwhelming support of congressional Republicans, while a majority of congressional Democrats voted against it.

Although the Republican and Democratic parties have been at odds on social welfare issues, they have also had reason to work together. Millions of Americans depend on the federal government to provide benefits to ease the loss of income caused by retirement, disability, unemployment, and the like. These benefit programs differ in whom they serve, what they provide, and how eligibility is acquired. In broad terms, they fall into two general categories: social insurance and public assistance. Programs in the first category enjoy broader public support, are more heavily funded, and provide benefits to individuals of all income levels. Programs in the second category have less public support, receive less funding, and are restricted to people of low income.

Programs in both categories involve **transfer payments,** government benefits given directly to individual recipients, such as the monthly social security checks that retirees receive. Some social welfare spending, such as federal grants for health research, is not in the form of a transfer payment because the money does not go to individual recipients. Most programs that support individuals directly are **entitlement programs,** meaning that any individual who meets the criteria for eligibility is entitled to the benefit. For example, upon reaching the legal retirement age, any senior citizen who has paid social security taxes for the required amount of time is entitled to receive social security benefits. In this sense, entitlement programs have the same force of law as taxes. Just as individuals are required by law to pay taxes on the income they earn, they are entitled by law to receive government benefits for which they qualify.

As indicated, individual-benefit programs fall into two broad groups: social insurance programs and public assistance programs. The next two sections discuss these two types of programs.

Social Insurance Programs

More than forty million Americans receive monthly benefits from social insurance programs—including social security, Medicare, unemployment insurance, and workers' compensation. The two major programs, social security and Medicare, cost the federal government more than $800 billion per year. Such programs are labeled **social insurance** because only those individuals who paid special payroll taxes when they were employed are eligible for these benefits.

Social Security   The leading social insurance program is social security for retirees. The program began with passage of the Social Security Act of 1935 and is funded through payroll taxes on employees and employers (currently set at 6.2 percent). Franklin D. Roosevelt emphasized that retiring workers would receive an insurance benefit that they had earned through their payroll taxes, not a handout from the government. In part because of this method of financing social security, the program has broad public support.[9] Opinion polls indicate that the large majority of Americans favor current or higher levels of social security benefits for the elderly. Social security is one of the few welfare programs run entirely by the federal government. Washington collects the payroll taxes that fund the program and sends monthly checks directly to the nearly forty million social security recipients, who receive on average about $900 a month.

Although people qualify for social security by paying payroll taxes during their working years, the money they receive upon retirement is funded by payroll taxes on current workers' salaries. This arrangement poses a long-term threat to the viability of the social security program because people are living longer than they once did. Three decades from now, about one in five Americans will be over age sixty-five, at which time—unless changes are made in the social security program—there will not be enough workers to pay for retiree benefits.

In 2005, President George W. Bush proposed a partial privatization of social security as an answer to the long-term problem. Workers would have been allowed to place roughly a third of social security tax payments into private individual stock accounts. Bush claimed that individuals would get a greater return on their money through the stock market, thereby reducing what government would need to pay when workers retired. Bush's proposal was attacked by congressional Democrats and by powerful groups including the American Association of Retired Persons (AARP), who argued that Bush's proposal would expose retirees to the risks of the stock market. Critics also said that the Bush plan would make the problem

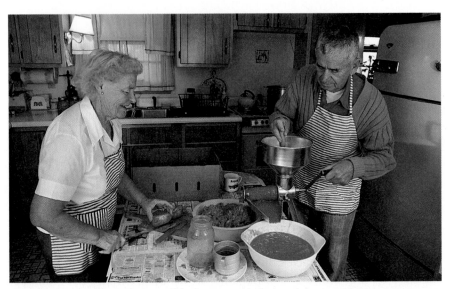

Social security benefits make it possible for many elderly Americans to maintain a secure, independent retirement.

of solvency worse, not better. Payroll taxes that otherwise would have been used to offset payments to retirees would instead be diverted into private accounts. Bush's plan failed to win congressional approval, but the need to overhaul social security remains. At some point, as happened in the 1980s, a bipartisan commission is likely to be formed to develop a compromise solution that will preserve America's commitment to its elderly retirees.

Unemployment Insurance The 1935 Social Security Act provides for unemployment benefits for workers who lose their jobs involuntarily. Unemployment insurance is a joint federal-state program. The federal government collects the payroll taxes that fund unemployment benefits, but states have the option of deciding whether the taxes will be paid by both employees and employers or by employers only (most states use the latter option). Individual states also set the tax rate, conditions of eligibility, and benefit level, subject to minimum standards established by the federal government. Although unemployment benefits vary widely among states, they average $350 a week, somewhat more than a third of what an average worker makes while employed. The benefits in most cases are terminated after twenty-six to thirty-nine weeks.

The unemployment program does not have the broad public support that social security enjoys. This situation reflects the widespread assumption that the loss of a job, or the failure to find a new one right away, is typically a personal failing. Unemployment statistics indicate otherwise. For example, U.S. Bureau of Labor statistics reveal that of those workers who lost their jobs in 2001, only 13 percent were fired or quit voluntarily. The rest became unemployed because of either a temporary layoff or the permanent elimination of a job position.

Medicare   After World War II, most European democracies created government-paid health care systems, and President Harry Truman, a Democrat, proposed a similar program for Americans. The American Medical Association (AMA) called Truman's plan "un-American" and vowed to mobilize local physicians to campaign against members of Congress who supported "socialized medicine." Truman's proposal never came to a vote in Congress. In 1961, President John F. Kennedy, also a Democrat, proposed a health care program restricted to social security recipients, but the AMA, the insurance industry, and congressional conservatives succeeded in blocking the plan.[10]

The 1964 elections swept a tide of liberal Democrats into Congress, and the result was Medicare. Enacted in 1965, the program provides medical assistance to retirees and is funded primarily through payroll taxes. Medicare is based on the insurance principle and because of this has gained as much public support as social security has. Medicare does not cover all hospital, nursing home, or physicians' fees, but enrollees in the program have the option of paying an insurance premium for fuller coverage of these fees. Enrollees who cannot afford the additional premium can apply to have the government pay it.

In 2006, a prescription drug benefit as part of the Medicare program went into effect. The program includes a recipient contribution and primarily benefits retirees who either are too poor to afford prescription drugs or have very high prescription drug costs. Retirees not in these categories receive a small benefit from the program but are required to pay most of the cost of their prescription drugs. The program's complicated rules have led to numerous complaints from senior citizens.

At some point soon, Congress will have to overhaul the Medicare program as a whole. The rising cost of medical care and the growing number of elderly have combined to threaten the solvency of the program; it is projected to run out of money within a decade unless new revenues and cost-cutting measures are devised. Among the options under consideration are increased payroll taxes, more cost-sharing by recipients, more use of managed care options, and further limits on government payments to doctors and hospitals.

Public Assistance Programs

Unlike social insurance programs, **public assistance** programs are funded through general tax revenues and are available only to the financially needy. Eligibility for these programs is established by a **means test;** applicants must prove that they are poor enough to qualify for the benefit. Once they have done so, they are entitled to the benefit, unless their personal situation changes or the government legislates different eligibility criteria. These programs often are referred to as "welfare" and the recipients as "welfare cases."

Americans are much less supportive of public assistance programs than they are of social insurance programs. Americans tend to look upon social insurance benefits as having been "earned" by the recipient, while they see public assistance benefits as "handouts." Because of their individualistic culture, Americans are less inclined than Europeans to believe that government should provide substantial help to the poor (see Figure 16–2). Support for public assistance programs also is weakened by Americans' perception that the government is already spending vast amounts on welfare. A poll found that Americans believe public assistance programs to be the second costliest item in the federal budget. These programs actually rank much farther down the list. In fact, the federal government spends hundreds of billions of dollars more on its two major social insurance programs, social security and Medicare, than it does on all public assistance programs combined.

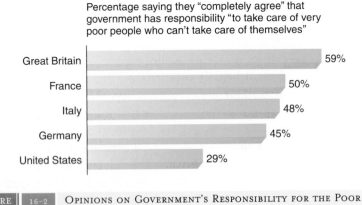

Percentage saying they "completely agree" that government has responsibility "to take care of very poor people who can't take care of themselves"

Great Britain	59%
France	50%
Italy	48%
Germany	45%
United States	29%

FIGURE 16-2   OPINIONS ON GOVERNMENT'S RESPONSIBILITY FOR THE POOR

Compared to Europeans, Americans are much less likely to believe that government has a responsibility for the poor. *Source: Pew Research Center for the People and the Press, Global Attitudes Survey, 2002.*

Supplemental Security Income   A major public assistance program is Supplemental Security Income (SSI), which originated as federal assistance to the blind and elderly poor as part of the Social Security Act of 1935. By the 1930s, most states had begun or were considering such programs. Although the federal legislation was designed to replace their efforts, the states have retained a measure of control over benefits and eligibility and are required to provide some of the funding. Because SSI recipients (who now include the disabled in addition to the blind and elderly poor) have obvious reasons for their inability to provide fully for themselves, this public assistance program is not widely criticized.

Temporary Assistance for Needy Families (TANF)   Before passage of the 1996 Welfare Reform Act (discussed in the chapter's introduction), needy American families had an open-ended guarantee of cash assistance. As long as their income was below a certain level, they were assured of government support. The program, Aid for Families with Dependent Children (AFDC for short), was created in the 1930s as survivors' insurance to assist children whose fathers had died prematurely. Relatively small at the outset, it became controversial as Americans increasingly linked it to welfare dependency and irresponsibility. AFDC was an entitlement program, which meant that any single parent (and in some states two parents) living in poverty could claim the benefit and keep it for as long as a dependent child was in the household. Some AFDC recipients were content to live on this assistance, and in some cases their children also grew up to become AFDC recipients, creating what was called "a vicious cycle of poverty." By 1995, AFDC was supporting fourteen million Americans at an annual cost of more than $15 billion.

The 1996 Welfare Reform Act abolished AFDC, replacing it with the program titled Temporary Assistance for Needy Families (TANF). TANF's goal is to reduce long-term welfare dependency by limiting the length of time recipients can receive assistance and by giving the states an incentive to get welfare recipients into jobs. Each state is given an annual federal bloc grant that it uses to help needy families meet their subsistence needs and to develop programs that will help the parents find employment. The state programs operate within strict federal guidelines, including the following:

- Americans' eligibility for federal cash assistance is limited to no more than five years in their lifetime.
- Within two years, the head of most families on welfare will have to find work or risk the loss of benefits.
- Unmarried teenage mothers are qualified for welfare benefits only if they remain in school and live with a parent or legal guardian.

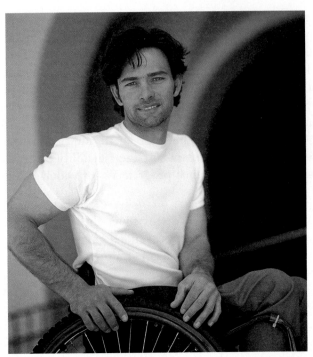

Supplemental Security Income (SSI) is a combined federal-state program that provides public assistance to blind and disabled people.

- Single mothers will lose a portion of their benefits if they refuse to cooperate in identifying for child-support purposes the father of their children.

Although states are allowed to make exceptions to some of the rules (for example, an unmarried teenage mother who faces sexual abuse at home is permitted to live elsewhere), the exceptions are limited. States can even choose to impose more restrictive rules in some areas. For example, states have the option of denying increased benefits to unwed mothers who give birth to another child.

The long-term effectiveness of TANF is not yet known. The trend so far is cause for mild optimism. The number of families on public assistance has declined sharply since passage of the 1996 Welfare Reform Act. The biggest challenge facing the states is developing welfare-to-work programs that will qualify people for jobs secure enough to free them from welfare dependency. Most welfare recipients who have found employment since 1996 had enough skills that they required little or no job training from their state. In contrast, most of those who have been unable to find long-term employment have limited education and few job-related skills. States are trying innovative ways to train these individuals for work; whether these programs will succeed is unclear.[11]

Food Stamps   The food stamp program, which took its present form in 1961, is fully funded by the federal government. The program provides an **in-kind benefit**—not cash, but food stamps that can be spent only on grocery items.

Food stamps are available only to people who qualify on the basis of low income. The program is intended to improve the nutrition of poor families by enabling them to purchase qualified items—mainly foodstuffs—with food stamps. Some critics say that food stamps stigmatize their users by making it obvious to onlookers in the checkout line that they are "welfare cases." More prevalent criticisms are that the program is too costly and that too many undeserving people receive food stamps.

Subsidized Housing   Low-income persons are also eligible for subsidized housing. Most of the federal spending in this area is on rent vouchers, an in-kind benefit. The government gives the individual a monthly rent-payment voucher, which the individual gives in lieu of cash to the landlord, who then hands the voucher over to the government in exchange for cash. About five million households annually receive a federal housing subsidy.

The U.S. government spends much less on public housing than on tax breaks for homeowners, most of whom are middle- and upper-income Americans. Homeowners are allowed tax deductions for their mortgage interest payments and their local property tax payments. The total of these tax concessions is three times as much as is spent by the federal government on housing for low-income families.

Medicaid   When Medicare, the health care program for the elderly, was created in 1965, Congress also established Medicaid, which provides health care for poor people who are already on welfare. It is considered a public assistance program, rather than a social insurance program like Medicare, because it is based on need and funded by general tax revenues. Roughly 60 percent of Medicaid funding is provided by the federal government, and about 40 percent by the states. More than twenty million Americans receive Medicaid assistance.

Medicaid is controversial because of its costs. As health care costs have spiraled far ahead of the inflation rate, so have the costs of Medicaid. It absorbs roughly half of all public assistance dollars spent by the U.S. government and has forced state and local governments to cut other services to meet their share of the costs. "It's killing us," is how one local official described the impact of Medicaid on his community's budget.[12] As is true of other public assistance programs, Medicaid has been criticized for supposedly helping too many people who could take care of themselves if they tried harder. This belief is contradicted, ironically, by the situation faced by many working Americans. There are roughly forty-five million Americans living in families with incomes that are too high to qualify them for Medicaid but too low to cover the cost of health insurance.[13]

Culture, Welfare, and Income

Surveys repeatedly show that most Americans are convinced people on welfare could get along without if they tried. As a consequence, there is constant political pressure to reduce welfare expenditures and to weed out undeserving recipients. The result is a welfare system that is both *inefficient*, in that much of the money spent on welfare never reaches the intended recipients, and *inequitable*, in that less than half of social welfare spending goes to the people who need it the most.

Inefficiency and Inequity   The United States has the most inefficient welfare system in the Western world. Because of the unwritten principle that the individual must somehow earn or be in absolute need of assistance, the U.S. welfare system is heavily bureaucratic. For example, the 1996 welfare reform bill—which limits eligibility to families with incomes below a certain level and, in most instances, to families with a single parent living in the home—requires that the eligibility of each applicant be checked periodically by a caseworker. This procedure makes such programs doubly expensive; in addition to payments to the recipients, the programs must pay local caseworkers, supervisors, and support staffs (see Figure 16–3). These costs do not include the costs of the state and federal agencies that oversee the programs.

FIGURE | 16-3   THE CUMBERSOME ADMINISTRATIVE PROCESS BY WHICH WELFARE RECIPIENTS GET THEIR BENEFITS

The bureaucratic costs of welfare are substantially lower in Europe because most European countries have unitary rather than federal systems, which eliminates a layer of government, and also because eligibility is more often universal, as in the case of government-paid health care. Caseworkers do not have to pore over records to determine who is and who is not eligible for medical treatment—everyone is.[14]

European welfare programs are also more equitable in the sense that the major beneficiaries are those individuals most in need, unlike the case in the United States. The federal government spends far more on social security and Medicare, which assist rich and poor alike, than it spends in total on all public assistance programs, which help only the needy. Of course, social insurance programs do help some who are needy. Monthly social security checks keep millions of Americans, mostly widows, out of poverty; about one-fourth of America's elderly have no significant monthly income aside from what they receive from social security. Nevertheless, families in the top fifth by income receive more in federal social insurance benefits than is spent on TANF, food stamps, and housing subsidies combined.

Income and Tax Measures   The American political culture's emphasis on individualism is also evident in its tax and income policies. Economic redistribution—the shifting of money from the more affluent to the less affluent—is an aspect of these policies, but it is a relatively small component.

The United States has substantial income inequality (see Figure 16–4). Americans in the top fifth by income receive half of total U.S. income, while those in the bottom fifth get less than a twentieth. According to 2006 Census Bureau figures, the typical American in the top fifth by income has an annual income fifteen times greater than that of the typical American in the bottom fifth by income. The imbalance is greater than that in any other industrialized democracy. One reason is that income taxes are not used for economic redistribution to the extent that they are in other democracies. In 2007, the top tax rate in the United States was 35 percent and applied to net income above $335,000. Income below that level is taxed at lower rates. Thus, a taxpayer with a net income of $500,000 pays the 35 percent rate on the amount above $335,000 and lower rates on the rest. In Europe, a top rate of 50 percent is not uncommon, and the top rate starts at a lower income level than in the United States.

The U.S. tax code also includes numerous tax deductions for upper-income individuals, such as the deduction for mortgage interest on a vacation home. Moreover, the well-to-do escape social security taxes on a large part of their income. The social security tax is a flat rate of about

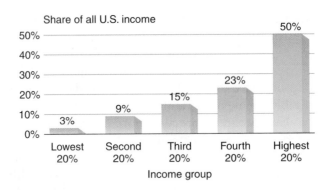

FIGURE   16-4   INCOME INEQUALITY IN THE UNITED STATES

The United States has the highest degree of income inequality of any industrialized democracy. Citizens in the top fifth by income get nearly half of all income; those in the bottom fifth get less than one-twentieth of all income. *Source: U.S. Bureau of the Census, 2006.*

6 percent that begins with the first dollar earned and stops completely after roughly $95,000 in earnings is reached. Thus, individuals earning less than $95,000 pay social security taxes on every dollar they make, while those earning more than $95,000 pay no social security taxes on the dollars they make over this amount.

The net result is that the **effective tax rate** (the actual percentage of a person's income spent to pay taxes) of high- and middle-income Americans is not greatly different. When all taxes (including personal income taxes, social security taxes, state sales taxes, and local property taxes) are combined, the average American family's effective tax rate is about three-fourths that of a family with an income over a million dollars. In Europe, where tax breaks for the well-to-do are few, the effective tax rate for high-income taxpayers is substantially greater than that for average taxpayers.[15]

Of course, although well-to-do Americans pay relatively low taxes, the fact that they earn a lot of money means that they contribute the large share of tax revenues in absolute dollars. The top 10 percent of U.S. earners pay about half the personal income taxes received by the federal government. On the other hand, they keep much more of what they earn than do high-income taxpayers elsewhere.

Over the past few decades, the trend has been toward reducing taxes on the wealthy, a development that began during the Reagan administration and continued under George W. Bush. Arguing that high taxes on the wealthy hurt economic growth (see Chapter 15), Bush persuaded Congress to enact phased-in tax cuts that sharply reduced taxes on high incomes. Capital-gains taxes were slashed, and marginal tax rates on personal income were reduced. The savings to Americans in the top 1 percent of income is $54,493 per year, compared with an average of $67 for those in the bottom 20 percent and $611 for those in the middle 20 percent. In terms of total dollars, less than 1 percent of the cuts are for those in the bottom fifth by income, while those in the middle fifth get 8 percent of the cuts and those in the top fifth receive 75 percent of the cuts.[16]

However, America's poorest working families have also received tax relief in recent decades. The vehicle for this relief is the Earned Income Tax Credit (EITC). About ten million low-income American families each year receive an EITC payment. The maximum yearly payment to any family is roughly $4,500, and eligibility is limited to families that include a wage earner. EITC payments result when individuals file their personal income taxes. The payment declines in amount as income rises and phases out entirely at a specified income level. The EITC program was started in 1975 and has been expanded to become the federal government's largest means-tested cash assistance program. According to U.S. Census Bureau calculations, EITC lifts about a third of low-income Americans above the poverty line. Moreover, because EITC payments are based on income tax returns, the program does not require a costly bureaucracy of caseworkers and support staff. EITC payments are processed at the same time and in the same way as tax refunds for employees who have paid too much withholding tax.

EDUCATION AS EQUALITY OF OPPORTUNITY

Although the Earned Income Tax Credit is subject to budgetary and political pressures, it enjoys more support than do most assistance programs. The reason is simple: EITC is tied to jobs. Only those who earn wages are eligible to receive the payment. Polls that span more than a half-century reveal that Americans consistently have favored work-based assistance over welfare payments as the answer to poverty. Work is believed to foster initiative and accountability, whereas welfare "handouts" are believed to breed dependency and irresponsibility.

At the same time, Americans believe that people should have a fighting chance to succeed in the job market. Although few Americans would support economic equality for all, most Americans endorse the principle of **equality of opportunity**—the idea that people should have a reasonable chance to succeed if they make the effort. The concept includes a commitment to equality in the narrow sense that everyone should have a fair chance to get ahead. But it is a form of equality shaped by liberty, because the outcome—personal success or personal failure—depends on what individuals do with that opportunity. The expectation is that people will end up differently; some will make a good living, and some will be poor. It has been said that equality of opportunity gives individuals an equal chance to become unequal.

Equality of opportunity is an ideal. Americans obviously do not start life on an equal footing. It was said of one successful American politician, whose father before him was a successful politician as well as a millionaire, that "he was born on third base and thought he hit a triple."[17] Some Americans are born into privilege, and others start life in such abject poverty that they have no realistic chance of escaping it. Nonetheless, equality of opportunity is more than a catch phrase. It is the philosophical basis for a number of government programs, none more notable than public education.

Public Education: Leveling Through the Schools

During the nation's first century, the question of a free education for all children was a divisive issue. Wealthy interests feared that an educated public would challenge their power. Egalitarians, on the other hand, saw education as a means of enabling ordinary people to get ahead. The egalitarians won out. Public schools sprang up in nearly every community and were open free of charge to children who could attend.

Today, as discussed in Chapter 1, the United States invests more heavily in public education at all levels than does any other country. The curriculum in American schools is also relatively standardized. Unlike those countries that divide children even at the grade school level into different tracks that lead ultimately to different occupations, the United States aims to educate all children in essentially the same way. Of course, public education is not a uniform experience for American children. The quality of education depends significantly on the wealth of the community in which a child resides. The Supreme Court has upheld this arrangement, saying that states are obliged to give all children an "adequate" education as opposed to an "equal" one across all communities.

The United States does have a federal education program, Head Start, dedicated to helping poor children. Established in the 1960s during the Johnson administration, it provides preschool education to low-income children in order to help them succeed when they begin kindergarten. At no time in its history, however, has the Head Start program been funded at a level that would allow all eligible children to participate. The low

POLITICAL CULTURE
Education and Equality

Public education has never been a uniform experience for American children. Cities in the late nineteenth century neglected the education of many immigrant children, who were thereby placed at a permanent disadvantage. During the first half of the twentieth century, southern public schools for black children were designed to keep them down, not lift them up. Today, many children in poorer neighborhoods attend overcrowded and understaffed public schools.

Nevertheless, the nation's public schools have been the primary means by which Americans of all nationalities, colors, creeds, and income levels have been brought together. At no time in most Americans' lives are they as thoroughly immersed in a socially diverse environment as when, as children and adolescents, they attend public schools.

America's broad-based system of public education stems from a melding of its egalitarian and individualistic traditions. Leon Sampson, a nineteenth-century socialist, noted the stark difference between the philosophy of public education in the United States and that in Europe. "The European ruling classes," he wrote, "were open in their contempt for the proletariat. But in the United States equality, and even class-lessness, the creation of wealth for all and political liberty were extolled in the public schools." Sampson concluded that American schools embodied a unique conception of equality. Everyone was being trained in much the same way so that each person would have the opportunity to succeed. "It is," he said, "a socialist conception of capitalism."

The making of one people out of many is fostered by the general philosophy of public education in America, which holds that students should share a common curriculum. A system that would seek instead to enhance the education of top students would work to the disadvantage of poor students and others who, for reasons of language or life circumstances, are less prepared to do well when they enter school. An elite-centered school system of the type found in some European societies would serve to widen the gap between the country's richer and poorer groups and to slow the assimilation into American society of its newer arrivals.

Of course, other institutions also contribute to the integration of American society, but no institution does it as well or as thoroughly as the public schools. This is not to say that the schools are mirrors of

(continued)

America's diversity. A great deal of ethnic, racial, and class segregation still exists in the schools. For example, in some suburban schools few of the children come from families earning less than $75,000 a year. And in some urban schools few of the children come from families earning more than $25,000 a year. Yet, were it not for public schools, America would be a substantially more stratified society, both in terms of one's classmates while in school and in terms of one's prospects for success after leaving school.

Public education in America was called "the great leveler" when it began in the early nineteenth century. Since then it has earned that label. Rarely has a public institution served so many so well for such a long period.

point was reached in the 1980s, when there was only enough money to allow the enrollment of one in ten of those eligible. Today, less than half of all eligible children participate.

Nevertheless, the United States through its public schools educates a broad segment of the population. Arguably, no country in the world has

The Head Start education program is designed to give preschool children from poorer homes a better chance to succeed when they enter kindergarten. Shown here is a teacher reading to a Head Start class in Austin, Texas.

made an equivalent effort to give children, whatever their parents' background, an equal opportunity in life through education. Per-pupil spending on public elementary and secondary schools is roughly twice as high in the United States as it is in Western Europe. America's commitment to broad-based education extends to college. The United States is far and away the world leader in terms of the proportion of adults receiving a college education.[18]

The nation's education system preserves both the myth and the reality of an equal-opportunity society. The belief that success can be had by anyone who works for it could not be sustained if the education system were tailored for a privileged elite. And educational attainment is related to personal success, at least as measured by annual incomes. In fact, the gap in income between those with and those without a college education is greater now than at any time in the country's history.

Public School Issues

Because America's public schools play such a key role in creating an equal-opportunity society, they are closely scrutinized. Parents of schoolchildren are not shy about saying what they think of their local schools. Interestingly, parents tend to rate their own children's schools more highly than they rate other schools. A national survey found that two-thirds of parents gave their children's schools a grade of A or B but only a fourth gave the nation's schools as a whole a grade that high.[19]

The issues facing public schools are far-ranging. Disorder in the schools is a major issue in some communities, as is student performance on standardized tests. American students do not even score in the top ten internationally on tests in science or math. Nevertheless, the most controversial policy issues involve proposals to reallocate money among schools. School choice is one such issue. Under this policy, the public schools compete for students, and schools that attract the most students are rewarded with the largest budgets. Advocates of the policy claim that it forces school administrators and teachers to do a better job and gives students the option of leaving a school that is performing poorly.[20] Parents favor such a policy by a wide margin, unless their children are harmed by it. Poor children in particular often have little choice but to attend the nearest school because their parents are unable to transport them to a better but more distant school.[21]

School vouchers are a related issue. A voucher system allows parents to use tax dollars to keep their children out of the public schools entirely. Parents receive a voucher from the government that they can give to a private or parochial school to cover part of the cost of their child's tuition.

Proponents say that vouchers force failing public schools to improve their instructional programs or face a permanent loss of revenue. Opponents, however, argue that vouchers weaken the public schools by siphoning off revenue and that vouchers subsidize many families that would have sent their children to private or parochial schools anyway. They note that vouchers are of little use to students from poor families because they lack the additional money required to pay the full tuition costs at a nonpublic school.

Although the courts have upheld the constitutionality of vouchers in some circumstances, polls indicate that Americans are divided over whether they would like to see a universal voucher system.[22] The question gets majority support when it is framed in the context of choice among public schools but is opposed by the majority when private and parochial schools are included among the choices. The issue of vouchers reflects the tensions inherent in the concept of equal opportunity. Vouchers expand the number of choices available to students. Yet, not all students are able to take advantage of the choices, and not all taxpayers want their tax dollars used to support private and parochial schools. (Another public school issue—uniform testing of all schoolchildren—is discussed in the next section.)

The Federal Role in Education: Political Differences

Education has traditionally been a state and local responsibility. Most school policies—from length of the school year to teachers' qualifications—are set by state legislatures and local school boards. Over 90 percent of the funds spent on schools are provided through state and local tax revenues.

Federal intervention in school policy has often been resisted by states and localities, as exemplified by their response to desegregation and busing directives (see Chapter 5). State and local governments have been less hesitant when it comes to federal education grants, but it is difficult to get congressional support for grant programs targeted at those schools that are most in need. Few members of Congress are willing to support large appropriations for education that do not benefit their constituents, a situation that has reduced Washington's contribution to a goal—quality education for every American child—that nearly every official endorses, at least in principle.

Indeed, not until 1965, with passage of the Higher Education Act and the Elementary and Secondary Education Act (part of President Johnson's Great Society initiatives), did the federal government become involved in

The Supreme Court has held that American children are entitled to an "adequate" education but do not have the right to an "equal" education. America's public schools differ greatly in quality primarily as a result of differences in the wealth of the communities they serve. Some public schools are overcrowded and have few facilities and little equipment. Others are very well equipped, have spacious facilities, and have small class sizes.

public education in a comprehensive way. Earlier federal efforts in the area of education had been either one-time or targeted interventions. In 1862, for example, Congress passed the Morrill Act, which provided states with free tracts of land if they used the land to establish colleges—the nation's great "land-grant" universities are the product of that legislation. Another one-time federal program was the G.I. Bill, enacted after World War II, giving financial assistance to enable military veterans to attend college or vocational school.

With passage of the 1965 federal legislation, the federal government assumed an ongoing role in public education. Federal grants to public schools and colleges became a regular part of their funding, though still a smaller part than that provided by state and local governments (see Chapters 3 and 18). The Higher Education Act became the foundation for Pell Grants, federal loans to college students, and federally subsidized college work-study programs. The Elementary and Secondary Education Act provides funding for items such as school construction, textbooks, special education, and teacher training. Federal funding is split almost evenly between support for colleges and support for elementary and secondary schools.

In recent years, education has increasingly become an issue of national debate, involving Washington officials ever more deeply in the issue.

President Bill Clinton rejected the idea of unrestricted school choice, arguing that it would weaken the nation's public schools and make them a repository of America's poorest children. Clinton persuaded Congress instead to appropriate billions in new funding to enable overcrowded schools to hire tens of thousands of new teachers.

President George W. Bush brought a different education agenda to the White House, persuading Congress in 2001 to enact the No Child Left Behind Act. The legislation requires national testing in reading, math, and science and ties federal funding to test results. Schools that show no improvement in students' test scores after two years of funding become eligible for additional funds. If these schools show no improvement by the end of the third year, however, their students become eligible to transfer elsewhere and their federal assistance is reduced.

Few federal education policies have provoked as much controversy as the No Child Left Behind Act. The National Education Association (NEA) claims that the law has forced teachers to teach to the national tests and thus has interfered with real learning in the classroom. Congressional Democrats say that the program has failed to provide struggling schools with enough funds to improve the quality of classroom education and has encouraged the flight of students from public to private schools. For their part, congressional Republicans have applauded the law, saying that it holds teachers and schools accountable for their students' performance. Congressman John Boehner (R-Ohio) said in 2003, "Money alone is not the answer to the problems facing our children's schools. High standards and accountability for results—not just spending—are the key to erasing the achievement gap in education."[23]

Some states and localities have embraced the No Child Left Behind Act as an answer to underperforming schools. Some schools have, in fact, improved in terms of their performance on the national tests. Other states and localities have opposed the act, saying that the federal government has not provided the funds necessary to fully implement the testing program and that penalizing schools for this failure is unfair. They also say that the legislation fails to account for the testing difficulties faced by special education children. Opinion polls show that Americans are split nearly 50-50 on the new law, with Democrats generally more opposed to it and Republicans more supportive of it.[24]

Thus, many of the partisan and philosophical differences that affect federal welfare policy also affect federal education policy. Democrats are more inclined to find the answer to how to improve schools in increased federal spending on education, particularly in less affluent communities, while Republicans are more inclined to look to marketlike mechanisms such as school choice and achievement tests.

THE AMERICAN WAY OF PROMOTING THE GENERAL WELFARE

All democratic societies promote economic security, but they do so in different ways and to different degrees. Economic security is a higher priority in European democracies than in the United States. European democracies have instituted programs such as government-paid health care for all citizens, compensation for all unemployed workers, and retirement benefits for all elderly citizens. As this chapter shows, the United States provides these benefits only to some citizens in each category. On the other hand, the American system of public education dwarfs those in Europe.

The policy differences stem from historical and cultural differences. Democracy in Europe developed in reaction to centuries of aristocratic rule, which brought the issue of economic privilege to the forefront. When strong labor and socialist parties emerged as a consequence of industrialization, European democracies initiated sweeping social welfare programs designed to bring about greater economic equality. Social inequality was harder to root out because it was thoroughly embedded in European society, shaping everything from social manners to education. Private schools and university training were the preserve of the elite, a relinquished tradition that nonetheless continues to affect how Europeans think about educational opportunity.

The American historical experience is different. Democracy in America grew out of a tradition of limited government that emphasized personal liberty, including a belief in self-reliance. This belief contributes to Americans' strong support for public education and their weak support for public assistance. Unlike political equality, the idea of economic equality never captured Americans' imagination. Try as they might during America's industrial age, labor and socialist parties were unable to gain large and loyal followings. Even today, Americans are as likely to make moral judgments as political ones when they think of the plight of poor people. Political scientists Stanley Feldman and John Zaller found that Americans' support for public assistance programs rests more on their compassion for the poor than on an ideological belief in economic sharing.[25] As political scientist Robert Lane expressed it, Americans have a preference for market justice, meaning they prefer that society's material benefits be allocated through the economic marketplace rather than through government policies.[26]

SUMMARY

The United States has a complex social welfare system of multiple programs addressing specific welfare needs. Each program applies only to those individuals who qualify for benefits by meeting the specific eligibility criteria. In general, these criteria are designed to encourage self-reliance or, when help is necessary, to ensure that laziness is not rewarded or fostered. This approach to social welfare reflects Americans' traditional belief in individualism.

Poverty is a large and persistent problem in the United States. About one in eight Americans falls below the government-defined poverty line, including a disproportionate number of children, female-headed families, minority-group members, and rural and inner-city dwellers. The ranks of the poor are increased by economic recessions and are reduced through government assistance programs.

Welfare policy has been a partisan issue, with Democrats taking the lead on government programs to alleviate economic insecurity and Republicans acting to slow down or decentralize these initiatives. Changes in social welfare have usually occurred through presidential leadership in the context of majority support for the change. Welfare policy has been worked out through programs to provide jobs and job training, education programs, income measures, and especially transfer payments through individual-benefit programs.

Individual-benefit programs fall into two broad categories: social insurance and public assistance. The former includes programs such as social security for retired workers and Medicare for the elderly. Social insurance programs are funded by payroll taxes paid by potential recipients, who thus, in a sense, earn the benefits they later receive. Because of this arrangement, social insurance programs have broad public support. Public assistance programs, in contrast, are funded by general tax revenues and are targeted toward needy individuals and families. These programs are not controversial in principle; most Americans believe that government should assist the truly needy. However, because of a widespread belief that most welfare recipients could get along without assistance if they tried, these programs do not have universal public support, are only modestly funded, and are politically vulnerable.

Social welfare is a contentious issue. In one view, social welfare is too costly and assists too many people who could help themselves; another view holds that social welfare is not broad enough and that too many disadvantaged Americans live in poverty. Because of these irreconcilable differences and because of federalism and the widely shared view that welfare programs should target specific problems, the existing system of multiple programs, despite its administrative complexity and inefficiency, has been the only politically feasible solution.

The balance between economic equality and individualism tilts more heavily toward individualism in the United States than in other advanced industrialized democracies. Other democracies, for example, have government-paid health care for all citizens, whereas the United States does not. Compared to other democracies, however, the United States attempts to more equally educate its children, a policy consistent with its cultural emphasis on equality of opportunity. Like social welfare, however, education is a contentious issue involving disputes over the federal government's role, school choice, spending levels, and mandatory testing.

KEY TERMS

effective tax rate (*p. 592*)
entitlement programs (*p. 582*)
equality of opportunity (*p. 593*)
in-kind benefit (*p. 589*)
means test (*p. 586*)
negative government (*p. 580*)

positive government (*p. 580*)
poverty line (*p. 577*)
public assistance (*p. 586*)
social insurance (*p. 583*)
transfer payments (*p. 582*)

SUGGESTED READINGS

Alesina, Alberto, and Edward Glaeser. *Fighting Poverty in the U.S. and Europe: A World of Difference.* New York: Oxford University Press, 2006. A comparison of poverty policies in the United States and Europe.

Diamond, Peter A. *Social Security Reform.* New York: Oxford University Press, 2002. A comprehensive look at the issue of social security reform.

Melnick, R. Shep. *Between the Lines: Interpreting Welfare Rights.* Washington, D.C.: Brookings Institution Press, 1994. An analysis of the intricate relationship between social welfare legislation and its interpretation in the courts.

Patterson, James T. *America's Struggle Against Poverty in the Twentieth Century.* Cambridge, Mass.: Harvard University Press, 2000. A careful study of poverty and its history.

Quadagno, Jill. *One Nation, Uninsured: Why the United States Has No National Health Insurance.* New York: Oxford University Press, 2005. A look at the politics of U.S. health care policy.

Reed, Douglas S. *On Equal Terms: The Constitutional Politics of Educational Opportunity.* Princeton, N.J.: Princeton University Press, 2003. An insightful analysis of school reform issues.

Reese, William J. *America's Public Schools: From the Common School to "No Child Left Behind."* Baltimore, Maryland: Johns Hopkins University Press, 2005. A history of U.S. public schools.

Van Dunk, Emily, and Anneliese M. Dickman, *School Choice and the Question of Accountability.* New Haven, Conn.: Yale University Press, 2003. A careful look at the voucher system as applied in the Milwaukee school system.

LIST OF WEBSITES

http://www.doleta.gov/ The U.S. Department of Labor's website on the status of the welfare-to-work program, including state-by-state assessments.

http://www.nea.org/ The home page of the National Education Association; provides information on the organization's membership and policy goals.

http://www.os.dhhs.gov/ The website of the Department of Health and Human Services—the agency responsible for most federal social welfare programs.

http://www.ssw.fordschool.edu/poverty The website of the University of Michigan's Program on Poverty and Social Welfare Policy; the program seeks to stimulate interest in policy issues and to transmit research findings to policymakers.

POLITICS IN THEORY AND PRACTICE

Thinking: How has welfare and education policy been influenced by Americans' belief in individualism? By America's federal system of government?

Participating: Although conservatives and liberals disagree on the question of how far government should go in helping the poor, virtually all Americans—on the right and on the left—support private efforts to help the poor. Numerous local religious, civic, social, and economic groups have programs for the poor, such as food kitchens or clothing drives. Consider volunteering some of your time to one of these groups.

ADDITIONAL RESOURCES

For quizzes, interactive simulations, games, graphics, and other study tools, visit the book's Online Learning Center at **www.mhhe.com/pattersonwtp7.**

Welfare Reform

By Bill Clinton

One of the most significant legislative initiatives of the late twentieth century was the Welfare Reform Act of 1996, which ended the decades-long family assistance program and replaced it with Temporary Assistance to Needy Families (TANF). On the tenth anniversary of that legislation, former President Bill Clinton wrote an op-ed piece in the New York Times *on what the passage of the Welfare Reform Act says about politics and policy. He argues that bipartisanship is a critical component of successful efforts to tackle large and controversial issues such as welfare reform.*

Ten years ago today I signed the Personal Responsibility and Work Opportunity Reconciliation Act. By then I had long been committed to welfare reform. As a governor, I oversaw a workfare experiment in Arkansas in 1980 and represented the National Governors Association in working with Congress and the Reagan administration to draft the welfare reform bill enacted in 1988.

Yet when I ran for president in 1992, our system still was not working for the taxpayers or for those it was intended to help. In my first State of the Union address, I promised to "end welfare as we know it," to make welfare a second chance, not a way of life, exactly the change most welfare recipients wanted it to be.

Most Democrats and Republicans wanted to pass welfare legislation shifting the emphasis from dependence to empowerment. Because I had already given 45 states waivers to institute their own reform plans, we had a good idea of what would work. Still, there were philosophical gaps to bridge. The Republicans wanted to require able-bodied people to work, but were opposed to continuing the federal guarantees of food and medical care to their children and to spending enough on education, training, transportation and child care to enable people to go to work in lower-wage jobs without hurting their children.

On Aug. 22, 1996, after vetoing two earlier versions, I signed welfare reform into law. At the time, I was widely criticized by liberals who thought the work requirements too harsh and conservatives who thought the work incentives too generous. Three members of my administration ultimately resigned in protest. Thankfully, a majority of both Democrats and Republicans voted for the bill because they thought we shouldn't be satisfied with a system that had led to intergenerational dependency.

The last 10 years have shown that we did in fact end welfare as we knew it, creating a new beginning for millions of Americans.

In the past decade, welfare rolls have dropped substantially, from 12.2 million in 1996 to 4.5 million today. At the same time, caseloads declined by 54 percent. Sixty percent of mothers who left welfare found work, far surpassing predictions of experts. Through the Welfare to Work Partnership, which my administration started to speed the transition to employment, more than 20,000 businesses hired 1.1 million former welfare recipients. Welfare reform has proved a great success, and I am grateful to the Democrats and Republicans who had the courage to work together to take bold action.

The success of welfare reform was bolstered by other anti-poverty initiatives, including the doubling of the earned-income tax credit in 1993 for lower-income workers; the 1997 Balanced Budget Act, which included $3 billion to move long-term welfare recipients and low-income, noncustodial fathers into jobs; the Access to Jobs initiative, which helped communities create innovative transportation services to enable former welfare recipients and other low-income workers to get to their new jobs; and the welfare-to-work tax credit, which provided tax incentives to encourage businesses to hire long-term welfare recipients.

I also signed into law the toughest child-support enforcement in history, doubling collections; an increase in the minimum wage in 1997; a doubling of federal financing for child care, helping parents look after 1.5 million children in 1998; and a near doubling of financing for Head Start programs.

The results: child poverty dropped to 16.2 percent in 2000, the lowest rate since 1979, and in 2000, the percentage of Americans on welfare reached its lowest level in four decades. Overall, 100 times as many people moved out of poverty and into the middle class during our eight years as in the previous 12. Of course the booming economy helped, but the empowerment policies made a big difference.

Regarding the politics of welfare reform, there is a great lesson to be learned, particularly in today's hyper-partisan environment, where the Republican leadership forces bills through Congress without even a hint of bipartisanship. Simply put, welfare reform worked because we all worked together. The 1996 Welfare Act shows us how much we can achieve when both parties bring their best ideas to the negotiating table and focus on doing what is best for the country.

The recent welfare reform amendments, largely Republican-only initiatives, cut back on states' ability to devise their own programs. They also disallowed hours spent pursuing an education from counting against required weekly work hours. I doubt they will have the positive impact of the original legislation.

We should address the inadequacies of the latest welfare reauthorization in a bipartisan manner, by giving states the flexibility to consider higher education as a category of "work," and by doing more to help people get the education they need and the jobs they deserve. And perhaps even more than additional welfare reform, we need to raise the minimum wage, create more good jobs through a commitment to a clean energy future and enact tax and other policies to support families in work and child-rearing.

Ten years ago, neither side got exactly what it had hoped for. While we compromised to reach an agreement, we never betrayed our principles and we passed a bill that worked and stood the test of time. This style of cooperative governing is anything but a sign of weakness. It is a measure of strength, deeply rooted in our Constitution and history, and essential to the better future that all Americans deserve, Republicans and Democrats alike.

What's Your Opinion?

Do you share former President Clinton's assessment of the 1996 Welfare Reform Act—was it the success he claims it to be? Do you agree or disagree with his claim about the importance of bipartisanship? Why?

CHAPTER 17

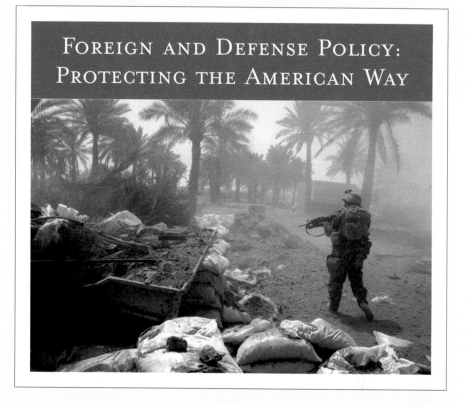

FOREIGN AND DEFENSE POLICY: PROTECTING THE AMERICAN WAY

❝We the people of the United States, in order to . . . provide for the common defense . . .❞

PREAMBLE, U.S. CONSTITUTION

As the sectarian violence continued in Iraq in 2007, U.S. policymakers worried that it was jeopardizing all that America had sacrificed during its four-year occupation of that country. Although three thousand U.S. soldiers had lost their lives and hundreds of billions of dollars had been spent, the situation in Iraq nonetheless seemed to have devolved into civil war. But if the military situation in Iraq was foremost in U.S. policymakers' minds, they also had their eye on a second issue: the economic consequences of the Iraq conflict. The cost of the war had contributed to massive budget deficits and a weakened dollar. The war also had raised tensions throughout the Middle East, leading to fears of a disruption in the flow of the region's oil that could destabilize world markets. The price of oil had already reached record heights, and a sharp reduction in Middle East oil production could send costs skyrocketing—with devastating consequences for the U.S. economy.

As America's involvement in Iraq illustrates, national security issues range from military strength to economic vitality. The primary goal of U.S. foreign policy is protection of the American state. This objective requires military readiness in order to safeguard the territorial integrity of the United States, and it rises to the fore with every immediate threat, such as the terrorist attacks of September 11, 2001. But the American state also represents a society of three hundred million people whose livelihood depends in significant part on the nation's position in the global economy. Through participation in economic policies that foster economic growth and international stability, the United States can secure the jobs and trade that contribute to the maintenance of a high standard of living.

National security, unlike other areas of government policy, rests on relations with actors outside rather than within the country. As a result, the chief instruments of national security policy differ markedly from those of domestic policy. One of these instruments is diplomacy, the process of negotiation between countries. The lead agency in U.S. diplomatic efforts is the Department of State, which is headed by the secretary of state and coordinates the efforts of U.S. embassies abroad, each of which is directed by a U.S. ambassador. American diplomacy also takes place through international organizations—such as the United Nations—to which the United States belongs. A second instrument of foreign policy is military power. The lead agency in military affairs is the Department of Defense, which is headed by the secretary of defense and oversees the three U.S. military branches—the Army, Navy, and Air Force. Here, too, the United States sometimes works through alliances, the most important of which is the North Atlantic Treaty Organization (NATO). NATO has twenty-six member nations, including the United States, Canada, and most Western and Eastern European countries. A third instrument of world politics is intelligence gathering, or the process of monitoring other countries' activities. For many reasons, but primarily because all countries pursue their own self-interest, each nation keeps a watchful eye on other nations. In the United States, the task of intelligence gathering falls to specialized federal agencies including the Central Intelligence Agency (CIA) and the National Security Agency (NSA). Because the intelligence budget is classified, the exact amount the United States spends annually in this area is unknown; it is estimated to be in the range of $40 billion to $50 billion. Economic exchange, the fourth instrument of foreign affairs, involves both international trade and foreign aid. U.S. interests in this area are promoted by a range of U.S. agencies, such as the Agriculture, Commerce, Labor, and Treasury Departments, as well as specialty agencies such as the Federal Trade Commission. The United States also pursues its economic goals through international organizations of which it is a member, including the World Trade Organization (WTO), the World Bank, and the International Monetary Fund (IMF).

The president is at the center of foreign policy activities. Although the president shares power and responsibility in the area of foreign and defense policy with Congress, the president's constitutional authority as commander-in-chief, chief diplomat, chief of state, and chief executive gives that office the lead role (see Chapter 12). For example, although President George W. Bush briefed congressional leaders on his plans for war with Iraq, they did not have full access to his intelligence reports, did not participate in the strategic planning for the war, and did not have a say in how the war plan was executed.

The national security policies of the United States include an extraordinary array of activities—so many, in fact, that they could not possibly be addressed adequately in an entire book, much less a single chapter. There are roughly two hundred countries in the world, and the United States has relations of one kind or another—military, diplomatic, economic—with all of them. This chapter narrows the subject by concentrating on a few main ideas:

★ *Since World War II, the United States has acted in the role of world leader, which has substantially affected its military, diplomatic, and economic policies.*

★ *The United States maintains a high degree of defense preparedness, which mandates a substantial level of defense spending and a worldwide deployment of U.S. conventional and strategic forces.*

★ *Changes in the international marketplace have led to increased economic interdependence among nations, which has had a marked influence on the U.S. economy and on America's security planning.*

The Roots of U.S. Foreign and Defense Policy

For nearly half a century, U.S. defense policy was defined by conflict with the Soviet Union. From the Berlin airlift in 1948 to the Vietnam escalation in 1965 to the Star Wars initiative in 1983, the United States seemed willing to pay any price to halt the spread of Soviet influence. Then, in the late 1980s, the Soviet empire dramatically began to fall apart. In December 1991, the Soviet

Historical Background

Union itself ceased to exist. For decades, there had been two superpowers, the Soviet Union and the United States. Now there is only one.

Since the fall of the Soviet Union, the United States has redefined its foreign and defense policies. The country is still at the center of world politics, but its challenges have changed. The terrorist attacks on the World Trade Center and the Pentagon in 2001 revealed to all what some analysts had been warning: the biggest threat to the physical security of the American people is not other nations but international terrorists who fight on behalf of causes. Developments in the previous decade had made another fact abundantly clear: a strong domestic base is the key to success in the increasingly important global economy.[1]

Although the age of superpower conflict is over, America's role in world affairs was shaped by that era. Accordingly, an understanding of the nation's foreign and defense policies and capabilities necessarily begins with an awareness of key developments during that period.

The United States as Global Superpower

Before World War II, the United States was an **isolationist** country, deliberately avoiding a large role in world affairs. A different America emerged from the war. It had more land, sea, and air power than any other country in the world, a huge military-industrial base, and several hundred overseas military bases. The United States had become an **internationalist** country, deeply involved in the affairs of other nations.

The shift away from isolationism was evident in Americans' attitude toward international organizations. After World War I, the United States refused to join the League of Nations, virtually guaranteeing that the League would be too weak to broker conflicts between the European powers. After World War II, the United States was the leading advocate of the United Nations, even granting it land in New York City for its headquarters. The UN Security Council—with the United States, France, Britain, the Soviet Union, and the Republic of China as its permanent members—was expected to create a new era of international cooperation.

This hope was derailed when the Soviet Union helped the communist parties in Eastern Europe capture state power, usually by coercive means. Poland, Hungary, and the other Eastern European countries were dragged into the Soviet orbit. The British wartime prime minister, Winston Churchill, said that an "iron curtain" had fallen across Europe.

U.S. security policy thereafter was designed to contain Soviet power. President Harry Truman regarded the Soviet Union as an implacable ideological foe bent on global domination that could be stopped only by the forceful use of U.S. power. Truman's view was based on assumptions

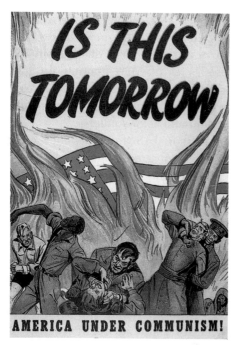

Cold war propaganda, like this poster warning of the danger of communism, contributed to a climate of opinion in the United States that led to public support of efforts to contain Soviet power.

derived from territorial concessions made to Germany's Adolf Hitler by Britain and France at a conference in Munich in 1938. Rather than appeasing Hitler, these concessions convinced him that Germany could bully its way to further gains. The idea that appeasement only encourages further aggression was the *lesson of Munich*, and it became the dominant view of U.S. policymakers in the postwar period. It contributed to the formulation of the doctrine of **containment,** which was based on the idea that the Soviet Union was an aggressor nation that had to be stopped from achieving its global ambitions.[2]

The Cold War and Vietnam

Developments in the late 1940s embroiled the United States in a **cold war** with the Soviet Union. The term refers to the fact that the two countries were not directly engaged in actual combat (a "hot war") but were locked in a deep-seated hostility that lasted forty-five years. The structure of international power was **bipolar:** the United States against the Soviet Union. Each side was supreme in its sphere and was blocked from expanding its influence by the power of the other.

The cold war included U.S. support for governments threatened by communist takeovers. In China, the United States backed the Nationalist government, which nevertheless was defeated in 1949 by the Soviet-supplied communist forces of Mao Zedong. In June 1950, when the Soviet-backed North Koreans invaded South Korea, President Truman sent troops into the conflict, which ended in stalemate and resulted in the death of thirty-five thousand U.S. soldiers.

A major turning point in U.S. foreign policy was the Vietnam War. Responding to the threat of a communist takeover, the United States became ever more deeply involved in the civil war in Vietnam. By the late 1960s, 550,000 Americans were stationed in South Vietnam. U.S. forces were technically superior in combat to the communist fighters, but they were fighting an enemy they could not easily identify in a society they did not fully understand.[3] Vietnam was a guerrilla war, with no front lines and few set battles. As the conflict dragged on, American public opinion, most visibly among the young, turned against the war, contributing to President Lyndon Johnson's decision not to run for reelection in 1968. Public opinion forced Richard Nixon, who became president in 1969, to aim not for victory but for a gradual disengagement. U.S. combat troops left Vietnam in 1973, and two years later North Vietnamese forces concluded their takeover of the country. Vietnam was the most painful and costly application of the containment doctrine: fifty-eight thousand American soldiers lost their lives in the fighting.

Disintegration of the "Evil Empire"

America's defeat in Vietnam forced U.S. policymakers to reconsider the country's international role. The *lesson of Vietnam* was that there were limits to the country's ability to assert its will in the world. Nixon claimed that the United States could no longer act as the "Lone Ranger" for the free world, and he sought to reduce tensions with communist countries. In 1972, Nixon took a historic journey to the People's Republic of China, the first official contact with that country since the communists seized power in 1949. Nixon also initiated the Strategic Arms Limitation Talks (SALT), which presumed that the United States and the Soviet Union each had an interest in retaining enough nuclear weapons to deter the other from an attack but that neither side had an interest in an arms race that could lead to their mutual destruction. This spirit of cooperation did not last. The Soviet invasion of Afghanistan in 1979 convinced U.S. leaders that the USSR was still bent on expansion and threatened Western interests in the oil-rich Middle East. Ronald Reagan, elected president in 1980, called for a renewed hard line toward the Soviet Union, which he described as the "evil empire."

Although U.S. policymakers did not fully realize it at the time, the Soviet Union was collapsing under its heavy defense expenditures, its isolation from Western technology and markets, and its inefficient centralized economy. In 1985, Mikhail Gorbachev became the Soviet leader and sought to restructure Soviet society, an initiative known as *perestroika*. He also ordered a Soviet withdrawal from Afghanistan (which had become his country's Vietnam).

Gorbachev's efforts came too late to save the Soviet Union. In 1989, the withdrawal of Soviet troops from Eastern Europe accelerated a pro-democracy movement that was already under way in the region. Poland initiated major reforms. Hungary dismantled the "iron curtain" that had blocked free travel to Austria. Then, in November, the Berlin Wall between East and West Germany—the most visible symbol of the separation of East and West—came down. The Soviet Union itself was also disintegrating. On December 8, 1991, the leaders of the Russian, Belarus, and Ukrainian republics declared that the Soviet Union no longer existed. The bipolar power structure that had dominated world politics since the end of World War II had collapsed. The new structure was **unipolar**—the United States was now the unchallenged world power.

A New World Order

The end of the cold war prompted the first President Bush in 1990 to call for a "new world order." His formulation abandoned the assumption that world affairs are a zero-sum game, in which for one nation to gain something, another nation has to lose. Bush championed **multilateralism**—the idea that major nations should act together in response to problems and crises. Included in Bush's plan was an enhanced status for the United Nations, which would assume a pivotal international role.

Multilateralism defined America's response to the Iraqi invasion of Kuwait in August 1990. President Bush obtained a UN resolution that imposed economic sanctions on Iraq and demanded its withdrawal from Kuwait. When Iraqi president Saddam Hussein did not comply, the UN authorized a military buildup in the Gulf. A half million troops, mostly American but including contingents from nearly two dozen other nations, were moved into positions facing the Iraqi army. When Iraq still refused to withdraw, the UN force attacked, first with an aerial bombardment and then with ground troops. The ground assault was spearheaded by U.S. Army and Marine units, flanked by French and British armored divisions. Four days into the ground fighting, Iraqi units fled the battlefield, ending the war.

The Gulf operation was a military triumph, prompting President Bush to declare that the United States had "kicked the Vietnam syndrome [the

In the jungle warfare of Vietnam, American soldiers had difficulty finding the enemy and adapting to guerrilla tactics.

legacy of America's defeat in Vietnam] once and for all." The Gulf War, however, was in another way less successful. Believing that an overthrow of Hussein's regime would destabilize Iraq, President Bush ordered a halt to the hostilities after Iraqi forces retreated. Hussein remained in power but was ordered by a UN resolution to dismantle his weapons programs, subject to UN inspections. However, Hussein constantly interfered with UN inspectors' attempts to verify the status of his weapons programs, raising concerns about his plans.

President Bush's multilateral approach to foreign affairs carried over into the Clinton administration. Confronting Serb atrocities in Bosnia— where tens of thousands of Muslims and Croats were murdered, raped, and driven from their homes—President Clinton pursued UN economic sanctions as a means of halting the slaughter. When sanctions failed, the United States and its NATO allies attacked Serb forces with air power. The result was a U.S.-negotiated peace agreement (the Dayton Accords) that included the deployment to Bosnia of nearly sixty thousand peace-keeping troops, including twenty thousand Americans. War in the Balkans flared again in 1999 when the Serbs undertook a campaign of "ethnic cleansing" in the Serbian province of Kosovo, whose population was 90 percent Albanian. When attempts at a negotiated settlement failed, NATO planes, including U.S. aircraft, attacked Serbia. After weeks of intensive bombing, Yugoslav president Slobodan Milosevic (who died in

2006 while on trial for war crimes) pulled his troops out of Kosovo. Ethnic Albanians moved back in and, despite the presence of UN peacekeeping troops, commenced revenge attacks on some of the Serbs who remained.

As these examples indicate, multilateralism has been only partly successful as a strategy for resolving international conflicts. With the deployment of enough resources, the world's major powers can intervene with some success in many parts of the developing world. However, these interventions offer no guarantee of long-term success. Regional and internal conflicts typically stem from enduring ethnic, religious, factional, or national hatreds or from chronic problems such as famine, over-crowding, or government corruption. Even if these hatreds or problems can be momentarily eased, they are often too deep-seated to be permanently resolved.

The War on Terrorism

When he assumed the presidency in 2001, George W. Bush made it clear that he would not follow the national security policy of his father. Bush declared that he had no plans to engage in "nation building" and that he would reduce America's military presence abroad as well as its reliance on the United Nations. He also announced that the United States would not participate in either the Kyoto Accord (a global climate treaty) or the International Criminal Court (the ICC, a permanent tribunal with jurisdiction over war crimes).

The terrorist attacks of September 11, 2001, on the World Trade Center and the Pentagon forced Bush to reverse course. Although he did not change his position on the ICC or the Kyoto Accord, he called upon the other nations of the world to join the United States in a global "war on terrorism." Unlike past wars, it targets not nations but groups engaged in terrorism that is aimed at U.S. interests at home and abroad. A war without sharply defined battlefronts, it is being waged through a wide variety of instruments, including military force, intelligence gathering, law enforcement, foreign aid, international cooperation, and immigration control. The tactics are also unusual. The rooting out of terrorist cells in the United States and Europe, for example, is entrusted to law enforcement agencies rather than to military units.

The war on terrorism resulted in the first major reorganization of the U.S. national security bureaucracy since the Department of Defense was formed after World War II to combine the previously separate War and Navy Departments. The new agency this time was the Department of Homeland Security (DHS), which was created in 2002 to coordinate domestic efforts to protect the United States against terrorist threats. The responsibilities of the homeland security agency include securing the nation's borders, enhancing defense against biological attacks, preparing emergency personnel (police, firefighters, and rescue workers) for their roles in responding to terrorist attacks, and coordinating efforts to stop domestic terrorism.[4]

The first U.S. military action in the war on terrorism was an attack on Afghanistan. Its Taliban-led government had provided training sites and protection to the Al Qaeda terrorist network, which had carried out the September 11 attacks. Backed by a UN resolution authorizing the use of force and supported by other NATO member countries, the United States toppled the Taliban government in early 2002; however, Al Qaeda leader Osama bin Laden and most of his top lieutenants evaded capture.

In 2002, President Bush labeled Iraq, Iran, and North Korea an "axis of evil," thereby signaling a widening of the war on terrorism. Shortly thereafter, he announced a new national security doctrine: the **preemptive war doctrine.** Speaking at West Point, President Bush said that the threat of international terrorism meant that the United States could not afford to wait until it was attacked by hostile nations. Bush declared that America was prepared to take "preemptive action."[5] This concept was not entirely new—U.S. officials had long maintained a right to strike first if faced with a serious and immediate threat. What was new

Secretary of State Condoleezza Rice speaks at a White House gathering. In her roles as secretary of state and, before that, national security advisor, Rice was one of the architects of the Bush administration's foreign and defense policies.

about the Bush doctrine was that it extended the option to include military action against remotely threatening countries.

The Iraq War

In the summer of 2002, Bush targeted the regime of Iraq's Saddam Hussein, claiming that it had weapons of mass destruction (WMDs)—chemical and biological weapons, and possibly even nuclear weapons. Bush asked Congress for a resolution authorizing the use of military force against Iraq if it did not fully disarm. In October, Congress passed the resolution.

Facing the possibility of a Middle Eastern war, America's European allies urged the disarmament of Iraq through UN weapons inspectors. In late 2002, the United Nations passed a resolution that required Iraq to accept weapons inspections. A two-track policy ensued. UN weapons inspectors entered Iraq in search of WMDs, while at the same time the United States deployed combat units to the Middle East.

Over the strenuous objections of the French, German, and Russian governments and despite a failure to get UN authorization for military action, President Bush in March 2003 ordered U.S. forces to attack Iraq. Although British units were also involved, the assault was essentially an act of **unilateralism**—the situation in which one nation takes action against another state or states. The Iraqi regime quickly collapsed—Hussein was deposed after less than a month of fighting. However, the post-combat phase proved deadlier than the Bush administration had anticipated. Roadside mines and suicide bombers took a heavy toll on U.S. soldiers, and the cost of rebuilding Iraq soon rose above $100 billion. Moreover, the WMDs that Bush had stated were the reason for the war could not be found. In early 2004, the chief U.S. weapons inspector, David Kay, testified before Congress that U.S. intelligence agencies had grossly exaggerated the extent of Iraq's weapons program.

The American public, which had strongly backed the invasion of Iraq, came to question the war. Americans also expressed doubts about Bush's preemptive war doctrine. One poll found that only 34 percent agreed that the "United States has the right and even the responsibility to overthrow dictatorships and help their people build a democracy."[6] Opinion elsewhere was more negative. For the first time since World War II, Western Europeans held that the United States should not be entrusted with world leadership. A year before the war, roughly 65 percent of Western Europeans had expressed a favorable opinion of the United States; fewer than half held that view after the U.S. invasion of Iraq (see Figure 17–1).

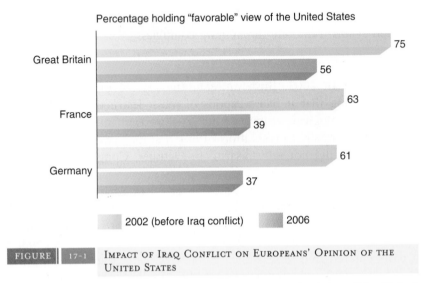

Percentage holding "favorable" view of the United States

Great Britain — 75 / 56

France — 63 / 39

Germany — 61 / 37

2002 (before Iraq conflict)   2006

FIGURE   17-1   IMPACT OF IRAQ CONFLICT ON EUROPEANS' OPINION OF THE UNITED STATES

The Iraq conflict has led to a sharp decline in Europeans' opinion of the United States. *Source: Pew Research Center for the People and the Press surveys.*

Public opinion in Europe hampered the postwar reconstruction of Iraq. America's request for assistance in rebuilding Iraq was not ignored by European governments, but they hardly jumped at the opportunity. Although some assistance was offered, it was limited by public opposition to what was seen as "America's war." Negative public opinion also led the Dutch and Spanish governments, which had backed the invasion, to withdraw their small troop units from Iraq.

Postwar reconstruction was also hampered by instability in Iraq. Age-old animosities between Sunni, Shiite, and Kurdish groups within Iraq blocked political compromise and fueled violence. As the sectarian killings escalated, the animosities deepened. Foreign-born fighters compounded the problem. Iraq's lengthy border with Iran and Syria—countries antagonistic to the United States—allowed Islamic militants from other countries to join the fighting in Iraq.

During White House deliberations before the war, Secretary of State Colin Powell had invoked what he called "the Pottery Barn rule." Powell warned that officials who believed Iraqis would welcome U.S. troops with open arms were engaging in wishful thinking. Foreseeing a difficult post-invasion phase, Powell said, "If you break it, you own it." Indeed, the United States has been forced to go it nearly alone in the reconstruction of Iraq at considerable cost in terms of American lives and dollars. An indicator of the price of unilateralism in Iraq is the fact that 90 percent of the casualties and monetary costs of the invading forces have been borne by the United States.

By 2007, it was apparent that the avowed goals of the Iraq invasion—the reduction of the terrorist threat, a democratic state in the Middle East, and regional stability—were in jeopardy, if not already lost. In response to growing criticism, President Bush replaced his secretary of defense, Donald Rumsfeld, with the less controversial Robert Gates. However, Bush then initiated a troop "surge" in Iraq, deploying an additional 21,000 U.S. soldiers in early 2007 in an effort to quell the rising violence. Public opinion was strongly opposed to the surge, as were nearly all congressional Democrats and some House and Senate Republicans. Only a few members of Congress, however, advocated an immediate withdrawal of U.S. forces from Iraq. The majority in Congress believed that the presence of U.S. troops in Iraq was fueling the insurgency, yet also believed that a hasty withdrawal would make matters worse. There was no clear-cut second-stage strategy for victory.

The difficulty of the reconstruction phase in Iraq has limited America's ability to respond to other fronts in the war on terrorism. Since the U.S. invasion, North Korea has acquired nuclear weapons, Iran is developing the technology that could lead to the acquisition of such weapons, and Taliban forces in Afghanistan have regrouped and are expanding the fighting in that country. Thus, as was true of multilateralism, unilateralism has been shown to have its limits. Even with the world's most powerful military, the United States has found it difficult to go it alone in Iraq. Wars like those in Iraq and Vietnam do not lend themselves to quick and tidy battlefield solutions. It is one thing to defeat a conventional army in open warfare and quite another to prevail in a conflict in which the fight is not for territory but for people's hearts and minds, especially when the people are not of one heart and one mind but instead are at each other's throats.

THE MILITARY DIMENSION OF NATIONAL SECURITY POLICY

The launching of the war on terrorism brought about the first major increase—tens of billions of dollars—in U.S. defense spending since the 1980s. The United States spends far more on defense, in both relative and absolute terms, than its allies do. On a per capita basis, U.S. military spending is more than twice that of other nations in the NATO alliance (see "How the United States Compares"). The U.S. defense budget is second to none in the world, but so is the military power it buys.

HOW THE UNITED STATES COMPARES

The Burden of Military Spending

The United States bears a disproportionate share of the defense costs of the NATO alliance. The U.S. military establishment is huge and is deployed all over the world, and taxpayers spend more than $400 billion per year to maintain it. These expenditures directly account for roughly 5 percent of the U.S. gross national product (GNP). By comparison, defense spending by Germany, Italy, and Canada accounts for 3 percent or less of their GNPs. The percentages for Great Britain and France are higher but not as high as for the United States. Japan, which is not part of NATO, spends only 1 percent of its GNP on defense. Japan's small military force is confined by World War II peace agreements to the country's islands and the adjoining waters.

The United States has pressured its allies to carry a larger share of the defense burden, but these countries have resisted, contending that the cost would be too high and that their security would not be substantially improved. A partial exception to this situation was the Persian Gulf War of the early 1990s. U.S. troops and equipment accounted for the bulk of the military strength arrayed against Iraq, but the financial cost of the war effort was borne by other countries. Germany, Japan, Saudi Arabia, and Kuwait were among those that helped fund the war. In fact, other countries gave the United States $20 billion more than it spent on the war.

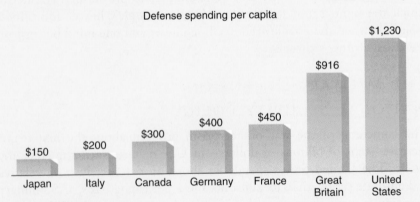

Source: OECD (Organization for Economic Cooperation and Development) and U.S. and British government statistics.

The war on terrorism has forced an increase in U.S. military spending that, except for Great Britain, has not been matched by increased spending by America's allies. However, some U.S. officials prefer the imbalance because it gives the United States more freedom to act on its own when it prefers to do so.

The United States accounts for nearly half of the total defense spending worldwide.

Military Power, Uses, and Capabilities

U.S. military forces are trained or called on for different types of military action, ranging from nuclear conflict to guerrilla warfare.

Nuclear War Capability Although the possibility of all-out nuclear war with Russia declined dramatically with the end of the cold war, the United States retains a nuclear arsenal designed to prevent such a war from ever happening. **Deterrence policy** is based on the notion that any nation would be deterred from launching a full-scale nuclear attack on the United States by the knowledge that, even if it obliterated the country, it would be destroyed as well. America's nuclear weapons are deployed in what is called the "nuclear triad." This term refers to the three ways nuclear weapons can be launched: by land-based missiles, by submarine-based missiles, and by bombers. The triad provides a second-strike capability, that is, the ability to absorb a first-strike nuclear attack and survive with enough nuclear punch for a massive retaliation (second strike). Since the end of the cold war, the United States and Russia have negotiated reductions in their nuclear arsenals and have created monitoring systems designed to reduce the possibility that either side, by mistake or by design, could launch a surprise attack with its remaining warheads.

A greater fear today than nuclear war with Russia is the possibility that a terrorist group or rogue nation could smuggle a nuclear device into the United States and detonate it. The technology and materials necessary to build a nuclear weapon (or to buy one clandestinely) are more readily available than ever before. Accordingly, the United States, Russia, and other nations are cooperating to halt the spread of nuclear weapons. This effort has had some success, but North Korea has recently acquired nuclear weapons and Iran could be moving in the same direction. Both nations have hostile relations with the United States.

★ ‖ STATES IN THE NATION

The All-Volunteer Military's Recruits

Until 1973, the United States had an active military draft. Upon reaching the age of eighteen, males were required to register for the draft. Local draft boards would then pick the draftees based on quotas that varied with the size of the local population. Accordingly, each state contributed equally to the military's manpower needs relative to its population size. Today's military is an all-volunteer force, and the states' contributions vary significantly. The map below indicates the degree to which each state is over- and underrepresented in the military as indicated by the ratio of military recruits from a state to the number of males ages eighteen to thirty-four in that state's population.

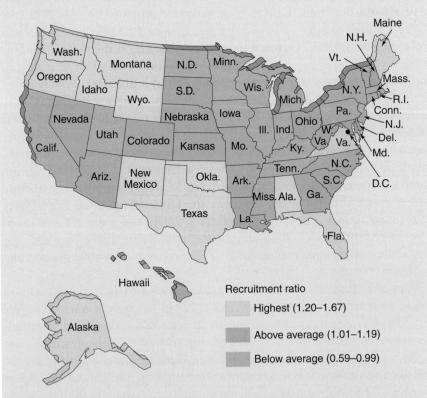

Recruitment ratio

Highest (1.20–1.67)

Above average (1.01–1.19)

Below average (0.59–0.99)

Source: Adapted from Tim Kane, "Who Bears the Burden? Demographic Characteristics of U.S. Military Recruits Before and After 9/11," Heritage Foundation, Center for Data Analysis Report #05-08, November 7, 2005.

Montana has the largest number of recruits relative to its population, followed in order by Alaska, Wyoming, and Maine. Utah, Rhode Island, and Massachusetts rank lowest, in that order.

Q: What might explain why military recruits come disproportionately from states like Montana, Alaska, Wyoming, and Maine as well as from the southern states?

A: According to Department of Defense data, recruits are more likely to come from rural areas, particularly areas where few well-paying jobs are available to young adults. The four states with the highest recruitment ratios have these characteristics. As for the South, higher recruitment levels there have been explained in terms of its stronger military tradition and its numerous military installations. Individuals from areas near these installations, as well as the sons and daughters of military personnel, are more likely to enlist in the military.

Conventional and Guerrilla War Capability   Nuclear preparedness is just one part of America's combat readiness. A second is conventional-force preparedness. Not since World War II has the United States fought an all-out conventional war, nor does it at present have the capacity to fight one. That type of war would require a reinstatement of the military draft and a full-scale mobilization of the nation's industrial capacity. Instead, the United States today has an all-volunteer military force with the training and armament needed to overwhelm any foe that would engage it in pitched battle (see "States in the Nation"). The U.S. Navy has a dozen aircraft carriers, scores of attack submarines, and hundreds of fighting and supply ships. The U.S. Air Force has thousands of high-performance aircraft, ranging from fighter jets to jumbo supply planes. The U.S. Army has roughly five hundred thousand regular troops and more than three hundred thousand Reserve and National Guard soldiers who are supplied with state-of-the-art tanks, artillery pieces, armored personnel carriers, and attack helicopters.

What makes these planes, tanks, and other weapons doubly lethal are the high-tech systems that support them. Surveillance devices (such as satellites), high-speed computers, and sophisticated software give U.S. military commanders an unrivaled ability to gather, process, and disseminate tactical information. No other nation has anywhere near the advanced weapons systems that the United States possesses. The full combat phases of the Afghanistan and Iraq wars demonstrated that modern warfare rests both on sheer firepower and on the capacity to direct it for maximum effect. In Iraq, U.S. forces were outnumbered by three to one yet took only three weeks to seize control of Baghdad, at which point the remaining Iraqi army units quit the field.

American forces had no particular advantage, however, in waging the type of armed conflict that followed—guerrilla action based on roadside explosive devices and suicide bombings. Such tactics are difficult to defend against and virtually impossible to stop by conventional military means. To defeat such an enemy requires the full support and cooperation of the local population. Without them, as was the case in Vietnam, the enemy has the capacity to sustain operations over a long period in an attempt to force a withdrawal of U.S. forces. As in Vietnam, U.S. military forces in Iraq have adapted their tactics to the demands of an unconventional war. Though unprepared for such combat when they went into Iraq, they have since learned how to wage it more effectively. However, such conflicts are not settled by the standards of conventional war. There is no visible enemy army to destroy or territory to be conquered. In some cases—some analysts believe Iraq is one of them—the mere presence of foreign troops in a country is a reason why some in the local populace take up arms against them.

Such situations require a political solution, not a military one, and political solutions are never as decisive as battlefield encounters. They require compromise and concessions from both sides. An occupying power, such as the United States, often is at a disadvantage in these negotiations because its interests include the withdrawal of its forces. If the occupier is dealing with a determined enemy that has the will and the capacity to continue the fight indefinitely, as was the case in Vietnam and might be the situation in Iraq, at some point it can be forced to accept an arrangement that is far less satisfying than the outcome that was anticipated upon entering into war.

The Politics of National Defense

Policy elites, public opinion, and special interests all play significant roles in national defense policy. The U.S. public typically supports the judgments of its political leaders on the use of military force. In virtually every conflict of the past half-century in which U.S. troops have been sent into battle, Americans have endorsed the action. When U.S. forces invaded Iraq in 2003 upon order of President George W. Bush, roughly 75 percent of Americans said they supported his decision. Such support invariably remains strong if the conflict is brief and not too costly. Public support might even hold up for years, as was the case during the first six

The publication of photos showing the abuse of Iraqi prisoners by U.S. soldiers weakened Americans' support for the Iraq war and fueled resentment of U.S. policy in the Arab world.

years of the Vietnam War. However, if a conflict seems endless and if the human and financial toll keeps rising, public support eventually declines. A swing in public opinion against the Vietnam War forced U.S. policy-makers to withdraw American troops in 1973. Public opinion on the Iraq War soured more quickly, partly because of indications that the stated justification for the war—to rid Iraq of its weapons of mass destruction—was not the full reason for the military action. As public opinion turned negative, the Bush administration's options narrowed. In 2004, for example, President Bush, who had planned to keep a U.S. administrator in charge of Iraq, concluded that he had no choice but to accelerate the timetable for turning the government over to Iraqis.

Even though public opinion places boundaries on what political leaders can do militarily, leaders have considerable latitude within these boundaries.[7] Policy debates and planning in the area of national security typically take place among political and policy elites. Most citizens are not informed enough about national security issues to contribute to the debate, particularly at the formative stage when critical first decisions are made. Moreover, early debates on critical issues—for example, whether to take the nation to war in the absence of a clear-cut and direct threat to the United States—take place behind closed doors in the Pentagon and the White House. The American people ordinarily trust their leaders to make the right decisions in such cases and will back them unless the decisions turn out badly.

The U.S. public assumes that great decisions about war and military might are driven by considerations of national security—doing what is necessary to protect and preserve the American nation and its interests. This view is not unwarranted, but it also is not the full picture. National defense is big business, involving the annual expenditure of hundreds of

★ | LEADERS

Dwight D. Eisenhower
(1890–1969)

One of four army generals to be elected to the presidency, Dwight D. Eisenhower left his mark on war and peace. Born in Abilene, Texas, Eisenhower was an accomplished athlete and student, and in his senior year of high school he received an appointment to West Point. During World War II, he commanded the Allied Forces that landed in North Africa and drove the German army back to the European mainland. He was Supreme Commander of the multinational force that on June 6, 1944 (D-Day), landed at Normandy, initiating the drive across Europe that eventually would force Germany to surrender. He declined an opportunity to run for the presidency in 1948 but accepted a Republican draft to run in 1952. Given his stature as the most popular figure in America, Eisenhower won easily.

Though trained in the art of war, Eisenhower sought throughout his presidency to reduce cold war tensions. He signed the truce that led to the end of the Korean conflict. Although he was unsuccessful in negotiating a thaw in the nuclear arms race with Soviet leaders, he convinced them that the United States was not seeking their country's destruction. In 1956, after Egypt nationalized the Suez Canal, a plan by the governments of Britain, France, and Israel to take it back by force was aborted when Eisenhower refused to support it, saying that Egypt had a right to self-determination and that the United Nations, not the force of arms, was the proper avenue for settling the dispute. As he was leaving the presidency, he used his farewell address to warn of the dangers of the military-industrial complex, arguing that sustained high levels of military expenditure and secrecy would only weaken America in the long run.

billions of dollars, and self-interested parties have a stake in maintaining permanently high levels of military spending and readiness.[8] In his 1961 farewell address, President Dwight D. Eisenhower, who had commanded U.S. forces in Europe during World War II, warned Americans against "the unwarranted influence" and "misplaced power" of what he termed "the military-industrial complex." The **military-industrial complex** has three components: the military establishment, the arms industry, and the members of Congress from states and districts that depend heavily on the arms industry. None of the three is predisposed to war, but neither are they, if the issue of war arises, adverse to it. If a president signals the likelihood of war, all three can be expected to endorse it. And all three benefit from a high level of defense spending, regardless of whether the expenditures are necessary. Without doubt, as Eisenhower knew, some proportion of U.S. defense strategy and spending reflects the power of the military-industrial complex rather than what is required to keep America safe. The problem is that no one knows exactly what that proportion is.

THE ECONOMIC DIMENSION OF NATIONAL SECURITY POLICY

Economic considerations are a vital component of national security policy. In the simplest sense, economic strength is a prerequisite of military strength—a powerful defense establishment can be maintained only by a country that is economically well off. In a broader and more important sense, economic prosperity enables a people to "secure" their way of life. As President Eisenhower said, it is folly to weaken at home what one is trying to strengthen abroad.

A Changing World Economy

Some aspects of the U.S. superpower policy have economic benefits. The clearest example is the European Recovery Plan, better known as the Marshall Plan. Proposed in 1947 and named after one of its chief architects, the widely respected General George Marshall, it is perhaps the boldest and most successful U.S. foreign policy initiative of the twentieth century. It called for $3 billion in immediate aid for the postwar rebuilding of Europe, with an additional $10 billion or so to follow. The

 Marshall Plan was unprecedented both in its scope (today, the equivalent cost would exceed $100 billion) and in its implica-

Historical   tions—for the first time, the United States had committed
Background   itself to an ongoing role in European affairs.

Apart from enabling the countries of Western Europe to better confront the perceived Soviet threat, the Marshall Plan was also designed to meet the economic needs of the United States. Wartime production had lifted the country out of the Great Depression, but the end of the war in 1945 brought a recession and renewed fears of hard times. A rejuvenated Western Europe furnished a market for U.S. goods. In effect, Western Europe became a junior partner within a system of global trade that worked to the advantage of the United States. Since then, major changes have taken place in the world economy. Germany has become an economic rival of the United States, and trade with Germany now results in a deficit for the United States. In addition, Western Europe, including Germany, has become a less receptive market for U.S. goods. European countries are now each other's best customers, trading among themselves through the European Union (EU).

In economic terms, the world today is tripolar—power is concentrated in three centers. One center is the United States, which produces roughly 20 percent of the world's goods and services. Another center is Japan and China, which account for more than 15 percent of the world's economy. The third and largest center, responsible for more than 25 percent of the world's economy, is the twenty-five-country EU. The EU is dominated by Germany, Britain, and France, which together account for more than half its economy.

By a few indicators, the United States is the weakest of the three economic centers. For example, it has the worst trade imbalance. Although the United States exports roughly $1 trillion annually in goods and services, the country imports an even larger amount. The result is a huge trade deficit that is easily the world's largest. The United States has not had a trade surplus since 1975 and in recent years has run deficits exceeding $500 billion (see Figure 17–2).

In other ways, however, the United States is the strongest of the three economic centers. For one thing, the American economy is the best balanced. Like the other economic powers, the United States has a strong industrial base, but it has a stronger agricultural sector and more abundant natural resources. Its vast fertile plains have made it the world's leading agricultural producer. The United States ranks among the top three countries worldwide in production of wheat, corn, potatoes, peanuts, cotton, eggs, cattle, and pigs. As for natural resources, the United States ranks among the top five nations in deposits of copper, uranium, lead, sulfur, zinc, coal, gold, iron ore, natural gas, silver, and magnesium.[9]

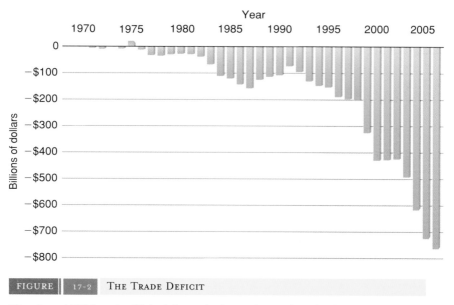

FIGURE 17-2 THE TRADE DEFICIT

Not since 1975 has the United States had a trade surplus; the deficit is now at a record level. *Source: U.S. Bureau of the Census. Trade Data Services, 2006.*

According to the Switzerland-based World Economic Forum, the United States also is more economically competitive than are its major trading rivals (see Chapter 15). The United States owes this position to factors such as the strength of its domestic economy and its technological know-how.[10] This competitive advantage has been evident since the early 1990s. As Japan and parts of Europe have at times struggled with slow growth rates, the United States has enjoyed economic growth without the accelerated inflation that normally accompanies such a period. The slowdown in the U.S. economy that began in 2000 tempered the belief that technological know-how had unleashed unstoppable growth. Nevertheless, other countries have looked to the United States, particularly its technology sector, for policy and market innovations that might spark their own economic expansion.

America's Global Economic Goals

The United States depends on other countries for raw materials, finished goods, and capital to meet Americans' production and consumption demands. Meeting this objective requires the United States to exert influence on world markets. The broad goals of the United States in the world economy include the following:[11]

- Maintaining access to energy and other natural resources vital to the strength of the U.S. economy
- Sustaining a stable and open system of trade that will promote prosperity at home
- Keeping the widening gap between the rich and poor countries from destabilizing the world economy

Access to Natural Resources   Although the United States is rich in natural resources, it is not self-sufficient. Oil is the main problem; domestic production provides only about half the nation's needs. Oil has been called "black gold," and even that description understates its significance. Oil is the engine of American society, powering the economy and providing fuel for automobiles and heat for homes and offices. For decades, the United States has used its economic and military power to protect its access to oil.

Outside the United States, most of the world's oil is found in the Middle East, Latin America, Africa, and Russia. Access to oil occurs through the world market for it. After World War II, the United States acquired a foothold in that market when its leading oil companies, with their technical expertise and huge amounts of capital, acquired a stake in Middle Eastern oil fields. Since then, U.S. firms have been leaders in worldwide oil exploration and production. Underpinning their activities is the military might of the United States. For example, the U.S. Navy patrols the world's shipping routes to ensure that oil tankers reach their destinations safely. The United States has also used its power to try to prevent oil-rich countries from being taken over by hostile interests. In 1951, for example, the Iranian government voted to nationalize its oil fields, threatening Western influence over that country's production and distribution. Two years later, the CIA helped orchestrate a coup that placed the pro-Western Shah of Iran, Mohammad Reza Pahlavi, in charge. The 1991 Gulf War was driven largely by a concern with oil. Iraq's invasion of Kuwait threatened access not only to Kuwait's oil fields but also to those of its neighbors, which persuaded Saudi Arabia and other Arab countries to back the use of force to drive Iraq from Kuwait. Some observers believe that oil was also a factor in President George W. Bush's decision to invade Iraq in 2003. Iraq's proven oil reserves of more than 100 billion barrels are second only to those of Saudi Arabia.

The issue of oil will grow in significance in coming years. Oil production may be nearing peak capacity. New oil fields are still being developed, but the world's major oil reserves are being depleted. Meanwhile, the demand for oil is rising as a result of the rapid economic growth of China, India, and other emerging industrialized countries. Oil topped seventy-five dollars a barrel for the first time in 2006. If a major disruption in the world's oil supply were to occur, oil prices would skyrocket, possibly causing a global recession and perhaps even triggering a regional war.

Promoting Global Trade   The American economy today depends more heavily on international commerce than at any time in the past. The domestic manufacturing sector that once was the source, directly or indirectly, of most U.S. jobs has shrunk, and many of the goods Americans buy, from their television sets to their automobiles, are produced by foreign firms. Indeed, nearly all large U.S. firms are themselves **multinational corporations,** with operations in more than one country. From a headquarters in New York City, a firm has no difficulty directing a production facility in Thailand that is filling orders for markets in Europe and South America. Money, goods, and services today flow freely and quickly across national borders, and large firms increasingly think about markets in global rather than national terms.

Economic globalization is a term that describes the increased interdependence of nations' economies. This development is both an opportunity and a threat to U.S. economic interests. The opportunity rests with the possibility of increased demand abroad for U.S. products and lower prices to U.S. consumers as a result of inexpensive imports. The threat lies in the fact that foreign firms also compete in the global marketplace and may use their competitive advantages, such as cheaper labor, to outposition U.S. firms.[12]

In general, international commerce works best when countries trade freely with one another. This situation keeps the prices of traded items, whether finished goods or raw materials, at their lowest level, resulting in economic efficiency (see Chapter 15). However, global trade is a political issue as well as an economic one, and different countries and interests have different views on how trade among nations should be conducted. The **free-trade position** holds that the long-term economic interests of all countries are advanced when tariffs and other trade barriers are kept to a minimum. Most free-trade advocates couple their advocacy with fair-trade demands, but they are committed philosophically and in practice to the idea that free trade fuels economic growth, results in a net gain for business, and provides consumers with lower-priced goods.

Recent U.S. presidents have been free-trade advocates. Large U.S. firms generally seek access to markets around the globe, and a president would have difficulty insisting that other countries open their markets to U.S. firms while simultaneously denying foreign firms open access to U.S. markets. Moreover, free trade can stimulate economic growth, which is always a presidential concern. The American people, when judging a president, base their judgment on whether the U.S. economy as a whole is doing well or poorly rather than on the basis of particular economic policies.

From a congressional perspective, free trade often is more appealing in theory than in practice. Although most members of Congress say they support free trade and some are unabashed advocates of it, many of them act differently when their state or district is threatened by foreign competition. Then they often try to protect their constituents' interests through measures such as favorable treatment of U.S. goods or tariffs on the goods produced by foreign firms.

Protectionism, as opposed to the free-trade position, emphasizes the immediate interests of domestic producers and includes measures designed to enable them to compete successfully with foreign competitors in the domestic market. For some protectionists, the issue is simply a matter of defending domestic firms against the actions of their foreign competitors. For others, the issue is one of fair trade; they are protectionists in those instances where foreign firms have an unfair competitive advantage, as, for example, when government subsidies allow them to market their goods at an artificially low price.

During the past two decades, the free-trade position usually has prevailed in U.S. policy disputes. In 1993, for example, Congress ratified the North American Free Trade Agreement (NAFTA), which creates a mostly free market among the United States, Canada, and Mexico. Although NAFTA was opposed by most congressional Democrats and by environmental and labor groups that objected to its weak protection of their interests, proponents prevailed due to the backing of President Bill Clinton and most congressional Republicans. The final votes needed for passage were gained by promises of trade protection for Florida citrus and vegetable growers. Another example of support for free trade is U.S. membership in the World Trade Organization (WTO). The WTO, created in 1995, is the formal institution through which most nations negotiate general rules of international trade. The WTO's mission is to promote a global free market through reductions in tariffs, protections for intellectual property (copyrights and patents), and similar policies. WTO members (roughly one hundred fifty in number) are committed to an open trade policy buttressed by regulations designed to ensure fair play among participating nations. Trade disputes among WTO members are settled by arbitration panels, which consist of representatives from the member nations. In 2003, for example, the WTO held that U.S. tariffs on imported steel, which were intended to protect U.S. steel makers, were illegal under WTO trade rules and had to be rescinded.

More recently, protectionist sentiment has gained strength in the United States. The WTO, for example, has been criticized for placing trade ahead of environmental protection and human rights. Some countries have gained a trade advantage through production processes that degrade the environment and exploit workers, including child laborers. Loss of jobs has also been an issue. Employment in U.S. textile factories, for example, has fallen sharply in the face of foreign competition. Even some high-tech jobs have been shipped abroad. Telephone-based technical services, for example, often can be provided at lower cost by hiring educated English-speaking technicians in India instead of their American counterparts.

The jobs issue did not receive much attention during the late 1990s, when the overall U.S. economy was growing at a rapid pace. However, in the economic downturn that began in 2000, nearly three million U.S. manufacturing jobs were lost, thrusting the issue into prominence and dramatically changing opinions on global trade. In polls taken during the late 1990s, a majority of respondents favored global trade, believing that it was good both for them and for the country as a whole. By 2005, Americans were of the opinion that international trade was hurting the country (see Figure 17–3).

U.S. officials have struggled to find an effective response to this development. Economists argue that the job losses are simply part of the "creative destruction" that occurs naturally in free markets. Firms have no choice but to adapt if they are to survive. Public officials, however, cannot so easily take such a long-range view, because they face immediate pressures from constituents who have lost jobs and from communities that have lost firms. In response to these pressures, U.S. officials have

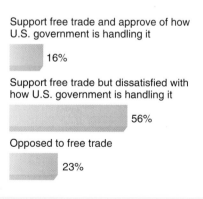

Support free trade and approve of how
U.S. government is handling it

16%

Support free trade but dissatisfied with
how U.S. government is handling it

56%

Opposed to free trade

23%

FIGURE 17-3 AMERICANS' OPINION OF FREE TRADE

Most Americans support free trade, but most of them also are dissatisfied with how the U.S. government is handling issues of job loss, the environment, and the exploitation of foreign workers. *Source: PIPA-Knowledge Networks survey, June 2005.*

sought to preserve free trade by insisting that foreign governments improve their labor and environmental practices and end whatever protectionist policies they still promote. The stated goal is to make global trade work in ways that will allow U.S. goods to compete on an even playing field. However, other countries are not always convinced that the United States itself plays fair. In 2006, WTO trade talks collapsed in part because the United States refused to reduce its hefty farm subsidies, which enable U.S. agricultural producers to keep their prices low, thereby giving them an advantage in world commodity markets.

Trade with China is an issue that looms ever larger with U.S. policymakers. In the past decade, America's trade deficit with China has increased more than thirty-fold and now exceeds $200 billion annually. The United States has provided China with a marketplace for its goods, which has helped fuel China's economic growth. China in turn has provided the United States with inexpensive goods, which has satisfied America's consumers and helped keep inflation in check. But Congress is increasingly signaling concern with the trade deficit. Many members of Congress from

In terms of its trade deficit, the United States' most significant trading partner is China. Shown here is China's president, Hu Jintao, on the South Lawn of the White House during his visit to the United States in 2006. Presidents Hu and Bush discussed U.S.–China relations during the visit.

GET INVOLVED!

Serve Your Country

In his 1961 inaugural address, President John F. Kennedy said, "Ask not what your country can do for you. Ask what you can do for your country." Kennedy called America's young people to service on behalf of their country. His call was not just a call to military service. One of Kennedy's early initiatives, the Peace Corps, offered Americans the opportunity to apply their skills to development projects in other countries. Under Kennedy's successor, President Lyndon Johnson, a domestic version of the Peace Corps—Volunteers in Service to America (VISTA)—was established.

Before the military draft ended in 1973, male Americans expected to serve their country. Not all did so, but millions served in the Army, Navy, Air Force, or Marines. Some gave their lives for their country. There was a shared sense of duty and sacrifice.

Since the end of the draft, Congress has from time to time considered establishing a National Service that would require every young American man and woman to serve the country in one way or another for a set period of time. However, you do not need an act of Congress if you want to serve your country. There is a wide range of opportunities. America's all-volunteer military seeks educated recruits for both its enlisted and its officer ranks. The Peace Corps, now four decades old, continues to send Americans to countries where their skills are needed. AmeriCorps, a network of local, state, and national service programs, places more than seventy thousand Americans each year in service positions in the areas of education, public safety, health, and the environment. These are just some of the numerous service programs to which you could apply.

both parties would like to see China increase the value of its currency, which would raise the price of its goods and thereby dampen consumer demand in the United States. Such a step would make U.S. goods more competitive with those produced in China and offer some protection to U.S. firms and workers. One thing is certain—trade between the United States and China is sure to remain a pressing political issue. China is the emerging giant in international trade.[13]

POLITICAL CULTURE

Foreign Policy and America's Ideals

During the 1950s, when the cold war was at a peak, President Dwight D. Eisenhower warned against actions that undermined the principles America stood for. He worried that threats originating abroad would lead Americans to support policies that compromised the ideals upon which the nation had been founded. Eisenhower believed that excessive government secrecy—justified in the name of national security—threatened liberty. He worried that a huge permanent military and the industrial firms that benefited from it would sap America of its resources and encourage the country to seek military solutions to international problems. If America was to remain a beacon of freedom for the world, it had to remain steadfast in its ideals.

Similar concerns have been raised in the context of the war on terrorism. Nearly all Americans agree that the terrorist threat cannot be met without making some adjustments in how government operates. However, disagreement has arisen over specific policies, such as the prolonged detention of noncitizens, the preemptive invasion of Iraq, and the wiretapping of phone calls without a judicial warrant.

How much leeway do you think policymakers should have in their pursuit of the war on terrorism? What compromises of principle do you find acceptable? Do you think noncitizens deserve the same constitutional protections as citizens? Do you think military force should be the nation's first response to terrorist threats? If not, what are the alternatives, and how, if at all, are they more consistent with America's founding ideals?

Relations with the Developing World   Although political instability in the less developed countries can disrupt world markets, less developed countries also offer marketplace opportunities. In order to develop further, they need to acquire the goods and services that more industrialized countries can provide. To foster this demand, the United States and the other industrialized countries provide developmental assistance to poorer countries. Contributions include direct foreign aid and also indirect assistance through international organizations such as the International Monetary Fund (IMF) and the World Bank. These two organizations were created by the United States and Great Britain at the Bretton Woods Conference near the end of World War II. The IMF makes short-term loans to prevent countries experiencing temporary problems from collapsing economically or resorting to destructive practices such as the unrestricted printing of paper money. The World Bank, on the other hand, makes long-term development loans to poor countries for capital investment projects such as dams, highways, and factories.

Since World War II, the United States has been the leading source of aid to developing countries. Although the United States still contributes the most in terms of total dollars, Canada, Japan, and the European countries spend more on a per capita basis than does the United States (see Figure 17–4). The United States has narrowed the gap since the events of September 11, 2001, which awakened some policymakers to the fact that global poverty generates resentment of the United States.[14] In the past few years, U.S. foreign aid spending has increased significantly.[15]

Public opinion is an obstacle to higher levels of spending on foreign aid. Polls show that most Americans believe the United States is already

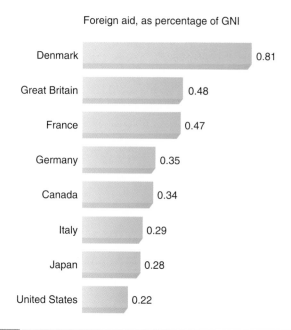

Foreign aid, as percentage of GNI

Denmark	0.81
Great Britain	0.48
France	0.47
Germany	0.35
Canada	0.34
Italy	0.29
Japan	0.28
United States	0.22

FIGURE 17-4   ASSISTANCE TO DEVELOPING COUNTRIES, AS PERCENTAGE OF GROSS NATIONAL INCOME

The United States ranks highest in terms of total amount spent on foreign aid to developing countries but ranks lower in terms of percentage of gross national income (GNI). Data exclude Iraq reconstruction spending. *Source: OECD (Organization for Economic Cooperation and Development), 2006.*

spending huge amounts on foreign aid. In a poll that asked Americans to name the largest federal programs, foreign aid topped the list, with 27 percent identifying it as the most expensive program.[16] In fact, foreign aid is far from the top. Nevertheless, Americans' perception makes foreign aid a potent political issue for politicians who would like to decrease it. Jesse Helms (R-N.C.), a past chair of the Senate Foreign Relations Committee, liked to say that foreign aid was nothing more than pouring billions of dollars "down foreign ratholes."[17]

A NEW WORLD

Although economic interests are a driving force in U.S. foreign policy, global terrorism has become America's top priority. "The world will never again be the same" became a common refrain after September 11, 2001. Subsequent developments have confirmed that judgment. Stopping terrorism has become the nation's most urgent policy goal, leading to massive increases in federal spending to combat the terrorist threat at home and abroad. The nation's intelligence and law-enforcement agencies have been reorganized to increase their capacity to blunt the threat. Shifts in policy toward the Middle East and South Asia have occurred. The U.S. attack on Iraq in 2003 was premised on the assumption that Iraq had chemical and biological weapons that could be funneled into the hands of anti-American terrorists. These are only a few examples of the changes brought about by the events of September 11. Virtually no area of U.S. foreign and defense policy has been unaffected.

One of the largest changes has been in a direction the terrorists had not predicted. With the September 11 attacks, they sought to force the United States to reduce its presence in the Middle East and in the Arab world generally. The effect has been the opposite. Just as Pearl Harbor ended Americans' isolationism, September 11 blunted a movement by some U.S. officials to reduce America's involvement in international affairs. As security analyst Philip Gordon noted, "The result of the September 11 attacks has not been an American return to isolationism, but a reinvigoration of engagement."[18]

However, the United States is struggling in its attempt to engage with the world in the aftermath of September 11, 2001. The global support that the United States received after the terrorist attacks on the World Trade Center and the Pentagon evaporated eighteen months later when the United States invaded Iraq. The conflict there also raised the risks for America. According to the National Intelligence Estimate that U.S. intelligence agencies compiled in 2007, the terrorist threat has worsened in the past few years, largely because the Iraq conflict has mobilized Islamic extremists around the globe. What analysts disagree about is the length of America's struggle with radical Islamists. Some analysts predict that the conflict will unwind within a decade or so. Others see it stretching across a far longer period, much like the religiously motivated Thirty Years War that consumed the first half of the seventeenth century in Europe. The challenge for Americans is to discover how to navigate this conflict in a way that preserves the integrity of the United States as a territorial state and as a vibrant democracy. It is the same challenge that President Dwight D. Eisenhower set forth near the start of the Cold War: "The problem in defense is how far you can go without destroying from within what you are trying to defend from without."

SUMMARY

The chief instruments of national security policy are diplomacy, military force, economic exchange, and intelligence gathering. These are exercised through specialized agencies of the U.S. government, such as the Departments of State and Defense, that are largely responsive to presidential leadership. National security policy has also relied on international organizations, such as the United Nations and the World Trade Organization, that are responsive to the global concerns of major nations.

From 1945 to 1990, U.S. foreign and defense policies were dominated by a concern with the Soviet Union. During most of this period, the United States pursued a policy of containment based on the premise that the Soviet Union was an aggressor nation bent on global conquest. Containment policy led the United States to enter into wars in Korea and Vietnam and to maintain a large defense establishment. U.S. military forces are deployed around the globe, and the nation maintains a large nuclear arsenal. The end of the cold war, however, made some of this weaponry and strategic planning less relevant to America's national security.

A first response to the post-cold-war world was multilateralism, the idea that major nations could achieve common goals by working together, including using force as a means of arresting regional conflicts. The interventions in the Persian Gulf and the Balkans during the 1990s are examples. They demonstrated that major nations can intervene with some success in global hot spots but also showed that the ethnic, religious, and national conflicts that fuel these flashes are not easily resolved.

The terrorist attacks on the World Trade Center and the Pentagon in 2001 led to broad changes in U.S. national security organization and strategy. Increased spending on defense and homeland security have been coupled with a partial reorganization of U.S. intelligence, law-enforcement, and immigration agencies, as well as new laws affecting the scope of their activities. The defining moment of the post–September 11 period was America's 2003 invasion of Iraq, which was rooted in President George W. Bush's preemptive war doctrine and his willingness to commit the United States to unilateral action. Iraq has largely been America's war—90 percent of the coalition casualties and monetary costs have been borne by the United States. Congressional and public support for the Iraq intervention has declined sharply.

In recent decades, the United States has increasingly taken economic factors into account in its national security considerations. For example, trade has played a larger part in defining its relationships with other countries. The trading system the United States helped erect after World War II has given way to a more global and more competitive system. Changes in communication, transportation, and computing have altered the way large corporations operate. As businesses have changed their practices, nations have had to adapt. The changes include the emergence of regional and international economic structures such as the European Union, NAFTA, and the WTO. Nevertheless, nations naturally compete for economic advantage, including access to natural resources. Accordingly, trade is a source of conflict as well as a source of cooperation. In the coming years, oil is likely to be at the center of the conflict.

KEY TERMS

bipolar (power structure) (*p. 609*)
cold war (*p. 609*)
containment (*p. 609*)
deterrence policy (*p. 619*)
economic globalization (*p. 629*)
free-trade position (*p. 629*)
internationalist (*p. 608*)
isolationist (*p. 608*)

military-industrial complex (*p. 625*)
multilateralism (*p. 611*)
multinational corporations (*p. 629*)
preemptive war doctrine (*p. 614*)
protectionism (*p. 630*)
unilateralism (*p. 615*)
unipolar (power structure) (*p. 611*)

SUGGESTED READINGS

Clarke, Richard A. *Against All Enemies: Inside America's War on Terror.* New York: Free Press, 2004. A best-selling book by the nation's former top-ranking presidential advisor on terrorism.

Fishman, Ted C. *China, Inc.: How the Rise of the Next Superpower Challenges America and the World.* New York: Scribner, 2005. A look at China's rapid economic growth and its implications.

Kegley, Charles W., and Gregory A. Raymond. *The Imperiled Imperium: America and the Erosion of Global Security.* New York: Oxford University Press, 2006. A pessimistic view of U.S. national security policy.

Lind, Michael. *The American Way of Strategy.* New York: Oxford University Press, 2006. An analysis that claims U.S. foreign policy works best when conducted in the context of America's ideals.

Nye, Joseph S. *Soft Power: The Means to Success in World Politics.* New York: PublicAffairs, 2004. An argument for making diplomacy, assistance, and other forms of "soft power" the basis of U.S. foreign policy.

Odom, William E. *Fixing Intelligence.* New Haven, Conn.: Yale University Press, 2003. A detailed critique of U.S. intelligence efforts by a former military intelligence officer.

Sobel, Richard. *The Impact of Public Opinion on U.S. Foreign Policy Since Vietnam.* New York: Oxford University Press, 2001. A careful account of how public opinion has affected foreign policy.

Woodward, Bob. *State of Denial: Bush at War, Part III.* New York: Simon & Schuster, 2006. An inside look at the Bush administration's Iraq policy.

LIST OF WEBSITES

http://www.defenselink.mil/ The U.S. Department of Defense's website; provides information on each of the armed services, daily news from the American Forces Information Service, and other material.

http://www.cfr.org/ Includes reports and assessments of the Council of Foreign Relations and transcripts of speeches by U.S. and world political leaders on topics of international interest.

http://www.igc.org/igc Website of the Institute for Global Communications (IGC); provides information and services to organizations and activists on a broad range of international issues, including human rights.

http://www.wto.org/ The World Trade Organization (WTO) website; contains information on the organization's activities and has links to related sites.

POLITICS IN THEORY AND PRACTICE

Thinking: What are the major objectives of U.S. foreign and defense policy? What are the mechanisms for pursuing those objectives?

Participating: International conflicts stem from real causes but also have roots in cultural misunderstandings. Americans are thought to be more prone than most peoples to such misunderstandings because they have not been forced by geography to take different cultures, languages, and national identities fully into account. British social scientist Harold Lasswell remarked that Americans tend to view the world through the lens of their own experiences. This perspective has become a greater handicap as trade and communication have made the countries of the world ever more interdependent. Even the war on terrorism will depend for its success on a greater sensitivity to the beliefs and aspirations of other peoples. Individual Americans can do their part by educating themselves about the world. Consider taking a college course in history, political science, language and culture, geography, religion, or any other subject that will introduce you to a part of the world you have not previously studied. Close attention to the foreign-affairs coverage in a quality newspaper or periodical can also deepen your understanding of other peoples and cultures.

ADDITIONAL RESOURCES

For quizzes, interactive simulations, games, graphics, and other study tools, visit the book's Online Learning Center at **www.mhhe.com/pattersonwtp7.**

The Preemptive War Doctrine

By George W. Bush

In a speech at West Point on June 1, 2002, President George W. Bush declared a new doctrine for U.S. military action—preemptive war. The United States had always reserved the right to make the first strike if directly and substantially threatened by a foreign adversary, but President Bush extended the principle to include more remote threats. His speech was a prelude to the U.S. invasion of Iraq in 2003, the first application of the preemptive war doctrine.

The nature of the Cold War threat required the United States—with our allies and friends—to emphasize deterrence of the enemy's use of force, producing a grim strategy of mutual assured destruction. With the collapse of the Soviet Union and the end of the Cold War, our security environment has undergone profound transformation.

Having moved from confrontation to cooperation as the hallmark of our relationship with Russia, the dividends are evident: an end to the balance of terror that divided us; an historic reduction in the nuclear arsenals on both sides; and cooperation in areas such as counterterrorism and missile defense that until recently were inconceivable.

But new deadly challenges have emerged from rogue states and terrorists. None of these contemporary threats rival the sheer destructive power that was arrayed against us by the Soviet Union. However, the nature and motivations of these new adversaries, their determination to obtain destructive powers hitherto available only to the world's strongest states, and the greater likelihood that they will use weapons of mass destruction against us, make today's security environment more complex and dangerous.

In the 1990s we witnessed the emergence of a small number of rogue states that, while different in important ways, share a number of attributes. These states brutalize their own people and squander their national resources for the personal gain of the rulers; display no regard for international law, threaten their neighbors, and callously violate international treaties to which they are party; are determined to acquire weapons of mass destruction, along with other advanced military technology, to be used as threats or offensively to achieve the aggressive designs of these regimes; sponsor terrorism around the globe; and reject basic human values and hate the United States and everything for which it stands.

At the time of the Gulf War, we acquired irrefutable proof that Iraq's designs were not limited to the chemical weapons it had used against Iran and its own people, but also extended to the acquisition of nuclear weapons and biological agents. In the past decade North Korea has become the world's principal purveyor of ballistic missiles, and has tested increasingly capable missiles while developing its own WMD arsenal. Other rogue regimes seek nuclear, biological, and chemical weapons as well. These states' pursuit of, and global trade in, such weapons has become a looming threat to all nations.

We must be prepared to stop rogue states and their terrorist clients before they are able to threaten or use weapons of mass destruction against the United States and our allies and friends. Our response must take full advantage of strengthened alliances, the establishment of new partnerships with former adversaries, innovation in the use of military forces, modern technologies, including the development of an effective missile defense system, and increased emphasis on intelligence collection and analysis. . . .

It has taken almost a decade for us to comprehend the true nature of this new threat. Given the goals of rogue states and terrorists, the United States can no longer solely rely on a reactive posture as we have in the past. The inability to deter a potential attacker, the immediacy of today's threats, and the magnitude of potential harm that could be caused by our adversaries' choice of weapons, do not permit that option. We cannot let our enemies strike first.

In the Cold War, especially following the Cuban missile crisis, we faced a generally status quo, risk-averse adversary. Deterrence was an effective defense. But deterrence based only upon the threat of retaliation is less likely to work against leaders of rogue states more willing to take risks, gambling with the lives of their people, and the wealth of their nations.

In the Cold War, weapons of mass destruction were considered weapons of last resort whose use risked the destruction of those who used them. Today, our enemies see weapons of mass destruction as weapons of choice. For rogue states these weapons are tools of intimidation and military aggression against their neighbors. These weapons may also allow these states to attempt to blackmail the United States and our allies to prevent us from deterring or repelling the aggressive behavior of rogue states. Such states also see these weapons as their best means of overcoming the conventional superiority of the United States.

Traditional concepts of deterrence will not work against a terrorist enemy whose avowed tactics are wanton destruction and the targeting of innocents; whose so-called soldiers seek martyrdom in death and whose most potent protection is statelessness. The overlap between states that sponsor terror and those that pursue WMD compels us to action.

For centuries, international law recognized that nations need not suffer an attack before they can lawfully take action to defend themselves against forces that present an imminent danger of attack. Legal scholars and international jurists often conditioned the legitimacy of preemption on the existence of an imminent threat—most often a visible mobilization of armies, navies, and air forces preparing to attack.

We must adapt the concept of imminent threat to the capabilities and objectives of today's adversaries. Rogue states and terrorists do not seek to attack us using conventional means. They know such attacks would fail. Instead, they rely on acts of terror and, potentially, the use of weapons of mass destruction—weapons that can be easily concealed, delivered covertly, and used without warning.

The targets of these attacks are our military forces and our civilian population, in direct violation of one of the principal norms of the law of warfare. As was demonstrated by the losses on September 11, 2001, mass civilian casualties is the specific objective of terrorists and these losses would be exponentially more severe if terrorists acquired and used weapons of mass destruction.

The United States has long maintained the option of preemptive actions to counter a sufficient threat to our national security. The greater the threat, the greater is the risk of inaction—and the more compelling the case for taking anticipatory action to defend ourselves, even if uncertainty remains as to the time and place of the enemy's attack. To forestall or prevent such hostile acts by our adversaries, the United States will, if necessary, act preemptively.

What's Your Opinion?

What's your view of President Bush's preemptive war doctrine? To what degree is your opinion affected by what has happened in the Middle East since the United States invaded Iraq in 2003? If you think the preemptive war doctrine is a flawed concept, what alternative would you recommend?

APPENDIXES

The Declaration of Independence
In Congress, July 4, 1776

The Unanimous Declaration of the Thirteen United States of America

When, in the course of human events, it becomes necessary for one people to dissolve the political bands which have connected them with another, and to assume, among the powers of the earth, the separate and equal station to which the laws of nature and of nature's God entitle them, a decent respect to the opinions of mankind requires that they should declare the causes which impel them to the separation.

We hold these truths to be self-evident, that all men are created equal; that they are endowed by their Creator with certain unalienable rights; that among these, are life, liberty, and the pursuit of happiness. That, to secure these rights, governments are instituted among men, deriving their just powers from the consent of the governed; that, whenever any form of government becomes destructive of these ends, it is the right of the people to alter or to abolish it, and to institute a new government, laying its foundation on such principles, and organizing its powers in such form, as to them shall seem most likely to effect their safety and happiness. Prudence, indeed, will dictate that governments long established, should not be changed for light and transient causes; and, accordingly, all experience hath shown, that mankind are more disposed to suffer, while evils are sufferable, than to right themselves by abolishing the forms to which they are accustomed. But, when a long train of abuses and usurpations, pursuing invariably the same object, evinces a design to reduce them under absolute despotism, it is their right, it is their duty, to throw off such government and to provide new guards for their future security. Such has been the patient sufferance of these colonies, and such is now the necessity which constrains them to alter their former systems of government. The history of the present King of Great Britain is a history of repeated injuries and usurpations, all having, in direct object, the establishment of an absolute tyranny over these States. To prove this, let facts be submitted to a candid world:

He has refused his assent to laws the most wholesome and necessary for the public good.

He has forbidden his governors to pass laws of immediate and pressing importance, unless suspended in their operation till his assent should be obtained; and, when so suspended, he has utterly neglected to attend to them.

He has refused to pass other laws for the accommodation of large districts of people, unless those people would relinquish the right of representation in the legislature; a right inestimable to them, and formidable to tyrants only.

He has called together legislative bodies at places unusual, uncomfortable, and distant from the depository of their public records, for the sole purpose of fatiguing them into compliance with his measures.

He has dissolved representative houses repeatedly for opposing, with manly firmness, his invasions on the rights of the people.

He has refused, for a long time after such dissolutions, to cause others to be elected; whereby the legislative powers, incapable of annihilation, have returned to the people at large for their exercise; the state remaining, in the meantime, exposed to all the danger of invasion from without, and convulsions within.

He has endeavored to prevent the population of these States; for that purpose, obstructing the laws for naturalization of foreigners, refusing to pass others to encourage their migration hither, and raising the conditions of new appropriations of lands.

He has obstructed the administration of justice, by refusing his assent to laws for establishing judiciary powers.

He has made judges dependent on his will alone, for the tenure of their offices, and the amount and payment of their salaries.

He has erected a multitude of new offices, and sent hither swarms of officers to harass our people, and eat out their substance.

He has kept among us, in time of peace, standing armies, without the consent of our legislatures.

He has affected to render the military independent of, and superior to, the civil power.

He has combined, with others, to subject us to a jurisdiction foreign to our Constitution, and unacknowledged by our laws; giving his assent to their acts of pretended legislation:

For quartering large bodies of armed troops among us:

For protecting them by a mock trial, from punishment, for any murders which they should commit on the inhabitants of these States:

For cutting off our trade with all parts of the world:

For imposing taxes on us without our consent:

For depriving us, in many cases, of the benefit of trial by jury:

For transporting us beyond seas to be tried for pretended offences:

For abolishing the free system of English laws in a neighboring province, establishing therein an arbitrary government, and enlarging its boundaries, so as to render it at once an example and fit instrument for introducing the same absolute rule into these colonies:

For taking away our charters, abolishing our most valuable laws, and altering, fundamentally, the powers of our governments:

For suspending our own legislatures, and declaring themselves invested with power to legislate for us in all cases whatsoever.

He has abdicated government here, by declaring us out of his protection, and waging war against us.

He has plundered our seas, ravaged our coasts, burnt our towns, and destroyed the lives of our people.

He is, at this time, transporting large armies of foreign mercenaries to complete the works of death, desolation, and tyranny, already begun, with circumstances of cruelty and perfidy scarcely paralleled in the most barbarous ages, and totally unworthy of the head of a civilized nation.

He has constrained our fellow citizens, taken captive on the high seas, to bear arms against their country, to become the executioners of their friends, and brethren, or to fall themselves by their hands.

He has excited domestic insurrections amongst us, and has endeavored to bring on the inhabitants of our frontiers, the merciless Indian savages, whose known rule of warfare is an undistinguished destruction of all ages, sexes, and conditions.

In every stage of these oppressions, we have petitioned for redress, in the most humble terms; our repeated petitions have been answered only by repeated injury. A prince, whose character is thus marked by every act which may define a tyrant, is unfit to be the ruler of a free people.

Nor have we been wanting in attention to our British brethren. We have warned them, from time to time, of attempts made by their legislature to extend an unwarrantable jurisdiction over us. We have reminded them of the circumstances of our emigration and settlement here. We have appealed to their native justice and magnanimity, and we have conjured them, by the ties of our common kindred, to disavow these usurpations, which would inevitably interrupt our connections and correspondence. They, too, have been deaf to the voice of justice and of consanguinity. We must, therefore, acquiesce in the necessity which denounces our separation, and hold them as we hold the rest of mankind, enemies in war, in peace, friends.

We, therefore, the representatives of the United States of America, in general Congress assembled, appealing to the Supreme Judge of the world for the rectitude of our intentions, do, in the name, and by the authority of the good people of these colonies, solemnly publish and declare, that these united colonies are, and of right ought to be, free and independent states: that they are absolved from all allegiance to the British Crown, and that all political connection between them and the state of Great Britain is, and ought to be, totally dissolved; and that, as free and independent states, they have full power to levy war, conclude peace, contract alliances, establish commerce, and to do all other acts and things which independent states may of right do. And, for the support of this declaration, with a firm reliance on the protection of Divine Providence, we mutually pledge to each other our lives, our fortunes, and our sacred honor.

The foregoing Declaration was, by order of Congress, engrossed, and signed by the following members:

JOHN HANCOCK

New Hampshire
Josiah Bartlett
William Whipple
Matthew Thornton

Massachusetts Bay
Samuel Adams
John Adams
Robert Treat Paine
Elbridge Gerry

Rhode Island
Stephen Hopkins
William Ellery

Connecticut
Roger Sherman
Samuel Huntington
William Williams
Oliver Wolcott

New York
William Floyd
Philip Livingston
Francis Lewis
Lewis Morris

New Jersey
Richard Stockton
John Witherspoon
Francis Hopkinson

John Hart
Abraham Clark

Pennsylvania
Robert Morris
Benjamin Rush
Benjamin Franklin
John Morton
George Clymer
James Smith
George Taylor
James Wilson
George Ross

Delaware
Caesar Rodney
George Reed
Thomas M'Kean

Maryland
Samuel Chase
William Paca
Thomas Stone
Charles Carroll, of
   Carrollton

Virginia
George Wythe
Richard Henry Lee
Thomas Jefferson
Benjamin Harrison
Thomas Nelson, Jr.
Francis Lightfoot Lee
Carter Braxton

North Carolina
William Hooper
Joseph Hewes
John Penn

South Carolina
Edward Rutledge
Thomas Heyward, Jr.
Thomas Lynch, Jr.
Arthur Middleton

Georgia
Button Gwinnett
Lyman Hall
George Walton

Resolved, That copies of the Declaration be sent to the several assemblies, conventions, and committees, or councils of safety, and to the several commanding officers of the continental troops; that it be proclaimed in each of the United States, at the head of the army.

The Constitution of the United States of America[1]

We the People of the United States, in Order to form a more perfect Union, establish Justice, insure domestic Tranquility, provide for the common defence, promote the general Welfare, and secure the Blessings of Liberty to ourselves and our Posterity, do ordain and establish this CONSTITUTION for the United States of America.

ARTICLE I

Section 1

All legislative Powers herein granted shall be vested in a Congress of the United States, which shall consist of a Senate and House of Representatives.

Section 2

The House of Representatives shall be composed of Members chosen every second Year by the People of the several States, and the Electors in each State shall have the Qualifications requisite for Electors of the most numerous Branch of the State Legislature.

No Person shall be a Representative who shall not have attained to the Age of twenty-five Years, and been seven Years a Citizen of the United States, and who shall not, when elected, be an Inhabitant of that State in which he shall be chosen.

[Representatives and direct Taxes[2] shall be apportioned among the several States which may be included within this Union, according to their respective Numbers, which shall be determined by adding to the whole Number of free Persons, including those bound to Service for a Term of Years, and excluding Indians not taxed, three fifths of all other Persons.][3] The actual Enumeration shall be made within three Years after the first Meeting of the Congress of the United States, and within every subsequent Term of ten Years, in such Manner as they shall by Law direct. The Number of Representatives shall not exceed one for every thirty Thousand, but each State shall have at Least one Representative; and until such enumeration shall be made, the State of New Hampshire shall be entitled to chuse three, Massachusetts eight, Rhode-Island and Providence Plantations one, Connecticut five, New York six, New Jersey four, Pennsylvania eight, Delaware one, Maryland six, Virginia ten, North Carolina five, South Carolina five, and Georgia three.

When vacancies happen in the Representation from any State, the Executive Authority thereof shall issue Writs of Election to fill such Vacancies.

---

[1]This version, which follows the original Constitution in capitalization and spelling, was published by the United States Department of the Interior, Office of Education, in 1935.
[2]Altered by the Sixteenth Amendment.
[3]Negated by the Fourteenth Amendment.

The House of Representatives shall chuse their Speaker and other Officers; and shall have the sole Power of Impeachment.

Section 3

The Senate of the United States shall be composed of two Senators from each State, chosen by the Legislature thereof, for six Years; and each Senator shall have one Vote.

Immediately after they shall be assembled in Consequence of the first Election, they shall be divided as equally as may be into three Classes. The Seats of the Senators of the first Class shall be vacated at the Expiration of the second Year, of the second Class at the Expiration of the fourth Year, and of the third Class at the Expiration of the sixth Year, so that one-third may be chosen every second Year; and if Vacancies happen by Resignation, or otherwise, during the Recess of the Legislature of any State, the Executive thereof may make temporary Appointments until the next Meeting of the Legislature, which shall then fill such Vacancies.

No Person shall be a Senator who shall not have attained to the Age of thirty Years, and been nine Years a Citizen of the United States, and who shall not, when elected, be an Inhabitant of that State for which he shall be chosen.

The Vice President of the United States shall be President of the Senate, but shall have no vote, unless they be equally divided.

The Senate shall chuse their other Officers, and also a President pro tempore, in the absence of the Vice President, or when he shall exercise the Office of President of the United States.

The Senate shall have the sole Power to try all Impeachments. When sitting for that purpose they shall be on Oath or Affirmation. When the President of the United States is tried, the Chief Justice shall preside: And no person shall be convicted without the Concurrence of two thirds of the Members present.

Judgment in Cases of Impeachment shall not extend further than to removal from Office, and disqualification to hold and enjoy any Office of honor, Trust, or Profit under the United States: but the Party convicted shall nevertheless be liable and subject to Indictment, Trial, Judgment and Punishment, according to Law.

Section 4

The Times, Place and Manner of holding Elections for Senators and Representatives, shall be prescribed in each State by the Legislature thereof; but the Congress may at any time by Law make or alter such Regulations, except as to the Places of Chusing Senators.

The Congress shall assemble at least once in every Year, and such Meeting shall be on the first Monday in December, unless they shall by Law appoint a different Day.

Section 5

Each House shall be the Judge of the Elections, Returns and Qualifications of its own Members, and a Majority of each shall constitute a Quorum to do Business; but a smaller number may adjourn from day to day, and may be authorized to compel the Attendance of absent Members, in such Manner, and under such Penalties, as each House may provide.

Each House may determine the Rules of its Proceedings, punish its Members for disorderly Behaviour, and, with the Concurrence of two thirds, expel a Member.

Each House shall keep a Journal of its Proceedings, and from time to time publish the same, excepting such Parts as may in their Judgment require Secrecy; and the Yeas and Nays of the Members of either House on any question shall, at the Desire of one fifth of those Present, be entered on the Journal.

Neither House, during the Session of Congress, shall, without the Consent of the other, adjourn for more than three days, nor to any other Place than that in which the two Houses shall be sitting.

Section 6

The Senators and Representatives shall receive a Compensation for their Services, to be ascertained by Law, and paid out of the Treasury of the United States. They shall in all Cases, except Treason, Felony, and Breach of the Peace, be privileged from Arrest during their Attendance at the Session of their respective Houses, and in going to and returning from the same; and for any Speech or Debate in either House, they shall not be questioned in any other Place.

No Senator or Representative shall, during the Time for which he was elected, be appointed to any civil Office under the Authority of the United States, which shall have been created, or the Emoluments whereof shall have been increased, during such time; and no Person holding any Office under the United States shall be a Member of either House during his continuance in Office.

Section 7

All Bills for raising Revenue shall originate in the House of Representatives; but the Senate may propose or concur with Amendments as on other bills.

Every Bill which shall have passed the House of Representatives and the Senate, shall, before it becomes a Law, be presented to the President of the United States; if he approve he shall sign it, but if not he shall return it, with his Objections, to that House in which it shall have originated, who shall enter the Objections at large on their Journal, and proceed to reconsider it. If after such Reconsideration two thirds of that House shall agree to pass the bill, it shall be sent, together with the objections, to the other House, by which it shall likewise be reconsidered, and if approved by two thirds of that House, it shall become a Law. But in all such Cases the Votes of both Houses shall be determined by Yeas and Nays, and the Names of the Persons voting for and against the Bill shall be entered on the Journal of each House respectively. If any Bill shall not be returned by the President within ten Days (Sundays excepted) after it shall have been presented to him, the Same shall be a Law, in like Manner as if he had signed it, unless the Congress by their Adjournment prevent its Return, in which Case it shall not be a Law.

Every Order, Resolution, or Vote to which the Concurrence of the Senate and House of Representatives may be necessary (except on a question of Adjournment) shall be presented to the President of the United States; and before the Same shall take Effect, shall be approved by him, or being disapproved by him, shall be repassed by two thirds of the Senate and House of Representatives, according to the Rules and Limitations prescribed in the Case of a Bill.

Section 8

The Congress shall have Power To lay and collect Taxes, Duties, Imposts and Excises, to pay the Debts and provide for the common Defence and general Welfare of the United States; but all Duties, Imposts and Excises shall be uniform throughout the United States;

To borrow money on the credit of the United States;

To regulate Commerce with foreign Nations, and among the several States, and with the Indian Tribes;

To establish a uniform rule of Naturalization, and uniform Laws on the subject of Bankruptcies throughout the United States;

To coin Money, regulate the Value thereof, and of foreign Coin, and fix the Standard of Weights and Measures;

To provide for the Punishment of counterfeiting the Securities and current Coin of the United States;

To establish Post Offices and post Roads;

To promote the Progress of Science and useful Arts, by securing for limited Times to Authors and Inventors the exclusive Right to their respective Writings and Discoveries;

To constitute Tribunals inferior to the Supreme Court;

To define and punish Piracies and Felonies committed on the high Seas, and Offenses against the Law of Nations;

To declare War, grant Letters of Marque and Reprisal, and make Rules concerning Captures on Land and Water;

To raise and support Armies, but no Appropriation of Money to that Use shall be for a longer Term than two Years;

To provide and maintain a Navy;

To make Rules for the Government and Regulation of the land and naval forces;

To provide for calling forth the Militia to execute the Laws of the Union, suppress Insurrections and repel Invasions;

To provide for organizing, arming, and disciplining the Militia, and for governing such Part of them as may be employed in the Service of the United States, reserving to the States respectively, the Appointment of the Officers, and the Authority of training the Militia according to the discipline prescribed by Congress;

To exercise exclusive Legislation in all Cases whatsoever, over such District (not exceeding ten Miles square) as may, by Cession of particular States, and the acceptance of Congress, become the Seat of the Government of the United States, and to exercise like Authority over all Places purchased by the Consent of the Legislature of the State in which the Same shall be, for the Erection of Forts, Magazines, Arsenals, Dock-yards, and other needful Buildings;—And

To make all Laws which shall be necessary and proper for carrying into Execution the foregoing Powers, and all other Powers vested by this Constitution in the Government of the United States, or in any Department or Officer thereof.

Section 9

The Migration or Importation of such Persons as any of the States now existing shall think proper to admit, shall not be prohibited by the Congress prior to the

Year one thousand eight hundred and eight, but a tax or duty may be imposed on such Importation, not exceeding ten dollars for each Person.

The privilege of the Writ of Habeas Corpus shall not be suspended, unless when in Cases of Rebellion or Invasion the public Safety may require it.

No bill of Attainder or ex post facto Law shall be passed.

No capitation, or other direct, Tax shall be laid unless in Proportion to the Census or Enumeration herein before directed to be taken.

No Tax or Duty shall be laid on Articles exported from any State.

No Preference shall be given by any Regulation of Commerce or Revenue to the Ports of one State over those of another: nor shall Vessels bound to, or from, one State, be obliged to enter, clear, or pay Duties in another.

No Money shall be drawn from the Treasury, but in Consequence of Appropriations made by Law; and a regular Statement and Account of the Receipts and Expenditures of all public Money shall be published from time to time.

No Title of Nobility shall be granted by the United States: And no Person holding any Office of Profit or Trust under them, shall, without the Consent of the Congress, accept of any present, Emolument, Office, or Title, of any kind whatever, from any King, Prince, or foreign State.

Section 10

No State shall enter into any Treaty, Alliance, or Confederation; grant Letters of Marque and Reprisal; coin Money; emit Bills of Credit; make any Thing but gold and silver Coin a Tender in Payment of Debts; pass any Bill of Attainder, ex post facto Law, or Law impairing the Obligation of Contracts, or grant any Title of Nobility.

No State shall, without the Consent of the Congress, lay any Imposts or Duties on Imports or Exports, except what may be absolutely necessary for executing its inspection Laws; and the net Produce of all Duties and Imposts, laid by any State on Imports or Exports, shall be for the use of the Treasury of the United States; and all such Laws shall be subject to the Revision and Control of the Congress.

No state shall, without the Consent of Congress, lay any duty of Tonnage, keep Troops, or Ships of War in time of Peace, enter into any Agreement or Compact with another State, or with a foreign Power, or engage in War, unless actually invaded, or in such imminent Danger as will not admit of delay.

ARTICLE II

Section 1

The executive Power shall be vested in a President of the United States of America. He shall hold his Office during the Term of four years, and, together with the Vice President, chosen for the same Term, be elected, as follows:

Each State shall appoint, in such Manner as the Legislature thereof may direct, a Number of Electors, equal to the whole Number of Senators and Representatives to which the State may be entitled in the Congress: but no Senator or Representative, or Person holding an Office of Trust or Profit under the United States, shall be appointed an Elector.

[The Electors shall meet in their respective States, and vote by Ballot for two persons, of whom one at least shall not be an Inhabitant of the same State with themselves. And they shall make a List of all the Persons voted for, and of the Number of Votes for each; which List they shall sign and certify, and transmit sealed to the Seat of the Government of the United States, directed to the President of the Senate. The President of the Senate shall, in the Presence of the Senate and House of Representatives, open all the Certificates, and the Votes shall then be counted. The Person having the greatest Number of Votes shall be the President, if such Number be a Majority of the whole Number of Electors appointed; and if there be more than one who have such Majority, and have an equal Number of Votes, then the House of Representatives shall immediately chuse by Ballot one of them for President; and if no Person have a Majority, then from the five highest on the List the said House shall in like Manner chuse the President. But in chusing the President, the Votes shall be taken by States, the Representation from each State having one Vote; a quorum for this Purpose shall consist of a Member or Members from two thirds of the States, and a Majority of all the States shall be necessary to a Choice. In every Case, after the Choice of the President, the Person having the greatest Number of Votes of the Electors shall be the Vice President. But if there should remain two or more who have equal votes, the Senate shall chuse from them by Ballot the Vice President.][4]

The Congress may determine the Time of chusing the Electors, and the Day on which they shall give their Votes; which Day shall be the same throughout the United States.

No person except a natural-born Citizen, or a Citizen of the United States, at the time of the Adoption of this Constitution, shall be eligible to the Office of President; neither shall any Person be eligible to that Office who shall not have attained to the Age of thirty-five years, and been fourteen Years a Resident within the United States.

In Case of the Removal of the President from Office, or of his Death, Resignation, or Inability to discharge the Powers and Duties of the said Office, the same shall devolve on the Vice President, and the Congress may by Law provide for the Case of Removal, Death, Resignation, or Inability, both of the President and Vice President, declaring what Officer shall then act as President, and such Officer shall act accordingly, until the disability be removed, or a President shall be elected.

The President shall, at stated Times, receive for his Services a Compensation, which shall neither be increased nor diminished during the Period for which he shall have been elected, and he shall not receive within that Period any other Emolument from the United States, or any of them.

Before he enter on the execution of his Office, he shall take the following Oath or Affirmation:—"I do solemnly swear (or affirm) that I will faithfully execute the Office of President of the United States, and will, to the best of my Ability, preserve, protect, and defend the Constitution of the United States."

Section 2

The President shall be Commander in Chief of the Army and Navy of the United States, and of the Militia of the several States, when called into the actual Service of

---

[4]Revised by the Twelfth Amendment.

the United States; he may require the Opinion, in writing, of the principal Officer in each of the executive Departments, upon any subject relating to the Duties of their respective Offices, and he shall have Power to Grant Reprieves and Pardons for Offenses against the United States, except in Cases of Impeachment.

He shall have Power, by and with the Advice and Consent of the Senate, to make Treaties, provided two thirds of the Senators present concur; and he shall nominate, and by and with the Advice and Consent of the Senate, shall appoint Ambassadors, other public Ministers and Consuls, Judges of the supreme Court, and all other Officers of the United States, whose Appointments are not herein otherwise provided for, and which shall be established by Law: but the Congress may by Law vest the Appointment of such inferior Officers, as they think proper, in the President alone, in the Courts of Law, or in the Heads of Departments.

The President shall have Power to fill up all Vacancies that may happen during the Recess of the Senate, by granting Commissions which shall expire at the End of their next Session.

Section 3

He shall from time to time give to the Congress Information of the State of the Union, and recommend to their Consideration such Measures as he shall judge necessary and expedient; he may, on extraordinary occasions, convene both Houses, or either of them, and in Case of Disagreement between them, with respect to the Time of Adjournment, he may adjourn them to such Time as he shall think proper; he shall receive Ambassadors and other public Ministers; he shall take care that the Laws be faithfully executed, and shall Commission all the Officers of the United States.

Section 4

The President, Vice President and all civil Officers of the United States, shall be removed from Office on Impeachment for, and Conviction of, Treason, Bribery, or other high Crimes and Misdemeanors.

ARTICLE III

Section 1

The judicial Power of the United States, shall be vested in one supreme Court, and in such inferior Courts as the Congress may from time to time ordain and establish. The Judges, both of the supreme and inferior Courts, shall hold their Offices during good Behaviour, and shall, at stated Times, receive for their Services, a Compensation, which shall not be diminished during their Continuance in Office.

Section 2

The judicial Power shall extend to all Cases, in Law and Equity, arising under this Constitution, the Laws of the United States, and Treaties made, or which shall be made, under their Authority;—to all Cases affecting ambassadors, other public ministers and consuls;—to all cases of admiralty and maritime Jurisdiction;—to Controversies to which the United States shall be a Party;—to Controversies between two or more states;—between a State and Citizens of another State;[5]—between Citizens of different States—between Citizens of the same State claiming Lands under Grants of different States, and between a State, or the Citizens thereof, and foreign States, Citizens, or Subjects.

In all Cases affecting Ambassadors, other public Ministers and Consuls, and those in which a State shall be Party, the supreme Court shall have original Jurisdiction. In all the other Cases before mentioned, the supreme Court shall have appellate Jurisdiction, both as to Law and Fact, with such Exceptions, and under such Regulations as the Congress shall make.

The trial of all Crimes, except in Cases of Impeachment, shall be by Jury; and such Trial shall be held in the State where the said Crimes shall have been committed; but when not committed within any State, the Trial shall be at such Place or Places as the Congress may by Law have directed.

Section 3

Treason against the United States, shall consist only in levying War against them, or in adhering to their Enemies, giving them Aid and Comfort. No Person shall be convicted of Treason unless on the Testimony of two Witnesses to the same overt Act, or on Confession in open Court.

The Congress shall have power to declare the Punishment of Treason, but no Attainder of Treason shall work Corruption of Blood, or Forfeiture except during the Life of the Person attainted.

ARTICLE IV

Section 1

Full Faith and Credit shall be given in each State to the public Acts, Records, and judicial Proceedings of every other State. And the Congress may by general Laws prescribe the Manner in which such Acts, Records and Proceedings shall be proved, and the Effect thereof.

Section 2

The Citizens of each State shall be entitled to all Privileges and Immunities of Citizens in the several States.

A Person charged in any State with Treason, Felony, or other Crime, who shall flee from Justice, and be found in another State, shall on demand of the executive Authority of the State from which he fled, be delivered up, to be removed to the State having Jurisdiction of the crime.

No Person held to Service or Labour in one State, under the Laws thereof, escaping into another, shall, in Consequence of any Law or Regulation therein, be discharged from such Service or Labour, but shall be delivered up on Claim of the Party to whom such Service or Labour may be due.

---

[5] Qualified by the Eleventh Amendment.

Section 3

New States may be admitted by the Congress into this Union; but no new State shall be formed or erected within the Jurisdiction of any other State; nor any State be formed by the Junction of two or more States, or parts of States, without the Consent of the Legislatures of the States concerned as well as of the Congress.

The Congress shall have Power to dispose of and make all needful Rules and Regulations respecting the Territory or other Property belonging to the United States; and nothing in this Constitution shall be so construed as to Prejudice any Claims of the United States, or of any particular State.

Section 4

The United States shall guarantee to every State in this Union a Republican Form of Government, and shall protect each of them against Invasion; and on Application of the Legislature, or of the Executive (when the Legislature cannot be convened) against domestic Violence.

ARTICLE V

The Congress, whenever two-thirds of both Houses shall deem it necessary, shall propose Amendments to this Constitution, or, on the Application of the Legislatures of two thirds of the several States, shall call a Convention for proposing Amendments, which, in either Case, shall be valid to all Intents and Purposes, as part of this Constitution, when ratified by the Legislatures of three-fourths of the several States, or by Conventions in three-fourths thereof, as the one or the other Mode of Ratification may be proposed by the Congress; Provided that no Amendment which may be made prior to the Year One thousand eight hundred and eight shall in any Manner affect the first and fourth Clauses in the Ninth Section of the first Article; and that no State, without its Consent, shall be deprived of its equal Suffrage in the Senate.

ARTICLE VI

All Debts contracted and Engagements entered into, before the Adoption of this Constitution, shall be as valid against the United States under this Constitution, as under the Confederation.

This Constitution, and the Laws of the United States which shall be made in Pursuance thereof; and all Treaties made, or which shall be made, under the Authority of the United States, shall be the supreme Law of the Land; and the Judges in every State shall be bound thereby, any Thing in the Constitution or Laws of any State to the Contrary notwithstanding.

The Senators and Representatives before mentioned, and the Members of the several State Legislatures, and all executive and judicial Officers, both of the United States and of the several States, shall be bound by Oath or Affirmation to support this Constitution; but no religious Tests shall ever be required as a qualification to any Office or public Trust under the United States.

ARTICLE VII

The Ratification of the Conventions of nine States shall be sufficient for the Establishment of this Constitution between the States so ratifying the same.

Done in Convention by the Unanimous Consent of the States present the Seventeenth Day of September in the Year of our Lord one thousand seven hundred and Eighty seven, and of the Independence of the United States of America the Twelfth. In Witness whereof We have hereunto subscribed our Names.[6]

George Washington
President and deputy
from Virginia

New Hampshire
John Langdon
Nicholas Gilman

Massachusetts
Nathaniel Gorham
Rufus King

Connecticut
William Samuel
  Johnson
Roger Sherman

New York
Alexander Hamilton

New Jersey
William Livingston
David Brearley
William Paterson
Jonathan Dayton

Pennsylvania
Benjamin Franklin
Thomas Mifflin
Robert Morris
George Clymer
Thomas FitzSimmons
Jared Ingersoll
James Wilson
Gouverneur
  Morris

Delaware
George Read
Gunning Bedford, Jr.
John Dickinson
Richard Bassett
Jacob Broom

Maryland
James McHenry
Daniel of St. Thomas
  Jenifer

Daniel Carroll

Virginia
John Blair
James Madison, Jr.

North Carolina
William Blount
Richard Dobbs Spaight
Hugh Williamson

South Carolina
John Rutledge
Charles Cotesworth
  Pinckney
Charles Pinckney
Pierce Butler

Georgia
William Few
Abraham Baldwin

Articles in Addition to, and Amendment of, the Constitution of the United States of America, Proposed by Congress, and Ratified by the Legislatures of the Several States, Pursuant to the Fifth Article of the Original Constitution[7]

AMENDMENT I

Congress shall make no law respecting an establishment of religion, or prohibiting the free exercise thereof; or abridging the freedom of speech, or of the press; or the

---

[6]These are the full names of the signers, which in some cases are not the signatures on the document.

[7]This heading appears only in the joint resolution submitting the first ten amendments, which are collectively known as the Bill of Rights. They were ratified on December 15, 1791.

right of the people peaceably to assemble, and to petition the Government for a redress of grievances.

AMENDMENT II

A well regulated Militia, being necessary to the security of a free State, the right of the people to keep and bear Arms shall not be infringed.

AMENDMENT III

No Soldier shall, in time of peace, be quartered in any house, without the consent of the Owner, nor in time of war, but in a manner to be prescribed by law.

AMENDMENT IV

The right of the people to be secure in their persons, houses, papers, and effects, against unreasonable searches and seizures, shall not be violated, and no Warrants shall issue, but upon probable cause, supported by Oath or affirmation, and particularly describing the place to be searched, and the persons or things to be seized.

AMENDMENT V

No person shall be held to answer for a capital or otherwise infamous crime, unless on a presentment or indictment of a Grand Jury, except in cases arising in the land or naval forces, or in the Militia, when in actual service in time of War or public danger; nor shall any person be subject for the same offence to be twice put in jeopardy of life or limb; nor shall be compelled in any criminal case to be a witness against himself, nor be deprived of life, liberty, or property, without due process of law; nor shall private property be taken for public use, without just compensation.

AMENDMENT VI

In all criminal prosecutions, the accused shall enjoy the right to a speedy and public trial, by an impartial jury of the State and district wherein the crime shall have been committed, which district shall have been previously ascertained by law, and to be informed of the nature and cause of the accusation; to be confronted with the witnesses against him; to have compulsory process for obtaining witnesses in his favour, and to have the Assistance of Counsel for his defence.

AMENDMENT VII

In suits at common law, where the value in controversy shall exceed twenty dollars, the right of trial by jury shall be preserved, and no fact tried by a jury, shall be otherwise reexamined in any Court of the United States, than according to the rules of the common law.

AMENDMENT VIII

Excessive bail shall not be required, nor excessive fines imposed, nor cruel and unusual punishments inflicted.

AMENDMENT IX

The enumeration of the Constitution, of certain rights, shall not be construed to deny or disparage others retained by the people.

AMENDMENT X

The powers not delegated to the United States by the Constitution, nor prohibited by it to the States, are reserved to the States respectively, or to the people.

AMENDMENT XI [1795]

The Judicial power of the United States shall not be construed to extend to any suit in law or equity, commenced or prosecuted against one of the United States by Citizens of another State, or by Citizens or Subjects of any Foreign State.

AMENDMENT XII [1804]

The Electors shall meet in their respective States and vote by ballot for President and Vice-President, one of whom, at least, shall not be an inhabitant of the same State with themselves; they shall name in their ballots the person voted for as President, and in distinct ballots the person voted for as Vice-President, and they shall make distinct lists of all persons voted for as President, and of all persons voted for as Vice-President, and of the number of votes for each, which lists they shall sign and certify, and transmit sealed to the seat of the government of the United States, directed to the President of the Senate;—The President of the Senate shall, in the presence of the Senate and House of Representatives, open all the certificates and the votes shall then be counted;—The person having the greatest number of votes for President, shall be the President, if such number be a majority of the whole number of Electors appointed; and if no person have such majority, then from the persons having the highest numbers not exceeding three on the list of those voted for as President, the House of Representatives shall choose immediately, by ballot, the President. But in choosing the President, the votes shall be taken by states, the representation from each state having one vote; a quorum for this purpose shall consist of a member or members from two-thirds of the states, and a majority of all the states shall be necessary to a choice. And if the House of Representatives shall not choose a President whenever the right of choice shall devolve upon them, before the fourth day of March next following, then the Vice-President shall act as President, as in the case of the death or other constitutional disability of the President.—The person having the greatest number of votes as Vice-President, shall be the Vice-President, if such number be a majority of the whole number of Electors appointed, and if no person have a majority, then from the two highest numbers on the list, the Senate shall choose the Vice-President; a quorum for the purpose shall consist of two-thirds of the whole number of Senators, and majority of the whole number shall be necessary to a choice. But no person constitutionally ineligible to the office of President shall be eligible to that of Vice-President of the United States.

AMENDMENT XIII [1865]

Section 1

Neither slavery nor involuntary servitude, except as a punishment for crime whereof the party shall have been duly convicted, shall exist within the United States, or any place subject to their jurisdiction.

Section 2

Congress shall have power to enforce this article by appropriate legislation.

AMENDMENT XIV [1868]

Section 1

All persons born or naturalized in the United States, and subject to the jurisdiction thereof, are citizens of the United States and of the State wherein they reside. No State shall abridge the privileges or immunities of citizens of the United States; nor shall any State deprive any person of life, liberty, or property, without due process of law; nor deny to any person within its jurisdiction the equal protection of the laws.

Section 2

Representatives shall be apportioned among the several States according to their respective numbers, counting the whole number of persons in each State, excluding Indians not taxed. But when the right to vote at any election for the choice of electors for President and Vice-President of the United States, Representatives in Congress, the Executive and Judicial officers of a State, or the members of the Legislature thereof, is denied to any of the male inhabitants of such State, being twenty-one years of age, and citizens of the United States, or in any way abridged, except for participation in rebellion, or other crime, the basis of representation therein shall be reduced in the proportion which the number of such male citizens shall bear to the whole number of male citizens twenty-one years of age in such State.

Section 3

No person shall be a Senator or Representative in Congress, or elector of President and Vice-President, or hold any office, civil or military, under the United States, or under any State, who, having previously taken an oath, as a member of Congress, or as an officer of the United States, or as a member of any State legislature, or as an executive or judicial officer of any State, to support the Constitution of the

United States, shall have engaged in insurrection or rebellion against the same, or given aid or comfort to the enemies thereof. But Congress may by a vote of two-thirds of each House, remove such disability.

Section 4

The validity of the public debt of the United States, authorized by law, including debts incurred for payment of pensions and bounties for services in suppressing insurrection or rebellion, shall not be questioned. But neither the United States nor any State shall assume or pay any debts or obligation incurred in aid of insurrection or rebellion against the United States, or any claim for the loss or emancipation of any slave; but all such debts, obligations, and claims shall be held illegal and void.

Section 5

The Congress shall have the power to enforce, by appropriate legislation, the provisions of this article.

AMENDMENT XV [1870]

Section 1

The right of citizens of the United States to vote shall not be denied or abridged by the United States or by any State on account of race, color, or previous condition of servitude.

Section 2

The Congress shall have power to enforce this article by appropriate legislation.

AMENDMENT XVI [1913]

The Congress shall have power to lay and collect taxes on incomes, from whatever source derived, without apportionment among the several States, and without regard to any census or enumeration.

AMENDMENT XVII [1913]

The Senate of the United States shall be composed of two Senators from each State, elected by the people thereof, for six years; and each Senator shall have one vote. The electors in each State shall have the qualifications requisite for electors of the most numerous branch of the State legislatures.

When vacancies happen in the representation of any State in the Senate, the executive authority of such State shall issue writs of election to fill such vacancies: Provided, That the legislature of any State may empower the executive thereof to make temporary appointments until the people fill the vacancies by election as the legislature may direct.

This amendment shall not be so construed as to affect the election or term of any Senator chosen before it becomes valid as part of the Constitution.

Amendment XVIII [1919]

Section 1

After one year from the ratification of this article the manufacture, sale, or transportation of intoxicating liquors within, the importation thereof into, or the exportation thereof from the United States and all territory subject to the jurisdiction thereof for beverage purposes is hereby prohibited.

Section 2

The Congress and the several States shall have concurrent power to enforce this article by appropriate legislation.

Section 3

This article shall be inoperative unless it shall have been ratified as an amendment to the Constitution by the legislatures of the several States, as provided in the Constitution, within seven years from the date of the submission hereof to the States by the Congress.

Amendment XIX [1920]

The right of citizens of the United States to vote shall not be denied or abridged by the United States or by any State on account of sex.

Congress shall have power to enforce this article by appropriate legislation.

Amendment XX [1933]

Section 1

The terms of the President and Vice-President shall end at noon on the 20th day of January, and the terms of Senators and Representatives at noon on the 3d day of January, of the years in which such terms would have ended if this article had not been ratified; and the terms of their successors shall then begin.

Section 2

The Congress shall assemble at least once in every year, and such meeting shall begin at noon on the 3d day of January, unless they shall by law appoint a different day.

Section 3

If, at the time fixed for the beginning of the term of the President, the President elect shall have died, the Vice-President elect shall become President. If a President shall not have been chosen before the time fixed for the beginning of his term or if the President elect shall have failed to qualify, then the Vice-President elect shall act as President until a President shall have qualified; and the Congress may by law provide for the case wherein neither a President elect nor a Vice-President elect shall have qualified, declaring who shall then act as President, or the manner in which one who is to act shall be selected, and such person shall act accordingly until a President or Vice-President shall have qualified.

Section 4

The Congress may by law provide for the case of the death of any of the persons from whom the House of Representatives may choose a President whenever the right of choice shall have devolved upon them, and for the case of the death of any of the persons from whom the Senate may choose a Vice-President whenever the right of choice shall have devolved upon them.

Section 5

Sections 1 and 2 shall take effect on the 15th day of October following the ratification of this article.

Section 6

This article shall be inoperative unless it shall have been ratified as an amendment to the Constitution by the legislatures of three-fourths of the several States within seven years from the date of its submission.

AMENDMENT XXI [1933]

Section 1

The eighteenth article of amendment to the Constitution of the United States is hereby repealed.

Section 2

The transportation or importation into any State, Territory, or possession of the United States for delivery or use therein of intoxicating liquors, in violation of the laws thereof, is hereby prohibited.

Section 3

This article shall be inoperative unless it shall have been ratified as an amendment to the Constitution by conventions in the several States, as provided in the Constitution, within seven years from the date of the submission hereof to the States by the Congress.

AMENDMENT XXII [1951]

No person shall be elected to the office of the President more than twice, and no person who has held the office of President, or acted as President, for more than two years of a term to which some other person was elected President shall be elected to the office of the President more than once.

But this Article shall not apply to any person holding the office of President when this Article was proposed by the Congress, and shall not prevent any person who may be holding the office of President, or acting as President, during the term within which this Article becomes operative from holding the office of President or acting as President during the remainder of such term.

This article shall be inoperative unless it shall have been ratified as an amendment to the Constitution by the legislatures of three-fourths of the several states within seven years from the date of its submission to the states by the Congress.

AMENDMENT XXIII [1961]

Section 1

The District constituting the seat of Government of the United States shall appoint in such manner as the Congress may direct:

A number of electors of President and Vice-President equal to the whole number of Senators and Representatives in Congress to which the District would be entitled if it were a State, but in no event more than the least populous State; they shall be in addition to those appointed by the States, but they shall be considered, for the purposes of the election of President and Vice-President, to be electors appointed by a State; and they shall meet in the District and perform such duties as provided by the twelfth article of amendment.

Section 2

The Congress shall have power to enforce this article by appropriate legislation.

AMENDMENT XXIV [1964]

Section 1

The right of citizens of the United States to vote in any primary or other election for President or Vice President, for electors for President or Vice President, or for Senator or Representative in Congress, shall not be denied or abridged by the United States or any state by reason of failure to pay any poll tax or other tax.

Section 2

The Congress shall have the power to enforce this article by appropriate legislation.

AMENDMENT XXV [1967]

Section 1

In case of the removal of the President from office or of his death or resignation, the Vice President shall become President.

Section 2

Whenever there is a vacancy in the office of the Vice President, the President shall nominate a Vice President who shall take office upon confirmation by a majority vote of both Houses of Congress.

Section 3

Whenever the President transmits to the President Pro Tempore of the Senate and the Speaker of the House of Representatives his written declaration that he is unable to discharge the powers and duties of his office, and until he transmits to them a written declaration to the contrary, such powers and duties shall be discharged by the Vice President as Acting President.

Section 4

Whenever the Vice President and a majority of either the principal officers of the executive departments or of such other body as Congress may by law provide, transmit to the President Pro Tempore of the Senate and the Speaker of the House of Representatives their written declaration that the President is unable to discharge the powers and duties of his office, the Vice President shall immediately assume the powers and duties of the office as Acting President.

Thereafter, when the President transmits to the President Pro Tempore of the Senate and the Speaker of the House of Representatives his written declaration that no inability exists, he shall resume the powers and duties of his office unless the Vice President and a majority of either the principal officers of the executive departments or of such other body as Congress may by law provide, transmit within four days to the President Pro Tempore of the Senate and the Speaker of the House of Representatives their written declaration that the President is unable to discharge the powers and duties of his office. Thereupon Congress shall decide the issue, assembling within forty-eight hours for that purpose if not in session. If the Congress, within twenty-one days after receipt of the latter written declaration, or, if Congress is not in session, within twenty-one days after Congress is required to assemble, determines by two-thirds vote of both Houses that the President is unable to discharge the powers and duties of his office, the Vice President shall continue to discharge the same as Acting President; otherwise, the President shall resume the powers and duties of his office.

AMENDMENT XXVI [1971]

Section 1

The right of citizens of the United States, who are eighteen years of age or older, to vote shall not be denied or abridged by the United States or by any State on account of age.

Section 2

The Congress shall have the power to enforce this article by appropriate legislation.

AMENDMENT XXVII [1992]

No law varying the compensation for the service of Senators and Representatives shall take effect until an election of Representatives shall have intervened.

GLOSSARY

affirmative action A term that refers to programs designed to ensure that women, minorities, and other traditionally disadvantaged groups have full and equal opportunities in employment, education, and other areas of life.

age-cohort tendency The tendency for a significant break in the pattern of political socialization to occur among younger citizens, usually as the result of a major event or development that disrupts preexisting beliefs.

agency point of view The tendency of bureaucrats to place the interests of their agency ahead of other interests and ahead of the priorities sought by the president or Congress.

agenda setting The power of the media through news coverage to focus the public's attention and concern on particular events, problems, issues, personalities, and so on.

agents of socialization Those agents, such as the family and the media, that have significant impact on citizens' political socialization.

air wars A term that refers to the fact that modern campaigns are often a battle of opposing televised advertising campaigns.

alienation A feeling of personal powerlessness that includes the notion that government does not care about the opinions of people like oneself.

Anti-Federalists A term used to describe opponents of the Constitution during the debate over ratification.

apathy A feeling of personal noninterest or unconcern with politics.

appellate jurisdiction The authority of a given court to review cases that have already been tried in lower courts and are appealed to it by the losing party; such a court is called an appeals court or appellate court. (See also **original jurisdiction**.)

authoritarian government A form of government in which leaders, though they admit to no limits on their powers, are effectively limited by other centers of power in the society.

authority The recognized right of an individual or institution to exercise power. (See also **power**.)

autocracy A form of government in which absolute control rests with a single person.

balanced budget When the government's tax revenues for the year are roughly equal to its expenditures.

bill A proposed law (legislative act) within Congress or another legislature. (See also **law**.)

Bill of Rights The first ten amendments to the Constitution. They include such rights as freedom of speech and trial by jury.

bipolar (power structure) A power structure dominated by two powers only, as in the case of the United States and the Soviet Union during the cold war.

block grants Federal grants-in-aid that permit state and local officials to decide how the money will be spent within a general area, such as education or health. (See also **categorical grants**.)

brief A written statement by a party in a court case that details its argument.

budget deficit Situation when the government's expenditures exceed its tax and other revenues.

budget surplus Situation when the government's tax and other revenues exceed its expenditures.

bureaucracy A system of organization and control based on the principles of hierarchical authority, job specialization, and formalized rules. (See also **formalized rules; hierarchical authority; job specialization**.)

bureaucratic accountability The degree to which bureaucrats are held accountable for the power they exercise.

bureaucratic rule The tendency of large-scale organizations to develop into the bureaucratic form, with the effect that administrators make key policy decisions.

cabinet A group consisting of the heads of the (cabinet) executive departments, who are appointed by the president, subject to confirmation by the Senate. The cabinet was once the main advisory body to the president but no longer plays this role. (See also **cabinet departments.**)

cabinet (executive) departments The major administrative organizations within the federal executive bureaucracy, each of which is headed by a secretary (cabinet officer) and has responsibility for a major function of the federal government, such as defense, agriculture, or justice. (See also **cabinet; independent agencies.**)

candidate-centered politics Election campaigns and other political processes in which candidates, not political parties, have most of the initiative and influence. (See also **party-centered politics.**)

capital-gains tax Tax that individuals pay on money gained from the sale of a capital asset, such as property or stocks.

capitalism An economic system based on the idea that government should interfere with economic transactions as little as possible. Free enterprise and self-reliance are the collective and individual principles that underpin capitalism.

categorical grants Federal grants-in-aid to states and localities that can be used only for designated projects. (See also **block grants.**)

checks and balances The elaborate system of divided spheres of authority provided by the U.S. Constitution as a means of controlling the power of government. The separation of powers among the branches of the national government, federalism, and the different methods of selecting national officers are all part of this system.

citizens' (noneconomic) groups Organized interests formed by individuals drawn together by opportunities to promote a cause in which they believe but that does not provide them significant individual economic benefits. (See also **economic groups; interest group.**)

civic duty The belief of an individual that civic and political participation is a responsibility of citizenship.

civil law Laws governing relations between private parties where no criminal act is alleged and where the parties are making conflicting claims or are seeking to establish a legal relationship.

civil liberties The fundamental individual rights of a free society, such as freedom of speech and the right to a jury trial, which in the United States are protected by the Bill of Rights.

civil rights (equal rights) The right of every person to equal protection under the laws and equal access to society's opportunities and public facilities.

civil service system See **merit system.**

clear-and-present-danger test A test devised by the Supreme Court in 1919 to define the limits of free speech in the context of national security. According to the test, government cannot abridge political expression unless it presents a clear and present danger to the nation's security.

clientele groups Special-interest groups that benefit directly from the activities of a particular bureaucratic agency and therefore are strong advocates of the agency.

cloture A parliamentary maneuver that, if a three-fifths majority votes for it, limits Senate debate to thirty hours and has the effect of defeating a filibuster. (See also **filibuster.**)

cold war The lengthy period after World War II when the United States and the Soviet Union were not engaged in actual combat (a "hot war") but were nonetheless locked in a state of deep-seated hostility.

collective (public) goods Benefits that are offered by groups (usually citizens' groups) as an incentive for membership but that are nondivisible (e.g., a clean environment) and therefore are available to nonmembers as well as members of the particular group. (See also **free-rider problem; private goods.**)

commerce clause The clause of the Constitution (Article I, Section 8) that empowers the federal government to regulate commerce among the states and with other nations.

common-carrier role The media's function as an open channel through which political leaders can communicate with the public. (See also **public-representative role; signaling role; watchdog role.**)

communism An economic system in which government owns most or all major industries and also takes responsibility for overall management of the economy.

compliance The issue of whether a court's decisions will be respected and obeyed.

concurring opinion A separate opinion written by a Supreme Court justice who votes with the majority in the decision on a case but who disagrees with their reasoning. (See also **dissenting opinion; majority opinion; plurality opinion.**)

confederacy A governmental system in which sovereignty is vested entirely in subnational (state) governments. (See also **federalism; unitary system.**)

conference committees Temporary committees formed to bargain over the differences in the House and Senate versions of a bill. A committee's members are usually appointed from the House and Senate standing committees that originally worked on the bill.

conservatives Those who believe government does too many things that should be left to firms and individuals but look to government to uphold traditional social values. (See also **liberals; libertarians; populists.**)

constituency The individuals who live within the geographical area represented by an elected official. More narrowly, the body of citizens eligible to vote for a particular representative.

constitution The fundamental law that defines how a government will legitimately operate.

constitutional democracy A government that is democratic in its provisions for majority influence through elections and constitutional in its provisions for minority rights and rule by law.

constitutionalism The idea that there are definable limits on the rightful power of a government over its citizens.

containment A doctrine, developed after World War II, based on the assumptions that the Soviet Union was an aggressor nation and that only a determined United States could block Soviet territorial ambitions.

cooperative federalism The situation in which the national, state, and local levels work together to solve problems.

criminal law Laws governing acts deemed illegal and punishable by government, such as robbery. Government is always a party to a criminal law case; the other party is the individual accused of breaking the law.

decision A vote of the Supreme Court in a particular case that indicates which party the justices side with and by how large a margin.

de facto discrimination Discrimination on the basis of race, sex, religion, ethnicity, and the like that results from social, economic, and cultural biases and conditions. (See also **de jure discrimination.**)

deficit spending Situation when the government spends more than it collects in taxes and other revenues.

de jure discrimination Discrimination on the basis of race, sex, religion, ethnicity, and the like that results from a law. (See also **de facto discrimination.**)

delegates Elected representatives whose obligation is to act in accordance with the expressed wishes of the people they represent. (See also **trustees.**)

demand-side economics A form of fiscal policy that emphasizes "demand" (consumer spending). Government can use increased spending or tax cuts to place more money in consumers' hands and thereby increase demand. (See also **fiscal policy; supply-side economics.**)

democracy A form of government in which the people govern, either directly or through elected representatives.

demographic representativeness The idea that the bureaucracy will be more responsive to the public if its employees at all levels are demographically representative of the population as a whole.

denials of power A constitutional means of limiting governmental action by listing those powers that government is expressly prohibited from using.

deregulation The rescinding of excessive government regulations for the purpose of improving economic efficiency.

détente A French word meaning "a relaxing" and used to refer to an era of improved relations between the United States and the Soviet Union that began in the early 1970s.

deterrence policy The idea that nuclear war can be discouraged if each side in a conflict has the capacity to destroy the other with nuclear weapons.

devolution The passing down of authority from the national government to states and localities.

direct primary See **primary election.**

dissenting opinion The opinion of a justice in a Supreme Court case that explains his or her reasons for disagreeing with the majority's decision. (See also **concurring opinion; majority opinion; plurality opinion.**)

diversity The principle that individual and group differences should be respected and are a source of national strength.

dual federalism A doctrine based on the idea that a precise separation of national power and state power is both possible and desirable.

due process clause (of the Fourteenth Amendment) The clause of the Constitution that has been used by the judiciary to apply the Bill of Rights to the actions of state governments.

economic depression A very severe and sustained economic downturn. Depressions are rare in the United States; the last one was in the 1930s.

economic globalization The increased interdependence of nations' economies. The change is a result of technological, transportation, and communication advances that have enabled firms to deploy their resources around the globe.

economic groups Interest groups that are organized primarily for economic reasons but that engage in political activity in order to seek favorable policies from government. (See also **citizens' groups; interest group.**)

economic recession A moderate but sustained downturn in the economy. Recessions are part of the economy's normal cycle of ups and downs.

economy A system of production and consumption of goods and services that are allocated through exchange among producers and consumers.

effective tax rate The actual percentage of a person's income that is spent to pay taxes.

efficiency An economic principle that holds that firms should fulfill as many of society's needs as possible while using as few of its resources as possible. The greater the output (production) for a given input (for example, an hour of labor), the more efficient the process.

elastic clause See **"necessary and proper" clause.**

Electoral College An unofficial term that refers to the electors who cast the states' electoral votes.

electoral votes The method of voting that is used to choose the U.S. president. Each state has the same number of electoral votes as it has members in Congress (House and Senate combined). By tradition, electoral voting is tied to a state's popular voting; thus, the presidential candidate with the most popular votes overall usually has also had the most electoral votes.

elitism The view that the United States essentially is run by a tiny elite (composed of wealthy or well-connected individuals) who control public policy through both direct and indirect means.

entitlement programs Any of a number of individual benefit programs, such as social security, that require government to provide a designated benefit to any person who meets the legally defined criteria for eligibility.

enumerated (expressed) powers The seventeen powers granted to the national government under Article I, Section 8 of the Constitution. These powers include taxation and the regulation of commerce as well as the authority to provide for the national defense.

equality The notion that all individuals are equal in their moral worth, in their treatment under the law, and in their political voice.

equality of opportunity The idea that all individuals should be given an equal chance to succeed on their own.

equality of result The objective of policies intended to reduce or eliminate the effects of discrimination so that members of traditionally disadvantaged groups will have the same benefits of society as do members of advantaged groups.

equal-protection clause A clause of the Fourteenth Amendment that forbids any state to deny equal protection of the laws to any individual within its jurisdiction.

equal rights See **civil rights.**

equity (in relation to economic policy) The situation in which the outcome of an economic transaction is fair to each party. An outcome usually can be considered fair if each party enters into a transaction freely and is not unknowingly at a disadvantage.

establishment clause The First Amendment provision that government may not favor one religion over another or favor religion over no religion, and that prohibits Congress from passing laws respecting the establishment of religion.

exclusionary rule The legal principle that government is prohibited from using in trials evidence that was obtained by unconstitutional means (for example, illegal search and seizure).

executive departments See **cabinet departments.**

executive leadership system An approach to managing the bureaucracy that is based on presidential leadership and presidential management tools, such as the president's annual budget proposal. (See also **merit system; patronage system.**)

expressed powers See **enumerated powers.**

externalities Burdens that society incurs when firms fail to pay the full cost of resources used in production. An example

of an externality is the pollution that results when corporations dump industrial wastes into lakes and rivers.

facts (of a court case) The relevant circumstances of a legal dispute or offense as determined by a trial court. The facts of a case are crucial because they help determine which law or laws are applicable in the case.

federalism A governmental system in which authority is divided between two sovereign levels of government: national and regional. (See also **confederacy; unitary system.**)

Federalists A term used to describe supporters of the Constitution during the debate over ratification.

filibuster A procedural tactic in the U.S. Senate whereby a minority of legislators prevent a bill from coming to a vote by holding the floor and talking until the majority gives in and the bill is withdrawn from consideration. (See also **cloture.**)

fiscal federalism A term that refers to the expenditure of federal funds on programs run in part through states and localities.

fiscal policy A tool of economic management by which government attempts to maintain a stable economy through its taxing and spending decisions. (See also **demand-side economics; monetary policy; supply-side economics.**)

formalized rules A basic principle of bureaucracy that refers to the standardized procedures and established regulations by which a bureaucracy conducts its operations. (See also **bureaucracy.**)

freedom of expression Americans' freedom to communicate their views, the foundation of which is the First Amendment rights of freedom of conscience, speech, press, assembly, and petition.

free-exercise clause A First Amendment provision that prohibits the government from interfering with the practice of religion or prohibiting the free exercise of religion.

free-rider problem The situation in which the benefits offered by a group to its members are also available to nonmembers. The incentive to join the group and to promote its cause is reduced because nonmembers (free riders) receive the benefits (e.g., a cleaner environment) without having to pay any of the group's costs. (See also **collective goods.**)

free-trade position The view that the long-term economic interests of all countries are advanced when tariffs and other trade barriers are kept to a minimum. (See also **protectionism.**)

gender gap The tendency of women and men to differ in their political attitudes and voting preferences.

gerrymandering The process by which the party in power draws election district boundaries in a way that advantages its candidates.

government corporations Bodies, such as the U.S. Postal Service and Amtrak, that are similar to private corporations in that they charge for their services, but different in that they receive federal funding to help defray expenses. Their directors are appointed by the president with Senate approval.

graduated personal income tax A tax on personal income in which the tax rate increases as income increases; in other words, the tax rate is higher for higher income levels.

grants-in-aid Federal cash payments to states and localities for programs they administer.

grants of power The method of limiting the U.S. government by confining its scope of authority to those powers expressly granted in the Constitution.

grassroots lobbying A form of lobbying designed to persuade officials that a group's policy position has strong constituent support.

grassroots party A political party organized at the level of the voters and dependent on their support for its strength.

Great Compromise The agreement of the constitutional convention to create a two-chamber Congress with the House apportioned by population and the Senate apportioned equally by state.

hard money Campaign funds given directly to candidates to spend as they choose.

hierarchical authority A basic principle of bureaucracy that refers to the chain of command within an organization whereby officials and units have control over those below them. (See also **bureaucracy.**)

hired guns The professional consultants who run campaigns for high office.

honeymoon period The president's first months in office, a time when Congress, the press, and the public are more inclined than usual to support presidential initiatives.

ideology A consistent pattern of opinion on particular issues that stems from a core belief or set of beliefs.

imminent-lawless-action test A legal test that says government cannot lawfully suppress advocacy that promotes lawless action unless such advocacy is aimed at producing, and is likely to produce, imminent lawless action.

implied powers The federal government's constitutional authority (through the "necessary and proper" clause) to take action that is not expressly authorized by the Constitution but that supports actions that are so authorized. (See also **"necessary and proper" clause.**)

inalienable (natural) rights Those rights that persons theoretically possessed in the state of nature, prior to the formation of governments. These rights, including those of life, liberty, and property, are considered inherent and as such are inalienable. Because government is established by people, government has the responsibility to preserve these rights.

independent agencies Bureaucratic agencies that are similar to cabinet departments but usually have a narrower area of responsibility. Each such agency is headed by a presidential appointee who is not a cabinet member. An example is the National Aeronautics and Space Administration. (See also **cabinet departments.**)

individual goods See **private goods.**

individualism The idea that people should take the initiative, be self-sufficient, and accumulate the material advantages necessary for their well-being.

inflation A general increase in the average level of prices of goods and services.

in-kind benefit A government benefit that is a cash equivalent, such as food stamps or rent vouchers. This form of benefit ensures that recipients will use public assistance in a specified way.

inside lobbying Direct communication between organized interests and policymakers, which is based on the assumed value of close ("inside") contacts with policymakers.

interest group A set of individuals who are organized to promote a shared political interest. (See also **citizens' groups; economic groups.**)

interest-group liberalism The tendency of public officials to support the policy demands of self-interested groups (as opposed to judging policy demands according to whether they serve a larger conception of "the public interest").

intermediate-scrutiny test A test applied by courts to laws that attempt a gender classification. In effect, the test eliminates gender as a legal classification unless it serves an important objective and is substantially related to the objective's achievement.

internationalist A person who holds the view that the country should involve itself deeply in world affairs. (See also **isolationist.**)

iron triangle A small and informal but relatively stable group of well-positioned legislators, executives, and lobbyists who seek to promote policies beneficial to a particular interest. (See also **issue network.**)

isolationist A person who holds the view that the country should deliberately avoid a large role in world affairs and, instead, concentrate on domestic concerns. (See also **internationalist.**)

issue network An informal network of public officials and lobbyists who have a common interest and expertise in a given area and who are brought together temporarily by a proposed policy in that area. (See also **iron triangle.**)

job specialization A basic principle of bureaucracy that holds that the responsibilities of each job position should be explicitly defined and that a precise division of labor within the organization should be maintained. (See also **bureaucracy.**)

judicial activism The doctrine that the courts should develop new legal principles when judges see a compelling need, even if this action places them in conflict with the policy decisions of elected officials. (See also **judicial restraint.**)

judicial conference A closed meeting of the justices of the U.S. Supreme Court to discuss and vote on the cases before them; the justices are not supposed to discuss conference proceedings with outsiders.

judicial restraint The doctrine that the judiciary should be highly respectful of precedent and should defer to the judgment of legislatures. The doctrine claims that the job of judges is to work within the confines of laws set down by tradition and by lawmaking majorities. (See also **judicial activism.**)

judicial review The power of courts to decide whether a governmental institution has acted within its constitutional powers and, if not, to declare its action null and void.

jurisdiction (of a congressional committee) The policy area in which a particular congressional committee is authorized to act.

jurisdiction (of a court) A given court's authority to hear cases of a particular kind. Jurisdiction may be original or appellate.

laissez-faire doctrine A classic economic philosophy that holds that owners of businesses should be allowed to make their own production and distribution decisions without government regulation or control.

large-state plan See **Virginia Plan.**

law (as enacted by Congress) A legislative proposal, or bill, that is passed by both the House and the Senate and is either signed or not vetoed by the president. (See also **bill.**)

lawmaking function The authority (of a legislature) to make the laws necessary to carry out the government's powers. (See also **oversight function; representation function.**)

laws (of a court case) The constitutional provisions, legislative statutes, or judicial precedents that apply to a court case.

legitimacy (of judicial power) The issue of the proper limits of judicial authority in a political system based in part on the principle of majority rule.

libel The publication of material that falsely damages a person's reputation.

liberals Those who believe government should do more to solve the nation's problems but reject the notion that government should favor a particular set of social values. (See also **conservatives; libertarians; populists.**)

libertarians Those who believe government tries to do too many things that should be left to firms and individuals and who oppose government as an instrument of traditional values. (See also **conservatives; liberals; populists.**)

liberty The principle that individuals should be free to act and think as they choose, provided they do not infringe unreasonably on the rights and freedoms of others.

limited government A government that is subject to strict limits on its lawful uses of powers and hence on its ability to deprive people of their liberty.

lobbying The process by which interest-group members or lobbyists attempt to influence public policy through contacts with public officials.

logrolling The trading of votes between legislators so that each gets what he or she most wants.

majoritarianism The idea that the majority prevails not only in elections but also in determining policy.

majority opinion A Supreme Court opinion that results when a majority of the justices are in agreement on the legal basis of the decision. (See also **concurring opinion; dissenting opinion; plurality opinion.**)

material incentive An economic or other tangible benefit that is used to attract group members.

means test The requirement that applicants for public assistance demonstrate that they are poor in order to be eligible for the assistance. (See also **public assistance.**)

merit (civil service) system An approach to managing the bureaucracy whereby people are appointed to government positions on the basis of either competitive examinations or special qualifications, such as professional training. (See also **executive leadership system; patronage system.**)

military-industrial complex The three components (the military establishment, the industries that manufacture weapons, and the members of Congress from states and districts that depend heavily on the arms industry) that mutually benefit from a high level of defense spending.

momentum (in campaigns) A strong showing by a candidate in early presidential nominating contests, which leads to a buildup of public support for the candidate.

monetary policy A tool of economic management, available to government, based on manipulation of the amount of money in circulation. (See also **fiscal policy.**)

money chase A term used to describe the fact that U.S. campaigns are very expensive and that candidates must spend a great amount of time raising funds in order to compete successfully.

multilateralism The situation in which nations act together in response to problems and crises.

multinational corporations Business firms with major operations in more than one country.

multiparty system A system in which three or more political parties have the capacity to gain control of government separately or in coalition.

national debt The total cumulative amount that the U.S. government owes to creditors.

natural rights See **inalienable rights.**

"necessary and proper" clause (elastic clause) The authority granted Congress in Article I, Section 8 of the Constitution "to make all laws which shall be necessary and proper" for the implementation of its enumerated powers. (See also **implied powers.**)

negative government The philosophical belief that government governs best by staying out of people's lives, thereby giving individuals as much freedom as possible to determine their own pursuits. (See also **positive government.**)

neutral competence The administrative objective of a merit-based bureaucracy. Such a bureaucracy should be "competent" in the sense that its employees are hired and retained on the basis of their expertise and "neutral" in the sense that it operates by objective standards rather than partisan ones.

New Jersey (small-state) Plan A constitutional proposal for a strengthened Congress but one in which each state would have a single vote, thus granting a small state the same legislative power as a larger state.

news The news media's version of reality, usually with an emphasis on timely, dramatic, and compelling events and developments.

news media See **press.**

nomination The designation of a particular individual to run as a political party's candidate (its "nominee") in the general election.

noneconomic groups See **citizens' groups.**

North-South Compromise The agreement over economic and slavery issues that enabled northern and southern states to settle differences that threatened to defeat the effort to draft a new constitution.

objective journalism A model of news reporting that is based on the communication of "facts" rather than opinions and that is "fair" in that it presents all sides of partisan debate. (See also **partisan press.**)

oligarchy A form of government in which control rests with a few persons.

open party caucuses Meetings at which a party's candidates for nomination are voted on and that are open to all the party's rank-and-file voters who want to attend.

open-seat election An election in which there is no incumbent in the race.

opinion (of a court) A court's written explanation of its decision, which serves to inform others of the legal basis for the decision. Supreme Court opinions are expected to guide the decisions of other courts. (See also **concurring opinion;**

dissenting opinion; majority opinion; plurality opinion.)

original jurisdiction The authority of a given court to be the first court to hear a case. (See also **appellate jurisdiction.**)

outside lobbying A form of lobbying in which an interest group seeks to use public pressure as a means of influencing officials.

oversight function A supervisory activity of Congress that centers on its constitutional responsibility to see that the executive carries out the laws faithfully and spends appropriations properly. (See also **lawmaking function; representation function.**)

packaging (of a candidate) A term of modern campaigning that refers to the process of recasting a candidate's record into an appealing image.

partisan press Newspapers and other communication media that openly support a political party and whose news in significant part follows the party line. (See also **objective journalism.**)

party caucus A group that consists of a party's members in the House or Senate and that serves to elect the party's leadership, set policy goals, and determine party strategy.

party-centered politics Election campaigns and other political processes in which political parties, not individual candidates, hold most of the initiative and influence. (See also **candidate-centered politics.**)

party coalition The groups and interests that support a political party.

party competition A process in which conflict over society's goals is transformed by political parties into electoral competition in which the winner gains the power to govern.

party discipline The willingness of a party's House or Senate members to act as a cohesive group and thus exert collective control over legislative action.

party identification The personal sense of loyalty that an individual may feel toward a particular political party. (See also **party realignment.**)

party leaders Members of the House and Senate who are chosen by the Democratic or Republican caucus in each chamber to represent the party's interests in that chamber and who give some central direction to the chamber's deliberations.

party organizations The party organizational units at national, state, and local levels; their influence has decreased over time because of many factors. (See also **candidate-centered politics; party-centered politics; primary election.**)

party realignment An election or set of elections in which the electorate responds strongly to an extraordinarily powerful issue that has disrupted the established political order. A realignment has a lasting impact on public policy, popular support for the parties, and the composition of the party coalitions. (See also **party identification.**)

patronage system An approach to managing the bureaucracy whereby people are appointed to important government positions as a reward for political services they have rendered and because of their partisan loyalty. (See also **executive leadership system; merit system; spoils system.**)

pluralism A theory of American politics that holds that society's interests are substantially represented through the activities of groups.

plurality opinion A court opinion that results when a majority of justices agree on a decision in a case but do not agree on the legal basis for the decision. In this instance, the legal position held by most of the justices on the winning side is called a plurality opinion. (See also **concurring opinion; dissenting opinion; majority opinion.**)

policy implementation The primary function of the bureaucracy; it refers to the process of carrying out the authoritative decisions of Congress, the president, and the courts.

political action committee (PAC) The organization through which an interest group raises and distributes funds for election purposes. By law, the funds must be raised through voluntary contributions.

political culture The characteristic and deep-seated beliefs of a particular people.

political movements See **social movements.**

political participation Involvement in activities intended to influence public policy and leadership, such as voting, joining political parties and interest groups, writing to elected officials, demonstrating for political causes, and giving money to political candidates.

political party An ongoing coalition of interests joined together to try to get their candidates for public office elected under a common label.

political socialization The learning process by which people acquire their political opinions, beliefs, and values.

political system The various components of American government. The parts are separate, but they connect with each other, affecting how each performs.

politics The process through which society makes its governing decisions.

population In a public opinion poll, the people (for example, the citizens of a nation) whose opinions are being estimated through interviews with a sample of these people.

populists Those who believe government should do more to solve the nation's problems and who look to it to uphold traditional values. (See also **conservatives; liberals; libertarians.**)

pork-barrel projects Legislative acts whose tangible benefits are targeted at a particular legislator's constituency.

positive government The philosophical belief that government intervention is necessary in order to enhance personal liberty when individuals are buffeted by economic and social forces beyond their control. (See also **negative government.**)

poverty line As defined by the federal government, the annual cost of a thrifty food budget for an urban family of four, multiplied by three to allow also for the cost of housing, clothes, and other necessities. Families below the poverty line are considered poor and are eligible for certain forms of public assistance.

power The ability of persons or institutions to control policy. (See also **authority.**)

precedent A judicial decision in a given case that serves as a rule of thumb for settling subsequent cases of a similar nature; courts are generally expected to follow precedent.

preemptive war doctrine The idea, espoused by President George W. Bush, that the United States could attack a potentially threatening nation even if the threat had not yet reached a serious and immediate level.

presidential approval ratings A measure of the degree to which the public approves or disapproves of the president's performance in office.

presidential commissions Organizations within the bureaucracy that are headed by commissioners appointed by the president. An example is the Commission on Civil Rights.

press (news media) Those print and broadcast organizations that are in the news-reporting business.

primary election (direct primary) A form of election in which voters choose a party's nominees for public office. In most states, eligibility to vote in a primary election is limited to voters who designated themselves as party members when they registered to vote. A primary is direct when it results directly in the choice of a nominee; it is indirect (as in the case of presidential primaries) when it results in the selection of delegates who then choose the nominee.

prior restraint Government prohibition of speech or publication before the fact, which is presumed by the courts to be unconstitutional unless the justification for it is overwhelming.

private (individual) goods Benefits that a group (most often an economic group) can grant directly and exclusively to the individual members of the group. (See also **collective goods.**)

probability sample A sample for a poll in which each individual in the population has a known probability of being selected randomly for inclusion in the sample. (See also **public opinion poll.**)

procedural due process The constitutional requirement that government follow proper legal procedures before a person can be legitimately punished for an alleged offense.

procedural law Laws governing the legal process that define proper courses of action by government or private parties.

proportional representation A form of representation in which seats in the legislature are allocated proportionally according to each political party's share of the popular vote. This system enables smaller parties to compete successfully for seats. (See also **single-member districts.**)

prospective voting A form of electoral judgment in which voters choose the candidate whose policy promises most closely match their own preferences. (See also **retrospective voting.**)

protectionism The view that the immediate interests of domestic producers have a higher priority (through, for example, protective tariffs) than free trade between nations. (See also **free-trade position.**)

public assistance A term that refers to social welfare programs funded through general tax revenues and available only to the financially needy. Eligibility for such a program is established by a means test. (See also **means test; social insurance.**)

public goods See **collective goods.**

public opinion The politically relevant opinions held by ordinary citizens that they express openly.

public opinion poll A device for measuring public opinion whereby a relatively small number of individuals (the sample) is interviewed for the purpose of estimating the opinions of a whole community (the population). (See also **probability sample.**)

public policy A decision of government to pursue a course of action designed to produce an intended outcome.

public policy process The political interactions that lead to the emergence and resolution of public policy issues.

public-representative role A role whereby the media attempt to act as the public's representatives. (See also **common-carrier role; signaling role; watchdog role.**)

purposive incentive An incentive to group participation based on the cause (purpose) that the group seeks to promote.

realignment See **party realignment.**

reapportionment The reallocation of House seats among states after each census as a result of population changes.

reasonable-basis test A test applied by courts to laws that treat individuals unequally. Such a law may be deemed constitutional if its purpose is held to be "reasonably" related to a legitimate government interest.

redistricting The process of altering election districts in order to make them as nearly equal in population as possible. Redistricting takes place every ten years, after each population census.

registration The practice of placing citizens' names on an official list of voters before they are eligible to exercise their right to vote.

regulation Government restrictions on the economic practices of private firms.

regulatory agencies Administrative units, such as the Federal Communications Commission and the Environmental Protection Agency, that have responsibility for the monitoring and regulation of ongoing economic activities.

representation function The responsibility of a legislature to represent various interests in society. (See also **lawmaking function; oversight function.**)

representative democracy A system in which the people participate in the decision-making process of government not directly but indirectly, through the election of officials to represent their interests.

republic Historically, the form of government in which representative officials met to decide on policy issues. These representatives were expected to serve the public interest but were not subject to the people's immediate control. Today, the term *republic* is used interchangeably with *democracy.*

reserved powers The powers granted to the states under the Tenth Amendment to the Constitution.

retrospective voting A form of electoral judgment in which voters support the incumbent candidate or party when its policies are judged to have succeeded and oppose the candidate or party when its policies are judged to have failed. (See also **prospective voting.**)

rider An amendment to a bill that deals with an issue unrelated to the content of the bill. Riders are permitted in the Senate but not in the House.

sample In a public opinion poll, the relatively small number of individuals interviewed for the purpose of estimating the opinions of an entire population. (See also **public opinion poll.**)

sampling error A measure of the accuracy of a public opinion poll. It is mainly a function of sample size and is usually expressed in percentage terms. (See also **probability sample.**)

selective incorporation The absorption of certain provisions of the Bill of Rights (for example, freedom of speech) into the Fourteenth Amendment so that these rights are protected from infringement by the states.

self-government The principle that the people are the ultimate source and proper beneficiary of governing authority; in practice, a government based on majority rule.

senatorial courtesy The tradition that a U.S. senator from the state in which a federal judicial vacancy has arisen should have a say in the president's nomination of the new judge if the senator is of the same party as the president.

seniority A member of Congress's consecutive years of service on a particular committee.

separated institutions sharing power The principle that, as a way to limit government, its powers should be divided among separate branches, each of which also shares in the power of the others as a means of checking and balancing them. The result is that no one branch can exercise power decisively without the support or acquiescence of the other branches.

separation of powers The division of the powers of government among separate institutions or branches.

service relationship The situation in which party organizations assist candidates for office but have no power to require them to accept or campaign on the party's main policy positions.

service strategy Use of personal staff by members of Congress to perform services for constituents in order to gain their support in future elections.

signaling (signaler) role The accepted responsibility of the media to alert the public to important developments as soon as possible after they happen or are discovered. (See also **common-carrier role; public-representative role; watchdog role.**)

single-issue politics The situation in which separate groups are organized around nearly every conceivable policy issue and press their demands and influence to the utmost.

single-member districts The form of representation in which only the candidate who gets the most votes in a district wins office. (See also **proportional representation.**)

slander Spoken words that falsely damage a person's reputation.

small-state plan See **New Jersey Plan.**

social capital The sum of face-to-face interactions among citizens in a society.

social contract A voluntary agreement by individuals to form a government, which is then obligated to act within the confines of that agreement.

social insurance Social welfare programs based on the "insurance" concept, so that individuals must pay into the program in order to be eligible to receive funds from it. An example is social security for retired people. (See also **public assistance.**)

socialism An economic system in which government owns and controls many of the major industries.

social (political) movements Active and sustained efforts to achieve social and political change by groups of people who feel that government has not been properly responsive to their concerns.

soft money Campaign contributions that are not subject to legal limits and are given to parties rather than directly to candidates.

solicitor general The high-ranking Justice Department official who serves as the government's lawyer in Supreme Court cases.

sovereignty The ultimate authority to govern within a certain geographical area.

split ticket The pattern of voting in which the individual voter in a given election casts a ballot for one or more candidates of each major party.

spoils system The practice of granting public office to individuals in return for

political favors they have rendered. (See also **patronage system.**)

standing committees Permanent congressional committees with responsibility for a particular area of public policy. An example is the Senate Foreign Relations Committee.

stewardship theory A theory that argues for a strong, assertive presidential role, with presidential authority limited only at points specifically prohibited by law. (See also **Whig theory.**)

strict-scrutiny test A test applied by courts to laws that attempt a racial or ethnic classification. In effect, the strict scrutiny test eliminates race or ethnicity as legal classification when it places minority group members at a disadvantage. (See also **suspect classifications.**)

suffrage The right to vote.

sunset law A law containing a provision that fixes a date on which a program will end unless the program's life is extended by Congress.

supply-side economics A form of fiscal policy that emphasizes "supply" (production). An example of supply-side economics would be a tax cut for business. (See also **demand-side economics; fiscal policy.**)

supremacy clause Article VI of the Constitution, which makes national law supreme over state law when the national government is acting within its constitutional limits.

suspect classifications Legal classifications, such as race and national origin, that have invidious discrimination as their purpose and are therefore unconstitutional. (See also **strict-scrutiny test.**)

symbolic speech Action (for example, the waving or burning of a flag) for the purpose of expressing a political opinion.

totalitarian government A form of government in which the leaders claim complete dominance of all individuals and institutions.

transfer payment A government benefit that is given directly to an individual, as in the case of social security payments to a retiree.

trustees Elected representatives whose obligation is to act in accordance with their own conscience as to what policies are in the best interests of the public. (See also **delegates.**)

two-party system A system in which only two political parties have a real chance of acquiring control of the government.

tyranny of the majority The potential of a majority to monopolize power for its own gain and to the detriment of minority rights and interests.

unilateralism The situation in which one nation takes action against another state or states.

unipolar (power structure) A power structure dominated by a single powerful actor, as in the case of the United States after the collapse of the Soviet Union.

unitary system A governmental system in which the national government alone has sovereign (ultimate) authority. (See also **confederacy; federalism.**)

unit rule The rule that grants all of a state's electoral votes to the candidate who receives the most popular votes in the state.

unity The principle that Americans are one people and form an indivisible union.

veto The president's rejection of a bill, thereby keeping it from becoming law unless Congress overrides the veto.

Virginia (large-state) Plan A constitutional proposal for a strong Congress with two

chambers, both of which would be based on numerical representation, thus granting more power to the larger states.

voter turnout The proportion of persons of voting age who actually vote in a given election.

watchdog role The accepted responsibility of the media to protect the public from deceitful, careless, incompetent, and corrupt officials by standing ready to expose any official who violates accepted legal, ethical, or performance standards. (See also **common-carrier role; public-representative role; signaling role.**)

Whig theory A theory that prevailed in the nineteenth century and held that the presidency was a limited or restrained office whose occupant was confined to expressly granted constitutional authority. (See also **stewardship theory.**)

whistle-blowing An internal check on the bureaucracy whereby individual bureaucrats report instances of mismanagement that they have observed.

writ of certiorari Permission granted by a higher court to allow a losing party in a legal case to bring the case before it for a ruling; when such a writ is requested of the U.S. Supreme Court, four of the Court's nine justices must agree to accept the case before it is granted certiorari.

NOTES

CHAPTER 1

[1]Alexis de Tocqueville, *Democracy in America (1835–1840)*, ed. J. P. Mayer and A. P. Kerr (Garden City, N.Y.: Doubleday/Anchor, 1969), 640.

[2]See John Harmon McElroy, *American Beliefs: What Keeps a Big Country and a Diverse People United* (Chicago: I. R. Dee, 1999); but see also Michael B. Katz and Mark J. Stern, *One Nation Divisible: What America Was and What It's Becoming* (New York: Russell Sage Foundation, 2006).

[3]Clinton Rossiter, *Conservatism in America* (New York: Vintage, 1962), 67; see also Robert A. Ferguson, *Reading the Early Republic* (Cambridge, Mass.: Harvard University Press, 2004).

[4]Tocqueville, *Democracy in America*, 310.

[5]James Bryce, *The American Commonwealth*, vol. 2 (New York: Macmillan, 1960), 247–54. First published in 1900.

[6]See Gabriel Almond and Sidney Verba, *The Civic Culture* (Boston: Little, Brown, 1965); Richard Merelman, *Making Something of Ourselves: On Culture and Politics in the United States* (Berkeley: University of California Press, 1984); but see also John Kenneth White, *The Values Divide* (Washington, D.C.: CQ Press, 2002).

[7]Paul Gagnon, "Why Study History?" *Atlantic Monthly*, November 1988, 47.

[8]Ralph Barton Perry, *Puritanism and Democracy* (New York: Vanguard, 1944), 124–25; see also Peter D. Salins, *Assimilation, American Style* (New York: Basic Books, 1996).

[9]Louis Hartz, *The Liberal Tradition in America* (New York: Harcourt, Brace, 1953), 12; see also Jeffrey Stout, *Democracy and Tradition* (Princeton, N.J.: Princeton University Press, 2004).

[10]James Bryce, *The American Commonwealth*, vol. 2 (Indianapolis, Ind.: Liberty Fund, 1995), 1419.

[11]The Pew Research Center for the People and the Press's Global Attitudes Survey, 2002.

[12]See Douglas Muzzio and Richard Behn, "Thinking About Welfare," *The Public Perspective*, February/March 1995, 35–38.

[13]See Seymour Martin Lipset, *American Exceptionalism: A Double-Edged Sword* (New York: Norton, 1996); Claude Levi-Strauss, *Structural Anthropology* (Chicago: University of Chicago Press, 1983); Clifford Geertz, *Myth, Symbol, and Culture* (New York: Norton, 1974).

[14]U.S. Census Bureau, 2006.

[15]Quoted in Ralph Volney Harlow, *The Growth of the United States*, vol. 2 (New York: Henry Holt, 1943), 497.

[16]Survey of American Political Culture, James Davison Hunter and Carol Bowman, directors, University of Virginia, 1996; Debra L. DeLaet, *U.S. Immigration Policy in an Age of Rights* (Westport, Conn.: Praeger Publishers, 2000).

[17]Harold D. Lasswell, *Politics: Who Gets What, When, How* (New York: McGraw-Hill, 1938).

[18]See Charles H. McIlwain, *Constitutionalism: Ancient and Modern* (Ithaca, N.Y.: Cornell University Press, 1983).

[19]Alan S. Rosenbaum, ed., *Constitutionalism: The Philosophical Dimension* (Westport, Conn.: Greenwood, 1988), 4; see also Russell Hardin, *Liberalism, Constitutionalism, and Democracy* (New York: Oxford University Press, 1999).

[20]Tocqueville, *Democracy in America*, ch. 6.

[21]Harold D. Lasswell and Abraham Kaplan, *Power and Society* (New Haven, Conn.: Yale University Press, 1950), 75–77.

[22]Benjamin I. Page and Robert Shapiro, "Effects of Public Opinion on Policy," *American Political Science Review* 77 (March 1983): 178; see also Lawrence R. Jacobs and Robert Shapiro, *Politicians Don't Pander* (Chicago: University of Chicago Press, 2000).

[23]See Robert Dahl, *On Democracy* (New Haven, Conn.: Yale University Press, 2000).

[24]C. Wright Mills, *The Power Elite* (New York: Oxford University Press, 1965).

[25]G. William Domhoff, *Who Rules America? Power and Politics*, 4th ed. (New York: McGraw-Hill, 2002).

[26]See, for example, Dahl, *On Democracy*.

[27]See H. H. Gerth and C. Wright Mills, eds., *From Max Weber: Essays in Sociology* (New York: Oxford University Press, 1958).

[28]Roberto Michels, *Political Parties* (New York: Collier Books, 1962). First published in 1911.

[29]David Easton, *The Political System* (New York: Knopf, 1965), 97.

[30]E. E. Schattschneider, *Two Hundred Million Americans in Search of a Government* (New York: Holt, Rinehart & Winston, 1969), 42.

CHAPTER 2

[1]Quoted in Charles S. Hyneman, "Republican Government in America," in George J. Graham Jr. and Scarlett G. Graham, eds., *Founding Principles of American Government*, rev. ed. (Chatham, N. J.: Chatham House, 1984), 19.

[2]See Russell Hardin, *Liberalism, Constitutionalism, and Democracy* (New York: Oxford University Press, 1999); A. John Simmons, *The Lockean Theory of Rights* (Princeton, N. J.: Princeton University Press, 1994).

[3]George Bancroft, *History of the Formation of the Constitution of the United States of America*, 3d ed., vol. 1 (New York: D. Appleton, 1883), 166.

[4]Quoted in "The Constitution and Slavery," Digital History Website, December 1, 2003.

[5]Gaillard Hunt, ed., *The Writings of James Madison* (New York: Putnam, 1904), 274; see also Garret Ward Sheldon, *The Political Philosophy of James Madison* (Baltimore: Johns Hopkins University Press, 2000).

[6]*Federalist* No. 47.

[7]See *Federalist* Nos. 47 and 48.

[8]Richard Neustadt, *Presidential Power* (New York: Macmillan, 1986), 33.

[9]Henry J. Abraham, *The Judicial Process*, 6th ed. (New York: Oxford University Press, 1993), 320–22.

[10]*Marbury v. Madison*, 1 Cranch 137 (1803).

[11]Martin Diamond, *The Founding of the Democratic Republic* (Itasca, Ill.: Peacock, 1981), 62–71.

[12]*Federalist* No. 10.

[13]Leslie F. Goldstein, "Judicial Review and Democratic Theory: Guardian Democracy vs. Representative Democracy," *Western Political Quarterly* 40 (1987): 391–412.

[14]Benjamin Ginsberg, *The Consequences of Consent* (New York: Random House, 1982), 22.

[15]Robert Dahl, *Pluralist Democracy in the United States* (Chicago: Rand McNally, 1967), 92.

[16]This interpretation is taken from Walter Lippmann, *Public Opinion* (New York: Free Press, 1965), 178–79; for a general discussion of the uncertain meaning of the Constitution, see Lawrence H. Tribe and Michael C. Dorf, *On Reading the Constitution* (Cambridge, Mass.: Harvard University Press, 1991).

[17]Michael McGeer, *A Fierce Discontent: The Rise and Fall of the Progressive Movement in America, 1870–1920.* (New York: Free Press, 2005).

[18]Charles S. Beard, *An Economic Interpretation of the Constitution* (New York, Macmillan, 1941). First published in 1913.

[19]See Randall G. Holcombe, *From Liberty to Democracy* (Ann Arbor: University of Michigan Press, 2002).

Chapter 3

[1]Woodrow Wilson, *Constitutional Government in the United States* (New York: Columbia University Press, 1908), 173.

[2]*Gonzales, Attorney General, et al. v. Oregon, et al.*, No. 04-623 (2006).

[3]See Samuel Beer, *To Make a Nation: The Rediscovery of American Federalism* (Cambridge, Mass.: The Belknap Press of Harvard University, 1993).

[4]*Federalist* No. 2; for the Anti-Federalist view, see Saul Cornell, *The Other Founders* (Chapel Hill: University of North Carolina Press, 1999).

[5]*McCulloch v. Maryland*, 4 Wheaton 316 (1819).

[6]*Gibbons v. Ogden*, 22 Wheaton 1 (1824).

[7]Oliver Wendell Holmes Jr., *Collected Legal Papers* (New York: Harcourt, Brace, 1920), 295-96.

[8]See John C. Calhoun, *The Works of John C. Calhoun* (New York: Russell & Russell, 1968).

[9]*Dred Scott v. Sanford*, 19 Howard 393 (1857).

[10]*U.S. v. Cruikshank*, 92 U.S. 452 (1876).

[11]*Slaughter-House Cases*, 16 Wallace 36 (1873); *Civil Rights Cases*, 109 U.S. 3 (1883).

[12]*Plessy v. Ferguson*, 163 U.S. 537 (1896).

[13]*Santa Clara County v. Southern Pacific Railroad Co.*, 118 U.S. 394 (1886).

[14]*U.S. v. E. C. Knight Co.*, 156 U.S. 1 (1895).

[15]*Hammer v. Dagenhart*, 247 U.S. 251 (1918).

[16]*Lochner v. New York*, 198 U.S. 25 (1905).

[17]Alfred H. Kelly, Winifred A. Harbison, and Herman Belz, *The American Constitution*, 7th ed. (New York: Norton, 1991), 529.

[18]James E. Anderson, *The Emergence of the Modern Regulatory State* (Washington, D.C.: Public Affairs Press, 1962), 2–3.

[19]*Schechter Poultry Co. v. United States*, 295 U.S. 495 (1935).

[20]*NLRB v. Jones and Laughlin Steel*, 301 U.S. 1 (1937).

[21]*American Power and Light v. Securities and Exchange Commission*, 329 U.S. 90 (1946); see also Richard A. Maidment, *The Judicial Response to the New Deal: The U.S. Supreme Court and Economic Regulation* (New York: Manchester University Press, 1992).

[22]Louis Fisher, *American Constitutional Law*, 6th ed. (Durham, N. C.: Carolina Academic Press, 2005), 390.

[23]See Maidment, *Judicial Response to the New Deal*.

[24]*Brown v. Board of Education*, 347 U.S. 483 (1954).

[25]*Miranda v. Arizona*, 384 U.S. 436 (1966).

[26]See Thomas Anton, *American Federalism and Public Policy* (Philadelphia: Temple University Press, 1989).

[27]Morton Grodzins, *The American System: A New View of Government in the United States* (Chicago: Rand McNally, 1966).

[28]Rosella Levaggi, *Fiscal Federalism and Grants-in-Aid* (Brookfield, Vt.: Avebury, 1991).

[29]Timothy J. Conlan, *From New Federalism to Devolution* (Washington, D.C.: Brookings Institution, 1998).

[30]*Garcia v. San Antonio Authority*, 469 U.S. 528 (1985).

[31]See Tinsley E. Yarbrough, *The Rehnquist Court and the Constitution* (New York: Oxford University Press, 2000).

[32]*United States v: Lopez*, 514 U.S. 549 (1995).

[33]*Printz v. United States*, 521 U.S. 98 (1997).

[34]*Kimel v. Florida Board of Regents*, 528 U.S. 62 (2000).

[35]*Board of Trustees of the University of Alabama v. Garrett*, 531 U.S. 356 (2002).

[36]*Nevada Department of Human Resources v. Hibbs*, No. 01-1368 (2003).

[37]See Pran Chopra, *Supreme Court Versus the Constitution: A Challenge to Federalism* (Thousand Oaks, Calif.: Sage Publications, 2006).
[38]See Robert F. Nagel, *The Implosion of American Federalism* (New York: Oxford University Press, 2001).
[39]*Gonzales v. Raich,* No. 03-1454 (2005).
[40]Andrew W. Dobelstein, *Politics, Economics, and Public Welfare* (Englewood Cliffs, N. J.: Prentice-Hall, 1980), 5.
[41]Lloyd A. Free and Hadley Cantril, *The Political Beliefs of Americans* (New York: Simon & Schuster, 1968), 21; see also William Lunch, *The Nationalization of American Politics* (Berkeley: University of California Press, 1987).
[42]Survey for the Times Mirror Center for the People and the Press by Princeton Survey Research Associates, July 12–27, 1994; see also Tommy Thompson, *Power to the People* (New York: HarperCollins, 1996).
[43]Daniel J. Boorstin, *The Americans: The Democratic Experience* (New York: Vintage Books, 1974).

CHAPTER 4

[1]Julian P. Boyd, ed., *The Papers of Thomas Jefferson*, vol. 12 (Princeton, N. J.: Princeton University Press, 1955), 440.
[2]*Anderson v. Creighton*, 483 U.S. 635 (1987).
[3]*Bose Corp. v. Consumers Union of the United States*, 466 U.S. 485 (1984).
[4]*Schenck v. United States*, 249 U.S. 47 (1919).
[5]*Dennis v. United States*, 341 U.S. 494 (1951).
[6]See, for example, *Yates v. United States*, 354 U.S. 298 (1957); *Noto v. United States*, 367 U.S. 290 (1961); *Scales v. United States*, 367 U.S. 203 (1961).
[7]*United States v. Carolene Products Co.*, 304 U.S. 144 (1938).
[8]*United States v. O'Brien*, 391 U.S. 367 (1968).
[9]*Texas v. Johnson*, 109 S. Ct. 2544 (1989).
[10]*United States v. Eichman*, 496 U.S. 310 (1990).
[11]*New York Times Co. v. United States*, 403 U.S. 713 (1971).
[12]*Nebraska Press Assn. v. Stuart*, 427 U.S. 539 (1976).
[13]*Barron v. Baltimore*, 7 Peters 243 (1833).
[14]*Gitlow v. New York*, 268 U.S. 652 (1925).
[15]*Fiske v. Kansas*, 274 U.S. 30 (1927); *Near v. Minnesota*, 283 U.S. 697 (1931); *Hamilton v. Regents, U. of California*, 293 U.S. 245 (1934); *DeJonge v. Oregon*, 299 U.S. 253 (1937).
[16]*Near v. Minnesota*, 283 U.S. 697 (1931).
[17]*Brandenburg v. Ohio*, 395 U.S. 444 (1969).
[18]*R.A.V. v. St. Paul*, No. 90-7675 (1992).
[19]*Wisconsin v. Mitchell*, No. 92-515 (1993).
[20]*National Socialist Party v. Skokie*, 432 U.S. 43 (1977).
[21]*Forsyth County v. Nationalist Movement*, No. 91-538 (1992).
[22]*Milkovich v. Lorain Journal*, 497 U.S. 1 (1990); see also *Masson v. The New Yorker*, No. 89-1799 (1991).
[23]*New York Times Co. v. Sullivan*, 376 U.S. 254 (1964).
[24]*Roth v. United States*, 354 U.S. 476 (1957).
[25]*Miller v. California*, 413 U.S. 15 (1973).
[26]*Barnes v. Glen Theatre*, No. 90-26 (1991).
[27]*Stanley v. Georgia*, 394 U.S. 557 (1969).
[28]*Osborne v. Ohio*, 495 U.S. 103 (1990).
[29]*Ashcroft v. Free Speech Coalition*, No. 00-795 (2002).
[30]*Denver Area Consortium v. Federal Communications Commission*, No. 95-124 (1996); *Reno v. American Civil Liberties Union*, No. 96-511 (1997); *Ashcroft v. ACLU*, No. 03-0218 (2004).
[31]*Engel v. Vitale*, 370 U.S. 421 (1962).

[32]*Abington School District v. Schempp,* 374 U.S. 203 (1963).

[33]*Wallace v. Jaffree,* 472 U.S. 38 (1985).

[34]*Santa Fe Independent School District v. Does,* No. 99-62 (2000).

[35]*Van Orden v. Perry,* No. 03-1500 (2005).

[36]*McCreary County v. American Civil Liberties Union,* No. 03-1693 (2005).

[37]*Board of Regents v. Allen,* 392 U.S. 236 (1968).

[38]*Lemon v. Kurtzman,* 403 U.S. 602 (1971).

[39]Ibid.

[40]*Mitchell v. Helms,* No. 98-1648 (2000).

[41]*Zelman v. Simmons-Harris,* No. 00-1751 (2002).

[42]*Locke v. Davey,* No. 02-1315 (2004).

[43]*Wisconsin v. Yoder,* 406 U.S. 295 (1972); see also *Church of the Lukumi Babalu Aye v. City of Hialeah,* No. 91-948 (1993).

[44]*Edwards v. Aguillard,* 487 U.S. 578 (1987).

[45]*Griswold v. Connecticut,* 381 U.S. 479 (1965).

[46]*Roe v. Wade,* 401 U.S. 113 (1973).

[47]*Webster v. Reproductive Health Services,* 492 U.S. 490 (1989); see also *Rust v. Sullivan,* No. 89-1391 (1991).

[48]*Planned Parenthood v. Casey,* No. 91-744 (1992).

[49]*Ayotte v. Planned Parenthood of Northern New England,* No. 04-1144 (2006).

[50]*Stenberg v. Carhart,* No. 99-830 (2000).

[51]*Bowers v. Hardwick,* 478 U.S. 186 (1986).

[52]*Lawrence v. Texas,* 539 U.S. 558 (2003).

[53]*Vacco v. Quill,* 117 S.C. 36 (1996); *Washington v. Glucksberg,* No. 96-110 (1997).

[54]*Gregg v. United States,* No. 00-939 (2001).

[55]*Powell v. Alabama,* 287 U.S. 45 (1932).

[56]*Palko v. Connecticut,* 302 U.S. 319 (1937).

[57]*Mapp v. Ohio,* 367 U.S. 643 (1961).

[58]*Gideon v. Wainwright,* 372 U.S. 335 (1963).

[59]*Malloy v. Hogan,* 378 U.S. 1 (1964).

[60]*Miranda v. Arizona,* 384 U.S. 436 (1966); see also *Escobedo v. Illinois,* 378 U.S. 478 (1964).

[61]*Pointer v. Texas,* 380 U.S. 400 (1965).

[62]*Klopfer v. North Carolina,* 386 U.S. 213 (1967).

[63]*Duncan v. Louisiana,* 391 U.S. 145 (1968).

[64]*Benton v. Maryland,* 395 U.S. 784 (1969).

[65]*Dickerson v. United States,* No. 99-5525 (2000).

[66]*Missouri v. Siebert,* 542 U.S. 600 (2004).

[67]*Michigan v. Sitz,* No. 88-1897 (1990).

[68]*Indianapolis v. Edmund,* No. 99-1030 (2001).

[69]*Kyllo v. United States,* No. 99-8508 (2001).

[70]*Ferguson v. Charleston,* No. 99-936 (2001).

[71]*Board of Education of Independent School District No. 92 of Pottawatomie County v. Earls,* No. 01-332 (2002).

[72]*Weeks v. United States,* 232 U.S. 383 (1914).

[73]*Nix v. Williams,* 467 U.S. 431 (1984); see also *United States v. Leon,* 468 U.S. 897 (1984).

[74]*Whren v. United States,* 517 U.S. 806 (1996).

[75]*Hudson v. Michigan,* No. 04-1360 (2006).

[76]*Townsend v. Sain,* 372 U.S. 293 (1963).

[77]*Keeney v. Tamaya-Reyes,* No. 90-1859 (1992); see also *Coleman v. Thompson,* No. 89-7662 (1991).

[78]*Brecht v. Abrahamson,* No. 91-7358 (1993); see also *McCleskey v. Zant,* No. 89-7024 (1991).

[79]*Felker v. Turpin,* No. 95-8836 (1996); but see *Stewart v. Martinez-Villareal,* No. 97-300 (1998).

[80]*Williams v. Taylor,* No. 99-6615 (2000).

[81]*Miller-El v. Cockrell,* No. 01-7662 (2003); *Wiggins v. Smith,* No. 02-311 (2003).

[82]Kurt Heine, "Philadelphia Cops Beat One of Their Own," *Syracuse Herald-American*, January 15, 1995, A13.

[83]*Wilson v. Seiter*, No. 89-7376 (1991).

[84]*Harmelin v. Michigan*, No. 89-7272 (1991).

[85]*Lockyer v. Andrade*, No. 01-1127 (2003); see also *Ewing v. California*, No. 01-6978 (2003).

[86]*Atkins v. Virginia*, No. 01-8452 (2002); see also Roger Hood, *The Death Penalty: A Worldwide Perspective* (New York: Oxford University Press, 2003).

[87]*Roper v. Simmons*, No. 03-633 (2005).

[88]*Hill v. McDonough*, No. 05-8794 (2006).

[89]*Ring v. Arizona*, No. 01-488 (2002).

[90]*Blakely v. Washington*, No. 02-1632 (2004).

[91]*Korematsu v. United States*, 323 U.S. 214 (1944).

[92]Case cited in Charles Lane, "In Terror War, 2nd Track for Suspects," *Washington Post*, December 1, 2001, A1.

[93]Bill Mears, "Supreme Court Rejects Appeal over Secret 9/11 Detentions," *Washington Post*, January 12, 2004. Internet copy.

[94]*Rasul v. Bush*, No. 03-334 (2004); see also *al-Odah v. United States*, No. 03-343 (2004).

[95]*Hamdi v. Rumsfeld*, No. 03-6696 (2004); see also *Rumsfeld v. Padilla*, No. 03-1027 (2004).

[96]*Hamdan v. Rumsfeld*, No. 05-184 (2006).

[97]Quoted in "Feds Get Wide Wiretap Authority," CBSNEWS.com, November 18, 2002.

[98]Lane, "In Terror War, 2nd Track for Suspects," A1.

[99]See Alpheus T. Mason, *The Supreme Court: Palladium of Freedom* (Ann Arbor: University of Michigan Press, 1962); see also Henry J. Abraham, *Freedom and the Court* (New York: Oxford University Press, 1998).

CHAPTER 5

[1]Speech of Martin Luther King Jr. in Washington, D.C., August 2, 1963.

[2]*Washington Post* wire story, May 14, 1991.

[3]"African-American Health," amednews.com (online newspaper of the American Medical Association), May 1, 2000.

[4]Robert Nisbet, "Public Opinion Versus Popular Opinion," *Public Interest* 41 (1975): 171.

[5]See, for example, John R. Howard, *The Shifting Wind* (Albany: State University of New York Press, 1999).

[6]The classic analysis of this system of legalized segregation is C. Vann Woodward, *The Strange Career of Jim Crow*, 3d rev. ed. (New York: Oxford University Press, 1974).

[7]*Plessy v. Ferguson*, 163 U.S. 537 (1896).

[8]Ada Lois Sipuel Fisher, Danney Gable, and Robert Henry, *A Matter of Black and White: The Autobiography of Ada Lois Sipuel Fisher* (Norman: University of Oklahoma Press, 1996).

[9]*Brown v. Board of Education of Topeka*, 347 U.S. 483 (1954).

[10]See Sar Levitan, William Johnson, and Robert Taggert, *Still a Dream* (Cambridge, Mass.: Harvard University Press, 1975).

[11]Data from National Office of Drug Control Policy, 1997.

[12]See Keith Reeves, *Voting Hopes or Fears?* (New York: Oxford University Press, 1997); Tali Mendelberg, *The Race Card* (Princeton, N. J.: Princeton University Press, 2001).

[13]See Glenna Matthews, *The Rise of Public Women* (New York: Oxford University Press, 1994).

[14]*Tinker v. Colwell*, 193 U.S. 473 (1904).

[15]See Jane Mansbridge, *Why We Lost the ERA* (Chicago: University of Chicago Press, 1986).

[16]*Pennsylvania State Police v. Suder*, No. 03-95 (2004).

[17]*Burlington Northern and Santa Fe Railroad Company v. White*, No. 05-259 (2006).

[18]Linda Witt, Karen M. Paget, and Glenna Matthews, *Running as a Woman* (New York: Free Press, 1994).

[19]Timothy Bledsoe and Mary Herring, "Victims of Circumstance: Women in Pursuit of Political Office," *American Political Science Review* 84 (1990): 213–24.

[20]U.S. Department of Education, 2006.

[21]See Sara M. Evans and Barbara Nelson, *Wage Justice* (Chicago: University of Chicago Press, 1989).

[22]See Joane Nagel, *American Indian Ethnic Renewal* (New York: Oxford University Press, 1996).

[23]James G. Gimpel, "Latinos and the 2002 Election: Republicans Do Well When Latinos Stay Home," Center for Immigration Studies, University of Maryland, January 2003, web download; see also Louis DeSipio, *Counting on the Latino Vote* (Charlottesville: University of Virginia Press, 1996).

[24]James Truslow Adams, *The March of Democracy*, vol. 4 (New York: Scribner's, 1933), 284–85.

[25]*Lau v. Nichols*, 414 U.S. 563 (1974).

[26]See Gordon Chang, ed., *Asian Americans and Politics* (Stanford, Calif.: Stanford University Press, 2001).

[27]*Kimel v. Florida Board of Regents*, No. 98-791 (2000).

[28]*Board of Trustees of the University of Alabama v. Garrett*, No. 99-1240 (2002); *Tennessee v. Lane*, No. 02-1667 (2004).

[29]*Romer v. Evans*, 517 U.S. 620 (1996).

[30]*Lawrence v. Texas*, 539 U.S. 558 (2003).

[31]*Boy Scouts of America v. Dale*, No. 99-699 (2000).

[32]*Rumsfeld v. Forum for Academic and Institutional Rights*, No. 04-1152 (2006).

[33]Kaiser Family Foundation poll, 2001.

[34]*Craig v. Boren*, 429 U.S. 190 (1976).

[35]*Rostker v. Goldberg*, 453 U.S. 57 (1980).

[36]*United States v. Virginia*, No. 94-1941 (1996).

[37]U.S. Conference of Mayors Report, 1998; see also Survey by Federal Financial Institutions Examination Council, 1998.

[38]V. O. Key Jr., *Southern Politics* (New York: Knopf, 1949), 495.

[39]*Smith v. Allwright*, 321 U.S. 649 (1944).

[40]*Muller v. Johnson*, No. 94-631 (1995); *Bush v. Verg*, No. 94-805 (1996); *Shaw v. Hunt*, No. 94-923 (1996).

[41]*Easley v. Cromartie*, No. 99-1864 (2001).

[42]*League of United Latin American Voters v. Perry*, No. 05-204 (2006).

[43]Terry H. Anderson, *The Pursuit of Happiness: A History of Affirmative Action* (New York: Oxford University Press, 2005).

[44]*University of California Regents v. Bakke*, 438 U.S. 265 (1978).

[45]*Steelworkers v. Weber*, 443 U.S. 193 (1979); *Fullilove v. Klutznick*, 448 U.S. 448 (1980).

[46]*Local No. 28, Sheet Metal Workers v. Equal Employment Opportunity Commission*, 478 U.S. 421 (1986); see also *Local No. 93, International Association of Firefighters v. Cleveland*, 478 U.S. 501 (1986); *Firefighters v. Stotts*, 459 U.S. 969 (1984); *Wygant v. Jackson*, 476 U.S. 238 (1986).

[47]*Adarand v. Pena*, No. 94-310 (1995).

[48]*Gratz v. Bollinger*, No. 02-516 (2003).

[49]*Grutter v. Bollinger*, No. 02-241 (2003).

[50]See J. Edward Kellough, *Understanding Affirmative Action: Politics, Discrimination, and the Search for Justice* (Washington, D.C.: Georgetown University Press, 2006).

[51]*Swann v. Charlotte-Mecklenburg County Board of Education*, 402 U.S. 1 (1971).

[52]Christopher Jencks and Meredith Phillips, eds., *The Black-White Test Score Gap* (Washington, D.C.: Brookings Institution Press, 1998).

[53]*Milliken v. Bradley*, 418 U.S. 717 (1974).

[54]*Board of Education of Oklahoma City v. Dowell*, 498 U.S. 237 (1991).

[55]Sam Dillon, "Schools' Efforts Hinge on Justices' Ruling in Cases on Race and School Assignments," *New York Times*, June 24, 2006, A11.

[56]Gunnar Myrdal, *An American Dilemma: The Negro Problem and Modern Democracy* (New York: Harper, 1944).

CHAPTER 6

[1]V. O. Key Jr., *Public Opinion and American Democracy* (New York: Knopf, 1961), 8.

[2]See Brandice Canes-Wrone, *Who Leads Whom? Presidents, Policy, and the Public* (Chicago: University of Chicago Press, 2005).

[3]See Jeremy Bentham, *An Introduction to the Principles of Morals and Legislation* (Oxford, England: Clarendon Press, 1996; originally published in 1789).

[4]Jerry L. Yeric and John R. Todd, *Public Opinion*, 3d ed. (Itasca, Ill.: Peacock, 1996), 3.

[5]Elisabeth Noelle-Neumann, *The Spiral of Silence*, 2d ed. (Chicago: University of Chicago Press, 1993), ch. 1.

[6]"Study Finds Widespread Misperceptions on Iraq Highly Related to Support for War," web release of the Program on International Policy Attitudes, School of Public Affairs, University of Maryland, October 2, 2003.

[7]Times-Mirror Center for the People and the Press survey, 1994.

[8]Survey of students of the eight Ivy League schools by Luntz & Weber Research and Strategic Services, for the University of Pennsylvania's Ivy League Study, November 13–December 1, 1992.

[9]See R. Michael Alvarez and John Brehm, *Hard Choices, Easy Answers* (Princeton, N. J.: Princeton University Press, 2002); see also Samuel L. Popkin, *The Reasoning Voter* (Chicago: University of Chicago Press, 1991).

[10]See Herbert Asher, *Polling and the Public*, 6th ed. (Washington, D.C.: Congressional Quarterly Press, 2004).

[11]Example from Adam Clymer, "Wrong Number: The Unbearable Lightness of Public Opinion Polls," *New York Times*, July 22, 2001. Internet copy.

[12]M. Kent Jennings and Richard G. Niemi, *Generations and Politics* (Princeton, N. J.: Princeton University Press, 1981).

[13]See Orit Ichilov, *Political Socialization, Citizenship Education, and Democracy* (New York: Teachers College Press, 1990).

[14]Thomas E. Patterson, *Out of Order* (New York: Vintage, 1994), ch. 2.

[15]Noelle-Neumann, *Spiral of Silence*.

[16]Jon Western, *Selling Intervention and War: The Presidency, the Media, and the American Public* (Baltimore, Md.: Johns Hopkins University Press, 2005).

[17]See, however, Dietram A. Scheufele, Matthew C. Nisbet, and Dominique Brossard, "Pathways to Political Participation: Religion, Communication Contexts, and Mass Media," *International Journal of Public Opinion Research* 15 (Autumn 2003): 300–324.

[18]John L. Sullivan, James E. Pierson, and George E. Marcus, "Ideological Constraint in the Mass Public," *American Journal of Political Science* 22 (May 1978): 233–49.

[19]CNN/USA Today poll conducted by the Gallup Organization, 1997.

[20]Philip Converse, "The Nature of Belief Systems in Mass Publics," in David Apter, ed., *Ideology and Discontent* (New York: Free Press, 1965), 206.

[21]Susan A. MacManus, *Young v. Old: Generational Combat in the Twenty-first Century* (Boulder, Colo.: Westview Press, 1996).

[22]See Angus Campbell, Philip Converse, Warren Miller, and Donald Stokes, *The American Voter* (New York: Wiley, 1960), chs. 3 and 4.

[23]Martin P. Wattenberg, *The Decline of American Political Parties, 1952–1996* (Cambridge, Mass.: Harvard University Press, 1998).

[24]Donald Green, Bradley Palmquist, and Eric Schickler, *Partisan Hearts and Minds* (New Haven, Conn.: Yale University Press, 2002).

[25]See William Domhoff, *Who Rules America?* 4th ed. (New York: McGraw-Hill, 2001).

[26]Benjamin I. Page and Robert Y. Shapiro, "Effects of Public Opinion on Policy," *American Political Science Review* 77 (March 1983): 178; see also Richard Sobel, *The Impact of Public Opinion on U.S. Foreign Policy* (New York: Oxford University Press, 2001); James Stimson, *Tides of Consent: How Public Opinion Shapes American Politics* (New York: Cambridge University Press, 2004).

[27]Lawrence R. Jacobs and Robert Y. Shapiro, *Politicians Don't Pander* (Chicago: University of Chicago Press, 2000).

CHAPTER 7

[1]Walter Lippmann, *Public Opinion* (New York: Free Press, 1965), 36.

[2]Quoted in Ralph Volney Harlow, *The Growth of the United States* (New York: Henry Holt, 1943), 312.

[3]Example from Gus Tyler, "One Cheer for the Democrats," *New Leader,* November 3, 1986, 6.

[4]Turnout figures provided by Washington, D.C., embassies of the respective countries, 2000.

[5]Thomas E. Patterson, *The Vanishing Voter* (New York: Knopf, 2002), 134.

[6]Russell Dalton, "The Myth of the Disengaged American," web publication of the Comparative Study of Electoral Systems, October 2005, 2.

[7]Ivor Crewe, "Electoral Participation," in David Butler, Howard R. Penniman, and Austin Ranney, eds., *Democracy at the Polls* (Washington, D.C.: American Enterprise Institute, 1981), 251–53.

[8]Malcom Jewell and David Olson, *American State Politics and Elections* (Homewood, Ill.: Irwin Press, 1978), 50.

[9]A. Karnig and B. Walter, "Municipal Elections," in *Municipal Yearbook, 1977* (Washington, D.C.: International City Management Assn., 1977).

[10]Richard Boyd, "Decline of U.S. Voter Turnout," *American Politics Quarterly* 9 (April 1981): 142.

[11]G. Bingham Powell, "Voting Turnout in Thirty Democracies," in Richard Rose, ed., *Electoral Participation: A Comparative Analysis* (Beverly Hills, Calif.: Sage, 1980), 6.

[12]See Joseph Nye, David King, and Philip Zelikow, *Why People Don't Trust Government* (Cambridge, Mass.: Harvard University Press, 1997).

[13]John M. Strate, Charles J. Parrish, Charles D. Elder, and Coit Ford III, "Life Span Civic Development and Voting Participation," *American Political Science Review* 83 (June 1989): 443–65.

[14]See M. Margaret Conway, *Political Participation in the United States*, 3d ed. (Washington, D.C.: Congressional Quarterly Press, 2000), 23–25; Sidney Verba, Kay Schlozman, and Henry Brady, *Voice and Equality* (Cambridge, Mass.: Harvard University Press, 1995); Jan Leighley, *Strength in Numbers* (Princeton, N. J.: Princeton University Press, 2001).

[15]Vanishing Voter Survey, 2000; but see Jeffrey Stonecash, *Class and Party in American Politics* (Boulder, Colo.: Westview Press, 2000).

[16]W. Russell Neuman, *The Paradox of Mass Politics* (Cambridge, Mass.: Harvard University Press, 1986), 176.

[17]Samuel H. Barnes et al., eds., *Political Action* (Beverly Hills, Calif.: Sage, 1979), 541–42.

[18]Theda Skocpol, *Diminished Democracy: From Membership to Management in American Civic Life* (Norman: University of Oklahoma Press, 2003).

[19]Russell J. Dalton, *Citizen Politics*, 4th ed. (Washington, D.C.: CQ Press, 2005).

[20]Robert Putnam, *Bowling Alone* (New York: Simon & Schuster, 2000); but see Cliff Zukin et al., *A New Engagement: Political Participation, Civic Life, and the Changing American Citizen* (New York: Oxford University Press, 2006).

[21]Pew Research Center for the People and the Press, "Cable and Internet Loom Large in Fragmented Political News Universe," January 11, 2004, 1; web release.

[22]See Bruce Bimber and Richard Davis, *Campaigning Online* (New York: Oxford University Press, 2003); Bruce Bimber, *Information and American Democracy* (New York: Cambridge University Press, 2003); Joe Trippi, *The Revolution Will Not Be Televised* (New York: HarperCollins, 2004).

[23]See Benjamin Ginsberg, *The Consequences of Consent* (New York: Random House, 1982), ch. 2.

[24]See Laura R. Woliver, *From Outrage to Action* (Urbana: University of Illinois Press, 1993).

[25]ABC News/Washington Post poll, March 23, 2003.

[26]Dalton, *Citizen Politics*, 38.

[27]Gallup poll, January 2003.

[28]William Watts and Lloyd A. Free, eds., *The State of the Nation* (New York: University Books, Potomac Associates, 1967), 97.

[29]Robert E. Lane, "Market Justice, Political Justice," *American Political Science Review* 80 (1986): 383; see also Jennifer Nedelsky, *Private Property and the Limits of American Constitutionalism* (New York: Oxford University Press, 1990).

[30]Sidney Verba and Norman Nie, *Participation in America* (New York: Harper & Row, 1972), 131.

[31]See Verba and Nie, *Participation in America*, 332; V. O. Key Jr., *Southern Politics* (New York: Vintage Books, 1949), 527; Lawrence Jacobs and Robert Shapiro, *Politicians Don't Pander* (Chicago: University of Chicago Press, 2000).

CHAPTER 8

[1]E. E. Schattschneider, *Party Government* (New York: Rinehart, 1942), 1.

[2]See John Aldrich, *Why Parties? The Origin and Transformation of Political Parties in America* (Chicago: University of Chicago Press, 1995); L. Sandy Maisel, *Parties and Elections in America*, 4th ed. (Latham, Md.: Rowman and Littlefield, 2004), 27.

[3]E. E. Schattschneider, *The Semisovereign People: A Realist's View of Democracy in America* (New York: Holt, Rinehart & Winston, 1961), 140.

[4]Thomas E. Patterson, *The Vanishing Voter* (New York: Knopf, 2002), ch. 2.

[5]See Richard P. McCormick, *The Second American Party System: Party Formation in the Jacksonian Era* (Chapel Hill: University of North Carolina Press, 1966).

[6]Alexis de Tocqueville, *Democracy in America (1835–1840)*, ed. J. P. Mayer and A. P. Kerr (Garden City, N.Y.: Doubleday/Anchor, 1969), 60.

[7]Aldrich, *Why Parties?* 151.

[8]See Kristi Andersen, *The Creation of a Democratic Majority, 1928–1936* (Chicago: University of Chicago Press, 1979).

[9]See Kevin Phillips, *The Emerging Republican Majority* (New Rochelle, N.Y.: Arlington House, 1969).

[10]See Harold W. Stanley, "Southern Partisan Changes: Dealignment, Realignment or Both?" *Journal of Politics* 50 (1988): 64–88; Earl Black and Merle Black, *Politics and Society in the South* (Cambridge, Mass.: Harvard University Press, 1987); Robert H. Swansbrough and David M. Brodsky, eds., *The South's New Politics: Realignment and Dealignment* (Columbia: University of South Carolina Press, 1988); Dewey L. Grantham, *The Life and Death of the Solid South* (Lexington: University of Kentucky Press, 1988).

[11]Pew Research Center for People & the Press Poll, January 2007.

[12]William H. Flanigan and Nancy Zingale, *Political Behavior of the American Electorate*, 9th ed. (Washington, D.C.: Congressional Quarterly Press, 1998), 58–63.

[13]See Lewis L. Gould, *Grand Old Party* (New York: Random House, 2003); but see also Jacob S. Hacker and Paul Pierson, *Off-Center: The Republican Revolution and the Erosion of American Democracy* (New Haven, Conn.: Yale University Press, 2006).

[14]See John B. Judis and Ruy Teixeira, *The Emerging Democratic Majority* (New York: Scribner, 2002).

[15]CNN exit polls, November 2004.

[16]Clinton Rossiter, *Parties and Politics in America* (Ithaca, N.Y.: Cornell University Press, 1960), 11.

[17]Nancy Gibbs and Michael Duffy, "Fall of the House of Newt," *Time*, November 16, 1998, 47.

[18]John F. Bibby, *Politics, Parties, and Elections in America*, 5th ed. (Belmont, Calif.: Wadsworth, 2002), 275–83.

[19]John Green, Mark Rozell, and William Clyde Wilcox, eds., *The Christian Right in American Politics* (Washington, D.C.: Georgetown University Press, 2003).

[20]Micah L. Sifrey, *Spoiling for a Fight: Third-Party Politics in America* (New York: Routledge, 2003).

[21]Daniel A. Mazmanian, *Third Parties in Presidential Elections* (Washington, D.C.: Brookings Institution, 1984), 143–44.

[22]See Lawrence Goodwyn, *The Populist Movement* (New York: Oxford University Press, 1978).

[23]Anthony King, *Running Scared* (New York: Free Press, 1997).

[24]See Alan Ehrenhalt, *The United States of Ambition* (New York: Times Books, 1991).

[25]See Paul S. Herrnson and John C. Green, eds., *Responsible Partisanship* (Lawrence: University Press of Kansas, 2003).

[26]See Sarah McCally Morehouse, "Money Versus Party Effort," *American Journal of Political Science* 34 (1990): 706–24.

[27]David Adamany, "Political Parties in the 1980s," in Michael J. Malbin, ed., *Money and Politics in the United States* (Chatham, N.J.: Chatham House, 1984), 114.

[28]*Senator Mitch McConnell et al. v. Federal Election Commission et al.*, No. 02-1674 (2003).

[29]Joseph Napolitan, *The Election Game and How to Win It* (New York: Doubleday, 1972).

[30]Federal Elections Commission data, 2006.

[31]David B. Magleby and Candice J. Nelson, *The Money Chase: Congressional Campaign Finance Reform* (Washington, D.C.: Brookings Institution, 1990); see also David B. Magelby, J. Quin Monson, and Kelly D. Patterson, eds., *Dancing Without Partners: How Candidates, Parties and Interest Groups Interact in the New Campaign Finance Environment* (Provo, Utah: Brigham Young University Press, 2005).

[32]David Chagall, *The New King-Makers* (New York: Harcourt Brace Jovanovich, 1981).

[33]Lawrence R. Jacobs and Robert Y. Shapiro, *Politicians Don't Pander: Political Manipulation and the Loss of Democratic Responsiveness* (Chicago: University of Chicago Press, 2000).

[34]Darrell M. West, *Air Wars: Television Advertising in Election Campaigns, 1952–2000* (Washington, D.C.: Congressional Quarterly Press, 2001), 140–46.

[35]Stephen Ansolabehere and Shanto Iyengar, *Going Negative* (New York: Free Press, 1995), ch. 5.

[36]West, *Air Wars*, 12.

[37]Peter J. Peterson, *Running on Empty: How the Democratic and Republican Parties Are Bankrupting Our Future and What Americans Can Do About It* (New York: Farrar, Straus, and Giroux, 2005).

CHAPTER 9

[1]E. E. Schattschneider, *The Semisovereign People: A Realist's View of Democracy in America* (New York: Holt, Rinehart & Winston, 1960), 35.

[2]Alexis de Tocqueville, *Democracy in America (1835–1840)*, ed. J. P. Mayer and A. P. Kerr (Garden City, N.Y.: Doubleday/Anchor, 1969), bk. 2, ch. 4.

[3]Mancur Olson, *The Logic of Collective Action*, rev. ed. (Cambridge, Mass.: Harvard University Press, 1971), 147; see also Theda Skocpol, *Diminished Democracy* (Norman: University of Oklahoma Press, 2003).

[4]See Jack L. Walker, *Mobilizing Interest Groups in America* (Ann Arbor: University of Michigan Press, 1991).

[5]See Jeffrey M. Berry, *The New Liberalism: The Rising Power of Citizen Groups* (Washington, D.C.: Brookings Institution Press, 1999).

[6]Olson, *Logic of Collective Action*, 64.

[7]Christopher J. Bosso, "The Color of Money: Environmental Groups and the Pathologies of Fund Raising," in Allan J. Cigler and Burdett Loomis, *Interest Group Politics*, 4th ed. (Washington, D.C.: Congressional Quarterly Press, 1995), 101–3.

[8]Kay Lehman Schlozman and John T. Tierney, *Organized Interests and American Democracy* (New York: Harper & Row, 1986), 54.

[9]Norman J. Ornstein and Shirley Elder, *Interest Groups, Lobbying, and Policymaking* (Washington, D.C.: Congressional Quarterly Press, 1978), 82–86.

[10]See John Mark Hansen, *Gaining Access* (Chicago: Chicago University Press, 1991); Bruce Wolpe and Bertram Levine, *Lobbying Congress* (Washington, D.C.: Congressional Quarterly Press, 1996).

[11]Robert H. Salisbury and Paul Johnson, "Who You Know Versus What You Know," *American Journal of Political Science* 33 (February 1989): 175–95; see also William P. Browne, *Cultivating Congress* (Lawrence: University Press of Kansas, 1995).

[12]Quoted in Ornstein and Elder, *Interest Groups, Lobbying, and Policymaking*, 77.
[13]Paul J. Quirk, *Industry Influence in Federal Regulatory Agencies* (Princeton, N. J.: Princeton University Press, 1981); John E. Chubb, *Interest Groups and the Bureaucracy: The Politics of Energy* (Stanford, Calif.: Stanford University Press, 1983), 200–201; Charles T. Goodsell, *The Case for Bureaucracy*, 3d ed. (Chatham, N.J.: Chatham House, 1994), 55–60.
[14]Lee Epstein and C. K. Rowland, "Interest Groups in the Courts," *American Political Science Review* 85 (1991): 205–17.
[15]Hugh Heclo, "Issue Networks and the Executive Establishment," in Anthony King, ed., *The New American Political System* (Washington, D.C.: American Enterprise Institute, 1978), 87–124.
[16]Ornstein and Elder, *Interest Groups, Lobbying, and Policymaking*, 88–93.
[17]Quoted in Mark Green, "Political PAC-Man," *The New Republic*, December 13, 1982, 20; see also Frank J. Sorauf, *Inside Campaign Finance* (New Haven, Conn.: Yale University Press, 1992).
[18]Quoted in Larry Sabato, *PAC Power: Inside the World of Political Action Committees* (New York: Norton, 1984), 72.
[19]Federal Elections Commission data, 2006.
[20]See Thomas L. Gatz, *Improper Influence* (Ann Arbor: University of Michigan Press, 1996); Gene M. Grossman and Elhanan Helpman, *Interest Groups and Trade Policy* (Princeton, N.J.: Princeton University Press, 2002).
[21]Walker, *Mobilizing Interest Groups in America*, 112.
[22]Theodore J. Lowi, *The End of Liberalism: The Second Republic of the United States* (New York: Norton, 1979).

CHAPTER 10

[1]Theodore H. White, *The Making of the President, 1972* (New York: Bantam Books, 1973), 327.
[2]See Richard Davis, *The Press and American Politics*, 3d ed. (Upper Saddle River, N.J.: Prentice-Hall, 2000), 24–27.
[3]See Geneva Overholser and Kathleen Hall Jamieson, eds., *The Press* (New York: Oxford University Press, 2005).
[4]Frank Luther Mott, *American Journalism, a History: 1690–1960* (New York: Macmillan, 1962), 114–15.
[5]Culver H. Smith, *The Press, Politics, and Patronage* (Athens: University of Georgia Press, 1977), 163–68.
[6]Doris A. Graber, *Mass Media and American Politics*, 6th ed. (Washington, D.C.: Congressional Quarterly Press, 2001), 36; Mark Wahlgren Summers, *The Press Gang* (Chapel Hill: University of North Carolina Press, 1994).
[7]Mott, *American Journalism*, 122–23, 220–27.
[8]Ibid., 220–27, 241, 243.
[9]Edwin Emery, *The Press and America: An Interpretive History of the Mass Media* (Englewood Cliffs, N. J.: Prentice-Hall, 1977), 350.
[10]Quoted in Mott, *American Journalism*, 529.
[11]See Bill Kovach and Tom Rosenstiel, *The Elements of Journalism* (New York: Three Rivers Press, 2001).
[12]Quoted in David Halberstam, *The Powers That Be* (New York: Knopf, 1979), 208–9.
[13]See Ben Bagdikian, *The New Media Monopoly* (Boston: Beacon Press, 2004).
[14]See Timothy E. Cook, *Governing with the News* (Chicago: University of Chicago Press, 1997); Bartholomew Sparrow, *Uncertain Guardians* (Baltimore: Johns Hopkins University Press, 1999).
[15]Bernard Goldberg, *Bias: A CBS Insider Exposes How the Media Distort News* (New York: Harper Paperbacks, 2003).
[16]David H. Weaver, Randal A. Beam, Bonnie J. Brownlee, Paul S. Voakes, and G. Cleveland Wilhoit, *The American Journalist in the 21st Century* (Mahwah, N.J.: LEA, 2006).
[17]Center for Media and Public Affairs, *Media Monitor*, various dates.

[18]Michael Robinson, "Public Affairs Television and the Growth of Political Malaise," *American Political Science Review* 70 (1976): 409–32.

[19]Center for Media and Public Affairs, *Media Monitor,* various dates.

[20]*Ibid.*

[21]Thomas Patterson, *Out of Order* (New York: Knopf, 1993), ch. 4.

[22]Project for Excellence in Journalism, "The Debate Effect," web release, October 27, 2004.

[23]William Cole, ed. *The Most of A. J. Leibling* (New York: Simon, 1963), 7.

[24]Walter Lippmann, *Public Opinion* (New York: Free Press, 1965), 214. First published in 1922.

[25]Donald Shaw and Maxwell McCombs, *The Emergence of American Political Issues: The Agenda-Setting Function of the Press* (St. Paul, Minn.: West Publishing, 1977).

[26]Bernard C. Cohen, *The Press and Foreign Policy* (Princeton, N.J.: Princeton University Press, 1963), 13.

[27]Figures from Center for Media and Public Affairs, various dates.

[28]Kiku Adatto, "Sound Bite Democracy," Joan Shorenstein Center on the Press, Politics, and Public Policy, Research Paper R-2, Harvard University, Cambridge, Mass., June 1990.

[29]Quoted in Doreen Carvajal, "For News Media, Some Introspection," *New York Times,* April 5, 1998, 28.

[30]Quoted in Max Kampelman, "The Power of the Press, *Policy Review* 6 (1978): 19.

[31]James Reston, "End of the Tunnel," *New York Times,* April 30, 1975, 41.

[32]Quoted in Edward J. Epstein, *News from Nowhere* (New York: Random House, 1973), ix.

[33]See Matthew Baum, *Soft News Goes to War* (Princeton, N.J.: Princeton University Press, 2003); James T. Hamilton, *All the News That's Fit to Sell* (Princeton, N.J.: Princeton University Press, 2004).

[34]Study Finds Widespread Misperceptions on Iraq," Program on International Policy Attitudes, University of Maryland, October 2, 2003.

[35]Lippmann, *Public Opinion,* 221.

CHAPTER 11

[1]Roger H. Davidson and Walter J. Oleszek, *Congress and Its Members,* 9th ed. (Washington, D.C.: Congressional Quarterly Press, 2004), 4.

[2]See Paul S. Herrnson, *Congressional Elections: Campaigning at Home and in Washington,* 4th ed. (Washington, D.C.: Congressional Quarterly Press, 2003).

[3]See Gary C. Jacobson, *The Politics of Congressional Elections,* 5th ed. (New York: Longman, 2001).

[4]Bruce Cain, John Ferejohn, and Morris P. Fiorina, *The Personal Vote* (Cambridge, Mass.: Harvard University Press, 1987).

[5]Information provided by Clerk of the House.

[6]U.S. Code online, 2006.

[7]Edward Sidlow, *Challenging the Incumbent: An Underdog's Undertaking* (Washington, D.C.: Congressional Quarterly Press, 2003).

[8]Jennifer Babson and Kelly St. John, "Momentum Helps GOP Collect Record Amounts from PACs," *Congressional Quarterly Weekly Report,* December 3, 1994, 3456.

[9]Quoted in "A Tale of Myths and Measures: Who Is Truly Vulnerable?" *Congressional Quarterly Weekly Report,* December 4, 1993, 7; see also Dennis F. Thompson, *Ethics in Congress* (Washington, D.C.: Brookings Institution Press, 1995).

[10]James E. Campbell, *The Presidential Pulse of Congressional Elections* (Lexington: University Press of Kentucky, 1993).

[11]Robert Erikson, "The Puzzle of Midterm Losses," *Journal of Politics* 50 (November 1988): 1011–29.

[12]Linda L. Fowler and Robert D. McClure, *Political Ambition* (New Haven, Conn.: Yale University Press, 1989).

[13]Keith R. Poole and Howard Rosenthal, "Patterns of Congressional Voting," *American Journal of Political Science* 35 (February 1991): 228.

[14]*Congressional Quarterly Weekly Report,* various dates.

[15]Linda Witt, Karen M. Paget, and Glenna Matthews, *Running as a Woman: Gender and Power in American Politics* (New York: Free Press, 1993); Sue Thomas, *How Women Legislate* (New York: Oxford University Press, 1994); Tali Mendelberg, *The Race Card* (Princeton, N.J.: Princeton University Press, 2001).

[16]See Barbara Sinclair, *Legislators, Leaders, and Lawmaking* (Baltimore, Md.: Johns Hopkins University Press, 1998).

[17]Barbara Sinclair, *Majority Leadership in the U.S. House* (Baltimore, Md.: Johns Hopkins University Press, 1983); Barbara Sinclair, *Unorthodox Lawmaking: New Legislative Processes in the U.S. Congress*, 2nd ed. (Washington, D.C.: Congressional Quarterly Press, 2000).

[18]See Stephen E. Frantzich and Steven E. Schier, *Congress: Games and Strategies* (Dubuque, Iowa: Brown & Benchmark, 1995), 127.

[19]David King, *Turf Wars* (Chicago: University of Chicago Press, 1997).

[20]See Gerald S. Strom, *The Logic of Lawmaking* (Baltimore, Md.: Johns Hopkins University Press, 1990).

[21]See Sinclair, *Unorthodox Lawmaking.*

[22]See Jon R. Bond and Richard Fleisher, eds., *Polarized Politics: Congress and the President in a Partisan Era* (Washington, D.C.: Congressional Quarterly Press, 2000).

[23]See Gary Orfield, *Congressional Power: Congress and Social Change* (New York: Harcourt Brace Jovanovich, 1975).

[24]James L. Sundquist, "Congress and the President: Enemies or Partners?" in Lawrence C. Dodd and Bruce I. Oppenheimer, eds., *Congress Reconsidered* (New York: Praeger, 1977), 240.

[25]Keith Krehbiel, "Are Congressional Committees Composed of Preference Outliers?" *American Political Science Review* 84 (1990): 149–64; Richard L. Hall and Bernard Grofman, "The Committee Assignment Process and the Conditional Nature of Committee Bias," *American Political Science Review* 84 (1990): 1149–66.

[26]Joel A. Aberbach and Mark A. Peterson, eds., *The Executive Branch* (New York: Oxford University Press, 2005), 534–35.

[27]Davidson and Oleszek, *Congress and Its Members*, 7.

CHAPTER 12

[1]Woodrow Wilson, *Constitutional Government in the United States* (New York: Columbia University Press, 1908), 67.

[2]Sidney Milkis and Michael Nelson, *The American Presidency: Origins and Development, 1790–2002*, 4th ed. (Washington, D.C.: Congressional Quarterly Press, 2003).

[3]James W. Davis, *The American Presidency* (New York: Harper & Row, 1987), 13; see also Bruce Ackerman, *The Failure of the Founding Fathers* (Cambridge, Mass.: Belknap Press of Harvard University Press, 2005).

[4]See Barry M. Blechman and Stephen S. Kaplan, *Force Without War* (Washington, D.C.: Brookings Institution, 1978); Arthur M. Schlesinger, Jr., *War and the American Presidency* (New York: W. W. Norton, 2004).

[5]*United States v. Belmont*, 57 U.S. 758 (1937).

[6]Robert DiClerico, *The American President*, 5th ed. (Englewood Cliffs, N.J.: Prentice-Hall, 1999), 47.

[7]Quoted in Wilfred E. Binkley, *President and Congress*, 3d ed. (New York: Vintage, 1962), 142.

[8]Theodore Roosevelt, *An Autobiography* (New York: Scribner's, 1931), 383.

[9]See Richard M. Pious, *The American Presidency* (New York: Basic Books, 1979), 83.

[10]Harry S Truman, *Years of Trial and Hope* (New York: Signet, 1956), 535.

[11]See Joseph A. Pika and John Anthony Maltese, *The Politics of the Presidency*, 6th ed. (Washington, D.C.: Congressional Quarterly Press, 2004).

[12]James Bryce, *The American Commonwealth* (New York: Commonwealth Edition, 1908), 230.

[13]Hugh Heclo, "Introduction: The Presidential Illusion," in Hugh Heclo and Lester M. Salamon, eds., *The Illusion of Presidential Government* (Boulder, Colo.: Westview Press, 1981), 6.

[14]James W. Ceaser, *Presidential Selection: Theory and Development* (Princeton, N.J.: Princeton University Press, 1979).

[15]Thomas E. Patterson, *The Vanishing Voter* (New York: Vintage, 2003); John S. Jackson and William J. Crotty, *The Politics of Presidential Selection* (New York: Longman, 2001).

[16]Sidney Kraus, ed., *The Great Debates* (Bloomington: Indiana University Press, 1962), 190.

[17]John P. Burke, *The Institutionalized Presidency* (Baltimore: Johns Hopkins University Press, 1992); Charles E. Walcott and Karen M. Hult, *Governing the White House* (Lawrence: University Press of Kansas, 1995).

[18]Quoted in Stephen J. Wayne, *Road to the White House, 1992* (New York: St. Martin's Press, 1992), 143.

[19]See Shirley Anne Warshaw, *Powersharing: White House–Cabinet Relations in the Modern Presidency* (Albany: State University of New York Press, 1995).

[20]See Jeffrey E. Cohen, *The Politics of the United States Cabinet* (Pittsburgh: University of Pittsburgh Press, 1988).

[21]James Pfiffner, *The Modern Presidency* (New York: St. Martin's Press, 1994), 123.

[22]Quoted in James MacGregor Burns, "Our Super-Government—Can We Control It?" *New York Times*, April 24, 1949, 32.

[23]See Paul C. Light, *Thickening Government: Federal Hierarchy and the Diffusion of Accountability* (Washington, D.C.: Brookings Institution, 1995).

[24]Erwin Hargrove, *The Power of the Modern Presidency* (New York: Knopf, 1974); see also John H. Kessel, *Presidents, the Presidency, and the Political Environment* (Washington, D.C.: Congressional Quarterly Press, 2001).

[25]James P. Pfiffner, *The Strategic Presidency: Hitting the Ground Running*, 2d ed. (Chicago: Dorsey Press, 1996).

[26]Aaron Wildavsky, "The Two Presidencies," *Trans-Action*, December 1966, 7.

[27]Pfiffner, *The Modern Presidency*, ch. 6.

[28]Thomas P. (Tip) O'Neill, with William Novak, *Man of the House: The Life and Political Memoirs of Speaker Tip O'Neill* (New York: Random House, 1987), 297.

[29]Fred I. Greenstein, ed., *Leadership in the Modern Presidency* (Cambridge, Mass.: Harvard University Press, 1988), ch. 10.

[30]Richard E. Neustadt, *Presidential Power and the Modern Presidents* (New York: Free Press, 1990), 71–72.

[31]Ibid., 33.

[32]Charlie Savage, "Senator Considers Suit Over Bush Law Challenge," *Boston Globe*, June 28, 2006, Internet copy.

[33]John E. Mueller, "Presidential Popularity from Truman to Johnson," *American Political Science Review* 64 (March 1970): 18–34; Kathleen Frankovic, "Public Opinion in the 1992 Campaign," in Gerald M. Pomper, ed., *The Election of 1992* (Chatham, N.J.: Chatham House, 1993).

[34]Samuel Kernell, *Going Public: New Strategies of Presidential Leadership*, 3d ed. (Washington, D.C.: Congressional Quarterly Press, 1997), 1; see also Robert M. Eisinger, *The Evolution of Presidential Polling* (New York: Cambridge University Press, 2003).

[35]Heclo, "Introduction: The Presidential Illusion," 2.

[36]Theodore J. Lowi, *The "Personal" Presidency: Power Invested, Promise Unfulfilled* (Ithaca, N.Y.: Cornell University Press, 1985).

CHAPTER 13

[1]Norman Thomas, *Rule 9: Politics, Administration, and Civil Rights* (New York: Random House, 1966), 6.

[2]James P. Pfiffner, "The National Performance Review in Perspective," working paper 94-4, Institute of Public Policy, George Mason University, 1994, 2.

[3]Ibid., 12.

[4]Max Weber, *Economy and Society*, trans. Guenther Roth and Claus Wittich (New York: Bedminster Press, 1968), 23; see also Paul Du Gay, *The Values of Bureaucracy* (New York: Oxford University Press, 2005).

[5]See Cornelius M. Kerwin, *Rulemaking*, 3d ed. (Washington, D.C.: Congressional Quarterly Press, 2003).

[6]Michael Lipsky, *Street-Level Bureaucracy* (New York: Russell Sage Foundation, 1980); see also George Serra,"Citizen-Initiated Contact and Satisfaction with Bureaucracy," *Journal of Public Administration* 5 (April 1995): 175–88.

[7]Paul Van Riper, *History of the United States Civil Service* (Evanston, Ill.: Peterson, 1958), 36.

[8]David H. Rosenbloom, *Federal Service and the Constitution* (Ithaca, N.Y.: Cornell University Press, 1971), 83.

[9]Herbert Kaufman, "Emerging Conflicts in the Doctrine of Public Administration," *American Political Science Review* 50 (December 1956): 1060.

[10]Ibid., 1062.

[11]Quoted in Hugh Heclo, *A Government of Strangers* (Washington, D.C.: Brookings Institution, 1977), 225.

[12]Norton E. Long, "Power and Administration," *Public Administration Review* 10 (Autumn 1949): 269; Joel D. Aberbach and Bert A. Rockman, *In the Web of Politics* (Washington, D.C.: Brookings Institution Press, 2000).

[13]See Heclo, *A Government of Strangers*, 117–18.

[14]Quoted in Aaron Wildavsky, *The Politics of the Budgetary Process*, 4th ed. (Boston: Little, Brown, 1984), 19; see also Dennis D. Riley, *Bureaucracy and the Policy Process: Keeping the Promises* (Latham, Md.: Rowman & Littlefield, 2005).

[15]Joel D. Aberbach and Bert A. Rockman, "Clashing Beliefs Within the Executive Branch," *American Political Science Review* 70 (June 1976): 461.

[16]See B. Dan Wood and Richard W. Waterman, *Bureaucratic Dynamics* (Boulder, Colo.: Westview Press, 1994); Edward C. Page and Bill Jenkins, *Policy Bureaucracy: Government with a Cast of Thousands* (New York: Oxford University Press, 2005).

[17]See John Brehm and Scott Gates, *Working, Shirking, and Sabotage* (Ann Arbor: University of Michigan Press, 1996).

[18]Long, "Power and Administration," 269; see also John Mark Hansen, *Gaining Access* (Chicago: University of Chicago Press, 1991).

[19]Charles T. Goodsell, *The Case for Bureaucracy*, 2d ed. (Chatham, N.J.: Chatham House, 1985), 55–60; see also B. Guy Peters, *The Politics of Bureaucracy*, 5th ed. (New York: Routledge, 2001).

[20]William T. Gormley Jr. and Steven J. Balla, *Bureaucracy and Democracy* (Washington, D.C.: Congressional Quarterly Press, 2003).

[21]See Paul Light, *Thickening Government* (Washington, D.C.: Brookings Institution, 1995).

[22]James G. March and Johan P. Olson, "Organizing Political Life: What Administrative Reorganization Tells Us About Government," *American Political Science Review* 77 (June 1983): 281–96.

[23]Kenneth J. Meier, *Regulation* (New York: St. Martin's Press, 1985), 110–11.

[24]See Heclo, *A Government of Strangers*.

[25]See Donald Kettl, *Deficit Politics* (New York: Macmillan, 1992).

[26]See Joel D. Aberbach, *Keeping a Watchful Eye* (Washington, D.C.: Brookings Institution, 1990).

[27]David Rosenbloom, "The Evolution of the Administrative State, and Transformations of Administrative Law," in David Rosenbloom and Richard Schwartz, eds., *Handbook of Regulation and Administrative Law* (New York: Marcel Dekker, 1994), 3–36.

[28]See *Vermont Yankee Nuclear Power Corp. v. National Resources Defense Council, Inc.*, 435 U.S. 519 (1978); *Chevron v. National Resources Defense Council*, 467 U.S. 837 (1984); *Heckler v. Chaney*, 470 U.S. 821 (1985); but see *FDA v. Brown & Williamson Tobacco Co.* (2000).

[29]*Pigeford v. Veneman*, U.S. District Court for the District of Columbia, Civil Action No. 97-1978 (1999).

[30]"Clark: Bush Didn't See Terrorism as 'Urgent,'" *CNN.com*, March 25, 2004.

[31]See Brian J. Cook, *Bureaucracy and Self-Government* (Baltimore, Md.: Johns Hopkins University Press, 1996).

[32]Ibid.

[33]David Osborne and Ted Gaebler, *Reinventing Government: How the Entrepreneurial Spirit Is Transforming the Public Sector* (New York: Addison-Wesley, 1992); see also Michael Barzelay and Babak J. Armajani, *Breaking Through Bureaucracy* (Berkeley: University of California Press, 1992); Robert D. Behn, *Leadership Counts* (Cambridge, Mass.: Harvard University Press, 1991).

[34]Pfiffner, "The National Performance Review in Perspective," 7.

[35]Ronald C. Moe, "The 'Reinventing Government' Exercise: Misinterpreting the Problem, Misjudging the Results," *Public Administration Review*, March/April 1994, 125–36.

CHAPTER 14

[1]*Marbury v. Madison*, 5 U.S. 137 (1803).

[2]*Bush v. Gore*, No. 00-949 (2000).

[3]Rebecca Mae Salokar, *The Solicitor General: The Politics of Law* (Philadelphia: Temple University Press, 1992); see also Cornell W. Clayton, *The Politics of Justice: The Attorney General and the Making of Legal Policy* (Armonk, N.Y.: Sharpe, 1992).

[4]See Bernard Schwartz, *Decision: How the Supreme Court Decides Cases* (New York: Oxford University Press, 1996).

[5]Henry Glick, *Courts, Politics, and Justice*, 3d ed. (New York: McGraw-Hill, 1993), 214.

[6]Lawrence Baum, *The Supreme Court*, 8th ed. (Washington, D.C.: Congressional Quarterly Press, 2003), 120.

[7]*Gideon v. Wainwright*, 372 U.S. 335 (1963).

[8]From a letter to the author by Frank Schwartz of Beaver College; this section reflects substantially Professor Schwartz's recommendations to the author, as does the later section that addresses the federal court myth. See also Robert A. Carp and Ronald Stidham, *The Federal Courts*, 4th ed. (Washington, D.C.: Congressional Quarterly Press, 2001).

[9]*Hutto v. Davis*, 370 U.S. 256 (1982).

[10]*Lawrence v. Texas*, No. 02-102 (2003).

[11]*Bowers v. Hardwick*, 478 U.S. 186 (1986).

[12]See Richard Davis, *Electing Justices* (New York: Oxford University Press, 2005).

[13]See Lee Epstein and Jeffrey Segal, *Advice and Consent: The Politics of Judicial Appointments* (New York: Oxford University Press, 2005).

[14]Robert Scigliano, *The Supreme Court and the Presidency* (New York: Free Press, 1971), 146; see also Lee Epstein and Jack Knight, *The Choices Justices Make* (Washington, D.C.: Congressional Quarterly Press, 1998).

[15]Quoted in Baum, *The Supreme Court*, 37.

[16]See Virginia A. Hettinger et al., *Judging on a Collegial Court: Influences on Federal Appellate Decision Making* (Charlottesville, Va.: University of Virginia Press, 2006).

[17]John Gottschall, "Reagan's Appointments to the U.S. Courts of Appeals," 70 *Judicature* 48 (1986): 54.

[18]Carp, *The Federal Courts*.

[19]Joseph B. Harris, *The Advice and Consent of the Senate* (Berkeley: University of California Press, 1953), 313.

[20]Quoted in Louis Fisher, *American Constitutional Law* (New York: McGraw-Hill, 1990), 5.

[21]Quoted in Charles P. Curtis, *Law and Large as Life* (New York: Simon & Schuster, 1959), 156–57.

[22]See Lee Epstein and Jack Knight, *The Choices Justices Make* (New York: Longman, 1995); Thomas G. Hansford and James F. Spriggs II, *The Politics of Precedent on the Supreme Court* (Princeton, N.J.: Princeton University Press, 2006).

[23]*Faragher v. City of Boca Raton*, No. 97-282 (1998).

[24]Stephen L. Wasby, *The Supreme Court in the Federal Judicial System*, 4th ed. (Chicago: Nelson-Hall, 1993), 53.

[25]Linda Greenhouse, "Sure Justices Legislate. They Have To," *New York Times*, July 5, 1998, sect. 4, p. 1.

[26]John Schmidhauser, *The Supreme Court* (New York: Holt, Rinehart & Winston, 1964), 6.

[27]Linda Greenhouse, "In a Momentous Term, Justices Remake the Law, and the Court," *New York Times*, July 1, 2003, A1.

[28]*Bush v. Gore*, No. 00-949 (2000).

[29]See, however, James L. Gibson, Gregory A. Caldeira, and Lester Kenyatta Spence, "The Supreme Court and the U.S. Presidential Election of 2000," *British Journal of Political Science* 33 (2003): 535–56.

[30]David M. O'Brien, *Storm Center: The Supreme Court in American Politics*, 7th ed. (New York: Norton, 2005), 14–15.

[31]Ross Sandler and David Schoenbrod, *Democracy by Decree* (New Haven, Conn.: Yale University Press, 2003).

[32]Some of the references cited in the following sections are taken from Henry J. Abraham, "The Judicial Function Under the Constitution," *News for Teachers of Political Science* 41 (Spring 1984): 12–14; see also Louis Michael Seidman, *Our Unsettled Constitution* (New Haven, Conn.: Yale University Press, 2002).

[33]Abraham, "The Judicial Function," 14.

[34]Alexander M. Bickel, *The Supreme Court and the Idea of Progress* (New Haven, Conn.: Yale University Press, 1978), 173–81; see also Antonin Scalia, *A Matter of Interpretation* (Princeton, N.J.: Princeton University Press, 1997).

[35]Abraham, "The Judicial Function," 13.

[36]*Colegrove v. Green*, 328 U.S. 549 (1946).

[37]*Baker v. Carr*, 369 U.S. 186 (1962).

[38]Frank H. Easterbrook, "Do Liberals and Conservatives Differ in Judicial Activism?" *University of Colorado Law Review* 73 (2002): 1401.

[39]Randy E. Barnett, "Is the Rehnquist Court an 'Activist' Court? The Commerce Clause Cases," *University of Colorado Law Review* 73 (2002): 1275.

[40]Quoted in Linda Greenhouse, "The Justices Decide Who's in Charge," *New York Times*, June 27, 1999, sect. 4, p. 1.

[41]Epstein and Knight, *The Choices Justices Make*; see also Mark Tushnet, *A Court Divided* (New York: W. W. Norton, 2005).

[42]*Vieth v. Jubelirer*, 504 U.S. 267 (2004).

[43]Quoted in Curtis, *Law and Large as Life*, 157.

CHAPTER 15

[1]E. E. Schattschneider, *The Semisovereign People* (New York: Holt, Rinehart and Winston, 1960).

[2]Aaron Wildavsky, *The Politics of the Budgetary Process*, 4th ed. (Glenview, Ill.: Scott Foresman & Co., 1984).

[3]John W. Kingdon, *Agendas, Alternatives, and Public Policies*, 2nd ed. (New York: Longman, 2002).

[4]James Kuhnhenn, "Lawmakers Fear Another Senior Citizens' Revolt Against Medicare Bill," Knight Ridder newspapers, November 23, 2003; Internet copy.

[5]The section titled "Efficiency Through Government Intervention" relies substantially on Alan Stone, *Regulation and Its Alternatives* (Washington, D.C.: Congressional Quarterly Press, 1982).

[6]See Marc Allen Eisner, *Regulatory Politics in Transition*, 2d ed. (Baltimore: Johns Hopkins University Press, 1999).

[7]Paul Portney, "Beware of the Killer Clauses Inside the GOP's 'Contract,'" *The Washington Post National Weekly Edition*, January 23–29, 1995, 21.

[8]See Richard A. Harris and Sidney M. Milkis, *The Politics of Regulatory Change* (New York: Oxford University Press, 1996).

[9]Lawrence E. Mitchell, *Corporate Irresponsibility* (New Haven, Conn.: Yale University Press, 2003).

[10]H. Peyton Young, *Equity: In Theory and Practice* (Princeton, N.J.: Princeton University Press, 1995).

[11]"Hill Foes of New Clean Air Rules Unite Behind Moratorium Bill," *Congressional Quarterly Weekly Report*, Spring 1998 (Washington, D.C.: Congressional Quarterly Press, 1998), 61.

[12]See Thomas Streeter, *Selling the Air* (Chicago: University of Chicago Press, 1996); Robert McChesney, *The Problem of the Media* (New York: Monthly Review Press, 2004).

[13]See Christopher J. Bosso, *Environment, Inc.: From Grassroots to Beltway* (Lawrence: University Press of Kansas, 2005).

[14]Rachel Carson, *The Silent Spring* (Boston: Houghton Mifflin, 1962); see also Lester R. Brown, *Plan B2.0: Rescuing a Planet Under Stress and a Civilization in Trouble* (New York: W. W. Norton, 2006).

[15]Robert B. Keiter, *Keeping Faith with Nature* (New Haven, Conn.: Yale University Press, 2003).

[16]*U.S. News & World Report*, June 30, 1975, 25.

[17]*Whitman v. American Trucking Association*, No. 99-1257 (2001).

[18]See Walter A. Rosenbaum, *Environmental Politics and Policy*, 6th ed. (Washington, D.C.: Congressional Quarterly Press, 2004); Norman J. Vig and Michael E. Kraft, eds., *Environmental Policy: New Directions for the Twenty-First Century* (Washington, D.C.: Congressional Quarterly Press, 2003).

[19]See Robert Lekachman, *The Age of Keynes* (New York: Random House, 1966); see also Richard Kopke, Geoffrey M. B. Tootell, and Robert K. Triest, eds., *The Macroeconomics of Fiscal Policy* (Cambridge, Mass.: MIT Press, 2006).

[20]See Bruce Bartlett, *Reaganomics: Supply-Side Economics* (Westport, Conn.: Arlington House, 1981).

[21]See Richard Duncan, *The Dollar Crisis: Causes, Consequences, Cures*, rev. ed. (New York: John Wiley & Sons, 2005).

[22]See Allen Schick, *The Federal Budget*, rev. ed. (Washington, D.C.: Brookings Institution Press, 2000).

[23]U.S. Senate clerk, 2002.

[24]Martin Mayer, *FED: The Inside Story of How the World's Most Powerful Financial Institution Drives the Markets* (New York: Free Press, 2001).

CHAPTER 16

[1]Quoted in E. J. Dionne Jr., "Reflecting on 'Reform,'" *Washington Post*, web download, February 15, 2004.

[2]Press releases of House Committee on Ways and Means and National Conference of State Legislatures, September 19 and June 26, 2002, respectively.

[3]Michael Harrington, *The Other America: Poverty in the United States* (New York: Macmillan, 1962); see also James T. Patterson, *America's Struggle Against Poverty in the Twentieth Century* (Cambridge, Mass.: Harvard University Press, 2000).

[4]Charles Murray, *Losing Ground: American Social Policy, 1950–1980* (New York: Basic Books, 1984).

[5]Signe-Mary McKernan and Caroline Ratcliffe, "Events That Trigger Poverty Entries and Exits," *Social Science Quarterly* 86 (2005): 1146–69.

[6]See Katherine S. Newman, *No Shame in My Game* (New York: Alfred A. Knopf and Russell Sage Foundation, 1999), 41.

[7]V. O. Key Jr., *The Responsible Electorate* (Cambridge, Mass.: Belknap Press of Harvard University, 1966), 43.

[8]Everett Carll Ladd, *American Political Parties* (New York: Norton, 1970), 205.

[9]Institute on Taxation and Economic Policy poll, 2002.

[10]For a general overview of 1950s and 1960s policy disputes, see James Sundquist, *Politics and Policy* (Washington, D.C.: Brookings Institution, 1968).

[11]See Jason DeParle, *American Dream: Three Women, Ten Kids, and a Nation's Drive to End Welfare* (New York: Penguin, 2005).

[12]Quoted in Malcolm Gladwell, "The Medicaid Muddle," *The Washington Post National Weekly Edition*, January 16–22, 1995, 31.

[13]Jill Quadagno, *One Nation, Uninsured: Why the United States Has No National Health Insurance* (New York: Oxford University Press, 2005).

[14]Alberto Alesina and Edward Glaeser, *Fighting Poverty in the U.S. and Europe* (New York: Oxford University Press, 2006).

[15]Robert D. Ebel, Tuan Minh Le, and Zicheng Li Swift, "National Tax Levels and the Rich vs. the Poor," publication of the Tax Policy Center, Washington, D.C., June 6, 2005.

[16]Paul Krugman, "Hey, Lucky Duckies," *New York Times*, December 3, 2002, A31.

[17]Said of George H. W. Bush at the 1988 Democratic Convention. The quote is variously attributed to Ann Richards or Jim Hightower.

[18]Based on Organization for Economic Cooperation and Development (OECD) data, 2006; see Douglas S. Reed, *On Equal Terms: The Constitutional Politics of Educational Opportunity* (Princeton, N.J.: Princeton University Press, 2003).

[19]Kaiser Family Foundation/Washington Post/Kennedy School of Government poll, September 1999.

[20]See John E. Chubb and Terry M. Moe, *Politics, Markets, and America's Schools* (Washington, D.C.: Brookings Institution, 1990); Tony Wagner and Thomas Vander Ark, *Making the Grade* (New York: Routledge, 2001).

[21]See Jeffrey R. Henig, *Rethinking School Choice* (Princeton, N.J.: Princeton University Press, 1995).

[22]Phi Delta Kappa/Gallup poll, 2002.

[23]Press release, Congressman John Boehner, January 4, 2003.

[24]Phi Delta Kappa/Gallup poll, 2005.

[25]Stanley Feldman and John Zaller, "The Political Culture of Ambivalence: Ideological Responses to the Welfare State," *American Journal of Political Science* 36, no. 1 (1992): 268–307.

[26]Robert E. Lane, "Market Justice, Political Justice," *American Political Science Review* 80 (1986): 383.

CHAPTER 17

[1]American Assembly Report (co-sponsored by the Council on Foreign Relations), *Rethinking America's Security* (New York: Harriman, 1991), 8.

[2]See Mr. X. (George Kennan), "The Sources of Soviet Conduct," *Foreign Affairs* 25 (July 1947): 566–82.

[3]David M. Barrett, *Uncertain Warriors: Lyndon Johnson and His Vietnam Advisors* (Lawrence: University Press of Kansas, 1993); see also Stanley Karnow, *Vietnam: A History* (New York: Penguin, 1983).

[4]See Mark Sauter and James Carafano, *Homeland Security* (New York: McGraw-Hill, 2005).

[5]West Point speech, June 1, 2002; for an opposing view, see Gary Hart, *The Shield and the Cloak: The Security of the Commons* (New York: Oxford University Press, 2006).

[6]PIPA-Knowledge Network survey, October 29–November 10, 2003.

[7]See Ole Holsti, *Public Opinion and American Foreign Policy* (Ann Arbor: University of Michigan Press, 1996); Richard Sobel, *The Impact of Public Opinion on U.S. Foreign Policy Since Vietnam* (New York: Oxford University Press, 2001).

[8]George C. Wilson, *This War Really Matters: Inside the Fight for Defense Dollars* (Washington, D.C.: Congressional Quarterly Press, 2000).

[9]U.S. government data, various agencies, 2006.

[10]*The World Competitiveness Yearbook* (Lausanne, Switzerland: International Institute for Management Development, 2006).

[11]American Assembly Report, *Rethinking America's Security*, 9.

[12]Manfred B. Steger, *Globalism: The New Market Philosophy* (New York: Rowman & Littlefield, 2002).

[13]Ted C. Fishman, *China, Inc.: How the Rise of the Next Superpower Challenges America and the World* (New York: Scribner, 2005).

[14]See Joseph S. Nye, *Soft Power: The Means to Success in World Politics* (New York: PublicAffairs, 2003); Michael Lind, *The American Way of Strategy* (New York: Oxford University Press, 2006).

[15]U.S. Department of State data, 2006.

[16]Hobart Rowen, "The Budget: Fact and Fiction," *The Washington Post National Weekly Edition*, January 16–22, 1995, 5.

[17]Tom Masland, "Going Down the Aid 'Rathole'?" *Newsweek*, December 5, 1994, 39.

[18]Philip Gordon, "September 11 and American Foreign Policy," website of the Brookings Institution, downloaded on June 21, 2002. The chapter's last section is based substantially on Gordon's observations.

CREDITS

PHOTO CREDITS

Chapter 1 p. 1: © Damian Dovarganes/Pool/Reuters/Corbis Images; p. 6: © Chromosohm Media/ Stock Boston; p. 9: © Ernest C. Withers, Courtesy, Panopticon Gallery, Waltham, MA; p. 20: Collection, The Supreme Court Historical Society. Photo by Richard Strauss, Smithsonian Institution; p. 21: © Bob Daemmrich/Image Works; p. 29: © John Neubauer/PhotoEdit

Chapter 2 p. 37: © The Granger Collection; p. 38: © Jim Wells; p. 43: © The Granger Collection; p. 60: Library of Congress, Prints & Photographs Division (LC-USZC4-2474); p. 62: © The Granger Collection; p. 68: © Bob Daemmrich/Image Works

Chapter 3 p. 73: © The Granger Collection; p. 75: © AP/Wide World Photos; p. 81: Library of Congress, Prints and Photographs Division (LC-USZ62-62-1304); p. 83, p. 87: © The Granger Collection; p. 92: Library of Congress, Prints and Photographs Division; p. 97: © Rick Wilking/Reuters/Corbis Images; p. 104: © AP/Wide World Photos

Chapter 4 p. 109: © AP/Wide World Photos; p. 114: © Paul Conklin/PhotoEdit; p. 117: Library of Congress, Prints & Photographs Division (LC-USZ62-47817); p. 121, p. 123, p. 128, p. 130: © AP/Wide World Photos; p. 137: © Jeff Cadge/Getty Images; p. 146: © Joe Raedle/Getty Images

Chapter 5 p. 151: © AP/Wide World Photos; p. 154: © Charles Moore/Black Star; p. 164, p. 166: © AP/Wide World Photos; p. 168: © Underwood and Underwood/Corbis Images; p. 174, p. 184: © AP/Wide World Photos

Chapter 6 p. 191: © Charles Gupton/Corbis Images; p. 195: © University College London; p. 197, p. 199: © Bettmann/Corbis Images; p. 211: © Ann Johansson/Corbis Images; p. 218: © Mario Tama/Getty Images; p. 219: © AP/Wide World Photos

Chapter 7 p. 223: © Jonathan Nourok/Getty Images; p. 225: © Culver Pictures; p. 226: © The Granger Collection; p. 235: © AP/Wide World Photos; p. 239: © Michael Newman/PhotoEdit; p. 241: © Frederic Larson/Corbis Images; p. 243: © AP/Wide World Photos

Chapter 8 p. 251: © Bob Daemmrich/Corbis Images; p. 257: Library of Congress, Prints and Photographs Division (LC-USZ62-13016); p. 258: © Bettmann/Corbis Images; p. 270, p. 275: © AP/Wide World Photos; p. 280: © Alex Wong/Gettty Images; p. 287: © AP/Wide World Photos

Chapter 9 p. 293: © AP/Wide World Photos; p. 299: Library of Congress, Prints & Photographs Division; p. 302, p. 307, p. 310: © AP/Wide World Photos; p. 316: © Chip Somodevilla/Getty Images; p. 321: © Greg Smith/Corbis Images

Chapter 10 p. 327: © AP/Wide World Photos; p. 329: Photo courtesy U.S. Army; p. 332: © Stock Montage; p. 338: © Brown Brothers; p. 342: © Patrick Olear/Photo Edit; p. 343: © AP/Wide World Photos; p. 351: © Thorne Anderson/Corbis Images; p. 353: © AP/Wide World Photos

Chapter 11 p. 359: © Vanessa Vick/Photo Researchers; p. 362, p. 367: © Bettmann/Corbis Images; p. 370: © James Leynse/Corbis Images; p. 379, p. 389: © AP/Wide World Photos; p. 395: © John Van Hasselt/Corbis Images; p. 400: © Allan Tannenbaum

Chapter 12 p. 407: © James P. Blair; p. 409: © AP/Wide World Photos; p. 413: © Christie's Images/Corbis Images; p. 415: © UPI/Bettmann/Corbis Images; p. 427, p. 432, p. 445: © AP/Wide World Photos

Chapter 13 p. 449: © Medioimages/Getty R-F Website; p. 451: © AP/Wide World Photos; p. 459: © Bob Daemmrich/Stock Boston; p. 468: © Don Perdue/Getty Images; p. 472: White House Historical Association (White House Collection) (22); p. 477: © Mark Wilson/Getty Images

Chapter 14 p. 487, p. 491: © Collection of the Supreme Court of the United States; p. 498: © AP/Wide World Photos; p. 500: Collection, The Supreme Court Historical Society. Photo by Steve Petteway, Supreme Court; p. 509: © Landon Nordeman/Getty Images; p. 512, p. 517 (both): © AP/Wide World Photos; p. 521: Library of Congress, Prints & Photographs Division (LC-USZ62-54940)

Chapter 15 p. 527: © Najlah Feanny/Corbis Images; p. 531, p. 541: © AP/Wide World Photos; p. 544: © Alfred Eisenstaedt/Time Life Pictures//Getty Images; p. 545: © John M. Roberts; p. 549: © Win McNamee/Getty Images; p. 566: © Bill Nation/Corbis Images

Chapter 16 p. 573: © AP/Wide World Photos; p. 581: Library of Congress, Prints and Photographs Division (LC-USA62-117 121); p. 584: © William Johnson/Stock Boston; p. 588: © Dana Fineman; p. 596: © Bob Daemmrich/Stock Boston; p. 599: © Bob Daemmrich/Image Works

Chapter 17 p. 605: © Robert Nickelsberg/Getty Images; p. 609: © Michael Barson/Past Perfect; p. 612: © Bettmann/Corbis; p. 614: © AP/Wide World Photos; p. 623: © AFP/Getty Images; p. 624: © Ed Clark/Life Magazine/Time & Life Pictures/Getty Images; p. 632: © AP/Wide World Photos

TEXT AND LINE ART CREDITS

Chapter 1, Table 1-2: From *Survey of American Political Culture*, vol. 2, Institute for Advanced Studies in Culture, University of Virginia, James Davison Hunter and Carl Bowman, survey directors. Used with permission. R1: James Carroll, "What We Love About America," *Boston Globe*, July 3, 2006, p. A11. Reprinted with permission by the author. **Chapter 3,** R3: Reprinted by permission of the publisher from *To Make A Nation: The Rediscovery of American Federalism* by Samuel H. Beer, pp. 1–5, Cambridge, Mass.: The Bellknap Press of Harvard Press. Copyright © 1993 by the President and Fellows of Harvard College. **Chapter 5,** Figure 5-2: Global Attitudes Survey (2002) by the Pew Global Attitudes Project. Used with permission. Figure 5-4: Global Attitudes Survey (2002) by the Pew Global Attitudes Project. Used with permission. Figure 5-6: Pew Research Center for the People and the Press. May 14, 2003. Used with permission. R5: "Letter from Birmingham Jail" by Dr. Martin Luther King, Jr. Reprinted by arrangement with the Estate of Martin Luther King, Jr., c/o Writers house as agent for the proprietor New York, NY. Copyright © 1963 by Martin Luther King, Jr., copyright renewed 1991 by Coretta Scott King. Used with permission. **Chapter 6,** Figure 6-1: Used by permission of National Opinion Research Center, University of Chicago. R6: "The Iraq Syndrome" by John Mueller. Reprinted by permission of *Foreign Affairs*, (Nov/Dec 2005). Copyright © 2005 by the Council on Foreign Relations, Inc. **Chapter 7,** Table 7-1: From *Survey of American Political Culture* (1996), vol. 2, Institute for Advanced Studies in Culture, University of Virginia, James Davison Hunter and Carl Bowman, survey directors. Used with permission. Figure 7-2: The Vanishing Voter Project Shorenstein Center on the Press, Politics and Public Policy, Harvard University. Published by permission of project director. Figure 7-4: From Russell J. Dalton in "The Myth of the Disengaged American," *CSES Report*, October 25, 2005. Used with permission. Figure 7-5: From Russell J. Dalton in "The Myth of the Disengaged American," *CSES Report*, October 25, 2005. Used with permission. **Chapter 8,** R8: Ronald Brownstein, "GOP Has Lock on South, and Democrats Can't Find Key," *Los Angeles Times*, December 15, 2004. Reprinted with permission. **Chapter 9,** R9: Jonathan D. Salant, "The Lobbying Game Today," excerpted from *Extensions*, A Journal of the Carl Albert Center, Fall 2006. Used with permission. **Chapter 10,** p. 335–336: Thomas E. Patterson, Media and Democracy Project, in progress. Reprinted by permission of the author. Figure 10-2: Adapted from Daniel C. Halin, "Sound Bite News: Television Coverage of Elections 1968–1988," *Journal of Communication* 42 (Spring 1992): 6. Used with permission by Blackwell Publishing Ltd. The 1991–2004 data are from the Center for Media and Public Affairs. P. 342 With permission from Rock the Vote Education Fund. R10: Alex Jones, "To Publish or Not to Publish," Shorenstein Center on the Press, Politics and Public Policy. Used with permission. **Chapter 11,** p. 373: Center for American

INDEX